Baedeker

Israel

211 illustrations, 36 special plans, 25 town plans, 17 ground-plans, 7 general maps, 6 drawings, 1 large map of Israel at the end of the book

Original German text: Dr Otto Gärtner, Birgit Borowski, Prof. Wolfgang Hassenpflug
Editorial work: Baedeker-Redaktion (Birgit Borowski)
General direction: Dr Peter Baumgarten, Baedeker Stuttgart

Cartography: Gert Oberländer, Munich; Hallwag AG, Berne (large map of Israel)
Source of illustrations: Bader (10); Bildagentur Schuster (2); Bilderdienst Süddeutscher Verlag (1); Borowski (153); Brödel (3); CESA Diaarchiv (3); Hoene (16); Lade (Fotoagentur) (2); Rudolph (Diaarchiv) (1); Sperber (13); Stetter (1); Ullstein Bilderdienst (5).

English language edition: Alec Court
English translation: James Hogarth

3rd English edition 1995

© Baedeker Stuttgart: original German edition 1994

© 1995 Jarrold and Sons Ltd: English language edition worldwide

© 1995 The Automobile Association: United Kingdom and Ireland

Published in the United States by:
Macmillan Travel
A Simon & Schuster Macmillan Company
15 Columbus Circle
New York, NY 10023

Macmillan is a registered trademark of Macmillan, Inc.

Distributed in the United Kingdom by the Publishing Division of the Automobile Association, Fanum House, Basingstoke, Hampshire RG21 2EA

Licensed user: Mairs Geographischer Verlag GmbH & Co., Ostfildern-Kemnat bei Stuttgart

The name Baedeker is a registered trademark

A CIP catalogue record of this book is available from the British Library

Printed in Italy by G. Canale & C.S.p.A – Borgaro T.se –Turin

ISBN 0–02–860484–9 US and Canada

Library of Congress Catalog Card Number: 92–083956

Contents

Large Map of Israel at end of book

The Principal Sights at a Glance

(Continued on page 446)

N.B.: The spelling of Hebrew and Arabic names gives rise to some difficulty, since there are no generally accepted systems for the transcription of modern Hebrew (Ivrit) and Arabic into English, and variant spellings are found even in reliable Israeli sources.

Preface

This guide to Israel is one of the new generation of Baedeker guides.

These guides, illustrated throughout in colour, are designed to meet the needs of the modern traveller. They are quick and easy to consult, with the principal places of interest described in alphabetical order, and the information is presented in a format that is both attractive and easy to follow.

This guide covers the whole of Israel together with the Israeli-occupied areas of the West Bank of the Jordan, the Gaza Strip and the Golan Heights. Since many visitors to Israel make an excursion to St Catherine's Monastery in Sinai the guide also includes a description of the Sinai peninsula, which is in Egyptian territory.

The guide is in three parts. The first part gives a general account of Israel, its topography, climate, flora and fauna, population, religion, language, government and society, educational system, economy and transport, history, famous people, art and architecture. A selection of literary quotations and a number of suggested itineraries lead in to the second part, in which towns, regions and features of tourist interest are described. The third part contains a variety of practical information. Both the sights and the practical information are listed in alphabetical order.

The new Baedeker guides are noted for their concentration on essentials and their convenience of use. They contain numerous specially drawn plans and colour illustrations; and at the end of the book is a large map making it easy to locate the various places described in the "A to Z" section of the guide with the help of the co-ordinates given at the head of each entry.

How to use this book

Following the tradition established by Karl Baedeker in 1844, sights of particular interest are distinguished by either one ★ or two ★★.

To make it easier to locate the various sights listed in the "A to Z" section of the Guide, their co-ordinates on the large map of Israel are shown in red at the head of each entry.

Only a selection of hotels and restaurants can be given: no reflection is implied, therefore, on establishments not included.

The symbol ⓘ on a town plan indicates the local tourist office from which further information can be obtained. The post-horn symbol indicates a post office.

In a time of rapid change it is difficult to ensure that all the information given is entirely accurate and up to date, and the possibility of error can never be completely eliminated. Although the publishers can accept no responsibility for inaccuracies and omissions, they are always grateful for corrections and suggestions for improvement.

Facts and Figures

The Middle Eastern state of Israel lies in an area which is holy ground for the three great monotheistic religions – Judaism, Christianity and Islam. Judaism and Christianity originated here, and Jerusalem, from which Mohammed is believed to have ascended into heaven, is Islam's most important shrine after Mecca and Medina. The Holy Land is thus of supreme significance to the adherents of these three religions.

Although Israel was never a great power and for many centuries had no independent existence as a state, it lies at a focal point of Middle Eastern history and is richly stocked with remains of a long and eventful past reaching far back into prehistory – to the 8th millennium B.C., when Jericho was one of the world's earliest urban settlements, and even farther back to the remote times when Palaeolithic man began laboriously developing his primitive culture. In this relatively small area a whole succession of peoples have left evidence of their existence – the people of Jericho, the Canaanites, the Israelites of the Old Testament, Greeks, Romans, Byzantines, Arabs, European crusaders, Mamelukes, Turks and finally the Christians from Europe and Russia who in more recent centuries have built their churches and religious houses in many places in this country.

But the country has a present as well as a past. In the few decades since its establishment as an independent state (the movement toward which began in the 19th century) Israel, though surrounded by enemies, has a tremendous constructive achievement to its credit, astonishing in both quantity and quality – testimony to an elemental will to survive and assert itself, fired both by the sufferings of the 19th and even more so of the 20th century and by the ancient religious forces which have enabled the Jewish people to survive the long years of dispersion and persecution.

All this exists within a small country which is a kind of microcosm of wider regions of the globe in which very different climatic zones and landscape types lie side by side: the blossoming countryside of Galilee and the arid Negev, mountains and coastal plains and deserts.

Whether a visitor comes to Israel as a pilgrim, as an art-lover or as one interested in history or in the problems of our own day, he will find much to fascinate him. Even those who come only for a bathing holiday on the Mediterranean or the Red Sea coast cannot but feel something of the special qualities of this country.

General

Situation

The land of Israel (Eretz Yisrael) lies on the eastern coast of the Mediterranean between latitude 29°30′ and 33°20′ north and between longitude 34°20′ and 35°40′ east. It extends for 420km/260 miles from north to south, with a breadth of only between 20km/12½ miles and 116km/72 miles. It is bounded on the north by Lebanon, on the east by Syria and Jordan and on the south and south-west by Egypt. Its southern tip reaches down to the Gulf of Aqaba (Gulf of Elat; Red Sea). The only frontiers recognised by both parties are those with Lebanon and with Egypt.

Territory

The state of Israel, the homeland of the Jewish people, has an area (including East Jerusalem and inland waters) of 20,770sq.km/8020sq.miles, or rather more than half the area of Switzerland. This figure relates to the country's *de jure* frontiers. In addition there are the territories under

◀ *The Sea of Galilee from the Mount of the Beatitudes*

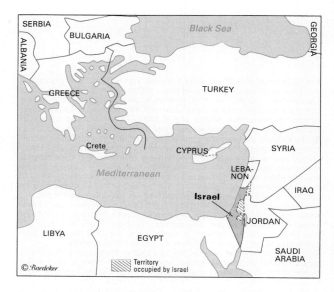

Territory occupied by Israel

Israeli administration since 1967 and partly annexed to Israel – the West Bank of the Jordan (5572sq.km/2151sq.miles), the Golan Heights (1150sq.km/444sq.miles) and the Gaza Strip (202sq.km/78sq.miles). The Sinai peninsula, which was also occupied by Israel in 1967, was returned to Egypt by 1982 under the Egyptian-Israeli peace treaty of 1979.

Capital

In 1950 West Jerusalem was declared capital of Israel in place of Tel Aviv. Most other countries have failed to recognise this decision and have left their embassies in Tel Aviv. (The United Nations had proposed the internationalisation of Jerusalem in 1947.)

During the Six Day War in 1967 Israel occupied the eastern part of Jerusalem, and East Jerusalem was then combined with West Jerusalem by unilateral annexation. Israel declared the reunited Jerusalem capital of Israel.

Topography

General

The landscape of Israel is marked by an alternation between uplands and lowlands. The southern part of the country is occupied by the desert region of the Negev, while the north consists of three different regions – the coastal plain, the western uplands and the Jordan rift valley.

Coastal plain

An extensive coastal plain stretches along the Mediterranean coast of Israel, interrupted only by the cliffs of Rosh Haniqra on the northern frontier and Cape Carmel at Haifa. From Lebanon in the north to the Sinai desert in the south the plain extends for some 270km/170 miles. The Bay of Haifa, with the country's principal port, is the only major indentation in the coastline, which curves gently from north to south-west. The coastal plain, only 16km/10 miles wide on average, broadens out from north to south to

The plain of Sharon, one of the most fertile areas in Israel

some 40km/25 miles. It consists of drifted sands and recent marine sediments, forming a landscape which alternates between gently sloping country covered with sand dunes and sheer cliffs.

The plain, which is traversed by a number of rivers, like the Kishon at Haifa and the Yarqon at Tel Aviv–Jaffa, is made up of a number of different sections. The coastal strip between Rosh Haniqra and Akko is no more than 7km/4½ miles wide. To the south of this is the Zevulun plain. The narrow coastal plain of Carmel to the south of Haifa is a popular holiday area, with many seaside resorts. To the south of this again is the Sharon plain, a 55km/35 mile long stretch of coast bounded by the river Yarqon extending to Tel Aviv–Jaffa. This region, formerly forest-covered and later a swamp which was subsequently drained, is now a fertile area of great importance to the Israeli economy, with many towns and rural settlements, agricultural units and industrial installations. Hadera, Netanya, Kefar Sava and Herzliya are the main urban centres in the region, whose development has been promoted by its excellent communications. To the south of Tel Aviv, along the Gaza Strip, is the Shefela plain, extending for some 90km/55 miles from north to south and 25–30km/15–20 miles from east to west.

Inland from the coastal plain are the western uplands, consisting mainly of limestones and dolomites: in the north the hills of Galilee, reaching a height of 1208m/3963ft in Mount Meron, and to the south the hills of Samaria, rising to 1018m/3340ft, and the Judaean Hills (1020m/3347ft), which extend south towards the Negev desert. The average height of these upland regions is around 850m/2800ft.

Uplands

In geological structure and petrographic composition the Israeli uplands, forming part of the Syrian Shelf, are a continuation of the hills of Lebanon. The hills of Galilee and Samaria are broken up by tectonic fault-lines, the most striking example being the Jezreel plain (Emeq Yizre'el), which cuts

In the Judaean uplands

diagonally across the strike of the hills. This 20km/12½ mile long valley separates the uplands of Galilee from those of Samaria. The Galilean hills in Upper Galilee, with great expanses of basalt, are the highest in the area (Mount Meron); in southern Galilee the land is flatter, reaching a height of only 588m/1929ft in Mount Tabor. The Samarian uplands include Mount Carmel (546m/1791ft) in the north-west and Mount Gilboa (518m/1700ft) in the north-east. The hills of Samaria and Judaea are separated by the rivers Yarqon and Shilo.

The Judaean Hills, Israel's most massive range of hills, are 80km/50 miles long and between 15km/9½ miles and 20km/12½ miles across. Forming the watershed for much of its length, the range is characterised by terraced slopes. At its south end are the hills of Hebron, and to the north of these are the Jerusalem hills, on the crest of which are the Mount of Olives and Mount Scopus. At the north end of the range are the Bet El hills. In these sparsely wooded upland regions there are fewer towns than in the coastal plain; most of the settlements are Arab villages.

Jordan rift valley

To the east the hills fall down to the Jordan rift valley. This begins in the north of the country, to the south of the Mount Hermon range (whose peaks rise to over 2800m/9000ft), with the Hule plain (Emeq Hula). This was once a lake surrounded by marshland, but after the draining of the marshes around the middle of this century the lake also dried up, and the plain is now one of the most intensively cultivated areas in the country.

The rift valley then follows the upper Jordan, and in the Sea of Galilee (Lake Tiberias; Yam Kinneret) lies 210m/690ft below sea level. The lake, over 20km/12½ miles long (area 170sq.km/65sq.miles) and up to 60m/200ft deep, is richly stocked with fish.

From the Sea of Galilee the valley, the southern part of which is known as the Ghor ("hollowed out"), then follows the Jordan to the Dead Sea, the lowest point on earth (surface 396m/1299ft below sea level, bed up to

The river Jordan

A wadi in Negev

829m/2720ft below sea level), continues through the Wadi Arava depression and reaches the Red Sea at Elat.

The Jordan rift valley is part of the Syro-African rift system, filled up by sediments of the Quaternary era.

The Jordan (Yarden), Israel's and the kingdom of Jordan's longest and most abundant river, is formed by three source streams, the Banyas, the Dan and the Hazbani, in the northern Hule plain and flows into the Dead Sea. It has a number of tributaries, the largest of which is the Yarmouk, coming in on the east below the Sea of Galilee. The Jordan valley is 252km/157 miles long, but the river's winding course has a total length of 330km/205 miles. Its flow varies with the time of year, and its meandering course makes it unsuitable for navigation. At present it forms the frontier between Israel and Jordan, which continues through the Dead Sea.

Beyond the Jordan depression the land rises in Jordan to heights of up to 1736m/5696ft in the eastern Jordanian hills, with the Biblical regions of Gilead and Ammon to the north, Moab in the centre and Edom to the south.

The desertic southern part of Israel, the Negev, extends in a wedge running south from Beersheba to the Red Sea, with a narrow spur reaching west to the Mediterranean. The northern part, consisting of Cretaceous sediments with a covering of loess, has an annual rainfall of only 200mm/8in., but artificial irrigation has made it possible to bring large areas into cultivation. To the south is an upland region traversed by folded rocks of the Upper Cretaceous, reaching a height of 1035m/3396ft in Mount Ramon. Erosion has formed numbers of corries or craters (*makhtesh*) in the rock. The southernmost part of the Negev, a rugged upland region of ancient rocks, is a continuation of the mountains of Sinai. In this area there are occasional outcrops of Nubian sandstone, often eroded into bizarre mushroom-shaped or columnar forms. Here too there are expanses of *serir* (sandy desert) and *hamada* (stony desert). In the east the Negev falls down to the Arava depression and the Jordan rift valley.

Negev

Climate

Judaean Desert

Between the hills of Samaria in the west and the Dead Sea and Jordan valley to the east extends the Judaean Desert, whose aridity results from its situation on the lee side of the hills – though it has a higher rainfall than the Negev. It is a region of canyons and valleys, with only a sparse growth of vegetation. On its east side are the famous site of Masada and the Qumran caves.

Dead Sea

The Dead Sea (Yam Hamelach), an inland sea without an outlet, extends from the inflow of the Jordan in the north to the Wadi Arava in the south for a distance of 78km/48 miles, with a maximum breadth of 18km/11 miles, giving it a total area of 980sq.km/378sq.miles. On the west it is bordered by the Judaean Hills, on the east by the hills of eastern Jordan. The Lashon (Arabic Lisan) peninsula (the "Tongue") divides it into a deep northern part (up to 400m/1300ft deep) and a shallow southern part (4–6m/13–20ft deep). As a result of high evaporation the water has a salt content of up to 25%, and it yields minerals like potassium and bromine salts. Round its shores are various hot springs (sulphurous and radioactive), and as a result Newe Zohar and En Boqeq on the south-east side of the Dead Sea have developed into health resorts.

Climate

General

Israel lies in a zone of transition between Mediterranean and desertic climate, and its climate is also influenced by its southerly situation (latitude 29°30' to 33°20' north) and sharp differences in altitude. The movement of air is markedly influenced by the trade winds and the antitrades overlying them.

Climatic zones

The Mediterranean climate is characterised by dry, hot summers, while thanks to the moderating influence of the heat stored in the sea the winters are mild and relatively humid. This seasonal pattern results from the fact that the weather is determined in summer by the subtropical zone of high pressure and drought, in winter by the extra-tropical west-wind zone of the temperate latitudes. Winter lasts from November to April, summer from May to October. During the winter there may be falls of snow in the mountains. In summer the desert wind known as the *sharav* (Arabic *khamsin*) brings heat waves with temperatures of up to 50°C/122°F. The farther south a place is, the more dominant and long-lasting is the influence of the subtropical high-pressure zone, with correspondingly lower rainfall and higher temperatures. To the south of a steppe-like area of transition extending from the Gaza Strip and tapering eastward towards the Dead Sea a hot desert climate, with wide fluctuations in temperature over the day, prevails, reaching its most extreme form in the Jordan rift valley and the Negev.

Apart from this change of climate from north to south there is also a variation from west to east. On the coast the moderating influence of the Mediterranean is predominant; inland, towards the east, the fluctuations in temperature become greater. On the western slopes of the hills rainfall increases, while the eastern slopes are markedly arid.

Uplands

In the upland regions temperatures are below the national average, and climatic variations are less affected by the moderating influence of the sea. As a result of the phenomenon of temperature inversion found in many mountain regions it is sometimes warmer on the hills than in the valleys. The winter rains begin later than in the coastal areas and reach a maximum in January and February.

Coastal plain

In general the coastal plain is warmer. Frost is rare, but the *sharav* (*khamsin*) also blows less frequently. Nevertheless it can become very hot in towns with high-rise buildings which hinder the free movement of air,

Climatic Zones in Israel

Nahariya
Akko
Haifa
Tiberias
Sea of Galilee
Nazareth
Netanya
Nablus
Tel Aviv–Yafo
Jericho
JERUSALEM
Ashdod
Ashqelon
Gaza
Hebron
En Gedi
Dead Sea
Beersheba
Elat

© Baedeker

Mediterranean climate
Steppe climate
Desert climate
Extreme desert climate

Climate

particularly since the buildings store up heat during the day and release it after the sun goes down. The highest winter rainfall is in December and January, which account for some two-thirds of total annual rainfall.

Jordan rift valley

The continental climate is even more marked in the Jordan rift valley than in the upland regions. The Hule plain, on the lee side of the hills, is sheltered from wind and rain. The summer is hot, but in winter cold winds blow down from Mount Hermon. Here too temperature inversion brings night frosts at low levels, so that tropical plants cannot survive but temperate crops like apples thrive.

Sea of Galilee

The area round the Sea of Galilee has a variant micro-climate, since the water stores heat during the summer, leading to winter temperatures of around 14°C/57°F. As a result crops which require warmth, like dates and bananas, flourish here. Rainfall is low, and decreases still further in the lower Jordan valley.

Dead Sea

The Dead Sea and surrounding area also have a particular climate of their own, mainly because the capacity of the water to store heat is unusually high as a result of its high concentration of salt. This is particularly noticeable round the deeper northern part of the sea, where temperatures fluctuate less markedly over the year than round the shallower southern part, which was cut off by salt deposits in the dry summer of 1979.

Negev

The Negev, the desert region in southern Israel, is divided into a semi-arid zone round Beersheba and a larger arid zone. Here summer temperatures rise to 30°C/86°F; at Elat they can be over 45°C/113°F. The climate is markedly continental, with temperature fluctuations of up to 16°C/29°F over the day in summer. Rainfall is very low (an annual 200–300mm/8–12in. at Beersheba, 50mm/2in. in the Arava plain).

Rivers

As a result of the long dry summers and the high rate of evaporation caused by the heat most of Israel's rivers flow only for part of the year and are known as wadis. The Jordan has a constant flow of water from its source streams on Mount Hermon.

Day and night

For visitors planning their day – particularly for photographers – it is often important to know how many hours of daylight there are at a particular time of year. Sunrise ranges between 5am (local time) in June and 7am in December, sunset between 7pm in June and 5pm in December. The period of twilight lasts barely half an hour.

Climatic diagrams

The climatic characteristics of different parts of Israel are reflected in the diagrams of temperature and rainfall on page 17. The blue columns show annual rainfall in millimetres month by month in accordance with the blue scale on the right. The temperatures are shown in the red band, the upper edge of which shows average maximum day temperatures and the lower edge average minimum night temperatures in accordance with the red scale on the right.

The figures for the three selected weather stations apply also to the surroundings of the stations. For other parts of the country rainfall and temperature figures are likely to lie between those for the two nearest weather stations – though it must be borne in mind that differences in altitude may produce considerable differences of climate over a relatively short distance.

Central uplands Jerusalem weather station

Jerusalem lies at an altitude of 750m/2460ft in a hollow in the central upland region, which reaches heights of just over 1000m/3280ft to the north and south of the town. The diagram clearly shows the sharp distinction between the cool, humid winter and the hot, dry summer. Most of the rain falls between November and March, during which period there are normally between seven and eleven days with rain per month. Between

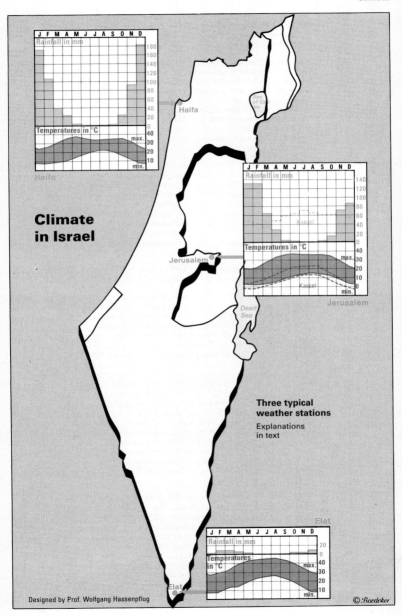

**Climate
in Israel**

**Three typical
weather stations**

Explanations
in text

Designed by Prof. Wolfgang Hassenpflug

© Baedeker

Climate

June and September there is less than one day with rain per month; in the intermediate seasons there are three days per month. Even on rainy days it is unlikely to rain all day: a day with even a brief shower (producing over 1mm of rain) counts as a day with rain.

Because of the town's altitude temperatures are considerably lower than in the coastal plain. Fluctuations in temperature over the day and over the year are greater, since the moderating influence of the sea is less strongly felt here. Even so the range of temperature over the day is two or three times as great as in Central Europe, and visitors from more northern latitudes should take account of this in deciding what to wear. In winter temperatures at night are only barely above freezing point, while at midday it can be almost as warm as in a Central European summer. In winter masses of cold air travelling from southern Russia may even bring frost and snow.

Coastal plain Haifa weather station

The Haifa weather station shows the climatic characteristics of the central coastal region; farther south rainfall decreases. These characteristics are typical of the Mediterranean climate with its mild, humid winters and hot, dry summers. Fluctuations in temperature are less than in the interior, while – as a result of the barrier effect of the Mount Carmel range, which has the highest rainfall in Israel – rainfall is higher than at Jerusalem. The relative humidity of the air lies between 60 and 70% throughout the year, compared with 40–50% at Jerusalem in summer. Inflows of cold air in winter may bring brief frosts, but average minimum temperatures are well above freezing point.

In winter sea temperatures fall to 16°C/61°F; in summer they reach 28°C/82°F. In summer there are frequent cooling northerly winds.

Desert Elat weather station

The climatic diagram for Elat, which lies at the southernmost tip of Israel, reflects the hot, subtropical desert climate typical of extensive areas in the south of the country (the Negev, the Jordan rift valley), with high temperatures, wide fluctuations in temperature and minimal rainfall.
The annual rainfall of around 25–40mm/1–1½in. is concentrated in a few heavy showers during the winter months. Most of the time the sky is cloudless, and days without sunshine are very rare. "Winter" temperatures between November and May, with cool nights and warm days, are very agreeable. Even the absolute minimum night temperatures are well above freezing point. During the rest of the year it is extremely hot, with absolute maxima exceeding 45°C/113°F. In contrast to the more southerly coasts of the Red Sea the relative humidity of the air at Elat is low (20% during the day in summer and 40% during the night, 45% during the day in winter and 60% during the night). The reason for this is the wind which constantly blows from the north through the Jordan rift valley. Without this wind life in this area in summer would be much less agreeable: the wind reduces the humidity of the air, making the heat more tolerable, and calms the sea, creating excellent conditions for water sports. When the wind turns, as it does for some days in May and June, the air becomes intolerably close and the swell at sea increases.

The southern part of the Jordan rift valley, extending to north of the Dead Sea, also has a hot, desertic climate. This is particularly true of the Dead Sea itself. As a result of its low altitude (396m/1299ft below sea level) and its situation in the lee of the mountains it has much reduced rainfall and much higher temperatures. The annual rainfall of 50–100mm/2–4in., concentrated in the winter months, is of little importance because of the high temperatures. In summer maximum temperatures exceed 40°C/104°F; even in winter minimum temperatures rarely fall below 12°C/53°F, while midday temperatures are around 20°C/68°F. So anyone wishing to avoid a rainy winter day in Jerusalem or elsewhere in the upland regions need only go down to the Dead Sea to exchange the rain for the sun, the cold for warmth.

Flora and Fauna

Flora

The composition of the flora of Israel is influenced by two factors: first the country's situation at the meeting-place of three continents (Europe, Asia and Africa) and secondly the Mediterranean climate and the fact that the boundary of the arid climatic zone passes through the southern and eastern parts of the country, making it necessary for vegetation to adapt to long periods of drought and low humidity.

General

In order to survive in semi-arid and arid climates plants have developed various methods of reducing water loss and evolved efficient means of taking in water. Thus in some plants (succulents) surface evaporation is inhibited by a fine layer of wax on the leaves, while others have an elaborately ramified root system, enabling them to take in moisture from lower levels within the soil. Some species, like the Persian cyclamen (*Cyclamen persicum*) and the crown anemone (*Anemone coronaria*), store water in bulbs or corms for the dry summer and after the end of the dry period develop rapidly and bloom during the rainy winter. Others, like the sea squill (*Urginea maritima*), produce long, broad leaves in spring but blossom only in autumn.

Adaptation to climatic conditions

Most plants adapt their life cycle to the rainy period, when no protection is needed against excessive loss of moisture. The drier the climate, the shorter the blossoming time. In the Negev and the Judaean Desert the seeds of some plants often lie in the soil for years, waiting for a rainy winter; then, all at once, they shoot up, bloom and within a few weeks produce fresh seed. Particularly unusual are the halophytes (salt-loving plants), whose sap is enriched with salt. Plants of this type are found in the Arava valley, the Dead Sea area and the lower Jordan valley.

Two thousand years ago much of the country was forest-covered which was then cleared to provide land for agriculture, and as a result the upper layers of soil, no longer held together by the roots of the trees, were washed away, leaving the bare rock exposed. These areas reverted to wasteland, and with further erosion and grazing by goats the old forest areas gave place to thorny scrub, macchia and garrigue.

Steppe formation; reafforestation

When the Zionist movement brought new settlers to Israel in the early 20th century they soon realised that it was necessary to increase the stock of trees by reafforestation. Eucalyptus trees were planted, and it was quickly discovered that these fast-growing trees could flourish in arid regions. The commonest species grown in Israel is *Eucalyptus rostrata*. *Eucalyptus gomphocephala* also grows in upland regions.

After the First World War reafforestation was pursued on an increasing scale, particularly on rocky hillsides where the soil was too exhausted to grow fruit trees or cereals. In the areas planted with conifers pines (particularly Aleppo pines) predominate, since they do not need good soil and require little moisture. Other trees planted include acacias, robinias and poplars.

Round sand dunes and fields much exposed to wind and erosion eucalyptuses and tamarisks are grown to prevent the soil from being blown away or otherwise destroyed.

Four large vegetation zones can be distinguished in Israel: the Mediterranean zone, the Irano-Turanian zone, the Saharo-Sindinian zone and the Sudano-Deccanian zone (see map, page 22).

Vegetation zones

The Mediterranean zone comprises those areas which have an annual rainfall of 350mm/14in. or more, including large expanses in the coastal plain and the upland regions.

Mediterranean zone

The characteristic plant of the central and northern parts of the coastal plain and the south-west of Lower Galilee is the Tabor oak (*Quercus ithabu-*

Wherever there is enough water . . .

rensis), a tall tree with a wide crown. The oak forests have been almost completely destroyed, often giving place to scrub vegetation. There are, however, large numbers of evergreen, narrow-leaved and long-leaved shrubs, tulips, anemones and annual grasses, oleanders and myrtles, pines, olives and the mulberry fig or Pharaoh's fig (*Ficus sycomorus*).

In upland regions over 300m/1000ft, where there has been much refforestation, there are Aleppo pines (*Pinus halepensis*), gall-oaks, the evergreen kermes oak, laurels, terebinths, cypresses, strawberry trees (*Arbutus andrachne*), Judas trees (*Cercis siliquastrum*) and carob-trees (*Ceratonia siliqua*). There are also expanses of garrigue in which the cistus predominates.

Irano-Turanian zone

The Irano-Turanian zone is confined to the region round Beersheba, where the average annual rainfall ranges between 150mm/6in. and 300mm/12in. and the upper layers of soil consist predominantly of loess or chalk. The vegetation consists of low-growing bushes and dwarf shrubs, including particularly wormwood. To the east this zone extends into the Judaean Desert and the Jordan valley.

Saharo-Sindinian zone

The Saharo-Sindinian zone lies in southern Israel, taking in most of the Negev, the Judaean Desert, the Arava depression and the area round the Dead Sea. These regions, where the annual rainfall lies between 50mm/2in. and 150mm/6in., have true desert vegetation, consisting predominantly of bushes with small thick leaves or thorns. Frequently there is on average no more than one plant per square metre. The areas of stony desert (*hamada*) are mostly without any vegetation at all. Thorny shrubs grow in the wadis, where plants can sometimes draw water from the soil. Acacias – a plant native to the African savannas – can also occasionally be encountered in the desert.

A narrow strip of the Saharo-Sindinian zone extends along the Mediterranean coast in the form of sand dunes. Since water rapidly runs away into

. . . Israel is a green and flowering land

the sand, the conditions for plant life in this area are very similar to those of the extreme desertic climate. Here are found plants which also occur in the Negev, like wormwood and broom. Other plants, like the sea daffodil (*Pancratium maritimum*), grow only in the dunes on the Mediterranean coast.

The Sudano-Deccanian zone is restricted to oases with tropical and sub-tropical vegetation in the eastern desert areas, for example at En Gedi on the Dead Sea and at Jericho. Here are found more than 40 species of plants requiring both high temperatures and plenty of water. The best known of these plants is Christ's thorn (*Paliurus spina Christi*), of which the crown of thorns is said to have been composed.

Sudano-Deccanian zone

Tropical and subtropical plants are also found in marshy areas and in shallow lakes. Before the draining of the Hule plain, which was completed in 1958, most plants of this kind grew in the Hule valley. Nowadays they are to be found only in the Hule Nature Reserve and along the canals which traverse the plain. Notable among them is the papyrus plant (*Cyperus papyrus*), which now grows only in Egypt and Israel and at Syracuse in Sicily.

Fauna

Israel's coastal waters and its various regions support a wide range of fauna (reptiles, fish, birds, mammals, etc.). As in other parts of the world, however, many species have died out in the course of the centuries, as a result either of a sudden change in climate or of changes in their habitat by the action of man. Thus many creatures mentioned in the Bible are no longer to be found in this area – lions, tigers, bears, antelopes, ostriches, crocodiles.

General

A variety of fish and other marine fauna live in the coastal waters of the Mediterranean and in the Red Sea, but because of its high salt content (up

Marine fauna

21

Vegetation zones in Israel

Nahariya
Akko
Haifa
Sea of Galilee
Nazareth
Netanya
Nablus
Tel Aviv – Yafo
Jericho
JERUSALEM
Ashdod
Ashqelon
Hebron
Dead Sea
Beersheba
Elat

© Baedeker

Mediterranean zone
Irano-Turanian zone
Saharo-Sindinian zone
Dune vegetation
Sudano-Deccanian enclaves

to 4%) the Mediterranean is unsuitable for many species found in the open sea. In the immediate vicinity of the coast, however, the salt content is only around 3.1%, thanks to a current from the south-west which carries water here from the Nile. The water temperature ranges between 16°C/61°F and 29°C/84°F. Off the Mediterranean coasts there are sponges, sea anemones, bristle-worms, shrimps, crabs, starfish and sea-urchins. At greater depths there are leather, horn and stone corals, lobsters, crayfish and moray eels, as well as numerous species of shellfish, often buried in the sea-bed. In open waters, sometimes directly off the coast, are cuttlefish, rays, hake, bass and bream. Weever fish bury themselves in the sand in the shallows; the spines supporting their fins contain poison-glands and can inflict a dangerous wound. Farther out to sea there are tunny and the larger species of sharks, which may come closer to land in the wake of ships. Turtles, dolphins and toothed whales are also occasionally found.

With its rich marine fauna the Red Sea is a happy hunting ground for scuba divers. Off the coast are coral reefs which are the haunt of brilliantly coloured fish belonging to the Chaetodontidae (butterfly fish), Acanthuridae (surgeon fish) and Ostraciontidae (cow fish) families. In addition to numerous sharks there are also sawfish (a type of ray).

The largest expanse of fresh water in Israel is the Sea of Galilee, in which there are carp, catfish and various perch-like fish, including St Peter's fish, a cichlid (mouthbreeder). **Freshwater fish**

With its high temperatures and intense sunlight, Israel has large numbers of reptiles. There are seven species of tortoises, four of which live in water and three on land. The gecko, a kind of lizard, is common, and often makes its way into houses. The chameleon, which can change its colour to match its surroundings, is a slow mover but can catch insects by suddenly shooting out its long tongue. Among the commonest non-poisonous snakes are the sand boa and the black snake, which grows to a length of over 2 metres (6½ft). The most dangerous of the poisonous snakes is the Palestinian viper (*Vipera palaestinensis*). **Reptiles**

Israel has more than 300 species of birds. Some of them live here throughout the year, others only in summer. Some species like the hawk and the vulture have withdrawn from the regions inhabited by man to more remote parts of the country, while others, like the blackbird, have made their homes in the newly planted gardens and woodland or, like the swallow and the crested lark, on arable land. On the Mediterranean coast there are gulls and other waterfowl. Of the few species of birds which live in the desert the best known are the fantailed raven (*Corvus rhipidurus*) and the common courser (*Cursorius cursor*), which is found on sandy soil. Bare rocks are the preferred habitat of the trumpeter finch (*Rhodopechys githaginea*), whose colouring merges so well into the desert floor that its presence can often be detected only by its call. Some species are confined to small areas, like the Dead Sea sparrow (*Passer moabiticus*) and the mourning wheatear (*Oenanthe lugens*). **Birds**

In spring the flight path of the birds is generally from the south to the north of the country, in autumn in the reverse direction. Most of the larger birds fly by day, the smaller ones at night. An interesting phenomenon – which is referred to in the Bible – is the autumn arrival of enormous flocks of quail on the coasts of the Negev and the Sinai peninsula. The birds fall exhausted to the ground, and are then caught in their thousands by the local Bedouin and fellahin.

Israel has some 60 species of mammals – a large number for a relatively small country. Formerly there were many more. Most of Israel's mammals are to be found in other parts of the world, but there are also a number of indigenous species, like the lesser Egyptian jerboa (*Jaculus jaculus*) and various gazelles. The animals living in Israel have largely adapted to the conditions of an arid or semi-arid climate. Most of the mammals are **Mammals**

The people of Israel: of different origins and different faiths

nocturnal, and since they rest during the day require only a minimum of water. There are also species which require plenty of water and live in swamp areas or round lakes; an example is the wild pig (*Sus scrofa*), which often causes considerable damage in orchards, fields and vegetable plots in the Hule plain and round the Sea of Galilee.

With the steady growth of settlement in Israel the number of mammals living in the wild is declining. As a result the howling of the jackal, which is a common sound at night in most country areas, is no longer heard round the towns.

Among the large felines which once inhabited the area were leopards. While at the end of the 19th century numbers of leopards could still be seen, by 1948, when the state of Israel was founded, only a few isolated specimens remained. In 1964 the Knesset passed an act on the protection of nature, to which a clause for the protection of wild animals was added. Thereupon a zoologist scoured the country with the object of making an inventory of beasts of prey. Finding what looked like the tracks of a leopard in the Judaean Desert, he staked out an animal as bait one night and in the morning found that it had been eaten. Eventually he managed to get a photograph of a leopardess with her young. Recent observation indicates that there are some twenty adult leopards with their young in an area of 1000sq.km/385sq.miles to the west of the Dead Sea. They live mainly by hunting hares, and because of the intense heat in the Judaean Desert go out in quest of prey at night.

Population

After the destruction of the Temple by the Romans in A.D. 70 and their repression of the Bar Kochba rising in the 2nd century the Jewish population of what was then Palestine fell at an increasing rate. By the beginning of the 19th century the total population was no more than 250,000 of all ethnic groups.

Development of population

The Jews living in the Diaspora formed minorities, often persecuted, in the countries in which they had settled. After 1870 Jews began to return and settle in deserted areas of Palestine, away from the towns. Between 1882 and the foundation of the state of Israel in 1948 there were several waves of immigrants (Aliyah) which led to a sharp increase in the proportion of Jews in the population. In 1948 the total population of Israel was 878,000; thereafter it rose rapidly to 1,174,000 in 1949, 2,032,000 in 1958, 3,780,000 in 1979 and 4,375,000 in 1987. This figure included 3,590,000 Jews and 785,000 non-Jews (excluding the occupied territories); the non-Jews were predominantly Arabs, together with other small groups (Druze, etc.).

Between 1972 and 1985 the annual rate of population growth was 2.3%, only about a third of which was due to natural growth. In subsequent years immigrants continued to come to Israel in large numbers. As a result of the political changes in the former Soviet Union and the fact that the prospects of immigration to the United States are now restricted there are expected to be large numbers of immigrants from now until the end of the century. By 1993 more than 250,000 Jews from the former Soviet Union arrived in Israel; many of them are now encountering serious social problems in their "Promised Land".

The majority of Israel's Jews have now been born in the country; they are known as Sabras. At the end of 1986 there were some 1.37 million Jews living in Israel (31.7% of the total population) who had not been born there. The largest group (49.2%) came from European countries, more than a quarter of them from the former Soviet Union. Other immigrants came from Africa (mainly Morocco), Asia (particularly Iran, Iraq, Yemen and Turkey), America and Oceania.

Population structure

Israel also has a small ethnic minority in the Circassians, who emigrated from Russia around 1880 and settled in the eastern territories of the Ottoman Empire, in Amman and Jerash (now in Jordan) and in the Galilean villages of Kefar Kama and Rihaniye (Israel), In which some 1200 members of this population group still live.

Among Jews a distinction is made between the Ashkenazim and the Sephardim. The Ashkenazim are Jews from Central and Eastern Europe and their descendants. They have their own traditions and spoke (and to some extent still speak) Yiddish, a language based on an older form of German. The Sephardim are, properly speaking, the descendants of the Jews who were expelled from Spain and Portugal and during the 15th and 16th centuries settled in various European countries, North Africa and the Near East; nowadays the term is applied, improperly, to all Oriental Jews. Factors promoting the integration of people from so many different cultural backgrounds have been the introduction of modern Hebrew (Ivrit) as the national language, the schools, military service and the establishment of settlements inhabited by Jews from many different countries. Nevertheless differences between Jews of western and eastern origin can still be detected in many fields of life. While the leaders of the country tend to be Ashkenazim, the Sephardim form the majority of the population, and they are now demanding a greater share in directing the country's political and economic life. Some also view with mistrust the massive influx of Russian Jews, which they fear may threaten their numerical superiority.

The main problem of the Jewish state, however, is still the Israeli-Arab conflict. In addition to the 800,000 Arabs living in Israel there are another 1.5 million Palestinians on the West Bank and in the Gaza Strip. While these Arabs largely cooperated with the occupying forces until the end of 1987, their desire for independence has found vigorous expression since the outbreak of the *intifada* (see History, 1987).

A minority within the Arab population is formed by the Bedouin, some 70,000 of whom live in Israel. Many of them still lead a nomadic existence, living in tents (illustration, page 27), while others have settled in villages which are little different from other Arab settlements.

Expectation of life

The life expectancy of Israelis rose between 1965 and 1985 from 71 years for men and 74 for women to 73 and 77 years respectively.

Age structure

At the end of 1986 children under 15 accounted for 32.4% of the total population, a slight fall from the 1972 figure of 32.7%. Between 1972 and 1986 the proportion of older people (over 65) in the population rose from 7.1% to 8.8%.

Types of Settlement

General

The population of Israel is concentrated mainly in the towns: some 87% of the country's inhabitants live in towns and urban settlements, 50% of them in Jerusalem, Tel Aviv-Jaffa and Haifa. There are 28 Jewish towns, two Arab towns and six mixed Jewish and Arab. Population density ranges between 5800 inhabitants to the sq. kilometre (15,022 to the sq. mile) in Tel Aviv and less than 30 to the sq. kilometre (78 to the sq. mile) in the Negev. In planning settlements for new immigrants, therefore, the desire to achieve a more even distribution of the population has been an important factor.

In addition to the town (*ir*, plural *arim*) and the village of traditional type (*moshava*, plural *moshavot*) there are three characteristic types of village settlement which have been developed since the turn of the century and now accommodate some 8% of the Jewish population of Israel.

Kibbutz

The *kibbutz* (plural *kibbutzim*) is a village which is communally owned and run by all the inhabitants. The members of the kibbutz (kibbutzniks) contribute their labour and receive in return board, lodging and pocket money. The kibbutz also looks after the education of the children.

The first kibbutz, Deganya (at the south end of the Sea of Galilee), was established in 1909. Many kibbutzim are now occupied by the second and third generations of inhabitants, in some cases by the fourth generation.

The number of inhabitants ranges between 60 and 2000, with the average lying around 200 to 400. There are now some 230 kibbutzim in Israel; but whereas in 1948 the kibbutzniks accounted for 7.6% of the total population the proportion has now fallen to 2.8%. The kibbutzim are run on democratic lines: there is a weekly meeting of all members at which important decisions are taken, and the various economic activities of the kibbutz are directed by committees.

The kibbutz movement played a leading role during the building up and establishment of the state of Israel. For most Jews the return home to Israel from the Diaspora meant more than the restoration of national independence: they wanted to form a society which was closely bound to the soil of

A Bedouin encampment in the desert

the country. Many leading figures in public life, therefore, have been and are members of kibbutzim.

Many kibbutzim are now confronting the problem of industrialisation. In order to maintain their position in commercial terms many settlements have supplemented their agricultural activities by establishing processing industries and running kibbutz hotels.

Moshav

The *moshav* (plural *moshavim*) is organised on a cooperative basis. Each family runs its own household, with ownership of house and garden, and works its own land. Machinery and large items of equipment, however, are acquired collectively, and the products are marketed by the cooperative. The first moshav was established at Nahalal in the Jezreel valley in 1921. The average moshav has a population between 100 and 1000. There are now 350 moshavim, accounting for 4% of the total population.

Moshav-shitufi

The *moshav-shitufi*, like the kibbutz, is based on collective ownership and cultivation of the land, but each family runs its own household. Work and pay are geared to individual requirements. The first settlement of this kind was established in 1936 at Kefar Hittim. There are now 45 settlements of this type in Israel, with a total of 7000 inhabitants.

Many countries in Asia, Africa and Latin America have sent students to Israel to learn about the cooperative way of life and have invited Israeli advisers to help them in setting up similar organisations.

Religion

General

The state of Israel guarantees the free practice of religion to members of all faiths. In this relatively small country Jews, Muslims, Druze, Christians and adherents of other beliefs live side by side.

Jews

The Jews, with 85.2% of the population, are by far the largest religious group in Israel. The supreme Jewish religious authority is the Chief Rabbinate, which consists of the Chief Rabbis of the Ashkenazi and Sephardi communities together with the Supreme Rabbinical Council. The Chief Rabbinate has authority in questions of Jewish law and the prescriptions on ritual purity, and the rabbinical courts are subject to its jurisdiction. Israel has both secular and religious courts. The Supreme Court, the country's highest judicial authority, sits in Jerusalem. The marriage and divorce of Jews resident in the state of Israel falls within the competence of the rabbinical courts, and there are similar provisions applying to the courts of other religious communities.

The sacred books of the Jews are the Torah (the five books of Moses, the Pentateuch) and other books of holy scripture, the Talmud, which consists of two collections of texts, the Mishnah and the Gemara are commentaries. The weekly day of rest is the Sabbath, which extends from Friday evening to Saturday evening. The most important place of prayer is the Western (Wailing) Wall, the Herodian boundary wall of the Temple precinct in Jerusalem, to which the Jews have had access again since 1967.

Since the time when the Temple was still standing the Jewish people has traditionally been divided into three groups: a distinction which is mainly of importance in religious life. The Cohanim (singular Cohen), who trace their descent from the sons of Aaron, have certain privileges in the synagogue, but also have to perform certain duties in the service of the Temple. The Levites (singular Levi), who are descended from Levi, the son of Jacob and Leah, occupy a lower level in the religious hierarchy, with auxiliary functions in the service of the Temple. Israel, the ordinary people, have no part in the service of the Temple. Many family names – Cohen (Kahn), etc. – are inherited, others such as Levi are derived from ancient tribal designations.

In questions of religious belief, too, the Jews are by no means homogeneous. The Chief Rabbinate represents the orthodox school of Judaism, to

The Western Wall: the holiest Jewish place of prayer

which something like a sixth of the population belong. They are distinguished from other Israelis by the *kipa,* the embroidered cap worn by men. Many live in districts in towns in which the rules of Judaism are strictly observed; but most orthodox Jews live in the same way as secular Jews. Very different are the ultra-orthodox Jews, readily distinguishable by their black clothing, side curls (*peiyot*) and felt-trimmed hats (*streimel*). Some speak mainly Yiddish, since they regard Hebrew as a sacred language, to be used only for religious purposes. This does not prevent them from taking an active part in political life. Considering their small numbers they have considerable influence in political decisions and in the formation of governments: frequently they hold the balance of power. The way of life of this extreme religious group differs sharply from that of other Jews. In general they avoid the use of modern technology; television and newspapers are frowned on; their (numerous) children attend private religious schools, where they receive only a minimum of secular education; they do not do military service; and their whole life is governed by their religious principles.

In addition to these groups there are conservative Jews and liberal or Reform Jews, as well as non-religious and anti-religious Jewish groups.

The Karaites (Karaim), a sect founded in Persia in the 8th century A.D. by Anan Ben David, recognise only the Law of Moses and reject the rabbinical tradition. The sect now has some 11,000 adherents, half of them in Israel, with 3000 living in and around Ramla alone. | Karaites

The Samaritans, a small group whose sacred place is Mount Gerizim near Nablus (Shekhem, Biblical Shechem), broke away from the rest of Jewry after the Babylonian captivity. Their sacred writings are the five books of Moses and the book of Joshua. | Samaritans

Most of the Arabs living in Israel are Muslims, predominantly Sunnites. Their principal holy places in Israel are the Dome of the Rock and the | Muslims

El-Aqsa Mosque in Jerusalem, which is the most important Islamic shrine after Mecca and Medina. The Haram El-Khalil in Hebron is another important Islamic holy site.

The canonical book of the Muslims is the Koran (the "Reading" or "Recitation"), which consists of 114 suras or chapters and is venerated as God's revelation to the Prophet Mohammed (571–632). It is supplemented by two collections of texts, the Hadith ("Tradition") and the Sunna ("Custom"). Islam (which means "submission to the will of God") acknowledges the holy books of Judaism and Christianity as preliminary stages of the final revelation, and also recognises the prophets of the two other great monotheistic religions, Christ being considered as the greatest prophet after Mohammed.

The five duties imposed on the believer by Islam are to believe in Allah as the one God, to pray five times daily, to give alms, to observe the fast of Ramadan and to make the pilgrimage to Mecca. The weekly holy day is Friday.

The leaders of the Muslims in Israel are the Kadis (judges of the religious courts).

Druze

The Druze, who live in Syria and parts of Israel, split off from Islam in the reign of Caliph El-Hakim (996–1021); they take their name from Imam Ismail el-Darazi (b. 1019). Their secret doctrine is described as Gnostic mysticism; their basic dogma is the oneness of God, who reveals himself in human incarnations, most recently in the person of El-Hakim. They are divided into the "ignorant" members of the sect (*juhhal*), who form the majority, and the "intelligent" (*uqqal*), who are initiated into the doctrine and lead the services held in their house of worship, the *khilwah,* on Thursdays. The Druze are not considered in Israel to be Arabs.

Christians

The Christians in Israel belong to many different communities, some of which have been established here since early Christian or Byzantine times. From these other creeds later split off (mostly in 451, following the condemnation of Monophysitism as a heresy at the 4th Oecumenical Council, held in Chalcedon). In addition there are the Roman Catholics, the Uniat churches (Orthodox but in communion with Rome) and the Protestants, who have been represented in Israel only since the 19th century.

The Greek Orthodox church has had a Patriarchate in Jerusalem since 451; it has some 80,000 members. Greek Catholics are Orthodox but have been united with Rome since 1709; they observe the Greek rite but recognise the Pope as head of the church (Melchites).

The Copts (Egyptian Christians) have had their own church since 451. The Coptic Catholic church (not represented in Jerusalem) has been united with Rome since 1741.

The Syrian Orthodox church (Jacobites), whose liturgy is conducted in Old Syriac, has also existed since 451. The Patriarch resides in Damascus. The Syrian Catholic church (Patriarch of Antioch, with seat in Beirut) has existed since 1662.

The Armenian Orthodox church, the national church of the Armenians, also dates from 451. The Armenian Catholic church has existed since 1740.

The Roman Catholic (Latin) church has a Patriarchate in Jerusalem. The holy places belonging to the church are maintained by Franciscan friars.

The Abyssinians are also represented in Jerusalem. They belong to the monophysite Church of Ethiopia, which is headed by the Abuna of Gondar (for the secular clergy) and the Etchagué (for the monastic clergy). Until the end of the monarchy the Etchagué was also the Emperor's confessor.

The Protestant churches, including the Anglicans, have been represented in Jerusalem since the 19th century. From 1841 to 1881 there was an Anglo-German bishopric, but since then the Anglicans have had their own hierarchy. For German and Arab Lutherans there is a provostry, established in 1898 for the consecration of the Church of the Redeemer. It now belongs to the Evangelical Lutheran church in Jordan, established in 1959, which in 1979 received its first Arab bishop.

The Bahai, adherents of a faith which originated in Persia, live mainly in Haifa, their spiritual headquarters.

The Ahmadiya, members of a movement stemming from India, live in the village of Kababir on Mount Carmel.

Pilgrimage to the Holy Land

The greatest Father of the Latin church, St Augustine (354–430), rejected pilgrimages to the places of origin of Christianity as having no relevance to a believer's faith. His contemporary St Jerome (347–420), however, considered that prayer at a place where Christ had been was an effective act of faith; and it was the view of this doctor of the church from Dalmatia, who founded a monastery in Bethlehem and there translated the Bible into Latin, which prevailed.

As early as the 3rd century devout Christians began to go to Bethlehem and Jerusalem to pray at the scenes of Christ's Nativity, Passion and Resurrection. After Constantine the Great made Christianity the religion of the Roman Empire his mother St Helen (see Famous People) made a pilgrimage to Palestine and became the first successful Christian archaeologist. During her visit to the Holy Land in 326 she demolished Hadrian's temple of Venus on Golgotha and brought to light the site of Christ's crucifixion and burial, where she discovered the cross which was thereafter revered as the True Cross, one of the most important relics in Christendom. Her son then built on the site the Church of the Holy Sepulchre, which still exists in a much altered form, and also erected the Church of the Nativity in Bethlehem.

In subsequent years increasing numbers of pilgrims made their way to the Holy Land, undeterred by the complaint by St Gregory of Nyssa (d. 394) that Jerusalem was a den of adulterers, thieves, idolators and murderers. Around 400 a French nun named Aetheria travelled to the Holy Land and Sinai, and – as her diary, found at Arezzo in 1884, records – was able to locate many of the holy places with the aid of the Biblical narrative.

In 438–439 the Empress Eudoxia, the daughter of a pagan philosopher of Athens who became the wife of Theodosius II, made a pilgrimage to Jerusalem, accompanied by a brilliant retinue. Bishop Juvenal presented her with a number of relics, including two chains which were said to have been Peter's fetters in prison. She gave one of them to the church of the Holy Apostles in Constantinople; the other was taken by her daughter, also called Eudoxia, to Rome, where it can still be seen in a Renaissance tabernacle under the high altar of the 5th century church of San Pietro in Vincoli (St Peter in Chains). After Theodosius's death in 450 Eudoxia returned to Jerusalem, where there were now numerous religious houses and hospices for pilgrims, and lived there until her death in 460.

The cult of relics which had been established by Helen was given further impetus by Eudoxia, and this concern with relics led to increased western interest in the Near East. "When a lady of Maurienne brought back from her travels the thumb of Saint John the Baptist, her friends were all inspired to journey out to see his body at Samaria and his head at Damascus" (Steven Runciman). Many pilgrims travelled to Palestine in trading vessels until shipping became unsafe during the Arab wars of conquest in the 7th century. Even then, however, the stream of pilgrims continued. Among the pilgrims were both secular and ecclesiastical dignitaries, like the Frankish bishop Arculf, who travelled in Egypt, Palestine and Syria in 670, and the English monk (St) Willibald, later bishop of Eichstätt in Germany (d. 787), who travelled to Rome in 720 and to Palestine in 723. Charlemagne, who was able to establish good relations with Caliph Haroun al-Rashid, caused hospices for pilgrims to be built. Around the same period Spanish nuns served for a time as guardians of the Holy Sepulchre.

In the 10th century, when the Byzantines, under their general (later Emperor) Nicephorus Phocas, achieved some successes in their conflict with the

Arabs, the number of pilgrims again increased. Among those recorded as having made the pilgrimage were Judith of Bavaria, sister-in-law of the Holy Roman Emperor Otto I (970), the Count of Anhalt and Bishops Conrad of Constance and John of Parma. Pilgrims either followed the land route via Constantinople and through the Byzantine Empire or took ship from Venice or Bari.

Pilgrimages were now recognised by the Catholic church as a form of penance for sins. This view was promoted particularly by the Cluniacs, who not only compelled the Abbot of Stavelot (990) and the Count of Verdun (997) to make the pilgrimage to the Holy Land but concerned themselves with organising and facilitating journeys for numbers of ordinary people. Among the pilgrims were Frenchmen, Germans, Englishmen and increasing numbers of Scandinavians, particularly after they formed the Emperor's Varangian Guard in Constantinople (11th century onwards).

When the Seljuks advanced towards Constantinople in the 11th century and gained control of territories in Asia Minor and Palestine, however, the pilgrims were exposed to great difficulty and danger, and this led to the First Crusade in 1096.

Later
Middle Ages

After the end of the crusading era (1291) pilgrims continued to make their way to the Holy Land, and now some of them recorded their experiences in books. Thus in 1283 Brother Brocardi wrote a description of his pilgrimage in Latin which was published in Venice in 1519 and in 1584 in a German edition as the "Book of Travel to the Holy Land". In 1382–84 Count Solms and Bernard von Breidenbach went on pilgrimage, a journey described by Breidenbach in his "Itinerarium Hierosolymitanum". In 1519 Ludwig von Tschudi, a Swiss, travelled to Palestine and wrote an account of his journey in his "Journey and Pilgrimage to the Holy Sepulchre". In 1573 Hans Ulrich von Krafft made a pilgrimage in the course of which he spent several years in prison, describing his experiences in his "Memorabilia".

Modern times

In the 16th century the motives for travel changed. Travels of a secular nature were now prompted by the discovery of new lands like America and India or were undertaken for commercial or scientific reasons. In the 18th and 19th centuries the Christian motive for pilgrimage lost ground to the interests of archaeological and historical research. A further religious impulse came to the fore, however, in 1846, when Christian Friedrich Spittler, founder of the Basle Mission, sent members of his community to Jerusalem, where they established the Syrian Orphanage.

Christian pilgrims of many denominations still form part of the scene in the Holy Places. But even those who visit Israel for non-religious reasons will feel this to be a special land which promotes new spiritual and intellectual insights.

Languages

Official languages

Modern Hebrew (Ivrit) is the first official language of Israel; Arabic is the second. Hebrew and Arabic both belong to the Semitic language family. Both are written from right to left, but their scripts are very different.

Hebrew

Hebrew is a West Semitic language related to Assyrian and Aramaic. After the Babylonian exile (587–538 B.C.) the influence of Aramaic became increasingly strong. Aramaic was the language of administration in the Persian Empire, and from the 6th century B.C. to the 6th century A.D. it served as a lingua franca throughout the Near East. Aramaic (and in Hellenistic times Greek) became the ordinary language of the Jewish people, displacing Hebrew – which, however, continued to be used in religious services and by scholars and writers. The Mishnah, which was completed about A.D. 200, is largely written in an Aramaic-influenced form of Hebrew with the addition of words from Greek and Latin.

Hebrew enjoyed a great flowering in Moorish Spain from the 11th century to 1492. Its revival began in Germany in the late 18th century during the

Enlightenment (Haskalah), and from there it spread to Italy, Poland and Russia.

With the emergence of the Zionist movement in the 19th century efforts were made to heal the ancient breach between the sacred and the secular language: Hebrew was no longer to be restricted to the religious field but was to become the ordinary language of the people. This unique development has largely been realised in Israel. A major part in the movement was played by Eliezer Ben Yehuda (see Famous People), who also helped to coin new terms and concepts to meet the needs of a modern society.

An Israeli is able to read the Hebrew Bible with ease; but anyone brought up on Biblical Hebrew will have some difficulty in reading an Israeli newspaper.

Many Israelis also speak other languages like English, French, German, Russian, Polish, Spanish, Hungarian and Yiddish.

Arabic

Arabic belongs to the south-western branch of the Semitic languages. Northern Arabic established its predominance with the advance of Islam, and is now spoken in numerous dialects throughout North Africa and the Near East. The most important of these dialects, which is spoken by the Arab population of Israel, is Egyptian Arabic.

Glossary of Jewish Terms

Ark of the Covenant (Aron Hakodesh)

On Moses' instructions (Exodus 37) Bezaleel made the Ark of the Covenant, the portable shrine of shittim (acacia) wood, overlaid with pure gold within and without, which the Jews carried with them on their wanderings. The symbol of the presence of God, it was borne on a throne flanked by golden cherubim. According to a later interpretation the Ark contained the Tables of the Law which Moses received on Sinai. In the time of the Judges the Ark was in Shiloh. Subsequently it was carried off by the Philistines. Recovered by David, it was taken to Jerusalem, where David's son Solomon built the Temple to house it. When Jerusalem was destroyed by Titus in A.D. 70 the Ark, along with other cult objects, was carried off to Rome.

Ashkenazim

(From Ashkenaz = Germany). The term applied to Jews (and their descendants) originating from central and eastern Europe who came to Palestine via the Balkans.

Berakhah

Blessing, prayer.

Bet hamidrash

A Talmudic school and house of prayer.

Chassidim (the "Pious")

1. In the Maccabean period (2nd c. B.C.), the term applied to pious Jews.
2. Adherents of Chassidism, a movement which developed in Ukraine and Poland in the 18th century, who took the Ukrainian Rabbi Israel Ben Eliezer (1699–1760) as their model and venerated holy men (*zadik*) and wonderworkers.

Gabbai

The men who help with the functions of the synagogue.

Gemara

A kind of encyclopedia compiled about A.D. 500 containing explanations and interpretations of the Mishnah.

Haggadah ("Narration")

The non-legal part of the Talmud (see below); it is used at Passover, telling the story of that holiday.

Languages

Halakhah ("Regulation")	The legal part of the Talmud, a system of law mostly derived from the Torah and formulated in a series of prescriptions; the basis of religious practice.
Hazzan	The leader of prayer in the synagogue.
Kabbalah ("Tradition")	In Talmudic times this was the term for the oral tradition which existed alongside the written laws; in the Middle Ages it meant the mystical Jewish philosophy of religion, made up of reflections on the essence and the action of God, the creation of the world and the last days. Interest in the Kabbalah reached its peak in the 13th century in Spain, where the mystical "Zohar" was written.
Karaites (Karaim)	A Jewish sect, established in Persia in the 8th century A.D., which rejects the Talmud and the rabbinical tradition and recognises only the Old Testament. Around 850 a group of Karaites settled in Ramla, in what is now Israel, and have remained there ever since.
Kashrut	The concept of "kosher" is related to the humane killing of animals and other prescriptions on eating and drinking. The whole body of ordinances on purity and cleanliness, known as Kashrut, may have been laid down by Moses with hygienic and aesthetic considerations in mind or a concern to establish a clear distinction between the Israelites and other peoples. Leviticus, the third book of Moses, contains in chapter 12 rules of cleanliness for women in childbed and for the circumcision of male children; chapter 18 lays down laws on marriage and chastity, chapter 19 on the consecration of daily life and the observance of the Sabbath. Chapter 17 of Deuteronomy, the fifth book of Moses, bans the worship of pagan gods, while chapter 24 prescribes laws on the conduct of marriage. The laws on clean and unclean food and animals are laid down in chapters 11 and 17 of Leviticus and chapter 14 of Deuteronomy. The ban on eating pork and mixing meat and milk were reactions to the sacrificial customs of the Canaanites, known to us through the Ugarit archives. The rules on the preparation of food are adhered to by government institutions, public bodies and the armed forces as well as by most hotels and restaurants.
Kehillah ("Congregation")	Jewish religious community.
Kibbutz	A self-governing settlement in communal ownership: see page 26.
Menorah	The seven-branched candlestick fashioned by Bezaleel (Exodus 37). A large bronze menorah carved by Benno Elkan and presented by the British to the Israeli Parliament stands in front of the Knesset in Jerusalem.
Midrash	Midrash (plural Midrashim) means "interpretation". The Midrashim are collections of rabbinical commentaries on the Bible dating from between 30 B.C. and A.D. 900. The Halakhite Midrash contains interpretations of religious laws, the Haggadite Midrash ethical and contemplative texts.
Mikve	Ritual bath.
Minyan	The quorum of ten adult males required for the purposes of formal worship.
Mishnah ("Repetition")	A compilation of Jewish religious laws completed about A.D. 200. It is divided into six parts (*sedarim*).
Mitzvah	A religious commandment or duty.
Moshav	A co-operative settlement in Israel: see page 28.

A Jewish religious teacher chosen by the congregation (not ordained). His (or her) duties include taking part in the service of worship in conjunction with the prayer leader (*hazzan),* directing and supervising religious instruction and performing various religious ceremonies such as weddings. The term *rabbi* ("my teacher") is derived from the Aramaic and Hebrew word *rab* ("great" in learning), and is an honorific title given to Hebrew scholars. The still more honourable style of Rabboni ("Master") is used in John 20,16.

Rabbi

The Sanhedrin, a Hebraised form of the Greek Synhedrion, was the supreme council of the Jews, presided over by the chief priest. In Maccabean times the Sanhedrin was the highest court of law. After the destruction of Jerusalem and the Temple in A.D. 70 Rabbi Yohanan Ben Zakkai was granted permission to transfer the seat of the Sanhedrin to Jamnia. Around A.D. 140 it moved to Usha in Galilee and later to Tiberias.

Sanhedrin

(From Sepharad = Spain). A term applied to Jews expelled from Spain and Portugal in 1492 who settled in various European countries, North Africa and the Near East; now wrongly applied to all Middle Eastern and North African Jews.

Sephardim

A ram's horn which is blown on the Day of Atonement and at the New Year.

Shofar

A code of religious law compiled in the 16th century.

Shulhan Arukh

A Greek term for a community or congregation; later also the building in which it met. Probably originating during the Babylonian exile (587–538), it subsequently increased in importance. The oldest synagogues for which there is evidence, in Egypt, date from about 250 B.C. In Hellenistic times synagogues were the centres of Jewish life throughout the Mediterranean area. Most of the synagogues found in Israel and Syria date from the 3rd–7th centuries. The prayer hall faced in the direction of Jerusalem, and the Torah scrolls were kept in wooden shrines in a recess or in subsidiary rooms.

Synagogue

During the Israelites' sojourn on the Sinai peninsula after the Exodus a tent was fashioned of linen curtains, as a form of portable temple in which the Ark of the Covenant, the table for the twelve loaves of shewbread and a seven-branched candlestick (menorah) were kept. See Exodus chapters 25–31 and 35–40.

Tabernacle

A large light-coloured prayer shawl with dark borders worn by orthodox Jews.

Tallith

The most important compilation of the teachings of post-Biblical Judaism. Begun in the 6th century B.C. and completed in the 5th century A.D., it contains the religious laws, previously handed down by oral tradition, which supplemented the written Mosaic Law. It consists of the Mishnah and the Gemara. A distinction is made between the Babylonian Talmud, compiled in the East Aramaic language about A.D. 500, which has become the authoritative guide to religious practice, and the Jerusalem (properly Palestinian) Talmud, compiled in the 4th century A.D.

Talmud ("Teaching")

A leather strap with a small box containing Torah texts (phylactery), worn from Sunday to Friday for the morning prayer.

Teffelin

The five books of Moses (the Pentateuch).

Torah ("Doctrine")

A higher school for all Jewish studies.

Yeshiva

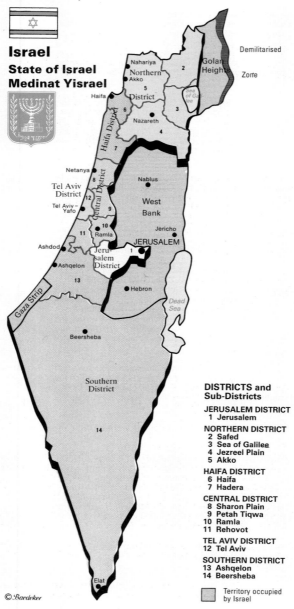

Israel
State of Israel
Medinat Yisrael

Demilitarised

Zorfe

Nahariya
Akko
Northern
District
Haifa
Golan Heights

2

Sea of Galilee

5

6

3

Nazareth

4

7

Netanya

8

Nablus

Tel Aviv District

12

West Bank

Tel Aviv–Yafo

9

11

10

Jericho

Ramla

JERUSALEM

Ashdod

Jeru-salem District

1

Ashqelon

13

Hebron

Dead Sea

Beersheba

Southern District

14

DISTRICTS and Sub-Districts

JERUSALEM DISTRICT
1 Jerusalem

NORTHERN DISTRICT
2 Safed
3 Sea of Galilee
4 Jezreel Plain
5 Akko

HAIFA DISTRICT
6 Haifa
7 Hadera

CENTRAL DISTRICT
8 Sharon Plain
9 Petah Tiqwa
10 Ramla
11 Rehovot

TEL AVIV DISTRICT
12 Tel Aviv

SOUTHERN DISTRICT
13 Ashqelon
14 Beersheba

Territory occupied by Israel

Gaza Strip

Elat

© Baedeker

Government and Society

The state of Israel (Medinat Yisrael), founded in 1948, is a parliamentary democracy. There is, so far, no written constitution, but the framework of the state is laid down in a series of basic laws passed by the Israeli parliament in 1958, and at some point in the future, not yet decided, these will form the basis of the country's constitution.

The head of state is the President, who is elected by Parliament for a five-year term (with the possibility of re-election for a second term) and has mainly formal and representational functions. The President appoints ambassadors, judges and the Auditor-General. He also recommends to Parliament a State Comptroller, who must be elected by Parliament and is answerable to it. The Comptroller is responsible for the oversight of all organs of government.

The Israeli Parliament, the Knesset, consists of 120 members, who are elected by proportional representation for a four-year term; electors have the vote at the age of 18. The Knesset is the country's highest authority and legislature. Draft laws are usually put forward by the government, but they can also be tabled by individual members of parliament or parliamentary groups. All parliamentary debates are conducted in modern Hebrew (Ivrit), but Arab members may submit motions and questions in their mother tongue.
Legislation is not subject to judicial review.
The government is formed by a member of the Knesset who is invited by the President to do so. It consists of the prime minister and other ministers and forms the country's executive. All members of the government are responsible to Parliament and must retain its confidence.
The first prime minister of Israel was David Ben-Gurion, appointed in 1948. The present incumbent is Yitzhak Rabin.

In October 1984 the Provisional Council of State adopted the national flag, with two blue stripes on a white ground enclosing the star of David. It reproduces the flag hoisted at the first Zionist Congress at Basle in 1897. It was designed by the Zionist leader David Wolffsohn.

National flag and emblem

The official emblem of the state, adopted in 1949, is the Menorah, the ancient symbol of the Jewish people, as it appears on the Arch of Titus in Rome. The menorah is flanked by two olive branches, linked with the inscription "Israel" in Hebrew script below the menorah. The olive branches symbolise the Jewish people's longing for peace.

Israel's democracy is based on a multi-party system which reflects the ethnic, cultural and ideological diversity of Israeli society. Since the foundation of the state of Israel the smaller religious parties have often held the balance of power in the formation of government coalitions.
The two largest party groupings are the nationalist Likud bloc and the Labour bloc (Mapai, Mapam, etc.). To the left of the Labour parties are the Israeli Communist Party, which espouses the cause of the Palestinian refugees, and the New Communist Party, influenced by Moscow. A general election in 1992 returned the Labour party and its allies to power.

Parties

The Israeli courts are independent. The highest court is the Supreme Court in Jerusalem. In matters of personal status (divorce, etc.) each religious group has its own jurisdiction.

Administration of justice

The Law of Return, passed in 1950, gives all Jews the right to come to Israel and become Israeli citizens. The minister of the interior, however, has

Immigration

power to withhold this right from persons with a criminal record and those whose presence would endanger public health or public order.

Armed forces

The Israeli armed forces (Zahal, Israel Defence Forces) developed out of Haganah, the self-defence organisation established during the British Mandate. The prime duty of the army is to maintain the independence of the state.

The regular army consists of a small nucleus of professional officers, non-commissioned officers and men. In addition there is compulsory military service (36 months for men, 24 months for women) for Jews, Druzes and Circassians; Muslims and Christians may volunteer for service. Although no state in the world makes such demands on its citizens as Israel, there are practically no conscientious objectors to military service, though a few soldiers have refused to serve in southern Lebanon and the occupied territories. 60% of all women serve in the army; the rest are exempted from service (wives, mothers, women with a strictly orthodox religious upbringing). Women soldiers are not sent to the front, and most of them serve their time in administration.

The great bulk of the army consists of reservists (400,000 of whom can be mobilised within 24 hours). Men under 55 and women, without children, under 34 can be called up once a year for four weeks in the reserve. Thus the Israeli armed forces can be converted at short notice from a small standing army into a formidable fighting force.

The Pioneer Fighting Youth (Nahal), who are volunteers, are subject to military discipline and are given practical agricultural training. They are deployed in frontier areas where it is planned to establish a settlement or where living conditions are unsuitable for the civilian population.

Trade unions

Histadrut, the General Federation of Labour (founded 1920; headquarters in Tel Aviv), is the largest workers' organisation in Israel. It is open to members of the liberal professions, who can join as individual members. It has a total of around 1.6 million adult members, including 170,000 Arabs and Druzes. There are also a number of other workers' organisations (young people in employment, students, religious organisations) under the general aegis of Histadrut, which altogether represents some 85% of the working population. Wage rates, which are tied to the cost of living index, are fixed by the government in association with the workers' organisations. Histadrut administers a health insurance scheme (Kupat Holim) and a welfare fund (Mish'an) which grants loans to members in cases of need, and also runs old people's and children's homes.

Histadrut organises professional training courses and evening classes for adults and provides cultural and sporting facilities for its members.

Jewish Agency

The Jewish Agency, founded in 1922 as the Jewish Agency for Palestine and renamed in 1948 the Jewish Agency for Israel, has a special role in Israeli life. It is concerned with questions of immigration (organisation, transport) and settlement (help in resettlement, reafforestation and extension of agricultural land). The organisation is financed mainly by voluntary contributions, property taxes, government subsidies and loans.

Administration

For administrative purposes the country is divided into six districts, which are further divided into sub-districts (see map, page 36). The West Bank of the Jordan and the Gaza Strip, which have been occupied by Israel since 1967, are under military administration. The Golan Heights, also conquered in 1967, were annexed by Israel in 1981.

District	Area in sq.km. (sq.mile)	Population (1986)	Chief town	Inhabitants per sq.km. (sq.mile)
Jerusalem	627[1] (242)	518,000	Jerusalem	826 (2,139)
Northern	3,325 (1,284)	695,000	Nazareth	209 (541)
Haifa	854 (330)	596,000	Haifa	698 (1,808)
Central	1,242 (480)	908,000	Ramla	731 (1,893)
Tel Aviv	170 (66)	1,019,000	Tel Aviv–Jaffa	5,993 (15,522)
Southern	14,107 (5,447)	518,000	Beersheba	37 (96)
Israel	20,325[2] (7,847)	4,254,000[3]		209 (541)

[1] including East Jerusalem (70sq.km/27sq.miles)
[2] excluding inland waters
[3] excluding areas administered by Israel

Israel is a member of the United Nations (UN) and the General Agreement on Tariffs and Trade (GATT), and since 1975 has had a free trade agreement with the European Union (EU).

International organisations

Freedom of opinion is guaranteed in the Declaration of Independence. Reporting on military matters is, however, subject to censorship.

Mass media

All Israel's daily newspapers are published in Tel Aviv or Jerusalem. There is no real local press. The papers with the highest circulations are "Yediot Aharonot", "Ma'ariv" and "Ha'aretz" and the Arabic "El-Quds". The English-language "Jerusalem Post" is well respected beyond the bounds of Israel. In addition there are foreign-language papers catering for different language groups and a number of weeklies. The Israel Broadcasting Authority (IBA), founded in 1965, runs both radio and television services. The Kol Israel station has three radio services, transmitting programmes in Hebrew, Arab, English and French (as well as news bulletins in nine other languages). There is also a station for the army and various private stations. Television came to Israel in 1968; there are both Hebrew and Arabic channels.

Israel's health services are comparable with those of western countries. This is reflected in expectation of life (see Population), in infantile mortality rates and in the high proportion of doctors to population (1:346).

Health services

Health insurance is run by the trade unions; some 66% of the population are covered.

Men are entitled to a retirement pension at 65 if they actually retire at that age, otherwise at 70; the corresponding ages for women are 60 and 65. The state social security system also provides a widow's pension and industrial accident insurance. Mothers are entitled to six weeks' maternity leave before and after the birth and to a maternity allowance. Family allowances are paid to families with more than three children (there are different regulations for government employees).

Social security

Housing was a major problem after the foundation of the state of Israel, and the immediate need for new houses was met by the erection of multi-storey blocks of no great architectural quality. In the 1980s some 30,000 new dwellings a year were built, but this was insufficient to meet the demand. Houses to rent are particularly difficult to find, since property-owners are subject to high taxes when they let their houses. In view of the large numbers of immigrants from the former Soviet Union (see Population) the housing problem is likely to get worse.

Housing

Education

Schools
The Israeli education system is of a high standard. School attendance is obligatory for children between 5 and 15. Schooling is free. Some 65% of children attend state schools; the others go to religious schools or state-approved private schools. There are separate schools for Arab children. The state educational system comprises a kindergarten and a pre-school year, six years in primary school, three years in junior school and three years in secondary school.

Since the population of Israel comes partly from under-developed countries like Yemen and Morocco and partly from the USA and Western Europe there are considerable differences in educational level. The proportion of pupils from Asian and African countries falls sharply in the successive stages of the system from primary school to university. It is a prime object of the educational system to get rid of such differences: thus, for example, children from poorer families are given financial assistance for the purchase of schoolbooks.

Illiteracy
A survey in 1972 showed that 12.4% of the population over the age of 14 were illiterate; the rate for the Jewish population was 9.2%, for the Arab population 36.5%. By 1986 the illiteracy rate had been reduced to 6.5%.

Universities
There are universities in Jerusalem, Tel Aviv, Ramat Gan, Haifa and Beersheba. In addition there are the Technion (College of Technology) in Haifa, the Weizmann Institute in Rehovot and the Bezalel Academy of Art and Design in Jerusalem.
The total number of university students is approximately 60,000.
Some 20,000 students attend Talmudic schools (*yeshivot,* singular *yeshiva*).

Beersheba University

Library of the College of the Negev, Sede Boqer

In proportion to population Israel has more academics than any other country in the world. Many of them are of great distinction and have helped to make Israel the great centre of scientific research which it now is. It devotes 3% of its budget to research and development (though 60% of this goes to projects of military importance). In addition Israeli scientists have great achievements to their credit in the fields of medical technology, molecular biology, biotechnology and micro-electronics and have secured impressive results in the development of irrigation systems and solar energy installations.

Research

The Israeli armed forces have an important educational role, and not merely in the military field. Provision is made, for example, for the further education and admission to university of soldiers from under-privileged classes of the population, and no soldier leaves the army without a basic education.

Education in the armed forces

Economy

Since the foundation of the state of Israel in 1948 the country's economy has had to contend with a variety of difficulties and disadvantages. The land was under-developed; many immigrants arrive in Israel with neither training nor possessions; conflicts with Arabs and Palestinians have kept defence costs high; and the country has few mineral resources. In spite of all this Israel achieved a considerable economic upswing: in the fifties and sixties the growth rate of the Israeli economy was one of the highest in the world. The main causes were a rapid increase in the labour force, a high influx of capital (including reparations from Germany and loans from the United States and the World Bank) and high rates of taxation.
Although Israel's economic strength is still much greater than that of its non-oil-exporting neighbour states the general economic situation of the

General

41

country has continued for many years to be bad. Inflation, which reached a peak of 444% in 1984 and was then brought down, by a freeze on wages, prices, exchange rates and government spending, to an annual 15%, flared up again in 1989 to 20.6%. The growth rate per head in that year was only 1.2%, and unemployment rose to 9% (compared with only 5.6% in 1987). Contributing to these economic difficulties, Israel's defence costs are enormously draining on the economy, swallowing up 20% of the budget. In addition sales of goods in the occupied territories have declined drastically; the West Bank and the Gaza Strip no longer provide a reservoir of cheap labour; and the *intifada* has had a detrimental effect on the tourist trade. A further problem is the increasing number of immigrants, with thousands of people, particularly from Russia, still seeking residence in Israel. Given the present high unemployment rate, it is difficult to find a place for these incomers on the labour market.

Israel has both private, state and trade union enterprises. Histadrut, the country's largest trade union organisation, is the second biggest owner of businesses after the state.

In terms both of turnover and numbers employed the services sector is the leading branch of the economy, a major role being played by banks and insurance corporations. Some 63% of the working population are employed in this sector; commerce accounts for 12% and agriculture for 6%, while the rest are employed in industry.

Agriculture

Irrigation

A crucial factor in Israeli agriculture is that as a result of the unfavourable climatic conditions, particularly in the south of the country, only 20% of the total area can be brought into cultivation, much of it only with the aid of artificial irrigation. To bring water to the arid regions conduits and pipelines (the National Water Carrier) have been laid carrying water from the Sea of Galilee and the river Yarqon (Kinneret-Negev and Yarqon-Negev lines) to the southern coastal plain and the northern Negev. The rain which occasionally falls on the fringes of the desert is channelled from the hillsides to lower-lying fields which are surrounded by embankments to preserve the water. In order to reduce evaporation many of the crops are grown under plastic sheeting. Another means of reducing evaporation to the minimum is sub-surface irrigation, in which hoses laid in the fields and plantations convey water direct to the roots of the plants. By this means the consumption of water can be reduced by 50% for the same crop yield.

In spite of this system for the collection, transport, distribution and effective use of water Israel now on average consumes 20% more water than is supplied by rainfall. Since further economies are not possible efforts are being made to increase the available supplies. Some success has been achieved by bombarding rain clouds with deep-frozen silver iodide, which enlarges the cloud and causes it to discharge its water sooner. In some areas this has led to an increase in rainfall of some 20%. Attention is also being devoted to the recycling of water, which in the most favourable conditions is expected to meet up to 10% of total consumption. It remains doubtful, however, whether these methods will be sufficient to meet the country's requirements. Since Israel's neighbours are no better off, it is to be feared that water may become a political problem. The Palestinians are already accusing the Israelis of theft in taking two-thirds of the West Bank's water resources to meet the needs of the Israeli heartland.

Agricultural areas

Bananas and citrus fruits are grown on the fertile soil of the coastal plain. The plantations in this area, intensively cultivated and for the most part artificially irrigated, produce high yields. In addition to lemons, which were introduced from California, there are the famous Jaffa oranges and grapefruit. The plantations in the coastal region cover an area of 500sq.km/

Fertile land in the Negev, created by irrigation

195sq.miles and supply Israel's most important agricultural produce, which is exported in canned or fresh form, particularly to Britain and Germany.

The agricultural produce of the upland regions goes – with the exception of tobacco – to meet domestic needs. Thanks to the winter rains the farmers, who are mostly Arabs, can grow cereals, particularly wheat, in terraced fields. Other crops are vines, olives, figs, almonds and peaches.

Three regions in the Jordan rift valley are of agricultural importance: the Hule plain, the area round the Sea of Galilee and the valley of the Wadi Arava. Cotton, cereals and groundnuts are grown in the drained marshland of the Hule plain, and there are plantations of peaches, apples and pears on the slopes of the valley. Dates and bananas, together with avocados, vines and citrus fruits, flourish on the good soil round the Sea of Galilee. In the Wadi Arava tomatoes and vegetables are grown in irrigated fields, and in winter flowers.

Cereals are grown in the Negev, on the borders of the arid zone, and with artificial irrigation fruit can also be grown. In this area, as in the southern part of the Jordan rift valley, shelter belts of tamarisks, eucalyptus and acacias are built to protect the crops from wind. In recent years sisal has also been grown here, yielding fibres which are used in making ropes and other products.

The Jezreel plain to the south of Haifa, with its fields of cotton, cereals and sugar-beet, is one of Israel's most productive agricultural regions. The karstic terrain on the hillsides is being reafforested.

Many crops – citrus fruits, sugar-beet, groundnuts and cotton – are grown on a large scale, on a carefully planned basis, to increase agricultural production. Although less than 6% of the working population are employed in agriculture, which is highly mechanised, Israel is largely self-sufficient in agricultural produce, requiring to import only grain, oil and fats.

Productivity

43

Important crops: bananas . . .   *. . . and grapefruit*

Agricultural
exports

In addition to traditional agricultural produce like fruit (particularly citrus fruits), vegetables and poultry Israel now exports increasing quantities of dates, Japanese persimmons, pomegranates, medlars and pecan nuts, as well as improved varieties of fruit and vegetables like seedless table grapes and melons. Organically grown products are also increasingly being exported.

Another special feature made possible by the Israeli sun is the production of young plants which are then exported to nurseries in Europe for growing on. Numerous experiments in the growing of other crops (sweet potatoes, bananas, etc.) are also in progress.

Stock-farming

While in the past the livestock reared in Israel consisted predominantly of sheep and goats, the main emphasis is now on milk and egg production. The scope for beef production is limited because of the shortage of fodder crops. On the insistence of the religious parties pig-farming is generally prohibited; only Christian Arabs are allowed to keep pigs. In order to increase the production of meat the breeding of turkeys has been developed in recent years.

Fisheries

Fish-farming has also been stepped up to provide animal protein for the domestic consumer, and the carp ponds in the northern coastal plain, the Hule plain and the Sea of Galilee area yield considerable quantities of fish. The Mediterranean fisheries have so far proved less productive, but it is planned to develop them further. Overall Israel cannot meet the demand for fish from domestic production.

Forestry

Israel has few forests, and accordingly forestry makes little contribution to the economy. Reafforestation is being actively pursued by the state. In addition to native species quick-growing trees from other parts of the world (conifers, acacias, etc.) are being planted in many areas.

Israeli fisheries: catches insufficient to meet the country's needs

Mining and Energy Production

Since the foundation of the state Israel has intensified the search for mineral resources. Large quantities of minerals are won from the Dead Sea. In consequence of the high rate of evaporation (some 6–8 million cu.m/1.3–1.8 billion gallons a day) the clear, deep blue sea forms a saturated salt solution (about 25% salt), making it difficult to dive and impossible to sink in its waters. The Dead Sea Works, near Sodom, at the south end of the Dead Sea, are one of the world's largest producers of potash and bromine and potassium salts, and also produce common salt. The brine is pumped into shallow artificial salt-pans, with a high rate of evaporation, on the northern and southern shores of the sea. The larger the salt-pans, the greater is the yield of minerals. In 1963, therefore, with aid from the World Bank, the Israelis began to construct huge new salt-pans in the southern basin of the Dead Sea. Asphalt and bitumen, which are also found on the shores of the Dead Sea, make a contribution to Israel's exports.

Israel's largest resources of minerals are in the Negev. At Timna, near Elat, copper has been mined since 1955; as a result of falling copper prices on the world market the mines were temporarily closed down in the seventies, but production was resumed in 1980. Makhtesh Hagadol has quarries of quartz sand which supply the country's glassworks. Other products are kaolin, used in the ceramics industries, and phosphates, which are used as fertilisers. The phosphate-bearing rocks also contain uranium. The Negev also has deposits of iron ore, as has Galilee.

In order to transport the minerals of the Negev to Israel's industrial centres new roads are being built, and a railway line to Beersheba has been completed. The port of Elat plays an important part in the export of minerals.

Israel is poorly supplied with primary sources of energy like coal, oil and hydroelectric power. There has been much drilling for oil, but with little

Minerals

Energy production

45

success. Since nuclear power cannot, on political grounds, be contemplated as an alternative, Israel is obliged to import 97% of its energy requirements. Crude oil is brought in through the port of Elat and conveyed in a 400km/250 mile long pipeline to Haifa, where there are large refineries. There is another pipeline from Elat to Ashqelon, south-east of which, in the Shefela plain, drilling in the fifties produced some signs of oil.

Over 90% of Israel's energy is produced in thermal power stations at Haifa, Tel Aviv-Jaffa, Ashdod and Elat, largely powered by oil.

An alternative source of power which is being actively developed is solar energy. Experiments are under way in the Jordan depression with a "sun pool" and in the Negev with a "solar plantation". In towns like Jerusalem, too, the sun is already making a considerable contribution to the production of energy. In these towns it is obligatory to install solar panels on any building of less than eight storeys.

Israeli scientists believe that domestic sources of energy (in addition to solar power they are thinking of oil shale, which occurs in the south of the country) will meet between 10 and 20% of Israel's energy requirements until the year 2000.

Industry

Although Israel has only limited supplies of raw materials and is largely lacking in energy resources, its industry stands high in comparison with other Middle Eastern countries.

The production of building materials has fallen in recent years as a result of the economic recession, but this is still one of the country's most important industries. Prefabricated sections, asbestos sheets, concrete pipes, etc., are produced in numerous specialised factories. Cement production also occupies an important place. The port towns of Akko and Ashqelon, with their steel works, are centres of heavy industry. Other towns in the coastal region produce machinery and machine tools; there are shipyards at Haifa and aircraft factories in Lod. The chemical, precision engineering and electrical industries have experienced a considerable boom, with the electronics industry (micro-computers, telecommunications, measuring instruments and medical apparatus) showing a particularly high growth rate.

Diamond-cutting

After the Second World War many diamond-cutting establishments were transferred from Belgium to Israel, and now a high proportion of the gem diamonds sold on the world market come from Israel. The centre of the diamond-cutting industry is Netanya; the Diamond Exchange is in Tel Aviv (Ramat Gan). Imported raw diamonds are processed in some 650 establishments, which have largely automated their production processes. In recent years quite large stones (1 to 10 carats) have been cut in Israel – work which was formerly done almost exclusively in Belgium and the United States.

In the early eighties, as a consequence of the worldwide recession, the export of diamonds fell sharply. Recovery began in 1985, and 1986 was a record year, in which diamonds to a value of 1.7 billion US dollars were exported, representing 24% of Israel's total income from exports.

Foreign Trade

In spite of all efforts there is still a deficit on Israel's balance of trade, with the value of imports far exceeding that of exports. The most important exports are gem diamonds, citrus fruits, canned fruit, chemicals and fertilisers, hardware, aircraft, machinery and telecommunications equipment. Israel's principal trading partners are the United States, Germany, Britain, the Netherlands, France, Italy, Belgium, Switzerland and Japan. A treaty of 1975 with the European Union provides for the progressive reduction of duties on Israeli imports into the EU.

Tourism

Tourism is one of Israel's major industries. Most visitors still come out of religious or cultural interest, but there has been an increase in the number drawn by the country's holiday attractions. Particularly during the winter season many thousands of sun-lovers come to enjoy a holiday on the beaches of Elat. Many come also for health reasons, for the area round the Dead Sea offers a unique variety of spas and health-promoting facilities. 1987 was a record year for the Israeli tourist trade, with 1.37 million foreign visitors, who spent an average of eleven days in Israel. Most of the visitors came from the United States (21.6%), followed by Germany (12.5%), France (12.4%) and Britain (11%). The outbreak of the *intifada* in December 1987 dealt a blow to the tourist trade, with a reduction of 20% in numbers of visitors and in income in 1988. There was a slight upward trend in 1989 and the first half of 1990, but the Gulf crisis in the summer of that year brought a further setback, from which there has since been a recovery.

Transport

Israel has a network of over 4000km/2500 miles of asphalt roads, with a particular concentration in the coastal plain. Almost all passenger traffic goes by road, as does much of the country's freight traffic. **Road traffic**
Car ownership has risen sharply in recent years, and between 1980 and 1986 the number of vehicles registered rose by 60%. The development of the road system has not kept pace with this rapid increase, and as a result there are often catastrophic bottlenecks, particularly in and around Tel Aviv and Jerusalem.

Israel's rail network is relatively undeveloped – partly for political reasons, since trains are a favourite target for terrorists. Only 5% of passenger traffic is carried on the railways, which are mainly of importance for the transport of bulk goods. The total length of the network is 865km/537 miles (main lines 528km/328 miles, branch lines 337km/209 miles). The most important line is the coastal line between Tel Aviv and Haifa, with its continuation by way of Beersheba to Elat. Passengers are carried only between Tel Aviv and Haifa. **Railways**

Almost the whole of Israel's foreign trade goes by sea. The busiest port is Haifa, with almost 60% of the total traffic. Ashdod exports fertilisers from its eastern hinterland and citrus fruits. The port of Elat handles trade with Asia. **Shipping**

International services are flown by the national airline, El Al (Israel Airlines); domestic traffic is carried by the state-owned Arkia airline. The Ben-Gurion Airport near Lod links Israel with the international network of air services. There are also charter flights from various foreign countries to Elat airport. There are regional airports at Tel Aviv, Jerusalem, Haifa, Rosh Pinna, Beersheba and Sodom. **Air services**

History

Stone Age

The beginnings of human history cannot be precisely dated, and the materials used in the making of tools and implements therefore serve as a basis for establishing a chronology. In the Palaeolithic or Old Stone Age man had only crude stone tools. In the Mesolithic or Middle Stone Age more refined weapons and implements fashioned from flint or tipped with flint made hunting and tilling of the ground possible. In the Neolithic or New Stone Age man had learned to make vessels from clay; and finally in the Chalcolithic or Copper Age he had discovered how to work with metal.

1,000,000–14,000 B.C.	Palaeolithic era, in which three stages can be distinguished.
1,000,000–300,000	Primitive hunters and gatherers use river or lake pebbles as tools. Remains of this pebble culture have been found at El-Ubeidiyya, to the south of the Sea of Galilee.
300,000–70,000	Humid climate, with jungle flora and fauna. In various caves, particularly on Mount Carmel, fossils have been found with anatomical features enabling them to be identified as an early form of modern man. Recent research has dated them to 90,000 years ago.
70,000–14,000	A climatic change leads to the disappearance of the tropical forests and the animals which lived in them. During this period there seems to have existed in the territory of Israel, alongside the "modern man" already mentioned, a type of Neanderthal man. Remains of this late archaic form of Homo sapiens, which later died out, have been found in a number of caves and are dated to 60,000 years ago. It is not known why the two types of man did not mingle or why modern man appeared in Europe only 40,000 years ago.
14,000–7500	In the Mesolithic era, with the use of the bow and the trap, hunting becomes more productive, and dogs are used as hunting dogs. Flint sickles point to the beginnings of agriculture. Beginning of the "Stone Age revolution", the transition from the gathering of useful plants to their regular cultivation. Man takes to a settled existence (beginnings of house-building), thus creating the conditions for more advanced cultural development.
7500–4000	Neolithic era: continuation of the development which began in the Mesolithic. Homo sapiens works the land according to the seasons (upper Jordan plain, Yarmouk valley, oasis of Jericho). Because yields differ, a social stratification develops and larger communities are formed. Discovery of the craft of pottery, marking progress in cultural development; emergence of a rural fertility cult (figurines found at Sha'ar Hagolan on the Yarmouk). A temple is built in Jericho to a divine triad (man, woman, child). Skulls with modelled plaster features reflect a belief in a life after death.
4000–3000	Chalcolithic era: the art of working metal is discovered. Material of this period has been found in the Jordan valley, in the Beersheba area, at En Gedi on the Dead Sea and in the coastal plain. A temple was found at En Gedi, a temple treasure in the "Treasure Cave" in the Judaean Desert.

Bronze Age (Canaanite Period)

City states inhabited by Semites come into being in Canaan; at times they are under Egyptian rule. Abraham, forefather of the Israelites, journeys from Mesopotamia to the land later known as Judah. Around 1700 B.C. the Israelites travel into Egypt, returning to Canaan 500 years later.

Early Bronze Age: emergence of early advanced cultures in Egypt and Mesopotamia, influencing the territory of Israel from the south and east. The land occupied by the West Semitic Amorites (Amurru, the "people of the West") on the Mediterranean coast and the upper Jordan valley (Canaan) is divided into city states. The towns are fortified: in the north Hazor, in the Jezreel plain Megiddo and Bet Shean, in the uplands Shechem, Gezer, Jerusalem and Hebron. Each town has its Baal, its divine owner, who is represented by its king or priest.
From the 3rd millennium onwards Egypt gains influence on the Canaanite towns.

3000–2000

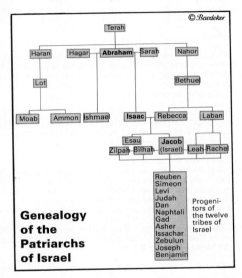

© *Baedeker*

Genealogy of the Patriarchs of Israel

Middle Bronze Age. The journey of Abraham, who according to the Old Testament account came from Ur in Chaldaea, round the "fertile crescent" (that is, up the Euphrates and then south by way of Shechem to Hebron and Beersheba) can be dated to the 18th century B.C. From reports by Pharaoh Amenhotep (Amenophis) II (1438–12) it is known that at this period, in addition to the sedentary Hurrite tribes, there was a nomadic people, the Apiru or Habiru, which probably included the early Hebrews.
The Exodus of the Israelites, their journey to Egypt, which the Bible associates with Abraham's grandson Jacob and his son Joseph, may possibly have coincided with the campaign of the Hyksos, the Asiatic kings who conquered Egypt around 1650 B.C., after the great days of the Middle Kingdom.

2000–1600

Late Bronze Age. In the 2nd millennium B.C. the Pharaohs of the New Kingdom, like Tuthmosis I (1528–10) and Tuthmosis III (1468–36), control the most important roads and towns; some towns have Egyptian governors. The kings of Canaanite city states take advantage of Egypt's decline under the "heretical" Pharaoh Akhenaton (1364–47) to extend their power.

1600–1200

Battle of Kadesh (near present-day Homs in Syria) between the Egyptians, led by Ramesses II (1290–24), and the Hittites, who had been living in

1285

northern Canaan and Syria for several hundred years. This leads to a demarcation of the spheres of influence of the two sides.

c. 1250 Different dates (15th and 13th c. B.C.) have been advanced for the return of the Israelites to Canaan. Present-day opinion favours the later date. On this basis the Israelites leave the Nile delta in the reign of Ramesses II and, according to the Biblical account, travel under the leadership of Moses through the Sinai peninsula and eastern Jordan, where the kingdoms of Ammon, Moab and Edom had been established in the 14th century. From there, led by Joshua, they advance into Canaan. "The Israelites' seizure of the western Jordan lands was a lengthy process, during which different tribes (the sons of Leah in the north and south, the sons of Rachel in the centre) settled one after another" (Avi-Yonah). Jericho and Hazor are conquered; the Canaanites hold on to Jerusalem and parts of the coastal plain.

Early Iron Age (Israelite Period)

Under the Judges, and later under the Kings, the Israelites war with the Philistines. The kingdom reaches its peak in the time of David and Solomon, builder of the Temple. After Solomon's death the country is divided into two kingdoms. In their conflicts with the Assyrians and later with the Babylonians the Israelites are defeated. The Babylonian Captivity begins in 587.

1200–1025 Period of the Judges. The beginning of the Israelite period sees incursions by the Philistines, one of the "Sea Peoples" who also threaten Egypt. They gain control of the coast and establish strongholds in Gaza, Ashkelon, Ashdod, Ekron, Gath and Jaffa, later extending their dominion to the southern shore of the Sea of Galilee.
In the 12th century the Israelite tribes, only loosely organised, fight the Philistines, who have an advantage over them with their iron weapons. The Israelites are led by the "Judges" (Deborah, Gideon, Samson, etc.). At the end of the 11th century the Philistines defeat the Israelites at Eben-ezer, capture the Ark of the Covenant and destroy the tabernacle of Shiloh.

1025–587 The period of the Kings begins when the last of the Judges, Samuel, anoints Saul as king at Gilgal, near Jericho. It lasts until the capture of Jerusalem by Nebuchadnezzar II in 587.

1025 Saul becomes king of the Israelites. He and his son Jonathan defeat the Philistines.

1006 Saul falls in battle against the Philistines. The tribe of Judah elect David, born in Bethlehem, as Saul's successor and crown him as king in Hebron. After the elimination of Saul's son Ish-bosheth David becomes king of the whole of Israel.

1000 David conquers Jerusalem and makes it his capital. After the Ark of the Covenant is housed on the Temple Mount Jerusalem also becomes the religious centre of the Jews.
David recovers the Jezreel plain from the Philistines, defeats the Moabites at Madaba and captures the Ammonite capital, Rabbath Ammon, and Damascus, capital of the Aramaeans. A victory over Edom enables him to extend his territory to the Red Sea.

965 Solomon, David's son, becomes king of the enlarged kingdom, which now enjoys a period of prosperity. Solomon ensures the safety of the country with strongholds like Hazor and Megiddo, establishes a strong administration and carries on trade from Elat with Ophir (in East Africa?). He conquers Gezer but loses Damascus.

953 Solomon builds the Temple in Jerusalem.

Death of Solomon. The kingdom falls into two parts, Israel to the north and Judah to the south (with Jerusalem as its capital). Solomon's son Rehoboam rules the kingdom of Judah, with the tribes of Judah and Benjamin. Jeroboam I (982–907) rules the kingdom of Israel, with the other ten tribes. — 928

Campaign of Pharaoh Seshonq I (the Shishak of the Old Testament). Jerusalem is sacked. — 924

Rehoboam, king of Judah, dies. His successors are of no particular note. — 910

Omri becomes king of Israel. He consolidates the state and establishes his capital in Samaria. The marriage of his son Ahab with Jezebel, daughter of the king of Sidon, brings in Phoenician influences, including the worship of Baal, against which Elijah and other prophets inveigh. — 878

Ahab becomes king of Israel. He wages three wars against the Aramaean state of Damascus (Aram) but is killed in 852. — 871

Jehu overthrows the Omrid dynasty and becomes king of Israel (842–814). He fights Damascus, which is destroyed in 806 by the Assyrians under Adan Nirari III.
In Judah Athaliah, mother of King Ahaziah, introduces the worship of Baal, leading to popular unrest. — 842

Joash seizes power in Judah. — 836

Amaziah succeeds Joash as king of Judah. He defeats the Edomites. — 801

Uzziah king of Judah. Attempts to develop the Negev. — 769–733

Ahaz, son of Uzziah, becomes king of Judah. He submits to the growing power of the Assyrians and introduces their religious practices in Judah. — 733

In the reign of King Pekah Israel is defeated by the Assyrians under Tiglath-pileser III. Much of the country is annexed by the Assyrians. — 732

Hezekiah becomes king of Judah. He purifies the Temple of alien cults and carries through economic reforms. — 727

Conquest of Samaria, capital of the northern kingdom, by Sargon II of Assyria. Many inhabitants of Israel are carried off into captivity and are replaced by settlers from Babylon. The mingling of Jews and Babylonians, gives rise to the Samaritans. — 721

The Assyrians establish the province of Philistia, centred on Ashdod. Hezekiah secures Jerusalem's water supply by the construction of a tunnel. He forms an alliance with Egypt, Babylon and Ashkelon against the Assyrians. — 712

Unsuccessful siege of Jerusalem by Sennacherib of Assyria. Hezekiah becomes a vassal of the Assyrians. — 701

Manasseh, Hezekiah's son, is also an Assyrian vassal. — 696–642

Amon, king of Judah, is assassinated on account of his pro-Assyrian policy. — 641/640

Josiah becomes king of Judah. When the Babylonians inflict an annihilating defeat on the Assyrians he annexes Samaria and Galilee. He purifies the temple and in a centralising religious reform, largely inspired by the prophet Jeremiah, he closes all Jewish places of worship outside Jerusalem. — 639

Josiah dies and is succeeded by his son Joachim, who is at first dependent on the Egyptian Pharaoh Necho and then on Nebuchadnezzar II of Babylonia. — 609

598	Zedekiah becomes king of Judah.
597	After an attempted rebellion by Joachim Nebuchadnezzar captures Jerusalem, deposes Joachim and carries off his son Jehoiachin and members of the country's ruling classes to Babylon. This is the first Exile.
589	Zedekiah rebels against the Babylonians.
587	After a siege lasting a year and a half Nebuchadnezzar recaptures Jerusalem and destroys the Temple. This is the end of the kingdom of Judah and the beginning of the Babylonian Captivity (the second Exile). Judah becomes a Babylonian province. The Edomites conquer the territory round Hebron and Beersheba, which is now called Idumaea.

Persian Rule and Hellenistic Influence

	After the return from the Babylonian Captivity Judah becomes a Persian province.
539	Cyrus II of Persia conquers the Babylonian empire.
538	Cyrus allows the Jews to return home. Rebuilding of the Temple. Akko and Gaza become royal strongholds; the coastal region is divided between the Phoenician cities of Tyre and Sidon; the rest of the country is divided into provinces.
520	Building of the Second Temple in Jerusalem.
519	Sheshbazzar, a descendant of Joachim, the second-last king, is appointed governor of Judah. He and his successors are aided by the high priest and a council of elders. Consecration of the Second Temple during the governorship of Nehemiah.
445	Jerusalem gets new town walls.
5th and 4th c.	Increase in Greek influence, long before the conquest of the country by Alexander. In the 4th century there are Greeks living in Akko; mercenaries settle in Atlit.

Hellenistic Period

	Alexander the Great brings Judaea under Macedonian rule. With increasing Hellenisation of the country there is conflict between the Greek Seleucid rulers and the Jews who remain faithful to their Law. Antiochus IV orders the Jews to worship Greek gods and suspends Jewish services in the Temple.
336	Alexander the Great becomes king of Macedonia.
333	Alexander defeats Darius III's Persian army in the battle of Issus.
332	Alexander conquers Tyre, Syria and Egypt. Judaea comes under Macedonian rule.
323	Death of Alexander. His successors, the Diadochi, contend for possession of Judaea. Antigonus Monophthalmus fights the Nabataeans, an Arab people who live in the Petra area (now in Jordan).
312	Ptolemy I, ruler of Egypt, takes Jerusalem; Judaea becomes part of the Ptolemaic empire. Many Jews, either by force or of their own free will, go to

Egypt. Judaea is governed by high priests of the Oniad dynasty. There is a Macedonian colony in Samaria. Galilee is administered from Mount Tabor. The Phoenician towns on the coast become independent. The Tobiads, a powerful family of eastern Jordan, gain increased influence in the Near East and promote the process of Hellenisation, which is reflected in new Greek names, like Ptolemais for Akko and Philadelphia for Rabbath Ammon. The Jewish colony in Egypt is also Hellenised, and in the 3rd century the books of the Bible which form the Old Testament are translated into Greek (the Septuagint).

In the battle of Paneion (now Banyas) Ptolemy V is defeated by Antiochus III (223–187), the Seleucid ruler of Syria. Antiochus combines the conquered territories in the satrapy of Coele Syria and Phoenicia, and creates four eparchies in Palestine – Samaria, Idumaea, Gilead (east of the Jordan) and Paralia (the coastal region). He grants the Jews the right to live "according to the laws of their fathers" and allots funds to the Temple. When Syria loses a war with Rome and has to pay heavy reparations one of Seleucus IV's ministers tries to gain control of the Temple treasury, and this leads to tension between the Seleucid rulers and the Jews.   **198**

The next Seleucid, Antiochus IV (175–163), pursues a thoroughgoing policy of Hellenisation which brings him into even sharper conflict with those of the Jews who remain faithful to their Law. He replaces the high priest, Onias III, by his brother Jason, an advocate of Hellenisation, who builds a gymnasium at the foot of the Temple Mount and incurs the displeasure of the priests. His period of office is short.

Menelaus, brother of Simeon, keeper of the Temple, manages to get himself appointed high priest even though he is not an Oniad. He misappropriates Temple vessels to enable him to pay his tribute to the king and has the former high priest, Onias III, murdered.   **172/171**

Antiochus IV appropriates the rest of the Temple treasury. A conflict between Menelaus and the Tobiads leads Antiochus to intervene militarily. Menelaus is ordered to suppress the practice of the Jewish religion; he erects an altar dedicated to Dionysos Sabazios in the Temple in Jerusalem and plans to build a temple of Zeus.   **169**

The Temple in Jerusalem is closed down.   **167**

The Maccabean Rising and the Hasmonean State

Under the Hasmonean rulers Mattathias and Judas Maccabeus there is a rising against Antiochus IV. Thereafter Antiochus withdraws the anti-Jewish laws and allows the Jews to practise their religion. After the Hasmoneans have held the offices of governor and high priest in Judaea for over a hundred years conflicts arise between them and the Jewish population. Some years later the Roman general Pompey captures Jerusalem.

Religious oppression leads to a rising by the Jews against their foreign ruler. The Hasmonean priest Mattathias kills a royal official and one of the sacrificing priests during a pagan service in the town of Modein near Lydda (present-day Lod) and then flees to the mountains along with other rebels. After his death in the same year his son Judas Maccabeus takes over the leadership of the rising. The rebels, rapidly increasing in strength, launch a war against Antiochus IV.   **166**

Antiochus withdraws the anti-Jewish laws.   **165**

Judas Maccabeus cleanses the Temple: an event commemorated by the Jewish festival of Hanukkah.   **164**

After several years of fighting with Antiochus IV and Demetrius I Judas Maccabeus falls in a battle at Elasa. His brother Jonathan continues the struggle.   **160**

152	Demetrius appoints Jonathan governor of Judaea.
150	The Seleucid king Alexander Balas appoints Jonathan high priest. "Thus the Hasmoneans held power in Judaea as governors and high priests both *de facto* and *de jure,* and the object of their revolution was largely achieved" (Avi-Yonah). Jonathan takes advantage of the tensions among the Seleucid rulers and between the Seleucids in Syria and the Ptolemies in Egypt to extend his territory and his authority.
147	In the battle of Jamnia the Hasmonean army, led by Jonathan, defeats the Seleucid forces.
142	Jonathan is taken prisoner and killed. His brother Simeon succeeds him as high priest and secures recognition of the independence of Judaea (with the Jewish Hasmonean dynasty holding both secular and spiritual authority).
135	Simeon is succeeded by John Hyrcanus I, who seeks to re-establish the kingdom of David (compulsory conversion of the Idumaeans to Judaism, defeat of the Samaritans).
104	End of John Hyrcanus's reign.
103	Alexander Jannaeus (Yannai), who has the support of the Hellenised citizens, comes to power. He conquers some of the coastal towns, Galilee and part of the eastern Jordanian lands, taking the Hasmonean kingdom to its largest extent. Jewish resistance to the Hasmonean dynasty, which had already been directed against Jonathan's assumption of the office of high priest, increases when Jannaeus declares himself king.
76	End of Alexander Jannaeus's reign. Unrest grows during the reigns of his sons Hyrcanus II and Aristobulus II.
63	The Roman general Pompey, under orders to end the third Mithradatic War, takes advantage of the conflicts within the Hasmonean dynasty to capture Jerusalem. The Hasmonean kingdom becomes a Roman vassal state.
37	The Romans execute the last Hasmonean king, Mattathias Antigonus.

Roman Rule

During the reign of King Herod, who is half Jewish, Jesus is born. After Herod's death Judaea is governed by Roman procurators. Tensions between Jews and Romans lead to military conflict (destruction of the Temple in Jerusalem). After the Bar Kochba rising the Jews are expelled from Jerusalem; thereafter Tiberias in Galilee becomes the centre of Judaism and the Patriarchate which is now established. Formation of the first Christian communities.

37	Herod (the Great), son of an Idumaean father and a Nabataean mother, gains control of the country with Roman assistance. To buttress his unpopular rule he builds a series of powerful fortresses (Machaerus to the east of the Jordan, Masada, Herodeion and Cyprus). The Temple is rebuilt within an enlarged precinct. Herod builds palaces in Jerusalem, the Antonia Fortress, a theatre and a hippodrome on the Greek and Roman model.
30	Augustus (until the year 27 Octavian) becomes Roman Emperor. He confirms Herod I as king of Judaea. In honour of the Emperor Herod builds a harbour at Caesarea, rebuilds Samaria under the name of Sebaste (Sebastos in Greek = Augustus) and erects a temple of Augustus there.

Jesus is born in Bethlehem. (The year of his birth was incorrectly calculated in the 6th century). 7/6

On Herod's death his kingdom is divided between his three surviving sons. Archelaus receives Idumaea and Samaria, with the style of Ethnarch; Philip rules over the northern and east Jordanian territories as Tetrarch and founds the city of Caesarea Philippi at Paneas (now Banyas); while Herod Antipas becomes Tetrarch of Galilee and Peraea and founds the city of Tiberias. Herod Antipas causes John the Baptist to be killed on the instigation of his wife Herodias. 4 B.C.

Beginning of the Christian era. Year 1

Augustus deposes Archelaus. A.D. 6

End of Augustus's reign. 14

Pontius Pilate becomes procurator and prefect of Judaea. 26

First appearance of John the Baptist. 29

Jesus is crucified in Jerusalem. c. 33

Philip, son of Herod, dies. 34

Pilate loses his post as procurator and prefect of Judaea. 36

Agrippa I, a grandson of Herod the Great, becomes king of Judaea. Persecution of the first community of Christians in Jerusalem. The Emperor Caligula exiles Herod Antipas. 37

After Agrippa's death Judaea becomes the Roman province of Palaestina. 44

The Roman procurators have little understanding of the Jews' way of life, governed as it is by their religion, and particularly of their expectation of the coming of a Messiah; they are cruel and corrupt. Growing tensions lead to a Jewish rising against the Romans, led by the fanatically religious Zealots. 66

The soldiers of the Roman garrison in the royal palace are massacred after surrendering.

69	Vespasian becomes Emperor.

70   Vespasian's son Titus captures Jerusalem. Destruction of the Temple, the religious and political centre of the Jews. 600,000 Jews are killed in the uprising.

74   Masada, the last Jewish stronghold, is taken by the Romans after a long siege. The Jewish defenders commit mass suicide.
After the destruction of Jerusalem and of the Temple the leading role passes from the priests to the Pharisees. The Sanhedrin, presided over by Rabbi Yohanan, moves to Jamnia (Yavne). The study of the Law which is pursued there ensures the survival of Judaism.
Rome strengthens the position of the governor of Judaea, giving him command of the legion stationed in Jerusalem. Caesarea becomes a Roman colony. Vespasian founds the military colony of Flavia Neapolis (now Nablus) near Samaria-Sebaste.

79   End of Vespasian rule.

79–81   Titus becomes Emperor.

81–96   Reign of Domitian. The Jewish king Agrippa II dies; his kingdom is divided between Judaea and Syria.

98   Trajan becomes Emperor.

106   The Nabataean kingdom is incorporated in the Roman Empire.

115   Jewish risings in Cyrene, Egypt and Cyprus spread to Judaea, where a number of rabbis are executed.

117   Hadrian becomes Emperor.

130   Hadrian prohibits the Jewish practice of circumcision.

132   Jewish rising led by Bar Kochba (Simeon Bar Kosiba).

135   The Romans put down the Bar Kochba rising. Some of the rebels take refuge in caves on the west side of the Dead Sea (where letters from Bar Kochba have been found).
Jerusalem becomes the Roman military colony of Aelia Capitolina. The Romans erect an equestrian statue of Hadrian on the site of the Temple and expel the Jews from Aelia Capitolina. The centre of Judaism now becomes Usha in Galilee.

138   Antoninus Pius becomes Emperor. He permits the practice of the Jewish religion, which had been banned after the Bar Kochba rising.

c. 140   The Sanhedrin, meeting in Usha, elects Simeon II as Patriarch. The Jews are granted their own legal jurisdiction and municipal self-government. Roman urban culture spreads through much of the country.

2nd–3rd c.   Under Judah I the Patriarchate takes on an almost monarchic character. Judah's grave in Bet Shearim becomes the centre of a large Jewish cemetery. The seat of the Patriarch and the Sanhedrin is transferred from Usha to Tiberias.
There is a Christian community in Jerusalem, where Bishop Alexander (212–251) founds a library. There are other communities at Caesarea, Ptolemais (Akko), Joppa (Jaffa), Lydda (Lod) and Pella in the 1st century, at

Flavia Neapolis in the 2nd century and at Caesarea Philippi, Bostra, Sebaste, Philadelphia (Amman), Bethlehem, Gaza, Jericho and other places in the 3rd. The leading Christian community is Caesarea, the base of two Doctors of the Church, Origen (c. 185–254) and Eusebius (c. 260–339).

East Roman/Byzantine Rule

In the reign of the Emperor Constantine, who grants toleration to Christianity, many Jews become Christians. Palestine becomes the "Holy Land". Always an area of conflict among the great powers of the day, in the 7th century it comes within the Arab sphere of influence.

After the division of the Roman Empire into four Constantine, son of Constantius, eliminates his rivals and rules over the whole Empire as Constantine the Great. His reign is a turning point in the destinies of Palestine. "Not merely did Christianity now become a *religio licita,* but this hitherto unimportant province became the 'Holy Land' of the predominant religion" (Avi-Yonah). **324**

In Jerusalem and the surrounding area churches are built on sites with important Christian associations (Church of the Nativity in Bethlehem, Church of the Holy Sepulchre on Golgotha in Jerusalem). The Jews are still allowed to enter the town only once a year, on the anniversary of the destruction of the Temple.

In the reign of Theodosius I Christianity spreads widely through the Empire. Theodosius divides the Empire into the Western and the Eastern Empires. **379–395**

By the end of Theodosius II's reign the majority of the population of Palestine are Christian. **408–450**

On the death of Gamaliel IV the office of Jewish Patriarch lapses. **before 429**

The Bishop of Jerusalem is granted the status of a Christian Patriarch. At the Council of Chalcedon the differences between the orthodox imperial church and the Monophysites, who reject the doctrine of the dual nature of Christ, become evident. Large numbers of people in Palestine are Monophysites and at odds with the Byzantine Empire and its church. **451**

A rising by Samaritans and Jews is repressed by the Byzantine authorities. **484**

In the reign of the Byzantine Emperor Justinian there is further conflict with rebellious Samaritans and Jews. Justinian promotes settlement in the Negev and the cultivation of the desert lands with the help of Nabataean irrigation techniques. **527–565**

Birth of Mohammed. **570**

The Persians, the greatest power in the eastern Mediterranean, conquer Palestine in the reign of Chosroes II. Patriarch Zacharias and 37,000 other Christians are carried off to Persia, along with the True Cross from the Church of the Holy Sepulchre. **614**

The Emperor Heraclius (601–640) defeats the Persians, releases their prisoners and restores the Cross to the Church of the Holy Sepulchre. **628**

Two years after the death of the Prophet Mohammed (571–632) the Byzantine governor is killed in a battle with the advancing Arabs. **634**

The Byzantine army is defeated by the Arabs on the river Yarmouk. **636**

Arab Rule

The Arab Caliphs conquer Jerusalem and rule Palestine first from Ramleh (Ramla), later from Damascus and finally from Baghdad. Most Caliphs are tolerant of believers in other faiths like Jews and Christians. In the 11th century the Seljuks, a Turkish people, move into Palestine. Their brutal treatment of Christian pilgrims sparks off the Crusades.

638	Patriarch Sophronius surrenders Jerusalem to Caliph Omar.

c. 640   The Arab administrative centre is Emmaus (Latrun), and later the new foundation of Ramleh. Jews and Christians, as "peoples of the Book", are tolerated, being required only to pay a poll tax.

661–750   Under the Omayyad Caliphs, residing in Damascus, Palestine (except the towns in the Negev) enjoys a period of prosperity.

c. 700   Caliph Abd el-Malik builds the Dome of the Rock on the Temple platform. The Dome of the Rock and the El-Aqsa Mosque make Jerusalem the most important Muslim city after Mecca and Medina. The foot of the Rock on the Temple Mount is believed to be the spot where Mohammed tied up his horse Burak and ascended into heaven.

750   The Abbasid Caliphs, residing in Baghdad, succeed the Omayyads.

807   Caliph Haroun el-Rashid recognises Charlemagne as protector of the Holy Places.

878   The Turkish mercenary leader Ahmed Ibn Tulun becomes the most powerful man in Palestine. After his death Turkish mercenaries continue to oppress the population of the country.

c. 977   The Fatimid Caliphs, who had conquered Egypt in 969, rule in Palestine.

1004   El-Hakim, the new Caliph (whom the Druze regard as the founder of their religion), persecutes the non-Muslim inhabitants of Palestine.

1009   Destruction of the Church of the Holy Sepulchre.

1021   End of El-Hakim's reign.

1055   The Seljuks, a Turkish people, take Baghdad and thrust into the Near East.

from 1078   The Seljuks attack Christian pilgrims from the Byzantine Empire and Europe. Their brutality leads to the launching of the Crusades.

The Age of the Crusades

From the end of the 11th century, on the call of Pope Urban II, Catholic Christians from Europe undertake a series of Crusades to Palestine in order to protect the holy places from Islam. Jerusalem becomes capital of a Crusader state which continues to exist until 1291.

1095   At the Council of Clermont Pope Urban II calls on all Christians to take up arms against Islam: "Dieu le vult" ("God wills it"). There is an overwhelming response.

1096   Beginning of the first Crusade, with a force consisting mainly of French knights and Normans from southern Italy. The Crusaders travel through the Byzantine Empire and reach the Mediterranean at Tripoli (now in Lebanon).

1099   After a siege lasting 39 days the Crusaders take Jerusalem on July 15th; they slaughter the Muslim and Jewish inhabitants. Godfrey of Bouillon, who had played a decisive part in the storming of Jerusalem, assumes the style of "Advocatus sancti sepulchri" (Protector of the Holy Sepulchre).

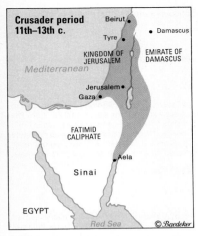

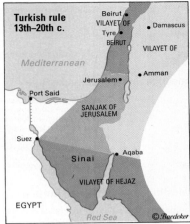

Death of Godfrey of Bouillon. His brother has himself crowned as king of Jerusalem under the title of Baldwin I. The Christian kingdom of Jerusalem is organised as a feudal state on the French model. Baldwin captures the coastal towns from Ashkelon to Akko (Acre), the lands west of the Jordan and an area extending from Kerak to Aila (Elat) on the east bank of the Jordan.	1100
The Order of the Knights Templar is founded by Hugo of Payens to protect pilgrims to Jerusalem. The Grand Master resides in Jerusalem. The knights wear a white cloak with a red Maltese cross.	1119
Fulk, Count of Anjou, as king of Jerusalem, builds numerous castles to defend his kingdom. His central authority is restricted, however, by the feudal system and the existence of numerous principalities (in Tripoli, Edessa, Antioch and Galilee).	1131–43
Second Crusade: battles with the Turks, quarrelling among the Crusaders.	1147–49
King Amalric I tries to conquer Egypt.	1162–74
The Egyptian Sultan Saladin defeats the Crusaders' army at the Horns of Hittim and three months later occupies Jerusalem.	1187
Third Crusade, led by the Emperor Frederick I Barbarossa.	1189–92
Acre (Akko) is recovered by the Crusaders and becomes capital of the Crusader kingdom.	1191
Fourth Crusade.	1202–04
Fifth Crusade, led by the Emperor Frederick II Hohenstaufen. He makes a treaty with the Egyptian Sultan under which he receives Jerusalem, where he has himself crowned as king, together with Bethlehem, Nazareth and a corridor between Jerusalem and the Mediterranean.	1228/1229
Jerusalem is reconquered by Egyptian forces.	1244
Sixth Crusade.	1248–54

1261–72	Sultan Baibars, a Mameluke, conquers almost all that is left of the Crusader state.
1270	Seventh Crusade.
1291	Sultan El-Ashraf Khalil captures Acre. End of the Crusader state.

Palestine under Mameluke Rule

The Mamelukes (freed slaves of Turkish or Circassian origin) gain power in Egypt around 1250 and from there extend their power still further. The Egyptian Mameluke dynasty consists of two lines, the Bahrites (1252–1390) and the Burjites (1382–1517). The age of the Mamelukes, who rule Palestine after the dissolution of the Crusader state, is a period of domestic unrest; but they improve the roads and build bridges, caravanserais and mosques.

1492	Jews expelled from Spain come to Palestine.

Palestine in the Ottoman Empire

With the conquest of Jerusalem by Sultan Selim I Palestine becomes part of the Ottoman Empire. After the death of Suleiman the Empire declines and the European great powers gain increasing influence in the eastern Mediterranean area. At the end of the First World War Palestine becomes a British Mandate. Around the turn of the 19th century the Zionist movement begins to make headway.

1516/1517	Sultan Selim I defeats the Mamelukes at Aleppo, takes Jerusalem and then occupies Egypt.
1520–66	In the reign of Selim's son Suleiman II (the Magnificent) Palestine enjoys a period of development and domestic consolidation. The walls of Jerusalem are rebuilt, partly on a new line, the Dome of the Rock is faced with faience tiles and the water supply is improved. The age of the great Kabbalists (exponents of the mystical doctrine of the Kabbalah) begins in Safed. After Suleiman's death the decline of the Ottoman Empire sets in.
c. 1660	The Druze emir Fakhr ed-Din rebuilds Akko, which had been destroyed in 1291.
1730–70	Daher el-Amr rules the whole of Galilee from Akko.
1775–1804	Ahmed el-Jazzar (the "Butcher") defeats Daher el-Amr and makes Akko his capital.
1805	Mohammed (Mehmed) Ali, an Albanian officer of Macedonian origin, declares himself Pasha of Egypt in place of the expelled Turkish governor.
1833	Ibrahim Pasha, son (or adoptive son?) of Mohammed Ali, rules Palestine and Syria after a successful military campaign.
1840	Under pressure from the Quadruple Alliance (Britain, Russia, Prussia and Austria) Ibrahim Pasha gives up Palestine and Syria, and with European support Turkey resumes control. France regards itself as protector of the Catholics in Palestine, Russia as protector of the Orthodox.
1841	Britain and Prussia, as protectors of the Protestants in Palestine, jointly establish a bishopric of Jerusalem.
1848	An Ashkenazi community (i.e. a community of Jews from Central and Eastern Europe formed in earlier times) builds a synagogue in Jerusalem.

The German Society of the Temple establishes its first settlement in Haifa. **1868** This Pietist movement (not to be confused with the order of the Templars) seeks to establish the Kingdom of God on earth. Subsequently further settlements are established, including one in Jerusalem in 1873. Some of the settlements are abandoned before the First World War, while others continue to exist until the Second World War; thereafter the British Mandatory authorities evacuate the settlers to Australia.

Jews from Jerusalem establish the first Jewish agricultural settlement at **1878** Petah Tiqwa, east of Jaffa.

The first large wave of foreign immigrants, mainly from Russia, Poland and **1882** Yemen (the First Aliyah), begins, with the support of Baron Edmond de Rothschild.
Egypt is occupied by British forces.

Theodor Herzl publishes his book "The Jewish State", which calls for the **1896** creation of a Jewish state in Palestine (Zionism).

First Zionist Congress in Basle, which formulates the programme of the **1897** Zionist movement in these words: "Zionism aims to create for the Jewish people a home in Palestine secured by public law."

Second wave of Jewish immigrants (the Second Aliyah). **1904–14** In 1914 the population of Palestine consists of 600,000 Arabs and some 100,000 Jews.

Foundation of Tel Aviv as a purely Jewish town. **1909**

The first kibbutzim (communal settlements on a voluntary basis) are *c.* **1910** established.

The murder of the heir to the Austrian throne in Sarajevo (June 28th) **1914** precipitates the First World War. On November 1st Turkey enters the war on the side of the Central Powers (Germany and Austria-Hungary). Declaration of a British protectorate of Egypt (December 18th).

The British High Commissioner in Egypt promises Sherif Hosain of Mecca **1915** that in the event of a victory over Turkey an Arab state will be established in the Arabic-speaking provinces of the Ottoman Empire.

The Sykes-Picot agreement sets out the spheres of influence and territorial **1916** acquisitions of the Entente powers (Britain and France) in Turkey. Under the agreement Palestine is to come under international administration.

In a letter to Lord Rothschild the British foreign secretary, A. J. Balfour, **1917** confirms his government's intention to facilitate the creation of a national home for the Jews in Palestine, it being clearly understood that the rights of non-Jewish communities are not thereby prejudiced (the Balfour Declaration).

Palestine is occupied by British forces and comes under British military **1917/1918** administration.

End of the First World War. The Ottoman Empire capitulates on October **1918** 30th.

The British Mandate

After the First World War Palestine becomes a British mandated territory. There are increasing tensions between Arabs and Jews, particularly when the numbers of Jewish immigrants increase after 1933. In 1947 the General Assembly of the United Nations approves the partition of Palestine into two states, a move rejected by the Arabs. A year later Britain gives up its mandate.

History

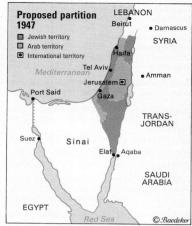

1920	Under the treaty of San Remo Britain is given the League of Nations' mandate to administer Palestine. Growing tensions between Arabs and Jews, with violent confrontations. Foundation of Haganah, a military organisation for the protection of Jewish settlements (incorporated in the Israeli army on the establishment of the state of Israel in 1948).
1921	Arab attacks on Jews.
1922	Formation of the Jewish Agency for Palestine to represent Jewish interests in dealings with the British authorities. (Renamed the Jewish Agency for Israel in 1948, it concerns itself with immigration into Israel and settlement problems.)
1929	Arab massacre of Jews in Hebron, attacks on Jews in Safed.
1933	Beginning of a massive surge of immigration following the persecution of Jews in Germany, after Hitler comes to power.
1936	An Arab rising against the rapid growth of the Jewish population is repressed by British troops.
1937	The Peel Report proposes the division of Palestine between Jews and Arabs. The Arabs, however, call for an independent Palestine under the prevailing Arab majority.
1939	A "White Paper" issued by the British government introduces restrictions on the immigration of Jews into Palestine.
1941–45	Six million Jews are exterminated by the Nazis, chiefly in the occupied territories of Poland and the Soviet Union. There is no escape route to Palestine, as the British have cut off Jewish immigration in 1939. There is no escape from the Holocaust.
1947	The General Assembly of the United Nations adopts a resolution calling for the partition of Palestine into a Jewish state (in the predominantly Jewish-occupied areas) and an Arab state (the predominantly Arab-occupied areas). Jordan annexes the West Bank and East Jerusalem. Jerusalem is to come under international administration.

The State of Israel

After the proclamation of the state of Israel in May 1948 there are four wars within twenty-five years between Israel and the neighbouring Arab states. In 1967 Egypt, which has launched many terrorist attacks on Israel, closes the Suez Canal and masses troops on the Israeli frontier. in the ensuing Six Day War Israel occupies large tracts of territory belonging to Arab states. Jordan also attacks Israel in the same year. In 1973 Egypt attacks Israel; this, the Yom Kippur War, is ended by a ceasefire as a result of United Nations mediation. Years of peace conferences and the efforts of the United States finally lead in 1979 to a peace treaty between Egypt and Israel, under which the Israeli-occupied Sinai peninsula is returned to Egypt. Relations with other neighbouring Arab states, however, remain tense. The Israeli attempt in 1982 to destroy the Palestine Liberation Organisation (PLO) by military action fails. The outbreak of the *intifada* in December 1987 intensifies the conflict between Jews and Palestinians.

On May 14th, one day before the end of the British mandate, David Ben-Gurion proclaims the sovereign state of Israel (Medinat Yisrael). Jordan, Egypt, Iraq, Syria and Lebanon immediately launch a war to prevent the establishment of the new state. East Jerusalem and the Arab territories on the west bank of the Jordan are occupied by the Hashemite kingdom of Jordan.

1948

A ceasefire between Israel and Lebanon, Jordan and Syria is agreed on January 15th. Jordan retains the territory it has conquered. The Gaza Strip remains under Egyptian control. The Jewish quarter of Jerusalem, the Old City and the Holy Sites fall to Jordan, Israel acquires almost the whole of Galilee. The boundary lines existing at the time of the ceasefire form the frontiers of the young state of Israel, but these and the existence of the state itself are not recognised by the Arabs.

1949

The Knesset, the Israeli Parliament, meets for the first time on February 4th. The largest political party is the social democratic Mapai. The first President of Israel is Chaim Weizmann.

Israel becomes a member of the United Nations on May 11th.

President Nasser of Egypt nationalises the Suez Canal Company (June 26th). When he goes on to close the Strait of Tiran at the south end of the

1956

Gulf of Aqaba to Israeli shipping the British and French, with Israeli support, attacks Egypt (October 29th). Israel occupies the Gaza Strip and the Sinai peninsula (the Suez War).

1957 Both the United States and the Soviet Union are anxious, though for different reasons, to settle the Suez conflict, and following United Nations mediation hostilities end in March. The Gaza Strip is put under United Nations control, the Gulf of Aqaba is internationalised and Israel withdraws from the territory it had occupied in Sinai.

1958 The parliamentary republic of Israel, which has no written constitution, passes the first Basic Law, under which supreme authority is vested in the Knesset, to which the government is responsible.

1967 The Six Day War (June 5th–11th). Egypt again closes the Strait of Tiran to Israeli shipping (May 22nd). Following mobilisation in Egypt and attacks by Jordan and Syria Israel destroys the air forces of Egypt, Jordan, Syria and Iraq on the ground. Under the command of Moshe Dayan Israeli forces occupy the Gaza Strip, the Sinai peninsula as far as the Suez Canal, the Golan Heights, the west bank of the Jordan and East Jerusalem.
In November the UN Security Council adopts Resolution 242, which states that after peace is declared withdrawal can occur according to the decision of the interested parties.

1968–72 The Palestine Liberation Organisation (PLO), founded in 1964, which claims to represent all Palestinians, sees violence as the only means of freeing Palestine. From bases in Syria, Jordan and Lebanon the PLO launches terrorist attacks on Israel, which responds with military action.

1972 Arab terrorists attack the Israeli team at the summer Olympic Games in Munich, taking hostages. An attempt to free them fails and 11 Israeli athletes are killed.

1973 The Yom Kippur War. On the Jewish Day of Atonement (Yom Kippur, October 6th), the holiest day of the year for Jews, Egypt and Syria attack Israel. Egyptian troops advance far into the Sinai peninsula, while Syrian forces attack Israeli positions on the Golan Heights. After hard fighting with

great losses on both sides the Egyptian army is surrounded and defeated on the Egyptian side of the Suez Canal and the Syrians are pushed back from the Golan. With the help of the United Nations a ceasefire is agreed (October 22nd–26th).

In November the US Secretary of State, Henry Kissinger, begins a campaign of "shuttle diplomacy" aimed at consolidating the ceasefire and resolving the conflict. At his suggestion Israel sends humane aid to the Egyptian army.

An Egyptian-Israeli agreement on the disengagement of troops is signed on January 18th and comes into force on the 24th. Israel evacuates the west bank of the Suez Canal. (UN troops subsequently occupy a buffer zone.) **1974**
On May 31st a Syrian-Israeli disengagement treaty is signed in Geneva. Israel returns territories occupied during the Yom Kippur War, together with the towns of Quneitra and Rafid; exchange of prisoners. UN troops police the neutral buffer zone.

After the failure of further attempts at mediation between Israel and Egypt by Henry Kissinger (March) a second disengagement treaty between the two countries is signed in September: Israel evacuates the Gidi and Mitla passes on Sinai and Abu Rodeis (oilfields). Both states express their desire to settle their differences by peaceful means. Egypt guarantees free passage of non-military goods to and from Israel on the Suez Canal and Israel makes gestures of good will. **1975**

After a general election in May in which the right-wing Likud bloc wins a majority in Parliament Menachem Begin becomes prime minister and Moshe Dayan foreign minister (until 1979). **1977**
In November President Sadat of Egypt makes an unprecedented visit to Jerusalem and addresses the Knesset in a speech which attracts much attention (peace initiative).

After long negotiations between Begin, Sadat and US President Carter at Camp David (Maryland, USA) draft agreements on peace in the Middle East and on the conclusion of a peace treaty between Egypt and Israel are signed in Washington on September 17th. Sadat and Begin are awarded the Nobel Peace Prize. **1978**

A peace treaty between Israel and Egypt is signed in Washington on March 26th. The Israelis are to withdraw from Zones A and B on Sinai by the end of 1979 and from Zone C by April 1982. The agreement is condemned by all the other Arab states and Egypt is expelled from the Arab League. **1979**

Israeli forces in Sinai withdraw to a line from El-Arish to Cape Ras Mohammed by January 25th. Israel and Egypt resume diplomatic relations on February 26th and exchange ambassadors. **1980**
On July 30th Jerusalem, including the Old City, is declared by the Knesset to be the "eternal capital of Israel". The Arabs, and other countries, condemn this move as making a resolution of the Arab-Israeli conflict more difficult.

In February the UN Commission on Human Rights condemns the Israeli annexation of East Jerusalem. **1981**
Israeli air attacks on Palestinian positions in southern Lebanon, in retaliation for shelling from Lebanon.
In a general election in June Begin's Likud bloc wins by a narrow margin. Formation of a coalition government of Likud and three religious parties, with Begin as prime minister.
The difficult economic situation compels the government to adopt drastic economy measures.

Negotiations in Cairo between representatives of Egypt, Israel and the United States on granting autonomy to the Palestinians on the West Bank of the Jordan and in the Gaza Strip.

Assassination of President Sadat of Egypt (October 6th). Prime Minister Begin attends his funeral in Cairo and meets President-Designate Mubarak. The Knesset resolves on December 14th to annex the Golan Heights, which have been occupied by Israel since 1967.

1982

Complete evacuation of Sinai by Israel (April).
After continued attacks by Palestinians from southern Lebanon Israeli troops enter Lebanon on June 6th with the object of destroying the PLO as a political and military force in the Middle East. Lebanese Christian militias massacre 2000 civilians in two Palestinian camps, Sabra and Chatila (September 16th–18th).

1983

Economic recession and high inflation in Israel.
President Reagan of the USA asks Begin to evacuate the Golan Heights; Begin resigns as prime minister and is succeeded by Yitzhak Shamir.

1984

Lebanon denounces the treaty of May 1983 with Israel on the withdrawal of troops.
The Likud bloc, the Labour parties and a number of smaller parties form a "government of national unity", headed for the first 25 months by Shimon Peres.
17,000 Ethiopian Jews rescued (Operation Moses).

1985

Israel puts forward a three-stage plan for the withdrawal of its forces from southern Lebanon. The withdrawal is largely completed by the beginning of June.
Currency reform (September 4th): "new shekel" introduced, worth 1000 old shekels.

1986

During a visit to King Hassan II of Morocco in Rabat Prime Minister Peres puts forward a ten-point programme for peace in the Middle East.
Under the coalition agreement of 1984 Shimon Peres, a socialist, hands over the prime ministership to the conservative Yitzhak Shamir (October).

1987

After an Israeli army articulated truck runs down a vehicle full of Palestinians in the Gaza Strip there are mass demonstrations, which soon spread to the West Bank, East Jerusalem and the Golan Heights. This Palestinian resistance movement, the *intifada*, hits the headlines in the world press. Since then violent disturbances have continued, with frequent confrontations between women and young people, armed only with stones, and Israeli forces. Protest also takes the form of boycotts and strikes.

1988

A general election on November 1st shows a movement towards the right. A new coalition government is formed by Likud, the Labour party and three religious parties; Yitzhak Shamir remains prime minister.
In December the PLO issues a declaration recognising Israel's right to exist. In a speech to the United Nations the PLO leader Yasser Arafat renounces all forms of terrorism. Nevertheless terrorist activities continue.

1989

The conflict between Egypt and Israel over the Taba enclave on the Red Sea 8km/5miles south-west of Elat is settled in February. This little patch of land (area 1 sq.km/250 acres), with a luxury hotel and a holiday village, now belongs to Egypt, though the hotel is to remain under Israeli management for 20 years.
In September Hungary resumes diplomatic relations with Israel, broken off during the Six Day War – the first Warsaw Pact country to do so.

1990

After the collapse of the coalition the Likud bloc and seven ultra-right-wing religious splinter parties form a new coalition, still with Yitzhak Shamir as prime minister.
Israel directly threatened by the Gulf crisis, sparked off by the Iraqi occupation of Kuwait on August 2nd. As a prerequisite to Iraqi withdrawal from

Kuwait Saddam Hussein demands that Israel gives up all the Occupied Territories. His words find positive support among the Palestinians. *Intifada* again attracts popular support, and there are frequent violent clashes between Palestinians and Israelis.

After the outbreak of the Gulf War (January 17th) a state of emergency is declared in Israel. Rocket attacks on Israel by the Iraqis begin on January 18th, but in order to prevent the United States' Arab allies from backing out of the anti-Iraq coalition Israel does not respond in kind. By the time the war ends on February 28th many Israelis have been killed and injured. **1991**

In a general election in June the Labour party and its allies gain a convincing victory over Likud. Yitzhak Rabin forms a coalition with 62 of the 120 seats in the Knesset. **1992**
The stream of Jewish refugees from the Gulf states (30,000 emigrate to Israel in the first half of 1992 alone) leads to economic problems and Palestinian resistance.

In March Ezer Weizmann is elected the new state president. **1993**
PLO chief Yassir Arafat and prime minister Rabin sign documents in September mutually recognising Israel and Palestine. This is followed by agreements on the partial autonomy of the Palestinians in the Gaza strip and in Jericho.

Early in the year PLO chief Arafat and Israel's foreign minister Perez meet several times in an attempt to establish a basis for Palestinian self-government. **1994**

Famous People

This section contains brief biographies of notable people who were born, lived and worked in Israel or died there.

Shmuel Yosef Agnon (1888–1970)

Shmuel Yosef Agnon ranks as the most important Hebrew novelist and short-story writer of the 20th century. The son of a rabbi in Buczacz (Galicia), he attended a Talmudic school and a teachers' training college, and began by writing poetry in Yiddish and later in Hebrew. In 1907 he emigrated to Palestine, where he soon became known for his writings. Between 1913 and 1924 he lived in Berlin, Wiesbaden and Bad Homburg, and finally settled in Jerusalem in 1924.

In a long series of legends, short stories and novels Agnon described mainly Jewish life in eastern Europe, but also in modern Israel. Among his finest works are the picaresque novel "The Bridal Canopy" (1931; revised version 1953), "Yesteryear" (1936, in German), a novel on the life of young pioneers in Israel at the beginning of the 20th century, and "A Guest for the Night" (1938–39, in German), which is concerned with the decline of the Jewish communities in Poland after the First World War. His works are written in an archaic-seeming Hebrew, but Agnon uses modern narrative techniques and shows considerable psychological finesse. Characteristic of his heroes is an inability to realise their plans.

Agnon was a member of the Hebrew Academy and won many prizes; he was the first Hebrew writer to be awarded the Nobel Prize for Literature (in 1966).

Menachem Begin (1913–92)

Menachem Begin achieved what none of his predecessors as prime minister had been able to – a peace treaty with the most powerful of Israel's Arab neighbours, Egypt. For this he received, jointly with President Sadat of Egypt, the Nobel Peace Prize.

Begin was born in Brest-Litovsk, the son of a Jewish community leader. As an adolescent he got to know the Zionist leader Vladimir Jabotinsky, who profoundly influenced his later life. During his schooldays and his subsequent law studies he became a committed supporter of the radical Zionist movement Betar, which gave young people a military training in preparation for the establishment of a Jewish state. When German forces thrust into Poland Begin's parents were murdered before his eyes. He himself was able to flee to the Soviet Union, but his underground activity there resulted in his being sent to a camp in Siberia. In May 1942 he went to Palestine as a member of the Polish liberating army, but a year later he went underground in order to fight against the British occupation. From 1943 to 1948 he was leader of the underground terrorist organisation known as Irgun Zvai Leumi, which was involved in the bombing of the King David Hotel in Jerusalem, headquarters of the British administration, with the loss of over a hundred lives.

After the establishment of the state of Israel Begin was one of the founders of the Herut (Freedom) party and in 1973 built up the right-wing Likud bloc. As leader of the opposition he suffered eight electoral defeats; only between 1967 and 1970 was he a minister without portfolio in the government of national unity. Finally he came to power as prime minister in June 1977 after Likud's electoral victory. The basis of his policy continued to be the creation and consolidation of an Israeli state within the boundaries of the Biblical Palestine. He pressed on, therefore, with Jewish settlement on the West Bank and in the Gaza Strip. His period of office also saw the annexation of the Golan Heights and the entry of Israeli forces into Lebanon. All this brought him under increasing international and national pressure. After the death of his wife in November 1982 Begin rarely appeared in public, and in August 1983 he announced his resignation on the ground

Shmuel Yosef Agnon   *David Ben-Gurion*   *Moshe Dayan*

that he no longer had the strength to carry on the business of government. Thereafter he lived a reclusive life in a Jerusalem flat until his death.

Ben-Gurion, Israel's first prime minister, was born in Poland as David Gruen and from 1906 lived in Palestine. He earned his living by working on the land, and then in 1912 took up the study of law in Istanbul. He returned to Palestine in 1914, but was expelled by the Turkish government and went into exile in the United States, where he married his wife Paula in 1917. After the end of the First World War Ben-Gurion played a leading part in the organisation of the Labour movement in Palestine. He was one of the founders of the trade union organisation Histadrut, of which he was Secretary-General from 1921 to 1935, and during this period promoted the settlement of the country by Jewish immigrants. The foundation of the socialist Labour Party, Mapai, was also his work. In 1935 he became chairman of the Jewish Agency (until 1948) and in 1944 of the World Zionist Organisation. As prime minister of a provisional government he declared the independence of the state of Israel in Tel Aviv on May 14th 1948. In his diary he referred to this event in sober terms: "At 4 the declaration of independence. All over the country immense joy and celebration, but once again I feel myself to be . . . bereaved, though surrounded by jubilant multitudes."
In his subsequent years in government, during the War of Independence, Ben-Gurion succeeded in asserting the existence of Israel in face of the neighbouring Arab states and in doubling the population of the country by mass immigration. Worn down by cabinet crises and feuds within his own party, he resigned his office in 1953 and joined the recently founded kibbutz of Sede Boqer. His withdrawal from politics, however, lasted only 14 months, after which he felt bound in view of the military situation to take up political office again, first as defence minister and then as prime minister again. He continued as prime minister until 1963, when he resigned – again because of internal party disputes. The new party, Rafi, which he founded in 1965 achieved no great electoral success in subsequent elections, and he increasingly withdrew from politics. He resigned from the Knesset in 1970. Ben-Gurion spent the last years of his life mainly in Sede Boqer, where he selected the site of his grave, on the highest point of a crag looking out on the Wilderness of Zin.

David Ben-Gurion
(1886–1973)

The Jewish philologist Eliezer Ben Yehuda is honoured as the "inventor" of modern Hebrew (Ivrit).
Born in Lithuania, Ben Yehuda lived in Jerusalem from 1881 as a teacher and journalist, and also played a leading part in the Zionist movement. His main concern was to re-establish Hebrew as an everyday spoken language, and for this purpose he began to reconstruct a modern tongue from Biblical

Eliezer Ben
Yehuda
(1858–1922)

and other classical sources and compiled a dictionary of Old and New Hebrew. In 1890 he founded a Hebrew Language Committee, which later developed into the Academy of the Hebrew Language.

There are streets named after Ben Yehuda in a number of Israeli towns. In Jerusalem, where he died in 1922, Ben Yehuda Street is in the centre of the modern city.

Max Brod
(1884–1968)

Born in Prague, Max Brod studied law and was at first a government official, then a theatre and music critic and a writer. He is best known as a friend of Franz Kafka and the publisher of his works – posthumously and against Kafka's express wish. Brod himself wrote Expressionist works like "On the Beauty of Ugly Pictures" (1913), "A Pugnacious Life" (autobiographical; 1960, enlarged edition 1969) and "Of the Immortality of the Soul" (1969).

The political situation in Prague led Brod at an early stage to become involved in the Zionist movement. In 1939 he emigrated to Palestine, where he worked for many years as literary director of the Habimah Theatre in Tel Aviv. He also wrote essays, biographical works and numerous novels, many of them with Jewish settings. He spent the last years of his life in a modest flat in Tel Aviv and was buried in a cemetery on the south side of the city.

David
(ruled 1004 to
965 B.C.)

After the death of Saul David was anointed in Hebron as king of Judah, and soon afterwards was recognised by the twelve tribes as king of the whole kingdom. The two books of Samuel describe the rise of the shepherd boy of Bethlehem, his first anointing by Samuel, his skill as a player on the harp, his appointment as Saul's armour-bearer, his fight with the Philistine giant Goliath and the jealousy of Saul, who soon began to regard the successful David as a hated rival.

The constant tensions between the northern kingdom of Israel and the southern kingdom of Judah pointed to the desirability of a neutral site for the capital of the united kingdom. Thereupon David conquered the Jebusite city of Jebus (Jerusalem); the Jebusites, allowed to remain in their town, supported the new king; and Jerusalem became the capital and was surrounded by a wall. The Jebusite acropolis, known as Zion, was given the name of the City of David.

The Ark of the Covenant, the symbol of the presence of God, was then transferred to Jerusalem, which thus became the political and spiritual centre of a kingdom extending from the Mediterranean to the Arabian Desert.

In the Bible David is depicted as the epitome of a ruler pleasing to God, a statesman and a poet, a general and a musician. All later kings are measured against his standard. He had his lapses, like his dancing before the Ark of the Covenant, but he never turned away from the Lord, and his greatest sin – his adultery with Bathsheba and his murder of Uriah – was forgiven him after he repented. After a period of mourning he married Bathsheba, who bore him a son: Solomon, his successor (see below).

David desired to build a temple in which to house the Ark of the Covenant but, as the prophet had foretold, this task was reserved for Solomon. David died at the age of 70.

Moshe Dayan
(1915–81)

General Moshe Dayan made a major contribution to the legend of the invincibility of the Israeli army, but was also active as a leading politician for many years.

Moshe Dayan was born in the first kibbutz established in Israel at Neganya near the Sea of Galilee. He began by earning his living as an agricultural worker, and at an early age joined Haganah, the Jewish self-defence organisation. He gained his first military experience as company commander in a "troop for the protection of Jewish communities against Arab raids and for the support of special operations by the British army". In one such operation a bullet destroyed his left eye, which thereafter was concealed under his characteristic black eye-patch. During the War of Independence he played a major part in numerous successful military operations and was finally appointed commandant of the city of Jerusalem. He also proved himself as a politician when he conducted the negotiations for a ceasefire in 1948–49. Appointed chief of the general staff by Ben-Gurion in 1953, he was supreme commander of Israeli troops in the Sinai campaign of 1956. After his term as chief of staff Dayan, then 41 years old, began to study political science at Jerusalem University. His two years of study, which he himself regarded as a period of "leave", gave him the theoretical basis for his later political offices. In 1959 he became minister of agriculture in Ben-Gurion's government, a post which he held until 1964. In 1965 he was involved in the founding of the Rafi party, still retaining his seat in the Knesset; but in 1967, when the political situation in Israel became increasingly critical, he felt called on to take an important military job again and was appointed minister of defence.

His services in the Six Day War won Dayan a high reputation, but he was severely criticised for alleged failings in the Yom Kippur War in 1973 and lost his post as defence minister in 1974. He returned to political life as foreign minister in 1977–79, when he played an important part in the conclusion of the Israeli-Egyptian peace treaty. He resigned from this post because of serious differences with Begin over foreign policy and settlement policy.

After his retirement he enjoyed only a brief period of private life, dying in Tel Aviv in 1981.

As a botanist and one of the best known specialists in desert ecology Michael Evenari has played an important part in the development of Israel. It is thanks to his work that parts of the Negev and other deserts throughout the world can be brought into intensive cultivation through a carefully devised irrigation system.

Michael Evenari
(b. 1904)

Evenari was born in Metz in 1904 as Walter Schwarz. After taking his degree in botany he became a lecturer in the universities of Frankfurt, Prague and Darmstadt. Increasing anti-semitism and his dismissal from his university post compelled him in 1933 to leave Germany and emigrate to Israel. A period of fruitful scientific work now began, interrupted by five years in the Jewish Brigade of the British army and much foreign travel. Evenari specialised in research into the reactions and adaptations of desert plants and the history of settlement in the Negev. What had been possible thousands of years ago – flourishing desert towns with no water problems – could surely, he thought, be reproduced in modern times. He successfully reconstructed ancient desert farms and irrigated their fields and fruit plantations, using the ancient "run-off" method.

St Helen, mother of Constantine the Great, was the founder of almost all the early Christian buildings in and around Jerusalem. Originally the owner of an inn in Bithynia, Helen married the future Emperor Constantius Chlorus and in the year 312, after his death, became a Christian. In 313 Constantine promulgated the Edict of Milan, which granted tolerance to Christians. Accounts of Constantine's conversion are embroidered with legend: it is said that a cross with the inscription "Under this sign you will conquer" appeared to him before a decisive battle. In 325 Helen, now raised to the status of Augusta, made a pilgrimage to Jerusalem at Constantine's behest and there found the True Cross.

St Helen
(c. 257–c. 337)

Her discoveries in the Holy Land – mainly of various relics – led to the building of many churches, the most important of which were the Church of the Holy Sepulchre in Jerusalem and the Church of the Nativity in Bethlehem. The relics of the Cross were taken to Rome, where they were displayed annually on Good Friday and May 3rd in the church of Santa Croce in Gerusalemme.

Helen died at the age of 80, probably in Rome, and was buried on the Via Labicana. Constantine had her remains transferred to Constantinople. Her sarcophagus is now in the Vatican Museum. In the 9th century her relics were conveyed to the abbey of Hautvilliers in France; they are now in the church of Santa Maria in Aracoeli in Rome.

Famous People

Herod the Great
(c. 73 B.C.
to 4 B.C.)

Herod I – one of the greatest builders of the ancient world, the most hated and the most complex of the rulers of Judaea and the only one to bear the style of "the Great" – was born in Idumaea which had come under the control of the Jewish Hasmonean (Maccabee Dynasty), the son of the royal governor Antipater and an Arabian princess, Cyprus. After Antipater was murdered the Roman triumvir Mark Antony appointed Herod Tetrarch in 42 B.C.; but during the struggle for the Jewish throne Herod was compelled to flee to Rome, where in 40 B.C. the Senate proclaimed him King of the Jews. After the conquest of Jerusalem and the execution of many members of the Jewish nobility Herod took up his post in 37 B.C. His policy was based on close links with Rome and a constant attempt to realise the Roman concept of the *pax romana* combined with the ideas of Hellenism. During his reign Palestine enjoyed a period of unexampled prosperity and over thirty years of peace. The Jews were left almost undisturbed in the practice of their religion, though they considered Hellenisation and Herodian control to be a basic interference with their society. Revolts against Rome occurred in A.D. 66–70 and again in A.D. 132–135 and there were many smaller revolts during Herod's reign.

The country's prosperity was reflected in much building activity, which Herod contrived to carry out without raising taxes. In addition to building the towns of Samaria and Caesarea (the largest port in the ancient world) he was particularly concerned to enlarge and embellish Jerusalem. The Antonia Fortress was built above the Temple platform and a new district grew up on the north of the city, with a theatre and circus. The three towers of the citadel in the western part of the city survived even the destruction of Jerusalem by the Romans. The city's water supply was also considerably improved. Around 20 B.C. Herod altered and rebuilt the Temple in a form which far surpassed the older building in size and splendour. Other buildings of Herod's reign were the rock stronghold of Masada on the Dead Sea, the luxurious fortress of Herodeion near Bethlehem, the complex of structures above the Patriarchs' Cave at Machpelah in Hebron and the winter palace at Jericho.

In Christian tradition, in literature and often in historical writing Herod is depicted as a bloodthirsty tyrant who sought to win over the Jews by grandiose display and the creation of general prosperity, the builder of strongholds to cow the people, the murderer of his wife Mariamne and the inhuman monster who ordered the massacre of the infants of Bethlehem. Herod died in Jericho. The Jewish historian Flavius Josephus describes the ceremonial transfer of his remains from Jericho to the Herodeion, where Herod had already erected his mausoleum. A number of burials have been discovered in the Herodeion, but the grave of Herod himself has not been found.

Theodor Herzl
(1860–1904)

Theodor Herzl was the founder of political Zionism, and the establishment of the state of Israel was essentially the consequence of the ideas he put forward.

Born in Budapest, Herzl graduated as a doctor of philosophy in Vienna in 1884, at a time when anti-Jewish disturbances were a daily occurrence at Vienna University. From 1891 to 1895 he worked as a foreign correspondent in Paris, where the anti-Semitic attitude of much of the population, particularly during the Dreyfus affair, made him a confirmed supporter of Zionism. After his return from Paris, in 1896, Herzl published in Vienna the Zionist manifesto "The Jewish State", in which he called for the establishment of a sovereign Jewish state on the ground that the Jews were not only a religious community but a separate people. As possible countries to which they might emigrate he mentioned Argentina and Palestine. He saw the constitution of the future Jewish state as a form of constitutional monarchy or aristocratic republic.

In 1897 Herzl convened the first Zionist Congress in Basle, at which the "creation for the Jewish people of a home in Palestine secured by public law" was adopted as the Zionist programme. Herzl wrote in his diary on September 30th 1897: "In Basle I have founded the Jewish state. Perhaps in

Theodor Herzl

Else Lasker-Schüler

Golda Meir

five years, certainly in fifty, everyone will realise that." The negotiations on the foundation of a Jewish state which Herzl, as President of the World Zionist Organisation, conducted with the Sultan and a number of European rulers ended, however, in failure.

After the establishment of the Jewish state in 1948 Herzl's body was transferred from Vienna to Mount Herzl in Jerusalem. Every year the inaugural ceremonies on Israel's National Day are conducted here.

The importance of Flavius Josephus lies in his work as a historian. His "Jewish War" and "Jewish Antiquities" are still valuable sources on the history of Israel and the Jews in the 1st century A.D. Both works were addressed to a readership in the Roman and Hellenistic world. His "Jewish War" was designed to support the Jewish cause and at the same time to glorify his Roman patrons Vespasian and Titus. In the "Antiquities" he was concerned to explain Jewish life and religion to non-Jews.

Flavius Josephus (A.D. 37/38 to after 100)

Although Flavius Josephus was highly regarded by the Romans his ideas at first had no great influence. After he was acclaimed by the doctors of the Church as one of the great historians of antiquity he remained until the 18th century one of the most read ancient authors. 19th and 20th century scholars, however, have identified inaccuracies and literary defects in his writings, and his work is now regarded more critically.

Born in Jerusalem in A.D. 37 or 38, Flavius Josephus (Joseph Ben Mattathias) was a scion of the Jewish priestly nobility. He first made his mark during a visit to Rome (64–66), when he secured the release from prison of a number of Jewish priests. During the Jewish War he fought against the Romans in Galilee and was finally taken prisoner. His prophecy that Vespasian would become Emperor brought him imperial favour: whereupon he adopted the Emperor's family name of Flavius and thereafter fought on the Roman side. In the year 70 he was present when Titus captured Jerusalem. At the end of the war Josephus settled in Rome, where he enjoyed the favour of Vespasian, Titus and Domitian, who granted him Roman citizenship and an annual pension, and devoted himself to his historical writing. Josephus married four times, his last wife being a Jewish woman from Crete, and had five sons. He is believed to have died in Rome after 100.

The satirical writer Ephraim Kishon was born in Budapest, where he studied art history and qualified as a teacher. He spent the Second World War in Hungarian, German and Russian camps. In 1948 he won a literary prize for a novel which could not be published in Hungary. He emigrated to Israel in 1949 and at first earned his living as an electrician and motor mechanic. He learned Hebrew and in 1952 began to write political and satirical pieces, many of them published in Israel's most popular newspaper.

Ephraim Kishon (b. 1924)

His first longer works were published in Germany in the early sixties ("Turn Round, Mrs Lot", 1961; "Noah's Ark, Tourist Class", 1963, etc.). These and his later satirical works, like "The Case of Cain and Abel" (1976), "Just in Case" (1987) and "Linked to the Network" (1989), show a strong sense for situation comedy. Kishon directs his satire against common human foibles, political and bureaucratic absurdities and the follies of contemporary life, though he is not really concerned to seek remedies for what is wrong. In addition to his short stories and novels he also writes plays and scripts for films and television.

Now a popular and successful author, Kishon sees himself as "an Israeli writer who spends a lot of time in Europe". His works, written in Hebrew, have been translated into many languages.

Teddy Kollek
(b. 1911)

As Mayor of Jerusalem Teddy Kollek is known far beyond the bounds of his city and ranks as one of the most popular and most progressive of Jewish politicians.

Born in Vienna, the son of a Jewish office-worker, Kollek became involved in the Zionist Socialist youth movement, attended various congresses from 1923 onward and in 1930 entered an agricultural training centre for Jewish settlement in Palestine. In 1935 he emigrated to Palestine and founded the En Gev kibbutz on the east side of the Sea of Galilee.

After various missions on behalf of the Zionist movement, including intelligence activity in Istanbul during the Second World War, he went in 1947 to New York, where he prepared for the establishment of the state of Israel by purchasing and smuggling arms and above all by collecting money from American Jews. From 1952 to 1964 he was head of the prime minister's office in the new state, and in 1965 became mayor of Jerusalem, an office he held until 1993. Teddy Kollek is regarded as the creator of present-day Jerusalem. No other politician has done so much to transform the former British provincial administrative centre into a flourishing metropolis, making efforts to maintain co-existence among Jerusalem's many peoples. There are no commemorative tablets to Teddy Kollek in Jerusalem, but almost all the modern achievements in Jerusalem, as well as the restoration and refurbishment of its older buildings, are to be attributed to him. He also played a major part in the building up of the Israel Museum and initiated the Spring Festival.

Else Lasker-
Schüler
(1869–1945)

Else Lasker-Schüler, one of the great German women lyric poets, died in poverty, almost forgotten, in Jerusalem in 1945.

She was born in Wuppertal-Elberfeld in the Rhineland, the daughter of a Jewish banker and architect. A happy childhood was followed by two failed marriages. In 1933 the rise of National Socialism compelled her to leave Germany and she moved to Zurich, where she continued her unsettled bohemian life. In 1934 friends financed her first visit to Jerusalem, of which she had already written enthusiastically in her poems (e.g. "Hebrew Ballads", 1913). She visited Jerusalem again in 1937, intending to return to Switzerland, but was prevented from doing so by the outbreak of the Second World War. Her life in Jerusalem was unhappy, and her letters to relatives and friends reflect bitterness and despair. She lived in a modest furnished room, spending her days in the Café Sichel in the centre of Jerusalem, and scraped a meagre living by giving readings, with the help of subsidies from a few friends. The volume of poems which she wrote during this period ("My Blue Piano", 1943) was published in an edition of only a few hundred copies.

In the last years of her life Lasker-Schüler was working on a drama entitled "Ichundich" ("I-and-I"), which she was unable to complete. In January 1945 she collapsed in her favourite café, and died a few days later in the hospital on Mount Scopus. Her friends arranged for her burial on the Mount of Olives.

Golda Meir
(1897–1978)

One of the few women to play a leading role in the history of Israel was Golda Meir, prime minister from 1969 to 1974.

Born in Kiev, she had an unhappy childhood: her early years were a time of poverty, cold, hunger and fear. The situation improved when the family emigrated to the United States in 1906. Golda Meir completed a course of higher education, worked as a librarian and in other jobs, and found time to become involved in the Zionist movement. With her husband Morris, whom she had married in 1917, she emigrated to Palestine in 1921 and lived for some time in a kibbutz and then in Tel Aviv and Jerusalem.

She became a member of the Mapai party and of the trade union organisation Histadrut. From 1946 to 1948 she was chairman of the political section of the Jewish Agency for Palestine, and in 1948 she was one of the signatories of the proclamation on the foundation of the state of Israel. In 1948–49 she was Israeli ambassador in Moscow; thereafter she became head of the Ministry of Labour, and finally spent eleven years as foreign minister. In March 1969 she was elected prime minister by the Knesset, and remained in office after a general election in December 1973. She resigned in April 1974 on account of the continuing controversy over deficiencies revealed in the Yom Kippur War, and died in Jerusalem in 1978.

The internationally known architect Moshe Safdie was born in Haifa and emigrated at the age of 15 to Canada. After his studies at Montreal University he opened his own architectural office in Montreal. In 1975 he was invited to take up a chair at Beersheba University, where he became head of the department of desert architecture and the environment. Three years later, however, he moved to Cambridge University.

Moshe Safdie (b. 1938)

Safdie's breakthrough as an architect came in 1967 with his Habitat project, a residential complex built for the international exhibition of that year in Montreal, Expo 67. Subsequently he was responsible for numerous major buildings, including some in Israel. He was concerned in the redevelopment of the Jewish Old City in Jerusalem and was responsible for the building of Yeshivat Porat Yosef College and for the Mamilla project. Safdie likes to form his buildings from loose and irregular combinations of standard units made from prefabricated parts, in a manner reminiscent of medieval European towns on sloping sites and of closely packed North African and Middle Eastern towns.

Solomon, son of David (see above) and Bathsheba, became king during his father's lifetime. During his reign the kingdom of Israel attained its greatest extent, reaching from the Mediterranean (excluding Philistia) to the Euphrates and southward to the frontiers of Egypt.

Solomon (reigned 965 to 926 B.C.)

Solomon's reorganisation of the kingdom into twelve administrative units, with the court and the army alternating between them, the rearmament of his forces, now equipped with chariots, and the building of numerous fortresses all had a defensive purpose, but he also contrived to extend his territories by diplomatic means and above all by his marriage policy: he had no fewer than 700 principal and subsidiary wives (1 Kings 11,3). The expansion of the kingdom brought with it control over almost all trade with Arabia. The wealth resulting from this trade, together with the income from the copper- and iron-mines on the Red Sea, was spent mainly on the development and embellishment of Jerusalem, including in particular the building of the Temple.

Apart from the building of the Temple and his successes in foreign and domestic policy Solomon is mainly famed for his wisdom. He is described in the Old Testament as "wiser than all men" (1 Kings 4,31); and "there came of all people to hear the wisdom of Solomon, from all kings of the earth." To him too are attributed the book of Proverbs, the book of Ecclesiastes and the Song of Solomon.

Like his father David, Solomon was torn between obedience to God and sin; but while David's sins were forgiven him God's judgment on Solomon was never withdrawn, for he had turned to other gods. Under the influence of his foreign wives Solomon had worshipped the Phoenician fertility and love goddess Ashtoreth, the Ammonite god Moloch, to whom children were sacrificed (see Sights from A to Z, Jerusalem, Hinnom valley), and other foreign deities. God's punishment was that after his death his kingdom would fall apart.

Solomon died after a reign of forty years, and his kingdom was divided into the northern state of Israel and the southern state of Judah.

Yigael Yadin
(1917–84)

Yigael Yadin was one of Israel's leading archaeologists. He took part in the excavation of the Biblical city of Hazor, investigated the Qumran caves, where the first of the "Dead Sea scrolls" were discovered by a Bedouin shepherd in 1948, and became world-famous as director of the excavations at Masada from 1963 onwards.

Yadin's life, however, was not solely dedicated to archaeology. Born in Jerusalem, he was actively involved in the Haganah during the British Mandate, and after the declaration of independence and the subsequent attack by Arab forces he became deputy chief of staff of the army, establishing and organising the Israeli system of an army of reservists.

At the age of 35 he abandoned his military career and thereafter devoted himself to archaeology. In 1973, however, he was called on to head a commission of investigation into the Yom Kippur War. The commission's report brought an inglorious end to the political careers of Golda Meir and Moshe Dayan. Some years later Yadin decided to become personally involved in politics, and in 1976 he founded the "Party of Change", which sought to bring a "fresh wind" into political life. At first the new party attracted considerable numbers of supporters, but after the change of government in 1977 support fell off. Yadin became deputy prime minister in Menachem Begin's government and concerned himself particularly with improving housing conditions in the poorer quarters of the towns. Political work did not, however, bring the successes he hoped for, and in 1981 he retired into private life.

Art and Architecture

The first structures pointing to the emergence of an urban culture appear in Jericho in the 8th millennium B.C. in the form of a number of circular houses and a round tower 8.5m/28ft high with an internal staircase abutting on a 4m/13ft high wall, 3m/10ft thick at the base, which may be a town wall. In the 7th millennium houses on a rectangular plan were built in Jericho containing skulls modelled in plaster – an early form of portrait. After a long period during which Jericho and other settlements were abandoned the sites were reoccupied by nomads in the 5th millennium. In the Negev, near Beersheba, semi-nomads lived in oval underground dwellings entered from above (the Beersheba culture). In the Megiddo area (Jezreel plain) a Canaanite settlement with a shrine was established in the 4th millennium. Other Canaanite towns, farther south, were Gezer (site of Tel Gezer) and Arad. In the 2nd millennium Canaanites founded in the north of the country the considerable town of Hazor and Bet Shean with its impressive temples. The Canaanites, a sedentary people, had a polytheistic religion with over thirty gods – the most important being Baal – to whom they erected temples. In the religious field there was thus a fundamental difference between the indigenous population and the Israelite tribes pushing into the country, who recognised only one God, Yahweh. The "residence" of Yahweh was the portable tabernacle which housed the Ark of the Covenant. The Canaanite temple which has been excavated at Lachish has a main hall with an altar at one end.

When the Israelites, coming from Egypt, settled in Canaan in the 13th century B.C. they had no art or architecture of their own. The book of Exodus (chapter 37) contains an account of craft activity in the construction and decoration of the Ark of the Covenant. The Biblical ban on graven images or other likenesses (Exodus 20,4; Deuteronomy 5,8) was intended, according to the Mishnah, to prevent the worship of idols. "The fiercely dogmatic attitude of the Jews and the continuing struggle against neighbouring peoples and foreign rule militated against the development of art" (Carel J. du Ry). The religious component in the intellectual life of the people led to a fixation on written texts (the Old Testament and later theological works).

In the reigns of Solomon and his successors there was much building activity. Thus the town of Megiddo, frequently mentioned in the Old Testament, was rebuilt and fortified. The most important building of this period was the Temple in Jerusalem (953 B.C.), in which thereafter the Ark of the Covenant was preserved. For the building of this First Temple Solomon brought in Phoenician craftsmen from Tyre.

After the division of the kingdom following Solomon's death (928 B.C.) a number of towns were successively capital of the northern state of Israel. In 878 King Omri founded Samaria as the future capital. The city was built on a hill and the area containing the palace and the administrative buildings was surrounded by a wall. The excavation of the surviving remains of this wall, built of flat dressed stones, was the first in Palestine to yield evidence of Phoenician influence in masonry techniques. The excavations in Samaria also brought to light ivory carvings which may have been ornaments on furniture.

Following Alexander's conquest of Judaea at the end of the 4th century B.C. Greek cultural influences begin to appear in the 3rd century. Theatres, hippodromes, temples and aqueducts of a type familiar throughout the ancient world are built, but some of them show the influence of local styles of building. Thus in Bet Shean large marble columns belonging to a

Excavations of the Nabataean city of Mamshit

3rd century Greek temple were found. The most impressive remains at Bet Shean, however, are the ruins of the Roman theatre, the largest and best preserved in Israel.

Before Palestine was incorporated in the Roman Empire the kingdom of the Nabataeans, extending from Petra into the Negev, enjoyed a great flowering of art and architecture. The Nabataeans, who were gifted artists and architects, built a series of towns like Avdat, Shivta and Mamshit along their trade routes.

Roman period

With the beginning of Roman rule in the 1st century B.C. Palestine was increasingly influenced by the architectural styles of late antiquity. Herod the Great covered the country with monumental structures (Hebron, Herodeion, Masada, Caesarea, Samaria/Sebaste, Ascalon). In Jerusalem he built the Antonia Fortress and rebuilt the Temple. The ban on graven images, however, remained in force, and accordingly the representations of animals in the palace of Herod Antipas in Tiberias were judged to be contrary to the Law and were removed at the earliest opportunity.

After the destruction of the Temple the practice of worship was the bond which united all Jews. Many synagogues – meeting-places in which the community could worship – were built. These were usually rectangular or on a centralised plan, with a recess facing east and curtained off in which the shrine containing the Torah scrolls was housed. The scrolls were (and are) rolled round rods with crowns or finials (*rimonim*) at the ends.

The oldest surviving synagogue is believed to be the one at Capernaum, built in the 2nd or 3rd century. To the same period belongs the ruined synagogue in Chorazin, which is built of black basalt. Both of these have three aisles. There are also remains of an early synagogue at Gush Halav. In the 3rd century the Jews began to move away from their aniconic attitude. In synagogues in Galilee there are representations of angels, human beings and animals, and even of the Greek god Helios in the centre of the Zodiac; and the walls of the 3rd century synagogue at Dura Europos

Roman remains, Ashqelon and Masada

North Church, Avdat

79

on the Euphrates (now Es-Salahiye in Syria) are completely covered with paintings on Biblical themes.

Greco-Roman, and also Palmyrene, influence is also evident in tombs. The representation of mythological scenes on sarcophagi was no longer objected to, as numerous examples at Bet Shearim demonstrate.

Early Christian and Byzantine period

Christian influence began to make itself felt in Palestine in the 4th century. From the time of Constantine the Great, who erected the Church of the Nativity in Bethlehem and the Church of the Holy Sepulchre in Jerusalem, numerous churches and religious houses were built, together with hospices for the many thousands of pilgrims. This development reached its peak in the 6th century, in the reign of Justinian, with more religious buildings and extensive urban developments in the Negev, using the building and irrigation techniques of the Nabataeans.

At Tabgha, where the feeding of the five thousand was believed to have taken place, a three-aisled basilica was erected on the foundations of an earlier church; its mosaic pavements, with representations of fish and a basket containing bread, have been preserved. Mosaics belonging to Christian churches (5th/6th c.), with representations of animals and symbols of the seasons, have been brought to light at Ben Guvrin.

Jewish synagogues of this period are also decorated with mosaics. Mosaic pavements belonging to a synagogue of the 5th/6th century have been preserved in Jericho, and at Bet Alfa the mosaic pavement of a 6th century synagogue was discovered in 1928.

Arab period

Between the 7th and the 11th century Arab Islamic culture left its mark on Palestine. The Omayyad Caliphs built mosques, palaces and fortresses. The ban on images which Islam shares with Judaism was not yet in operation in the Omayyad period, until the middle of the 8th century. In Jerusalem the Dome of the Rock with its rich mosaic decoration and the El-Aqsa Mosque were built during this period, in Jericho Hisham's Palace, built as a winter residence of the Omayyad Caliphs. Numbers of caravanserais (khans) were also built.

Age of the Crusades

During the Crusades (12th/13th c.) the Crusaders, many of them French knights, built strongholds in the Holy Land. There are Crusader castles, for example, at Akko (Acre), Atlit, Belvoir, Caesarea and Montfort. The Crusaders also built churches, particularly in Jerusalem (St Anne's Church, Church of the Assumption). The Crusader church at Abu Ghosh – a three-aisled basilica with remains of frescoes – is one of the best preserved in the country.

The buildings of the crusading period combine western elements with Oriental features. The churches and castles show a transition from the compact architecture of the 12th century to the lighter Gothic of the 13th.

Ottoman period

Numerous buildings survive from the period of Turkish rule (1517–1917), like the mosque of 1781 in Akko and the Mahmudiye Mosque in Jaffa (1810). During the Ottoman period Christian influence gradually increased again, and many churches were built, including the Protestant Church of the Redeemer (1898) in Jerusalem.

From the 16th century onwards artistic furnishings and utensils for the synagogues were produced, including metalwork (Torah crowns and candlesticks), ceramics (dishes for the Purim festival), fabrics (Torah curtains) and wooden articles (Torah shrines).

British Mandate

During the period of the British Mandate (1920–48) buildings were erected in a pseudo-Oriental style, like the Rockefeller Museum in Jerusalem. In an effort to develop a national style Alexander Baerwald, an architect from Berlin, also used Oriental elements in his design for the Technion (1914–24)

Modern architecture: the Shrine of the Book and the Knesset, Jerusalem ▶

Crusader castle, Caesarea

Khan el-Umdan, Akko

in Haifa. After the Nazis came to power in Germany in 1933 hundreds of architects emigrated to Israel, including Arieh Sharon, a former student of the Bauhaus, whose workers' dwellings in Tel Aviv (1935–40) were much imitated, Joseph Neufeld, Max Loeb and architects of international reputation like Erich Mendelsohn, Alexander Klein and Johann Ratner. The buildings they designed transformed whole districts of Tel Aviv and Haifa into Bauhaus-style settlements.

1948 to the present

After the foundation of the state of Israel in 1948 the main problem, given the great wave of immigrants, was to provide sufficient housing accommodation. There was no time for interesting architectural ideas: the important considerations were speed, economy and quantity. As a result the dwellings built during this period are notable for their plainness and uniformity. There was a gradual change in the sixties: the house types were now more varied, the standard of comfort and amenity higher. In addition to the housing developments on the outskirts of the larger towns (for example East Talpiot and Ramot in Jerusalem) entirely new towns like Arad were built. At the same time a beginning was made with the restoration and rehabilitation of the old town centres. Attractive results of this work can be seen, for example, in Safed and Jaffa as well as in Jerusalem.

In addition to these various housing developments new public buildings were erected in cosmopolitan architectural styles. Interesting examples of modern architecture are the Universities of Beersheba and Jerusalem (Givat Ram and Mount Scopus), the Israel Museum in Jerusalem (by Al Mansfield and Dora Gat), the Tel Aviv Museum of Art (by Dan Eitan and Yitzhak Yashar) and the Mann Auditorium in Tel Aviv, which combines monumentality with functional efficiency.

New religious buildings have also been erected, like the Church of the Annunciation in Nazareth (1969), one of the largest Christian churches in the Middle East.

Painting and Sculpture

The influence of modern trends in the West is also seen in painting and sculpture. The landscapes of Israel, whether a hill with trees or a region in the desert, provide the themes for paintings by Anna Ticho (1894–1980), Raffi Kaiser (b. 1931), Tamara Rikman (b. 1934) and others. From purely representational pictures of the landscape some artists have moved on, in their different ways, to projects concentrating on a particular field. Thus in October 1970 a number of artists carried out the "Jerusalem River Project" in a valley in the arid hills round Jerusalem, using a recording of the sound of falling water, relayed through loudspeakers, to create the impression of a river flowing down the valley. Other painters are concerned with the problems of the towns: thus a picture by Yossef Asher (b. 1946) depicts the featurelessness of a house-front ("Apartment Building", 1971).

In the seventies abstract painting came increasingly to the fore. An outstanding figure in this connection is Moshe Kupferman (b. 1926), whose works are of great expressive quality. Alima (born in Haifa) goes in for geometric abstractions, Reuven Berman (b. 1929) for contrasting areas of colour.

Wood and metal are the materials used for works of sculpture reminiscent of Naum Gabo (Nahum Tevet, b. 1946) or arrangements of pieces of sculpture which are related to one another and thus achieve a powerful spatial effect (Michael Gitlin, b. 1943).

During the seventies numbers of large works of sculpture were set up in squares and in public buildings. Among the creators of these sculptures – mostly abstract works – were Yehiel Shemi (b. 1922), Israel Hadani (b. 1941), Michael Gross (b. 1920), Igael Tumarkin (b. 1933) and Ezra Orion (1934), whose 18m/59ft high stepped sculpture "Ma'alot" (1979–80) stands in a busy street in Jerusalem. The steel sculpture "Ma'agalim" on Mount Scopus, by the well-known sculptor Menashe Kadishman (b. 1932), is in the form of a ring with one section displaced and another missing.

Israeli painting of the seventies was much concerned with political and social themes, and numerous pictures reflect the artists' reactions to current events. Leading representatives of this trend are Zvi Goldstein (b. 1947), Pinchas Cohen Gan (b. 1942), Tamar Getter (b. 1953) and Micha Ullmann (b. 1940). Moshe Gershuni (b. 1936) creates works which suggest war, sorrow and death but also contain elements of consolation ("Shalom Soldier", 1981).

Archaeology

Israel has preserved extraordinary numbers of remains of the past spanning many thousands of years, even though so much has been destroyed down the centuries. Many such monuments of the past have remained standing; others have been excavated by archaeologists during the 19th and 20th centuries.

After earlier investigations by Ulrich Seetzen and J. L. Burckhardt the American scholar Edward Robinson began in 1824–25 to study the topography of Palestine. The first exact cartographic survey of the country from Dan to Beersheba was undertaken in 1871–77 by Condor and Kitchener (the future Lord Kitchener) on behalf of the Palestine Exploration Society. Excavations were carried out in Jerusalem by Caignart de Saulcy (1864), Charles Warren (1867–70), H. Guthe (1882) and F. J. Bliss and R. A. S. Macalister (1891–94), who also worked in the Zevulun plain; in 1902–09 Macalister directed excavations at Gezer.

At the beginning of the 20th century, when Palestine was still under Ottoman rule, Ernst Sellin worked at Taanach (1902–04), Jericho (1907–08) and Shechem (1913–14). Synagogues in Galilee were investigated by H. Kohl and C. Watzinger (1905). G. A. Reisner and C. S. Fisher carried out excavations at Samaria (1908–11), G. Weill in Jerusalem (1914, 1923–24).

During the British Mandate most excavation work was done by British and American archaeologists – at Bet Shean by G. M. Fitzgerald and A. Rower

(1921–23), at Megiddo by P. L. O. Guy and G. Loud (1925–29), in Jerusalem and Samaria by J. W. Crowfoot (1923–27 and 1931–35). Flinders Petrie, who had developed the method of dating occupation levels by pottery finds at Tell el-Hesi in the south of the country in 1891, excavated various sites in south-western Palestine between 1926 and 1936. In southern Judaea W. F. Albright carried out what Avi-Yonah has called a "model excavation" at Tel Beit Mirsim (1926–32), which established the stratification for almost the whole of the Bronze and Iron Ages.

Archaeological work was suspended for many years during the Second World War and the post-war period. Kathleen Kenyon made major new discoveries at Jericho (1955–58) and Jerusalem (1961–67). L. Harding and R. de Vaux investigated the Essenian settlement at Qumran between 1951 and 1958. At Bet Shearim N. Avigad (1953–59) continued the work of B. Mazar (1936–40). Yigael Yadin carried out important excavations at Hazor (1955–58, 1968–69) and Masada (1963–65). From 1967 onwards Mazar and Avigad carried out excavations in Jerusalem, mainly on the outer side of the walls enclosing the Temple platform. Since then there have been excavations at many sites, for example on the tell of Akko, at Ashdod, Ramat Rahel, Beersheba and Lachish, and in recent years particularly at Bet Shean.

At present there are some 250 professional archaeologists working on the most important sites throughout the country – in proportion to population by far the highest number in any country in the world.

Quotations

So Joshua took all that land, the hills, and all the south country, and all the land of Goshen, and the valley, and the plain, and the mountain of Israel, and the valley of the same; even from the mount Halak, that goeth up to Seir, even unto Baal-gad in the valley of Lebanon under mount Hermon: and all their kings he took, and smote them, and slew them. Joshua made war a long time with all those kings. There was not a city that made peace with the children of Israel, save the Hivites the inhabitants of Gibeon: all other they took in battle . . .

So Joshua took the whole land, according to all that the Lord said unto Moses; and Joshua gave it for an inheritance unto Israel according to their divisions by their tribes. And the land rested from war.

Joshua 11,16–19 and 11,23

Old Testament

Masada:
A rock of no small girth and considerable height is surrounded on all sides by steep gorges whose depth cannot be measured from above and in which neither men nor animals can gain a foothold; only at two points can the rock be climbed, and then with difficulty. One access runs up from the asphalt lake to the east; the other, on the west, is less difficult. The first one is known as the Snake because of its narrowness and its many windings. At a point where the rock projects this path describes a bend, and it often turns back on itself and then stretches out again, so that it can be followed only with great difficulty. When you are on this path you must balance first on one foot and then on the other: otherwise you are lost, for on either side yawn deep abysses, the sight of which will terrify the boldest. When you have climbed 30 stades up this path you come to the summit, which does not narrow to a sharp point but forms a plateau. Here the high priest Jonathan built a fortress which he called Masada. Later Herod devoted much effort to improving this stronghold: he surrounded the higher part, measuring seven stades round, with a wall of white stone twelve cubits in height and eight cubits in breadth, with thirty-seven towers, each 50 cubits high. Through this there was access to the dwellings built round the whole inner side of the wall.

"Jewish War", VII,8 (written at the end of the 1st century A.D.).

Flavius Josephus
Jewish historian

Palestine sits in sackcloth and ashes. Over it broods the spell of a curse that has withered its fields and fettered its energies. Where Sodom and Gomorrah reared their domes and towers, that solemn sea now floods the plain, in whose bitter waters no living thing exists – over whose waveless surface the blistering air hangs motionless and dead – about whose borders nothing grows but weeds, and scattering tufts of cane, and that treacherous fruit that promises refreshment to parching lips, but turns to ashes at the touch. Nazareth is forlorn; about that ford of Jordan where the hosts of Israel entered the Promised Land with songs of rejoicing, one finds only a squalid camp of Bedouins of the desert; Jericho the accursed lies a mouldering ruin today, even as Joshua's miracle left it more than three thousand years ago; Bethlehem and Bethany, in their poverty and their humiliation, have nothing about them now to remind one that they once knew the high honour of the Saviour's presence; the hallowed spot where the shepherds watched their flocks by night, and where the angels sang Peace on earth, good will to men, is untenanted by any living creature, and unblessed by any feature that is pleasant to the eye. Renowned Jerusalem itself, the stateliest name in history, has lost its ancient grandeur, and is become a pauper village; the riches of Solomon are no longer there to compel the

Mark Twain
American writer

admiration of visiting Oriental queens; the wonderful temple, which was the pride and glory of Israel, is gone, and the Ottoman crescent is lifted above the spot where, on that most memorable day in the annals of the world, they reared the Holy Cross. The noted Sea of Galilee, where Roman fleets once rode at anchor and the disciples of the Saviour sailed in their ships, was long ago deserted by the devotees of war and commerce, and its borders are a silent wilderness; Capernaum is a shapeless ruin; Magdala is the home of beggared Arabs; Bethsaida and Chorazin have vanished from the earth, and the "desert places" round about them, where thousands of men once listened to the Saviour's voice and ate the miraculous bread, sleep in the hush of a solitude that is inhabited only by birds of prey and skulking foxes.

Palestine is desolate and unlovely. And why should it be otherwise? Can the *curse* of the Deity beautify a land?

Palestine is no more of this work-day world. It is sacred to poetry and tradition — it is dream-land.

From "The Innocents Abroad", 1869.

Conrad von Orelli
(1846–1917)
Swiss theologian

Nablus:

Since we did not wish to disturb them we climbed up to the "ash hills" at the foot of Mount Gerizim, from which there is a magnificent view of the town and its hills. When one comes from the arid south one is surprised by the abundance of water in the town. True, one no longer hears the murmuring of streams in the streets of which earlier descriptions speak: the channels have been covered over. But numerous streams still flow down the slopes of Mount Gerizim, and in consequence there are dense growths of cactuses, olives and fruit-trees of all kinds, more or less uncared-for. One is reminded of Jotham's fable of the trees which set out to appoint a king over them (Judges 9,8); for here they all grow intermingled and in republican sovereignty.

From "Durchs Heilige Land. Tagebuchblätter" ("Through the Holy Land: Leaves from a Diary").

Baedeker
"Palestine and
Syria"

Nazareth:

The appearance of the little town, especially in spring, when its dazzling white walls are embosomed in the green of cactus-hedges, fig-trees and olive-trees, is very charming. The rapidly increasing population amounts to about 15,000, including 5000 Moslems, 5000 Orthodox Greeks, 1000 United Greeks, 2000 Latins, 200 Maronites and 250 Protestants. The town enjoys a certain measure of prosperity; most of the inhabitants are engaged in farming, gardening or cattle-raising, some of them in handicrafts (particularly in the manufacture of knives, sickles, ploughshares and so on), and in the cotton and grain trade. The inhabitants are noted for their turbulent disposition. The Christian farmers have retained many peculiarities of costume. At festivals the women, many of whom are beautiful, wear gay embroidered jackets and have their foreheads and breasts laden with coins, while the riding-camel which forms an indispensable feature in such a procession is smartly caparisoned with shawls and strings of coins.

From Baedeker's "Palestine and Syria", 5th English edition, 1912.

The Balfour
Declaration

His Majesty's Government view with favour the establishment in Palestine of a national home for the Jewish people, and will use their best endeavours to facilitate the achievement of this object, it being clearly understood that nothing shall be done which may prejudice the civil and religious rights of existing non-Jewish communities in Palestine, or the rights and political status enjoyed by Jews in any other country.

From a letter written on November 2nd 1917 by A. J. Balfour, British Foreign Secretary, to Lord Rothschild.

And so we come to Safed, the highest town in the country. It is an old Kabbalist town, surrounded by the smaller dwelling-places of medieval teachers like Rabbi Meir. From the ruins of the old castle of the knights of St John we have wide views over Galilee, the land of miracles, which now lies at our feet. From here the road runs up to a pass from which we have views taking in the lake, the Mediterranean and the snow-covered peak of Mount Hermon. This is one of the most magnificent viewpoints in the world. We are favoured by the sun: when we passed this way two years ago the sky was covered with clouds. Today the country glows in the most cheerful golden light. A finer farewell and conclusion cannot be imagined . . .

And now the way down from the pass to Akko is a quite new world. The breath of the Mediterranean rises up to us, more authentic and more concentrated than at Jaffa. The road is flanked on both sides by wondrously venerable, rich red-earthy olive-trees. The air is infused with Homeric/Greek light effects of the sun. What is it that at once calls up the odour of Greece? It is not merely the marriage of air and light: somehow the etherisation of the liquid element is also aromatically involved. It cannot be described. It has a divinely light quality which communicates itself at once to our senses.

Then we are in the Crusader city of Akko: a city on the sea which gives us a distant impression of Tyre and Sidon. The air is imbued with the atmosphere and the brightness of the sea. We walk through the streets, visit the mosque with its beautiful verdant arcaded courtyard, we see the vaulting of the old Crusader church in the cellars of adjoining houses and spend a long time on the fortress walls, battered by the sounding surf. The crusading period is overlaid by the history of Napoleonic times; but on the horizon the image of the Crusades and the spirit of chivalry rise gently up. We now drive towards the long ridge of Mount Carmel which closes off the bay on the south . . .

Haifa is now a great city which has grown tremendously. In the last two years its aspect has been totally changed. It has acquired a large harbour surrounded by quays, and European-style blocks of flats cover the whole length of the high ridge which slopes down to the bay.

From "Reisetagebücher" ("Travel Diaries"), Stuttgart, 1986 (referring to a journey to Palestine in 1934).

Emil Bock
German
theologian

Jerusalem:
The beauty of Jerusalem in its landscape can be compared with that of Toledo. The city stands in the mountains, a scape of domes and towers enclosed by crenellated walls and perched on a table of rock above a deep valley. As far as the distant hills of Moab the contours of the country resemble those of a physical map, sweeping up the slopes in regular, stratified curves, and casting grand shadows in the sudden valleys. Earth and rock reflect the lights of a fire-opal. Such an essay in urban emplacement, whether accidental or contrived, has made a work of art . . .

Yet Jerusalem is more than picturesque, more than shoddy in the style of so many Oriental towns. There may be filth, but there is no brick or plaster, no crumbling and discolourment. The buildings are wholly of stone, a whitish cheese-like stone, candid and luminous, which the sun turns to all tones of ruddy gold. Charm and romance have no place. All is open and harmonious. The associations of history and belief, deep-rooted in the first memories of childhood, dissolve before the actual apparition. The outpourings of faith, the lamentations of Jew and Christian, the devotion of Islam to the holy Rock, have enshrouded the *genius loci* with no mystery. That spirit is an imperious emanation, evoking superstitious homage, sustained thereby perhaps, but existing independently of it. Its sympathy is with the centurions rather than the priests. And the centurions are here again. They wear shorts and topees, and answer, when addressed, with a Yorkshire accent.

From "The Road to Oxiana", 1937.

Robert Byron
English writer

Quotations

Leon Uris
American writer

The Negev Desert composed half the area of Israel. It was for the most part a wilderness, with some areas which resembled the surface of the moon. This was the wilderness of Paran and Zin where Moses wandered in search of the Promised Land. It was a broiling mass of denuded desolation where the heat burned down at a hundred and twenty-five degrees over the endless slate fields and deep gorges and canyons. Mile after mile of the rock plateaus would not give life to so much as a single blade of grass. No living thing, not even a vulture, dared penetrate.

The Negev Desert became Israel's challenge. The Israelis went down to the desert. They lived in the merciless heat and they built settlements on rock. They did as Moses had done: they brought water from the rocks, and they made life grow.

They searched for minerals. Potash was pulled from the Dead Sea. King Solomon's copper mines, silent for eternities, were made to smelt the green ore again. Traces of oil were found. A mountain of iron was discovered. The northern entrance to the Negev, Beersheba, became a boom town with a skyline springing up on the desert overnight.

The greatest hope of the Negev was Elath, at the southern tip on the Gulf of Akaba. When Israeli troops arrived at the end of the War of Liberation it consisted of two mud huts. Israel had the dream of making a port there with a direct route to the Orient, someday when the Egyptians lifted the blockade of the Gulf of Akaba. They built in preparation for that day.

From "Exodus", 1958.

Ephraim Kishon
Israeli writer

The history of Tel Aviv, too, is quite notable. It dates back only fifty years. Once upon a time, fifty years ago, there were two Jews in a desolate sandy waste. One of them gave it as his opinion that no human being could live there. The other maintained that where there was a will there was a way. They made a bet on it. And so Tel Aviv was founded.

Conditions were so wretched, however, that for a very long time no one settled there. Those who tried to were soon driven away by the infernal heat and scattered in all directions. Even the handful of Jews who felt compelled, for reasons that were not always clear, to build their miserable shacks on the site and carry on their questionable businesses there fled to more hospitable regions when circumstances permitted.

Tel Aviv came into being without any planning but with a great deal of noise. When the population rose to 15,000 the noise was so great that 5000 of them made good their escape.

The lack of planning had increasingly distressing effects. The streets, laid out with a population of 10,000 in view, were much too cramped to allow even a semi-satisfactory flow of traffic for 50,000 people. As a result even the greatest optimists despaired of the future of Tel Aviv. And certainly the dismal and unsightly town had a depressing effect on its 100,000 inhabitants, not least because of the almost complete absence of open spaces. When it is considered, too, that the town had only inadequate rudiments of a drainage system, so that when it rained whole districts were under water, it is easy to understand why the population never rose above 150,000. Tel Aviv, we must regretfully admit, is not an attractive town. How many Jews can we expect to live in an intolerably overcrowded huddle of houses in catastrophic housing conditions? Well, how many? 250,000? All right; but that is the absolute maximum.

I am no grumbler, I assure you, but I cannot help wondering how it is possible for a city of 400,000 inhabitants to have no zoo and to do practically nothing else for its children. Why, for example, is there no decent bathing station? Why are there no nice places where people can enjoy a day in the country? These are not trifling questions: the justified complaints of 700,000 Jews are no trifle.

It is high time the city fathers did something about these things. Otherwise it will be at least three years before the population of Tel Aviv reaches the million mark . . .

From "Drehn Sie sich um, Frau Lot" ("Turn Round, Mrs Lot"), Munich, 1965.

The bus runs past the old town walls of Jerusalem, past the Arab quarter, past the Russian Orthodox church with its golden onion-towers, past the Church of All Nations, with the Garden of Gethsemane, past the mosque with the green dome and then up the Mount of Olives. The whole hill is a cemetery, a huge and ancient cemetery with graves dating from the time of the Second Temple. "The dead are keeping watch," I think. At the point where the road to Jericho branches off I get out and walk up the hill, passing old, fallen gravestones, wading through thistles, with here and there a new grave. It is all overgrown, unkempt, abandoned. Opposite is the Old City with the golden and silver domes of the Mosque of Omar and the El-Aqsa Mosque; to the left extends the Judaean Desert, bathed in a gentle pinkish-purple light; and, looking up, I see the sky, overarching Jerusalem like a light and airy canopy. The colours are brilliantly luminous and yet not garish. The chalk-white of the tombs mingles with the gold of the sun and the blue of the sky. The view ends on the horizon of the desert; the world seems open and endless, with no walls, no houses, no trees to restrict it. It is quiet on the hill, but not oppressive. There is a feeling of unspoiled primeval nature. Grass and thistles cover the gravestones, relieving the solemn seriousness of the cemetery. The dead have been buried, and their fate now lies in God's hands. They don't need any fine tombs, they need no flowers. They are now concerned with other values; and we, the living, leave them in peace.

Lea Fleischmann
German-Israeli
writer

From "Ich bin Israelin" ("I am an Israeli Woman"), Munich, 1982.

Ashdod:

A small Mediterranean city is Ashdod, a pleasant city, unpretentious, with a port and a lighthouse, and a power station and factories and many land-scaped avenues. Not pretending to be Paris or Zurich or aspiring to be Jerusalem. A city planned by social democrats: without imperial boule-vards, without monuments, without grandiose merchants' homes. A city living entirely in the present tense, a clean city, almost serene. The horns of passing cars do not squeal, the pedestrians do not run. It seems that almost everybody here knows almost everybody. If there is poverty it is not glaring. Even the wealth of the suburb of villas near the beach is not ostentatious. A city of workers and businessmen and artisans and house-wives. Of the sixty or seventy thousand souls here, about half are immi-grants from North Africa, approximately one-third come from Western Europe and the Americas, and the remainder are native-born. At this morning hour, a weekday serenity rests on Ashdod: the men at work, some of the women at work, some at home. The children have gone off to day-care centers or to school. You will find no Light unto the Nations here, but also no ghetto or slum – only a small, bright port city rapidly growing and expanding to the south and east.

Amos Oz
Israeli writer

From "In the Land of Israel", London, 1983.

Suggested Routes

The routes suggested in this section are designed to help visitors travelling by car to plan their trip, while leaving them free to vary the routes according to their particular interests and the time available.

The suggested routes take in the main places of interest described in this guide, though some of them involve a side trip or detour off the main route. The routes can be followed on the map at the end of the guide, which will facilitate detailed planning of the trip.

In the description of the routes, places for which there is a separate entry in the A to Z section of this guide are shown in **bold** type. Descriptions of other places can be found by reference to the Index at the end of the guide.

The distances shown in brackets at the head of each route relate to the main route. Where suggested side trips or detours add significantly to the mileage the additional distance is indicated.

Tour of Northern Israel (330km/205 miles)

This tour of northern Israel gives a good impression of the varied topography of the country. It is particularly to be recommended for visitors who are more interested in natural scenery than in archaeological sites or towns.

Visitors who want only to do a little walking and see the main sights can easily do the tour in three days. The starting-point is Haifa; possible overnight stops are Tiberias, on the Sea of Galilee, and a kibbutz hotel in the extreme north of the country (eg. at Kfar Giladi, Hagoshrim or Kfar Blum).

Haifa via
Nazareth to
Tiberias

Much more interesting than the direct road to Nazareth is the longer route through the Mount Carmel range. Leave **Haifa** by way of the attractive Central Carmel district and continue south-east on the Moriah road. The road runs past Haifa University and then climbs to the highest point in the Mount **Carmel** range. Soon after the Druze village of Daliyat a road goes off to Mount Muhraka, with the Carmelite house of St Elias. Returning to the main road, we continue south for another 7km/4½ miles to join the main road coming from Zikhron Ya'aqov. Turning left into this road, we continue north-east; then in 6km/4 miles turning left and soon afterwards right we come to **Bet Shearim**, which in the 2nd and 3rd centuries A.D. was a place of great importance as the seat of the Sanhedrin (interesting catacombs with the tombs of members of the Sanhedrin). A short distance beyond Bet Shearim we join the main road from Haifa to Nazareth. This runs east over the plain and comes in just under 20km/12½ miles to **Nazareth**, with the Church of the Annunciation, the Fountain of Mary and other sites associated with Jesus and his parents.

9km/6 miles north-east of Nazareth is the village of **Cana**, scene of the marriage in Cana. Continuing towards Tiberias, we see on the left of the road the **Horns of Hittim**, where in 1184 the Crusaders suffered an annihilating defeat at the hands of Saladin. The road then runs down to **Tiberias** on the **Sea of Galilee**. A pleasant place to pause is one of the lakeside restaurants, all of which offer the local speciality, St Peter's fish. Two particular features of interest in Tiberias are the spa establishment and the old synagogue in the Hammat district. If you are spending the night in Tiberias a boat trip on the Sea of Galilee in the late afternoon is an attractive possibility. There are regular ferries to the kibbutz of **En Gev** on the other side of the lake.

Bathing lake, Mount Gilboa ▶

Suggested Routes

Tiberias via Capernaum to the northern frontier of Israel

From Tiberias the route continues north on the lakeside road. It is worth stopping at the kibbutz of Ginnosar, situated directly on the lake, which displays a "fishing boat from the time of Christ". On the right of the road can be seen the Kinneret pumping station, which pumps water from the Sea of Galilee into a channel which conveys it to the Negev. From the pumping station a road running in the direction of the lake leads to the ruins of the palace of Minya (1km/¾ mile), which belonged to the Omayyad Caliph El-Walid (705–715), builder of the Omayyad Mosque in Damascus and the El-Aqsa Mosque in Jerusalem.

Immediately north of this are a number of sites associated with the Christian tradition: **Tabgha**, scene of the feeding of the five thousand, with the Church of the Multiplication of the Loaves (5th c. mosaic pavement), the nearby St Peter's Church and Mensa Christi ("Christ's Table"), and **Capernaum**, with a partly rebuilt synagogue and other excavations.

At Tabgha the road leaves the shores of the lake and climbs north into the hills, passing on the right the **Mount of the Beatitudes**. Soon afterwards another road goes off on the right to **Chorazin**.

Farther north is **Rosh Pinna**, where a winding road goes off on the left to **Safed** (8km/5 miles).

Beyond this again, to the left of the road, is the tell of **Hazor**, where 23 occupation levels were identified by the excavators. Just beyond this, to the right, is the kibbutz of Ayelet Hashahar, with a guest-house and a museum displaying finds from Hazor. The road now runs along the **Hule plain**, an area of former marshland which has been drained and brought into cultivation. The Hule Nature Reserve gives an impression of what it was originally like; it is reached on a road which goes off a few kilometres beyond the kibbutz.

The route continues north through the little town of Qiryat Shemona and then turns east. On this road a visit can be paid to the **Dan** Nature Reserve, with waymarked footpaths leading to the springs of Dan and the ancient site of Tel Dan. A few kilometres north-east is another beautiful spot – **Banyas**, where one of the three source streams of the Jordan rises.

From here the road winds its way up the **Golan Heights**, passing Israel's winter sports centre of Newe Ativ, to Nimrod's Castle at Banyas, from which there are magnificent views.

From Qiryat Shemona along the northern frontier to Rosh Haniqra

From Banyas return to Qiryat Shemona, and from there take a road on the right to Metulla; then turn into a road on the left which runs past Tel Hay. On this mound is the grave of Joseph Trumpeldor, a leading Zionist who in 1920 conducted a heroic defence of the settlement against an Arab attack but was killed in the fighting. The building in which the settlers entrenched themselves is now a museum. The road now climbs and turns south, running parallel with the Lebanese frontier and affording superb views of the fertile **Hule plain**.

Soon after the kibbutz of Yiftah turn right at a T junction and continue along the frontier with Lebanon to a point where a road goes off on the left to Bar'am, with the well restored remains of a synagogue of the 2nd or 3rd century. From Bar'am the road runs south-west to Sasa.

If you are pressed for time the best plan is to take the better main road via Hurfeish to Nahariya (c. 40km/25 miles).

Scenically more attractive, though with many bends, is the narrow road which runs north-west from Sasa by way of the remote settlements of Netu'a, Even Menahem and Shomera to the Goren Natural Forest near the kibbutz of Elon. From here there is a footpath (3km/2 miles) to the Crusader castle of **Montfort**. A few kilometres beyond Elon the road runs into the main road along the Mediterranean coast. Along this road to the north is the village of Rosh Haniqra, on the Lebanese frontier. From the village a cableway runs down to the beach, on which are a number of caves.

Rosh Haniqra to Haifa

The return to Haifa is on the coast road, which runs past the archaeological site and holiday area of Akhziv and soon afterwards comes to the seaside resort of **Nahariya**, founded in 1936 by German immigrants. Near the moshav of Shave Zion, also founded by settlers from Germany in 1938, a mosaic pavement in an early Christian basilica (before 422) has been excavated. Beyond this is the kibbutz of Lohamei Hageta'ot, with a museum commemorating those who perished in the Holocaust.

Farther down the coast is **Akko**, a town of Oriental aspect. In addition to a number of buildings dating from the crusading period and from Ottoman times its attraction lies in the atmosphere of its busy bazaar quarter and picturesque harbour. Beyond Akko the road runs round the Bay of Haifa with its industrial installations and finally comes to the port of **Haifa** itself.

Tour of Central Israel (350km/220 miles)

This tour of central Israel, starting from Jerusalem, takes in a number of important archaeological sites but also gives a good impression of the varied landscapes of the Holy Land.

Much of the route runs through the Israeli-occupied West Bank. In spite of the *intifada* this does not usually offer any hazards for tourists, but it is advisable to check on the current situation before setting out and if conditions are unsettled to avoid the main centres of the Palestinian uprising, Ramallah and Nablus.

At least three days should be allowed for the trip. Good places for overnight stops are Tiberias on the Sea of Galilee, Netanya and Tel Aviv.

The route runs past the **Jerusalem** airport and beyond Ain Sinya enters the fertile "Valley of Robbers" (Wadi el-Haramiye). It then climbs into the hills, passing Sinjil, and runs down to Lubban, the Biblical Lebonah. A little way east was Shiloh, where the Ark of the Covenant was kept before the building of the Temple in Jerusalem.

Jerusalem to the Sea of Galilee

Shortly before **Nablus** (Hebrew Shekhem), the chief town of the West Bank, a road turns sharply off on the right to Jacob's Well (Bir Yakub), traditionally believed to have been dug by Jacob, where Jesus met the woman of Samaria. Some 13km/8 miles north-west of Nablus, on the right of the road, is the extensive ancient site of **Samaria** (Arabic Sebastiya, Hebrew Shomron), with imposing remains of the Israelite, Herodian, Roman and early Christian periods. The road continues north through the hills of Samaria, passing a number of Arab villages, runs down into the valley of Dothan, where Joseph was sold by his brothers to the Ishmaelite merchants, and comes to the Arab town of **Jenin**. Beyond the village of Jalama the road leaves the West Bank and, 11km/7 miles from Jenin, comes to a junction, where we take the road to the right, signposted to Bet Shean. Near the village of Gidona (founded 1949), at the foot of **Mount Gilboa**, is the Ma'ayan Harod National Park. Soon after this we leave the main road and turn into a side road which runs south to **Bet Alfa**, noted for the mosaic pavement in its old synagogue.

Beyond Bet Alfa is the National Park of Gan HaShelosha ("Park of the Three"), whose name commemorates three settlers killed during the conquest of this area in 1938. Above the impressive waterfalls (Arabic Sakhne) is a bathing lake.

4km/2½miles east is the important archaeological site of **Bet Shean**, with a Roman theatre opposite the tell once occupied by Canaanite temples. From here the route continues north towards the Sea of Galilee.

10km/6 miles farther on a road goes off on the left and winds its way up, with many hairpin bends, to the Crusader castle of **Belvoir**, 500m/1650ft higher up.

Soon after the turn-off for Belvoir the road cuts across the Tavor valley. 2km/1¼ miles beyond this, at Gesher, a side road goes off on the right to the Naharayim hydraulic power station. Here the river Yarmouk, on which in 636 the Byzantine army suffered a crushing defeat at the hands of Caliph Omar, flows into the Jordan. The road now follows the Jordan valley to the southern tip of the **Sea of Galilee**.

Suggested Routes

From here a side trip can be made to **Hamat Gader**, 10km/6 miles south-east. This was already frequented as a bathing resort in ancient times, and visitors still come to enjoy the healing effects of its waters in a series of pools at different temperatures.

From the Sea of Galilee via Afula and Caesarea to Netanya

The main route runs north-west for a short distance along the shores of the Sea of Galilee. At Bet Yerah a side road goes off to the kibbutz of Deganya, at the outflow of the Jordan into the lake; this was the first of the kibbutzes, founded in 1909. In front of the main entrance is a Syrian tank, knocked out at the gates of the settlement by a Molotov cocktail in 1948. Although it is not the place where Christ was baptised, many pilgrims have themselves baptised in the water of the **Jordan** at Yardenit, 1km/¾ mile west of Bet Yerah. Beyond the archaeological site of Tel Bet Yerah, where extensive remains dating from the 4th–6th centuries have been brought to light, the road leaves the shores of the Sea of Galilee and runs west in the direction of Afula. (Visitors who are not doing the tour of northern Israel should make a side trip to the north end of the lake: see page 98.)

The road now begins to climb. From the car park at the sign marking sea level there is a magnificent view of the Sea of Galilee. Soon afterwards the road passes a tell which is thought to be the site of the Bronze Age settlement of Yin'an. Beyond this are Yavne'el, a little township founded in 1901, and the village of Kafr Kama, occupied by Circassian settlers in 1880. Soon after Kefar Tavor a side road goes off to **Mount Tabor**, the highest hill in Lower Galilee, with a Franciscan church and magnificent views.

Returning to the main road, we continue to **Afula**, the agricultural centre of the **Jezreel plain**, which has little to offer the tourist. Of more interest is the tell of **Megiddo** (12km/7½ miles west of Afula), a strategic site which was fortified from the 3rd millennium B.C. onwards. There are extensive excavations and an instructive museum. From Megiddo the route continues north-west, takes a left turn at Yoqne'am and finally runs into the road to **Zikhron Ya'aqov**, a well-known wine-growing town in a beautiful setting.

Crusader city, Caesarea

Beyond Zikhron Ya'aqov the road runs downhill, cuts across a secondary road running north–south and joins the expressway which runs close to the coast. Along this road to the south is **Caesarea**, which enjoyed its last great period of prosperity in the time of the Crusaders.

A good place for a bathing holiday is **Netanya**. With its beautiful long sandy beaches, its many large hotels and its well planned town centre (partly pedestrianised) it has developed into Israel's leading tourist resort on the Mediterranean coast.

From Netanya the coast road (best avoided during the morning rush) continues south. Soon after **Herzliya**, which has a good beach and attractive residential areas but nothing of particular interest for the visitor, it enters the outskirts of **Tel Aviv**, the largest city in Israel, with many features of interest and an attractive Mediterranean atmosphere.

Netanya via Tel Aviv to Jerusalem

From Tel Aviv an expressway runs south-east, passing the Ben-Gurion Airport near **Lod** and the monastery of **Latrun**, on a hill to the right of the road. Beyond this is the Arab hill village of **Abu Ghosh**, dominated by a massive Crusader church. 10km/6 miles beyond this is Jerusalem.

To the Dead Sea (260km/160 miles)

Since many visitors to Israel make Jerusalem their main base, the description of this trip starts from there. It can be done in a day, but to do justice to the features of interest on the way at least two days are required. Sufficient time should be allowed in particular for the En Gedi Nature Park and the extraordinary archaeological site of Masada. Possible overnight stops are the kibbutz guest-house at En Gedi and one of the hotels in En Boqeq on the Dead Sea.

Leave Jerusalem on the excellent expressway which runs east, signposted to Jericho. In the hot climate no crops flourish here, and there is no human habitation apart from a few Bedouin tents. In 20km/12½ miles a road goes off on the left to St George's Monastery in the **Wadi Qilt**. From a parking place with an outlook terrace there is a fine view of the romantic Qilt gorge. Farther along the main road an asphalted side road goes off on the right to the Islamic shrine of **Nabi Musa**. The next place of interest is the oasis town of **Jericho**. Although the town itself has little of interest to offer except for the archaeologically minded, it is worth visiting for the sake of the earliest remains of human settlement to be seen here.

Jerusalem via Jericho to Qumran

From Jericho the route runs south, then turns left at a road junction to reach the **Dead Sea** at Ma'aganit Hamelach. There is a large leisure park, with bathing beach, designed to attract visitors, but otherwise the area is not particularly inviting. The scars left by artillery fire are a reminder of the fierce fighting that has taken place in this part of the West Bank. From here the road continues south, running close to the shores of the Dead Sea. The next place of interest is **Qumran**, where the Dead Sea Scrolls were discovered in caves round a former Essenian monastery.

This section of the route runs along the shores of the Dead Sea. Some 20km/12½miles beyond Qumran a side road goes off on the right to the kibbutz of Metzoke Dragot, from which there are organised trips into the desert; there is a guest-house. At **En Gedi** the austerity of the landscape is relieved by palm-groves and gardens. The beauty of the scenery can be enjoyed on walks in the En Gedi Nature Park. Farther south again is one of the high spots of a visit to Israel, the fortress of **Masada**, protected by sheer rock faces 400m/1300ft high. The site was excavated and partly restored by Yigael Yadin in the 1960s. Access is by the steep path known as the Snake or by cableway.

Qumran to Newe Zohar

Returning to the lakeside road, we continue south to **En Boqeq** and Newe Zohar. In these two places are concentrated most of the Dead Sea's spa and bathing facilities. Since the level of the Dead Sea is steadily falling because of the reduced inflow of water from the Jordan the roads from the hotels to the beaches are growing continually longer.

Newe Zohar via
Arad and Hebron
to Jerusalem

The road running west from Newe Zohar climbs rapidly and comes to two fine viewpoints lying close together. From the first there is a superb view, particularly in the evening, of the Dead Sea and the hills of Moab; the second offers views of the rugged background of hills and, lower down, the Nabataean and later Byzantine stronghold of Mezad Zohar, which guarded the valley road between Judaea and Edom. The road continues north-west to **Arad**, a resort favoured by asthma sufferers because of its desert situation and high altitude. 10km/6 miles beyond the town a road goes off to the important archaeological site of Tel Arad. In another 15km/9 miles we turn right into the road to **Hebron**. (Since there have been disturbances in Hebron since the declaration of the *intifada* it is advisable to check in advance that it is safe to go there.) The town's main tourist sight is the monumental building erected over the cave in which Abraham was buried. Shortly before reaching Bethlehem the road runs past (on right) Solomon's Pools, three large open cisterns which have been used from Roman times down to the present day for the storage of water. Then comes **Bethlehem**, the birthplace of David and of Jesus. Its main tourist attractions are the Church of the Nativity and Manger Square.

From Bethlehem side trips can be made to the **Herodeion** (11km/7 miles south-east), the hill on which Herod the Great built a sumptuous palace, and to the Greek Orthodox monastery of **Mar Saba**.

At the far end of Bethlehem, to the left of the road, can be seen Rachel's Tomb. Beyond this, on the right, is the monastery of St Elias. Then, before continuing into central Jerusalem, it is worth while making a short detour to the Haas Promenade, a beautifully laid out viewing terrace in the district of East Talpiot; it is reached by way of a street which turns right off Hebron Road.

Through the Negev (500km/310 miles)

A trip through the Negev does not offer a succession of tourist sights as do other circuits in the Holy Land, and there is little variety in the scenery; but few visitors will find a journey through the Negev monotonous. The rocks in the desert present an endless range of bizarre forms amd shimmer, particularly in the evening light, in an ever-changing spectrum of colour. Here and there are agricultural settlements which contrive to wring harvests from the desert soil with the aid of artificial irrigation.

The route suggested here starts from Beersheba. Since there are few traffic hold-ups in the Negev it can be done without difficulty in two days. Elat, on the Red Sea, is a well equipped resort for an overnight stop.

Beersheba via
Avdat to Elat

Leave **Beersheba** on the road which runs south-east to Yeroham, and from there take a road south-west to **Sede Boqer** (19km/12 miles), a kibbutz founded in 1952 which was the home of David Ben-Gurion. 3km/2 miles beyond this, to the left, can be seen the College of the Negev (Midreshet Sede Boqer), founded by Ben-Gurion. In front of the library is his grave. The complex lies above the Wadi Zin, with a road leading down into the valley. From the car park a footpath leads to the spring of **En Avdat**, named after the Nabataean and later Byzantine town of **Avdat**, the remains of which (partly restored) lie 5km/3 miles south to the left of the road.

At the far end of the settlement of Mizpe Ramon (pop. 2000), founded in 1953, is an outlook terrace (restaurant) from which there is a fine view into the largest crater-valley in Israel, **Makhtesh Ramon**. Beyond Mizpe Ramon we turn off into a road on the right which runs west, passing below Mount Ramon (1035m/3396ft), and just before reaching the Egyptian frontier runs into a new north-south road, which we follow southward. 10km/6 miles before Elat a side road (signposted) goes off to the spring of En Netafim,

Bizarre rock formations in the Negev

which is a short walk from the end of the road. The main road then continues to **Elat**, Israel's tourist centre on the Red Sea.

The main road north from Elat runs through the Arava depression, following the frontier between Israel and Jordan. It reaches an altitude of 200m/650ft at Gav Zaarava and then runs gradually down to 398m/1306ft below sea level at the Dead Sea.

From Elat through the Arava depression to Beersheba

In 25km/15 miles a road goes off on the left to the copper-mines of Timna, which have been brought back into production in recent years. 2km/1¼ miles beyond this another road leads to **Timna** Park, an area of bizarre rock formations, notably "Solomon's Pillars", which can be explored by car.
17km/10½ miles farther north, to the right of the road, is the Hai Bar Nature Reserve, established in 1963 as a safe refuge for antelopes, wild asses, ostriches and other desert animals. This too can be explored by car or on a coach trip starting from the visitor centre of the Yotvata kibbutz (founded in 1951 as an army settlement). At Gerofit, 8km/5 miles beyond Yotvata, a road goes off on the left to Beersheba: our route, however, continues north towards the Dead Sea. At the village of Paran (45km/28 miles) the road crosses the broad Wadi **Paran**; later (65km/40 miles) it crosses the Wadi Zin, at the head of which is the spring of En Avdat. Soon after this we turn left into the road to Beersheba and come in another 27km/17 miles to the remains of the Nabataean town of **Mamshit**. From there the road continues by way of the town of Dimona (founded in 1955) to Beersheba.

Grand Tour of Israel (1300km/800 miles)

The routes described above can be combined into a grand tour covering the whole of the country and taking in all the principal towns, historical sites and scenic beauties. For this trip at least two weeks should be allowed. In the following description places and features of interest are referred to in

Beach, Netanya

From Jerusalem to the northern frontier

detail only where the grand tour follows a different route from the regional tours.

Leave **Jerusalem** on the main road running east. After affording a brief view on the **Wadi Qilt** it comes to **Jericho**. From here a side trip (45km/28 miles there and back) can be made to **Qumran** on the **Dead Sea** (unless you intend to return by way of Qumran: see page 107). The road now runs north, close to the frontier with Jordan. The region is thinly populated, with only the occasional settlement surrounded by barbed wire. Just beyond Mehola we leave the occupied West Bank, and soon after this **Mount Gilboa** rises above the road to the left. There is good bathing to be had in one or other of the nature parks in this area; for those interested in thr history and archaeology of Israel **Bet Alfa** and **Bet Shean** are musts. Farther north, to the left of the road, can be seen the Crusader castle of **Belvoir**. The road then continues to the **Sea of Galilee**. The main tourist centre here is **Tiberias**, from which other places of interest in the area – **Tabgha**, **Capernaum** and **Hamat Gader** – can be visited.

From here the road runs past the **Mount of the Beatitudes** and the archaeological site of **Chorazin** and then continues by way of **Rosh Pinna** to **Hazor**. A few kilometres farther north the **Hule plain** begins. In the extreme north of the country, in the **Dan** Nature Reserve and round **Banyas**, is country of great scenic beauty.

Banyas via Safed and Akko to Haifa

From Banyas we follow the hill road running close to the Lebanese frontier above the Hule plain. After passing the archaeological site of Bar'am this continues by way of Sasa and **Meron** to **Safed**. Returning to Meron, we head west, passing through the little townships of Parod and Rama, to **Akko**, with its picturesque old town and fishing harbour. The route then continues down the coast to **Haifa**. Possible excursions from here are to the Mount **Carmel** National Park, the necropolis of **Bet Shearim**, the archaeological site of **Megiddo** and **Nazareth**.

Memorial park in the kibbutz of Yad Mordekhay

There are two roads running south from Haifa. From the old road, running a little way inland, a side road goes off in 10km/6 miles to En Hod, a former Arab village now occupied by artists.

The new expressway runs close to the coast. A side road on the right leads to the Crusader castle of **Atlit** (in military occupation). Farther south another road goes off to the moshav of **Dor**. Beyond the railway line, to the right, can be seen the kibbutz of Nahsholim, beside the remains of a glassworks established by Baron Edmond de Rothschild; to the right is the village of Dor, founded by immigrants from Greece. Farther south the expressway comes to the ancient city and Crusader strongold of **Caesarea**. To the south of this is the attractive bathing resort of **Netanya**, on the Mediterranean. The road then continues via **Herzliya** to **Tel Aviv**.

Immediately south of Tel Aviv is the town of Rishon LeZion, and beyond this again is **Rehovot**, with the Weizmann Institute, founded by the statesman of that name, whose work ranges from biology to atomic research. Southwest of Rehovot is **Yavne** (ancient Jamnia), with its harbour 8km/5 miles north-west at the kibbutz of Palmahim. Beyond this are the port of **Ashdod** and **Ashqelon**, with interesting excavations. 10km/6 miles south of Ashqelon is the kibbutz of Yad Mordekhay, with memorials to the rising in the Warsaw ghetto and the repulse of Egyptian attacks in 1948.

From Haifa along the Mediterranean coast to Ashqelon

Tourists are well advised to avoid the Gaza Strip, and should take the road via Nir'am and Netivot to **Beersheba**. Thereafter the route continues to **Sede Boqer**, **En Avdat** and **Avdat**. Beyond Mizpe Ramon there is a magnificent view of **Makhtesh Ramon**. Soon afterwards a road goes off on the right and runs along the Egyptian frontier to **Elat**.

Ashqelon via Beersheba to Elat

To the north of Elat are the **Timna** Park and the Hai Bar Nature Reserve, near the kibbutz of Yotvata. Beyond this the road crosses the dried-up valley of the river **Paran** and runs through the Arava depression, passes the Dead Sea Works and the salt caves of Sedom and reaches the **Dead Sea** at Newe Zohar. A high spot of any tour of Israel is a visit to the fortress of **Masada**.

Elat to the Dead Sea

Suggested Routes

Farther north is the **En Gedi** Nature Reserve (there and back from Newe Zohar 80km/50 miles). The road then continues north along the shores of the Dead Sea to **Qumran** and from there to Jerusalem.

Newe Zohar via Hebron to Jerusalem

Before following this route it is advisable to check that it is safe to go through Hebron, which is one of the centres of the Palestinian uprising. The road runs via the desert town of **Arad** and Tel Arad to **Hebron** and from there continues to **Bethlehem**, from which excursions can be made to the **Herodeion** and the desert monastery of **Mar Saba**.

Alternative route via Qiryat Gat and Bet Shemesh to Jerusalem

An alternative route avoiding the occupied West Bank is via **Arad** and Qiryat Gat, a town with agricultural industries. The northern part of the town is believed to have been the site of Gath, one of the five cities of Phoenicia. From here the road runs east through a fertile and attractive region to the tell of **Lachish** and then passes the site of **Mareshah** and the kibbutz of **Bet Guvrin**. 10km/6 miles beyond Bet Guvrin is the tell with the site of Biblical Azekah, to the north of which the prophet Zechariah is said to have been buried. Just after the moshav of Zekharya a road goes off on the right to Beth Gamal (2km/1¼ miles), with an orphanage of the Salesian order; in the cloister are a number of Byzantine fragments. The road continues north to **Bet Shemesh**, founded in 1950 to house new immigrants, which is now an industrial town with a population of 12,000. Beyond this the road runs into the expressway from Tel Aviv to Jerusalem, on which – with an intermediate stop at **Abu Ghosh** – we return to the Holy City.

The Old City of Jerusalem, with the Dome of the Rock ▶

Sights from A to Z

Abu Ghosh G/H 4

District: Jerusalem
Altitude: 610–720m/2000–2360ft
Population: 2000

Situation and characteristics

Abu Ghosh is an Arab village 13km/8 miles west of Jerusalem, just north of the expressway to Tel Aviv. Its main feature of interest is its Crusader church.

Abu Ghosh is named after a sheikh from the Hejaz who settled here with his four sons about 1800 and was granted the right to protect the pilgrim route from the coast to Jerusalem. In return for his services he levied a toll which was the foundation of his fortune. The present inhabitants of the village regard themselves as his descendants.

History

The site was inhabited before the coming of the Bedouin, for there was a spring here with an abundant flow of water. In the 1st century the Romans established a fort here for units of the Tenth Legion (Fretensis), which is believed to have been involved in the crucifixion of Christ. In the Islamic period a caravanserai was built, and in 1099 the Crusaders passed through the village on their way to Jerusalem. The spring led them to believe that this was ancient Emmaus. They built the castle of Fontenoide and a church (1142), which was abandoned in 1187 after the battle at the Horns of Hittim (see entry).

Sights

★Crusader church

The village is dominated by the Crusader church, whose builder took over from the Muslim caravanserai the idea of the pointed arch – a feature that was to become characteristic of Gothic architecture. For many years the church was used as a stable; then in 1899 the French government purchased the building and handed it over to the Benedictine order. Since 1956 it has belonged to the Lazarists. Built on to the church is a mosque.

In the wall of the church near the entrance is a stone with the inscription "Vexillatio Leg(ionis) Fret(ensis)" – a reminder that the site was occupied more than a thousand years earlier by a Roman fort. Like the rather older church of Notre Dame in Tartus (Syria) and the contemporary church of St Anne in Jerusalem, this is a fine example of the monumental church architecture of the Crusaders in the 12th century. With its 4m/13ft thick walls the church (three-aisled; 20m/66ft long, 15m/49ft across) has a fortress-like character.

The interior of the church is plain but full of atmosphere. In the crypt is the spring which has been an important feature of the site since its earliest days.

Notre Dame de l'Arche d'Alliance

On a hill above the village is the church of Notre Dame de l'Arche d'Alliance (Our Lady of the Ark of the Covenant), conspicuous with its commandingly situated statue of the Virgin. Built in 1924 over the remains of a 5th century Byzantine church, it belongs to the French order of the Sisters of St Francis. The name of the church reflects the belief that this was the site of Kirjathjearim, where the Ark of the Covenant was kept for a time.

Abu Ghosh: in the foreground the Crusader church

Surroundings of Abu Ghosh

Just outside the village on the Jerusalem road a side road goes off to Qiryat Anavim ("Village of Grapes"), beautifully situated above a valley. Founded in 1920, this was the first kibbutz in the Judaean uplands. The spacious guest-house, with a swimming pool set in carefully tended gardens, is a pleasant quiet place to stay before or after a visit to Jerusalem.

Qiryat Anavim

The youth village of Qiryat Yearim ("Village of the Forest"), 1km/¾ mile west of Abu Ghosh, was founded in 1952. It takes its name from the Biblical Kirjath-jearim, which may have been situated on the tell 3km/2 miles north-east but is thought by some to have occupied the site of present-day Abu Ghosh.

Qiryat Yearim

The name of Kirjath-jearim occurs several times in the Old Testament in connection with the Ark of the Covenant. During their struggle with the Philistines in the 11th century B.C. the Israelites carried with them the Ark of the Covenant, which was normally kept in Shiloh. It was captured at Eben-ezer by the Philistines, who took it to Ashdod (see entry) and then to Gath and Ekron (1 Samuel 4 and 5); but since they believed that it brought them ill-fortune they returned it to the Israelites, who took it to Kirjath-jearim. There it stayed for twenty years in the house of Abinadab (1 Samuel 6 and 7). Then when David became king of the whole of Israel and captured Jerusalem he took it there. At first, however, it went only as far as Perez-uzzah on Mount Qastel (4km/2½ miles east of Abu Ghosh); then three months later it was taken to Jerusalem, where it was greeted "with shouting, and with the sound of the trumpet" (2 Samuel 6).

An attractive trip from Abu Ghosh is to Aqua Bella, an idyllic spot a few kilometres south-east of the village. It is reached by leaving on the Jerusa-

Aqua Bella

103

lem road, following the expressway for a short distance and then turning right at the Hemed intersection. Aqua Bella (Hebrew En Hemed, the Well of Grace) is known to the Arabs as Deir el-Benat ("House of the Women") after a 12th century convent which was destroyed in 1187. The buildings in the square complex have been restored. The surrounding country, with a grove of pomegranates round the well which gave the place its Latin name, is now a much frequented National Park with picnic areas and a camping site.

Acre

See Akko

Afula   H 3

District: Northern
Altitude: 60–80m/200–260ft
Population: 20,000

Situation and characteristics

The town of Afula, founded in 1925 on the site of the Arab village of Afule, to the west of Mount Hamore (Givat Hamore, 515m/1690ft), is situated at an important road intersection in the Jezreel plain. The inhabitants live by farming, trade and various crafts.

History

The place is not mentioned in the Bible. The Crusaders built the castle of La Fève (later destroyed by Sultan Baibars) to protect the old roads which met here. In the later Turkish period the Arab village was a station on the railway line from Haifa via Bet Shean and through the Yarmouk valley to Damascus. During the First World War the Turks and Germans built the branch line from Afula via Jenin to the south.

The town

Afula is a modern and not particularly attractive little town, the principal market centre for the Jezreel plain. There are only scanty remains of the older Arab settlement.

2km/1¼ miles east of the town centre, in the kibbutz of Merhavya (founded 1911), are the ruins of the Crusader castle of La Fève.

Surroundings of Afula

Sunam

To the east of Afula is the Arab village of Sunam (Hebrew Shunem), the Biblical Shunam. This was the home of the "fair damsel" Abishag who was brought in to minister to the aged king David (1 Kings 1,1–4). The village fountain, En Avishag, bears her name.

En Dor

14km/8½ miles north-east of Afula is the kibbutz of En Dor, founded in 1941 and named after the Biblical Endor, situated on a tell to the east of the kibbutz. Faced with the Philistine armies drawn up at Shunam, King Saul consulted the witch of Endor, who prophesied his doom (1 Samuel 28). The prophecy was fulfilled on the following day, when Saul and his sons were killed in a battle on Mount Gilboa, south-east of Afula, and his body was hung from the walls of Bet Shean.

Mount Tabor

A side road runs south from En Dor to Mount Tabor (see entry) with its imposing church.

10km/6 miles south-east of Afula near the village of Gidona (founded 1949), at the foot of Mount Gilboa, is the Ma'ayan Harod National Park (camping site, youth hostel), with an artificial lake (swimming pool) surrounded by eucalyptus trees. At the well of Harod Gideon selected his 300 warriors to fight the Midianites (Judges 7,5–7).

Ma'ayan Harod

Also within easy reach of Afula are Megiddo, Nazareth, Jenin and the Jezreel plain (see entries).

Akko

G 2

District: Northern
Altitude: 20m/65ft
Population: 36,800

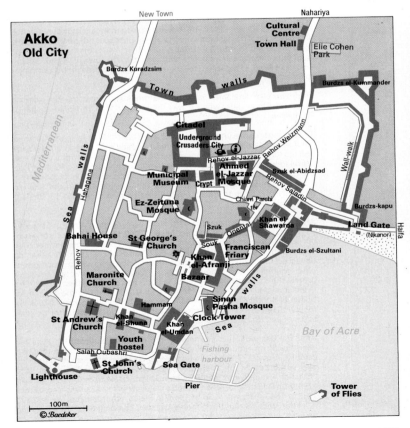

Akko

Situation and
characteristics

From ancient times until the 19th century Akko (better known in English as
Acre) was Palestine's leading port, and it has preserved an abundance of
remains dating from the Middle Ages and the early modern period. The
densely populated Old City, with its mosques, caravanserais, fortifications,
Crusader buildings, bazaar and old harbour, is in striking contrast to the
modern city of Haifa, only 23km/14 miles away.

Akko has an iron and steel works and chemical, ceramic and metalworking
industries.

History

The history of Akko goes back to the Canaanite period. It was originally
situated on Tell el-Fukhtar (2km/1¼ miles east, near the stadium), on which
excavations were carried out from 1973 onwards by an international team
of archaeologists. Under Hellenistic and Persian occupation levels were
revealed remains of a Canaanite settlement which the most recent findings
suggest may have been occupied as early as 3000 B.C. The town was
conquered by Pharaohs Tuthmosis III and Ramesses II, who recognised the
strategic importance of its site. The Phoenicians who had settled here were
deported in 640 B.C. by Assurbanipal. From 532 B.C. to the Greek conquest in
332 B.C. Akko was Persian. In 261, while under the sway of the Egyptian
ruler Ptolemy II, it was renamed Ptolemais. In 219 it passed into the hands
of the Seleucids, rulers of Syria, but was able to maintain its independence
as a city-state. The Hasmoneans made two unsuccessful attempts to take
Akko. In 30 B.C. Herod the Great received Octavian, the future Emperor
Augustus, here, and later built a gymnasium in the town. In A.D. 67 Vespasian used Akko, along with Caesarea (see entry), as a base for his campaign
in Palestine.

The town also prospered in Byzantine times and, from the 7th century,
under the Omayyads, when it was the port for the Ommayad capital of
Damascus.

The Crusaders were unable to take the town until 1104, five years after their
conquest of Jerusalem. They renamed it St Jean d'Acre and built a palace
and the massive vaulted structure known as the Crypt of St John (Acre was
the headquarters of the Knights of St John). The Italian cities of Genoa, Pisa
and Venice established trading posts in the town, and it developed into a
busy and flourishing port town. In 1187 the Crusaders were compelled to
surrender the town to Saladin, but it was recovered in 1191 by Richard
Coeur de Lion.

After the loss of Jerusalem in 1187 Acre became capital of the Crusader
kingdom, with a population estimated at 50,000. In 1219 St Francis of Assisi
visited the town and established a nunnery. In 1228 the Emperor Frederick
II landed here during his Crusade, as did Louis IX of France in 1250 after his
unsuccessful campaign against Damietta. Soon afterwards there was a
bitter conflict, almost amounting to civil war, between the two religious
orders, the Knights Hospitallers of St John and the Templars. In 1290 the
Crusaders slaughtered large numbers of Muslims. When the Mameluke
Sultan El-Ashraf Khalil captured the town in the following year he took his
revenge, and the Crusader kingdom came to a bloody end after an existence of just under 200 years.

After the destruction of the town it remained uninhabited for over 200
years, until its rebuilding by the Druze emir Fakhr ed-Din in the 17th
century. Around 1750 it was enlarged by Daher el-Amr, and this process
was continued by his murderer and successor Ahmed el-Jazzar (the
"Butcher"), a native of Bosnia, who ruled as Pasha from 1775 to 1805. In
1799, with British help, he withstood a siege of the town by Napoleon. From
1833 to 1840 Akko was held by Ibrahim Pasha, who defeated the Turks in
Palestine with his Egyptian forces but was compelled by the European
powers to withdraw. In the latter part of the 19th century Akko lost its

Ahmed el-Jazzar Mosque, Akko

Ablutions fountain

importance as a port to Beirut and then Haifa. When British forces captured the town from the Turks in 1918 it had a population of 8000, most of them Arabs. In 1920 and again during the Second World War the British authorities used the Citadel as a prison for Jewish underground fighters. The town was occupied by Israeli troops on May 17th 1948.

The most interesting part of Akko is the walled Old City with its Arab and Oriental atmosphere. Outside the massive town walls are extensive residential areas in plain and unpretentious style developed since the Israeli conquest.

★★Townscape

Ancient Akko (Tell el-Fukhtar) lies 2km/1¼ miles east of the Old City. To the south-east of the Old City extends a long sandy beach (Argaman Beach), with a number of large hotels and restaurants.

Sights

The sights of the Old City are described in the form of a walk round the town.

From the central bus station Weizmann Street runs past the Cultural Centre and the Town Hall to a breach in the town walls, which were given their present form by Ahmed el-Jazzar in the 18th century. From here we go up the ramp and walk along the walls to the Land Gate.

Town walls

At the north-east corner is a massive tower, the Burj el-Kummander, which defied Napoleon in 1799. It stands on the foundations of the "Accursed Tower", from which Richard Coeur de Lion hauled down the Duke of Austria's banner in 1191.

Akko

★Ahmed el-Jazzar
Mosque

Until the opening of a breach in the walls for Weizmann Street in 1910 the Land Gate was the only entrance to the town on the landward side.

From the Land Gate Saladin Street leads to the Ahmed el-Jazzar Mosque, the largest of Akko's four mosques. Occupying the site of the Crusader cathedral, it was built by Ahmed el-Jazzar in 1781 on the model of the Ottoman domed mosques.

The courtyard of the mosque is entered by a flight of steps, on the right of which is a small Rococo kiosk. The courtyard is rectangular, with arcaded halls round three sides. The rooms round the courtyard once provided accommodation for pilgrims and Islamic ecclesiastics. In the arcaded gallery on the east side are steps leading down to a cistern dating from the time of the Crusaders which provided a water supply for the population when the town was under siege.

In front of the main entrance to the mosque is a fountain for ritual ablutions with a copper roof borne on elegant columns. A small plain domed building to the right of the entrance contains the sarcophagi of Ahmed el-Jazzar (d. 1804) and his successor Suleiman Pasha (d. 1819).

The mosque itself, with its tall, slender minaret, is a fine example of Turkish Rococo architecture. The huge interior is decorated in blue, brown and white.

Akko (Acre)

Underground Crusader city

Knights' Halls

Court- yard

Offices

Entrance Hall

Entrance

Refectory

Underground passage

Bosta

Exit

© Baedeker

Khan el-Umdan, Akko

Opposite the mosque is the entrance to the massive complex of buildings occupied by the Knights of St John, the "Crusader city", which now lies underground. It was buried under a great mound of earth on which Ahmed el-Jazzar built his Citadel (see page 105). Much of the complex was excavated between 1955 and 1964. In the northern part were found seven rooms, presumably belonging to the seven "tongues" (national groups) of which the order of St John was composed. One of them is now used as a concert hall. These rooms and a very large hall (perhaps the dormitory) have been only partly excavated in order to avoid endangering the stability of the Citadel built over them. One part of the complex which has been completely exposed is the refectory, often erroneously called the crypt, because before the excavations it was entered by descending from a window at street level. It is a large rectangular hall with groined vaulting borne on three massive round piers. An indication of its date is provided by the fleur-de-lis carved on two consoles, which are associated with Louis VII of France's stay in the town in 1148. More important than such details, however, is the extraordinary spatial effect of this monumental structure. From the refectory we descend into a lighted underground passage, originally 350m/380yds long, which dates from the Persian period and was used by the Crusaders as a secret means of access to the harbour. It now runs for only 65m/70yds to the Bosta, a part of the building which was used by the Knights as a refuge and hospice for pilgrims.

★ Crusader city

Opposite the Crusader city is the entrance to the Municipal Museum, housed in the old Pasha's Baths (Hammam el-Basha) which were built by Ahmed el-Jazzar in 1780 and remained in use until 1947. The numerous rooms, mostly quite small, house a number of permanent exhibitions on the history of the town and surrounding area – collections of archaeological finds from Akko, Islamic art, costumes, weapons and other material, together with photographs illustrating more recent history.

Municipal Museum

Akko

Khan el-Afranji

Turning right from the Museum in the direction of the old harbour, we pass through the bustling streets of the bazaar into the southern part of the Old City, with two large caravanserais (khans). The Khan el-Afranji (Khan of the Franks, i.e. of the Europeans), the town's oldest khan, was built by Fakhr ed-Din around 1600. Here there is a small Franciscan convent, occupying the site of the house of Poor Clares founded by St Francis in 1219, whose nuns disfigured their faces in order to avoid attracting the interest of the Arab conquerors.

Khan el-Umdan

A little way south is the Khan el-Umdan ("Khan of the Columns"), so called because of the granite and porphyry columns which Ahmed el-Jazzar brought from Caesarea (see entry) when building this khan on the site of the Crusaders' Dominican monastery. Over the north entrance is a clock-tower commemorating Sultan Abdul Hamid's jubilee in 1906.

Fishing harbour

Immediately east of the Khan el-Umdan is the harbour. A busy port in ancient times and the Middle Ages – sometimes occupied by as many as eighty ships in the time of the Crusaders – it is now silted up and is used only as a fishing harbour.

Continuing west along a street in which are the youth hostel and the church of St John, we come to the lighthouse and the sea wall. The breach in the sea wall was the result of an earthquake in 1837.
Going north along the sea wall and turning right at the Greek Catholic church of St Andrew, we come to the Maronite church (on left).

St George's Church

From the Khan esh-Shuna a street runs north to the Greek Orthodox church of St George, which is built on medieval foundations. There is a memorial tablet to Major Oldfield, a British officer killed during Napoleon's siege of Acre.

Burj Kurajim

Returning from here to the sea wall and following it northward, we come, at the north-west corner of the walls, to the Burj Kurajim (Tower of the Vine), a Turkish bulwark against attack from the sea built on foundations dating from the Crusader period.

Citadel

From the wall beyond the sea wall a little street leads to the entrance to Ahmed el-Jazzar's Citadel (18th c.), which was used during the British Mandate as a prison. A memorial room with a collection of photographs and documents commemorates the Jewish underground fighters who were imprisoned or executed here by the British authorities.

Surroundings of Akko

Bahji

3km/2 miles north of Akko, on the east side of the road to Nahariya, are the Persian Gardens of Bahji. In these beautifully laid out gardens is the shrine containing the remains of Baha Ullah ("Glory of God"; 1817–92), founder of the Bahai faith. He was exiled to Akko in 1868 and spent the last years of his life in the red-roofed house which is also in the gardens.

★Lohamei Hageta'ot

On the road from Akko to Nahariya, shortly before Regba, is the kibbutz of Lohamei Hageta'ot, founded in 1949 by survivors from Nazi concentration camps, with a richly stocked museum. In addition to a cultural centre and a documentary collection named after the poet Beit Katznelson, murdered in Auschwitz in 1944, the building, which is of several storeys, contains a collection of material and documents on the various concentration camps and on Jewish resistance to the Nazis in Poland and Lithuania. Every year on April 19th, the anniversary of the rising in the Warsaw ghetto in 1943, there are special exhibitions and lectures here.
On the ground floor are displays illustrating the history of Vilnius, the "Jerusalem of Lithuania", and the town's Jewish community from 1551 to

1940. In addition to small wooden figurines there is material on the early days of the socialist and Zionist movement at the end of the 19th century and objects illustrating the everyday life of Polish Jews. From the entrance hall stairs lead down to two underground rooms. On the staircase are plans and Nazi insignia recalling the extermination camps of eastern Europe. In one of the rooms is a large plan of Treblinka, in the other a portrait of Janusz Korczak (1879–1942), doctor and teacher, and some two thousand drawings and paintings by prisoners, including portraits of concentration camp inmates. On the first floor of the museum are documents on anti-semitism under the Nazis, the ghettoes and the deportation of Jews, a plan of Anne Frank's house in Amsterdam, pictures of the Terezín (Theresienstadt) camp and some thousand photographs of the Warsaw rising.

Allone Abba

See Haifa

Arad   H 5

District: Southern
Altitude: 640m/2100ft
Population: 16,000

Arad is a rising modern town a few kilometres north-west of the Dead Sea. Founded only in 1961, it has attractive residential districts and in its barren surroundings has something of the aspect of a green oasis. Its altitude and desert climate, with dry and pollen-free air, make it an ideal resort for sufferers from asthma. The existing spa facilities are to be developed to make Arad an international medical centre.

Situation and characteristics

The town is best known, however, for the important archaeological site on Tel Arad.

★Tel Arad

10km/6 miles west of Arad on the road to Beersheba a side road goes off to Tel Arad, where excavations between 1962 and 1984 brought to light two major complexes – a Canaanite town and an acropolis dating from Israelite and Roman times.

Situation and characteristics

On a site occupied since the Chalcolithic (4th millennium B.C.) a large Canaanite town was built here in the 2nd millennium B.C. Its king drove the Israelites back when they sought to advance into the Promised Land from the south (Numbers 21,1). After its capture by Joshua (Joshua 12,14) it passed to the tribe of Judah, and the "children of the Kenite" (Moses' father-in-law) dwelt in the town. The further development and fortification of the town are probably to be attributed to Solomon, who built a temple to Jehovah on the site of a hilltop sanctuary of the Kenites. Soon afterwards, in 920 B.C., Arad was taken by Pharaoh Seshonq, the Shishak of the Old Testament. It was soon recovered by the kingdom of Judah, however, to which it belonged until the fall of Judah in 586 B.C. Arad retained its importance, thanks to its situation on important trade routes, into the Roman period, and was abandoned only after the first Islamic campaign of conquest in the 7th century.

History

The Canaanite town which has been excavated on the tell dates back to the 2nd millennium B.C. In the north-west of the site are palace and temple precincts, to the south-west residential quarters. The line of the walls,

Canaanite town

Temple, Arad: the holy of holies

which were reinforced by round towers and extended up to the citadel on the acropolis, can still be traced for considerable stretches.

Acropolis

The structures on the acropolis date from the post-Canaanite period. They were built over a period of more than a thousand years, extending from early Israelite to Roman times. The massive walls of the citadel have been rebuilt, using original material. The complex is entered through the east gate, which is flanked by massive towers. Within the walls can be seen remains of various store-rooms and a Hellenistic tower.

The most important building, however, is the Jewish temple in the north-west of the citadel. A number of small rooms surround the courtyard, in which, to the right, is the altar for burnt offerings, built up of undressed stone and mud brick. In the direction of the holy of holies were discovered the bases for two cult pillars (cf. the pillars known as Jachin and Boaz in Solomon's Temple in Jerusalem: 1 Kings 7,21). Two low horned altars flank the entrance to the small rectangular holy of holies (*hekal*), in which two aniconic cult stones are still in situ. Within the temple precinct channels and basins have been hewn from the rock for the purpose of water supply and storage, including a channel the height of a man which cuts through the town walls to the left of the holy of holies.

The temple is the only Jewish sacred building of its kind so far brought to light by excavation. Since excavation is not permitted on the Temple platform in Jerusalem information about the Temple can be obtained only from the written sources. The Arad temple, several times destroyed but each time rebuilt, is therefore of great importance to archaeology and the history of religion. It contributes to the evidence for the decentralisation of worship in the first century after the Israelite occupation of Canaan, since it is now known that there were temples not only in Shiloh, Bethel and Dan but also in Arad. This came to an end when King Josiah of Judah, in his wide-ranging reform of religious life, concentrated worship in the Temple in Jerusalem.

Ashdod

District: Southern
Altitude: 0–10m/0–35ft
Population: 65,700

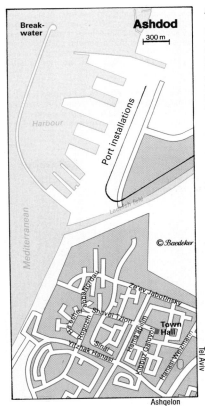

Ashdod, founded only in 1957, lies some 40km/25 miles south of Tel Aviv-Jaffa (Yafo). Within a very short period it has developed into the largest Israeli port after Haifa. As a result numerous industrial and transport installations have been established in the town.

Situation and characteristics

Ancient Ashdod, which lay to the south of the modern town, is mentioned along with Gaza and Gath in the 12th–11th centuries B.C. as a town of the Anakims, and it appears along with Gaza, Ashkelon, Gath and Ekron as one of the five lordships of the Philistines (Joshuah 13,3). When the Philistines carried off the Ark of the Covenant they took it first to Ashkelon and then to the temple of Dagon in Ashdod (1 Samuel 5,1–5). Although conquered by the Assyrians in 732 B.C., Ashdod remained an independent city state. Then in the 6th–5th centuries, under the Persians, it developed into an important port town. In the Hellenistic period (3rd c. B.C.) it was known as Azolus – a name which was also used by the Crusaders in the 12th century. The Arabs called it Minat el-Qala ("castle harbour"). For more recent centuries it was a modest little village: its development began in 1957, when the Israeli government decided to establish the industrial settlement of Ashdod, with a deep-sea harbour, on a site 3km/2 miles north of the ruins of the old town.

History

113

Ashqelon

Ashdod is a modern town with a well planned street layout, but it has little to offer the tourist. The best general view of the town and the port installations is to be had from the hill on the northern edge of the town centre (photography forbidden).

Ashqelon   F 5

District: Southern
Altitude: 0–10m/0–35ft
Population: 53,000

Situation and characteristics

The town of Ashqelon (Askelon, Ashkelon in the Old Testament) lies on the Mediterranean 56km/35 miles south of Tel Aviv-Jaffa (Yafo). With a history going back to the time of the Canaanites and Philistines, it has preserved interesting remains of the past and is now also a popular seaside resort with a long sandy beach. It has hitherto been frequented mainly by Israeli holidaymakers, but it is now planned to develop it into an international tourist centre.

History

The Canaanite trading town of Ashkelon is referred to in Egyptian texts as early as the 18th–15th centuries B.C. When the Philistines came here around 1200 B.C. during the movement of the Sea Peoples Ashkelon became one of their five lordships. Of these the sites of Gaza, Ashkelon and Ashdod are

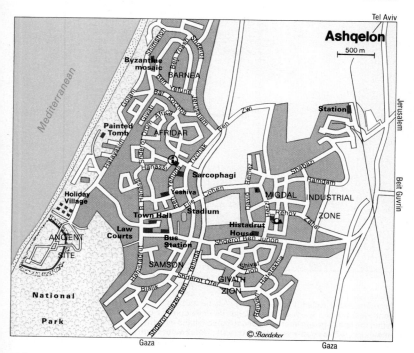

known but Ekron and Gath have not been located. Ashkelon was probably the most important of the five.

Until the time of the Jewish rising against Rome in the 1st century A.D. there was enmity between Ashkelon and the Israelites. This is reflected in the Biblical story of Samson (Judges 13–16). An angel promised that Samson, son of Manoah, would "begin to deliver Israel out of the hand of the Philistines." After marrying a Philistine woman from Timnath (Timna) he quarrelled with the Philistines and slew thirty of them in Ashkelon. The Philistines burned his wife to death, whereupon Samson killed a thousand Philistines with the jawbone of an ass (Judges 14 and 15). Becoming enamoured of Delilah, he betrayed to her the secret of his strength: he was of invincible force so long as his hair remained unshorn. When Delilah then cut off his seven locks he was taken prisoner, bound in fetters of brass and blinded. But as his hair grew again his strength returned, and when he was brought to a festival in the temple of Dagon to make sport for the people he pulled down the temple, killing all who were in it; and so "the dead which he slew at his death were more than they which he slew in his life" (Judges 16,30).

The Philistines adopted the worship of the Phoenician deities – the grim fertility god Dagon, who was venerated in Ugarit as the father of Baal and in Byblos as the brother of El (temple in Ashdod), and the mighty god Baal (Baal-zebub, a name which the Israelites interpreted as "lord of the flies") and his consort Astarte. About the middle of the 1st millennium B.C. the Philistines were absorbed into the Phoenician population, which was growing in numbers as a result of an influx from the northern coastal regions.

Ashkelon was captured in 732 B.C. by the Assyrian king Tiglath-pileser and in 701 by Sennacherib. In the 6th century, under Persian rule, it was controlled by the Phoenician city of Tyre. After 332 B.C. it was Hellenised. Under the Seleucid ruler Antiochus IX, in 104 B.C., Ashkelon was granted self-government and its own calendar. That it was a considerable intellectual centre is shown by the career of Antiochus of Ashkelon (born about 120 B.C.), who became head of the Platonic Academy in Athens, founded the "Fifth Academy" and became Cicero's teacher.

About 73 B.C. the future king Herod I is believed to have been born in Ashkelon, the son of an Idumaean father and a Nabataean mother (and thus a non-Jew). Flavius Josephus tells us that he "embellished the town with baths and fountains and with pillared halls of astonishing size and craftsmanship."

Under Roman rule, thanks to its situation on the important north–south road, the Via Maris, Ashkelon developed into a prosperous trading town, famed for its festival.

Two basilicas are known to have been built in the town in Byzantine times. After the Islamic conquest, in 685, the Omayyad Caliph Abd el-Malik, builder of the Dome of the Rock in Jerusalem, erected a mosque.

In 1099 Godfrey of Bouillon defeated the army of the Fatimid ruler of Egypt at Ashkelon, opening up the road to Jerusalem, but the city itself was captured only in 1135 by King Baldwin II. In 1187 it fell to Saladin, but five years later, during the third Crusade, Richard Coeur de Lion recovered the town and rebuilt it; the town walls date from his time. Finally it was taken by the Mameluke Sultan Baibars in 1290 and thereafter declined.

In the late 18th century Ahmed el-Jazzar used stone from the ruins of Ashkelon and Caesarea for his building operations in Akko. The Arab village of Migdal (the "Tower") grew up on the site of the ancient port.

In 1952 Jews from South Africa founded the settlement of Afridar (the present business district) to the east of Migdal, and this developed into the modern town of Ashqelon.

Ashqelon consists of five districts (Migdal, Givath Zion, Samson, Afridar and Barnea), lying some distance apart. The modern town is traversed by wide streets designed to carry a considerable volume of traffic. It is remark-

The town

ably well equipped with open spaces; four-fifths of the town's area is said to be occupied by parks and gardens.

From the main north–south road (Tel Aviv–Gaza) Sderot Ben-Gurion runs west into the town. To the north of this road, immediately west of the railway, are the industrial zone, with the terminal of the oil pipeline from Elat (see entry), and the former Arab village of Migdal, which was incorporated in the young town of Ashqelon in 1955. This is the scene of a busy market on Mondays and Thursdays.

The street continues past the Histadrut offices into the town centre, with the bus station, hospital and law courts, where Hanassi Street goes off on the right. This street, in which is the Town Hall, runs into the Afridar district, the nucleus of the modern town and now a busy shopping and commercial quarter (clock-tower, tourist information office).

Sights

Roman sarcophagi

In the Afridar district, diagonally opposite the tourist information office, under a protective roof, are two magnificent Roman sarcophagi discovered here during site works in 1972. One has reliefs of fighting scenes, the other the rape of Persephone. On the lids are two reclining figures, the heads of which are unfinished – evidently awaiting purchase and completion in the likeness of the person to be buried.

★ National Park, ancient Ashkelon

Some 2km/1¼ miles south of the town centre, in a National Park (camping site, picnic areas, restaurants, beautiful bathing beach), are the remains of ancient Ashkelon, separated from the modern town by a broad belt of gardens and orange plantations. The whole area, which contains numerous remains ranging in date from the Philistine period to the Middle Ages, is bounded by a semicircular wall of the Crusader period, both ends of which reach down to the sea.

Roman remains: the goddess Isis . . .   *. . . and a capital*

The excavations of Ashqelon, in a beautiful National Park

The wall, built by Richard Coeur de Lion in 1192, had four gates – the Jaffa Gate in the north, the Jerusalem Gate in the east, the Gaza Gate in the south and the Sea Gate in the west. From the entrance at the north end of the site a road leads to a large car park. Just south of this are remains of the Roman period, notably large Corinthian capitals, column bases and other fragments from the huge Hundred-Columned Stoa built by Herod the Great. The apse at the south end of the stoa was much altered in later centuries, most recently as the prayer niche of a mosque. In this is a large relief depicting the kneeling Atlas bearing the globe, with a goddess of Victory hovering over him. Another relief shows the goddess Isis with her son Horus. Elsewhere in the park, which is beautifully laid out, are numerous other ancient remains, mainly columns and fountain-houses.

At the south end of the site, by the old harbour, is the mound on which the Philistine town once stood; it is reached by taking a path which bears right off the main avenue. Projecting from the wall running along the old harbour, which has no facing, can be seen Roman columns built into the wall to strengthen it.

In Hatayasim Street, near the Shulamit Gardens Hotel, is the Painted Tomb, which dates from the Roman period (3rd c.). Four steps lead down into the barrel-vaulted tomb chamber, which is decorated with frescoes. On the wall opposite the entrance are two naked nymphs sitting amid trees and animals in a stream. On the ceiling is a female figure (Demeter or Kore), above which are a dog chasing a hare and a Gorgon's head. The scene also includes boys with a basket and grapes, Pan with his flute, gazelles and birds, all this enclosed within a pattern of intertwining vine tendrils.

Painted Tomb

Farther north, in the district of Barnea, are the remains of a Byzantine basilica and, adjoining this, a mosaic pavement, probably from a church (both 5th–6th c.).

Barnea

Surroundings of Ashqelon

Yad Mordekhay

10km/6 miles south of Ashqelon is the kibbutz of Yad Mordekhay (illustration, page 99), which was founded in 1943 and named after the leader of the rising in the Warsaw ghetto. In 1948, during the War of Independence, the members of the kibbutz held up the advance of the Egyptian army for five days, allowing the Israeli forces to regroup in Tel Aviv. There are a reproduction of the battle site and a museum commemorating the resistance in the Warsaw ghetto.

Atlit   G 3

District: Haifa
Altitude: 25m/80ft

Situation and
characteristics

The large Crusader castle of Atlit lies 16km/10 miles south of Haifa on a peninsula projecting into the Mediterranean. Since this is a military area closed to the public it is possible to get only a distant view of the remains of the castle.

History

The history of Atlit begins in 1187, when the Crusaders lost Jerusalem to Saladin. The Grand Master of the Templars thus had to leave his palace on the Temple Mount (the Omayyad Dome of the Rock), from which the Order took its name, and the Templars had to build new quarters at Akko (see entry), Atlit and elsewhere. The castle which they built at Atlit in 1218 was given the name of Castrum Peregrinorum or Château des Pèlerins (Castle of the Pilgrims); the name Atlit dates from a later period.

After the unsuccessful attack on Damietta in the Nile delta (1249) the French king Louis IX stayed for some time in Acre (Akko) and Atlit. Atlit was attacked by the Arabs for the first time in 1265. The outlying districts were destroyed and the Templars were required to pay tribute to the Arabs, though they were allowed to retain possession of the castle. In 1291, however, Sultan Melik el-Ashraf stormed Acre, capital of the Christian kingdom. This was the end of the Crusader state, though a few strongholds still held out for a short time, among them Tortosa (Tartus in Syria) and Atlit. After the fall of Tortosa on August 3rd 1291 the Templars decided to return to France, and in the middle of August they evacuated the Castle of the Pilgrims.

In later centuries the castle fell into decay, though considerable remains were left even after an earthquake in 1837. In 1898, when the German Emperor William II called in at Atlit on his way from Haifa to Jerusalem, the only inhabitants were two Arab families. The land round Atlit was owned by Baron Edmond de Rothschild, who initiated the development of the area. In 1903 he founded the Arab village of Atlit 1km/¾ mile south of the castle, and in 1911 Aaron Aaronsohn established an experimental agricultural station in an area of marshland, where salt was produced by the evaporation of sea-water. (Most of the salt consumed in Israel now comes from here.) Since 1948 many immigrants have settled in Atlit.

During the Second World War the British authorities used the ruins of Atlit as a camp for German and Italian prisoners of war, and after the war for illegal Jewish immigrants. In 1956 and 1967 Egyptian prisoners were confined here.

The castle
No access!

The Crusader castle occupies a rectangular area measuring 200m/220yds by 450m/490yds on a rocky peninsula projecting westward into the sea. The entrance is at the east end. In front of it was an outlying settlement, partly excavated before 1938. The castle itself is defended by a ditch (cut through a Phoenician cemetery) and by a stout double wall.

On the inner wall is the principal tower or keep, El-Karnifeh, built of massive square blocks with quoins of dressed stone. Adjoining this tower is the chapterhouse, which is preserved to the springing of the vaulting, borne on consoles with saints' heads. At the west end of the castle, where steps run down to the landing-stage, can be seen the foundations of the octagonal Templar church. Like other Templar churches, it was a small-scale copy of the Dome of the Rock in Jerusalem. Unusually, the altar stood not in an apse but in the centre of the church.

Avdat   G 6

District: Southern
Altitude: 625m/2050ft

The remains of the city of Avdat (Arabic Avda), prominently situated on a hill, lie 65km/40 miles south of Beersheba, immediately to the left of the road to Elat. Now partly rebuilt, they are one of the most important sites of the Nabataean, Roman and Byzantine periods in the Negev.

Situation and characteristics

The first excavations, begun in 1870, were followed from 1953 onwards by systematic archaeological investigation of the site under the direction of Michael Avi-Yonah and Abraham Negev. They showed that the town was not founded, as had been thought, in the reign of the Nabataean king Obodas or Obidath II (30–9 B.C.) but dated from the 3rd century B.C., when the nomadic Nabataeans, coming from north-western Arabia and first recorded in 312 B.C., had taken to a settled life. Their capital of Petra, famed for its rock-cut monuments, lay to the east of the Arava depression. The Nabataeans owed their wealth to trade along the old caravan routes, and in order to protect the route from Petra to the Mediterranean port of Gaza they established a number of settlements – Nizzana, Subeita (see Shivta), Obodas (Avdat) and Mampsis (see Mamshit) – and a series of guard posts along the way. These settlements are among the more than 2000 Nabataean sites identified by Nelson Glueck in southern Jordan, the Negev and Sinai. They could exist only thanks to advanced irrigation methods ("run-off" irrigation) which allowed the Nabataeans to cultivate the land in these arid areas and supply the population with water and food.

History

Towards the end of the 1st century B.C. the town was given the name of king Obodas or Obidath, from which the present name Avdat is derived. Obodas was buried in the town and revered as a god. In his reign and that of his successor Aretas IV (9 B.C.–A.D. 40) Avdat enjoyed its first great period of prosperity.

In A.D. 106 the Romans conquered the region of Nabatene and incorporated it in the Empire as the province of Arabia Petraea. The road which they built from Elat to Damascus bypassed Avdat, and as a result the town declined. It recovered in the late 3rd century when a military camp was established to the north of the town and a temple of Jupiter replaced the temple dedicated to Obodas on the acropolis. In the reign of Theodosius I (379–395) the Nabataeans were Christianised. The Byzantine Emperor Justinian (527–564) settled monks in the Negev who devoted themselves to the development of irrigation systems and agriculture. New buildings were erected, including two churches and a monastery in the old temple precinct on the acropolis, and the town enjoyed a second period of prosperity. Then the capture of Avdat by the Persians in 614 and by the Arabs in 634 led to its final decline. The site was abandoned and the irrigation system collapsed. After the establishment of the state of Israel in 1948 the botanist Michael Evenari studied the old Nabataean and Byzantine irrigation system, reconstructed it and succeeded in creating an experimental farm, using the old methods and growing plants cultivated in Nabataean times. His success encouraged him to establish similar farms at Beersheba and Shivta.

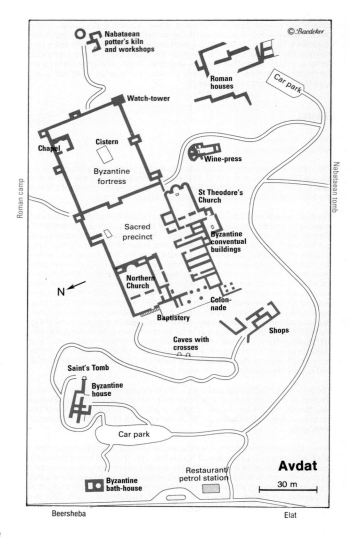

© Baedeker

Avdat

30 m

Beersheba   Elat

The ★ Site

An access road branches off the Beersheba–Elat road and ends at a car park (kiosk, rest-house) on the west side of the site. From here there is a road to another car park immediately south of the ancient city.

Nabataean tomb

Half way along the road between the two car parks a footpath goes off on the right to a Nabataean tomb. It is entered through a vaulted antechamber of dressed stone. Straight ahead is a doorway, on the lintel of which is a

Church of St Theodore on the acropolis of Avdat

Terrace on the west side

relief depicting a horned altar flanked by the moon, with a star (left), and the sun (right) and by two columns. The door leads into the burial chamber, which in the Nabataean fashion is hewn from the rock, with numerous narrow grave recesses in the walls (five to the left, eight straight ahead, nine to the right).

From in front of the tomb there is a good view of Michael Evenari's experimental "Nabataean" farm.

Roman houses, wine-press

From the upper car park a path leads north through a Roman residential quarter to a Nabataean wine-press which continued to be used into Byzantine times, with a semicircular upper section and a rectangular lower section. Nearby is a stone with a Nabataean inscription.

Byzantine fortress

The path now runs through the south gate into the rectangular Byzantine fortress. A vantage point in the south-east corner offers a view over the whole extent of the site with its (partly restored) walls and towers, a large cistern in the centre of the courtyard and the remains of a Late Byzantine chapel against the north wall. A passage in the north wall gives access to the Roman military camp, which measures 90m/100yds each way.

Sacred precinct

Adjoining the west side of the fortress is another courtyard, the sacred precinct. This dates from Byzantine times and contains two churches, built on the sites of Nabataean and Roman temples.

Church of St Theodore

To the left is the church of St Theodore, a three-aisled pillared basilica with three apses dedicated to a Greek martyr of the 4th century. The central doorway is embellished with two Nabataean horned capitals. In the floor of the lateral aisles are grave slabs with Greek inscriptions. One slab in the south aisle shows the Jewish seven-branched candlestick side by side with the Christian cross; another records that Zacharias, son of John, was buried here "in the martyrium of St Theodore". The sanctuary, in front of which, to the left, is the circular base of an ambo (reading desk), is two steps higher than the nave. It still preserves the old altar table. On the right-hand side of the principal apse and in front of the lateral apses are fragments of the templon (the low screen between the nave and the sanctuary). At the west end of the church are various conventual buildings.

Terrace, colonnade

At the west end of the sacred precinct, where the ground falls steeply away, is a broad terrace with a colonnade on the inner side. It is reached through a doorway which – like the central doorway of St Theodore's Church – has Nabataean capitals. On the terrace is a cruciform baptismal font (restored).

North Church

Adjoining the terrace is the entrance to the atrium of the North Church, the dedication of which is not known. This is also a three-aisled basilica with three apses. In the south aisle the consoles supporting the roof beams have been preserved. In front of the sanctuary, to the left, is the square base of an ambo. Two steps lead up into the sanctuary with its square altar.

The return to the lower car park is by way of a flight of steps leading down from the terrace beside the font, from which a path continues past two tomb chambers and the so-called Saint's Tomb (named after the image of a saint with a Greek inscription) near the remains of a Byzantine house. To the west of the car parks is a Byzantine bath-house which was still in use in Arab times.

Surroundings of Avdat

En Avdat

A little way north of the site of Avdat is the spring of En Avdat (see entry), one of the most abundant sources of water in the Wilderness of Zin, which extends from Avdat to the Arava depression.

Sede Boqer

To the north of En Avdat is the kibbutz of Sede Boqer (see entry), with the grave of David Ben-Gurion in the grounds of Sede Boqer College.

Banyas

Golan Territory
Altitude: sea level
Population: 200

The village of Banyas lies in a setting of extraordinary natural beauty and abundant vegetation 13km/8 miles east of Qiryat Shemona on the river Banyas (one of the source streams of the Jordan), under the south side of Mount Hermon. The area, which has been occupied by Israel since 1967, is now a nature reserve and a favourite place of resort with Israeli families and groups, particularly on the Sabbath.

Situation and characteristics

The name Banyas is derived from the Greek Paneas. From Hellenistic times this was the site of an important temple of the shepherd god Pan, whose cult had replaced the older worship of Baal. In 200 B.C. Antiochus III defeated a Ptolemaic army here and added Coele Syria and Palestine to his Seleucid kingdom. Augustus presented the area to Herod, whose son Philip established the capital of his tetrarchy here, naming it Caesarea in honour of the Roman Emperor. To distinguish it from other towns with the same name it was known as Caesarea Philippi. It was in this area that Jesus called Peter the rock on which he would build his church and promised to give him the keys of the kingdom of heaven (Matthew 16,13–20). In the 4th century Caesarea became the see of a bishop; in the 7th century it was conquered by the Arabs; it was taken by the Crusaders, who held it until 1165; and thereafter, until 1967, it was an Arab village.

History

Sights

Following the river Banyas upstream to the reddish-grey rock wall from which it emerges, we see a number of recesses with Greek inscriptions, once occupied by statues of Pan. To the left is the large cave where the river had its source until it was blocked by an earthquake.

★Source of the Banyas

On a hill farther to the left is the Weli (Tomb) of Sheikh El-Khidr, a Muslim holy man.

Weli

1km/¾ mile west of the source of the Banyas, at the kibbutz of Snir, is a beautiful waterfall, 10m/35ft high.

Waterfall

On a ridge of hill 3km/2 miles east, to the left of the road to Mount Hermon, is a castle built by the Arabs in 1226 under the name of Qalat Sudeiba and later occupied by the Crusaders. It is now known as Qalat Nimrod (Nimrod's Castle).

Qalat Nimrod

Beersheba/Be'er Sheva

District: Southern
Altitude: 240m/790ft
Population: 115,000

Beersheba (Be'er Sheva), famed in the Old Testament as the city of the Patriarchs, has developed within a few decades into the "capital of the Negev" and one of the largest cities in Israel, lying on the boundary between the arid pastureland to the south and the arable land to the north. It is a university town and an important industrial centre.
Beersheba has no outstanding tourist attractions to offer. Visitors come here mainly to see the great Bedouin market held every Thursday.

Situation and characteristics

Beersheba/Be'er Sheva

© Baedeker

Beersheba
Be'er Sheva

500 m

Tel Aviv, Jerusalem

History

The earliest settlement in the Beersheba area (Tel Sheva) lay on the Wadi Be'er Sheva, in the eastern outskirts of the modern city. Excavation on the banks of the river has brought to light a Chalcolithic settlement of the 4th millennium B.C. occupied by semi-nomads who constructed cisterns and underground dwellings entered from above. During the dry season they left these dwellings and moved northwards with their flocks and herds. A number of finds from the site are displayed in the Municipal Museum, and a fertility idol carved from bone can be seen in the Israel Museum in Jerusalem. The Horites encountered by Abraham also lived in underground dwellings. The Old Testament tells how Abraham and Abimelech of Gerar made a covenant at the well of Beersheba under which Abraham was to have unimpeded use of the well which he had dug (Genesis 21,32): an agreement which was repeated in the time of Abraham's son Isaac (Genesis 26,33).

In the time of the Judges Beersheba, which lay within the grazing lands of the Amalekites, formed the southern boundary of Israelite territory, which extended "from Dan even to Beersheba" (Judges 20,1). Around 1100 B.C. an Israelite town was built on Tel Sheva, 6km/4 miles east of the present city. The site was excavated in 1969 by Yohanan Aharoni, who brought to light an Israelite fort and material of the Aramaean, Edomite, Persian and Hellenistic periods. Later Beersheba became a garrison town, successively occupied by Maccabean, Roman and Byzantine forces. Thereafter for many

Abraham's Well, Beersheba

centuries the town was abandoned, though the well was still frequented by the Bedouin and their flocks and herds.

A new era in the history of Beersheba began around 1900, when the Turkish authorities made it the administrative centre for the Bedouin tribes of the Negev. A new town – now the old town – was laid out in 1907, with straight streets and the Bedouin market. In 1915, during the First World War, a railway line was constructed to supply the Turkish and German forces and a mosque (now occupied by the Municipal Museum) was built. Beersheba was the first Palestinian town taken by General Allenby, and a police fort was built here. During the period of British rule which now began the "Hunger Road", an asphalted road from Beersheba to Gaza, was built in order to provide employment in the region.

The first Jews settled in Beersheba around 1900, but during the Arab disturbances in 1929 they left the town. After Israel became independent in 1948 there was a fresh influx of Jews. At that time the town had a population of 3000. Beersheba is now a purely Jewish city, its inhabitants coming from countries all over the world.

Beersheba has the air of a young town, which still preserves a little of the "Wild West" character of its early days. The hub of the city's life is the old town of the Turkish period with its rectangular street grid, numerous shops, modest restaurants and snack bars. To the north of the old town are extensive new residential districts. To the east are the industrial installations, which use raw materials from the Negev.

The town

Sights

The main artery of the old town is Ha'atzmaut Street, in which is the Municipal Museum, housed in a mosque of the Turkish period. The collec-

Municipal Museum

125

tion includes material ranging right back to the early settlement on Tel Sheva (4th millennium B.C.). From the minaret of the former mosque there are fine views of the city and surrounding area.

Abraham's Well   At the south-east end of Ha'azmaut Street, where it joins Hebron Road (Derekh Hevron), is an old well (restored) known as Abraham's Well (see History, above), though it probably dates only from the Turkish period. Even the name, however, has commercial value: round the well a restaurant has set out its tables and there is a profitable trade in souvenirs.

Bedouin market   On the south side of Beersheba, in Elat Road (Derekh Elat), the Bedouin market is held every Thursday. It is frequented by Bedouin from far and wide, and its colourful bustle of activity attracts many tourists. The main wares of interest to visitors are carpets, finely embroidered cushions and camel saddles, copperware and numerous other craft products; the local people, on the other hand, come to buy articles of clothing, domestic requisites, skins and also live goats and hens.

Advice for visitors: Whatever you want to buy, you must never pay the seller's first asking price: haggling is an essential part of the process.

Other sights   Ha-Nesim Road (Sderot Ha-Nesim) branches off Elat Road and runs north past the Municipal Park to the Town Hall, in the immediate vicinity of which are the Bet Ha'am Cultural Centre (film shows, concerts, drama, lectures, exhibitions, etc.) and the Arid Zone Research Institute. Ha-Nesim Road continues north to the Soroka Medical Centre and the Ben-Gurion University, founded in 1968. (Conducted tours of the University site by appointment, made by telephone.)

Surroundings of Beersheba

Negev Brigade Memorial   The memorial to the Negev Brigade, which distinguished itself in the War of Independence, is reached by leaving the city on Hebron Road and soon after crossing the railway taking a road on the left.

Tel Sheva   South-east of the Negev Brigade Memorial (some 4km/2½ miles north-east of modern Beersheba) is Tel Sheva, with the remains of ancient Beersheba (defensive walls, water channels). There is a small site museum on the theme "Man in the Desert".

Near the site is a Bedouin settlement established in 1969 to rehouse Bedouin who had hitherto lived as nomads. At first the Bedouin were reluctant to live there, and it was only after they were allowed to build their own houses that they became reconciled to this new way of life. The settlement has one of the country's few Bedouin schools, and now also a secondary school.

Lahav kibbutz, Bedouin Museum   In the kibbutz of Lahav, 20km/12½ miles north-east of Beersheba, is a Bedouin Museum opened in 1985. The exhibits (clothing, domestic equipment, tools and implements, jewellery, etc.) are well presented and give a good impression of the art and culture of the various Bedouin tribes of Sinai and the Negev desert.

Beit Lahm

See Bethlehem

District: Northern
Altitude: 312m/1024ft

High above the Jordan valley rise the ruins of this great Crusader castle, built by French Knights Hospitallers and named Belvoir for its view of the valley. Its Hebrew name is Kokhav HaYarden ("Star of the Jordan").

Situation and characteristics

There are two routes to Belvoir. Coming from the north, turn off the Tiberias–Bet Shean road just beyond the Tavor valley (13km/8 miles south of the Sea of Galilee) into a road on the right which winds its way up to the castle, 500m/1650ft above the road. Alternatively, turn off the Bet Shean–Afula road at En Harod (14km/8½ miles from Bet Shean) into a very poor road on the right which runs up via the villages of Ramat Zevi and Bene Brit to Ramot Yissakhar and from there to Belvoir (13km/8 miles from En Harod).

The territory in which the castle stands was acquired in 1168 by the Knights Hospitallers, who then built one of the strongest frontier fortresses in the Frankish kingdom. In 1187 it withstood an attack by Saladin after his victory over the crusading army at the Horns of Hittim (see entry). Two years later, however, the knights were forced to surrender the castle on the promise of safe passage to Tyre. Fearing that the Crusaders might regain possession of the castle, the Arabs slighted it in 1219; and although the Crusaders did in fact recover it in 1241 it was never rebuilt.
In 1966–67 the ruins were cleared of soil and partly restored.

History

The castle, which covers an area of 100m/110yds by 140m/155yds, is surrounded on three sides by a moat 25m/80ft wide and up to 12m/40ft deep. The outer walls, in the form of a pentagon, are reinforced by seven towers, four at the corners and one in the middle of three of the sides. The east side, where the hill falls steeply down to the Jordan valley, was protected by a large projecting tower, which was destroyed in the last siege of the castle.

The ★castle

The castle walls enclose a fortress within a fortress. The square inner stronghold, measuring 40m/130ft each way, could still hold out even if the outer works were taken (though this situation never actually arose). On the ground floor of this inner castle were store-rooms, the kitchen and a dining room. The inner courtyard is thought to have been roofed over.
The main entrance to the castle was in the tower at the south-east corner of the complex. On the west side there was an entrance approached over a drawbridge (now replaced by a footbridge).

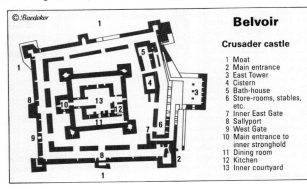

© Baedeker

Belvoir

Crusader castle

1 Moat
2 Main entrance
3 East Tower
4 Cistern
5 Bath-house
6 Store-rooms, stables, etc.
7 Inner East Gate
8 Sallyport
9 West Gate
10 Main entrance to inner stronghold
11 Dining room
12 Kitchen
13 Inner courtyard

Benot Ya'aqov Bridge

See Rosh Pinna

Bet Alfa

H 3

District: Northern
Altitude: 75m/245ft
Population: 800

Situation and characteristics

The kibbutz of Bet Alfa, at the foot of Mount Gilboa, 6km/4 miles west of Bet Shean (see entry) and 19km/12 miles east of Afula (see entry), was established in 1921. Its main claim to fame is the almost completely preserved mosaic pavement found nearby in a 6th century synagogue.

The mosaic, found by chance in 1928 during the construction of an irrigation canal on the neighbouring kibbutz of Hefzi Bah (see Tiberias) as one of the most important evidences of synagogue-building in the Byzantine period. The synagogue, which lies within the area of the Hefzi Bah kibbutz, bears the name of Bet Alfa since it belonged to the ancient settlement of that name.

Synagogue

The synagogue, a three-aisled building with a semicircular apse for the Torah shrine at the south end, has been re-roofed. There are mosaic pavements in the central and western aisles; the one in the central aisle has figural scenes, the other purely ornamental patterns. At the entrance to the central aisle is a Greek and Aramaic dedicatory inscription flanked by a lion and an ox.

★Mosaic in central aisle

The mosaic in the central aisle is in three parts.
Just inside the old central doorway is a representation of Abraham's sacrifice. To the left are two men leading Abraham's ass; in the centre is the bearded figure of Abraham in a long robe, holding the sacrificial knife in his right hand and the boy Isaac in his left; behind him is the ram, tied to a tree, and above is the Hand of God, directing Abraham to sacrifice the ram rather than his son, while to the right is the altar of sacrifice.

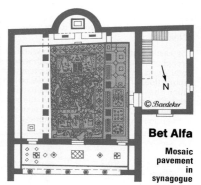

Bet Alfa

Mosaic
pavement
in
synagogue

The central panel of the mosaic is dominated by a cosmological theme. In the middle, presented frontally, is the sun god Helios in a chariot drawn by four horses; round him are the twelve signs of the Zodiac, and in the corners are the four Seasons.

The panel at the far end shows the Torah shrine in the centre, flanked by seven-branched candlesticks, incense scoops, two birds and two lions and framed by curtains on either side.

The themes of the Zodiac and the Torah shrine are also found in the mosaics of the synagogue at Tiberias-Hammat; but while the Tiberias mosaics are works of consummate artistic skill, those of Bet Alfa are in a plainer, more popular style.

Bet Guvrin

District: Southern
Altitude: 275m/900ft
Population: 200

The kibbutz of Bet Guvrin lies in the western Judaean hills, 36km/22 miles east of Ashqelon on the road to Jerusalem via Qiryat Gat and Bet Shemesh. It was established on the ruins of an Arab village in 1949 to protect Israel's frontier with Jordan and given an old Hebrew name.

Situation and characteristics

In the 6th century B.C. Bet Guvrin was an outpost of the Edomite capital of Mareshah (see entry), 2km/1¼ miles away. In the 1st century B.C., under Roman rule, it developed into an important fortified settlement, to which the Emperor Septimius Severus (193–211) gave the name of Eleutheropolis ("Free City"). In Byzantine times it was the administrative centre of the largest region in Palestine, which extended as far west as Gaza. The Crusaders built the castle of Gibelin here to protect the southern approach to Jerusalem. After being captured by Saladin in 1187 it was recovered by the Crusaders but finally fell to the Mamelukes in 1244.

History

In 1921 excavations on a site 1km/¾ mile south-east of the village brought to light two mosaic pavements from Christian churches of the 5th–6th centuries with representations of deer, birds, the Seasons and a hunting scene. (Conducted visits on application to the kibbutz.)

Sights

The excavators also found a 3rd century synagogue. Among the remains (now mostly in the Rockefeller Museum in Jerusalem) were a column with a Hebrew inscription and a capital carved with a seven-branched candlestick.

By the roadside is a building of the Crusader period which was occupied by Arabs until 1948.

Bethany

See El-Azariya

Bethlehem/Beit Lahm

West Bank
Altitude: 750m/2460ft
Population: 20,000

Bethlehem (Arabic Beit Lahm), birthplace of David and of Jesus, lies 10km/6 miles south of Jerusalem in a hilly and very fertile region. This fertility is reflected in the popular derivation of the name Bethlehem from the Hebrew word *lehm* ("bread"): Bethlehem is the "House of Bread". The Arabs interpret the name as "House of Meat" (Beit Lahm).

Situation and characteristics

Bethlehem has an Arab population consisting half of Christians and half of Muslims. Many of the inhabitants now make their living from the tourist trade. The main sources of income are the manufacture and sale of souvenirs, sacred images and sculpture of all kinds in mother-of-pearl, wood and

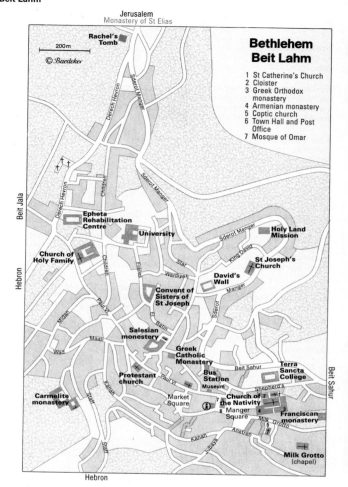

Jerusalem
Monastery of St Elias

Rachel's
Tomb

200m
© *Baedeker*

Bethlehem
Beit Lahm

1 St Catherine's Church
2 Cloister
3 Greek Orthodox
  monastery
4 Armenian monastery
5 Coptic church
6 Town Hall and Post
  Office
7 Mosque of Omar

Beit Jala

Hebron

Derech Hevron
Sderot Manger
Children
Erdves
Star
Wardiyeh
Paul VI
Midan
Maali
Wad
Kanah
Starr
Starr
Hebron

Epheta
Rehabilitation
Centre
University

Church of
Holy Family

Convent of
Sisters of
St Joseph

Salesian
monestery

Protestant
church

Carmelite
monastery

Sderot Manger
Holy Land
Mission

King David
St Joseph's
Church

David's
Wall
Manger

Sderot
Batin

Greek
Catholic
Monastery

Beit Sahur
Bus
Station
Museum

Market
Square

Church of
the Nativity
Manger
Square
Milk
Grotto
Anatren

Jubava

Kanah

Terra
Sancta
College

Shepherd's

Franciscan
monastery

Beit Sahur

Milk Grotto
(chapel)

bituminous limestone ("Dead Sea stone"), embroidered blouses, Crusader jackets and so on, as well as farming and sheep-rearing, craft production and trade.

Biblical tradition

Bethlehem is first mentioned in the account of the death of Rachel. On her way from Bethel to the south she died in giving birth to her second son Benjamin and "was buried in the way to Ephrath, which is Bethlehem" (Genesis 35,19).

Centuries later the widowed Ruth returned from Moab with her mother-in-law Naomi to her home town of Bethlehem. She was gleaning in a field belonging to Boaz when he encountered her. He then married her and she bore his son Obed, "the father of Jesse, the father of David" (Ruth 4,17).

In due time David, Jesse's youngest son, was anointed by Samuel in Bethlehem as king (1 Samuel 16,13).

Jesus, of the lineage of David, was born in Bethlehem, to which his parents had travelled from their home in Nazareth for a census in the reign of the Emperor Augustus (Luke 2,1–7), and an angel announced his birth to the shepherds in the field (Luke 2,10).

After the repression of the Bar Kochba uprising, in 135, the Emperor Hadrian built a temple of Adonis over the Grotto of the Nativity, which is not referred to in the Gospels but is mentioned by Justin Martyr about 155. By around 200 it had become an established place of pilgrimage, and in 325 the Emperor Constantine built a church over the grotto in place of Hadrian's temple. The plan of this church was reconstructed by R. W. Hamilton on the basis of contemporary descriptions and an excavation in 1934. A colonnaded atrium (under the present forecourt of the church) led into a five-aisled basilica with mosaic pavements and marble facing on the walls, from which three steps at the east end led into an octagon at a higher level. This stood immediately above the grotto, into which pilgrims could look down through an opening in the floor. It is not known whether the entrance to the grotto was at the west or the east end. A few decades after the building of the church, in 386, St Jerome, a native of Dalmatia, came to Bethlehem, settled in a cave adjoining the Grotto of the Nativity and composed his Latin translation of the Bible, the Vulgate, there. Thereafter hosts of pilgrims travelled to Bethlehem from many lands, and Jerome recorded that "men sang God's praises in many different tongues".

History

The Constantinian church was destroyed in 529 by rebellious Samaritans. St Sabas, who lived in his nearby monastery (see Mar Saba), travelled to Constantinople and sought the Emperor Justinian's support for the building of a new church. The Emperor's architect retained the original plan of a five-aisled nave but replaced the octagon by a trefoil sanctuary and omitted the atrium.

Miraculously, this church has survived to the present day. The Persians, advancing in 614 against Byzantium, spared it because they took the figures of the three kings from the East clad in Oriental garb in a relief over the entrance for fellow-countrymen. In the time of the Crusaders, who captured Bethlehem before taking Jerusalem, the Byzantine Emperor Manuel had the church thoroughly restored (1161–69). Previously, at Christmas 1100, Baldwin I had been crowned here as the first king of Jerusalem. In the 13th century the Mamelukes also left the church unscathed, but thereafter it fell increasingly into disrepair. In 1479 the roof had to be shored up, and from 1516 onwards the Turks used the marble facing in their buildings on the Temple platform in Jerusalem. In 1670, however, the Greek Orthodox church, with the permission of the Ottoman authorities, began work on the restoration of the church.

During the 18th and 19th centuries there were frequently bitter and sometimes violent conflicts between Greek Orthodox, Catholic and Armenian believers, which were still further aggravated by the intervention of the protecting powers, Russia and France. The Sublime Porte sought to settle these conflicts by means of the law on property rights originally introduced in 1757 and renewed in 1852 – a law which has outlived the Ottoman Empire and remains in force to this day.

Bethlehem still retains much of the atmosphere of an Oriental country township, with its Arab markets, colourful bazaar and countryfolk driving their sheep out to pasture.

The town

Side by side with this, however, the military presence in this Israeli-occupied area is very obvious. On the roofs of many houses can be seen soldiers on guard with sub-machine-guns, and military vehicles drive through the streets at almost hourly intervals. In the afternoon, when Arab shopkeepers close their shops in protest against the occupation, Bethlehem often looks like a dead town. The only signs of life then are in Manger Square in the town centre.

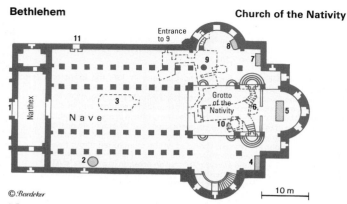

Bethlehem

Church of the Nativity

1 Entrance
2 Font
3 Mosaic pavement
4 Altar of Circumcision

5 High altar
6 Iconostasis
7 Altar of Three Kings
8 Altar of the Virgin

9 Grotto of Holy Innocents
10 Altar of the Manger
11 Doorway to St Catherine's Church

Sights

Manger Square

The life of Bethlehem centres on Manger Square, now serving as a car park. Visitors arriving in the square will be directed to a parking space by local children and young people – an offer of service which, on security grounds, should not be turned down. Round the square are cafés, restaurants and souvenir shops, a police station and a tourist information office and travel agency. On the west side of the square is the modern Mosque of Omar; the east side is dominated by the Church of the Nativity.

★★Church of the Nativity

The Church of the Nativity, seen from the square in front of it, is a fortress-like building on whose façade the pediment at the end of the nave can be distinguished only on close inspection. The central doorway shows the work of many centuries. The original door surround can be seen, as can the relief-decorated architrave and supporting consoles of the 6th century Justinianic church. The Crusaders reduced the size of the entrance, inserting a doorway with a pointed arch and walling up the upper part of the original doorway. The size of the doorway was later still further reduced in order to prevent the Mamelukes from riding into the church on horseback. It is now only 1.20m/4ft high, so that visitors must bend down to enter the church. The interior has essentially preserved the tranquil monumentality of the 6th century. The view towards the east end is unimpeded since the tall screen erected by the Greeks between the nave and choir was taken down on General Allenby's orders in 1917.

The nave is 54m/177ft long by 46m/151ft across. The roof of the lateral aisles and the clerestory of the nave are borne on four rows of eleven monolithic columns with Corinthian capitals, which were originally gilded. Two openings in the floor of the nave allow visitors to see mosaics on the floor of the Constantinian church of 325, which is 60cm/2ft below the present floor level. The font in the south aisle dates from the time of Justinian.
Parts of the mosaic decoration applied to the clerestory walls in the Crusader era (1261–69) has been preserved. On the south side are depicted the ancestors of Christ and the seven Oecumenical Councils recognised by the

Church of the Nativity, Bethlehem

In the Church of the Nativity

Grotto of the Nativity

Orthodox church – indicating that the mosaics were the work not of Western but of Greek artists – two mosaic artists from Constantinople, Basil and Ephraim, who were sent to Bethlehem by the Byzantine Emperor Manuel, a relative by marriage of Baldwin III, fourth king of the Frankish state. Paintings of the Crusader period have also been preserved on the columns in the nave. They include figures of saints (St George and King Canute of Denmark) and Baldwin I's helmet, with a swan as its crest. (Baldwin, who was crowned first king of Jerusalem in the Church of the Nativity in 1100, was held to be a descendant of Lohengrin, the Swan Knight.)

A few steps lead up to the crossing. The choir and transepts have semicircular apses. In the north transept are the Armenian altars of the Virgin and the Three Kings; in the south transept is the altar of the Circumcision, which, like the high altar behind the iconostasis, belongs to the Greeks.

From the south transept, in the apse of which is a door leading to the adjoining Greek Orthodox monastery, a finely carved doorway with a pointed arch dating from the Frankish period gives access to the stairs leading down to the Grotto of the Nativity (12.30m/40ft long by 3.15m/10ft across). The actual place where Jesus was born is marked by a silver star with the Latin inscription "Hic de virgine Maria Jesus Christus natus est" ("Here Jesus Christ was born of the Virgin Mary"). Above this is a recess containing an altar, with barely distinguishable 12th century mosaics. Opposite, three steps lower down, are the Manger Chapel and adjoining this the Altar of the Three Kings. The rear part of the grotto is not open to the public: the door leading to the other grottoes in the much ramified cave system is opened only on the occasion of special processions.

St Catherine's Church

The exit from the Grotto of the Nativity is by a second flight of steps leading into the north transept. A doorway in the north aisle leads into the neighbouring church of St Catherine, built by Franciscans in 1881 on the site of an earlier church. A flight of steps in the south aisle leads down to the northern part of the cave system. To the left is the Chapel of the Holy Innocents, commemorating Herod's massacre of the children of Bethlehem; straight ahead is St Joseph's Chapel; and to the right are the Chapel of St Eusebius, the tombs of St Paula and her daughter Eustochium and the tomb of St Jerome, with whom the two women came to Bethlehem. On the rear wall is the stone bench on which the remains of St Jerome (d. 420) rested until their translation to Rome and burial in the church of Santa Maria Maggiore. To the north is a room in which Jerome is said to have written the Vulgate.

Cloister

Adjoining St Catherine's Church is a cloister which originally dated from the Frankish period. It was excavated only in the middle of this century and then rebuilt by an Italian architect, Barluzzi, using the original material. In the cloister garth is a statue of St Jerome on a 2m/6½ft high column.

Milk Grotto

From the square in front of the Church of the Nativity a street runs southeast between houses and the Greek monastery and its associated buildings. This leads after a five minutes' walk to the Milk Grotto, a cave converted into a chapel (5m/16ft by 3m/10ft by 2.6m/8½ft) in which the Holy Family are said to have hidden before the flight into Egypt. According to the legend a drop of Mary's milk fell on the floor of the cave and whitened the stone.

Market Square

From Manger Square Paul VI Street runs west to Market Square and beyond this to the commercial districts of the town.

Museum of Old Bethlehem

A little way north-west of the Mosque of Omar is the Museum of Old Bethlehem, opened in 1972, with a collection of furniture, costumes, craft products and documents which present a vivid picture of 19th century Bethlehem.

David's Well

To the west of Manger Road (Sderot Manger), near St Joseph's Church, is David's Well, a rock-cut cistern. Excavations are being carried out in the area of "David's Wall", which surrounds it.

St Catherine's Church: interior . . .   *. . . and cloister*

Surroundings of Bethlehem

The little town of Beit Jala, to the west, is now almost continuous with Bethlehem. Of its four churches the most interesting is St Nicholas's.

Beit Jala

The road continues for another 2km/1¼ miles to Har Gillo (923m/3028ft), from which there is a magnificent view of Jerusalem.

Har Gillo

At the north end of the town, to the left, is the tomb of Rachel, who died in giving birth to Benjamin; it is a place of pilgrimage for pious Jews. The present domed structure dates mainly from the 18th and 19th centuries; the small vestibule containing a mihrab (Muslim prayer niche) was built in 1841.

Rachel's Tomb

On a hill 2km/1¼ miles north of Bethlehem, to the right of the main road to Jerusalem, is the Monastery of St Elias (Elijah), originally built in the 6th century and rebuilt by the Crusaders in the 11th century and the Greek Orthodox in the 17th century. From here there is a fine view of Bethlehem.

Monastery of St Elias

1km/¾ mile beyond this on the road to Jerusalem is the kibbutz of Ramat Rahel, founded in 1926, destroyed in 1948, when it was a front line post between Israeli and Jordanian forces, and rebuilt in 1950. The name refers to Rachel's Tomb. On the 818m/2684ft high hill a fortified palace of the kings of Judah has been excavated. Built in the 9th or 8th century B.C., it remained in use until the time of King Joachim (608–598 B.C.), was rebuilt in 535 B.C., after the Babylonian Captivity, and finally destroyed, probably in A.D. 70, by the Romans.

Ramat Rahel

South-east of Bethlehem is the village of Beit Sahur. A field here is said to be the one in which Boaz saw Ruth gleaning the ears of corn. Here too is the Shepherds' Field in which the angels announced the birth of Jesus (Luke

Beit Sahur

Monastery of St Elias, near Bethlehem

2,10). Adjoining the remains of a Byzantine church is a modern Franciscan church (1954). 1km/¾ mile away is a Greek Orthodox church where in 1972 archaeologists excavated a 4th century church with a very beautiful mosaic pavement which was known from the written sources.

On the eastern outskirts of Beit Sahur the road forks. The road to the left leads by way of the monastery of St Theodosius to the desert monastery of Mar Saba (8km/5 miles; see entry); the road to the left runs via the village of Za'tara, built in the sixties to house Bedouin of the Ta'amara tribe, to the Herodeion (11km/7 miles; see entry).

Solomon's Pools

The road which runs south-west from Bethlehem to Hebron (24km/15 miles; see entry) passes on the left, a few kilometres from Bethlehem, three large open cisterns known as Solomon's Pools, built in ancient times to provide water for Jerusalem. A reliable tradition dates them to the reign of Solomon in the 10th century B.C.: "I made me pools of water, to water therewith the wood that bringeth forth trees" (Ecclesiastes 2,6).

Artas

A side road which turns off on the left 5km/3 miles south of Bethlehem runs past Solomon's Pools, near which the Turks built a small fort in 1540, to the village of Artas (2km/1¼ miles), set in a lush green valley. The Hortus Conclusus nunnery below the village recalls the reference in the Song of Solomon (4,12) to a "garden inclosed": the *hortus conclusus* which later became a metaphor for virginity, a symbol of the Virgin Mary. The name of the village is derived from the Latin *hortus*.

Khadr

Shortly before the side road to Artas turns off the Bethlehem–Hebron road another road goes off on the right and runs north-west, passing the village of Khadr (4km/2½ miles), whose name comes from El-Chodr (St George). There is an old Greek Orthodox church dedicated to St George.

1km/¾ mile beyond Khadr a road goes off on the right to Battir (ancient Betar; 4km/2½ miles), on the southern slopes of the Ephraim valley, through which the Tel Aviv–Jerusalem railway line runs. Thanks to an abundantly flowing spring this is a flourishing agricultural region. Above the village are ancient remains (unexcavated) known to the Arabs as Khirbet el-Yahud (the Jew's Ruins). This is the site of a fortress which during the rising of 132–135 A.D. against the Romans held out until the last; the leader of the rising, Bar Kochba, was killed here.

Battir

Bet Shean

H 3

District: Northern
Altitude: 98m/322ft below sea level
Population: 15,000

Bet Shean (the Biblical Bethshan) lies on the river Harod 26km/16 miles south of the Sea of Galilee, in the eastern part of the Jezreel plain, which carefully regulated irrigation has made a fertile agricultural area. According to the Talmud "If the garden of Eden is in Israel, then its gate is in Bet Shean". In addition to such interesting remains as the Roman theatre there is evidence that the history of the site goes far back beyond Roman times into the 4th millennium B.C. It also has associations with King Saul.

Situation and characteristics

American archaeologists from the University of Pennsylvania carried out excavations here in 1921–23 and identified 18 occupation levels, the earliest dating back to the 4th millennium B.C. Bet Shean first appears in the records in Egyptian documents of the 19th century B.C. After his conquest of Canaan in the 15th century B.C. Pharaoh Tuthmosis III fortified the town. In the 11th century it was captured by the Philistines, advancing inland from the sea. After the Philistines defeated Saul and his sons in a battle on nearby Mount Gilboa in 1010 B.C. they "put [Saul's] armour in the house of Ashtaroth, and they fastened his body to the wall of Bethshan"; then during the night men from Gilead, beyond the Jordan, recovered the bodies and gave them burial (1 Samuel 31).

History

David, Saul's successor, conquered the Philistine town, which for some unknown reason was abandoned in the 8th century B.C. In the 3rd century B.C. it was resettled by Scythian veterans and renamed Scythopolis. In the Hasmonean period (2nd and 1st c. B.C.) numbers of Jews came to live in the town. In 63 B.C. Pompey declared it a free city and it became a member of the Decapolis, the League of Ten Cities. Under Roman rule, thanks to its productive agriculture and textile industry, it enjoyed a fresh period of prosperity, to which the numerous remains bear witness. In Byzantine times the town had a population of some 40,000; most of them were Christians, but there was also a Jewish community. This period came to an end with the Arab conquest in 639, and soon afterwards the town was destroyed by an earthquake and abandoned.

In the 12th century Bet Shean was held by Tancred, Prince of Galilee. After its conquest by Saladin in 1183 the town had a Jewish population, one member of which was Rabbi Estori Haparhi, who wrote the earliest work in Hebrew on the geography of Palestine. Later increasing numbers of Arabs settled in the town, and its name was changed to Beisan. A relic of the Turkish period is the Seraglio in the Municipal Park, an administrative building erected in 1905. Jews began to return to the town in 1937, and many more have come since 1948.

Bet Shean

Sights

Municipal Park, Seraglio

On the east side of the town, on the road from Tiberias, is the Municipal Park, with a small open-air theatre. In this park is the Turkish Seraglio of 1905, with antique columns framing the doorway.

From here King Saul Street (Rehov Shaul Hamelech) bears right, passes an area in which remains of the Roman hippodrome were found and comes to a road on the right which runs down to the Roman theatre.

★Roman theatre

The theatre, built in the late 2nd century, in the reign of Septimius Severus, is the best preserved Roman theatre in Israel. It had seating for 6000 spectators. The lower part of the structure with its semicircular tiers of seating was built into the ground; the upper part is borne on massive substructures, with nine entrances (vomitoria) leading to the horizontal gangway (diazoma) half way up the auditorium. From the vomitoria short, narrow passages branch off, leading to small rooms, originally domed, of unknown function. The upper tiers of seating have been partly destroyed, but the lower rows are excellently preserved. There are substantial remains of the stage wall, which was originally richly decorated with columns and statues; behind it are numerous architectural fragments.

★★Tell el-Husn

Immediately north of the theatre is Tell el-Husn, a settlement mound on which excavations in the 1920s brought to light mainly stelae, sculpture and other objects dating from the period of Egyptian rule. Most of the finds, including a stele of Pharaoh Sethos I (1318 B.C.) and a stele depicting the war goddess Anat (1250 B.C.), are now in the Rockefeller Museum in Jerusalem.

Further excavations since 1986 have yielded such impressive results that the tell now ranks as one of the most important archaeological sites in Israel. Since Bet Shean was destroyed by an earthquake shortly after the Arab conquest the building materials of the ancient town were not – as was the case, for example, at Caesarea – re-used in later buildings. This simplifies the work of the archaeologists, who have only to re-erect the walls which collapsed in the earthquake.

In the south part of the site another excellently preserved Roman and Byzantine theatre, also seating 6000 spectators, has been brought to light. North of this is a bath-house of the Byzantine period centred on an inner courtyard with colonnades round three sides and preserving remains of the original mosaic and marble decoration. Particularly fine is the Tyche mosaic (6th c. A.D.) found in a Byzantine building immediately north-east of the baths; it depicts Tyche, goddess of fate and of good fortune, with the cornucopia which was one of her attributes.

Roman theatre, Bet Shean

From the bath-house steps lead up to a colonnaded street linking the theatre and the baths with the centre of the city. At its north end is a broad flight of steps leading up the remains of a Roman temple of Dionysus. To the east of this temple were found foundations and architectural fragments belonging to a nymphaeum and a basilica which served in Roman times as a meeting-place and market-place and, south-east of the basilica, a row of monolithic Roman columns and part of a Byzantine street of shops leading to the southern part of the town.

Byzantine remains were also found to the north of Tell el-Husn, on the far side of the Harod valley. Here in 567 a noble lady named Mary and her son Maximus founded a monastery, with fine mosaics which are now under a protective roof.

Monastery of the Lady Mary

The entrance leads into a large trapezoidal courtyard, with a mosaic pavement depicting animals and birds, two Greek inscriptions and in the centre – within a circle of twelve figures representing the months, with Greek inscriptions – the sun god Helios and the moon goddess Selene. To the left is a rectangular room with a mosaic which an inscription records "was completed in the time of Abbot George and his deputy Komitas". Other mosaics (vine tendrils, hunters, animals) are in a small room opposite the entrance, in the east part of the monastery, in the narthex of the church and in the church itself. Within the doorway of the church are peacocks. In the sanctuary are gravestones inscribed in Greek.

Some of the material found in excavations round Bet Shean can be seen in the site museum, housed in a former mosque. Particularly notable is the Leontis mosaic (5th c. A.D.), named after a prosperous Jew from Alexandria who commissioned this mosaic, depicting a scene from the "Odyssey", for his magnificent villa in Bet Shean.

Museum

139

Surroundings of Bet Shean

Bet Alfa
6km/4 miles west of Bet Shean is Bet Alfa (see entry), famed for the mosaic in its ancient synagogue.

Gan HaShelosha National Park
The Gan HaShelosha National Park ("Park of the Three") lies on the road from Bet Shean to Bet Alfa: see Mount Gilboa.

Ma'ayan Harod National Park
10km/6 miles north-west of Gan HaShelosha is the Ma'ayan Harod National Park: see Mount Gilboa.

Newe Ur
12km/7½ miles north of Bet Shean is the kibbutz of Newe Ur, occupied by Jews from Iraq and accordingly named after Abraham's home town of Ur in Chaldaea (Mesopotamia).
On a hill to the north-west can be seen the remains of the Crusader castle of Belvoir (see entry), to which a winding road leads up.

Bet Shearim   H 3

District: Northern
Altitude: 138m/453ft

Situation and characteristics
The archaeological site of Bet Shearim, 20km/12½ miles south-east of Haifa, is reached by taking a side road which goes off the Haifa–Nazareth road on the right soon after Qiryat Tivon. Bet Shearim is an important site in the Jewish rabbinical tradition, particularly notable for the impressive catacombs excavated by B. Mazar in 1936 and later by N. Avigad. They lie in a beautiful setting, within an area of 2 hectares/5 acres which has been declared a National Park.

History
Bet Shearim acquired particular importance in 135, when, after the failure of the Bar Kochba rising, Rabbi Judah Hanassi moved his seminary here from Yavne (see entry), making Bet Shearim the spiritual centre of Jewry. The Sanhedrin, as leader of which Rabbi Judah bore the title of Hanassi ("Prince"), also met here for a time. Many members of the Sanhedrin were buried in Bet Shean, and its fame led other pious Jews to have themselves buried here.

Sights

Synagogue
Oil-press
Before the access road reaches the entrance to the National Park the remains of a large three-aisled synagogue of the 2nd or 3rd century, its façade oriented towards Jerusalem, can be seen on the left. Farther along is an oil-press, with two rooms.

Statue of Alexander Zaid
150m/165yds farther on, above the road on the left, on the highest point of the site, can be seen a statue of Alexander Zaid, who discovered the necropolis in 1936.

★★Necropolis
The access road then takes a sharp bend to the right and comes to the entrance to the site and the ticket kiosk. There is a car park inside the National Park.
The necropolis consists of a series of catacombs hewn from the rock on the hillside, each containing between 20 and 400 tombs. The catacombs had all been robbed, and the excavators found neither human remains nor grave goods. The sarcophagi, mostly of the local limestone, are decorated with Jewish symbols (seven-branched candlesticks, Torah shrines, etc.) but also

Bet Shearim: façade of Catacomb 20 ▶

Remains of synagogue, Bet Shearim

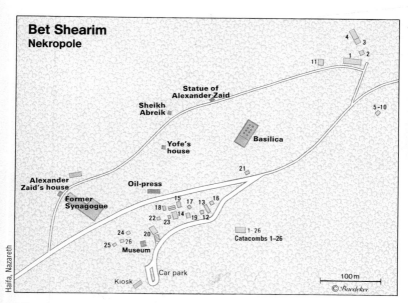

Bet Shearim
Nekropole

Statue of Alexander Zaid

Sheikh Abreik

Yofe's house

Basilica

Alexander Zaid's house

Oil-press

Former Synagogue

21

15 17 13 16
18   14 19 12
22 23

24
25   26
Museum

20

1–26
Catacombs 1–26

4
3
1 2
11
5–10

Car park

Kiosk

100 m

© Baedeker

Haifa, Nazareth

with figures of human beings and animals. The carving shows no great artistic skill. Many of the catacombs have a stone doorway preceded by an open forecourt.
Of the 26 catacombs so far discovered there are usually only two open to visitors, including No. 20, the largest of them all.

In one of the main chambers in Catacomb 20 is a museum displaying finds from the site, including a modern-looking relief of a menorah.

Museum

Catacomb 20 (illustration, page 141) has a façade, partly restored, with three arched stone doorways. There is a broad central corridor with a number of passages opening off it. In this underground palace were found over 200 sarcophagi, many of them weighing between 3 and 5 tons. At the far end of the first passage on the left note particularly the Hunting Sarcophagus (a lion hunting a gazelle) and the Lion Sarcophagus. In the first passage on the right is the Eagle Sarcophagus; in the second on the right a sarcophagus with the face of a bearded man; and in the third, at the far end, the Shell Sarcophagus, with particularly elaborate decoration.

Catacomb 20

Catacomb 14, which also has a triple-arched façade, contains a number of informative inscriptions in Hebrew, Greek and Aramaic, for example on the sarcophagi of Simon and Gamaliel, presumably sons of Rabbi Judah Hanassi, who was himself buried in Bet Shearim.

Catacomb 14

Bet Shemesh

G 4

District: Jerusalem
Population: 11,600

The town of Bet Shemesh, 30km/19 miles west of Jerusalem near the site of the Biblical Beth-shemesh, was founded in 1950. It is reached by turning off the Tel Aviv–Jerusalem road 5km/3 miles east of Latrun (10km/6 miles west of Abu Ghosh) into a road which runs south via Bet Guvrin to Qiryat Gad and Ashqelon.
Bet Shemesh has developed in a relatively short time from a tented settlement for new immigrants into a modern town. Since most of the settlers were employed on re-afforestation there are extensive pinewoods in the area. There is a cement factory, using limestone from quarries in the Judaean Hills.

Situation and characteristics

The new settlement was named after the Biblical Beth-shemesh, the site of which was identified in 1838 on a tell to the west of the town and excavated before and after the First World War. The excavations revealed the existence on this site of a Hyksos and later a Canaanite town dating back to the 18th century B.C. The name Beth-shemesh means "House of the Sun" – probably referring to a Canaanite temple, the foundations of which were found.
In the 13th century Joshua took the town (Joshua 21,16). In the 11th century the Philistines defeated the Israelites in a battle at Eben-ezer and captured the Ark of the Covenant; but its possession brought them ill luck and they returned it to the Israelites. The cart carrying the Ark, drawn by two milch kine, halted for a time in Beth-shemesh (1 Samuel 6,12) and then continued to Kirjath-jearim (Qiryat Yearim, near Abu Ghosh). About 800 B.C. there was a battle at Beth-shemesh between King Amaziah of Judah and King Jehoash of Israel (2 Kings 14,11).
The excavations showed that the site was still occupied in Hellenistic and Roman times. Over these remains the Mamelukes built a caravanserai in the 13th or 14th century.

History

Surroundings of Bet Shemesh

Beit Jimal

5km/3 miles south of Bet Shemesh, to the left of the road, is the monastery of Beit Jimal (Bet Gamal), built by Salesian monks in 1881. The few remaining monks grew some crops and also have a vineyard. In the cloister are a number of fragments of the Byzantine period, including a mosaic pavement from a church built in Bet Shemesh in the 5th or 6th century over the grave of a martyr called Stephen.

During archaeological digs carried out since 1989 a Byzantine church and a large oil-press have been found 2km/1¼ miles from the monastery

Caesarea   G 3

District: Haifa
Altitude: 20m/65ft

Situation and characteristics

The site of the ancient city of Caesarea, half way between Tel Aviv and Haifa, offers not only its fascinating ancient remains but also a variety of holiday and recreational facilities. In summer concerts are given in the restored Roman theatre as part of the Israel Festival.

The principal sights of Caesarea are the Crusader city and the Roman

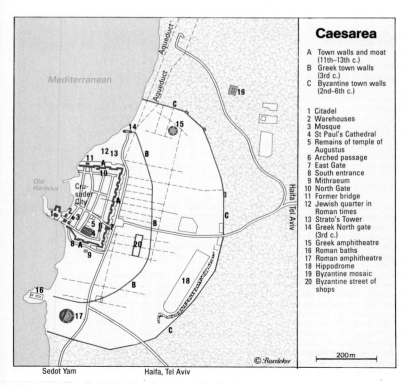

Caesarea

A Town walls and moat (11th–13th c.)
B Greek town walls (3rd c.)
C Byzantine town walls (2nd–6th c.)

1 Citadel
2 Warehouses
3 Mosque
4 St Paul's Cathedral
5 Remains of temple of Augustus
6 Arched passage
7 East Gate
8 South entrance
9 Mithraeum
10 North Gate
11 Former bridge
12 Jewish quarter in Roman times
13 Strato's Tower
14 Greek North gate (3rd c.)
15 Greek amphitheatre
16 Roman baths
17 Roman amphitheatre
18 Hippodrome
19 Byzantine mosaic
20 Byzantine street of shops

© Baedeker

200m

Sedot Yam   Haifa, Tel Aviv

theatre, both of which are now included in a National Park (single admission ticket for both sites). The remains of the ancient aqueduct on the beach to the north can be seen without a ticket; it is reached by way of a select residential area with beautiful gardens.

The site was first occupied by the Phoenicians, who built a harbour here in the 4th century B.C.; it is believed that their settlement lay to the north of the Crusader city, round Strato's Tower. After the conquest of the country by Alexander the Great in 332 B.C. the site was occupied by Greeks. In 22 B.C. Herod the Great began the construction of a large city which he named Caesarea in honour of Augustus. With its temple of Augustus, theatre, hippodrome and excellent water supply Caesarea developed into a considerable town with a busy harbour, occupied by both Jews and non-Jews. When Judaea became a Roman province Caesarea was from A.D. 6 the residence of the Roman procurators, including Pontius Pilate (A.D. 26–36), during whose term of office Christ was crucified, and Felix (52–60), who held the Apostle Paul prisoner here for two years (Acts 23,35). About A.D. 35, probably in the time of Pilate, Peter baptised the centurion Cornelius in Caesarea (Acts 10) – upsetting the "apostles and brethren" in Judaea, since this was the first time a non-Jew had been baptised (Acts 11,1–18).

Strife between the Jewish and the Greek population of the town led to the Jewish rising of 66, which was ruthlessly repressed by Vespasian and his son Titus in 70. In 69 Vespasian was proclaimed Emperor in Caesarea and granted the town the status of a Roman colony. After the repression of the second Jewish rising led by Bar Kochba its spiritual leader, Ben Akiba, was tortured to death in Caesarea in 135.

In the 1st century the Apostle Philip established a Christian community in the town, and by the end of the 2nd century it was the see of a bishop. In the 3rd century the theologian and spiritual writer Origen, a native of Alexandria, taught in Caesarea and founded his famous library. From 313 to 340 Eusebius, the first ecclesiastical historian, was bishop of Caesarea, of which he was probably a native. Around 500 Procopius, the historian of the age of Justinian, was born in the town.

This era ended with the Arab conquest in 637, and thereafter the harbour lost all importance.

The Crusaders occupied Caesarea in 1101, but it was not until 1254 that the French king Louis IX re-fortified the town – though the new walls enclosed only a fraction of the area of the ancient city. Only 21 years later the Mameluke Sultan Baibars captured the town, whose harbour now became completely silted up. At the end of the 19th century the Turkish authorities resettled Muslim refugees from Bosnia on the site of the Crusader city. Further Jewish settlement began in 1940 with the establishment of the kibbutz of Sedot Yam.

Archaeological investigation of the site began in 1951 and is still continuing. A number of important finds, including a figure of Artemis of the 3rd century B.C. and an important Byzantine mosaic, are now in the Israel Museum in Jerusalem.

Sights

The site of Caesarea is reached on a side road which turns left off the Tel Aviv–Haifa road. The first thing to be seen on entering the site of the Herodian town (on left) is the hippodrome, which was 230m/250yds long by 80m/90yds across and could accommodate 20,000 spectators. It is overgrown with vegetation and has not been excavated.

200m/220yds farther on, on the left, can be seen the remains of a Byzantine street of shops. A flight of steps on the north side leads up to a forecourt, with a mosaic containing a Greek inscription recording that the complex was built by Flavius Strategus during the governorship of Flavius Entolius. The entrance, flanked by columns, was later walled up. Behind this are two

Passage with pointed arches in the Crusader city, Caesarea

Caesarea: Roman theatre . . .

. . . and sculpture

Aqueduct, Caesarea

headless statues (2nd–3rd c.), one of white marble and the other of porphyry; the latter at least, because of the "purple" material used, is likely to be the figure of an Emperor, perhaps Hadrian (117–138).

Beyond this is the Crusader city, which was protected by stout walls and projecting bastions within a deep moat. These fortifications, enclosing a rectangular area with one side running along the sea, were built by Louis IX on a unified plan and completed in a very short time in 1254. The entrance is on the east side, through a gateway with 13th century groined vaulting. To the left can be seen the remains of houses containing cisterns with marble spouts. On the ground nearby are the shafts of columns and other fragments, closely packed together, showing how the Crusaders used materials from ancient buildings to provide bottoming for their streets and foundations for their buildings. A passage roofed by pointed arches leads to the south-east corner of the site, where it is possible to climb on to the walls and get an excellent general view of the area.

★★Crusader city

Within the fortified area the ground rises. Here can be seen remains of the ancient water supply and drainage system and the Herodian temple of Augustus. Nearby is the Crusader cathedral, with its three semicircular apses still standing. Dedicated to St Paul, it was built on the site of a Byzantine monastic church. This was probably the source of a famous trophy carried off by King Baldwin I when the Crusaders took the city in 1101. William of Tyre, the chronicler of the first Crusade, describes it as a shallow circular dish carved from a huge emerald and asserts that it was the Holy Grail, the chalice used at the Last Supper. Baldwin claimed to be descended from Lohengrin and thus to be following in the tradition of the knights of the Grail. He was obliged, however, to cede the precious object to the Genoese in payment for their help in providing ships for the Crusade. It is now preserved in the church of San Lorenzo in Genoa (though it has been shown to be a Roman glass dish).

On the seaward side of the cathedral can be seen a mosque built by Bosnian settlers at the end of the 19th century and the warehouses on the

Old Harbour. Here there are various restaurants and souvenir shops. The Old Harbour in its present form dates from the time of the Crusaders. The shafts of columns – remains of ancient Caesarea, used by the Crusaders to strengthen their breakwater – can be seen projecting from the harbour wall, eroded by the action of the sea. The Crusader citadel, with a keep (now totally destroyed) covering an area 19m/62ft square, stood on the tongue of land which projects into the sea; the site is now occupied by a restaurant.

★Roman theatre

To the south of the Crusader city, close to the Herodian south wall, is the Roman theatre. At the entrance to the area are various fragments of sculpture found here and a reproduction of a stone which bears the only inscription mentioning the name of Pontius Pilate, procurator from 26 to 36: "Tiberieum (Pon)tius Pilatus (praef)ectus Juda(eae)". The theatre, recently restored, is so designed that spectators have a view of the sea over the orchestra and the remains of the stage building. An unusual feature is that at some time after the original construction, and after the removal of the original stage wall, a second semicircular area was added to the semicircular orchestra, thus producing an elliptical arena, similar to that of an amphitheatre, suitable for fights with animals and gladiatorial contests.

★Aqueduct

A further relic of the Herodian period, at the northern tip of the site, is an aqueduct (now partly buried in drift sand) which brought water to Caesarea from a spring 6km/4 miles north of the town. There are two water conduits, and it can be seen at the broken south end that the right-hand channel was constructed first and the left-hand one added later. A second aqueduct was built some 100m/120yds farther inland.

Cana/Kafr Kanna   H 3

District: Northern
Altitude: 250–310m/820–1020ft
Population: 8500

Situation and
characteristics

The little town of Cana (Kafr Kanna), 8km/5 miles north-east of Nazareth on the road to Tiberias, is famed as the place where Jesus performed his first miracle, the changing of water into wine at the "marriage in Cana of Galilee" (John 2,1–11). In this attractive little town, with a population of both Christians and Muslims, there are two churches commemorating the event; and the wine sold here, labelled "Wine from Cana", reflects in its own fashion the Christian tradition.

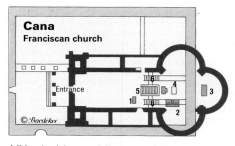

Cana
Franciscan church

Entrance

© Baedeker

1 Hebrew inscription
2 Well
3 Altar
4 Old jar
5 Stair down to crypt
6 Stair to upper floor

Sights

In the centre of the town is a Franciscan church consecrated in 1883. Tradition has it that it occupies the site of the house in which the marriage was celebrated. In the nave, just before the steps leading down to the crypt, is a Hebrew inscription commemorating "Joseph, son of Tanhum" (3rd or 4th c.). In the church visitors are shown an old jar, claimed to be one of the six in which the water was turned to wine.

Franciscan church

Opposite the Franciscan church is a rather dilapidated Greek Orthodox church, built in 1556 on the site of an earlier mosque. Here too there are two stone jars which are said to have been involved in the miracle (though in fact they are probably no more than 300 years old).

Greek Orthodox church

At the north end of the town is the Nathanael Chapel, which also belongs to the Franciscans. It was built at the end of the 19th century in honour of Nathanael, a man of Cana who was initially prejudiced against Jesus ("Can there any good thing come out of Nazareth?") but then worshipped him as the Son of God (John 1,46–49) and was also present when the risen Christ appeared to the disciples at the Sea of Tiberias (John 21,2).

Nathanael Chapel

Capernaum/Kefar Nahum

J 2

District: Northern
Altitude: 205m/673ft below sea level

Capernaum (Hebrew Kefar Nahum, the Village of Nahum; Arabic Tell Num), at the north end of the Sea of Galilee, is closely associated with

Situation and characteristics

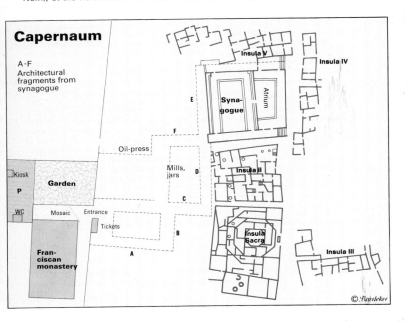

Christ's ministry, for after leaving his home town of Nazareth he taught mostly in this fishing village and the surrounding area.

The Franciscans of the monastery which was established here in 1894 have contributed, along with various archaeologists, to the investigation of this ancient site and the rebuilding of two important buildings, the House of Peter and the synagogue.

The Biblical story

Jesus left Nazareth and "came and dwelt in Capernaum, which is upon the sea coast, in the borders of Zabulon and Nephthalim" (Matthew 4,13). Here he called his first disciples, who were all fishermen: Simon Peter and his brother Andrew, James and his brother John (Matthew 4,18–22). He preached in the synagogue, where he healed a man with an unclean spirit (Mark 1,23–26). He also healed many who were lame, blind, dumb and maimed (Matthew 15,29–31), cured the centurion's servant (Luke 7,1–10) and brought back Jairus's daughter from the dead (Mark 5,35–42). Near Capernaum he fed the five thousand with five loaves and two fishes (Matthew 14,13–21; Mark 6,35–44), and on another occasion fed four thousand people with seven loaves and a few little fishes (Matthew 15,32–39: see Tabgha). In Capernaum he formulated his teaching in parables – the parable of the sower, of the tares among the wheat, of the grain of mustard-seed, of the leaven, of the treasure hidden in a field, of the net cast into the sea, and so on (Matthew 13) – and above all in the Sermon on the Mount (Matthew 5–7: see Mount of the Beatitudes).

History

Finds of coins suggest that the town – which is not mentioned in the Old Testament – was established in the 2nd century B.C. Capernaum was a small unfortified town which took no part in the uprisings against Rome in the 1st and 2nd centuries and as a result remained unscathed. Later it grew in size: originally extending only between the synagogue and the sea, it was enlarged in the 4th century by the development of new districts to the east and north of the synagogue. The prosperity of the town is indicated by the fact that the synagogue was not built of the local black basalt but of imported limestone. About 450 an octagonal church dedicated to St Peter, who was believed to have had a house on this spot, was built to the south of the synagogue on the site of earlier houses. After the Arab invasion in the 7th century the town's decline began. A pilgrim called Burchardus noted in the 13th century that "the once famous city of Capernaum is now a sad sight to behold: it consists only of seven wretched fishermen's huts".

A new phase began when Edward Robinson, an American, identified the site in 1838. The first soundings were carried out by Charles Wilson in 1866. In 1894 the Franciscans bought the site. In 1905 two German archaeologists, H. Kohl and C. Watzinger, brought to light the central and eastern aisles of the synagogue, which had collapsed in an earthquake; between then and 1914 Wendelin Hinterkeuser, a Franciscan, excavated the rest of the synagogue and the courtyard and investigated the surrounding area; and between 1921 and 1926 another Franciscan, Gaudentius Orfali, excavated the residential district, with the octagonal church of St Peter.

Further work on the site began in 1968. Excavations carried out by Stanislao Loffreda showed that from apostolic times onwards Capernaum and the surrounding area were continuously inhabited by Jewish Christians. These passed on their knowledge of the holy places in the area to the pilgrims who began to come to the Holy Land from the West in the 4th century and took home with them stories of what they had seen.

The Site

At the entrance to the site, between the Franciscan monastery and the gardens, is a kiosk selling tickets, slides and books, including Stanislao Loffreda's excellent guide "A Visit to Capernaum". Beyond this, in a kind of archaeological park, are numerous carved architectural fragments and mosaics; to the rear, straight ahead, is the Octagon of Peter, under an

Architectural fragments, Capernaum

Synagogue, Capernaum

unattractive modern concrete roof, and to the left the synagogue, which has been partly rebuilt.

Architectural fragments

Going round in an anti-clockwise direction, we come first, on the south side of the area, to a mosaic pavement from Cana and numerous carved stones from the synagogue, including columns from a window, a relief of vines, grapes and palm-fronds, a cornice carved with a sea-horse and two eagles bearing a garland, a column with an inscription in Aramaic "Alphaeus, son of Zebedee, son of John, made this column as a blessing unto himself", a relief of a wagon, probably the portable Ark of the Covenant, a cornice with grapes and figs, a shell surrounded by a garland (the keystone of an arch on the façade), stones with Greek key patterns and the star of David and another mosaic from Cana.

Octagon of Peter and insulae

Turning left and then right, we come to the "Insula Sacra", with the Octagon of Peter under its protective roof. The authenticity of this monument is established both by the literary sources and by archaeological investigation. It is built over the remains of earlier houses, laid out in regular square blocks (insulae), the oldest of which date from the 1st century B.C. These were humble dwellings, with small rooms surrounding a courtyard in which was a hearth; the fishing hooks found in them suggest that they were occupied by fishermen.

One of the houses was re-plastered at least three times, and on the remains of plaster were found 131 inscriptions in which the names of Christ and Peter frequently occur. It appears, therefore, that by the late 1st century the house was already revered as the house of the Apostle Peter.

Around 350 the building was surrounded by an enclosure wall and was given a new roof supported on an arch. The pilgrim Aetheria noted in the late 4th century that the house of the Prince of the Apostles in Capernaum had become a church and that its walls remained unaltered. This indicates that it was then a *domus-ecclesia*, a private house used for Christian worship.

Finally about 450 an octagonal church was built over the house (a round or octagonal building was the preferred form for a baptistery or – as here – a memoria). The mosaic pavement has a peacock, the symbol of immortality, in the centre. The semicircular apse at the east end served as a baptistery. To the north of the Insula Sacra is another insula.

★Synagogue

On the north side of the second insula is the synagogue. A few steps lead up to an open porch, from which three doors give access to the aisles of the synagogue and two others to the courtyard on its east side. The original consoles, carved with palm-trees, have been restored to the central doorway. Rows of columns run down between the three aisles and along the far end. Along the left-hand side are stone benches. On one of the Corinthian columns at the far end is a Greek inscription: "Herod, son of Monimus, and his son Justus, with their children, erected this column". The synagogue presumably had an upper gallery for women. There is no recess for the Torah, which must have been set up during worship at the south end (ie. at the entrance), facing in the direction of Jerusalem.

On the east side is the courtyard, which could be entered either from the synagogue itself or from the porch.

Watzinger dated the building, on stylistic and historical grounds, to the 2nd or early 3rd century, but more recent research, based on coins and pottery found under the synagogue, suggests that it was built about 400. While the building in the older level of the Octagon of Peter may well be the house in which Jesus stayed and in which he healed Peter's mother-in-law (Matthew 8,14–17; Mark 1,29–31; Luke 4,38–41), the synagogue is a much later building. It is hoped that further excavations may reveal the synagogue in which Jesus taught "as one that had authority, and not as the scribes" (Mark 1,22) and performed various miracles.

Carmel/Har Karmel

G 3

District: Haifa
Altitude: 546m/1791ft

The Mount Carmel range (Karmel = "God's Vineyard") is an outlier of the hills of Samaria, extending north-west for 23km/14 miles, with a breadth of up to 10km/6 miles, and falling steeply down to the sea in Cape Carmel. On the north-east its precipitous slopes descend to the Jezreel plain (see entry), and on the south-west it slopes down to the plain of Sharon (see entry).

Situation

Finds (now in the Rockefeller Museum in Jerusalem) in caves on Mount Carmel, for example at Bet Oren, have shown that this area was inhabited in Palaeolithic times, 130,000 years ago.

History

At least as early as Canaanite times Baal of Carmel was worshipped in hilltop shrines as the divine ruler of the region. Around 1000 B.C. David incorporated Carmel in his kingdom, but it was only in the 9th century that the prophet Elijah led the worship of Yahweh (Jehovah) to prevail over the cult of Baal which was favoured by King Ahab of Israel (1 Kings 18). In an act of great importance to the development of strict monotheism and to Jewish history Elijah confronted 450 priests of Baal and 400 priests of Astarte from Ahab's kingdom on Mount Carmel. There he and his adversaries offered up sacrifices in the sight of the people at one of the old "high places" and then waited for their respective gods to "answer by fire". From Baal there was no response, but the "fire of the Lord" fell on Elijah's altar. Thereupon Elijah took the priests of Baal and Astarte down to the brook Kishon and slew them there.

This event is believed to have taken place on the rocky hill of Muhraka (in Arabic "place of burning"; 482m/1581ft), on the south-east side of the range, where in 1886 a Carmelite monastery was built on the site of an earlier church (see below). Tell el-Kassis ("Priests' Hill"), in the plain below, is supposed to be the grave of the slaughtered priests. According to another version the confrontation took place on Cape Carmel, where there is a Carmelite house near Elijah's Cave (see Haifa).

The form of religious life introduced by Elijah came to an end only a hundred years later with the Assyrian conquest in 732 B.C. Baal of Carmel, whose worship was now restored, was identified by the Greeks under the rule of Alexander's successors with Zeus and was known to the Romans as Deus Carmelus. In the 2nd and 3rd centuries there was a cult here of Jupiter of Heliopolis (Baalbek – a name also associated with Baal), and a citizen of Caesarea erected a statue of this "Heliopolitan Zeus of Carmel". The Carmelite monastery has a fragment of the statue's foot, identified by an inscription.

The first Christians settled on Mount Carmel in the Crusader period. The Carmelite order was founded here in 1150; the monastery was several times destroyed and rebuilt, most recently in 1828.

Mount Carmel, which has two main ridges, consists of hard limestone and dolomite. Thanks to the abundant rainfall a great variety of plants and shrubs flourish in the depressions in the hills. This area of unspoiled natural beauty is now a National Park (several camping sites).
In the 20th century the rapidly developing city of Haifa has reached farther up the north-western slopes of Mount Carmel, with the University tower a prominent landmark on its hill. The Druze villages on the wooded slopes of the range attract many visitors from the city.

★Scenery

Sights

Monastery of St Elias

Leave Haifa (see entry) by way of the Central Carmel district, Moriah Street and Horev Street, going south-east. The road runs past the Biran Military Academy (on left), the village of Hod Karmel (on right) and the new University of Haifa (on left), and then climbs to the highest point on Mount Carmel (546m/1791ft). From there it continues to the village of Isfiya (14km/8½ miles), which is inhabited by both Druzes and Christians, and the Druze village of Daliyat (4km/2½ miles). From here a road runs southeast to Mount Muhraka (4km/2½ miles; 482m/1581ft), with the Carmelite monastery of St Elias (Elijah). It was here, according to the tradition, that Elijah set up an altar during his conflict with the priests of Baal (1 Kings 18,32).

Bet Oren

Bet Oren ("House in the Pinewood"), a kibbutz founded in 1939, lies to the south of Haifa on Mount Carmel but is only 6km/4 miles from the sea, so that holidaymakers here can enjoy a variety of scenery and of activity. There are two possible routes from Haifa to Bet Oren: either take the coast road to the south and at the turn-off for Atlit (13km/8 miles) turn into a road to the left, or alternatively take the Mount Carmel road and in 19km/12 miles turn right.

Remains of Carmel Man, who lived in the Palaeolithic era, 130,000 years ago, were found in caves 6km/4 miles west of the village. Finds from the site are now in the Rockefeller Museum in Jerusalem.

★En Hod

The artists' village of En Hod, 15km/9 miles south of Haifa on the western slopes of Mount Carmel, was founded in 1953 on the site of an abandoned Arab village by the Dadaist Marcel Janco. It is now occupied by 130 families, who form a village co-operative (agudat shitufi); at least one member of each family is an artist of some kind. The activities of the inhabitants cover a wide range: they include photographers, writers, actors, goldsmiths, painters and sculptors, who sell their works in various studios and galleries. There is also a museum mainly devoted to Dadaism.

Chorazin/Korazim

H 2

District: Northern
Altitude: 270m/885ft

Situation and characteristics

The site of Chorazin (Korazim), a small Jewish town which is mentioned in the New Testament, lies 4km/2½ miles north of the Sea of Galilee, 2km/1¼ miles east of the road from Tiberias to Rosh Pinna. It is reached by turning off the road to Rosh Pinna 19km/12 miles north of Tiberias into an asphalted side road on the right which leads to the kibbutz of Almagor. In 2km/1¼ miles, after passing a road on the left to the new settlement of Chorazin, the site of ancient Chorazin can be seen on the right.

History

Chorazin features in the New Testament as one of the cities upbraided by Jesus for their lack of faith (Matthew 11,21). The remains of buildings to be seen today belong to a town built in the 2nd century A.D. on the site of an earlier settlement. The town prospered, and in the late 2nd or early 3rd century could afford to build a synagogue. In the early 4th century, however – as the result either of an earthquake or of a conflict between Jews and Christians – the town was destroyed and thereafter remained unoccupied until the 16th century, when a small Jewish community was established here. Later they were joined by Muslims, who left the village in the mid 20th century.

Synagogue, Chorazin

Sights

Chorazin originally covered an area of 6 hectares/15 acres and was divided into four districts. The houses were built of the local black basalt, giving the settlement a rather sombre effect. Many of the houses have been restored. Within one building near the synagogue is an oil-press.

Houses

The most important building in Chorazin was – and is – the synagogue, built in the 2nd or 3rd century, also of black basalt. Like the synagogues of Capernaum and Bet Alfa (see entries), it has three aisles. The entrance was at the south end. Parts of the walls of the rectangular hall, the floor and the bases of ten of the original fourteen columns between the aisles still remain. The synagogue was richly decorated with architectural sculpture, like the one at Capernaum, but in less refined forms because of the harder material. The carving includes foliage, fruit, animals and human faces.
A particularly interesting find on the site of the synagogue was a finely carved stone seat with an Aramaic dedicatory inscription (now in the Israel Museum in Jerusalem). Seats of this kind were installed in old synagogues as places of honour for the head of the community.

★Synagogue

Dan

J 2

District: Northern
Altitude: 200m/650ft
Population: 450

The kibbutz of Dan, 8km/5 miles east of Qiryat Shemona near Israel's northern frontier, was founded in 1939 and named after Tel Dan, site of the ancient town of Dan, 1km/¾ mile north. At its foot rises the river Dan, one of the three source streams of the Jordan.

Situation and characteristics

History
The tell was the site of the Canaanite city of Leshem (Joshua 19,47), also called Laish, which is referred to in Egyptian texts of the 18th and 15th centuries B.C. It was conquered by the Jewish tribe of Dan, who set up a graven image which they had stolen on Mount Ephraim and built a shrine to house it (Judges 18,27–31). Another pagan shrine was established by Jeroboam I, first king of the northern kingdom of Israel. Since the Temple in Jerusalem was held by the kingdom of Judah he caused two shrines to be built, one in Bethel and the other in Dan, in which a golden calf was worshipped (1 Kings 12,28–30). He also built a palace in Dan. Two hundred years later the city was destroyed by Tiglath-pileser III.

Sights

Museum
The kibbutz has a natural history museum which illustrates the geology of the area and the draining of the Hule plain (see entry).

★★Dan
Nature Reserve
A walk through the Dan Nature Reserve, within which are the source of the river Dan and the ancient remains on Tel Dan, is a very rewarding experience. From the entrance to the reserve there are two waymarked trails, the longer of the two being particularly attractive. This runs through dense vegetation, over wooden bridges and a number of caves to the source of the Dan, which has been left in its natural, unspoiled state, and from there up to Tel Dan. Excavations which have been in progress here since 1965 have brought to light the remains of a town gate of the 10th century B.C. on the south side of the site, from which a flight of steps leads up to a platform measuring 18.7m/61ft by 18.2m/60ft, probably the remains of an Israelite shrine.

Dead Sea/Yam Hamelach   H/J 4–6

Southern District and West Bank
Altitude: 398m/1306ft below sea level

Situation and
characteristics
The Dead Sea (Hebrew Yam Hamelach, "Salt Sea"; Arabic Bahr Lut, "Sea of Lot") lies between Israel and Jordan, 398m/1306ft below sea level, making it the lowest point on the surface of the earth. It is a "dead" sea because of the high salt content (25–30%, compared with 3.5% in the Mediterranean) of its water, in which neither plants nor animals can live.
With a length of 76km/47 miles and a maximum breadth of 16km/10 miles, this inland lake has an area of some 1000sq.km/385sq.miles. It is divided by a peninsula projecting from the eastern shore into a smaller southern section with a depth of only 4–6m/13–20ft and a larger northern section up to 433m/1421ft deep.
The main inflow of water into the Dead Sea comes from the Jordan. It has no outlet, but in the hot climate of the area (annual mean temperature over 25°C/77°F) the rate of evaporation is so high that hitherto the water level has remained almost constant. In recent years, however, so much water has been diverted from the Sea of Galilee that the inflow of water into the Dead Sea from the Jordan has been reduced and the water level has fallen. As a result the northern and southern sections are now completely separated by the peninsula. The reduced inflow of fresh water means that the salt content is becoming even higher. In order to compensate for the loss of water it was planned to construct a canal from the Mediterranean to the Dead Sea, passing through the Gaza Strip; but there have now been second thoughts about the plan, and it is being considered whether water could be brought in from the Red Sea.

★Scenery
A trip to the Dead Sea is undoubtedly one of the great experiences of a visit to Israel. At many points round it, particularly in the southern part, where the salt content is even higher than in the northern part, there are bizarre

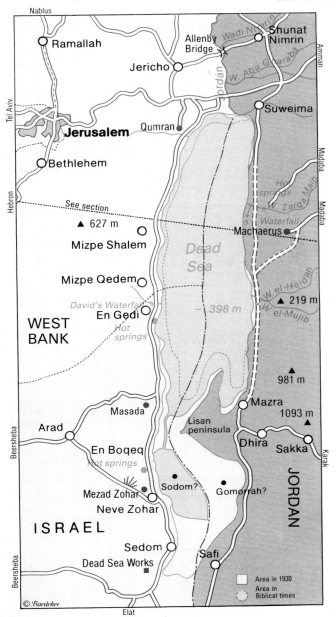

salt rock formations rising high above the water. As a result of the high rate of evaporation there is usually a veil of mist over the lake and the surrounding desert.

Bathing in the Dead Sea

A no less unusual experience is a dip in the Dead Sea. It is almost impossible to dive into the water, and it is perfectly possible to read a newspaper while floating on the surface. The best publicly accessible beaches are at En Boqeq and En Gedi (see entries). It is advisable when bathing in the Dead Sea to avoid immersing your eyes, nose or mouth; and after bathing a shower is essential to wash off the sticky salt water.

Biblical tradition

The salt landscape at the south end of the Dead Sea, with its salt caves, was the scene of the story of Sodom and Gomorrah, destroyed by fire and brimstone for their vices. On Abraham's intercession God spared only his nephew Lot and Lot's two daughters, who went to Zohar (to the west of the Dead Sea) and then to a cave in the hills, where the two sisters became pregnant by their father and bore Moab and Ben-ammi, progenitors of the Moabites and the Ammonites (Genesis 19). Above a salt cave near present-day Sedom (Sodom) is a pillar of salt, said to be Lot's wife.

Spa treatment

The water of the Dead Sea has not only the highest salt content in the world but also the highest mineral content, with an extraordinarily high concentration of bromine, magnesium, potassium and iodine. The air is also extraordinarily dry (maximum humidity in summer 35%) and pollen-free. The healing powers of the Dead Sea were already recognised in ancient times: it is said that Cleopatra "took the cure" here, and both Aristotle and Pliny the Elder refer to the beneficial effects of the water. In our own day numbers of people come to the Dead Sea seeking alleviation or cure for skin diseases like psoriasis, neurodermatitis, chronic eczema and parachroma, bronchial disorders and rheumatism of the muscles or joints. In recent years En Boqeq (see entry) and Newe Zohar (see En Boqeq) in particular, with their hot springs, have developed into popular spas.
Visitors who go to one of the Dead Sea resorts for the treatment of certain diseases have a prospect of an improvement in their condition – though this can, of course, be judged only by a doctor in a particular case – but prospective patients should be aware that spa treatment is not all pleasure. With the prevailing high temperatures the solar treatment which is frequently prescribed can be trying for many people, and the entertainment facilities, particularly for the young, are very limited indeed.

Industrial uses

The asphalt deposits which from time to time are washed up from under the Dead Sea were already exploited by the Egyptians and Nabataeans. Nowadays the Dead Sea Works at the south end of the Dead Sea extract potash and bromine from the water.

Sights

Places of interest on the west side of the Dead Sea are Masada, En Gedi and Qumran (see entries). There are also a number of ruined castles in the hills near its western shore. The most southerly of these, Mezad Zohar (see En Boqeq), which dates from Byzantine times, stands on a small rocky cone on the old valley road, in wild mountain country.
The road which runs up from Newe Zohar (see En Boqeq), near the south end of the Dead Sea, in the direction of Arad comes – before reaching the sign marking sea level – to two fine viewpoints. From the lower one there is

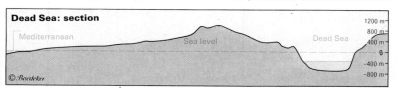

Dead Sea: section

Mediterranean   Sea level   Dead Sea

1200 m
800 m
400 m
0
−400 m
−800 m

© Baedeker

View of the Dead Sea from Masada

The Dead Sea: in the background En Boqeq

a breathtaking view, particularly at sunset, of the Dead Sea and the hills of Jordan; from the upper one there is a prospect of Mezad Zohar far below.

Dor   G 3

District: Haifa
Altitude: sea level
Population: 200

Situation and characteristics

Dor, a moshav with a beautiful beach, lies on the Mediterranean 29km/18 miles south of Haifa. It was founded in 1949 by immigrants from Greece on the ruins of the Arab village of Tantura.

It is reached by turning right off the Haifa–Tel Aviv road and, after crossing the railway, taking a little road on the left which leads to the moshav. To the right can be seen the kibbutz of Nahsholim, near the ruins of a glass factory built by Baron Edmond de Rothschild. A little way to the north are the remains of ancient Dor.

History

Dor was one of the 31 city states conquered by Joshua about 1200 B.C. (Joshua 12,23). One of the four islands lying off the coast bears the name of Solomon's daughter Taphath (Tafat), whose husband was appointed governor of the region of Dor (1 Kings 4,11). After the Assyrian conquest (8th c. B.C.) Dor was held for a time by the Phoenician kings of Sidon. From the 4th century A.D. it was occupied by Christians; then in the 7th century it was destroyed by the Arab invaders. In the 12th century the Crusaders built a castle here (Castellum Merle) which was destroyed by the Mamelukes in 1291.

Sights

Excavations to the north of the kibbutz of Nahsholim have brought to light remains of the old harbour, the Crusader castle and a 6th century Byzantine church. A 5th century basilica covering an area of 1000sq.m/1200sq.yds was excavated in 1979; a relic particularly revered in this church was a fragment of rock from Golgotha embedded in a marble column.

Elat (Eilat)   G 8

District: Southern
Altitude: 20m/65ft
Population: 21,000

Situation and characteristics

Elat (Eilat) is the most southerly town in Israel, situated at the northern tip of the Red Sea. Founded only in 1949, it rapidly developed from a police post into a town which at first preserved something of the atmosphere of a pioneer town but is now a major tourist resort. With its dry, hot climate (only eight days with rain a year, minimum winter temperature 10°C/50°F, summer temperature over 40°C/104°F), Elat now attracts holidaymakers both from Israel and from abroad. It can be reached either by driving through the Negev or by air.

Lying on a coastal strip only 11km/7 miles long between Mount Sinai in the west and the hills of Edom to the east which was incorporated in the new state of Israel in 1949, Elat has had since 1964 a harbour capable of handling ocean-going vessels, now an important oil terminal linked by a pipeline with Ashqelon on the Mediterranean coast.

Although Elat has no ancient remains, the surrounding area, with the adjoining Jordanian port of Aqaba, has a history going far back into the past.

History

After leaving Egypt under the leadership of Moses the Israelites wandered through Sinai and "the way of the plain from Elath, and from Ezion-gaber"

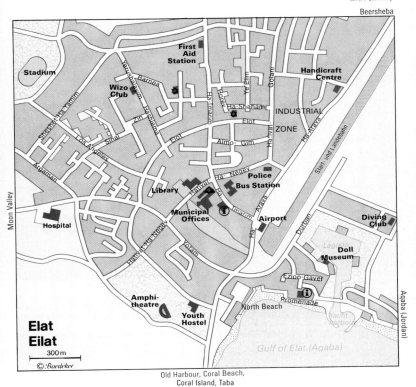

Beersheba

Stadium

First Aid Station

Handicraft Centre

Wizo Club

Ner Shaulon
Barnea
Ha-Tmarin
Zin
Zin Shelma
Sinai
Ha-Shalom
Ha-Shaham

INDUSTRIAL ZONE

Yotam
Yer Elim
Hova
Eilot
Almo-Gim

Sderot- und Landesbahn
Ha-Arava

Los Angeles
Sheshet Ha-Yamim
Argaman

Moon Valley

Library
Hativat Ha-Negev
Ha-Negev
Police
Bus Station

Municipal Offices
Ha-Tmarin
Airport

Hospital
Hativat Ha-Negev
Yotam
Ha-Arava
Durban

Diving Club

Lagoon
Doll Museum

Ezion-Gaver

Amphi-theatre

Youth Hostel

North Beach
Promenade

**Elat
Eilat**

300 m

© Baedeker

Gulf of Elat (Aqaba)

Yacht Harbour

Aqaba (Jordan)

Old Harbour, Coral Beach,
Coral Island, Taba

and then into the wilderness of Moab, which was held by the "children of Lot" (Deuteronomy 2,8–9). Thus it is clear that the two towns of Eilath (probably on the site of present-day Aqaba) and Ezion-gaber or -geber (excavated in 1934 on Tell el-Khalayfa in Jordan) were already in existence in pre-Israelite times. Ezion-geber, "Solomon's port", is thought to have been founded by the Edomites or by the Midianites who lived to the south of them, on the Saudi Arabian coast. It was also visited by Egyptian ships transporting copper from the mines of Timna (see entry). In the 10th century B.C. Solomon had ships built at Ezion-geber and manned them with his own people and with Phoenicians supplied by King Hiram of Tyre. These ships "came to Ophir and fetched from thence gold, four hundred and twenty talents, and brought it to king Solomon" (1 Kings 9,26–28). Here too the Queen of Sheba landed on her way to visit Solomon in Jerusalem and "try him with hard questions" (1 Kings 10,1 ff.).

In the 8th century B.C. the Israelites lost the port. In the 3rd century B.C. it passed to the Ptolemies who then ruled Egypt, then to the Nabataeans and finally to the Romans, to whom it was known as Aila. The architect who built the monastery of St Catherine on Sinai (see entry) in the 6th century was a native of Aila.

In 1116, during the reign of King Baldwin I of Jerusalem, the Crusaders built a castle on the island lying off present-day Elat. The castle was taken by

161

Elat: Israel's modern tourist metropolis on the Red Sea

Saladin in 1170, recovered by Reynald of Châtillon and thereafter was finally incorporated in the Muslim dominions, being held first by the Mamelukes and later by the Turks.

After the First World War Elat lay within the British mandated territory, and in 1949 became part of Israel. In that year was founded a new Jewish settlement, the kibbutz of Elot, which was later moved 3km/2 miles inland.

Free trade zone

In order to give a boost to the town's economy it was declared a free trade zone in 1985. The exemption from value-added tax and customs duties makes most goods, services and hotel tariffs considerably (about 15%) cheaper than in the rest of Israel.

The town

Elat is a modern town which is continually extending farther up the slopes of the surrounding hills. Most of the hotels (which in comparison with hotels in other parts of Israel are exceedingly luxurious) are on or near the North Beach, where there are also shopping arcades, a promenade and a yacht harbour which is already too small. The real centre of Elat, with numerous shops and restaurants, the tourist information office and the Town Hall, is north-west of the North Beach on Hatmarim Street. To the south of the town are the Old and New Harbours, which extend down the coast to Coral Beach.

In the centre of the town is its airport, with an alarmingly short runway, which is at present used only by El Al flights; charter flights normally use the military airport of Uvda, 60km/37 miles away. There are plans to build a new airport a few kilometres north of Elat; when this is brought into service the present terminal building will become part of a large shopping centre with boutiques and pavement cafés, and new hotels will be built on the runway.

Beaches

The North Beach (shingle) with its numerous hotels is usually crowded. Some of the hotels have their own stretches of beach, for residents only. On the beaches open to the public there are beach umbrellas and deck-chairs

162

(loungers) for hire. Much more beautiful is Coral Beach (5km/3 miles south of Elat) with its fine sand. It is part of the Coral Beach Nature Reserve (admission charge). Here swimmers, snorkellers and scuba divers can explore the fascinating underwater world of the banks of coral; there are underwater signposts drawing attention to the various species of coral and marine plants.

Sights

In the Coral Beach Nature Reserve is the very interesting Underwater Observatory. A pier 100m/110yds long leads to the Observatory, with twenty windows through which visitors can watch the teeming underwater life 6m/20ft below the surface. There is also an excellent aquarium with hundreds of Red Sea fishes in many different species. Other attractions are a shark pool and a turtle pool.

★★Underwater Observatory

Another way of seeing the underwater world of the Red Sea is a trip in a glass-bottomed boat (departures from the landing-stage a little way north of the Underwater Observatory).

Opposite the landing-stage used by the glass-bottomed boats is the Texas Ranch, which was originally built as a film set. Here visitors can live the life of the Wild West – or at any rate the organisers' version of it. Attached to the ranch is a riding school.

Texas Ranch

On the Ostrich Farm to the south of Elat, a little way inland, there are thirty ostriches, with periodic ostrich-riding shows. There are also a cafeteria and a souvenir shop.

Ostrich Farm

On the lagoon to the east of Elat, in the Caesar Hotel, is the Israel Palace Doll Museum, with a series of dioramas illustrating the life of the Jewish people in the past and present.

Israel Palace Doll Museum

Elat (Eilat)

Bird-watching   For bird-watchers there are guided walks on special paths with hides at intervals. These are particularly interesting in spring, when large numbers of migrant birds pass through the Elat area on their way from Africa to Europe. Information: International Bird-Watching Center, Etzion Hotel, Hatmarim Street.

Surroundings of Elat

En Netafim   10km/6 miles north-west of Elat is the spring of En Netafim. It is reached by turning off the road to Moon Valley, some 10km/6 miles from Elat, into an unsurfaced road signposted to En Netafim. In 800m (half a mile) the road comes to a car park, from which it is a 10-minute walk to En Netafim. It is the only spring in this area which flows throughout the year. The water gushes over a rock and falls into a pool below.

Moon Valley   5km/3 miles beyond the turning for En Netafim is the barren Moon Valley, lying at an altitude of 800m/2625ft flanked by granite hills.

Gorge of the Inscriptions   The Gorge of the Inscriptions, named after the numerous Nabataean, Hebrew and Greek inscriptions on its rock walls, is reached on a road (all-terrain vehicles only) which branches off the Moon Valley road on the left (22km/13½ miles from Elat).

Taba   The dispute between Egypt and Israel over the Taba enclave, 8km/5 miles south-west of Elat, was settled in 1989. This strip of land covering an area of 1 sq.km/250 acres, with a luxury hotel and a holiday village, now belongs to Egypt, though the hotel is to be under Israeli management for twenty years. The nude bathing which was formerly common here is now banned.
For a trip to Taba and farther along the Sinai peninsula regard must be had to the Egyptian entry regulations (see Practical Information, Travel Documents).

Coral Island   Some 5km/3 miles beyond the Israeli-Egyptian frontier, to the left of the road, can be seen the little offshore islet known as the Coral Island or Pharaoh's Island, a coral-fringed granite rock measuring 320m/350yds by 150m/165yds, with a small sheltered harbour (many starfish) on the south side. This is identified by some authorities with the Old Testament port of Ezion-geber. The island seems to have been inhabited since the time of the 20th Dynasty in Egypt and to have been used as a port for the shipment of copper from the mines of the Arava and Timna valleys (both now in Israel). It is crowned by the conspicuous ruins of a 12th century Crusader castle (illustration, page 165).

Sinai peninsula   The coast road down the west side of the Gulf of Aqaba continues south via Nuweiba, Dahab and the Sharira pass to the port of Sharm el-Sheikh (240km/150 miles from Elat). Some 15km/9 miles farther south as the crow flies is Ras Muhammad, the southern tip of the Sinai peninsula, from which there is a superb view of the Red Sea, the Gulf of Suez and Gulf of Aqaba opening off its northern end and the mountains along their shores.
For other features of interest in this area (eg. St Catherine's monastery) see Sinai Peninsula.

Timna Park   25km/15 miles north of Elat a road on the left branching off the main road to the Dead Sea leads to Timna Park (see Timna) with its bizarre rock formations.

Yotvata   Some 20km/12½ miles north of the turning for Timna is the oasis (date-palms) of the kibbutz of Yotvata, originally founded in 1951 as an army post. It is watered by an abundant spring, En Yotvata (Arabic Ain Radian), which is mentioned in the Old Testament ("Jotbath, a land of rivers of waters": Deuteronomy 10,7).

Crusader castle on the Coral Island, Elat

The kibbutz's visitor centre puts on an audio-visual show which illustrates the geography and way of life of the region. There is also an exhibition on the flora and fauna, the geology and history of the desert region.

From the Yotvata visitor centre there are excursions to the nearby Hai Bar Nature Reserve (open: mornings only). The reserve, which has an area of 10,000 acres, was established in 1963 as a home for the desert animals which lived in this area in Biblical times. It is now occupied by antelopes, wild asses, ostriches, etc., and has a new section in which leopards, wolves, foxes, hyenas and other predators can be watched in their natural surroundings. In the "Nocturnal Room" desert animals who are naturally nocturnal in their habits can be observed.

★Hai Bar

El-Azariya/Bethany

H 4

District: Jerusalem
Altitude: 660m/2165ft
Population: 2200

The Arab village of El-Azariya (or Eizariya), which has grown in the last few years from a small hamlet to a population of over 2000, lies on the eastern slopes of the Mount of Olives. It is the Bethany of the New Testament.

Situation and characteristics

Bethany was the home of the two sisters Martha and Mary who "received Jesus into their house" (Luke 10,38), when he brought their brother Lazarus back from the dead (John 11,11–45). When Christ travelled for the last time from Jericho to Jerusalem, where he was to suffer his Passion, he visited the house of Lazarus and his sisters six days before the Passover, and Mary anointed his feet (John 12,1–4); then on the next day he rode over the Mount of Olives to Jerusalem, mounted on an ass from Bethphage.

History

In the village of El-Azariya, which takes its name from Lazarus (El-Azar in Arabic), there are a number of places associated with events in the time of Jesus. In the 4th century a chapel was built over the supposed site of Lazarus's tomb. This fell into disrepair and was restored in the 12th century by the Crusaders, who built a monastery in commemoration of the house of Martha and Mary. Later the Muslims built a mosque over Lazarus's tomb, and it was only in the 17th century that Christians were again able to visit the site.

The Christian sites were restored in the 19th and 20th centuries. In 1953 the Franciscans built a new church dedicated to Lazarus on a site below his tomb which they had acquired in 1858. Nearby are remains of the Byzantine and Crusader periods.

Sights

Church of Lazarus

The new Church of Lazarus is in the form of a mausoleum on a Greek-cross plan surmounted by a dome. In the interior are inscriptions giving the Latin text of words spoken by Jesus in Bethany. On the wall behind the altar is "Ego sum resurrectio et vita" ("I am the resurrection and the life"), and in the dome is the continuation of the text: "He that believeth in me, though he were dead, yet shall he live" (John 11,25).

Tomb of Lazarus

Close to the church is the entrance to Lazarus's tomb, which is entered by a flight of 24 steps. It is held by the Muslims.

Greek Orthodox church

El-Azariya also has a modern Greek Orthodox church, readily recognisable by its light blue dome and its four-storey tower topped by a light lantern.

Emeq Hefer

See Hefer Plain

Emeq Hula

See Hule Plain

Emeq Sharon

See Sharon Plain

Emeq Yizre'el

See Jezreel Plain

En Avdat

G 6

District: Southern

Situation and characteristics

En Avdat, the spring near the ruined city of Avdat (see entry), is one of the most surprising natural phenomena in the Negev. Between Avdat and Sede Boqer (see entry), in the middle of a barren upland region of almost oppressive austerity, with only a few scattered settlements, four springs emerge from the rock. In order to preserve this unique and unspoiled area it has been declared a National Park.

The water from the spring of En Avdat falls into a pool and then enters a deep gorge. This is the origin of the Nahal Zin, which then flows through the Wilderness of Zin (Midbar Zin). After the tribe of Judah settled in the area this was the southern frontier of their kingdom (Joshua 15,1). Bounded on the north by hills rising to 500m/1650ft and on the south by hills almost 800m/2625ft high, it slopes down to the Arava depression, to the south of the Dead Sea.

From the wilderness of Paran the children of Israel, led by Moses, came into the wilderness of Zin, where they found themselves short of water. Then, on the Lord's command, Moses smote the rock with his staff and "the water came out abundantly, and the congregation drank, and their beasts also" (Numbers 20,1–11). We are not told whether this was the spring of En Avdat; but the story shows the importance of a spring in an arid region like the Negev.

History

There is a road to the spring from the College of the Negev, 3km/2 miles south of Sede Boqer. From here it is a full hour's drive to the site.

The ★spring

Going towards the College, take a track which goes off on the right just before the first houses and runs down into the gorge, with the surface getting steadily worse. Always keeping to the right, you come to a parking-place in the valley, from which there is a footpath to the spring. The valley becomes ever narrower, its rock walls reflecting the sun, and the stream flows down amid tumbles of rock and scrub vegetation. Finally the path comes to the pool into which the water of the spring flows over a rock wall. Every morning and evening the ibexes which live in this area come down to drink – though the water is fairly bitter.

On the way back to the parking-place the library of the College of the Negev can be seen on a high rocky cliff, with the trees surrounding David Ben-Gurion's grave in front of it.

The spring of En Avdat: an unexpected oasis in the Negev

En Boqeq
H 5

District: Southern
Altitude: 400m/1300ft below sea level

Situation and characteristics

En Boqeq, a tourist centre and spa on the south-western shore of the Dead Sea (see entry and illustration on page 159), has a warm mineral spring which has been used for therapeutic purposes since ancient times. Thanks to the extraordinary climatic conditions and the unique properties of the water of the Dead Sea, En Boqeq has had remarkable success in the treatment particularly of skin diseases.

The deeper layers of water in the Dead Sea, with their very high salt content, store up heat which is used in the production of electric power.

The town

En Boqeq is a town of hotels and spa establishments. To the north of the town are the remains of a fortress (Mezad Boqeq) built by the kings of Judah to provide protection against Moabite attacks.

Surroundings of En Boqeq

Newe Zohar

8km/5 miles south of En Boqeq, on the Dead Sea, is Newe Zohar, with several hot mineral springs. This is also a much frequented spa, with a lakeside restaurant and a petrol station. The Bet Hayozer Museum has informative displays on the characteristics and the economic value of the Dead Sea.

Mezad Zohar

A footpath (3km/2 miles) runs up the gorge of the river Zohar, which flows into the Dead Sea at Newe Zohar, to Mezad Zohar, a stronghold situated on a conical crag amid magnificent mountain scenery which was held by the

The gorge of the river Zohar, near En Boqeq

Nabataeans and later by the Byzantines. A fine view of the castle can be had by driving up the road from Newe Zohar to Arad as far as the second viewpoint (on right). From the lower viewpoint there is a magnificent prospect of the Dead Sea and the hills of Jordan.

12km/7½ miles north of En Boqeq up the shores of the Dead Sea is the fortress of Masada (see entry).

Masada

En Gedi

H 5

District: Southern
Altitude: 400m/1300ft below sea level
Population: 600

Thanks to the "Goats' Spring" (En-gedi) which is referred to in the Old Testament the kibbutz of En Gedi lies in an area of rich vegetation. The large En Gedi Nature Park with its flora and fauna and its historical remains ranks after Masada (see entry) as the great tourist attraction on the west side of the Dead Sea.

Situation and characteristics

The occupation of the site can be traced back to the Chalcolithic, the period of transition between the Stone and Metal Ages in the 4th millennium B.C. The remains of a temple above the Shulamite Spring date from this period. During an Egyptian campaign of conquest in Palestine the local inhabitants hid precious objects in a cave in the Nahal Mishmar valley (12km/7½ miles south of En Gedi), where excavation has brought to light, among other things, 240 heads from staffs of office and five ivory carvings, probably from the Chalcolithic temple.

History

After the Israelite occupation of the Promised Land En-gedi is referred to as a town held by the tribe of Judah (Joshua 15,62). When David fled from the wrath of the ageing Saul he sought refuge in the "holds at En-gedi". Then Saul set out with 3000 men to capture David and his followers, leading to a dramatic confrontation. Saul lay down to sleep in a cave, while "David and his men remained in the sides of the cave". In spite of the urging of his followers David did no harm to Saul, the anointed of the Lord, but merely cut off the skirt of his robe. When Saul left the cave David showed him the piece he had cut off to demonstrate that he had no evil intentions towards him. Then Saul said: "Thou art more righteous than I: for thou hast rewarded me good, whereas I have rewarded thee evil"; and he recognised David as his successor: "I know well that thou shalt surely be king, and that the kingdom of Israel shall be established in thine hand" (1 Samuel 24,2–23). The event is commemorated by the name of the river, Nahal David. En-gedi is referred to in the Song of Solomon (1,14) as a place of singular beauty: "My beloved is unto me as a cluster of camphire in the vineyards of En-gedi".

On Tel Goren, to the north of the kibbutz, excavations from 1961 onwards revealed five occupation levels extending from the 7th century B.C. to the 5th century A.D. – a period of some 1200 years.

The first settlement was destroyed by Nebuchadnezzar in 582 B.C., four years after the fall of Jerusalem. It was rebuilt after the Israelites returned from the Babylonian Captivity, and this town enjoyed a period of prosperity in the 5th and 4th centuries B.C. In the 2nd and 1st centuries the site was occupied by a third settlement, the Hellenistic city of the Hasmoneans, which was destroyed in a Parthian raid during the conflict between the Hasmoneans and Herod. Herod built and fortified the fourth town on the site, which was destroyed in 68 during the Jewish War. The fifth and last

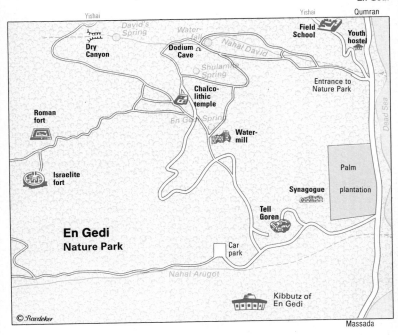

settlement lay north-east of the tell, its site marked by the remains of a synagogue; it was abandoned in the 5th century for reasons unknown. During the Bar Kochba rising which was crushed by the Emperor Hadrian in 135 the numerous caves round En Gedi played an important part, as excavations by Yigael Yadin have shown. Finds in the valley of the Nahal Hever, 5km/3 miles south of En Gedi, give evidence of the fate of the Jewish rebels who took refuge in this area. In the 150m/490ft deep Cave of Letters were found 15 letters written by Bar Kochba, a fragment from the Psalms, metal vessels, the keys of abandoned houses, human skulls, pieces of clothing and sandals. The Cave of Horrors opposite it is so called after the remains of the refugees who died here.

The site remained unoccupied from the 5th century until 1949, when an Israeli military camp was established here, only 4km/2½ miles south of the frontier with Jordan. In 1953 this became an agricultural settlement.

Sights

Immediately north of the kibbutz of En Gedi, running from west to east, is the valley of the Nahal Arugot. North of this again, near the shores of the Dead Sea, are large recently planted palm-groves and, a little way inland, Tel Goren. North-east of this, on the edge of the palm-groves, is the synagogue of the fifth settlement at En Gedi, with a mosaic pavement depicting several pairs of birds in the centre and in the corners, together with the star of David and an inscription of which eighteen lines survive.

Tel Goren

◀ In the En Gedi Nature Park

171

★★Nature Park

The great attraction of En Gedi, however, is the Nature Park, with a flora which includes both water plants and desert plants; it is the home of ibexes, hyenas, leopards and many species of birds. The entrance to the park is on a road which branches off the lakeside road to the north of the palm plantation (car park; plans of park on sale). From here a waymarked path runs up the Nahal David valley into an area of increasingly luxuriant vegetation, in striking contrast to the surrounding desert country, and comes to a pool into which the stream falls over a cliff. From the waterfall a track (difficult at some points) climbs southward to the En Gedi Spring, near which the remains of an old watermill were found. North-west of this are the remains of the Chalcolithic temple (4th millennium B.C.), dedicated to the cult of the moon and of the spring. In the centre of the building is the circular "Moon Stone". The two gates of the sacred precinct face towards the En Gedi Spring on one side and the Shulamite Spring on the other. From the Shulamite Spring a track continues north to the Dodim Cave, above the waterfall. From the Chalcolithic temple tracks run north-west to the Dry Canyon and west to a square Roman fort and a circular Israelite stronghold.

Time required for walks: from the entrance to the waterfall and back, 1¼ hours; to the En Gedi Spring, the Chalcolithic temple and the Dodim Cave, 4 hours; to the temple and the Dry Canyon, 5 hours.

Full information can be obtained from the park wardens and the field school (concerned with the study of the flora and fauna of the Judaean desert and the Dead Sea region), to the north of the entrance. For a trip of any length it is advisable to have a local guide, for the neighbouring desert is hot and dry and holds dangers for the inexperienced.

En Gev

J 3

District: Northern
Altitude: 200m/650ft below sea level
Population: 300

Situation and characteristics

The kibbutz of En Gev, founded in 1937, lies on the eastern shore of the Sea of Galilee, at the foot of a tell on which are the remains of ancient Susita. The kibbutz can be reached from Tiberias either by the land route (28km/17 miles) or by boat (9km/6 miles). Until 1967 it was accessible only by boat: a road built in 1941 was cut in 1948, when Syrian forces advanced to the shores of the lake.

Surroundings of En Gev

Susita

2km/1¼ miles east of En Gev, on a steep-sided hill rising 350m/1150ft above the Sea of Galilee, is the site of ancient Susita, whose name is derived from the Hebrew *sus* ("horse") and was altered in Hellenistic times to Hippos. In the 1st century it was a member of the Decapolis, a league of ten cities on the east bank of the Jordan; later it was incorporated in Herod's kingdom; in Byzantine times it was the see of a bishop; and in the 7th century it was destroyed by Persians or Arabs. On the summit of the hill are remains dating from Jewish, Roman and Byzantine times.

Kursi

Some 5km/3 miles north of En Gedi, at the junction with the road to Afiq, the remains of a Byzantine monastic church were discovered in 1970. The heyday of the monastery was from the end of the 5th century to the middle of the 6th; it was abandoned at the end of the 7th century for some unknown reason. The remains have been excellently restored.

En Karem

See Jerusalem

En Sheva

See Tabgha

Galilee/Galil

District: Northern
Altitude: up to 1208m/3963ft

Galilee (Hebrew Galil) is the most northerly part of Israel. Bounded by the Mediterranean coast, the Lebanese frontier, the Jordan valley and the Jezreel plain, it consists of a western coastal strip and the hills of Upper Galilee round Safed and Lower Galilee round Nazareth. It is the rainiest part of the country, a factor beneficial to its agriculture.

Situation and characteristics

The northern part of the region, Upper Galilee, rises to a height of 1208m/3963ft in Mount Meron; the southern part, Lower Galilee, is lower (Mount Tabor, 562m/1844ft). The boundary between Upper and Lower Galilee is the Bet Kerem plain.

When the Israelites took possession of the Promised Land the tribes of Naphtali, Zebulun and Asher settled in Galilee (Joshua 19), where they were later joined by the tribe of Dan (Judges 18). In the 8th century B.C. the country was occupied by the Assyrians; later came Babylonians, Persians and Greeks. After the Hasmonean conquest in 163 B.C. non-Jews lived in the coastal plain, Jews in the upland regions. When the Romans occupied Galilee it was ruled, along with Judaea, by the Hasmonean ruler Hyrcanus II and then by Herod the Great. Thereafter, in the lifetime of Jesus, it belonged to the tetrarchy of Herod Antipas, who made Tiberias his capital, and then, until 44, to the kingdom of Herod Agrippa. In 66 Galilee was a stronghold of the Jewish uprising against the Romans, and after the Bar Kochba rising (135) it replaced Judaea as the centre of Jewry, the towns of Bet Shearim, Sepphoris (Zippori) and Tiberias being of particular importance in this connection. In the 16th century Safed became the centre of a religious revival.

History

From the 7th century onwards the Arab population of Galilee increased steadily. The first Jewish settlements of modern times were established at Rosh Pinna (1878) and Metulla, the most northerly village in Israel (1886). In 1948 Galilee became part of the newly founded state of Israel.

Gaza/Azza

Gaza Strip
Altitude: 30m/100ft
Population: 175,000 (Gaza Strip 633,000)

The Arab town of Gaza, lying near the Mediterranean coast some 80km/50 miles south of Tel Aviv, is the commercial and industrial centre of the Gaza Strip, a stretch of territory 40km/25 miles long and up to 10km/6 miles across which has been occupied by Israel since the Six Day War.

Situation and characteristics

Of the 633,000 inhabitants of the Gaza Strip something like half live in refugee camps in appalling conditions. Not surprisingly, therefore, resistance to the Israeli occupiers finds particularly vigorous expression in this area, with frequent disturbances leaving a trail of dead and injured. Very few Israelis live in the Gaza Strip, and foreign visitors should be wary of staying there and before visiting it should inform themselves about the current political situation.

History

During the war of 1948–49 the Arab population of southern Palestine fled into the area round Gaza, which was then occupied by Egyptian forces. After the ceasefire of February 1949 this region was assigned to Egypt. In the Suez War (1956–57) Israel sought to gain control of the Gaza Strip, but in 1957 returned it to Egypt. In 1967 (the Six Day War) Israel occupied the Gaza Strip and put it under military administration. In the context of the Egyptian-Israeli peace agreements of 1979 the possibility of granting self-government to the Gaza Strip was considered but did not find favour with the local government authorities, and in 1982 the negotiations on self-government collapsed.

Sights

7km/4½ miles south-west of Gaza is Tel el-Ajjul, which has yielded evidence of a history going back 4000 years. Excavations in 1929–31 brought to light the remains of fortifications and tombs dating from around 1750 B.C.

In the busy and noisy town of Gaza the most interesting building is the Great Mosque, originally a 13th century Crusader church. Near the harbour are remains of a 5th century synagogue, with a mosaic pavement in the nave depicting King David as Orpheus, surrounded by wild beasts.

Gennesaret, Lake

See Sea of Galilee

Gilboa, Mount

See Mount Gilboa

Golan Heights   J 2/3

Situation and characteristics

The Golan Heights, which were annexed by Israel in 1981, lie to the east of the Jordan and the Sea of Galilee, extending from north to south between the foothills of Mount Hermon and the river Yarmouk for a distance of 50km/30 miles and reaching some 20km/12½ miles east of the Jordan. This high plateau reaches its greatest height in Mount Avital (Har Avital; 1204m/3950ft), to the west of Quneitra.

The Golan Heights consist mainly of volcanic basalt and are dissected by numerous wadis. The population comprises in addition to Jews a few remaining Arabs and some 10,000 Druze peasants. Since the area was occupied by the Israelis much has been done to improve the infrastructure, for example by the establishment of schools and the improvement of medical care.

History

In ancient times there were numbers of Jewish settlements in this area. In the 1st century A.D. it belonged to Herod's son Philip, who founded Caesarea Philippi (see Banyas). At the south end of the area, on the Yarmouk, was Gadara (see Hamat Gader), an important centre of Greek culture which was also frequented for its mineral springs.

From 1948 onwards the Israeli frontier with Syria ran along the Jordan. After the Israeli occupation of the Golan Heights in 1967 a number of Jewish settlements were established. United Nations troops are stationed in a buffer zone along the frontier. At the end of 1981 Israel declared the annexation of the Golan Heights.

Exhibition of agricultural machinery at Kefar Szold, on the edge of the Golan Heights

Sights

Organised coach and taxi trips to the Golan Heights usually take visitors to see conquered Syrian positions. Other reminders of the battles which raged here between 1967 and 1973 are the settlements with their barbed-wire defences, tanks abandoned by the roadside and the debris of war welded together to make primitive memorials of the fighting.

At the north end of the Golan Heights is the much visited nature reserve of Banyas (see entry). | Banyas

Also in the northern part of the area, in the foothills of Mount Hermon, is the moshav of Newe Ativ, Israel's winter sports centre (ski-lifts). | Newe Ativ

8km/5 miles south-east of the Benot Ya'aqov Bridge, in the centre of the Golan area, is Katzrin (Qazrin), a little town (pop. 2000) which is the administrative centre for the Israeli settlements on the Golan Heights. It has an interesting archaeological museum and, a short distance away, the excavated remains of a 4th century synagogue. | Katzrin/Qazrin

The site of the ancient city of Gamla, destroyed by the Romans in A.D. 68, was located in 1970 some 10km/6 miles south-east of Katzrin. Excavation has brought to light remains of dwelling-houses, a synagogue and water conduits. | Gamla

Other important archaeological finds have been made in the En Gev and Hamat Gader areas (see entries). | Other archaeological sites

175

Hadera

District: Haifa
Altitude: 20m/65ft
Population: 37,000

Situation and characteristics

Hadera is a rising town in the Sharon plain, half way between Haifa and Tel Aviv. Its name is derived from the Arabic word for "green". Its main features of interest are a number of tombs dating from the time

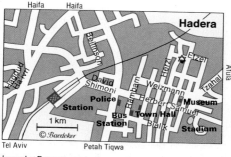

of the Second Temple and a Roman mausoleum.

History

The town has grown up round a caravanserai which was purchased, along with the surrounding land, in 1890. The old building now houses the Community Centre, with the Historical Museum, and a synagogue.

In 1891 an agricultural settlement was established and given the name of the old Arab village of Hudaira ("green"). The early settlers had to content with great difficulties in this malaria-ridden region, and living conditions improved only after the marshes had been drained with assistance from Baron Edmond de Rothschild. On its 20th birthday in 1911 the settlement had a population of 500, including immigrants from Russia and Yemen.

In 1920, under the British Mandate, Hadera was linked with the Tulkarm–Haifa railway line, and after Israel became independent the line between Hadera and Tel Aviv was built. Thereafter the area developed rapidly, some of the surrounding villages were incorporated in the town and paper-making and rubber industries were established.

Surroundings of Hadera

Caesarea

10km/6 miles north-west is the site of the ancient city of Caesarea (see entry).

Binyamina, Zikhron Ya'aqov

9km/6 miles north of Hadera is the village of Binyamina, named after the Hebrew forename of Baron Edmond de Rothschild, whose monumental tomb at Ramat Hanadiv is 5km/3 miles farther on, just before the wine-making town of Zikhron Ya'aqov (see entry).

HaEmeq

See Jezreel Plain

Haifa/Hefa

District: Haifa
Altitude: 0–300m/0–1000ft
Population: 227,000

Haifa (Hefa), Israel's chief port, lies on the northern slopes of Mount Carmel (see entry), which here juts out into the sea, climbing gradually up from the sheltered western corner of the Bay of Haifa. It handles an important trade in the export of Israeli products and is also an industrial centre and the seat of a college of technology and a university. Sites like the Bahai shrine and the "School of the Prophet" bear witness to the importance of the town to different faiths.

Haifa is not mentioned in the Bible. The site was originally occupied by two settlements. To the east was Salmona, on Tell Abu Hawam, beside the river Kishon, which in recent years has been levelled and is now occupied by industrial installations; to the west was Shiqmona, the remains of which, dating from the time of Solomon (10th c. B.C., have been excavated to the south of the Oceanographic Institute; finds from the site are in the Museum of Ancient Art in Haifa.

Between these two settlements was Haifa – a place named in the Talmud – whose name was applied to the settlement as a whole. Although it was destroyed in the 7th century, Haifa was famed in the 11th century for its shipbuilding and its Talmudic college. In 1099 it withstood a six-month-long siege by the Crusaders but was finally destroyed. In 1187 Saladin captured it from the Crusaders, but in 1191 it was recovered by Richard Coeur de Lion. The Crusaders were finally expelled from the town by Sultan Baibars. The monasteries of the Carmelite order, which was founded in Haifa in 1150 by a monk named Berthold, were destroyed after the fall of Acre in 1291, when the monks returned to Europe.

Under the Mamelukes and (from 1517) the Ottomans Haifa was an insignificant fishing village. In 1740 Daher el-Amr, lord of Galilee, took the place and founded a new settlement, the present Old City, between Kikar Paris (Paris Square) and the Head Post Office. He also developed the harbour for the export of grain to Egypt. Under Ahmed el-Jazzar, who

View of Haifa

© Baedeker

Haifa

400 m

Mediterranean

BAT GALIM

Rambam
Hospital

Pinhas Margolin Quay

Atlya

Shnla

Hahayl

West
Station

Bus
Station

Hahagana

QIRYAT ELIEZER

Stadium

Allenby

Jamal de Rothschild

Tel Aviv

Yafo

Stella

Maris

Pror

FRENCH
CARMEL

Tchernikovsky

Shaul

Hazionut

Yere

QIRYAT
ELIYAHU

GERMAN
COLONY

Allenby

Ben Haneglnim

Guvrin

WADI NISNAS

Hagefen

Abbas

Krourt

Central
Station

Dagon Silo
and Museum

Kikar
Plumer

Kikar
Yafo

Allenby
Hahagana

Kikar
Paris

Ha'azmaut

Landing-
stage

Harbour

Pier

Custom
House

Mosque

Bahai
Shrine

Russian
Church

Persian
Gardens

Hazionut

No.

Hanassi

Bahai
Archives

HERZLIYA

Chagall House

Haifa
Museum

Convent of
Sisters of
Nazareth

Herzliya

Herzl

Hassan Shukri

Shivat Zion

Gan
Haziqaron

WADI
SALIB

Hapalyam

Kikar
M. Faisal

East
Station

Nahal Lotem

Shoshanat

Derech

Tikotin Museum
of Japanese Art

Hacarmel

Hayam

Hazvi

Mare Katz
Museum

Arlozorov

Old
Technion

Arlozorov

Batrour

Hess

Town
Hall

HADAR
HACARMEL

Pevzne

Haym

Herzl

Hagvrom

Kibbutz Galuyot

David

Pinski

Moriah

Gan
Ha'em

Museum of Biology
and Prehistory

CENTRAL CARMEL

Bet Rothschild
and Auditorium

Wedgwood

Municipal
Theatre

Wingate

Rabi Aqiba

Great
Synagogue

Music
Library

Michael A

Carmelite
Railway

University,
New Technion

University, New Technion
Akko

Tel Aviv-Jaffa

Elijah's Cave, Carmelite Monastery, Naval Museum, Maritime Museum

Jewish Cemetery

Bet Shearim, Nazareth
Airport

succeeded Daher in 1775, the Carmelites were able to re-establish themselves near Elijah's Cave. In 1799, during Napoleon's advance on Akko
(Acre), their monastery was used as a military hospital, but after Napoleon's withdrawal the French wounded were killed by Ahmed el-Jazzar. On
the outbreak of the War of Greek Independence El-Jazzar's successor
Abdullah Pasha built a lighthouse (Stella Maris) at Elijah's Cave,
105m/345ft above the sea. He persecuted the Greek Orthodox but in 1828

allowed the French Carmelites to rebuild their monastery by the lighthouse.

The importance of Haifa increased with the coming of steamships, for which the nearby harbour of Akko was too small. In 1868 the Jewish population was increased by the arrival of German settlers, members of the Pietist Society of the Temple. Some of their houses have been preserved on both sides of Ben-Gurion Street, and north-west of this, in Jaffa Street, is their cemetery. When these German "Templars" sought to expand on Mount Carmel they came into conflict with the French Carmelites, who closed off much of the hill by building a wall: hence the name of "French Carmel" applied to the western part of the hill.

When the German Emperor, William II, visited Haifa in 1898 a jetty was constructed, and thereafter the development of the port continued. The Emperor promoted the idea of linking Haifa with the Hejaz railway and thus opening up the town's hinterland. The upswing in the economy led to the expansion of the Old City to the north-west, in the direction of the Germany Colony.

The first Jewish school had been established in 1881. Christians from Lebanon and Arabs also now moved into the town, and two sects which had broken away from Islam, the Bahai from Persia and the Ahmadiya from India, made Haifa their headquarters.

At the beginning of the 20th century a number of Jewish initiatives bore fruit. In 1902 Theodor Herzl, in his book "Old New Land" had hailed Haifa as the "city of the future"; and in 1903 the outlying suburb of Herzliya was established, in 1906 three Russian Zionists founded the Atid ("Future") soap factory, and in 1912 the Technion, an institute of technology, was founded, housed in a building which the Turks used as a military hospital in 1914. When the Technion reopened in 1925 the language of instruction was Hebrew (though the German founders had favoured German), and this sparked off a bitter conflict on the language question. Subsequently the Technion grew so rapidly that it became necessary by 1953 to develop a new site, Qiryat HaTechnion.

In September 1918 British forces occupied the town. Thereafter a new railway line was built, linking Haifa with Egypt by way of Gaza. In 1920 Histadrut, the trade union organisation, was founded in Haifa. The town developed new suburbs: Hadar HaKarmel ("Glory of Carmel") in 1920, Ahuzat Samuel in 1921, Bat Galim (the "Mermaid") in 1922, Geula ("Rescue") and Newe Sha'anan ("Home of Rest"). New industrial installations came into being. This development continued in spite of conflicts between the Jewish and the Arab populations. The modern deep-water harbour was completed in 1933, followed in 1934 by the development of the oil terminal at the end of the pipeline from Iraq.

In 1936, following further outbreaks of violence, the Jewish population left the eastern part of the lower town and concentrated in the Hadar HaKarmel district. Haifa was thus for all practical purposes divided into two. During the Second World War the German members of the Society of the Temple were evacuated. After the war there was continuing conflict between the Jewish underground organisation Haganah, the British naval base and the Arabs – a conflict from which Haganah emerged victorious.

After the proclamation of the Jewish state in 1948 Haifa acquired great importance as the port of entry for immigrants from Europe. The economic upswing was reflected in the aspect of the city, and the tourist trade was actively promoted.

Situated as it is on the slopes of Mount Carmel, the city is divided into three zones, one above the other. The Old City with its harbour and strip of coast forms the lower town; the central zone consists of the Hadar HaKarmel district, lying at a height of 120m/395ft, with Haifa's main shopping and commercial centre; and the upper town, Central Carmel (250–300m/820–985ft), with the town's handsomest residential district and a number of exclusive hotels and restaurants.

The ★town

These different zones were linked in 1959 by the Carmelite underground railway, which climbs with a gradient of 12% from the lower station in Kikar Paris (Paris Square) by way of four stations in the Hadar district to Gan Ha'em (alt. 280m/920ft), near the scenic Yefe Nof Street.

Opening Times

Bahai Shrine and Bahai Gardens
(Persian Gardens)
Gardens open: daily 9am–6pm, in winter to 5pm; Mausoleum of Bab: Sun.–Thur. 9am–noon (shoes must be taken off; photography forbidden)

Cable car to Carmelite monastery
Operates: Sat.–Thur. 10am–8pm, Fri. 9am–2pm

Carmelite Monastery
near lighthouse
Church and Museum open: Mon.–Sat. 8am–1.30pm and 3.30–5.30pm

Chagall House
24 Hazionut Street
Open: Sun.–Thur. 10am–2pm and 4–6pm, Sat. 10am–1pm

Dagon Silo and Museum
on harbour
Conducted tours: Sun.–Fri. at 10.30am; also by appointment (tel. 66 42 21)

Elijah's Cave
at south end of Haifa, near Carmelite monastery
Open: Sun.–Thur. 8am–4pm, Fri. 8am–noon

Ethnographic Museum
See Haifa Museum

Gan Ha'em Park
on Hanassi Boulevard, Central Carmel

Haifa Museum
26 Shabtai Levi Street
Open: Mon.–Thur. 5–9pm, Sat. 10am–1pm and 5–9pm, Sun. 10am–1pm

Mane Katz Museum
89 Yefe Nof Street
Open: Sun.–Thur. 10am–1pm and 4–6pm, Fri. and Sat. 10am–1pm
Pictures and sculpture by the Jewish artist Mane Katz, with his personal collection of Judaica and antique furniture

Maritime Museum
198 Allenby Street
Open: Sun.–Thur. 10am–4pm, Sat. 10am–1pm

Museum of Ancient Art
See Haifa Museum

Museum of Biology and Prehistory
in Gan Ha'em Park
Open: Sun.–Thur. 8am–2pm, Sat. 10am–2pm

Museum of Edible Oils
Shemen Oil Factory, Industrial Zone
Open: Sun.–Thur. 8am–2pm
Exhibits illustrating the history of edible oil production in Israel

Museum of Clandestine Immigration and Naval Museum
204 Allenby Street
Open: Mon., Wed. and Thur. 9am–3pm, Tues. and Sun. 9am–4pm, Fri.
9am–1pm

Museum of Modern Art
See Haifa Museum

Museum of Science and Technology
Balfour Street (on site of Old Technion)
Open: Mon., Wed. and Thur. 9am–5pm, Tues. 9am–7pm, Fri. 9am–1pm,
Sat. 10am–2pm

Prehistoric Museum
See Museum of Biology and Prehistory

Railway Museum
at Eastern Station
Open: Sun., Tues. and Thur. 10am–1pm
Old steam engines, luxuriously appointed carriages and restaurant cars

Reuben and Edith Hecht Museum
in Haifa University
Open: Sun.–Thur. 10am–4pm, Fri. and Sat. 10am–1pm

School of the Prophet
See Elijah's Cave

Tikotin Museum of Japanese Art
89 Hanassi Boulevard
Open: Sun.–Thur. 10am–5pm, Sat. 10am–2pm

University
Viewing platform in Eshkol Tower open: Sun.–Thur. 8am–3pm, Fri.
8am–1pm

Zoological Garden
in Gan Ha'em Park
Open: Sun.–Thur. 8am–6pm, Fri. 8am–1pm, Sat. 9am–4pm

Sights

Between 1929 and 1933 the harbour of Haifa was developed into a deep-water port. It is protected by two moles. The area required for port installations, administrative buildings, warehouses, roads and railway lines was provided by large-scale land reclamation schemes which have considerably altered the coastline.
Permits for admission to the harbour area can be obtained in the tourist information office to the right of the entrance. There are also boat trips round the harbour. (Photography is prohibited in the harbour area.) — Harbour

The most striking of the port installations are a 10,000 ton floating dock and the Dagon Silo, a grain elevator 68m/223ft high with a capacity of 100,000 tons. On the ground floor of the silo is a Grain Museum opened in 1955 (conducted visits). This presents a general survey of grain storage and processing; the oldest exhibits are millstones and other items from Jericho dating from the 8th millennium B.C. — Dagon Silo

Opposite the Dagon Silo is Ben-Gurion Street (formerly Sderot HaKarmel), the old main street of the German colony founded in 1868 by members of the Society of the Temple which continued to exist until the Second World War. The houses with their tiled roofs are very characteristic. — Ben-Gurion Street

(The cemetery of these modern Templars lies to the north-west, at 150 Jaffa (Yafo) Street, next to a British military cemetery of the First World War).

Paris Square

At the south end of Jaffa Street is Paris Square (Kikar Paris), with the lower station of the Carmelite underground railway (see p. 180) and a Maronite church.

Town Hall,
Gan Haziqaron

From Paris Square Khatib Street and Hanevi'im Street run south-west; then in 300m/330yds Hassan Shukri Street, on left, leads to the Town Hall and, opposite it, Gan Haziqaron (Memorial Park). The park lies at a height of 60m/200ft above sea level on the site of the citadel built by Daher el-Amr, ruler of Galilee from 1740 to 1775. The only relic of the citadel is an old cannon.

★Old Technion

A few hundred yards south-west of the Town Hall is the Old Technion (College of Technology; the larger New Technion is in the south-eastern district of Qiryat HaTechnion). The Old Technion was built between 1914 and 1924 to the design of a Berlin architect, Alexander Baerwald; it combines Oriental features with western ideas on the organisation of space. The Old Technion now houses the Institute of Architecture and the Museum of Science and Technology, which illustrates simple scientific principles and the results of recent Israeli research.

Central Carmel

From here it is a short walk uphill to Central Carmel, the highest and most select district of the city. In this area is the Gan Ha'em Park, with its small Zoo and the Museum of Biology and Prehistory.
Hanassi Boulevard (with the Tikotin Museum of Japanese Art at No. 89) and Yefe Nof Street now run downhill, affording superb views over the city and the harbour and across the bay to Akko.

★Bahai Shrine,
Persian Gardens

Below Yefe Nof Street, in Hazionut Street, are the beautiful Persian Gardens, with the Bahai Shrine, whose golden dome dominates the city. It contains the tomb of the founder of the Bahai faith, which has become its central shrine.
The founder of the faith was a Persian, Mirza Ali Mohammed, who in 1844 declared himself the Bab, the "Gateway" to God. After he was shot in Tabriz in 1850 his successor Mirza Hussein Ali, who took the name Baha-u-Illah, fled to the Ottoman Empire, where he proclaimed himself Imam in 1868. After being held in captivity in Akko for 24 years he died in 1892 and was buried near the present-day kibbutz of Shamerat, to the north of Akko. His followers secretly brought the remains of his predecessor Mirza Ali Mohammed from Persia to Palestine and in 1909 built his tomb in Haifa. The monumental dome over the tomb was completed in 1953.

Bahai Archives

On the other side of Hazionut Street, also in carefully tended gardens, is a neo-classical building erected in 1957 to house the archives of the Bahai faith, which has spread to Europe and America.

★Haifa Museum

A few hundred yards north-east of the Persian Gardens, at 26 Shabtai Levi Street, is the Haifa Museum, which since 1977 has included the Museum of Modern Art and the Museum of Ancient Art. The Museum also has departments of ethnography and folklore and a section devoted to Jewish ritual art. The collections of the Museum of Ancient Art include material from Caesarea and Byzantine mosaics from Shiqmona. The Museum of Modern Art displays pictures by Israeli and foreign (Western European, American, Japanese) artists from the 18th century to the present day.
There are several rooms used for special exhibitions, an auditorium and a reading room. Illustrated lectures are given in the evenings.

Chagall House

Diagonally opposite the Museum is Chagall House, which puts on periodic exhibitions of work by contemporary Israeli artists.

Bahai Shrine, Haifa

The Carmelite Monastery is situated on Cape Carmel, on the western outskirts of Haifa. It is reached from the harbour by way of Allenby and Stella Maris Streets or from Gan Ha'em Park by way of Hanassi Boulevard and Tchernikovsky Street. It lies close to the Stella Maris (Star of the Sea) lighthouse.

Carmelite Monastery

The first monastery built by the Carmelite order, founded on Mount Carmel in 1150, was destroyed in 1291 after the fall of Akko. After being rebuilt by Ahmed el-Jazzar in the late 18th century it was again destroyed in 1821 and once again rebuilt in 1828. It is dedicated to the Prophet Elijah and his disciple Elisha. The church contains paintings of scenes from their lives and a cedarwood figure of the Virgin with a porcelain head (1820), the Madonna of Mount Carmel.

Steps lead down to a grotto which is believed to be either the dwelling or the tomb of Elijah. There is a small museum in a room adjoining the entrance to the monastery.

In front of the monastery is the tomb of the wounded French soldiers who were killed on Ahmed el-Jazzar's orders in 1799.

Opposite the monastery is a path leading down to Elijah's Cave (also known as the School of the Prophet), at the foot of the cape. This is believed to be the cave in which Elijah hid from the kings of Israel and has been described by Zev Vilnay as "the holiest Jewish site in Haifa". Elijah is revered as El-Khidr by the Muslims, who had a mosque here until 1948.

Elijah's Cave

Also opposite the monastery is the upper station of the Cable Car, a cabin cableway running down to the sea. On the way down visitors are given a commentary on the leading buildings of Haifa.

Cable Car

Some 200m/220yds south-east of the lower cable car station, at 204 Allenby Street, is the Museum of Clandestine Immigration and Naval Museum. On the roof of the museum is the "Af Al Pi", an old tank landing craft which

Museum of Clandestine Immigration

Persian Gardens

Haifa Museum

broke through the British blockade and brought illegal Jewish immigrants to Palestine.

Maritime Museum

Next door to the Museum of Clandestine Immigration is the Maritime Museum, with a collection of ship models, maps and charts, prints, etc., illustrating the history of seafaring and harbours in the Holy Land.

University

To the south of Haifa, on the road running along the crest of Mount Carmel, is the University of Haifa, founded in 1972. The most eye-catching feature is the 30-storey Eshkol Tower, designed by the Brazilian architect Oscar Niemeyer. From the top of the tower there are breathtaking views.

Within the University complex is the Reuben and Edith Hecht Museum, with a display of archaeological material on the theme "The People of Israel and their Land" and a collection of Impressionist and Jewish painting.

Surroundings of Haifa

Allone Abba

Allone Abba, 25km/15 miles south-east of Haifa, is a moshav which was originally established by German settlers. It is reached on a road which turns left off the road to Nazareth 4km/2½ miles south of Qiryat Tivon. Originally called Waldheim, the settlement was founded in 1908 by members of the German Society of the Temple, who lived by farming, selling their produce in Haifa. The Germans were evacuated by the British authorities during the Second World War and the place was taken over by Israeli settlers. It was then renamed Allone Abba, after Abba Bardishev, who was dropped behind the German lines during the Second World War as a saboteur but was captured and executed. Some of the buildings of the original settlement have been restored, and the church has become the cultural centre of the moshav.

En Hod

The artists' village of En Hod lies 15km/9 miles south of Haifa on the western slopes of Mount Carmel (see entry).

Hamat Gader

District: Northern

Hamat Gader (Arabic El-Hamma) lies in the lower Yarmouk valley near the eastern shore of the Sea of Galilee. In ancient times it was much frequented – as it still is – for the sake of its medicinal springs of sulphurous water. It belonged to Gadara, a town on the east bank of the Yarmouk (now Jordanian territory), which in Hellenistic times became a centre of Greek culture in the territories to the east of the Jordan. The modern town of Hamat Gader has preserved impressive remains of Roman baths, a synagogue

Situation and characteristics

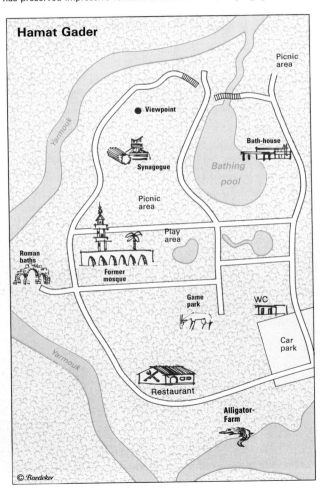

and a Roman theatre; but many visitors come to the town not for its archaeological interest but for the pleasure of relaxing in its mineral swimming baths, with a choice between hot and cold pools.

Hamat Gader is reached from Tiberias by taking a road which runs south, crosses the Jordan and passes through Ma'agan and the turning into a side road signposted to Sha'ar HaGolan. The distance from Tiberias is 20km/12½ miles.

History

Gadara was the home of the Greek satirical writer Menippus and the poet Meleager. In Roman times it was a member of the Decapolis, a league of ten cities including Scythopolis (Bet Shean) on the west bank of the Jordan and nine towns on the east bank, among them Damascus, Philadelphia (Amman), Pella and Gerasa (Jerash). For a time Gadara was the leading member of the league, which continued in existence into the 2nd century A.D. and is mentioned in the New Testament (Matthew 4,25; Mark 5,20 and 7,31).

Sights

★Modern spa facilities

In a beautifully laid out park with picnic areas, a restaurant, a children's playground and archaeological remains the principal attractions are the bathing pools, with water at different temperatures. The covered pool has water at a temperature of 42°C/108°F from a slightly radioactive mineral spring which is recommended particularly for relieving rheumatic complaints.

Synagogue

Near the bathing pools, on the highest point in the park, are the excavated remains of a synagogue of the 5th century, divided into three aisles by two rows of four columns. Remains of mosaics with simple geometric designs and representations of plants and animals were found here.

Roman baths, Hamat Gader

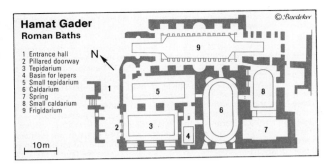

Hamat Gader
Roman Baths

1 Entrance hall
2 Pillared doorway
3 Tepidarium
4 Basin for lepers
5 Small tepidarium
6 Caldarium
7 Spring
8 Small caldarium
9 Frigidarium

© Baedeker

10m

There are only scanty remains of the Roman theatre, which could seat an audience of 2000. The site is now a game park.

Roman theatre

The Roman baths are unusually well preserved. From the entrance hall a pillared doorway of the 4th century (rebuilt) leads to the various rooms in the baths. The first room, the tepidarium, contains a large basin which would be filled with warm water; it seems to have been the most sumptuous room in the whole establishment. To the south of this is a small basin which may have been used by sufferers from leprosy. Beyond this again is the oval hot bath (caldarium), fed by an adjoining spring with water at a temperature of 52°C/126°F; since this was too hot for comfort, cold water had to be continually added. Other elements in the baths were another small caldarium, the pool containing the spring and a large cold bath (frigidarium), only partly excavated, housed in a spacious open hall.

★Roman baths

At the south end of the park is the Alligator Farm. The first alligators were flown in from Florida in 1981, and since then have flourished and multiplied.

Alligator Farm

Har Gilboa

See Mount Gilboa

Har Karmel

See Carmel

Har Tabor

See Mount Tabor

Hazor

H 2

District: Northern
Altitude: 330m/1080ft

Tel Hazor rises commandingly above the road which runs north from Tiberias to Metulla, at the point where it emerges from the hills into the Hule plain. After the first excavations by John Garstang in 1928 the history

Situation and characteristics

of the tell was extensively investigated by Yigael Yadin in excavations carried out between 1955 and 1969.

History

Excavation has revealed 21 occupation levels, the latest of which (I) is dated to the Hellenistic period (3rd–2nd c. B.C.), while the oldest (XXI) reaches back to the early Bronze Age (c. 2600 B.C.). This Canaanite city enjoyed a first period of prosperity in the 18th and 17th centuries B.C. (level XVII), when it is referred to in the archives of Mari on the Euphrates (Eastern Syria) along with Qatna, Babylon and other cities of similar size.

These facts, together with the extensive area of the site and the number of buildings of the Canaanite period, are in accord with the Biblical statement (Joshua 11,10) that Hazor was the "head" of many pre-Israelite kingdoms. The last king, Jabin, mustered the forces of many kings in the territory between Dor (see entry) on the Mediterranean coast and Mount Hermon in the north when the Israelites, led by Joshua, occupied the land in the 13th century B.C. But Joshua defeated the Canaanites "at the waters of Merom" (the present-day Hule region), conquered their cities and slew the defeated armies; the only city he burned down was Hazor (Joshua 11,13).

The first Israelite settlement on the territory of Hazor was established in the 12th century, but its real development began only in the 10th century, in the reign of Solomon (fortified gate, casemate walls), and still more actively in the reign of Ahab, whose capital was Samaria (9th c. B.C.). Level VIII in the citadel and the great store-room with its rows of pillars (formerly ascribed to Solomon) are testimonies to the magnificent architecture and economic importance of Hazor in the time of Ahab.

The town was destroyed by the Assyrian ruler Tiglath-pileser III in 732 B.C., but continued to exist as a fortress, with no economic importance, into the 2nd century B.C.

The ★Site

The entrance to the site, which covers a considerable area, is on the west side of the tell. The custodian who sells the tickets can also give information about the site. Further information is provided by large display boards with layout plans at the various excavated areas.

Hazor consisted of an upper town (600m/660yds long by up to 200m/220yds across) and a lower town (700m/765yds by 1000m/1100yds) to the north and east. The most impressive parts of the site for the ordinary visitor are sections A, B and L in the upper town and H in the lower town.

Section A

A general impression of Section A can be gained from a viewing platform. This was the site of the Canaanite royal palace and a broad ceremonial stairway leading up to it. After its destruction by Joshua in the 13th century B.C. Solomon built a new gateway of a type characteristic of his time, flanked by three rooms on each side and by a casemate wall (to the left of the staircase) and a barracks. Over this in the following century King Ahab built part of his large store-room, the other part of which had two rows of pillars, clearly visible from the viewing platform.

Section B

Section B contains the citadel. Remains found here included an Israelite place of prayer of the 11th century B.C. The citadel was rebuilt in monumental style in the reign of Ahab, but later alterations and additions have also been identified.

Section H

In Section H a tripartite temple built over the remains of three older temples was discovered. It dated from the time of the last king of Hazor, Jabin, and was destroyed when Joshua burned down the city. It consisted of a vestibule, a hall and the holy of holies laid out on the same axis. In the vestibule were two columns. In the holy of holies, which is surrounded by orthostats,

Hazor: King Ahab's pillared hall

the excavators found an altar for the burning of incense, libation offering tables, a basalt vessel, statuettes of seated figures (of the king?), a bronze bull, discs with a pattern of rays, etc. – all suggesting that the temple was dedicated to the weather god Hadad. Yadin saw in this Canaanite temple, which has a parallel in a temple of the 20th/19th century B.C. at Megiddo (see entry), a "prototype of the Solomonic Temple" in Jerusalem: a finding of particular importance, since Solomon's Temple is known only from descriptions in the literature, unsupported by archaeological evidence.

In Section F another temple was found, together with a 5-ton altar stone (15th c. B.C.), and in Section C a temple of the moon god with numerous stelae (14th c. B.C.). — Section F, Section C

In Section L the water supply system of Hazor was brought to light – a technological achievement dating from the reign of Ahab (9th c. B.C.) which is no less astonishing than the tunnel at Megiddo (see entry). A shaft, measuring 19m/62ft by 25m/82ft at the top, was driven through earlier occupation levels and then through the native rock to a depth of 30m/100ft. A flight of steps 3m/10ft wide runs round its four sides and is continued by a fifth flight which occupies the whole width of the shaft. This leads into a tunnel 25m/80ft long which ends in a 5m/16ft wide cistern 10m/33ft lower down, at the level of the natural water table. Hazor's water supply was thus assured even when the spring outside the town was cut off during a siege. A modern staircase of 150 steps laid over the original stone steps enables visitors to reach the cistern. — Section L

Finds from the Hazor excavations are now to be seen in the Israel Museum in Jerusalem, and also in the Hazor Museum at the kibbutz of Ayelet Hashahar, 1km/¾ mile away. This museum also has a model of ancient Hazor. — Hazor Museum

Hazor Museum in the kibbutz of Ayelet Hashahar

Hebron/Hevron

G/H 5

West Bank
Altitude: 926m/3038ft
Population: 38,500

Situation and characteristics

The town of Hebron (Hebrew Hevron, Arabic El-Khalil), situated in the Judaean Hills between Jerusalem (37km/23 miles) and Beersheba (48km/30 miles), is the religious centre of Islam in the southern part of the Israeli-occupied west bank of the Jordan, as Nablus is in the north. There is an Islamic university, which is periodically closed by the Israeli authorities on the grounds that it has provoked disturbances.

The monumental shrine erected over the cave in which Abraham was buried makes this one of the great sights for visitors with an interest in scriptural history; but since there are frequently violent clashes between Arabs and Israelis in Hebron it is essential before visiting the town to check up on the current situation with the tourist information office in Jerusalem.

History

Hebron is a very ancient city which has been continuously inhabited since its foundation by the Canaanites. The town's religious tradition goes back to Abraham, a patriarch to both the Jews and the Arabs. When his aged wife Sarah died here he bought from Ephron, son of Zohar, the field called Machpelah to the east of Mamre, together with "the cave which was therein, and all the trees that were in the field" (Genesis 23,17–20) and made it his family burial-place. After Sarah Abraham himself, his son Isaac, Isaac's wife Rebecca, his son Jacob and Jacob's wife Leah were likewise buried here. Jacob's son Joseph set out from Hebron to look for his brothers, who were conspiring to kill him (Genesis 37,14).

After the death of King Saul at the end of the 11th century B.C. the thirty-year-old David was anointed in Hebron as king of Judah. He lived here for

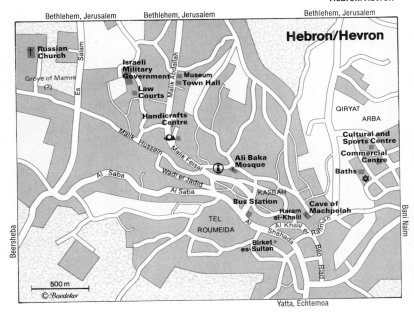

seven and a half years, until the conquest of Jerusalem, with his six wives (including Ahinoam from Jezreel, mother of his first-born son Amnon, Abigail from Carmel, mother of Chileab, and Maacah, mother of Absalom). During this period his general Joab killed Saul's general Abner in Hebron (2 Samuel 3,27). It was at the pool of Hebron that David ordered the execution of the two men who had murdered Ish-bosheth, Saul's last son, and had brought his severed head to David, who then had it buried in Abner's grave (2 Samuel 4,7–12).

When the Jews were carried off into captivity in Babylon Edomites from the Negev settled in Hebron in the 6th century B.C., and held the town until Judas Maccabeus attacked and destroyed it in 163 B.C. Herod the Great (37–4 B.C.) rebuilt the town and erected the great building which still stands over the cave of Machpelah.

In the 6th century A.D. the Emperor Justinian built a church over Machpelah, which was converted into a mosque in the 7th century, after the end of Byzantine rule. In 1215 the cave was opened by Crusaders, who, it is reported, saw the remains of the patriarchs. In 1267 the town was taken by the Mameluke Sultan Baibars, and thereafter Jews and Christians were banned from entering the sacred precinct – a prohibition which continued into modern times. It required a special firman from the Sultan to allow the Prince of Wales to enter the mosque in 1862.

At that time Hebron had a population of just under 10,000, including 500 Jews. The Jewish community increased in size at the end of the 19th century when Chassidic Jews from Eastern Europe settled in the town, and there was a further influx from Russia in 1925. In 1929, however, many Jews were killed in a pogrom. After the Six Day War, in 1967, Jews were able to enter the shrine of Machpelah for the first time in 700 years, but at the cost of frequent conflicts between Arabs and Jews.

View of Hebron

The town

The old town of Hebron has a markedly Oriental character. In the little streets round the Haram el-Khalil are numbers of shops and booths selling foodstuffs, pottery and glass.

North-east of the old town is the settlement of Qiryat Arba, founded in 1968, in which some 700 Israeli families live apart from the Arab population behind barbed wire barricades.

Sights

★Haram el-Khalil

The skyline of Hebron is dominated by the shrine over the cave of Machpelah, the Haram el-Khalil (Shrine of the Friend), so called because Abraham is known to Muslims as El-Khalil er-Rahman (Friend of the Lord). It stands near the Sultan's Pool (Birket es-Sultan), at which David had the murderers of Ish-bosheth, Saul's last son, executed (2 Samuel 4,7–12). The hovels which formerly surrounded the shrine were pulled down by the Jordanian authorities in 1960, and there is now an unimpeded view of the whole massive structure. The outer walls, their plain surface relieved by pilaster strips, were built by Herod the Great, enclosing an area measuring 65m/215ft by 35m/115ft. The top section of the wall with its battlements dates from the Islamic period, as do the two minarets which survive out of the original four.

A flight of steps on the north-east side leads up to the entrance, which gives access to the forecourt. Here there are four shrines or cenotaphs, under which are the tombs of the patriarchs. To the right are the mausolea built in the 14th century over the cenotaphs of Jacob (on left) and his wife Leah (on right). To the rear are the cenotaphs of Abraham (on right) and Sarah (on left). All these monuments are hung with richly embroidered cloths.

Beyond the forecourt is the three-aisled prayer hall of the mosque, 28m/92ft across and 24m/79ft deep. Originally this was probably a church built by Justinian and later used by the Crusaders; it was given its present form as a mosque by the Mamelukes in the 14th century. The roof is borne on four columns; half way along the south-east side is the mihrab (prayer niche), and just to the right of this is the richly carved minbar (pulpit), set up by Saladin in 1191. Here there are two other cenotaphs, those of Isaac (on right) and Rebecca. The right-hand part of the hall, which is uncarpeted, was assigned to the Jews in 1967 as a place for prayer, and is no longer regarded as forming part of the mosque. In the floor is an opening through which pious Jews drop into the cave of Machpelah slips of paper with prayers written on them.

A doorway on the west side of the mosque leads into a long corridor which serves as a mosque for women. On the left-hand side the Herodian outer wall has been breached and a square chamber built on. This contains a sarcophagus which is revered by Muslims as that of Joseph. The Jews, however, hold to the Biblical account that Joseph's remains, when brought from Egypt, were taken not to Hebron but to Shechem (see Nablus) and buried there (Joshua 24,32).

Before acquiring the cave of Machpelah Abraham had settled in the plain of Mamre. There he erected an altar (Genesis 13,18), and "the Lord appeared unto him" and he entertained the three angels unawares (Genesis 18,1–2). There too his wife Sarah died, and he buried her in the cave "before Mamre" (Genesis 23,17 and 49,30). This indicates that Mamre lay west of Hebron, and the likeliest site seems to be the Russian Orthodox community of Moskabia 1km/³⁄₄ mile west of the new bypass road, with a church of 1871 and the "Oak of Rest" (Balut es-Sebat), also known as Abraham's Oak.

Mamre/ Abraham's Oak

4km/2½ miles north of Hebron is another site linked by tradition with Mamre. This is Beit Ilanim, which lies 500m/550yds east of the road to Jerusalem at an altitude of 1024m/3360ft. Here there are remains of structures built of large blocks of dressed stone of the Herodian period. Excavations in 1926 established that the Herodian building was destroyed by Titus in A.D. 70 and rebuilt by Hadrian in 135, with a temple which Constantine replaced by a church in the 4th century. Until its destruction in the 7th century by Persians or Arabs this was regarded by Christian pilgrims as the dwelling-place of Abraham.

Mamre/ Beit Ilanim

Surroundings of Hebron

The upland region to the south and east of Hebron has many ancient remains which show that even after the destruction of Jerusalem in A.D. 70 there was a relatively large and prosperous Jewish population not only, as previously believed, in Galilee but also in Judaea. Some of their settlements were taken over by the Byzantines, and some still survive as Arab villages.

5km/3 miles east of Hebron, at an altitude of 951m/3120ft, is the Arab village of Bani Naim, with a mosque built over a Byzantine church which according to a local tradition contains the tomb of Lot. From here there is a fine view of the Dead Sea.

Bani Naim

A side road which turns off the Beersheba road 6km/4 miles south of Hebron leads in 6km to the large Arab village of Yatta, the Juttah of the Old Testament. Many of the houses are built of re-used ashlar blocks, and there are remains of a 6th century synagogue.

Yatta

5km/3 miles south-east of Yatta is the large and as yet unexcavated ancient site of Karmel. The Biblical Carmel, along with Maon (2km/1¼ miles south), where there are also extensive unexcavated remains, belonged to a rich man named Nabal, whose wife Abigail left Carmel after his death and married David (1 Samuel 25,2–42).

Karmel, Maon

Another road runs south from Yatta to Sammu, the Biblical Eshtemoa (Joshua 21,14). Near the village mosque the remains of a 3rd century

Sammu

synagogue, which seems to have continued in existence in the early Islamic period until the 8th century, were excavated in 1935.

Horvat Suseya

A country track runs east from Sammu to Horvat Suseya (Sussia; 5km/ 3 miles), where a large synagogue with a marble doorway, a women's gallery, a mosaic of a menorah (seven-branched candlestick) and a number of inscriptions was excavated some years ago. With their traditional farming methods, their flocks and herds and their whole way of life the people of this remote hill village seem still to be living in the world of the patriarchs.

Hefa

See Haifa

Hefer Plain/Emeq Hefer   G 3

Districts: Central, Haifa

Situation and characteristics

The plain of Hefer, formerly known as the Wadi Hawarith, extends along the Mediterranean coast between Hadera and Netanya, forming part of the plain of Sharon. Watered by streams flowing down from the hills of Samaria, it is a fertile and flourishing tract of land with numerous settlements.

History

During the occupation of the Promised Land by the Israelites the king of Hepher, along with thirty other Canaanite princes, was defeated by Joshua (Joshua 12,17). The Biblical town stood on the tell near the kibbutz of Mabarot. In the 10th century Solomon's court was supplied with victuals from the land of Hepher (1 Kings 4,10). Later the plain degenerated into marshland in which malaria was rife and permanent settlement impossible. In the 19th century this inhospitable region was inhabited only by a few Egyptian fellahin brought in by Ibrahim Pasha in 1830.

Settlements

In 1929 the Jewish National Fund acquired the area, and in the following year the draining of the marshes began. Thereafter the Hefer plain developed into one of the most fertile regions in Israel. Many settlements were established, beginning with Kefar Vitkin in 1933, and an agricultural college was founded. Some villages are named after famous personalities, like Kefar Monash (after the First World War general of that name) and Kefar Yedidia (after the Jewish philosopher Philo of Alexandria, known in Hebrew as Yedidia). The kibbutz of Mabarot has a museum containing archaeological finds from the area.

Herodeion   H 5

West Bank
Altitude: 758m/2487ft

Situation and characteristics

The hill known as the Herodeion, 11km/7 miles south-east of Bethlehem on the Israeli-occupied west bank of the Jordan, is a conspicuous landmark, rising sharply to a height of 100m/330ft above the surrounding country. It was given its characteristic form, like a volcano with its summit levelled off, when Herod, after whom it is named, built a fortified palace here. The excavation site on the Herodeion, which was declared a National Park in 1968, is now constantly guarded by Israeli troops. On the kiosk where visitors get their admission tickets is a plaque commemorating a park warden who was killed by Palestinians in 1988.

Peristyle and East Tower of Herod's palace on the Herodeion ▷

Herodeion

In 40 B.C., when in the course of the Roman-Parthian war the Hasmonean Antigonus became high priest and king, Herod took refuge here along with Mariamne and the rest of his family before withdrawing to Masada (see entry). After re-establishing his authority by his victory over Antigonus in 37 B.C. he built a fortress on the summit which he intended should be his mausoleum. After his death in 4 B.C. his son Archelaus brought his body from Jericho (see entry) in a splendid cortege to be buried in the mausoleum.

Excavations carried out from 1962 onwards confirmed the vivid account by Flavius Josephus in his "Jewish War". Herod had the summit of the hill cut away and dug out, the spoil being tipped over the edge of the circular plateau thus created, which was surrounded by a double ring of massive walls and towers. In the area within the walls he "built splendid palaces which were not only magnificent within but were surrounded without by walls, battlements and roofs of extravagant splendour". The excavations brought to light a garden laid out in a peristyle court, residential apartments, baths and a synagogue. Water was brought from Solomon's Pools to the south of Bethlehem. The fortress's only gate was approached by a flight of 200 white marble steps.

Herod's tomb has not been found. It is thought to have been destroyed at an early stage, perhaps during the Jewish War (A.D. 66–70), when Jewish zealots took refuge here, or during the Bar Kochba rising (132–135), when Bar Kochba established his headquarters on the hill.

Later the Herodeion was occupied by a few Byzantine monks, but in the 7th century, after the Persian and Arab invasions, the site was abandoned, and in subsequent centuries the palace fell into ruin.

In 1967, when resisting Jordanian attack, Israel captured Judea and Samaria.

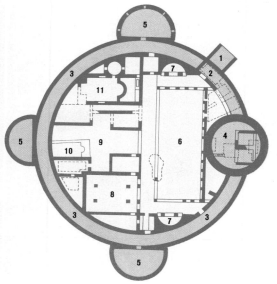

Herodeion Palace

1 Access ramp
2 Entrance hall
3 Double ring of walls
4 East Tower
5 Semicircular towers
6 Garden with peristyle
7 Exedra
8 Triclinium
  (later synagogue)
9 Cruciform courtyard
  (surrounded by bedrooms)
10 Byzantine chapel
11 Baths

20 m

© Baedeker

Herodeion: the lower town

The ★★Site

A broad footpath now runs up in a wide curve to the palace, though visitors usually climb up to it by way of a series of underground passages and cisterns. So far three large cisterns, with a total capacity of 2500 cu.m/550,000 gallons, have been found 25m/80ft below the palace complex.

Palace

From the top of the hill there are wide views, extending northward over the Judaean Hills to the towers on the Mount of Olives, near Jerusalem, and eastward to the Dead Sea, 1150m/3775ft below.

The double ring of walls surrounding the palace complex, reinforced by a round tower on the east side and three semicircular towers on the other sides, can be clearly distinguished. The outer wall has a diameter of 63m/207ft and, like the inner wall, stands to a height of 20–30m/65–100ft. The space between the two walls was occupied by passages and store-rooms. The round tower on the east side has a diameter of 18.3m/60ft and originally was probably 45m/150ft high.

The circular area within the walls is divided into two equal halves. The eastern part was occupied by a garden surrounded on three sides by Corinthian columns, with semi-columns engaged in the outer walls on the east side. At the north and south ends of the garden were semicircular recesses (exedrae).

The western part of the complex was occupied by residential apartments, mostly single-storied but with high ceilings. The triclinium (dining room), measuring 15m/49ft by 10.5m/34ft, is readily identifiable; it had a large doorway opening into the garden, with a window on either side. The columns and stone benches round three sides of the room were added in A.D. 70, when it was converted into a synagogue. Immediately north of the triclinium, on both sides of a cruciform courtyard, were bedrooms. The west side of the courtyard was occupied in Byzantine times by a chapel belonging to a small monastery built in the ruins of the palace. To the north of the courtyard were the palace baths, the largest room in which was the square caldarium; the circular tepidarium had a 4m/13ft high domed roof.

Lower town

At the foot of the hill are the excavated remains of the lower town built by Herod to house his courtiers and servants, which covers an area of 15 hectares/37 acres. Like the palace complex, it was aligned due north and south. It was in three parts – another large palace, of which only scanty remains survive; north of this an area with a large artificial pool; and farther north again a residential district. The pool in the centre of the lower town is clearly identifiable; measuring 70m/230ft by 46m/150ft, it was 3m/10ft deep and had a capacity of 10,000 cu.m/2,200,000 gallons. In the centre of the pool were found remains of a rotunda surrounded by columns. Presumably the pool served both as a reservoir of water and as a recreational area for bathing or boating. Round the pool was a large garden enclosed by massive walls.

Herzliya   G 4

District: Tel Aviv
Altitude: 10–40m/35–130ft
Population: 61,000

Situation and characteristics

Herzliya, 15km/9 miles north of Tel Aviv, was founded in 1924 and named after Theodor Herzl (see Famous People). Its population, only 500 in 1948, has increased more than a hundredfold since then. Its beautiful long sandy beach, now lined by hotels and bathing stations, has made it a popular seaside resort, frequented, particularly on the Sabbath, by large numbers of Israelis. (Buses run between Tel Aviv and Herzliya even on the Sabbath.)

The town

The town consists of two parts. The older part lies to the east of one of the large sandstone ridges which lie between the plain of Sharon and the coast. In ancient times a tunnel was cut through this ridge to allow water to drain

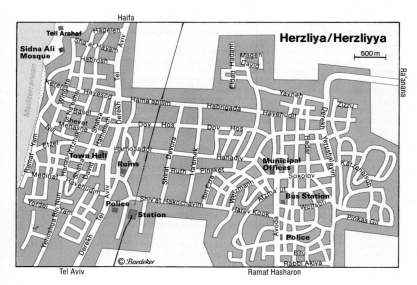

The beach of Herzliya, a popular seaside resort

away more easily into the sea and thus prevent the formation of marshes. After the foundation of Herzliya this was cleared of the detritus which had accumulated over the centuries; the mouth of the tunnel can be seen on the east side of the coast road, at the junction for Herzliya. To the east of this junction is the old town centre; to the west are the new districts above the beach.

Sights

On a hill on the north-west side of the town, beyond the little suburban districts of Nof Yam and Reshef, is the minaret of the shrine of Sidna Ali (Our Lord Ali), a Muslim holy man who was killed fighting the Crusaders.

Sidna Ali

Immediately north of the shrine of Sidna Ali is Tel Arshaf, site of the ancient port of Rishpon which is mentioned in Assyrian texts. The town was dedicated to Reshef, the Canaanite god of fire and fertility. The Greeks who settled here in the later 4th century B.C. equated Reshef with Apollo and named the town Apollonia. In 95 B.C. the town was captured by the Hasmonean king Alexander Jannaeus, but in 63 B.C. it was retaken by Pompey and again came under Hellenistic influence. In the 7th century the port was occupied by the Arabs, who called it Arsuf. In the 12th century it became known to the Crusaders as the castle of Arsur. Richard Coeur de Lion defeated Saladin here in 1191. In 1265 the town was destroyed by the Mamelukes.
Excavations from 1950 onwards brought to light various Roman buildings, including a theatre.

Tel Arshaf

Hevron

See Hebron

Horeshat Valley

See Hule Plain

Horns of Hittim/Qarne Hittim   H 3

District: Northern
Altitude: 326m/1070ft

Situation and characteristics

10km/6 miles west of Tiberias is a hill of moderate height which as a result of the collapse of its crater has taken on the characteristic form reflected in its name, the Horns of Hittim (Hebrew Qarne Hittim). This was the scene of a decisive battle during the Crusader period.

It is a half-hour walk to the top of the hill on a footpath running up from the main road. From the summit, on which there are Bronze Age remains, there are fine views of Eastern Galilee and the Sea of Galilee.

History

On July 4th 1187 Saladin inflicted an annihilating defeat on the Crusaders at the Horns of Hittim. The Latin kingdom of Jerusalem founded 88 years before now lost its capital, Jerusalem, and much of its territory; and for the remaining 104 years of its existence it was confined to a narrow coastal strip with its capital at Acre (Akko: see entry).

Saladin, a Kurd who had ruled Egypt since 1171 and in 1174 had incorporated Syria in his domains, crossed the Jordan in 1187 with a great army and set up camp near Tiberias, hoping to draw the crusading army into battle. The Crusaders had assembled on July 2nd 1187 at Sepphoris (see Zippori), 6km/4 miles north-west of Nazareth, where they had sufficient water for themselves and their horses. In a council of war held there the Grand Master of the Temple, Gerard of Ridfort, and Reynald of Châtillon, an adventurer, who favoured an immediate attack, prevailed over the more level-headed majority, and under their influence King Guy of Lusignan ordered the heavily armoured army to advance in the fierce heat through waterless country towards Hittim, 20km/12½ miles away as the crow flies. Arriving there, tormented by thirst, they found that the spring had dried up; and to make matters worse the Muslims had set fire to the withered undergrowth. The next morning the Crusaders launched their attack. The knights fought with the courage of despair, and some of them succeeded in breaking through to Tripoli. The bishop of Acre, who had carried the True Cross into the battle, was killed, and the precious relic was lost. Most of the Crusaders, including the king, were taken prisoner. Saladin offered King Guy water, but struck Reynald of Châtillon's head off, after reproaching him for his countless misdeeds, including his attacks on caravans during a truce and the robbing of pilgrims travelling to Mecca. The Knights Hospitallers and the Templars were killed by the fanatical Sufis, the secular barons were held captive and the common soldiers were taken to be sold in the slave market in Damascus, where as a result of this over-supply prices fell sharply.

The Horns of Hittim are thus a reminder of a futile military enterprise which had fateful consequences for those who initiated it. After his victory Saladin went on to take Jerusalem and Acre, though Acre was recaptured by the Christians four years later and remained in their hands for another hundred years.

Hule Plain/Emeq Hula   H/J 2

District: Northern

Situation and characteristics

The Hule plain (Emeq Hula) in northern Israel extends from Dan (see entry) on the Lebanese frontier to Hazor (see entry) in the south, and is bounded on the east by the Golan Heights (see entry) and on the west by the hills of Lebanon. The valley is one of the largest drainage basins and agricultural areas in Israel.

For many centuries the Hule plain was marshy and malaria-ridden. After the Egyptian general Ibrahim Pasha conquered Palestine from the Turks (1830–40) he had a passage blasted through the volcanic rocks to the south of the Benot Ya'aqov Bridge (see Rosh Pinna) to allow water to flow more readily into the Jordan. His programme for bringing the land into cultivation with the help of fellahin brought in from Egypt could not be carried out because of political developments, and the area was inhabited only by a few Bedouin with their water buffaloes.

In 1883 Jewish immigrants founded the village of Yesud HaMa'ala, 15km/9 miles north-east of Rosh Pinna. In the difficult early days Baron Edmond de Rothschild helped in the draining of the marshland by planting eucalyptus trees, which are great consumers of water. Large-scale drainage operations began, however, only after the acquisition of land by the Jewish National Fund in 1934, and this work was continued on a systematic basis between 1951 and 1958. More recently the drainage operations have been associated with the National Water Carrier which conveys water from Galilee to the southern parts of the country. The construction of canals and the deepening and straightening of the Jordan (see entry) have led to the disappearance of the marshes and the creation of fertile agricultural land. There are now also fish farms as well as fields.

Settlements

The improved living conditions have led to the establishment of several new farming settlements. 1940 saw the establishment, 6km/4 miles southeast of Qiryat Shemona, of the villages of Amir and Sede Nehemya, near which the rivers Hazbani, Dan and Banyas join to form the Jordan, and of Bet Hillel, 4km/2½ miles east of Qiryat Shemona. They were followed in 1946 by Ne'ol Mordekhay, 8km/5 miles south of Qiryat Shemona, and in 1948 by Hagoshrim, 5km/3 miles east of Qiryat Shemona on the northern edge of the Hule plain.

On the north-western edge of the Hule plain is Qiryat Shemona, now a town with a population of 15,500, which was founded in 1949 on the site of an abandoned Arab village as a camp for new immigrants. From here two roads run south, one in the valley and the other, to the west, skirting the Lebanese frontier, with fine views of the Hule plain.

★Hule Nature Reserve

15km/9 miles north of Rosh Pinna on the road to Qiryat Shemona a narrow road goes off on the right to the Hule Nature Reserve. The reserve (admission charge) has largely been left in its original state. Beyond the picnic areas at the entrance are paths leading through the marshy landscape with its unique flora and fauna, including a variety of waterfowl, wild cats, wild pigs, beavers and herds of water buffaloes. From an observation tower in the centre of the reserve there are views over its whole area.

Horeshat Valley National Park

In Upper Galilee, 5km/3 miles west of Qiryat Shemona, is the Horeshat (or Hurshat) Valley National Park (camping site), with a lake (bathing permitted) which is fed by the river Dan. Within the park are a number of gigantic oaks, some of which are said to be anything up to 2000 years old. Legend has it that they were planted by ten of Mohammed's soldiers who were encamped in this area and, finding no trees to tether their horses to, stuck stakes into the ground which grew overnight into tall oak-trees.

Jaffa

See Tel Aviv

Jenin   H 3

West Bank
Population: 13,200

Situation and
characteristics

At the Arab town of Jenin, lying between Afula (18km/11 miles) and Nablus (42km/26 miles) on the Israeli-occupied west bank of the Jordan, the old road going north from Jerusalem through the hills of Samaria runs through the Dotan valley into the Jezreel plain. From the earliest times, therefore, Jenin controlled this important line of communication.

History

In the 13th century the Mamelukes, fearing further incursions by the Crusaders, destroyed all the coastal towns and built Jenin up into a staging-point for caravans on the route between Damascus and Egypt. During the First World War Jenin was a station on the Afula–Nablus railway line, which it was planned to extend to Jerusalem and the Suez Canal; but when British forces gained control of the area the project was abandoned.
Until the early 1930s the road from Jerusalem to Haifa and Galilee ran through Jenin. With the development of Haifa as a port and the construction of the coast road via Hadera, however, the importance of Jenin declined.

Jericho/Yeriho   H 4

West Bank
Altitude: 260m/850ft below sea level
Population: 7000

Situation and
characteristics

Jericho (Hebrew Yeriho, Arabic Er-Riha), lying 36km/22 miles north-east of Jerusalem and 15km/9 miles north-west of the Dead Sea on the Israeli-occupied west bank of the Jordan, is an oasis town with agriculture supported by irrigation. Thanks to its abundant springs of fresh water and its mild climate bananas, dates and oranges do well here. In ancient times Jericho, which ranks as the oldest (and lowest-lying) city in the world, was the winter residence of various rulers, among them Herod the Great and Caliph Hisham.

History

The numerous occupation levels on Tel Jericho reach back to around 8000 B.C., in the Mesolithic period, when a nomadic people erected at the north end of the tell a remarkable rectangular building measuring 3.50m/11½ft by 6.50m/21½ft. Its stone walls were based on a 30cm/12in. thick layer of clay laid over the native limestone. Two of the blocks of stone, 75cm/30in. high, had holes bored through them from top to bottom for the insertion of poles, which it is suggested may have been totem poles. The building is believed, therefore, to have been a shrine of the nomadic people who erected it.
Another complex of structures in the centre of the tell is dated to the Neolithic period. Above a 3.90m/13ft thick layer of debris from the settlement of the 8th millennium the archaeologists found houses built of plano-convex bricks, some circular in plan, others rectangular with a semicircular end. This settlement was surrounded by a strong defensive wall, and can thus be regarded as a town. The wall is 1.95m/6½ft thick and on the west side is preserved to a height of 3.60m/12ft, and built against its inner side is a round stone tower 9m/30ft high. At a later period, around 7000 B.C., a ditch 2.70m/9ft deep and 8.10m/26½ft wide was dug in front of the wall, and the height of the wall was increased to 7.60m/25ft.

This indicates that between 8000 and 7000 B.C. a nomadic people of hunters and gatherers had made the transition to a settled way of life and now lived by farming and stock-herding. One man could thus produce food for many more people, and a division of labour developed, since each individual no longer had to look for his own food supply. These were the essential pre-conditions for the development of an advanced culture.

"The descendants of the Mesolithic hunters who had established the sanctuary by the spring at Jericho had therefore made remarkable progress. In the course of a period which Carbon-14 evidence suggests is about a thousand years, they had made the full transition from a wandering to a settled existence in what must have been a community of considerable complexity, for the imposing defences are evidence of an efficient communal organisation . . . The earliest villages known elsewhere were dated more than two thousand years later, and the pyramids of Egypt, the first great stone buildings of the Nile valley, are four thousand years younger than the great tower of Jericho" (Kathleen Kenyon).

The inhabitants of Jericho in this period had a cult of fertility and of the dead. They covered the skulls of their dead with a layer of plaster and set them up in their houses (finds in the Rockefeller Museum, Jerusalem, and Archaeological Museum, Amman).

After the destruction of the town, either by war or in an earthquake, the site was occupied in the 6th millennium B.C. by men of a different race who had mastered the craft of pottery but built very simple houses.

In the Chalcolithic period (5th millennium B.C.) the settlement moved west to the mouth of the Wadi Qilt (see entry), perhaps because the spring had altered its position, but it soon returned to the original site. Square houses were now built within a strong outer wall.

The period around 2000 B.C. is represented by pottery vessels in the form of human faces. In the Hyksos period (18th–16th c. B.C.) a new town wall was built of rammed earth, with a pronounced batter. This town was destroyed about 1400 B.C.

The Bible gives a detailed account (Joshua 2–6) of the conquest and destruction of Jericho by the Israelites, coming from east of the Jordan. This event was formerly dated to the 15th century B.C., but the 13th century (the time of Pharaoh Ramesses II) is now considered a more likely date. In the distribution of territory after the Israelites occupied the Promised Land the Jericho area was assigned to the tribe of Benjamin (Joshua 18,21). In the reign of King Ahab of Israel (9th c. B.C.) the destroyed city was rebuilt. During this period the prophet Elijah and his disciple Elisha came to Jericho (2 Kings 2). Elijah crossed the Jordan, and "there appeared a chariot of fire, and horses of fire . . . and Elijah went up by a whirlwind into heaven" (2 Kings 2,11). Elisha returned to Jericho, where the inhabitants complained that the water of the spring harmed the crops. Then he took some salt and "went forth unto the spring of the waters, and cast the salt in there, and said, Thus saith the Lord, I have healed these waters; there shall not be from thence any more death or barren land. So the waters were healed unto this day" (2 Kings 2,20–22). Accordingly the spring is known as Elisha's Spring.

In 586 B.C. the Babylonians held the last king of Judah, Zedekiah, who had fled from Jerusalem, as a prisoner in Jericho, blinded him and carried him off to exile in Babylon (2 Kings 25,7). During the Persian period the tell of Jericho was once again abandoned as it had been in the 5th millennium. After 332 B.C. the Hellenistic city of Jericho was built farther south, at the mouth of the Wadi Qilt. In 161 B.C. it was captured by the Maccabees. In 30 B.C. Octavian (the future Emperor Augustus) gave the oasis to Herod, who made it his winter residence, built the fortress of Cyprus (named after his mother) to defend it and died here in 4 B.C. His body was then conveyed in a splendid cortege to the Herodeion (see entry).

When Jesus was travelling for the last time from Galilee through the Jordan valley to Jerusalem he was hailed near Jericho by two blind men as "Son of David". He restored their sight, and "they followed him" (Matthew 20,30–34).

The Hellenistic/Herodian city of Jericho was destroyed by the Romans in A.D. 70. Later a settlement grew up on the site of the present town, to the south-east of the tell. A number of churches and a synagogue have been identified as dating from the Byzantine period. A new era began in 634 with the Arab conquest. The Omayyad Caliphs, ruling from Damascus, built a fortress and a mosque, and in 724 Caliph Hisham built a palace (Khirbet el-Mafyar). Thereafter Jericho gradually lost importance, declining into a modest village.

Under the British Mandate, between the two world wars, the old Roman road through the Wadi Qilt was replaced by a modern road from Jerusalem to the Dead Sea and Jericho. In 1940 the town had a population of 4000, who gained their living from the sale of bananas and citrus fruits grown in the oasis. The population has now risen to 7000.

The town

Jericho is a small, friendly town predominantly inhabited by Arabs. Thanks to its abundant springs of fresh water it is surrounded by lush green vegetation. The main street is lined by garden restaurants, but as a result of the *intifada* it frequently has a rather derelict air.

Sights

★Tel Jericho

Some 2.5km/1½ miles north-west of the town's central square, opposite Elisha's Spring (also known as the Sultan's Spring, Ain es-Sultan), is the tell which marks the site of ancient Jericho. Archaeological investigation of the site began in 1860, but at first was unrewarding (in his test dig Charles Warren just missed a stone tower). In 1906–07 Sellin and Watzinger continued the work, but no major successes were achieved until the British excavations of 1930–31. The thorough investigations of Kathleen Kenyon in the 1950s marked an important step forward.

On the tell of Jericho, standing 21m/69ft high and covering an area of 40,000sq.m/44,000sq.yds, Kathleen Kenyon identified 23 occupation

Neolithic tower, Jericho

levels. The oldest traces of human settlement date from around 8000 B.C. To the ordinary visitor the remains of this early period in human history will not appear particularly sensational. The most noticeable feature is the broad trench which the archaeologists cut through the hill in order to investigate the various occupation levels down to undisturbed soil. In the trench can be seen remains of the Neolithic town of around 7000 B.C., consisting of a section of the town wall and the 9m/30ft high round tower built against it. On the east side can be seen the entrance leading to the 22 steps of a spiral staircase and an opening higher up.

To the north of this Kathleen Kenyon found a shrine of the Mesolithic nomads, dating from about 8000 B.C.

Going north from Elisha's Spring and in 1km/⅝ mile turning right into an avenue of cypresses, we come to a house which has in the cellar a mosaic pavement from a synagogue of the Byzantine period (5th–6th c.). In the centre is a medallion containing a menorah, a palm branch, a ram's horn and the Hebrew inscription "Shalom al Israel" ("Peace for Israel").

Synagogue

Hisham's Palace (Khirbet el-Mafyar) lies 2km/1¼ miles north of Elisha's Spring, beyond a dry river-bed. It was built in 724 by Hisham, the tenth Omayyad Caliph and the last significant representative of the dynasty (724–743). The palace was left unfinished and was destroyed in an earthquake in 746. The site was covered over by sand and remained forgotten until British archaeologists located it in 1937 and excavated an area 160m/175yds by 130m/140yds. Numerous finds from the site, including the figural representations characteristic of early Islamic art, can be seen in the Rockefeller Museum in Jerusalem.

★Hisham's Palace (Khirbet el-Mafyar)

The palace is laid out on a square plan, with four ranges of buildings opening off an inner courtyard and no entrances on the outside. Immediately north is a large bath-house.

The palace is entered through a spacious forecourt containing a square pool, originally covered by a domed roof, and a gatehouse leading into a square inner courtyard. Set up here is a circular window which was originally in one of the rooms surrounding the courtyard. Straight ahead is the west wing, with steps leading down to an underground bath-house. To the right (north) are the remains of a mosque and beyond this the large bath-house, 40m/130ft square, the bareness of its outer walls relieved by semicircular recesses which originally contained alternating male and female figures. The roof was borne on sixteen pillars. Parts of the mosaic pavement have been preserved.

At the north-west corner of the bath-house is a small room with an apse, no doubt a rest room or reception room for the Caliph. It is famed for its completely preserved mosaic, a work of consummate craftsmanship depicting three gazelles under an orange-tree, one of them being attacked by a lion.

Jericho

1 Gatehouse
2 Small mosque
3 Underground bath-house
4 Large bath-house
5 Pool

Hisham's Palace Qirbat el-Mafyar

6 Room with mosaics
7 Caldarium (steam-bath)
8 Large mosque
9 Pool

25 m

© Baedeker

Inner courtyard

Forecourt

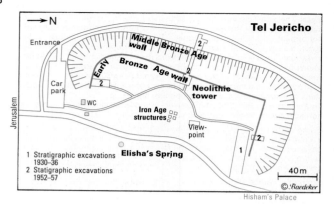

Tel Jericho

→ N

Entrance

Middle Bronze Age wall

Early Bronze Age wall

Neolithic tower

Car park

WC

Iron Age structures

View-point

Jerusalem

Elisha's Spring

1 Stratigraphic excavations 1930–36
2 Statigraphic excavations 1952–57

40 m

© Baedeker

Hisham's Palace

Mount of Temptation

North-west of Old Jericho is a prominent hill, known to the Arabs as Qarantal, which Christian tradition identifies as the Mount of Temptation, on which Jesus fasted after being baptised in the Jordan by John the Baptist and was tempted by the devil: "If thou be the Son of God, command that these stones be made bread. But he answered and said, It is written, Man shall not live by bread alone, but by every word that proceedeth out of the mouth of God" (Matthew 4,1–4).

In 340 St Chariton built a chapel on the summit of the hill, and another was built by the cave in which Jesus sheltered. The Greek Orthodox church

Hisham's Palace: columns . . .

. . . and window

acquired the site in 1875, and in 1895 built the Sarandarion monastery (a name which refers to the forty days of Jesus's fast) half way up the hill. From the monastery a steep path runs up to the summit, on which are the remains of St Chariton's chapel and the Hasmonean fortress of Dok (views).

2.5km/1½ miles west of Jericho, at the point where the Wadi Qilt enters the Jordan plain, recent excavations by Yehud Netzer have brought to light a large palace which shows clear signs of Hellenistic influence. It is thought to have been built by the Hasmonean king Alexander Jannaeus (103–76 B.C.) and to have been occupied by the last Hasmonean rulers and then by Herod, who enlarged and embellished it and died there. While the palace at Masada (see entry) was intended rather as a private residence this palace was designed for official and state occasions.

Hasmonean palace

The palace stood in a park laid out with terraces and water channels and was built on a symmetrical plan round a spacious courtyard. Among the structures identified are a large audience chamber, rooms decorated with frescoes, Roman baths and Jewish ritual baths. The most striking feature, however, is a large swimming pool measuring 32m/105ft by 18m/60ft and 4m/13ft deep which Netzer believes was the bath in which Herod had his 18-year-old brother-in-law Aristobulus drowned, only a year after he himself had appointed him high priest (Flavius Josephus, I,22,2). Soon afterwards he also caused his wife Mariamne, a Hasmonean princess and Aristobulus's sister, to be killed.

Jerusalem/Yerushalayim

H 4

District: Jerusalem
Altitude: 606–826m/1988–2710ft
Population: 415,000

The "high city" of Jerusalem (Hebrew Yerushalayim, "Abode of Peace"; Greek and Latin Hierosolyma; Arabic El-Quds, the "Sacred One"), once capital of the Jewish kingdom, is now capital of the state of Israel, the seat of a Greek Orthodox, an Armenian and a Roman Catholic Patriarch and the see of an Anglican bishop. As the city in which David and Solomon built their temples, the scene of Christ's Passion and the place from which Mohammed ascended into heaven Jerusalem is revered by Jews, Christians and Muslims alike. Its status as a holy city is uniquely reflected in the numerous holy places sacred to the three great monotheistic religions, which attract to Jerusalem hosts of pilgrims and tourists from all over the world.

Situation and characteristics

Jerusalem lies in latitude 31°47' north and longitude 35°14' east on an arid limestone plateau on the eastern slopes of the Judaean uplands which rises above the Kidron valley to the east and the Hinnom valley to the south and is divided by deep clefts into a narrow eastern hill (744m/2441ft), the Temple Mount, and a western hill (777m/2549ft), with the old upper town. Still higher is the north-west side, which is connected with the range of hills.

Finds of flint implements (in the Ephraim valley near the railway station) and of burials show that the site was occupied by man in the Palaeolithic period. From the 3rd millennium B.C. the centre of the settlement was on Mount Ophel, to the south of the Temple Mount. Here, near the Gihon Spring on which the existence of the settlement depended, was an early Canaanite town. In the time of Abraham (probably in the 18th century B.C.) the place was known as Salem, and its priest-king Melchizedek welcomed Abraham (Genesis 14,18). Towards the end of the 2nd millennium B.C. the town was held by the Jebusites, who were conquered by David about 1000 B.C. (2 Samuel 5,6–10). He then built the "City of David", again on Mount Ophel, and made Jerusalem the political and religious centre of the Israelite kingdom.

History

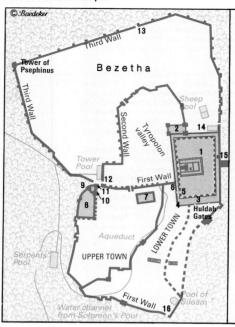

© Baedeker

Jerusalem in Ancient Times

1 Temple
2 Antonia Fortress
3 Stoa Basilike
4 Robinson's Arch
5 Barclay's Gate
6 Wilson's Arch
7 Hasmonean palace
8 Herod's Palace
9 Phasael's Tower
10 Mariamne's Tower
11 Hippicus's Tower
12 Garden Gate
13 Women's Gate
14 Israel Pool
15 Susa Gate
16 Gate of the Essenes

400 m

David's son Solomon (c. 969–930) built a palace and a temple for Yahweh (1 Kings 6–8). After his death Jerusalem became capital of the southern kingdom of Judah. Queen Athaliah (845–840) introduced the cult of Baal in the Temple, and in the reign of King Ahaz (733–727) Assyrian deities were also worshipped. His son Hezekiah (727–698) cleansed the Temple, built walls round the town and had a tunnel dug to secure its water supply. In 628 B.C. Josiah made Jerusalem the only legitimate Jewish place of worship (2 Kings 22f.). In 587 the town was captured by Nebuchadnezzar and many of the inhabitants were carried off to Babylon. After the end of the Babylonian Captivity, in 520 B.C., the Second Temple was built. In 445 B.C. Nehemiah built a new town wall.

In 332 B.C. Jerusalem came under Greek rule and was increasingly Hellenised. The desecration of the Temple by Antiochus IV sparked off the Maccabean rising of 167 B.C. Under the Maccabees and the Hasmoneans the town expanded westward on to Mount Zion. In 63 B.C. it passed into Roman control, and in 37 B.C. Herod, an Idumaean, became king of the Jews. He rebuilt and embellished the Temple platform and equipped the city with palaces, a citadel, a theatre, a hippodrome, an agora and other buildings on the Hellenistic and Roman model. After his death in 4 B.C. Jerusalem became the city of the high priests, under Roman procurators. From 41 to 44 it was ruled by Agrippa I, who extended the city northward, building the Third (North) Wall. In A.D. 70 Jerusalem was destroyed by Titus, to be rebuilt by Hadrian from 135 onwards under the name of Aelia Capitolina.

Jerusalem became a Christian city in 326, when the Emperor Constantine and his mother Helen built a number of churches. The Empress Eudoxia, wife of Theodosius II, who lived in Jerusalem from 444 to 460, and the Emperor Justinian (527–565) also built churches in the city. This era came to an end when Jerusalem was captured by the Persians in 614. It was recovered by the Byzantines in 627, but in 638 it was conquered by the armies of Islam. Thereafter the Omayyad Caliphs built the Dome of the Rock and the El-Aqsa Mosque.

A further period of Christian rule began in 1099 with the conquest of the city by the Crusaders, who built many churches, palaces and hospices. Islam returned to Jerusalem, however, when Saladin captured the city in 1187, and it remained in Muslim hands under the Mamelukes (1291–1517) and the Ottomans (1519–1917), who built the present town walls (1537).

In the 19th century the Christian powers of Europe, which had supported the Turkish Sultan against the Egyptian ruler Ibrahim Pasha, gained increasing influence from 1840 onwards, and numbers of churches, schools, hospitals and orphanages were now built. The Pope re-established the Latin Patriarchate, which had originally been founded in 1099 but was dissolved in 1291. In 1845 a joint Anglo-Prussian episcopal see was established. The German Society of the Temple founded a settlement in Jerusalem (near the station) in 1873, and in 1881 members of an American-Swedish group established the American Colony (north of the Damascus Gate).

After being banned for many centuries from living in Jerusalem, Jews began to return to the city in the 13th century. In 1267 Rabbi Moshe Ben Nahman Ramban (Nachmanides) founded a synagogue. In 1488 Jews from Egypt settled in Jerusalem, and they were followed from 1492 onwards by Sephardic Jews from Spain. The first Ashkenazis (500 Polish Jews led by Rabbi Hanassi) came in 1701. In the 18th century there were 1000 Sephardis (the Jewish elite) and 700 Ashkenazis in the city. The pace of immigration increased in the 19th century. The first Jewish hospital was established in 1854; in 1855 Sir Moses Montefiore founded the first Jewish settlement outside the Old City, still identifiable by its windmill; in 1868 Jews from North Africa built Mahane Israel (at the corner of King David and Agron Streets); and the settlement of Mea Shearim was established in 1874. The officially recognised representative of the Jews – divided as they were into different sects – was the Sephardic Chief Rabbi.

In December 1917 British forces under General Allenby entered the city, and on July 1st 1920 it became the seat of the British High Commissioner in the mandated territory of Palestine.

In 1925 the Hebrew University was established.

The United Nations resolved in 1947 that Palestine should be divided between the Arabs and the Jews and that Jerusalem should be internationalised. After the end of the British Mandate in 1948 Israeli and Jordanian forces fought for control of the city, and under a ceasefire agreement in 1949 it was partitioned. In 1950 the Israelis made West Jerusalem capital of their state; then after the Six Day War of 1967 they annexed East Jerusalem. There was further trouble in 1980, when the Israelis declared Jerusalem, including the Arab Old City, to be the "eternal capital of Israel".

The Israeli-Arab conflict intensified after the beginning of the *intifada* in December 1987. Since then Arab shopkeepers in the Old City have continued to close in the afternoon, and there are not infrequently violent clashes in Jerusalem between Palestinians and Israelis. The worst incident so far has been the massacre on the Temple Mount in October 1990.

The ★★town

The Old City is surrounded by a 4km/2½ mile long circuit of walls 12m/40ft high built in 1537 by Sultan Suleiman the Magnificent. Two main streets, David Street (in its eastern section called Chain Street), running east from the Jaffa Gate, and Suq Khan ez-Zeit, running south from the Damascus Gate, intersect in the centre of the Old City, dividing it into four quarters – the Christian Quarter to the north-west, the Armenian Quarter to the south-west, the Muslim Quarter to the north-east and the Jewish Quarter to the south-east. The streets are narrow, irregular and frequently vaulted.

The newer part of Jerusalem, to the west of the Old City, has a modern aspect, with office blocks, ministries and the Parliament Building,

Panoramic view of Jerusalem from the Haas Promenade

museums and also extensive parks and gardens. Here too is the main shopping district, centred on Ben Yehuda Street (pedestrian zone).

Since 1967, when the city was reunited, numerous satellite towns have been established in the surrounding area, usually distinguished by their functional but not particularly attractive architecture.

Bus route 99

The 99 bus is specially designed to cater for tourists. There are frequent services on a route which takes in all the city's main sights, with over thirty stops (including one at the Jaffa Gate).

Opening Times

Most museums, archaeological sites, etc., are closed or have restricted opening times on Friday afternoon and Saturday, the Jewish Sabbath. Admission tickets for these days must be bought in advance.

In the following list information about the individual sights, other than addresses and opening times, is given only where they are not mentioned in the descriptive section.

Agricultural Museum
13 Heleni Hamalka Street
Open: Sun.–Fri. 8am–1pm

Ammunition Hill Museum
Eshkol Boulevard
Open: Sun.–Thur. 9am–5pm (in winter to 4pm), Fri. 9am–1pm
A museum commemorating the Israeli dead of the Seven Day War.

Anna Ticho House
See Ticho House

Archaeological Museum
See Rockefeller Museum

Artists' House
See Bezalel School of Art

Bethesda, Pool of
See Pool of Bethesda

Bezalel School of Art
10–12 Shemu'el Hanagid Street
Open: Sun.–Thur. 10am–1pm and 4–7pm, Sat. 11am–2pm
Regular art exhibitions

Biblical Zoo
Yirmiyahu Street, Romema
Open: daily 9am to sunset

Burnt House
Jewish Quarter, Old City
Open: Sun.–Thur. 9am–5pm, Fri. 9am–1pm

Chaba Museum of Jewish Micrographic Art
43 Hanevi'im Street
Open: Sun.–Thur. 9am–5pm
Jewish miniature books, etc.

Chagall Windows
See Hadassah Medical Centre

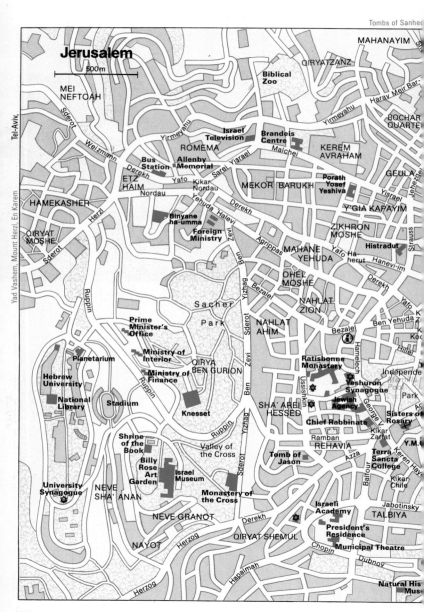

Jerusalem

500m

MEI NEFTOAH

Tombs of Sanhe

MAHANAYIM

QIRYAT ZANZ

Biblical Zoo

Harav Meir Bar

BOCHAR QUARTE

Tel-Aviv,

Sderot

Weizmann

Derekh

Yirmeyahu

Israel Television

Brandeis Centre

Malchei

KEREM AVRAHAM

ROMEMA

Bus Station

Allenby Memorial

Sarel Yisrael

Yafo

ETZ HAIM

Nordau

Kikar Nordau

Yehuda Halevi

MEKOR BARUKH

Porath Yosef Yeshiva

GEULA

Yisrael

HAMEKASHER

Herzl

Binyane ha-umma

Derekh

Y'GIA KAPAYIM

ZIKHRON MOSHE

Jehezke

QIRYAT MOSHE

Sderot

Foreign Ministry

Ben Zevi

Agrippas

MAHANE YEHUDA

Yafo Ha-herut

Histradut

Hanevi-im

Yad Vashem, Mount Herzl, En Karem

OHEL MOSHE

Derekh

Strauss

Ruppin

Sacher

Yizhag

Bezalel

NAHLAT ZION

Park

NAHLAT AHIM

Bezalel

Ben Yehuda

Prime Minister's Office

Planetarium

Ministry of Interior

QIRYA BEN GURION

Ratisbonne Monastery

Hamelech

Independe

Hebrew University

Ministry of Finance

Ussishkin

Yeshurun Synagogue

Koo

National Library

Stadium

Ruppin

Knesset

SHA'AREI HESSED

Jewish Agency

George

Sisters of Rosary

Chief Rabbinate

Ramban

Kikar Zarfat

Y.M.

Shrine of the Book

Ruppin

Yizhag

Ben Zevi

Sderot

Valley of the Cross

REHAVIA

Azza

Terra Sancta College

Keren Hay

University Synagogue

Billy Rose Art Garden

Israel Museum

Tomb of Jason

Balfour

Kikar Chile

NEVE SHA'ANAN

Monastery of the Cross

NEVE GRANOT

Israeli Academy

Jabotinsky

TALBIYA

NAYOT

Herzog

QIRYAT SHEMUL

Derekh

President's Residence

Chopin

Municipal Theatre

Dubnov

Hapalmah

Herzog

Natural His Mus

Atarot Airport **Ramallah, Nablus**

British
Military
Cemetery

Hadassah
Hospital

Eshkol

SHEIK JARRAH

Derekh Shekhem

Wadi

el

Ölbergstraße

NAHLAT
SHIMON

Tomb of Simon

Sderot Sir Winston Churchill

National Library
(Hebrew University)

Ölbergstraße

ISRAEL

Shemuel

Hanevi'im

St. Georg

Derekh Shekhem

Tombs of the
Kings

ibn

el

Waleed

WADI EL-JOZ

Joz

Mt Scopus

Mandelbaum
Gate

Khalid

Salah

ed

AMERICAN COLONY

ARIM

Shivte Yisrael

iopian
urch

Hanevi'im

St Stephen's
Church

Az-Zahara

Nur ed-

Din

El Mukadasi

Ben

Adaya

Garden
Tomb

Jeremiah's
Grotto

Rockefeller
Museum

Shmuel

SIAN
ARTER
alka

Shivte

Sultan

Suleiman

Jericho

Russian
Cathedral

Hatzanhanim

Damascus Gate

Herod's Gate

St Anne's Church

St Stephen's Gate
(Lion Gate)

EL-TUR

Law
Courts
Town
Hall

Notre-Dame
de France

MUSLIM

Tariq

al- Mujahedeen

St Stephen's
Church

Tomb of Virgin

Church of
All Nations

Chapel of
Ascension

New
Gate

Yisrael

Hativat

Suq Khan ez-Zeit

Via Dolorosa

QUARTER

Temple

Golden Gate

Dominus
Flevit

Kikar
Zahal

CHRISTIAN

Church of the
Khanqa

Church of
St Mary Magdalene

Pater Noster
Church

Mamila

QUARTER
Muristan

Church of
Holy Sepulchre

Dome of
the Rock

Church of
Redeemer

Tomb of
Absalom

© Baedeker

ERKAZ
S'HARI

Jaffa Gate
Citadel

Western Wall

Mount

Jacob's Cave

Tombs of
Prophets

Bethphage

ARMENIAN

Christ Church

JEWISH

Tomb of
Zachariah

erod's
amily Tomb

QUARTER

St James's
Cathedral

QUARTER

El-Aqsa
Mosque

Dung Gate

OPHEL

**Mount of
Olives**

YEMIN
MOSHE

Zion Gate

Church of
Dormition

Gihon
Spring

Derekh

Ha-Shiloah

Derekh Yeriho

ikar
ner

Montefiore
Windmill

Tomb of David

St. Peter
in Gallicantu

Matki Zedek

Shiloah

David

Hativat Yerushalayi

Mount Zion

SILWAN

St Andrew's
Church

Khan

Hinnom Valley

tation

Church of the Dormition
Mount Zion
Open: daily 8am–noon and 2–6pm

Church of the Holy Sepulchre
Old City
Open: daily 4.30am–8pm (in winter to 9pm)

Church of the Redeemer
Muristan, Old City
Open: Mon. 9am–12.45pm, Tues.–Sat. 9am–12.45pm and 2–4.45pm

Citadel
Old City, at Jaffa Gate
Open: Sun.–Thur. 10am–5pm (June–Aug. to 7pm), Fri. and Sat. 10am–2pm

City of David and Warren's Shaft
(excavation site)
Kidron valley, above Gihon Spring
Open: Sun.–Thur. 9am–4pm, Fri. 9am–2pm

Coenaculum
Mount Zion
Open: daily 8.30am to sunset

Convent of the Olive-Tree
Armenian Quarter, Old City
Open: Mon.–Fri. 8am–5pm

David Palombo Museum
Mount Zion
Visit by appointment (tel. 71 09 17)
Israeli sculpture

David's Tomb
Mount Zion
Open: Sun.–Thur. 8am to sunset, Fri. 8am–1pm

David's Tower
See Citadel

Dome of the Rock
Temple Mount, Old City
Open: Sat.–Thur. 8am–3pm (Ramadan 8–11am)

El-Aqsa Mosque
Temple Mount, Old City
Open: Sat.–Thur. 8am–3pm (Ramadan 8–11am)

Garden Tomb
Shechem (Nablus) Road
Open: Mon.–Sat. 8am–noon and 2.30–5pm

Gethsemane
at foot of Mount of Olives
Open: daily 8.30am–noon and 3–7pm (in winter 2 to 4 or 5pm)

Gihon Spring and Hezekiah's Tunnel
Kidron valley, at foot of Mount Ophel
Open: Sun.–Thur. 9am–4pm (in winter to 2pm), Fri. 9am–1pm

Hadassah Medical Centre
Qiryat Hadassah, En Karem
Open: Sun.–Thur. 8am–1.30pm and 2–4pm

Hall of Heroes
Russian Compound
Open: Sun.–Thur. 9am–4pm, Fri. 10am–1pm
The Hall of Heroes, in the former Central Prison with its cells and places of execution, commemorates the Jewish resistance fighters of the Mandate period.

Hall of Martyrs
Mount Zion
Open: Sun.–Thur. 9am–6pm, Fri. 9am–1.30pm
A memorial to the Jewish victims of the Nazis

Haram esh-Sharif
See Temple Mount

Hebrew University
Givat Ram campus
Conducted tours: Sun.–Fri. at 9 and 11am, starting from the administration building
Mount Scopus campus
Conducted tours: Sun.–Fri. at 11am, starting from the Allen Bronsman Family Reception Centre

Herodian houses
(excavation site)
Jewish Quarter, Old City
Open: Sun.–Thur. 9am–5pm, Fri. 9am–1pm

Herod's Family Tomb
Aba Siora (near King David Hotel)
Open: daily

Herzl Museum
Herzl Boulevard
Open: Sun.–Thur. 9am–5pm, Fri. 9am–1pm (park from 8am)

Hezekiah's Tunnel
See Gihon Spring and Hezekiah's Tunnel

Holocaust Museum
See Yad Vashem

Holy Sepulchre
See Church of the Holy Sepulchre

Hurva Synagogue
See Ramban and Hurva Synagogues

Islamic Museum
Temple Mount, Old City
Open: Sun.–Thur. 10am–1pm and 3.30–6pm, Sat. 10am–1pm

Israel Museum
Ruppin Road
Open: Sun., Mon., Wed. and Thur. 10am–5pm, Tues. 4–10pm (in summer from 10am), Fri. and Sat. 10am–2pm

Jason's Tomb
10 Alfasi Street
Open: Mon. and Thur. 10am–1pm

Jerusalem Museum
See Citadel

Ancient sarcophagus in the Israel Museum

Kings' Tombs
See Tombs of the Kings

Knesset (Israeli Parliament)
Ruppin Road
Conducted tours: Sun. and Thur. 8.30am–2.30pm

Last Supper, Room of the
See Coenaculum

Mayer Institute of Islamic Art
See Museum of Islamic Art

Model of Ancient Jerusalem
in garden of Holyland Hotel, Bayit WeGan
Open: daily 8am–5pm

Monastery of the Cross
Hayim Hazaz Boulevard
Open: Sat.–Thur. 9am–5pm, Fri. 9am–1pm

Montefiore Museum
in Montefiore Windmill, Yemin Moshe
Open: Sun.–Thur. 9am–4pm, Fri. 9am–1pm

Municipal Museum
See Citadel

Museum of Armenian Art and History
Old City, Armenian Quarter
Open: Mon.–Sat. 11am–4.30pm

Museum of the Divided City
See Turgemanposten Museum

Museum of Islamic Art
2 Palmach Street
Open: Sun.–Thur. 10am–5pm, Sat. 10am–1pm
Islamic art of many periods and from many countries, including ceramics,
carpets, textiles, miniatures and graphic art

Museum of Musical Instruments
(Rubin Academy of Music)
7 Smolenskin Street
Open: Sun.–Fri. 9am–1pm

Nahon Museum
27 Hillel Street
Open: Sun. 10am–noon, Wed. 4–7pm
Ancient Jewish cult objects, housed in an 18th century Italian synagogue

Natural History Museum
6 Mohiliver Street, German Colony
Open: Sun.–Thur. 8.30am–1pm, Wed. also 4–6pm
Birds, mammals; special anatomical section; numerous dioramas and
working models

Old Yishuv Court Museum
Or Hahayyim Street (Old City, Jewish Quarter)
Open: Sun.–Thur. 9am–4pm
In a restored 19th century house the way of life of the Jewish inhabitants of
the Old City from the 19th century to 1948 is illustrated with displays of
everyday objects, authentic interiors, etc.

Ophel Archaeological Park
(excavation site)
below the southern wall of the Temple precinct; entrance at Dung Gate
Open: Sun.–Thur. 9am–4pm, Fri. 9am–2pm

Papal Biblical Institute
2 Emile Botta Street
Open: Mon., Wed. and Fri. 9am–noon

Pool of Bethesda
(excavation site)
Old City, adjoining St Anne's Church
Open: daily 8am–noon and 2–6pm (in winter to 5pm)

Pool of Siloam
Kidron valley
Open: Sun.–Thur. 9am–4pm, Fri. 9am–1pm

Ramban and Hurva Synagogues
Jewish Quarter, Old City
Open: Sun.–Thur. 9am–5pm, Fri. 9am–1pm

Rockefeller Museum
1 Suleiman Street
Open: Sun.–Thur. 11am–5pm, Fri. and Sat. 10am–2pm

Roman Gate and Plaza
(excavation site)
at Damascus Gate
Open: Sat.–Thur. 9am–5pm, Fri. 9am–2pm

Rubin Academy of Music
See Museum of Musical Instruments

St Anne's Church
Old City, near Lion Gate
Open: daily 8am–noon and 2–6pm (in winter to 5pm)

St James's Cathedral
Armenian Quarter, Old City
Open: Mon.–Fri. 3–3.30pm, Sat. and Sun. 2.30–3.15pm

St Mark's Monastery
south-west of Old City
Open: Mon.–Sat. 9am–noon and 3.30–6pm

St Peter in Gallicantu
Malki Zedeq
Open: Mon.–Sat. 8.30–11.45am and 2–5.30pm (in winter to 5pm)

St Stephen's Monastery
Shechem (Nablus) Road
Open: daily 7.30am–1pm and 3–6pm

Schocken Institute
6 Balfour Street
Open: Sun.–Thur. 9am–1pm
Jewish illuminated manuscripts of the 13th century onwards; autographs;
some 50 incunabula

Sephardic Synagogues
Jewish Quarter, Old City
Open: Sun.–Thur. 9am–3pm, Fri. 9am–1pm

Siloam, Pool of
See Pool of Siloam

Solomon's Quarries
See Zedekiah's Cave

Taxation Museum
32 Agron Street
Open: Sun., Tues. and Thur. 1–4pm, Mon., Wed. and Fri. 10am–noon

Temple Mount
Old City
Open: Sat.–Thur. 8am to sunset

Ticho House
7–9 Harav Kook Street
Open: Sun., Mon., Wed. and Thur. 10am–5pm, Tues. 10am–10pm
Pictures by the artist Anna Ticho and a collection of Judaica

Tomb of the Virgin Mary
at foot of Mount of Olives
Open: daily 6.30am–noon and 2–5pm

Tombs of the Kings
Saladin Street
Open: daily 8am–12.30pm and 2–5pm

Tombs of the Prophets
on Mount of Olives
Opening times irregular (enquire of family living there)

Tombs of the Sanhedrin
Sanhedriya
Open: daily 9am to sunset

Town Walls (circuit)
Entrances at Jaffa and Damascus Gates
Open: Sat.–Thur. 9am–5pm, Fri. 9am–3pm

Turgemanposten Museum
1 Hel Hahandasa Street
Open: Sun.–Thur. 9am–4pm, Fri. 9am–1pm
The history of the divided and then reunited city of Jerusalem (photographs, documents, audiovisual shows), in a house which for nineteen years was a frontier post.

University
See Hebrew University

Warren's Shaft
See City of David and Warren's Shaft

Wilson's Arch
at Western Wall
Open: Sun., Tues. and Wed. 8.30am–3pm, Mon. and Thur. 12.30–3pm, Fri. 9am–1pm

Wolfson Museum
Chief Rabbinate, 58 King George Street
Open: Sun.–Thur. 9am–1pm, Fri. 9am–noon

Yad Vashem
Har Hazikkaron
Open: Sun.–Thur. 9am–4.45pm, Fri. 9am–1.45pm

Yishuv Court Museum
See Old Yishuv Court Museum

Zedekiah's Cave
Sultan Suleiman Street (between Damascus Gate and Herod's Gate)
Open: daily 9am–2pm

Zoo
See Biblical Zoo

Sights

From the Jaffa Gate to the Western Wall (Wailing Wall)

The Jaffa Gate (Hebrew Sha'ar Yafo; Arabic Bab el-Khalil, the Hebron Gate), through which the road to Jaffa leaves Jerusalem, is the link between the Old City and the new Jewish town to the west and apart from the Damascus Gate is the most important means of access to the Old City, declared by UNESCO in 1981 a cultural monument which must be preserved. The gate is set in the circuit of walls built by Sultan Suleiman the Magnificent in the 16th century. The gap in the walls to the right of the gate was opened up by the Turkish authorities in 1898 to allow the German Emperor and Empress to drive into the Old City; it now enables motor traffic to enter.

Jaffa Gate

Immediately south of the Jaffa Gate is the Citadel, popularly known as David's Tower (though strictly speaking this is only one of its towers). It has, however, no connection with David, having been erected by Herod to

★Citadel

Citadel in the Old City of Jerusalem

protect the palace he built around 24 B.C. to the south of the Citadel. Its three towers were named after Herod's brother Phasael, his wife Mariamne and his friend Hippicus. After Titus's conquest of Jerusalem in A.D. 70 the Romans stationed a garrison in the Citadel. Thereafter it fell into disrepair and was successively repaired and rebuilt by Crusaders, Mamelukes and Turks. What is now called David's Tower was built in the 14th century on the foundations of Phasael's Tower; the north-west tower occupies the site of Hippicus's Tower.

The Citadel now houses a museum on the history of Jerusalem and a folk museum and has some interesting excavations. From the Citadel, and particularly from David's Tower, there are superb views of the city.

In the evening (except on Friday) an impressive *son et lumière* show on the history of Jerusalem is presented in the Citadel.

Christ Church

Opposite the entrance to the Citadel is Christ Church (Anglican), built in 1849.

Armenian Quarter

Just beyond the Citadel we come into Armenian Patriarchate Street, which runs south through the Armenian Quarter of the Old City. After passing a police station (on right) we turn left into St James Street and then left again into Ararat Street, which leads to the Syrian monastery of St Mark.

St Mark's Monastery

The monastery's richly ornamented 12th century church is traditionally believed to occupy the site of the house belonging to Mary, mother of Mark the Evangelist, where Peter took refuge after escaping from the prison in which he had been confined by Herod Agrippa I (Acts 12,12–17). Just inside the church, to the right, is an inscription in Aramaic, and in the nave are a silver-mounted font and above this an icon of the Virgin which the monks ascribe to Luke the Evangelist (who is believed in the Eastern church to have painted the earliest, and therefore the authentic, icon of the Mother of God). There is also a richly carved patriarchal throne.

Returning to Armenian Patriarchate Street and continuing south, we come to the Monastery of the Armenian Patriarchate (on left), the largest monastic house in Jerusalem and the spiritual centre of the Armenians, of whom there are some 3500 in the city.

Monastery of the Armenian Patriarchate

St James's Cathedral dates from the time of the Crusades (12th c.). The porch on the south side has a fine doorway of that period.
The church has associations with two St Jameses. A chapel to the left of the entrance is believed to mark the spot where St James the Great, son of Zebedee, was beheaded in A.D. 44 on the orders of Herod Agrippa I (Acts 12,2). According to the traditional account his body was transported by his disciples to Spain, where it later became the centre of the cult of St James (Santiago) in the city which bears his name, Santiago de Compostela. Below the high altar is the tomb of the other St James, the Lord's Brother and the first bishop of Jerusalem, who was stoned to death in 62.
On the south side of the cathedral is a doorway leading into the Etchmiadzin Chapel, in which stones from Sinai and Mount Tabor are preserved.

St James's Cathedral

Near the south end of Armenian Patriarchate Street, approached by a flight of steps, is the Museum of Armenian Art and History, with a collection of documents on the history of the Armenian people, cult objects and works of art (including the sceptre of the last Armenian king, dating from the 14th century, liturgical vestments, crowns, etc.). The museum also possesses some 4000 illuminated manuscripts of the 10th–17th centuries.

Armenian Museum

Then, going past the Gulbenkian Library, through an arched gateway and turning right, we come to a chapel (1300) on the site of the house of Annas, father-in-law of the high priest Caiaphas, and the Convent of the Olive-Tree (Deir ez-Zeituni), where visitors are shown an olive-tree to which Christ is said to have been tied before appearing before the high priest.

House of Annas

Convent of the Olive-Tree

From here we continue south and then turn left (east) along the inside of the town walls, past the Zion Gate (from which roads run down into the Hinnom and Kidron valleys and up to Mount Zion), into the Jewish Quarter. This part of the Old City was laid in ruins during the Israeli–Arab fighting in 1948 and subsequently, and was rebuilt after 1967. Turning left into the second street of some size, Jewish Quarter Street (Rehov HaYehudim), and heading north, we pass a number of synagogues (on right) which have been rebuilt in recent years.

★**Jewish Quarter**

The first of these is the Ramban Synagogue, the first to be built in the Old City, founded in 1267 by Rabbi Moshe Ben Nahman Ramban (Nachmanides), who came to the Holy Land from Spain.

Ramban Synagogue

Immediately north of this are the remains of the Hurva Synagogue, founded by Rabbi Yehuda Hanassi, who came from Poland in 1701 with 500 Ashkenazis. The Jewish community in Jerusalem was now split in two, and the Ashkenazis built their own synagogue. After Rabbi Hanassi's death the synagogue fell into ruin (hurva = "ruin") and was rebuilt only in 1856. Thereafter, until its destruction in 1948, the synagogue again became the spiritual centre of Jerusalem's Ashkenazi Jews. After 1967 there were various plans for rebuilding it, but it was never fully restored. It now consists only of a domed central structure and a reconstructed arch, a landmark and emblem of the whole quarter and a reminder of the synagogue's former splendour

Hurva Synagogue

To the west of the Ramban and Hurva Synagogues are steps leading down to the Cardo Maximus, one of the city's two principal streets in Roman and Byzantine times. Excavated between 1976 and 1985 for a length of just under 200m/220yds, it now lies 6m/20ft below the modern ground level and accordingly runs underground for part of its course. As the reproduction of a 6th century mosaic pavement which is displayed here shows, it was a

Cardo Maximus

Jerusalem/Yerushalayim

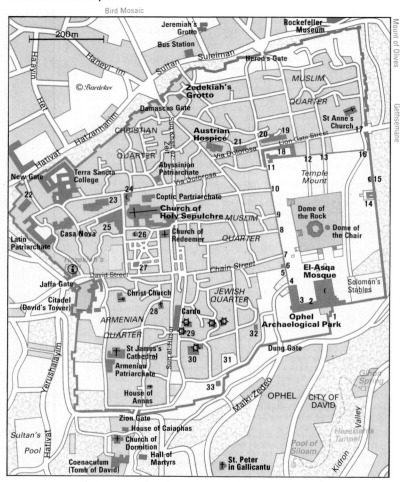

Jerusalem: Old City

In the Jewish Quarter

On the Roman cardo maximus

magnificent avenue flanked by columns supporting a roof and lined with shops; and indeed one section of the old cardo is now again a fashionable shopping street.

Turning south from the Ramban Synagogue, we come in a few yards to a little street on the left leading to the Sephardic synagogues, which were rebuilt in 1967 on the basis of old plans and have largely been restored to their original 17th and 18th century form. The Yohanan Ben Zakkai Synagogue is named after a rabbi of the Roman period. The name of the Eliahu Hanavi Synagogue commemorates the association of the site with the prophet Elijah. The Emtzai (Middle) Synagogue, the smallest of them all, was originally only the vestibule to the others. The Istanbuli Synagogue formerly belonged to Turkish Jews.

Sephardic synagogues

North-east of this complex is another important excavation site on which a number of houses built in the reign of Herod the Great (40–4 B.C.) and destroyed in A.D. 70 during the Jewish War have been brought to light. The size and magnificence of the houses, in particular the mosaic pavements (some of them excellently preserved) and the elaborate bath-houses, bear witness to the wealth of their owners. There is a site museum displaying frescoes, stucco decoration and remains of mosaic pavements as well as domestic equipment and luxury objects found in the excavations.

Herodian houses

Near here is the "Burnt House", which was also destroyed by the Romans in A.D. 70. There are relatively few archaeological finds to be seen here, but an audio-visual show which is presented several times daily gives a vivid picture of the history of the Jewish Quarter in the time of Herod and its destruction by the Romans.

Burnt House

Opposite the Burnt House are the remains of the Tiferet Israel ("Glory of Israel") Synagogue, the principal Chassidic synagogue, and the Court of the Karaites, the Jewish sect which rejects the authority of the Talmud.

Tiferet Israel

**★★Western Wall
(Wailing Wall)**

Continuing past the Porat Josef Synagogue, we come to the holiest Jewish site, the Wailing Wall or Western Wall (Kotel HaMa'aravi), as it is now officially known. This massive stretch of wall, 48m/52yds long by 18m/60ft high, is part of the retaining wall on the south-west side of the Temple platform. Since 1967 a densely built-up area in front of the wall has been cleared to make a large open space. The section of this area nearest the wall has been railed off and ranks as a synagogue, in which men go to the left and women to the right. This is where great religious ceremonies take place and army recruits are sworn in. The Wailing Wall was so called because of the Jews' laments for the destruction of the Temple. In the past it was the only part of the Temple area from which they were almost always excluded. Nowadays pious Jews do not go up on to the Temple Mount, as they are now able to do, since the position of the Holy of Holies, which could be entered only by the high priests, is not known.

Wilson's Arch

A vaulted passage at the north-east corner of the Western Wall leads along the Herodian walls to Wilson's Arch (below the present Chain Gate), which spanned the Tyropoeon valley and gave access to the Temple. A square shaft cut down under the arch allows visitors to see the massive foundations of the walls, with fourteen courses of dressed stone below the present ground level.

**Ophel
Archaeological
Park**

To the south and south-east of the Western Wall, below the south wall of the Temple precinct, is the Ophel Archaeological Park, an area in which Israeli archaeologists have made important discoveries since 1968. A little to the south of the Western Wall is Robinson's Arch (so called after its American discoverer), which was not, as originally thought, an arch carrying an access route to the Temple, like Wilson's Arch, but rather part of a flight of steps leading up to the Temple platform. In 1971 a 2m/6½ft high stone from the south-west corner of the Temple platform was found near here, 35m/115ft below the top of the enclosure wall, from which it had presum-

Jews at the Western Wall

ably tumbled during the destruction of the Temple in A.D. 70. This corner-stone, which is mentioned by Flavius Josephus, has a recess in which it is thought the priest stood to proclaim the beginning and end of the Sabbath. In the eastern part of the Archaeological Park can be seen the steps leading up to the Huldah Gates, from which there was access, under Herod's Stoa Basilike, to the Temple platform.

In the southern part of the area the remains of a two-storey palace covering an area of some 1000sq.m/1075sq.yds were discovered in 1975. It has been identified as the palace of Queen Helen of Adiabene (in northern Meso-potamia), who became a convert to the Jewish faith around A.D. 50 and came to live in Jerusalem.

From here we return to the open space in front of the Western Wall and take a narrow street at the north-east corner which runs into Chain Street. Turning left along this, we cross Khan ez-Zeit Street and continue along David Street, a busy thoroughfare lined with shops and cafés, to return to the Jaffa Gate. (An alternative possibility is to turn right into Khan ez-Zeit Street, which runs north to the Damascus Gate.)

Temple Mount

To the east of the Western Wall is the Temple Mount, the holiest place on earth for Jews. Yet Israel gave full administration of this area over to the Arabs after the 1967 war in the interests of peace. The old Temple precinct of the Jews (known to the Arabs as Haram esh-Sharif, the Noble Sanctuary) is also the most important Islamic shrine after Mecca and Medina.

Nowhere else do the holy places of the three monotheistic world religions lie so close together as here. Sacred both to Jews and Muslims, the precinct is also important to Christians, for it was here that the infant Jesus was presented in the Temple (Luke 2,22), that the twelve-year-old boy disputed with the scribes (Luke 2,46) and that he later cast out the merchants and money-changers (Matthew 21,12); and it was on a pinnacle of the Temple that he was tempted by the devil (Matthew 4,5).

The story of this sacred precinct, in which myth, miracle and history are combined, begins with Abraham. Having journeyed westward from Ur on the lower Euphrates, he and his tribe were living in Beersheba when God commanded him to sacrifice his son Isaac on Mount Moriah (Genesis 22). It is generally accepted that this was the hill on which the Temple was later built. Abraham followed the Lord's instructions, travelled the 85km/53 miles to Jerusalem in three days and prepared for the sacrifice; but follow-ing divine intervention Isaac was spared and a ram sacrificed in his place. This can be seen as a mythic account of the replacement of human by animal sacrifice. The event is probably to be dated to the 18th century B.C. About 1000 B.C. David took the Jebusite town which then occupied the site, built an altar on the threshing-floor of a Jebusite named Nachon and set up the Ark of the Covenant there (2 Samuel 6).

David's son Solomon (960–926 B.C.) built the First Temple on the site, along with a palace (1 Kings 5–6). This was the first large building erected by the Israelites, and since they had no experience in the practice of architecture Solomon sought the help of Hiram, the Phoenician king of Tyre. In return for 20,000 measures of wheat and 20 measures of pure oil a year Hiram supplied cedarwood from Lebanon and skilled builders. Accordingly the Temple showed the characteristics of Phoenician architecture: details like the pillars called Boaz and Jachin in the forecourt have their exact counter-parts in the temples of the pre-Israelite, Canaanite population (eg. the temple of the 20th–19th century B.C. at Hazor: see entry) as well as in much later temples of Baal like the one at Palmyra.

The Temple was begun in the fourth year of Solomon's reign and com-pleted in seven years (i.e. in 950 B.C.). It was 27m/89ft long, 10m/33ft wide and 14m/46ft high. In front of it was a forecourt 4.50m/15ft deep, and it had side chambers for the temple treasury and the priests' robes. The main

History

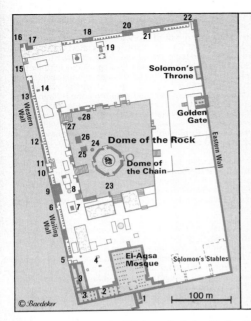

Jerusalem
Temple Mount

1 Double Gate
2 White Mosque
3 Islamic Museum
4 Dome of Yusuf
5 Bab el-Magharibeh
6 Bab es-Silsileh (Chain Gate)
7 Dome of Moses
8 Fountain of Qaitbay
9 Medrese
10 Bab-el-Mastarak
11 Bab-el-Qattanin
12 Bab-el-Hadid (Iron Gate)
13 Bab en-Nazir
14 Fountain of Ala ed-Din el-Basir
15 Bab el-Ghawanima
16 Minaret
17 Medrese el-Malakiyeh
18 Bab el-Atim
19 Fountain of Sultan Suleiman
20 Bab Hitta
21 Medrese el-Gahdiriyeh
22 Bab el-Asbat
23 Pulpit
24 Prayer Niche of the Prophet
25 Dome of the Ascension
26 Dome of Hebron
27 Dome of St George
28 Dome of the Spirits

chamber (hekal) was 18m/59ft long, the holy of holies (debis) beyond it 9m/29½ft long. The walls were panelled with cedarwood and gilded. In the main chamber was the altar, in the holy of holies the Ark of the Covenant, guarded by two golden cherubim whose wings stretched from wall to wall. In this sumptuously furnished temple the priests appointed by Solomon, the Zadoks, offered up prayers and sacrifices. The altar for burnt offerings was the topmost point of the rock of Mount Moriah, which was incorporated in the Temple.

Solomon's Temple stood for almost 400 years until its destruction by Nebuchadnezzar in 587 B.C. After the Israelites' return from the Babylonian Captivity they removed the debris and built the Second Temple, which was completed in 516 B.C. Its measurements are given in the book of Ezra (6,3); it was probably less sumptuously appointed than the First Temple.

In the course of time, particularly during the conflicts with the Seleucid rulers which led to the Maccabean rebellion, the Temple seems to have suffered severe damage, and Herod (37–4 B.C.), anxious to demonstrate to the Jews his piety and his respect for the Law, had it rebuilt. Like the First Temple, the third one borrowed ideas from another culture. Herod combined the requirements of Jewish worship with Hellenistic and Roman architectural features, as in other Semitic temples of the period (e.g. at Palmyra and Petra).

Herod began by enlarging the size of the Temple precinct to its present dimensions (300m/330yds by 480m/525yds). To achieve this it was necessary to build massive piers and substructures (now known as Solomon's Stables), since the ground fell steeply away on the south side, and build up

◄ *The Dome of the Rock and the El-Kas fountain*

the ground with imported soil. The enlarged area was surrounded by massive walls of dressed stone, which are still visible on the east and south sides and the southern half of the west side. At the south-east corner they rise to a height of 65m/215ft above the Kidron valley. Along these walls were colonnaded halls (stoas), the one on the south side, the Stoa Basilike (Royal Stoa), being particularly magnificent with its four rows of Corinthian columns. There were numerous entrances to the Temple precinct: one on the east side, at the point where the Golden Gate now stands; on the south side, under the Royal Stoa, the Huldah Gates which were brought to light by excavations from 1967 onwards; on the west side the Warren and Barclay Gates (named after their discoverers) and Wilson's Arch, carrying a causeway over the Tyropoeon valley; and at the south-west corner Robinson's Arch, recently re-excavated, to which a flight of steps led up.

The outer forecourt was a place for secular life and trade, open to all. On a higher level was the inner forecourt, which only Jews could enter. It was divided into three parts: the Women's Court, the Court of Israel (which only men could enter) and the Priests' Court. In the Priests' Court, probably over the sacred rock, stood the large horned altar on which animal sacrifices were offered.

Beyond this was the Temple, of which Flavius Josephus gives a detailed description ("Jewish War", V,4–6). The façade, of white marble, had golden capitals and a golden door lintel decorated with vine tendrils; it was 50m/165ft wide – 20m/65ft more than the building behind it – and 50m/165ft high. The front part had no doorways, for, according to Flavius Josephus, it was "designed to symbolise the infinite dimensions of heaven". In the rear part were a seven-branched candlestick and a censer and beyond these a curtain concealing the Holy of Holies, the dwelling-place of the invisible God. "The external aspect of the Temple offered everything that could delight the eye and the heart. Sheathed in heavy gold plate on every side, it shimmered at sunrise with the utmost brilliance and dazzled the eye like the rays of the sun": again the words of Flavius Josephus, who also describes the forms of worship in his time and the destruction of the Temple by the Romans in A.D. 70, barely a hundred years after its construction.

This was the last Temple. After its destruction the offering of sacrifices ceased; the priests gave place to rabbis; the synagogue became the place of meeting for prayer; and the only reminder of the Temple was the Wailing Wall. The Temple precinct is now a Muslim shrine.

Before the Muslims took over, however, Jerusalem was held by Christians. In the 4th century Constantine the Great built churches over the Holy Sepulchre and on the Mount of Olives, and in the 6th century Justinian dedicated a church to the Mother of God. Justinian's church had a roof structure of large cedar beams; according to Procopius (De Aedificiis, V,6) it stood on the Temple platform.

After the Muslim armies conquered Jerusalem in 638 Omar – originally a bitter opponent of Mohammed and later his second successor (Caliph = "Successor") – visited the city. Simply dressed, and accompanied by Archbishop Sophronius, he entered the Temple precinct and said a prayer on Abraham's rock. This to the Muslims was sacred, for the 17th sura of the Koran tells of the Prophet's miraculous night journey "from the holy temple in Mecca to the distant temple" in Jerusalem; from the rock of Moriah Mohammed ascended to the seven heavens, and from there returned to Mecca.

To the Muslims, therefore, the Haram esh-Sharif is a place of great significance. It has acquired further associations in the present century, for King

Hussein I (1853–1931), a pioneer of the contemporary Arab movement, was buried here and in 1951 his successor Abdullah was murdered here.

The brilliant period of the Omayyad Caliphs, whose capital was in Damascus, saw the erection on the Temple platform of the two buildings which have become the landmarks and emblems of Jerusalem – the Dome of the Rock, built over the rock of Moriah by Abd el-Malik in 687–691, and the El-Aqsa Mosque, converted by his son El-Walid I (705–715) from Justinian's church dedicated to the Mother of God.

The period of Muslim rule on the Temple Mount was interrupted by the coming of the Crusaders, who held Jerusalem from 1099 to 1187 and plundered the Dome of the Rock and the El-Aqsa Mosque (less generous than Caliph Omar, who had spared the church of the Holy Sepulchre). The first kings of Jerusalem resided in the El-Aqsa Mosque, but later made it over to the Order of the Temple (founded 1149), which took its name from the Templum Salomonis (El-Aqsa) and Templum Domini (Dome of the Rock).

After Jerusalem was recaptured for Islam by Saladin in 1187 there was much further building on the Temple platform, particularly by the Mamelukes. The Dome of the Rock was damaged by grenades during the fighting between Israelis and Arabs in 1948 but was restored, with a new golden dome, by Jordan, Egypt and Saudi Arabia between 1958 and 1964. During the Six Day War Israeli troops reached the Wailing Wall on June 7th 1967, since when it has been freely accessible again to Jews.

The walls enclosing the Temple Mount reach their highest point (65m/213ft) at the south-east corner, where there is a clear view of the massive blocks of dressed stone of the Herodian walls and the overlying courses of smaller stones of later restorations and rebuildings.   *The walls*
The entrances to the Temple Mount for non-Muslims are on the west side, in the 490m/535yd long stretch of wall extending southward from the Antonia fortress. In addition to Bab el-Magharibeh there are six other gates, the most important of which are the Chain Gate (Bab es-Silsileh), the Cotton-Merchants' Gate (Bab el-Qattanin) with its stalactitic corbelling, the Iron Gate (Bab el-Hadid) and the Watchman's Gate (Bab en-Nazir), the entrance for visitors coming from the Damascus Gate by way of King Solomon Street and Ala-ud-Din Street.

On the western and northern walls of the Haram esh-Sharif are four minarets, at the south-west corner (1278, altered 1622), above Bab es-Silsileh (1329), at the north-west corner (1297) and – the youngest of the four – on the north wall (1937).

Entering the Haram esh-Sharif by the Moroccans' Gate (Bab el-Magharibeh), we find ourselves in a spacious square. On the west side of the square are arcaded buildings of the Mameluke period occupied by various Muslim institutions. In the building between Bab el-Qattanin and Bab el-Hadid are a number of tombs, including that of King Hussein I Ibn Ali (1853–1931).   *Temple platform*
Hussein was a member of the Hashemite family, descended from Mohammed's grandfather Hashem, which ruled in Mecca from the 10th century. In 1916 he declared his independence from the Ottoman Empire, calling himself king of Arabia (though he was recognised only as king of the Hejaz), and in 1924 took the style of Caliph. In October 1924 he gave up both dignities in favour of his son Ali, who at the end of 1925 was compelled to resign authority over Arabia to Ibn Saud of the Wahabite tribe. Hussein's second son Abdullah (b. 1882), ruler of Transjordan from 1921 and king of Jordan from 1948, was assassinated in 1951 when entering the El-Aqsa Mosque with his grandson Hussein, the present king of Jordan. His younger brother Feisal (1883–1933) became king of Syria in 1920 and king of Iraq in 1921.

The principal buildings on the Temple platform are the El-Aqsa Mosque and the Dome of the Rock.

★El-Aqsa Mosque

The El-Aqsa Mosque (Masjid el-Aqsa) and its subsidiary buildings, the Museum of Islamic Art by the Moroccans' Gate and the prayer halls for women, occupy most of the south side of the Haram esh-Sherif. Its prayer niche (mihrab) faces south, in the direction of Mecca. The mosque was built by the Omayyad Caliph El-Walid I (705–715) on the site of Justinian's basilica dedicated to the Mother of God. The Crusaders took it for Solomon's Temple, and the Jews call it Solomon's School (Midrash Shelomo). It has been several times restored and renovated, most recently between 1938 and 1943, when columns of white Carrara marble supplied by Mussolini were installed and a new ceiling was built at the expense of King Farouk of Egypt.

The mosque (excluding the subsidiary buildings) is 80m/260ft long by 55m/180ft wide. In 1967 it was damaged by gunfire and in 1969 by fire, but has since been restored.

The interior with its seven aisles is impressive. The 12th century carved wooden pulpit, which was badly damaged in the 1969 fire (since restored), was a gift from Saladin, who also presented the beautiful mosaic on a gold ground in the drum supporting the dome. The mihrab (prayer niche) with its graceful marble colonnettes dates from the same period. Built on to the west side of the transept is the White Mosque (the women's mosque), which dates from the time of the Templars.

Ablutions fountain

Going north from El-Aqsa, we pass the large circular ablutions fountain (El-Kas) and climb a broad flight of steps leading to the upper platform.

"Scales"

The steps, like those on the other sides of the platform, are spanned by handsome pointed arches of the Mameluke period. They are known to Muslims as the "Scales", since it is believed that on the day of judgment the scales in which the souls of men will be weighed will be set up here.

The El-Aqsa Mosque on the Temple Mount

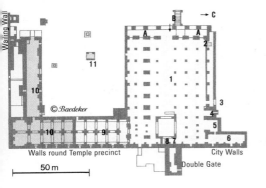

Jerusalem
El-Aqsa Mosque

A Porch
B Steps to underground rooms
C Steps to "Christ's Cradle"

1 Prayer hall
2 Fountain
3 Gate of Elias
4 Mihrab of Zechariah
5 Mosque of the Forty Martyrs
6 Mosque of Omar
7 Mihrab (prayer niche)
8 Minbar (pulpit)
9 White Mosque (Women's Mosque)
10 **Islamic Mosque**
11 Dome of Yusuf

Walls round Temple precinct   City Walls

50 m

Double Gate

At the top of the steps, on left, is a marble summer pulpit constructed during the Mameluke period, using colonnettes from a Crusader building.

We now come to the Dome of the Rock (Qubbet el-Sakhra), one of the greatest of Muslim monuments, still sometimes called the Mosque of Omar – wrongly, because it is not a mosque and does not date from the time of Caliph Omar. It was built by Abd el-Malik (685–705), the fifth Omayyad Caliph: an octagonal structure with a high dome over the sacred rock of Moriah. The impressive effect of the Dome of the Rock results from the combination of fine proportions and sumptuous decoration with an apparently simple ground-plan consisting of three concentric elements. Round the rock is a ring of piers and columns supporting the dome; a broad ambulatory separates this ring from an octagon, also formed by piers and columns; and this in turn is separated from the octagonal outer walls by a narrow ambulatory.

★★Dome of the Rock

K. A. C. Creswell discovered how the proportions of the building were worked out. Two squares were set out within the inner circle, one at an angle of 45 degrees to the other. If the sides of these squares were produced in both directions they met at eight points – the piers in the octagon between the two ambulatories. If the sides of the octagon were also produced in both directions they too met at eight points, forming two larger squares with sides parallel to the inner squares. If an outer circle was then described round the two larger squares and the sides of the inner octagon were extended outwards until they intersected this circle a larger octagon was formed, the line of the outer walls.

The diameter of the octagon is 54.8m/180ft, and each side of it has an external length of 20.5m/67ft (internal length 19.2m/63ft). The dome has a diameter of 23.7m/78ft and rises to 33m/108ft above the ground; it is topped by a crescent 3.6m/12ft high.

The exterior walls of the octagon were faced with superb faience tiles in the reign of Suleiman the Magnificent (1520–66); the elegant dome of gilded aluminium dates from the restoration of 1958–64.

Four doors, clad with copper by Qaitbay (1468–96), lead into the interior, which is exquisitely decorated, with richly ornamented wooden ceilings over the two ambulatories, magnificent marble piers and columns topped by antique capitals, two-coloured round-headed arches over the inner colonnade, stained glass windows filtering the light, mosaics on a gold ground in the inner rotunda and the ambulatories and luxuriant ornament on the dome. There is a striking contrast between the brightly coloured tiles which emphasise the solidity of the outer structure and the mysteriously shimmering mosaics in the interior.

Jerusalem

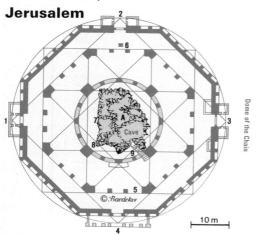

Dome of the Chain

Dome of the Rock

A **Holy Rock** (Es-Sakhra)

1 West Gate (Bab el-Gharb)
2 Gate of Paradise (Bab el-Jenneh)
3 David's Place of Judgment (Dome of the Chain)
4 South Gate (Bab el-Qibleh)
5 Mihrab (prayer niche)
6 Slab of jasper, said to have been the cover of Solomon's tomb, into which Mohammed drove twelve golden nails
7 Hand-print of the Archangel Gabriel, who prevented the Rock from following the Prophet in his ascension to heaven
8 Footprint of the Prophet
9 Steps down to the "Well of Souls" (Bir el-Arwah)

10 m

In the centre of the inner rotunda, rising to a height of 1.25–2m/4–6½ft above the floor, is Es-Sakhra, the Holy Rock, over which the Jews' altar for burnt offerings may have stood. Just under 18m/59ft long by 13.25m/43ft across, it is surrounded by a grille installed by the Crusaders in the 12th century to prevent relic-collectors from breaking off pieces of the stone. The best view of the Holy Rock is to be had from the high bench beside the

The Dome of the Rock: Islam's third most holy shrine

Dome of the Rock: detail of façade

Dome of the Ascension of the Prophet

Golden Gate

north-west gate in the grille. In Jewish belief the rock marks the spot where Abraham prepared to sacrifice Isaac, while the Muslims believe that it was from here that Mohammed ascended into heaven. Under the rock is a cave, known to Muslims as Bir el-Arwah ("Well of Souls"), where it is believed that the souls of the dead gather to pray.

Dome of the Chain

Immediately east of the Dome of the Rock is a small circular domed building known as David's Place of Judgment (Mehkemet Da'ud) or the Dome of the Chain (Qubbet es-Silsileh): so called because Solomon is said to have hung a chain over his father's place of judgment, from which a link would fall if any man appearing for judgment swore a false oath. The large mihrab (prayer niche) marking the direction of Mecca dates from the 13th century.

Other buildings round the Dome of the Rock

At the north-west corner of the raised platform on which the Dome of the Rock stands are a number of monuments (see plan, page 232): the Prayer Niche of the Prophet (Mihrab el-Nebi, 1538); the Dome of Hebron (Qubbet el-Khalil), a prayer hall built by the Sheikh of Hebron in the 19th century; and the Dome of the Ascension of the Prophet (Qubbet el-Miraj), built on the spot where, in Muslim tradition, Mohammed prayed before his ascent to heaven. In front of the arcading of the staircase at the north-west corner are the Dome of St George (Qubbet el-Khadir) and the Dome of the Spirits (Qubbet el-Arwah), which dates from the 15th century. The El-Kas fountain on the west side of the Dome of the Rock, below the broad flight of steps, was erected by the Mameluke Sultan Qaitbay in 1455.

Golden Gate

In the east wall of the Temple precinct is the Golden Gate, a double gateway built in the 7th century on the site of the Herodian Susa Gate. The Arabs call the southern entrance the Gate of Mercy (Bab el-Rameh), the northern one the Gate of Repentance (Bab el-Tobeh), reflecting the Jewish and Muslim belief that the Last Judgment would be held in the Kidron valley and on the Mount of Olives. The Jews believed that the Messiah would enter the city here; and accordingly – and undoubtedly also with strategic consider-ations in mind – the Arabs walled up both gateways and for good measure laid out a cemetery outside the gate.

Solomon's Stables

At the south-east corner of the sacred precinct is a flight of steps leading down to "Solomon's Stables" (usually closed), the substructures built by Herod to enlarge the Temple platform. Here 88 massive piers linked by arches form twelve parallel passages, which, as can be seen from the rings for tethering animals on many of the piers, were used by the Crusaders for stabling their horses.

From St Stephen's Gate to the Citadel

St Stephen's Gate (Lion Gate)

In the northern section of the wall on the east side of the Old City is St Stephen's Gate, where according to Christian tradition St Stephen suffered martyrdom. It is also known as the Lion Gate after the reliefs of lions on the outside, and in Arabic is called Bab Sitti Maryam, Gate of the Virgin Mary.

St Anne's Church

A few yards inside St Stephen's Gate, to the right, is St Anne's Church, a completely preserved church of the Crusader period. It was built in 1142 by Avda, widow of Baldwin I, the first king of Jerusalem, on the spot where the house of Joachim and Anne, Mary's parents, was believed to have stood. In 1192, a year after his conquest of Jerusalem, Saladin converted the church into a Koranic school. In 1856, in gratitude for French support during the Crimean War, the Ottoman Sultan Abdul Majid presented it to Napoleon III, and the interior was cleared of later additions.

A good view of the exterior, particularly the triangular apse, the transept and the shallow dome, from the east can be obtained by climbing a flight of steps on the town wall to the north of St Stephen's Gate. The church is built of small blocks of dressed stone, with small windows. It is entered through a severe doorway with a pointed arch between two buttresses. In the tympanum is an Arabic inscription dating from the time when the church was used as a Koranic school. The upper of the two windows above the doorway has similar decoration to the doorway of the Church of the Holy Sepulchre.

The interior of the church, a three-aisled basilica, is marked by austere monumentality. The nave, of three bays, is separated from the lower lateral aisles by arcades of pointed arches; the roof is groin-vaulted. There is a dome over the crossing, beyond which steps lead up to the sanctuary, with the high altar (by the French sculptor Philippe Kaeppelin, 1954). On the front of the altar are depicted the Nativity (left), the Descent from the Cross (centre) and the Annunciation (right); on the left-hand end is the teaching of Mary by her mother, on the right-hand end her presentation in the Temple. The decorative elements in the church are completely subordinated to the architecture and are confined to the capitals. On the first pillar on the left is a small cask, on the first on the right two sandals surmounted by a scroll (perhaps symbolising the marriage contract between Joachim and Anne). On other capitals are volutes and plant and leaf ornament, almost with the effect of Corinthian capitals. To the left of the principal apse is a human figure, to the right an ox (the attributes of the Evangelists Matthew and Luke), and on the semi-columns flanking the window in the apse are figures of animals.

In the south aisle is a flight of steps leading down to the crypt, in a grotto believed by the Crusaders to be Mary's birthplace (which according to tradition immediately adjoined the Pool of Bethesda).

The Pool of Bethesda lies in an excavated area immediately north-east of St Anne's Church. Here Jesus, who had come to Jerusalem for a Jewish feast, healed a man who had had an infirmity for 38 years (John, 5,1–9): "Jesus saith unto him, Rise, take up thy bed, and walk. And immediately the man was made whole." Jesus thus incurred the wrath of the pious Jews, for this took place on the Sabbath.

Pool of Bethesda

The pool by which the sick man lay was close to the Sheep Gate and was therefore known as the Sheep Pool (Piscina Probatica). John's reference to "five porches" at the pool seems to indicate that there was a portico on each side of the pool and a fifth on a rock division between its two halves, each 50m/165ft square and 13m/43ft deep. The water was credited with healing powers, and "an angel went down at a certain season into the pool and troubled the water", suggesting that the pool was fed by an intermittent spring.

By the pool, which no doubt originally served as a reservoir of water for the Temple precinct and in the time of Jesus was frequented by the sick and crippled, a temple of Aesculapius, the god of healing whose cult had spread from Epidaurus throughout the ancient world, was built in the 2nd century. The excavations which began in 1871 brought to light several votive offerings to the god, including a relief depicting the snake of Aesculapius and a model of a foot offered by a woman named Pompeia Lucilia.

In the 5th century the Byzantines built a three-aisled basilica here. The west end stood on the rock between the two halves of the pool, which was enlarged for the purpose by tall substructures, the east end on solid ground. This church was destroyed in the early 11th century; then in the 12th century the Crusaders built a chapel in the ruins of the north aisle.

The excavations have confirmed the topography as described in the New Testament and revealed remains of the various different periods: the two halves of the pool (now dry) and fragments of the rock division between the two halves, columns from the Roman temple of Aesculapius, the substructures and an arch from the façade of the Byzantine church, a mosaic with a representation of a gemmate cross from the martyrium in the church, etc. A general plan of the site, which is looked after by the French order of White Fathers, and labelling in French help visitors to find their way about.

Antonia Fortress

From here St Mary's Gate Street (Tariq Sitti Maryam) runs west to the site of the Antonia Fortress, built by Herod the Great and named after Mark Antony, who then ruled the eastern part of the Roman Empire.

The land here is higher than the Temple Mount to the south, and Herod accordingly chose this commanding situation for the erection of a strong fortress at the angle between the northern and western walls of the Temple precinct, on the site of the earlier Hasmonean stronghold of Baris.

The Antonia Fortress covered an area 100m/110yds by 160m/175yds and was surrounded by high battlemented walls. Flavius Josephus tells us in his "Jewish History" (V,5,8) that the fortress stood on a precipitous rock 33m/108ft high which was faced with polished stone slabs to a height of 27m/89ft. At the four corners were towers, the tallest of which, at the south-east corner, was almost 50m/165ft high, "so that from this tower the whole of the Temple precinct could be seen. Where it adjoined the Temple colonnades there were steps leading down to them, on which guards from the Roman unit which was always stationed in the fortress could descend, fully armed, to the colonnades in order to watch for any sign of disturbances among the population on days of festival". The interior "had the spaciousness and the appointments of a palace, for it was divided into apartments of every kind and purpose, with colonnades and baths and large courtyards, so that . . . in splendour it was like a royal palace".

The fortress stood for only a few decades. After Titus's conquest of Jerusalem in A.D. 70 it was pulled down. Parts of it, however, must have remained, for in the year 135, on the occasion of a visit by the Emperor Hadrian, a triumphal arch was built behind the main entrance on the west side. This, now known as the Ecce Homo Arch, still spans the Via Dolorosa. Other remains of the triumphal arch and of the Antonia (a cistern and the paving of the courtyard) can be seen in the Church of the Sisters of Zion.

Ecce Homo Arch

Continuing west from St Stephen's Gate along St Mary's Gate Street, we pass on the right the Chapel of the Flagellation (1927) and the Chapel of the Condemnation, marking the sites of events in Christ's Passion, and come to the Ecce Homo Arch, where, according to an old tradition, Pilate uttered the words "Behold the man!" (John 19,5).

Church of the Sisters of Zion

On the right is the entrance to the Church of the Sisters of Zion (Basilique des Dames de Sion). The church contains an explanatory model of the Antonia Fortress. A side arch of the Roman triumphal arch is built into the choir, producing a striking effect. Particularly impressive is a passage in the basement which runs past a large Herodian cistern into the crypt. Here we are on the original ground level: the floor of the crypt is the paving of a court in the Antonia Fortress, the pavement (*lithostrotos*) referred to in John 19,13. In the pavement are scratches made by Roman soldiers, including a kind of board game. It seems certain that on this pavement Christ stood before Pilate, was condemned, mocked and crowned with the crown of thorns (unless those scholars are right who believe that Pilate resided not in the Antonia Fortress but in the Citadel).

★Via Dolorosa

Here, continuing the line of St Mary's Gate Street, begins the Via Dolorosa, the first section of which runs along the east–west longitudinal axis of the Antonia Fortress. This "Way of Sorrow" was the route followed by Christ after his condemnation on his way to the place of execution on Golgotha. Every Friday at 3pm a procession led by Italian Franciscans makes its way along the Via Dolorosa, the course of which is marked by the fourteen Stations of the Cross, some of them based on the Gospels' accounts of the Passion and some on tradition.

Stations I–IX are on the Via Dolorosa, Stations X–XIV in the Church of the Holy Sepulchre, which is built over Golgotha and Christ's Tomb.

The Stations on the Via Dolorosa are not to be regarded as historical sites but as stages in the procession. The detritus of many centuries has raised the ground level much above its level in the time of Christ, and later building has altered the line of the streets in detail. The course of the Via

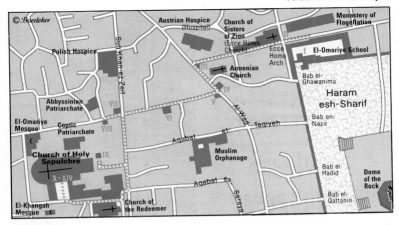

Via Dolorosa

I········XIV   **The Fourteen Stations of the Cross**

I   Jesus is condemned
    to death by Pilate
II Jesus takes up the Cross
III Jesus falls for the
    first time
IV Jesus meets his Mother
V   Simon of Cyrene helps
    Jesus to carry the Cross

VI   Veronica gives her
     handkerchief to Jesus
VII Jesus falls for the
     second time
VIII Jesus comforts the
     women of Jerusalem
IX   Jesus falls for the
     third time

IN CHURCH OF HOLY SEPULCHRE

X   Jesus is disrobed
XI   Jesus is crucified
XII Jesus dies on the Cross
XIII His body is taken down
     from the Cross
XIV His body is laid in
     the tomb

Golgotha

Dolorosa has thus frequently changed down the centuries, and the number of Stations has increased from the original seven to the present fourteen. The present route dates mainly from the 18th century; Stations I, IV, V and VIII were established only in the 19th century.

Station I (Christ is condemned to death) lies on the south side of the Via Dolorosa, in the courtyard of the El-Omariye Medrese, to which a flight of steps leads up. Here every Friday the Franciscan friars assemble for their procession. From window recesses in the south wall, on the line of the south wall of the Antonia, there is a very fine view of the Temple platform. Station II (Christ takes up the Cross) is on the other side of the Via Dolorosa at the entrance to the Chapel of the Condemnation. We now leave the site of the Antonia and continue west to Station III (Christ falls for the first time), on the left at the junction with King Solomon Street. Here we turn sharp left to reach Station IV (Christ meets his Mother) and then sharp right into a street at the near end of which is Station V (Simon of Cyrene helps Christ to carry the Cross). Farther along the street is Station VI (Veronica wipes the sweat off Christ's brow with her handkerchief).

Crossing a densely populated bazaar street (Suq Khan ez-Zeit), we come to Stations VII (Christ falls for the second time) and VIII (Christ speaks to the weeping women). Here we must turn back, since the direct route to Golgotha through one of the city gates has been walled up since the Middle Ages. Returning to Suq Khan ez-Zeit and turning right along this street, we come in some 60m/65yds to a broad flight of steps on the right which leads to Station IX (Christ falls for the third time), marked by a Roman column between the Coptic Patriarchate (on right) and the entrance to the Abyssinian Monastery (on left).

The Abyssinian Monastery is built over St Helen's Chapel in the Church of the Holy Sepulchre. The monks live in separate dwellings which together

Abyssinian
Monastery

The Via Dolorosa . . .

. . . street scene

form a laura (the term for a monastery in the Eastern church). They cele-brate the Nativity of Christ on the 24th of every month. The chapels of the monastery contain examples of Abyssinian folk art.

We can pass through the Abyssinian Monastery into the forecourt of the Church of the Holy Sepulchre, or alternatively we can return to the bazaar street, turn right and then into the first street on the right. In this street, on the right, is the Alexandra Hospice (Russian Orthodox), on a site occupied in the time of Christ by a section of the city wall (the excavations are shown to visitors by the nuns). Opposite are the Church of the Redeemer and the Muristan (see page 245). Continuing west past the Muristan (on left), we come to a narrow street leading to the forecourt of the Church of the Holy Sepulchre.

★★**Church of the Holy Sepulchre**

The Church of the Holy Sepulchre (Arabic Keniset el-Kiyaneh), with its conspicuous dome topped by a gilded cross, is one of the most sacred places in Christendom. built on the site of Christ's crucifixion and his tomb. Yet for many visitors it is a disappointment when they find, not a building of monumental scale and magnificence like Hagia Sophia in Istanbul or St Peter's in Rome but a church of moderate size surrounded by a confused huddle of other structures.

Authenticity

The question has frequently been raised whether the tomb in the Church of the Holy Sepulchre is really the one in which Christ was buried. Thus in the 19th century General Gordon – later the hero of Khartoum – disputed its authenticity on the ground that it lies within the city walls. He was right in thinking that tombs were considered unclean and were therefore always outside the walls of Jewish towns; but he overlooked the fact that the Ottoman walls of the 16th century, on the north side of which he discovered the "Garden Tomb" in 1882, ran farther north than the second circuit of walls which was standing in the time of Christ. Later research has shown that this second wall formed a re-entrant angle to the south and east of Golgotha, so that the place of execution lay outside the city walls.

Church of the Holy Sepulchre, seen from the tower of the Church of the Redeemer

Further arguments in favour of the authenticity of the site of the Holy Sepulchre are based on a historical tradition reaching back to the earliest days of Christianity. The original Christian community knew where Christ had been executed and buried; but, as Jews, they were prohibited from entering Jerusalem after its destruction by the Romans in A.D. 70. Yet the list of bishops of Jerusalem during this period is continuous, and the site of Christ's crucifixion was known even at a later date. Thus the decision by Hadrian (117–138) to eliminate the Christian churches is a clear indication that in his time the veneration of the Christian holy places was already widespread. The Romans built a temple of Venus over the tomb and erected a statue of Jupiter on Golgotha. The Christians still knew, however, of the existence of these places, and when the Empress Helen, Constantine the Great's mother, visited Jerusalem in 326 Bishop Macarius was able to give her information about their whereabouts; and Hadrian's temple was then replaced by a new church which became the central shrine of Christendom.

The removal of the temple and the terrace on which it stood revealed a tomb hollowed out of the rock, the hill of Golgotha and, to the east of this, an underground Roman cistern, into which a number of crosses used for executions had been thrown. Helen identified one of these as the True Cross on which Christ had been crucified, and it became one of the holiest relics of the Christian world. The discovery of the Cross is commemorated by the Roman Catholic feast of the Invention (Finding) of the Cross on May 3rd.

Architectural history

The top of the hill was then levelled by the removal of soil to provide a flat surface for building, leaving the Holy Sepulchre and Golgotha as projecting rocks. On this site was built the Church of the Holy Sepulchre.

The predominant type of church in the time of Constantine was a three- or five-aisled basilica, with a broad central aisle or nave and lower lateral aisles. The nave and aisles were separated by a horizontal architrave or by a

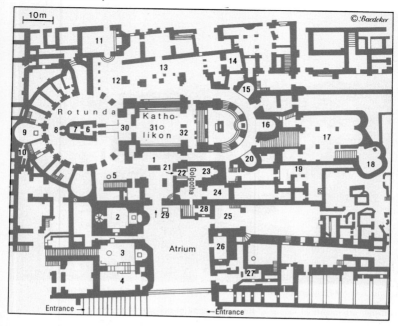

© Baedeker

Church of the Holy Sepulchre, Jerusalem

1 Stone of Unction
2 Chapel of Forty Martyrs and bell-tower
3 St John's Chapel and Baptistery
4 St James's Chapel
5 Place of the Three Marys (Armenian Orthodox)
6 Angel's Chapel
7 Holy Sepulchre
8 Coptic Chapel
9 Jacobite Chapel (Syrian Orthodox)
10 Tomb of Joseph of Arimathea (Abyssinian)
11 Franciscan Chapel (R.C.)

12 Altar of Mary Magdalene (R.C.)
13 Arches of the Virgin
14 Christ's Prison (Greek Orthodox chapel)
15 Chapel of Longinus (Greek Orthodox)
16 Chapel of Parting of Raiment (Armenian Orthodox)
17 St Helen's Chapel (Armenian Orthodox)
18 Chapel of Invention of Cross (R.C.) .
19 Medieval cloister
20 Chapel of the Mocking
21 Chapel of Adam (Greek Orthodox)
22 Site of tombs of Godfrey of Bouillon and Baldwin I

23 Altar of Crucifixion and Stabat Mater Altar (Greek Orthodox)
24 Altar of the Nailing to the Cross (R.C.)
25 St Michael's Chapel
26 St John's Chapel (Armenian Orthodox)
27 Chapel of Abraham
28 Chapel of the Agony of the Virgin and Chapel of St Mary of Egypt
29 Tomb of Philippe d'Aubigny
30 Latin Choir (R.C.)
31 Navel of the World
32 Greek Choir

row of arches. In front of the entrance was an atrium, and at the other end (which was usually oriented to the east) were the transept and an apse containing the altar. There were also circular or octagonal buildings roofed by a dome, mostly baptisteries and burial chapels.

The Church of the Holy Sepulchre built by Constantine combined both types. The rock containing Christ's tomb became the central point of a rotunda. To the east of this was a five-aisled basilica, and beyond this again an atrium. The entrance to the atrium was at the end of a street flanked by columns on the line of the present-day Khan ez-Zeit. In the open space between the basilica and the rotunda was the rock of Golgotha, topped by the True Cross.

Windows over the main entrance of the Church of the Holy Sepulchre

This building, begun in 326 and completed about 335, was destroyed when the Persians led by Chosroes conquered the country in 614. After its reconquest by the Byzantine Emperor Heraclius the church was rebuilt on its original plan by Abbot Modestus in 629. The Cross, which the Persians had carried off as booty, was returned and re-erected on Golgotha: an event commemorated by the feast of the Exaltation of the Cross on September 14th.

In 1009 the fanatical Fatimid Caliph El-Hakim almost completely destroyed the church, and in 1048, during the reign of the Byzantine Emperor Constantine IX Monomachus, it was rebuilt, though on a considerably smaller scale. The Constantinian basilica was abandoned and there remained only the rotunda, with a courtyard surrounded by small rooms on its east side. The Crusaders, who took Jerusalem in 1099, restored the bipartite layout. Their church was completed in 1149. The French architect, Jourdain, replaced the original basilica by a shorter nave with a semicircular east end and a vaulted roof in the style of the period. The rotunda containing the Holy Sepulchre was retained. Golgotha, which had hitherto stood by itself, was incorporated in the new nave as a raised side chapel, and in a cavity under Golgotha were constructed tombs for Godfrey of Bouillon, conqueror of Jerusalem, and Baldwin I, its first king. Thus the Church of the Holy Sepulchre has preserved, though in an altered form, the original arrangement with two sacred places and two separate sections related to one another. This pattern is reflected externally in the church's two domes. Since in the course of centuries the Church of the Holy Sepulchre had become shabby and unsightly, and in addition had suffered severe damage in the 1927 earthquake, the various Christian communities with rights in the church resolved in 1958 to restore it. Since then some restoration work has been done – thus some of the massive piers which surrounded the Holy Sepulchre have been replaced by a lighter arrangement of pillars and columns – but other urgently necessary work has not been carried out because the various communities have been unable to agree on what should be done. A dispute over the decorative patterns on the roof of the Rotunda, for example, has gone on for years.

Ownership

Ownership of the Church of the Holy Sepulchre is shared by six religious communities. The Greek Orthodox church owns the Katholikon (nave), the northern part of Golgotha, Adam's Chapel below it and "Christ's Prison". The Roman Catholics (the "Latins") have the southern part of Golgotha, the choir between the Rotunda and the Katholikon, the Chapel of the Apparition with the adjoining Franciscan friary, the Altar of Mary Magdalene and the Chapel of the Invention of the Cross. The Armenians have the Place of the Three Marys, the eastern chapel in the ambulatory and St Helen's Chapel. The Copts own the chapel on the west side of the Holy Sepulchre, the Syrians the western chapel in the Rotunda and the Abyssinians the "Tomb of Joseph of Arimathea" which is entered from that chapel. The Stone of Unction and the Holy Sepulchre itself are owned in common.

Exterior

On the entrance front (the south side) of the Church of the Holy Sepulchre the dominant features are the two doorways of the Crusader period with pointed arches; the right-hand one was walled up by Saladin in 1187. Over the doorways is a lavishly ornamented Corinthian cornice which dates from the Constantinian church.

Between the two doorways is a coat of arms with four quarters marking the tomb of Philippe d'Aubigny, tutor of King Henry III of England, who fell in 1236. His tomb is the only survivor of the many which once surrounded the church.

Interior

The left-hand doorway leads into the interior of the church, passing a recess on the left which was once occupied by the Muslim custodians, members of the Nuseibeh family who for centuries enjoyed the hereditary privilege of keeping the keys of the church. In order to get a general idea of the layout of the church it is a good idea to begin by going into the nave (Katholikon) or, if this is closed, into the little choir between the Katholikon and the Rotunda, both of which are on the central axis of the church.

Golgotha

To the right of the entrance is a flight of steps leading up to Golgotha (Mount Calvary), a rock which rises to 5m/16ft above floor level and, as excavation has shown, has a total height of 10m/33ft. On the rock are two chapels richly decorated with mosaics. We first enter the Chapel of the Nailing to the Cross (Roman Catholic), with copper reliefs of 1588 and realistic mosaics of 1937 showing how Christ was nailed to the Cross here. Through a window in the right-hand wall we can look into the Chapel of the Agony of the Virgin, which also belongs to the Roman Catholics. We now turn left and, passing the Stabat Mater Altar (Roman Catholic), where Mary is said to have stood during the crucifixion of her Son, enter the Greek Orthodox Chapel of the Crucifixion. On the wall above the altar is an almost life-size representation of the crucified Christ between Mary and his disciple John. Here too, behind bullet-proof glass, can be seen the rock in which the Cross is believed to have been set. It was previously faced with marble slabs, the removal of which in 1989 revealed nothing of particular significance. It can be seen that at some points the rock has been worked with a chisel; there is also a small slab of red marble which may have come from an earlier floor. To the right of the altar is a metal splint covering the cleft in the rock which occurred when Christ died (Matthew 27,51).

Chapel of Adam

From here we go down the steps on the north side to the Chapel of Adam (Greek Orthodox), in which there is also a cleft in the rock. The chapel gets its name from the legend that Adam's skull was found under the Cross at Christ's crucifixion. On either side of the entrance are stone benches marking the site of the tombs of the first two rulers of the Crusader kingdom, Godfrey of Bouillon and Baldwin I. Their remains were removed by Muslims in the 13th century, and the tombs themselves were broken up by fanatical Greek monks in 1808. The appearance of the tombs is known from drawings made before their destruction: low columns supported saddle roofs which bore Latin inscriptions, which also were recorded. One of them read (according to Zev Vilnay): "Here lies the famous Duke Godfrey of Bouillon, who won this whole country for the Christian faith. May his soul rest in Christ. Amen." The other read: "Here lies King Baldwin, a second Judas Maccabeus, the hope of his country, the pride of the Church and its strength. Arabia and Egypt, Dan and overweening Damascus feared his power and humbly brought him gifts and tribute. Alas! This poor sarcophagus covers him."

Going west from here, we pass the Stone of Unction, on which Christ's body was laid and anointed after his crucifixion (John 19,38–40), and the Place of the Three Marys (Armenian), from which the holy women watched the anointing, and come to the Rotunda containing the Holy Sepulchre. The exterior of the Rotunda was rebuilt after the 1808 fire by Kalfa Komnenos, a Greek from Smyrna, in the overcharged style of Turkish Rococo. In front of the entrance are huge candelabra, and over the doorway hang 43 lamps (thirteen each belonging to the Greeks, Latins and Armenians and four to the Copts). The structure of the tomb conceals the natural rock, which can be seen only in the Coptic chapel to the rear of the sepulchre.

Rotunda, Holy Sepulchre

In an antechamber, the Angel's Chapel, is a stone on which the angel who announced the resurrection of Christ to the holy women is said to have sat. It is probably a remnant of the round stone which closed the mouth of the sepulchre and was rolled away by the angel. A low door leads into the small tomb chamber, along the right-hand wall of which is a marble slab marking the empty burial-place. Apart from the marble cladding, this is a tomb similar to many others dating from the time of Christ, closed by a round stone like a millstone whose diameter determined the height of the entrance.

During the night before Easter Day the Holy Sepulchre is the scene of a ceremony in which the Greek Orthodox Patriarch of Jerusalem enters the

The Holy Sepulchre

Angel's Chapel, which has been closed since Good Friday, and lights the "holy fire" – a light from the darkness of the tomb which symbolises the Resurrection.

Chapel of the Jacobites

On the south, west and north sides of the Rotunda are semicircular conches. In the west conch, opposite the Coptic Chapel, is a chapel of the Syrian Christians (Jacobites), in which, on the left, is the entrance to a rock-cut tomb. It is traditionally ascribed to Joseph of Arimathea, who also provided the tomb for Christ (Matthew 27,60). It is still in its original condition, without marble cladding.

North aisle

The northern part of the Rotunda belongs to the Latins. Here are a chapel of the Franciscans, whose friary is immediately adjoining, and the Altar of Mary Magdalene. In the northern aisle are a number of columns of different periods, including richly decorated Corinthian columns from the original 4th century church. These are known as the Arches of the Virgin, because the risen Christ is said to have appeared to his Mother here. At the east end of the aisle is a small square chamber known, without any historical basis, as the Prison of Christ.

St Helen's Chapel

At the east end of the nave is a semicircular passage or ambulatory which runs past the Chapel of Longinus and the Chapel of the Parting of the Raiment to a flight of steps leading down to St Helen's Chapel (Armenian). In the rock face on the right are small crosses incised by pilgrims of the Crusader period. The chapel is roughly square, with four short columns of the Byzantine period carrying the high arches of the roof structure. Through the dome light falls from above into the large central square, giving the chapel its own special atmosphere, which is enhanced by the lamps, the decorative fabrics and the altar.

To the right of the principal apse is a recess from which Helen is said to have watched the bringing to light of the Roman cistern in which the True Cross was found.

Chapel of the Invention of the Cross

A further flight of steps leads down to the former cistern, now the plain little Chapel of the Invention of the Cross (Roman Catholic), its walls still showing signs of its original function. The statue of St Helen and the altar were gifted by Archduke Maximilian of Austria, the future ill-fated Emperor of Mexico.

Church of St John the Baptist

On leaving the Church of the Holy Sepulchre we turn right and continue west into Christian Quarter Street. Turning left along this street, we come in some 40m/45yds to the entrance (on right) of the Crusader church of St John the Baptist, built about 1170. It stands to the rear of a forecourt which is entered through a doorway marked with a cross. Built into the façade are re-used Roman stones. The church, on a trefoil plan without a nave, is now occupied by the Greek Orthodox. Facing the entrance, which is at the west end, is the wide iconostasis, behind which are the eastern conch and the altar. To left and right are the north and south conches.

The church occupies the site of an earlier building, a chapel of the 5th century. This is now the crypt of the later church, but, as the old window openings show, it originally stood on ground level. A crystal reliquary found here, originally hidden to save it from the Arabs, is said now to be preserved in the treasury of the Church of the Holy Sepulchre (not open to the public). This first church was dedicated to St John the Compassionate, Patriarch of Alexandria.

The church belonged to the pilgrim hospice which was founded here in 1073 – before the first Crusade – by merchants from the Italian maritime republic of Amalfi. Here too was founded the order of the Knights of St John or Knights Hospitallers (Ordo militiae Sancti Ioanni Baptistae hospitalis Hierosolymitani), the establishment of which was confirmed by Pope Pascal II in 1113, when the church was re-dedicated to St John the Baptist. It is venerated by the British Knights of St John as their mother church. The hospice complex occupies the area between David Street and the Church of the Holy Sepulchre and between Christian Quarter Street and Khan ez-Zeit Street. Vaulting belonging to the Hospitallers' establishment can still be seen in David Street. The tradition of the hospice was preserved in Jerusalem after the end of the Crusader period in 1187, and the area to the north of David Street is still known as the Muristan, a Persian/Arabic word meaning "hospital".

The Muristan is reached by turning left off David Street into the street leading to the Church of the Redeemer, which is seen on the left.

Muristan

In 1868 the Sultan presented the eastern part of this area to Crown Prince Frederick William of Prussia, and to secure equal representation the western part was assigned to the Greek Orthodox Patriarchate. It is now occupied by the Greek bazaar, which specialises in leather goods. In the centre of the bazaar area is an ornamental fountain (19th c.); at the north end is the Mosque of Omar, built in 1216 to commemorate Caliph Omar's visit to Jerusalem in 638.

On the eastern edge of the Muristan is the Lutheran Church of the Redeemer. Consecrated by the German Emperor William II on Reformation Day in 1898, it occupies a site with a long tradition behind it. The ground was presented to Charlemagne by Caliph Haroun el-Rashid and it became the site of the church of St Mary of the Latins, which was destroyed by El-Hakim in 1009 and rebuilt later in the same century. In the course of the centuries it fell into ruin; then in 1868 the site was acquired by Prussia, and in 1893 the foundation stone of a new church was laid. It was designed to perpetuate the old western tradition in the immediate vicinity of the Holy Sepulchre and serve as the spiritual centre of Protestantism in the Holy Land. Since then the church and adjoining buildings have been the seat of the Lutheran provostry of Jerusalem.

Church of
the Redeemer

The simple interior was renovated some years ago. To the right of the entrance is the door to the tower, which is well worth climbing for the sake

Church of the Redeemer

View from the tower

of the views it affords of the Old City and the Mount of Olives. Also of interest is the cloister, which incorporates some medieval architectural elements.

El-Khanqah Mosque

From the Church of the Holy Sepulchre a stepped lane to the right leads into Christian Quarter Street. At the north end of this street, at the corner of El-Khanqah Street (on right), is the El-Khanqah Mosque, which is believed to have originally been the palace of the Patriarch in Crusader times.

Monastery of Constantine

Shortly before this point, on the right, is Greek Orthodox Patriarchate Street, with the Patriarchate along its right-hand side. Opposite it is the Greek Orthodox Monastery of Constantine, which contains valuable icons. In a small museum in the monastery is the slender sarcophagus, with a decoration of plant ornament and rosettes on the front, of Queen Mariamne, who was murdered by her husband Herod I in 29 B.C. It was brought here from the Herodian family tomb near the King David Hotel, along with another sarcophagus, during the Second World War.

To the north of the monastery there once stood the palace occupied by the kings of Jerusalem after they made over their original residence, the El-Aqsa Mosque, to the Templars.

Turning left at the end of Christian Quarter Street, we enter the Roman Catholic (Latin) quarter. After passing the Terra Sancta Church (on right) we come, beyond the intersection with a street leading to the New Gate, to the Latin Patriarchate, immediately behind the town walls. From here a series of narrow lanes lead towards David Street, which is reached opposite the Citadel, at the Jaffa Gate.

From the Mount of Olives to Mount Zion

Tomb of the Virgin Mary

This walk over the Mount of Olives starts at a bend in Jericho Road below St Stephen's Gate. After passing a memorial to Israeli paratroops killed here in 1967, we come to the Tomb of the Virgin Mary (on left), which has a Gothic façade of the Crusader period (12th c.). It is one of many buildings in this area dating from three different periods: Early Christian (4th and 5th c.), the Crusaders (12th c.) and the 19th and 20th centuries.

A flight of 47 broad marble steps leads down to the dark underground shrine. Half way down are two recesses: the one on the right contains the tombs of Joachim and Anne, the Virgin's parents, the one on the left an altar over the tomb of Joseph. At the bottom of the steps, 12m/40ft below ground level, we turn right beyond a Greek Orthodox altar to reach the rock-cut tomb of the Virgin, at the east end of a long chamber. It is flanked on the left by an Armenian altar and on the right by a medieval Muslim prayer niche. At the west end of the chamber are a cistern, whose water is credited with healing powers, and an altar of the Abyssinian Christians. The first sanctuary on this site was established in the 5th century.

There is a house at Ephesus in Asia Minor in which the Virgin is said to have lived; but there is an early Christian tradition that she spent the last years of her life in Jerusalem, where she died 22 years after the death of her Son and was buried in the valley of Jehoshaphat.

The tomb is also known as the Church of the Assumption, in the belief that it was from here that Mary was carried up into heaven by angels.

★Garden of Gethsemane

To the left of the Tomb of the Virgin is a passage leading to the Grotto of the Agony, immediately south of which is the Garden of Gethsemane with its eight ancient olive-trees (the name Gethsemane is derived from the Hebrew Gath-shamma, "oil-press").

After Christ and his disciples had celebrated the Last Supper on the day later known as Maundy Thursday he went with them "unto a place called Gethsemane" (Matthew 26,36); "and he was withdrawn from them about a stone's cast, and kneeled down, and prayed . . . and being in an agony he

Garden of Gethsemane

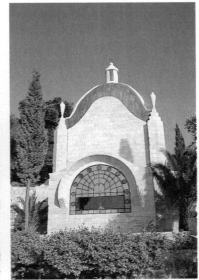

Dominus Flevit Church

prayed more earnestly'' (Luke 22, 41 and 44). The disciples slept and left him alone in this hour of agony, and soon afterwards he was arrested and taken into the city.

In the 4th century the Emperor Theodosius I built a basilica in the Garden of Gethsemane over the rock on which Christ was believed to have prayed. The ground-plan of this church is still visible on the floor of the modern church erected on the site in 1924. The present church is three-aisled like its predecessor, but on a larger scale. In marked contrast to the brightly coloured façade is the dim light in the interior. The roof, formed of twelve small domes decorated with mosaics, is borne on six columns. In front of the altar is the rock on which Christ prayed, surrounded by a low grille in the form of the crown of thorns. The church takes its name from the paintings, presented by many different nations, with which it is decorated.

Church of All Nations

Turning right from here, we come to the Russian Church of Mary Magdalene, a magnificent building with seven domes erected by Tsar Alexander III in memory of his mother Maria Alexandrovna. The church contains the tomb of Grand-Duchess Elizabeth, sister of the last Tsarina and wife of Grand-Duke Sergius, who was murdered in 1918.

Church of Mary Magdalene

Some 200m/220yds higher up, on left, is the entrance to a Franciscan property with the chapel of Dominus Flevit (''The Lord wept''), built in 1955 on the foundations of a church of the 5th century (a mosaic from which can be seen to the left of the entrance). In a large window above the altar is the outline of a chalice. The name of the chapel refers to the occasion when Christ, going to Jerusalem for the last time, wept over the fate that awaited the city (Luke 19,41).
During the construction of the chapel, in 1953, a number of Jewish and Byzantine graves were brought to light.

Dominus Flevit

200m/220yds farther on, on the right, are the Tombs of the Prophets, a complex of catacombs said to contain the tombs of the prophets Haggai,

Tombs of the Prophets

247

Mount of Olives: in the foreground the Church of All Nations

Zechariah and Malachi and their disciples but in fact much later than their time. The owner of the property in which they lie opens the tombs for visitors for a consideration (which should be agreed in advance!).

★★View

A little higher up, to the right, is a terrace from which there is a superb view of Jerusalem, extending over the Temple Mount and the Old City with its domes, minarets and church towers to the high-rise blocks of West Jerusalem.

Below the terrace is the large Jewish Cemetery (see below), with graves stretching back to Biblical times which suffered heavy damage at the hands of the Arabs in 1948.

Pater Noster Church

Going north from here, we turn right into a road leading to the Pater Noster Church, built on the site of a Constantinian basilica, the Eleona church (326–333), which was destroyed by the Persians in 614. Later the Crusaders built a chapel here. In 1874 the Princesse de la Tour d'Auvergne acquired the site, then abandoned and neglected, and founded a convent of Carmelite nuns. Here she was buried in 1957, long after her death. The chapel commemorates Christ's teaching of the Lord's Prayer (Luke 11,2–4), which appears on coloured tiles on the walls of the church in 80 different languages.

Bethphage

From the Pater Noster Church a side trip can be made to Bethphage (alt. 900m/2950ft), a short distance east, with a church commemorating the tradition that this was the Biblical Bethphage, to which Christ sent his disciples to fetch the ass on which he rode into Jerusalem on Palm Sunday (Luke 19,29). The remains of a Crusader church were found here in 1876. In the 19th century Franciscan church is a stone from this church with interesting Early Gothic paintings.

Chapel of the Ascension

We now come to the Arab village of Et-Tur, in which, within the precincts of a mosque, is the Chapel of the Ascension. The village lies on the road from

In the Pater Noster Church   *Chapel of the Ascension*

Jerusalem to Bethany (see El-Azariya), from which, according to Luke 24,50–51, Christ was carried up into heaven. In the 12th century the Crusaders built a chapel here, later converted by the Muslims into a tall domed building. The chapel was an octagonal structure with pointed arches on all eight sides and a narrow frieze round the top; the chapel was open to the sky, reflecting in its architecture the idea of the Ascension.

The Arab custodian also has the key to a tomb which lies a little to the west, opposite the Pater Noster Church. To the Jews this is the tomb of Huldah, a prophetess who lived in Jerusalem in the time of King Josiah (2 Kings 22,14) and has given her name to the southern doorways of the Temple platform. In Christian tradition – and the one tradition need not exclude the other – this was the cave of St Pelagia of Antioch, a repentant sinner who lived here and died in the year 280.

To the east of the Chapel of the Ascension is the Russian Monastery of the Ascension, with a 60m/200ft high tower which dominates the surrounding area (views).

Monastery of the Ascension

From Et-Tur we return to Gethsemane on one of the paths over the Mount of Olives. A little to the south of the church at Gethsemane the narrow and unsurfaced Siloam Road (Derekh HaShiloah) goes off on the right into the Kidron valley and its southward continuation the valley of Jehoshaphat, between the Mount of Olives and Mount Moriah (Temple Mount). This area is referred to in two Old Testament prophecies, by Zechariah and Joel. In the words of Joel (3,1–2): "For behold, in those days, and in that time, when I shall bring again the captivity of Judah and Jerusalem, I will also gather all nations, and will bring them down into the valley of Jehoshaphat, and will plead with them there for my people and for my heritage Israel", and (3,14) "Multitudes, multitudes in the valley of decision: for the day of the Lord is near in the valley of decision." (Jehoshaphat means "God will judge").

★Kidron valley

The Jews expect, therefore, that the Last Judgment will take place here, and this is also the Muslim belief: a rope will extend from the battlements of the Temple over the valley to the Mount of Olives, and the righteous will cross over, supported by their guardian angels, while the sinners will be cast down into damnation.

Jewish cemetery

The desire to be here on the Day of Judgment has led both Jews and Muslims to establish cemeteries on either side of the Kidron valley, on the slopes of the Mount of Olives and below the walls on the Temple Mount. The large Jewish cemetery dates back to Biblical times, and associated with it are the large funerary monuments to be seen along its lower edge, on the left of the road. They are attributed to various Old and New Testament figures but in fact all date from Hellenistic or Herodian times. They are not masonry-built but are almost entirely hewn from the rock, in the hybrid Hellenistic/Roman style of their period.

Tomb of Absalom

The series begins with the Tomb of Absalom, which it was formerly the practice to pelt with stones in memory of Absalom's revolt against his father David. The attribution to Absalom, however, is quite unhistorical. The square tomb chamber shows a characteristic mingling of styles, with a Doric frieze over Ionic half- and quarter-columns. Above this are an attic and a short drum topped by a pointed conical roof built up of dressed stone.

Other tombs

Farther south is a loggia-like façade with two Doric columns and a Doric architrave. In Christian tradition this was where St James the Less hid after the arrest of Christ. In fact it is a Jewish family tomb which, as an inscription on the architrave indicates, belonged to the Bene Hezir, a priestly family of the 1st century B.C. Next comes the Tomb of Zechariah, with a cube-shaped chamber topped by a pyramidal roof. To the right of this is another loggia-like tomb which was left unfinished.

Gihon Spring

400m/440yds farther on is the Gihon Spring. It lies under the east side of Mount Ophel, which slopes down from the wall on the south side of the

Jewish cemetery on the Mount of Olives

Tomb of Absalom

Tomb of Zechariah

Temple Mount to the junction of the Kidron and Hinnom valleys. On it was built the "City of David", successor to the earlier Jebusite town conquered by David.

Excavations recently carried out in this area (now the City of David Archaeological Garden) by a team of archaeologists led by Yigal Shiloh of the Hebrew University's Archaeological Institute reached occupation levels dated to the period of the foundation of the city by David around 1000 B.C. David's city was built on terraces on the hillside, like the present Arab village of Silwan opposite it. On the four man-made terraces, which were linked by flights of steps, the excavators found the remains of buildings and a drainage system. Individual finds from later periods show that Jews returning from the Babylonian Captivity settled here and that the site was also occupied in Persian, Hellenistic and Roman times. In the Middle Ages the City of David was abandoned, since Jerusalem had moved west to the area of the present Old City and the hill which then became known as Mount Zion.

City of David

In order to bring water to their town the Jebusites dug a tunnel from the Gihon Spring. At the end of the tunnel was a 13m/43ft deep shaft through which water was drawn up in buckets. The entrance to this shaft, named after its 19th century discoverer Charles Warren, is at the south end of the Archaeological Garden.

Warren's Shaft

Some centuries later King Hezekiah (727–698 B.C.) ordered the construction of another tunnel from the Gihon Spring. 540m/590yds long, 4m/13ft high and 1m/3ft 3in. wide, it ran under the south-eastern slopes of Mount Ophel to emerge at the Pool of Siloam. This ensured that the city could still get water even when it was under siege. It is necessary to stoop in some parts of the tunnel where the roof is low.

Hezekiah's Tunnel

The outflow of Hezekiah's Tunnel (which is still in use) into the Pool of Siloam can be seen some 500m/550yds from the Gihon Spring on the right

Pool of Siloam

of the road, below the minaret of a mosque belonging to the Arab village of Silwan. A Hebrew inscription found here in 1880 and now in Istanbul confirms the Biblical account of the construction of the tunnel. By the Pool of Siloam, which now measures 6m/20ft by 17m/56ft, Christ healed the man born blind (John 9,7). A church was built here in the 5th century, and some of its columns can be seen in the pool.

Hinnom valley

To the south of the Pool of Siloam extends the Hinnom valley. It is reached by returning from the Pool of Siloam to the road, continuing for another 200m/220yds and then taking a side road on the right.

In Canaanite times this valley was dedicated to the worship of Baal and Moloch, in which children "passed through the fire" (that is, were offered as burnt sacrifices to the god). This cruel cult, of which there is evidence throughout Phoenician territory, extending westward to Carthage, is the subject of a series of prohibitions in the books of Moses. In spite of this the cult of Moloch was practised in Israelite times: Manasseh, Hezekiah's son and successor, not only set up altars to Baal and Astarte but also "made his son pass through the fire" (2 Kings 21,6). The place where this occurred later came to be seen as the very essence of evil, and the name of Hinnom is derived from the Arabic word for hell, Gehenna.

The hill to the north-west became known in Crusader times as the "Mount of Evil Counsel", since this was believed to have been the meeting-place of the council held by the high priest Caiaphas at which it was resolved that Christ should be put to death (John 11,47–53). Here too, near the Monastery of St Onuphrius, is the Field of Blood (Aceldama), bought with the thirty pieces of silver which the repentant Judas cast down in the Temple (Matthew 27,6–8).

St Peter
in Gallicantu

From the Pool of Siloam a stepped path dating from the Roman period runs up Mount Zion. The tradition that Christ celebrated the Last Supper in a house in the upper town seems likely to be correct, and in that event he would have taken this path on his way to Gethsemane. The path leads to the Roman Catholic church of St Peter in Gallicantu ("at the place where the cock crew"), which commemorates Peter's three denials of Christ (Matthew 26,69–75). The monastic church (1931) contains archaeological finds from Jewish and early Christian times. Near the church is the so-called "Prison of Christ".

★Mount Zion

From here the road runs north to the Dung Gate and north-west to the Zion Gate. Turning left shortly before reaching the Zion Gate and then taking the first street on the right, we come to Mount Zion, with its Jewish, Christian and Muslim shrines. In Herodian times the hill lay within the upper town. Since the 4th century, as is demonstrated by churches built at that time, this has been revered as the place where Christ celebrated the Last Supper with his disciples and instituted the Eucharist (Matthew 26,17–30; Mark 14,12–25; Luke 22,7–20), where the Holy Ghost descended on the apostles at Pentecost (Acts 2), and where – as first affirmed by Patriarch Modestus in the 7th century – the Virgin spent the last years of her life and died.

The tomb of King David has been revered on Mount Zion since the 12th century, though it should rather be looked for in the old City of David on Mount Ophel. The churches built in the 4th and 5th centuries were in a state of ruin when the Crusaders arrived in Jerusalem in 1099. They rebuilt the old Minster of Zion and built a two-storey Romanesque house with the Room of the Washing of the Feet on the ground floor and the Room of the Last Supper on the upper floor. The church and the Room of the Last Supper were destroyed by the Egyptians in 1219, but the Room of the Last Supper was rebuilt in its present Gothic form by the Franciscans, to whom Pope Clement IV granted custody of the room in 1342. The Franciscans also built a small friary to the south of this. In the 16th century Sultan Suleiman the Magnificent expelled the Franciscans and a mosque was installed on the site. These older buildings were joined at the turn of the century by the Church of the Dormition, built on a site acquired by the German Emperor

Church of the Dormition on Mount Zion

Church of the Dormition: tower . . .

. . . and main doorway

William II and presented by him to the German Catholic Society of the Holy Land. At that time the Tomb of David was specially opened for the Emperor and Empress on the Sultan's command: Jews and Christians normally had no access to the tomb, and this remained the case until the British Mandate after the First World War.

Tomb of David

Remains of buildings of the Herodian period have been excavated at one site on the hill. On the right of the road is the entrance to the Room of the Washing of the Feet (John 13,1–11), now a synagogue. In an adjoining building is the Tomb of David, the dating of which is not certainly established. There are three theories: it is part of a Romanesque building of the Crusader period (12th c.), or of an early Christian church mentioned by the pilgrim Aetheria in 385, or of a synagogue referred to by the Pilgrim of Bordeaux in 333 as the only one in the area that had not been destroyed. (This last theory is supported by the fact that the apse faces north: that is, in the direction of the Temple Mount). In front of the apse, which is 2.48m/8ft wide and 2.44m/7ft 11in. high, is the cenotaph which is claimed to be David's tomb. It is draped in richly decorated cloths, and on it are silver Torah crowns and Torah scrolls. Jewish pilgrims pray here, particularly on Shavuot, the traditional day of David's death.

To the left of this building is the Chamber of Martyrs (Martet Hashoa), commemorating the Jews murdered by the Nazis.

Coenaculum

Leaving the Tomb of David and turning right into a narrow alley, we pass an arched doorway on the right and come to the steps leading up to the Room of the Last Supper (Coenaculum), which lies above the Room of the Washing of the Feet and the Tomb of David. The room, which was renovated by the Franciscans in the 14th century, measures 10m/33ft by 16m/52ft and has a vaulted roof borne on two Gothic columns. A block of dressed stone opposite the 16th century Muslim prayer niche is said to mark the place where Christ sat at the Last Supper.

Church of the Dormition

Farther along the alley is the commandingly situated Roman Catholic Church of the Dormition (the "Falling Asleep" of the Virgin), a neo-Romanesque building designed by Heinrich Renard and consecrated in 1908 which is served by Benedictine monks. Its centralised ground-plan betrays the influence of the Rotunda of the Church of the Holy Sepulchre. It has a beautiful mosaic pavement, in the centre of which are three intersecting circles, symbolising the Trinity; from this central point rays radiate outwards to the next two (concentric) circles, the first of which contains the names of the prophets Daniel, Isaiah, Jeremiah and Ezekiel, the second those of the twelve apostles. Round the outside are the signs of the Zodiac and an inscription (Proverbs 8,25–26). In the vaulting of the apse is a mosaic of the Virgin and Child. The chapels round the central area are dedicated to the English Benedictine St Willibald, the Three Kings, St Joseph, the Forefathers of Christ and St John the Baptist. In the centre of the crypt, under a mosaic dome, is a sculpture of the Dormition (the Virgin on her deathbed). Round the walls of the crypt are chapels endowed by various foreign countries.

From here we can either return to the Zion Gate or keep round the outside of the walls on the west side of the Old City to the Citadel and the Jaffa Gate.

From the Damascus Gate to Mount Scopus

Damascus Gate

The Damascus Gate serves as a link between the newer districts to the north and the Old City to the south. This is the starting-point of the road which runs by way of Nablus (Shekhem) to Damascus, and accordingly the first section of the road is known to the Arabs as Nablus Road and to the Jews as Shekhem Road. The gate itself is Sha'ar Shekhem (Shekhem Gate) to the Jews and Bab el-Amud (Gate of the Column), after a column from which the distance to Damascus was measured, to the Arabs.

The Damascus Gate, built in 1537, is the finest and most splendid of the gates built in the reign of Suleiman the Magnificent. With its two flanking towers and decorative battlements it is no less striking for its aesthetic qualities than for its defensive strength.

Here, as at the Jaffa Gate, a flight of steps leads up to the wall-walk round the Old City walls.

★Wall-walk

Under the bridge leading to the Damascus Gate is an archaeological site, the excavation of which was completed in 1982. There are remains of a Roman square or plaza, the Third Wall, built shortly before the destruction of Jerusalem by Titus in A.D. 70, and part of the Roman gate.

Roman Gate and Plaza

To the east of the Damascus Gate is a garden at the foot of the wall. 150m/165yds along this is an iron gate giving admission to Solomon's Quarries, a cave system with many ramifications extending under the Old City. According to an ancient tradition the stone for Solomon's buildings was quarried here. To the Jews this is known as Zedekiah's Grotto, in the belief that Zedekiah, the last king of Judah, hid here from the Babylonian forces in 587 B.C. before being captured and carried off with most of his people to Babylon.

Solomon's Quarries/ Zedekiah's Grotto

Opposite Solomon's Quarries is a short alley leading to Jeremiah's Grotto, believed to be the prison in which around 605 B.C. the prophet Jeremiah wrote his Lamentations on the forthcoming fall of Jerusalem, which actually occurred in 587 B.C. (Jeremiah 38,6).

Jeremiah's Grotto

Returning to the Damascus Gate, we turn right into Nablus (Shekhem) Road and almost immediately right again into an alley which leads to the Garden Tomb. Here, in a garden-like area in front of a low rocky hill which has been hewn into a vertical rock face, is a tomb which is entered through a doorway cut in the rock. This leads into a rectangular antechamber, to the right of which is the tomb chamber, with one burial place on the left and another, unfinished, on the right, under a small window. The tomb dates from the Roman or Byzantine period.
The tomb was found by General Gordon in 1882 and identified by him as Christ's tomb, since it lay outside the city wall in accordance with the requirements of Jewish law. He also saw in the shape of the rocky hill the likeness of a skull (in the New Testament Golgotha is described as "the place of a skull"). Gordon's theory, however, proved untenable, among other reasons because the course of the town walls in the time of Christ was different from their present line. Nevertheless some people, particularly Anglicans, still believe that it was here that Christ was buried and rose again.

Garden Tomb

Farther along Nablus Road, on the right, is the French Dominican monastery of St Stephen, on the spot where it is believed that St Stephen, the first Christian martyr, was stoned to death.

St Stephen's Monastery

Beyond this a street goes off on the left and runs into St George Street at the site of the Mandelbaum Gate, which from 1948 to 1967 was the only crossing-point between the Israeli and Jordanian sectors of Jerusalem. There was in fact no gate: merely a passage between barbed wire entanglements. It took its name from the owner of a nearby house, the site of which is marked by a plaque.

Mandelbaum Gate

Farther along St George Street a little street on the right runs past St George's Church (Anglican) into Nablus Road. Immediately north of this church, where Saladin Street runs into Nablus Road (on right), are the very interesting Tombs of the Kings, within the area of the American Colony founded in 1881. At the foot of 26 broad rock-cut steps, to the right, is a vertical face hewn from the rock in which can be seen two water channels

Tombs of the Kings

The Garden Tomb

and cisterns. To the left is a round-arched doorway in the rock leading into a spacious courtyard with the rock-cut façade of the tombs. Three steps lead down into an antechamber with a Doric frieze, and in the left-hand corner of this is the low entrance to the interior, once sealed by a round stone (which is still there). Beyond this is a central chamber giving access to a number of tombs on two levels.

The site was acquired by a French-Jewish Woman in 1874 and after her death passed to the French government. Sarcophagi from the tombs are now in the Louvre. The name "Tombs of the Kings" which was given to them was based on the assumption that this was the burial-place of the kings of Judah, but in fact the tombs date from a much later period. They were constructed by Queen Helen of Adiabene (present-day Kirkuk, between Mosul and Baghdad), a convert to the Jewish faith who came to live in Jerusalem about A.D. 45. Adiabene had won its independence after the fall of the Seleucid empire in the 2nd century and its governors had become kings. Helen, a great benefactress of the people of Jerusalem, took the Jewish name of Sara Melaka (Queen Sarah), and this name, in Aramaic script, appears on one of the sarcophagi in the Louvre.

★Rockefeller
Museum

We now return towards the Old City, following Saladin (Salah ed-Din) Street to Herod's Gate. Going east along the outside of the walls, we see, opposite the north-east corner of the Old City, the complex of the Archaeological or Rockefeller Museum, dominated by its massive tower. The museum is named after John D. Rockefeller, who financed its construction in 1927 with a gift of 2 million dollars. One of Israel's most important museums, it displays in chronological order archaeological material ranging in date from the Stone Age to the 18th century. Attached to the museum is a large library.

Beyond the entrance lobby is the Tower Hall, with casts of reliefs from the palace of Nineveh depicting the capture of Lachish by the Assyrian king

Rockefeller Museum

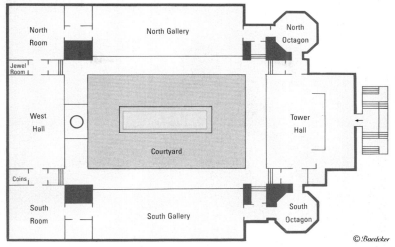

North Room

North Gallery

North Octagon

Jewel Room

West Hall

Courtyard

Tower Hall

Coins

South Room

South Gallery

South Octagon

© *Baedeker*

Sennacherib in 701 B.C. (Sennacherib also laid siege to Jerusalem but was unable to take it).

To the left of the Tower Hall is the South Octagon, with Egyptian and Mesopotamian material found in Palestine (much of it at Bet Shean). One of the finest pieces is a stele of Pharaoh Seti I (1319–04 B.C.).

The long South Gallery contains finds dating back to around 200,000 B.C. Among them are the Galilee Skull (*c.* 200,000 B.C.), human remains from Mount Carmel (*c.* 100,000 B.C.) and a skeleton found buried in a crouching position (*c.* 10,000 B.C.). Other exhibits include heads from Jericho (*c.* 6000 B.C.), a skull with added modelling in plaster (other examples in Amman Museum, Jordan) and a skull modelled in clay; a copper sword (*c.* 3500 B.C.), a pottery mould for casting bronze objects (*c.* 1600 B.C.), a game board with pottery men (also *c.* 1600 B.C.), a vessel from Cyprus (*c.* 1400 B.C.) and a bronze Hittite battleaxe (*c.* 1500 B.C.).

In the square South Room are wooden beams from the El-Aqsa Mosque (8th c.). The small adjoining room contains a collection of coins, including Jewish coins of the 1st and 2nd centuries A.D.

The West Hall displays finds from the palace at Jericho built in 724 by the Omayyad Caliph Hisham. They include windows and reconstructions of vaulted ceilings with rich ornament and many representations of human figures and animals showing the special characteristics and high quality of the early Islamic art of the Omayyad period. They show the influence of the art of the great neighbouring powers, Persia and Byzantium: Islam had not yet developed the aniconic art and the arabesque patterns of a later period. The small Jewel Room beyond the West Hall contains a collection of ancient jewellery, the oldest items in which date from about 2000 B.C. Particularly notable are the large gold earrings of the Roman period and a carved elephant's tusk.

The adjoining North Room contains material of the Crusader period (12th–13th c.), including relief carving from the Church of the Holy Sepulchre.

Beyond this is the long North Gallery, with material dating from 1200 B.C. onwards (i.e. following on chronologically from the South Gallery). The exhibits include a clay anthropomorphic sarcophagus (*c.* 1100 B.C.), a

257

Rockefeller Museum: courtyard

In the Rockefeller Museum

pottery incense burner decorated with human and animal figures (1100 B.C.), the "Lachish Letters" (clay tablets with Hebrew inscriptions, 588 B.C.) ivories from King Ahab of Israel's palace in Samaria (*c.* 850 B.C.), iron implements dating from about 1000 B.C. and Phoenician, Greek and Roman objects, including a bronze statuette of Herakles (2nd c. B.C.), a Nabataean dish dating from around the beginning of the Christian era, Roman glass (2nd–3rd c.) and a bronze coin of the time of Justinian (6th c.). Finally there is a family tomb of the Hyksos period (*c.* 1600 B.C.) found at Jericho in 1954. The North Octagon displays Jewish antiquities, including particularly candelabra and reliefs and a mosaic from the synagogue at En Gedi.

In the inner courtyard of the museum is a rectangular pool, round which are sarcophagi, capitals, mosaics, etc., and modern depictions of the history of Palestine.

From the Rockefeller Museum we go west along Shmuel Ben Adiya Street and turn left into Mount of Olives Street, which runs north to the older campus of the Hebrew University (opened 1925, with much recent building) on Mount Scopus (813m/2667ft). North of this are the Hadassah Clinics and the massive Augusta Victoria Hospital, which was financed by the German Emperor William II.

Mount Scopus

Districts North-West and South-West of the Old City

Outside the north-west corner of the Old City, 300m/330yds from the Jaffa Gate, is Zahal Square (Kikar Zahal). From here HaZanhanim Street runs north-east towards the Damascus Gate, passing the New Gate, opposite which is the Hospice of Notre Dame de France (1877), and Jaffa (Yafo) Road runs north-west to Bar Kochba Square and Zion Square, central features of the new town of Jerusalem.

From Bar Kochba Square a street goes off on the right into the Russian Compound, with the green-domed Russian Orthodox Cathedral. This part of the city grew up around 1860 as a large walled complex for the accommodation of the Russian pilgrims who came to Jerusalem in considerable numbers, particularly at Easter. On the north-east side of the complex were the Russian consulate and a hospice for women; to the south-west were a hospital, the mission house, with apartments for the archimandrite, the priests and well-to-do pilgrims, and, beyond the Cathedral, a large hospice for men. The buildings are now occupied by various government institutions (police headquarters, law courts, etc.).

Russian Compound

In ancient times there was a quarry here, and a relic of it is still to be seen in the form of a column fully 12m/40ft long which broke while it was being quarried and was left in situ, still embedded in the natural rock; it can be seen in a hollow in the ground opposite the entrance to the Cathedral. The column was presumably destined either for the colonnades of the Herodian Temple or – as a number of capitals found here suggest – for a building of the Theodosian period (second half of 4th c.).

From a side gate of the Russian Compound a street runs north-west into Prophets Street (Rehov HaNevi'im), beyond which is the Mea Shearim quarter. Turning left into Prophets Street, we take the first street on the right, Abyssinian Street (Rehov HaHabbashim), named after the Abyssinian Monastery founded and enlarged by Emperors John (1872–89) and Menelik (1889–1913). The church of the monastery is a round building with a green dome. The reliefs of lions above the doorway recall the style of Lion of Judah borne by the Abyssinian dynasty which traced its origins back to the Queen of Sheba; it was believed that the Queen of Sheba was also Queen of Abyssinia and that when she visited Solomon in Jerusalem he granted her a coat of arms with the lion of Judah. The church contains numbers of Abyssinian icons.

Abyssinian Church

Jerusalem/Yerushalayim

Ben Yehuda House

Adjoining the monastery is the house of Eliezer Ben Yehuda (see Famous People), who played a leading part in the creation of the modern Hebrew language; there is a commemorative plaque on the house.

★Mea Shearim

To the north of the Abyssinian Monastery is the Mea Shearim district, where the second Jewish settlement outside the Old City was established in 1875. At the entrances to this quarter are notices asking visitors to respect the customs of the strictly orthodox Jews who live here. This applies particularly to the Sabbath, but at all times visitors should avoid wearing "improper dress" (e.g. shorts, short-sleeved blouses and dresses) and taking photographs of the inhabitants. The name Mea Shearim ("a hundred gates") refers to Isaac's "hundredfold" harvest (Genesis 26,12). The ultra-orthodox Jews can be recognised by their old East European dress, their black clothes, felt hats (streimel) and side-curls (peiyot). They speak mostly Yiddish, since they regard Hebrew as a sacred language to be used only in religious services. An extreme group (Neturei Karta) refuses to recognise the state of Israel because it was not established by the Messiah and regard themselves as a ghetto of true orthodoxy within the Jewish state.

In this quarter there are numerous synagogues, ritual baths (mikvot), Talmudic schools and Torah scribes. The shops, particularly round the market square, sell religious articles, silverware, etc.

Bokharan Quarter

Going north from here along Yezekiel Street, we turn left into HaBuharim Street in the Bokharan Quarter, established in 1892 by Jews from Bokhara, in which picturesque old costumes are still worn, particularly on feast-days.

Tombs of the Sanhedrin

From Prophet Samuel Street (Rehov Shemuel HaNavi), which runs north-west from here, we take a road on the right which leads to the Tombs of the Sanhedrin, rock-cut tombs of the 1st century A.D. The triangular pediment over the entrance and the triangle over the doorway have delicate acanthus and pomegranate ornament. The principal chamber is two-storied, with steps leading down into a third (basement) storey. Recesses in the walls once held sarcophagi. It is believed that this handsome complex was the place of burial for members of the Sanhedrin, the Jewish supreme council.

Biblical Zoo

Returning to Prophet Samuel Street, we turn right along Bar Ilan Street and its continuation Jeremiah Street (Rehov Yirmiyahu). Shortly before reaching the Romema district we turn right into a street which leads to the Biblical Zoo, with a collection of birds, animals and reptiles mentioned in the Bible.

Allenby Memorial

Going south from here and turning right into Sarei Yisrael Street, we return to Jaffa Road at the memorial commemorating General Allenby's entry into Jerusalem in 1917.

Ben Yehuda Street

1km/¾ mile along Jaffa Road in the direction of the Old City we come into Jerusalem's main shopping and commercial centre. Particularly attractive is Ben Yehuda Street, which during the eighties, along with some of the side streets, was made a pedestrian zone, with numerous pavement cafés.

Yeshurun Synagogue

At the Eilon Tower Hotel Ben Yehuda Street runs into King George (HaMelekh George) Street, along the right-hand side of which are a number of important modern buildings, beginning with the Yeshurun Synagogue.

Ratisbonne Monastery

Beyond this is the Ratisbonne Monastery, founded in 1874 by Alfred Ratisbonne, which is occupied by a French order, the Pères de Sion.

Independence Park

To the east of King George Street at this point is the Independence Park (Gan HaAtsmaut). In this large park is the Lion's Cave, in which legend has it that a pious lion guarded the remains of martyrs. At the east end of the park,

Ben Yehuda Street, in the centre of Modern Jerusalem

in the grounds of an old Islamic cemetery, is the Mamilla Pool, a cistern which formed part of the water supply system of ancient Jerusalem.

Beyond this again is the Jewish Agency building, which also houses other Zionist institutions. The Jewish Agency, established by Theodor Herzl in 1897, occupies the central block, and in the side wings are the Jewish National Fund (Keren Kayemet), which was originally set up to acquire land for Jewish settlement and is now concerned with bringing land into cultivation, and the United Jewish Agencies. Here too are kept the Zionist archives and the Golden Books recording donations for land purchase. | *Jewish Agency*

Farther south is the Great Synagogue (consecrated 1982), a sumptuous building both externally and internally, the erection of which gave rise to a good deal of controversy. | *Great Synagogue*

On the south side of the Great Synagogue is the Chief Rabbinate (Hekhal Shelomo), the highest religious authority in the country. It is the seat of the Sephardi and Ashkenazi Chief Rabbis, who determine questions of Jewish law. On either side of the entrance to the building, which was donated by Sir Isaac Wolfson, are the scales of justice, with the Hebrew inscription "And they shall judge the people with just judgment" (Deuteronomy 16,18). On the façade is a representation of a menorah (seven-branched candlestick). Within the Rabbinate are a synagogue with an Ark of the Covenant from Padua, a museum of Jewish sacred and popular art bearing the name of the donor and a library. | *Chief Rabbinate*

A short distance beyond the Chief Rabbinate is Zarfat Square (Kikar Zarfat). Turning right from here into Ramban Street and in some 300m/330yds turning left along Ibn Ezra Street and its continuation Alfasi Street, we come (at No. 10) to the Tomb of Jason, a Hellenistic monument discovered during excavation work in 1956. The name of the occupant appears in an | *Tomb of Jason* inscription. The tomb, which is dated to the 2nd century B.C., has a façade of dressed stone and is topped by a pyramid. The entrance, divided into two by a squat column, leads into a passage flanked by tomb chambers with recesses for burials in the walls.

YMCA Building

Returning to Zarfat Square, we follow the continuation of King George Street, which runs south-east (at the near end, on right, the Franciscan Terra Sancta College), and take the first side street on the left, which leads to King David (David HaMelekh) Street. Here, on the right, is the YMCA Building (1928), with a 46m/150ft high tower which is a popular viewpoint. On the floor of the entrance lobby is a reproduction of the 6th century mosaic map in a church at Madaba (Jordan).

King David Hotel

Opposite the YMCA is the King David Hotel, which was the headquarters of the British forces during the Second World War and after the war. One wing of the building was blown up by a Jewish underground organisation in 1946. It was reopened as a hotel in 1948.

Herod's Family Tomb

In a side street to the east of the hotel is Herod's Family Tomb. Herod I built a monumental tomb for himself on the Herodeion (see entry) near Bethlehem and a separate tomb for his family above the Hinnom valley in which his wife Mariamne and other victims of his violent temper and persecution mania were buried. To the left of the entrance the foundations of a pyramid have been excavated. A flight of steps leads down to a rock-cut forecourt and the entrance passage, which could be closed by a round stone (still visible). Beyond this are a square chamber and behind it a smaller one, off which open three tomb chambers. Until the Second World War the sarcophagi were still in their original places, but when the British authorities used the tomb as an air raid shelter they were moved to the Monastery of Constantine, near the Church of the Holy Sepulchre.

Herod's Family Tomb

Montefiore Windmill

Farther south along King David Street, on the left, is the Montefiore Wind-mill, which contains a small museum on the life of the British philanthropist Sir Moses Montefiore (1784–1885).

In the middle of the 19th century Montefiore bought the area round the windmill and founded the first Jewish settlement outside the Old City (Mishkenot Sha'ananim). At the end of the century the area to the north, Yemin Moshe, was also built up; it is now an artists' quarter.

Diagonally opposite the windmill is Liberty Bell Park, a beautiful park laid out to mark the bicentennial of the United States, with a replica of the Liberty Bell in Philadelphia.

Farther south, on the far side of a street intersection, to the left, is St Andrew's Church (Church of Scotland; 1927). Beyond this is the Khan, an old Turkish caravanserai which has been converted into a theatre.

To the south of the Khan is a railway station, the terminus of the line from Jerusalem to Jericho constructed in 1891.

From the street intersection at St Andrew's Church Bethlehem Road runs south. Opposite the railway station Emeq Refaim Street branches off it on the right and runs through the territory of the German Templar Colony founded in 1873 by the German Protestant community of the Temple (no connection with the order of the Knights Templar). The community house with its apse and small bell-cote and the little houses set in gardens still give the area its particular stamp. At the far end of the Colony, immediately adjoining the American Cemetery, is the Templar Cemetery laid out in 1878. The members of the colony were evacuated by the British authorities during the Second World War.

On a hill a few hundred yards east is the district of Abu Tor. From this strategic point Titus launched his assault on Jerusalem in A.D. 70. From the hills there are fine views of the Hinnom valley, Mount Zion and the Old City.

Western New Town and Suburbs

Whereas the tours described so far can be done on foot, sightseeing in the western districts of the city, which extends beyond the village of En Karem, is best done by bus, taxi or private car.

Between the Rehavia district and the Israel Museum is the Valley of the Cross. Out of the olive-trees in the valley, on Hayim Hazaz Boulevard, rises the massive fortress-like bulk of the medieval Monastery of the Cross (Arabic Deir el-Musalliba).

According to the legend Lot came to live here after being separated from his daughters and planted cedar, cypress and pine seeds, which germinated and grew together to form the tree from whose wood Christ's cross was made. From this legend – which no doubt reflects an ancient tree cult – the monastery takes its name. Its early history is obscure. In Greek Orthodox tradition it was founded by the Empress Helen, mother of Constantine the Great, during her visit to Palestine. According to another tradition Constantine gave the site to the first Christian king of Georgia, Mirian (d. 342), who then built the monastery. Certainly there was a close connection over a long period between Georgia and the Monastery of the Cross, which had the same significance for the Christian peoples of Transcaucasia as the Georgian monastery of Iviron on Mount Athos.

During the Crusader period and the subsequent years of Muslim rule, until the 18th century, the monastery remained in Georgian hands. In the 16th century there were 365 monks' cells; in the 18th there were still 220. When, after the decline of Georgia in the latter part of the 18th century, the monastery found itself in financial difficulties it passed into the hands of the

Monastery of the Cross: a medieval fortified monastery

Greek Orthodox Patriarchate of Jerusalem, to which it still belongs. Valuable Georgian manuscripts are now preserved in the library of the Patriarchate. A few years after the foundation of the University of Athens the Greeks established a college here in which priests of eastern origin could pursue general and theological studies. The college, the first director of which was a Greek monk named Dionysios Kleophas, continued in existence until the First World War.

Until a few decades ago the monastery lay well to the west of Jerusalem, enjoying a seclusion which it has now lost with the steady expansion of the modern city.

The monastery is entered through a low doorway which leads into an extensive complex of courtyards, terraces and blocks of cells, with the church in the centre. The church dates from at least as far back as the 12th century and perhaps earlier; the tower shows Baroque features.

Behind the high altar is a round opening framed in silver marking the position of the tree which yielded the wood for the Cross. The wall paintings, which have largely been preserved but have sometimes been poorly restored, depict Biblical scenes, Georgian kings and saints. They include a representation of Shota Rustaveli, the great Georgian poet, who was sent here as a monk by Queen Tamara (1184–1211) and wrote his "Vapkis Takosani" ("The Man in a Panther's Skin", c. 1187) in the monastery. He is depicted as a small kneeling figure at the feet of St Maximus the Confessor and St John of Damascus.

★Knesset

Going north on Hayim Hazaz Boulevard and turning sharp left into Ruppin Road, we come to the Israeli Parliament, the Knesset (1966), the most striking building in the Hakirya district, the government quarter. Near the entrance is a 5m/16ft high bronze Menorah (seven-branched candlestick) by Benno Elkan, a gift from the British Parliament. It is decorated with 29 reliefs of figures and events in Jewish history.

Shrine of the Book

The interior is decorated with mosaics and tapestries by Marc Chagall. When Parliament is not sitting there are conducted tours of the building; when it is sitting visitors can usually get admission to the visitors' gallery (passport required).

North-west of the Knesset are three long ranges of government buildings – the Ministry of Finance, the Ministry of the Interior and the Prime Minister's Office.

On a hill to the south-west of the Knesset is the Israel Museum, a complex of low interconnected buildings and pavilions consisting of the Shrine of the Book, the Samuel Bronfman Biblical and Archaeological Museum, the Bezalel Art Museum and the Billy Rose Art Garden. The Museum, which was opened in 1965, is the only one in the country which collects and displays both archaeological material and art, conceived in the widest sense.

★★Israel Museum

To the right of the entrance is the Shrine of the Book, with a dome of light-coloured concrete modelled on the lids of the pottery jars containing the "Dead Sea scrolls". The scrolls were found from 1947 onwards in caves round the monastery of the Essenes at Qumran (see entry) and thanks to the efforts of the archaeologist Yigael Yadin were acquired for Israel; there are also some scrolls in the Archaeological Museum of Amman in Jordan. The scrolls are the earliest manuscripts of the Old Testament in the Hebrew language apart from two silver tablets engraved with a few words from the book of Numbers (see below, Bronfman Museum). In the centre of the rotunda are displayed scrolls containing extensive passages from the book of Isaiah (copies); written about 100 B.C., they show only slight variations from later manuscripts – evidence of the accuracy of the transmission of the Biblical text. Other texts are displayed round the walls of the rotunda. In

Shrine of the Book

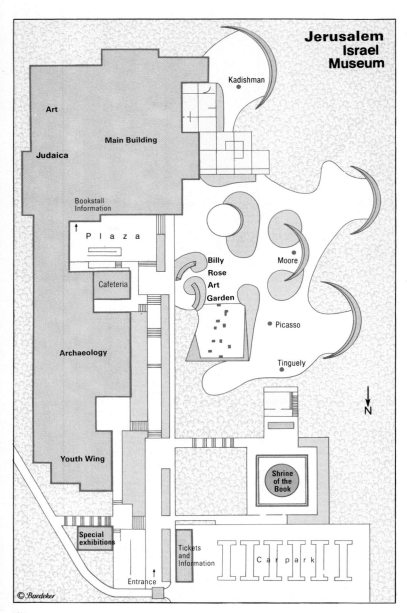

Jerusalem
Israel
Museum

Kadishman

Art

Main Building

Judaica

Bookstall
Information

Plaza

Cafeteria

Billy
Rose
Art
Garden

Moore

Picasso

Archaeology

Tinguely

N

Youth Wing

Shrine
of the
Book

Special
exhibitions

Tickets
and
Information

Car park

Entrance

© Baedeker

Israel Museum: sculpture in the Billy Rose Art Garden

cases on the lower floor are finds from Masada (see entry), material relating to the unsuccessful resistance by Jewish Zealots to the Roman besiegers in A.D. 73 found in excavations in 1964 and 1965 and the Bar Kochba letters found in the valley of the Nahal Hever in 1960 and 1961.

In the long main building are the Bronfman Biblical and Archaeological Museum (see below) and the Bezalel Art Museum, which has an impressive collection of Jewish sacred art. Many of the exhibits come from the Diaspora and show the stylistic influence of the various host countries. Items of particular interest include the Ark of the Covenant from the old synagogue in Cairo and the gates of Cairo's Maimonides Synagogue (11th c.), sculpture from the first synagogue in Tiberias (2nd–3rd c.) and reconstructions of the Venetian synagogue at Vittorio Veneto (end of 17th c.) and the synagogue of Horb (near Coburg in Germany). In the Ethnographic Wing are festival costumes from Morocco, Yemen, Bokhara and other regions of the Diaspora, brides' jewellery and a profusion of other material illustrating Jewish folk art and traditions.

Bezalel
Art Museum

Another section is devoted to the work of famous artists of the 16th–19th centuries. Although in this field the museum cannot match other great museums of international standing it does possess important works by Flemish and Dutch masters. Also of interest are the Rothschild Room, a salon in Louis XV style acquired by Baron Edmond de Rothschild in 1887, the Italian Pavilion (18th century Venetian furniture) and an 18th century English dining room.

The Israel Museum was enlarged in 1990 by the addition of a three-storey pavilion, the Nathan Cummings Building, to house 20th century art. It contains the museum's collections of modern and contemporary painting, sculpture, photography, graphic art and drawings, with examples of work by such internationally known artists as Klee, Dali, Picasso and Chagall and by present-day Israeli artists (Agam, Arikha, Aroch, Dagan, Engelsberg, Kupferman, Mokady, Paldi, Rubin, Witkin, Zaritsky, etc.).

Jerusalem/Yerushalayim

Samuel Bronfman Biblical and Archaeological Museum

The Samuel Bronfman Biblical and Archaeological Museum covers a wide range, from the Palaeolithic period to the Middle Ages: house-shaped funerary urns from Azor; the mould for making figures of a Canaanite goddess, from Nahariya; a town gate from Hazor, capitals from Ramat Rahel and the Holy of Holies from a temple at Arad; a small stone tablet with the name of Pontius Pilate, from Caesarea; mosaic pavements from old synagogues, etc. The collection is constantly being enlarged by finds from current excavations. Among recent acquisitions are two silver tablets inscribed with a few words from the book of Numbers, found in an excavation in the Hinnom valley and dated to the 6th century B.C. They are thus some 400 years older than the Dead Sea scrolls. A new pavilion was specially built to house a find made in 1986 – a 1700 year old mosaic from a Roman villa at Zippori with the figure of a woman which the American excavator declared to be the finest female figure in the whole Roman world and to which he gave the name of Mona Lisa. The representation of the "Mona Lisa" is built up from small pieces of stone in sixteen shades of colour, with, as a distinctive characteristic, a small piece of black stone amid the redness of her lips.

The museum has a Youth Wing with a Children's Museum which puts on special displays on ancient history and modern art, as well as exhibitions of work by children.

Billy Rose Art Garden

On the slopes of the Neveh Sha'anan is the Billy Rose Art Garden, in which a collection of sculpture donated by Billy Rose is displayed in a terraced garden laid out by the Japanese architect Isamo Noguchi. The collection, mostly of modern work, includes sculpture by Henry Moore, Victor Vasarely, Fritz Wotruba, Jacques Lipchitz, Aristide Maillol, Pablo Picasso, Jean Tinguely, Menashe Kadishman and Yehiel Shemi.

Hebrew University

Continuing west along Ruppin Road, we come to the extensive Givat Ram campus of the Hebrew University. To the right is the Administration Building, with a mosaic of the 5th–6th century from the Jezreel plain in the entrance lobby. Nearby is the Wise Auditorium. In the centre of the campus is the Jewish National and University Library, and to the south is the eye-catching white dome of the Synagogue (designed by a German-born architect, Rau) built in honour of Rabbi Israel Goldstein.

Mount Herzl

Ruppin Road runs into Herzl Boulevard (Sderot Herzl), which leads to a military cemetery with the remains of Israeli soldiers killed since 1948 and to Mount Herzl, which commemorates the founder of Zionism.

The remains of Theodor Herzl (see Famous People), who died in Austria in 1904, were brought to Israel in 1949, a year after the foundation of the independent Jewish state for which he had called, and buried in a free-standing sarcophagus on Mount Herzl. Here too, near the main entrance, is a reconstruction of Herzl's study and library. The large park also contains the graves of Herzl's parents and several leading Zionists. On the road to the military cemetery are the graves of two prime ministers of Israel, Levi Eshkol and Golda Meir.

★★Yad Vashem

From Mount Herzl Har HaZikkaron Street leads to Har HaZikkaron, the Hill of Remembrance, with Yad Vashem, the Holocaust Memorial to the Jews murdered by the Nazis.

The name Yad Vashem means "a memorial and a name" – referring to the words of the prophet Isaiah: "Thus saith the Lord, . . . Even unto them will I give in mine house and within my walls a place and a name better than that of sons and daughters: I will give them an everlasting name, that shall not be cut off" (Isaiah 56,4–5). The decision to create this memorial to the millions of victims of National Socialism was taken by the Knesset in 1953, and it was built by the Office for the Commemoration of Martyrs and Heroes and inaugurated in 1957.

We come first into the Avenue of the Righteous, which commemorates non-Jews who risked their own lives to save Jews. Israel bestows on them

Yad Vashem: the Children's Memorial

the honorary title of the "Righteous among the Gentiles", which carries with it the right to plant a carob-tree here bearing their name.

The Hall of Remembrance is built of large blocks of undressed stone and roofed with a massive concrete slab. In the spacious windowless interior the names of the Nazi death camps are set into the floor in Hebrew and Latin lettering, and an eternal flame burns in memory of the dead. Opening

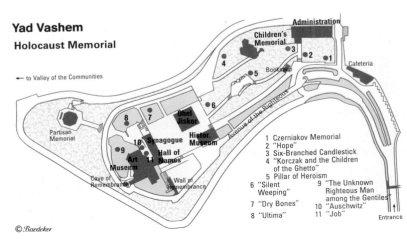

Yad Vashem
Holocaust Memorial

← to Valley of the Communities

Administration

Children's Memorial

Cafeteria

Bookshop

Avenue of the Righteous

Partisan Memorial

Ohel Jiskor

Synagogue

Histor. Museum

Art Museum

Hall of Names

Cave of Remembrance

Wall of Remembrance

Entrance

1 Czerniakov Memorial
2 "Hope"
3 Six-Branched Candlestick
4 "Korczak and the Children of the Ghetto"
5 Pillar of Heroism
6 "Silent Weeping"
7 "Dry Bones"
8 "Ultima"
9 "The Unknown Righteous Man among the Gentiles"
10 "Auschwitz"
11 "Job"

© Baedeker

off the main hall are a room containing the names of the victims, an exhibition, with photographs, a specialised library and an art museum with work by concentration camp inmates and by artists who have handled the theme of the Holocaust.

Particularly moving for most visitors will be the Children's Memorial created in 1987. In a completely dark underground room are glass walls reflecting to and fro the flames of five candles and creating the effect of countless flames, each symbolising the soul of a child. In the background can be heard a woman's voice giving the names of the children, their age and their place of birth.

A recent addition (1990) is the Valley of the Communities: a re-afforested area with high walls bearing tablets commemorating communities exterminated by the Nazis.

Within the extensive grounds of Yad Vashem are numerous works of sculpture and memorials on the theme of the Holocaust. Among the most impressive are Lea Michelson's "Silent Weeping", Ilana Gur's "Hope", Nandor Glid's "Dry Bones" and Boris Saktsier's "Korczak and the Children of the Ghetto" (commemorating a Polish teacher who went voluntarily into Treblinka extermination camp along with his children).

Near the entrance to the Administration Building is a six-branched candlestick which is the symbol of Yad Vashem. Its six arms represent the six million Jews who perished at the hands of the Nazis.

★En Karem

Returning to the main road, we turn right into En Karem Road, which runs down into the En Karem valley (4km/2½ miles). According to a Christian tradition going back at least as far as the 5th or 6th century the village of En Karem, set amid terraced vineyards, was the home of Zacharias and Elizabeth, where Mary visited her pregnant cousin Elizabeth (Luke 1,39–56) and where Elizabeth's son John the Baptist was born (Luke 1,57–66). From the main road a street on the right leads to the Franciscan friary of St John. The church was built in the 17th century over the Grotto of St John, traditionally

"Korczak and the Children of the Ghetto"

"Silent Weeping"

St John's Church, En Karem *Church of the Visitation*

John's birthplace. In another grotto near the entrance to the church is a mosaic of the 5th or 6th century depicting peacocks and doves, with a Greek inscription "Greetings to God's martyr". The church has fine wrought-iron screens. Steps lead down to the crypt, the Grotto of St John, with a marble slab bearing the inscription "Hic praecursor Domini natus est" ("Here the forerunner of the Lord was born"). Round the walls are reliefs of scenes from the life of John the Baptist.

On the opposite side of the main street, in the centre of the village, is a spring which has been known since Crusader times as the Spring of the Virgin. Beside it is a mosque, abandoned since the Arab population left the village in 1948. Steps lead up to the Franciscan Church of the Visitation, on the site of the house in which Mary is believed to have visited Elizabeth. The two-storey modern church, with a mosaic of the Visitation on the façade, was built over the ruins of a church of the Crusader period. In the lower church is an ancient cistern. The upper church preserves part of the apse of the Crusader church, beside which are crosses scratched in the stone by pilgrims. The furnishings of the church are modern.

From the Spring of the Virgin a narrow rocky path runs up the hill to a convent of Russian nuns with a small colourful church. Above the group of houses is an unfinished basilica.

From En Karem we take the road which runs north-west to Eitanim and in 2km/1¼ miles turn left into a road leading to the Hadassah Medical Centre (clinics of the Hebrew University), opened in 1962. Within the complex is a synagogue with twelve stained-glass windows (the tribes of Israel) by Marc Chagall.

Hadassah Medical Centre

Below, in the valley, is the little Franciscan monastery of St John in the Wilderness, recalling John the Baptist's early days in the desert (Luke 1,80).

St John in the Wilderness

On a hill to the south can be seen the Kennedy Memorial, the building of which was financed by contributions from American citizens. It can be

Kennedy Memorial

reached by taking the road which runs south-east from Hadassah and turning right into a road to the village of Ora; the monument is 3km/2 miles beyond the village.

★ Model of
Ancient
Jerusalem

From Mount Herzl Rav Uziel Street runs south to the Holyland Hotel, in the western suburb of Bayit VeGan. In the grounds of the hotel is a model of ancient Jerusalem.

The project was initiated and financed by the owner of the Holyland Hotel, Hans Kroch, the model was designed by the archaeologist Michael Avi-Yonah and it was executed between 1965 and 1968 by the sculptor E. Scheffler and by R. Brotze. The result is impressive, combining scientific accuracy with visual impact. This is what Jerusalem looked like in the time of the Second Temple, soon after the reign of Herod the Great: that is, in the time of Christ.

In an area of some 1000sq.m/1200sq.yds (= 1 dunam) the original topography was re-created in reinforced concrete and correctly oriented to the compass points (important for the effect of light and shade). The scale chosen was 1:50, so that 2 centimetres on the model represent 1 metre on the ground. This large scale made it possible to avoid the usual distortions between horizontal and vertical measurements. Between the highest point in the model, the Tower of Psephinus (815m/2674ft), and the lowest, in the Kidron valley (606m/1988ft), there is a difference in height of some 4 metres (13 feet). In constructing the model the original materials (stone, marble, metal) were used, so that a protective roof could be dispensed with. This enhanced the realistic effect of the model, though it meant that the details could not be so accurately reproduced as in plaster or plastic material.

The design of the model was based on a careful examination and evaluation of the archaeological evidence and the written sources. The most important of these sources were, for the structure and furnishings of the Temple, two treatises in the Mishnah, the "Midot" ("Survey") and the "Tamid" ("The Daily Temple Sacrifice"), and for the city as a whole Flavius

Model of Jerusalem in the time of Herod I in the grounds of the Holyland Hotel

Josephus's description in the "Jewish War". There are still gaps, however, in our knowledge of the city before its destruction in A.D. 70 – its detailed layout and, more particularly, the style of the larger buildings. This meant looking for analogies elsewhere. Thus the Hasmonean palace (2nd–1st c. B.C.) and the Herodian buildings (1st c. B.C.) were modelled on Hellenistic palaces, the palace of Queen Helen of Adiabene on Parthian buildings in her native Mesopotamia.

The entrance to the site (portable tape-recorded commentaries available) is on the west side, from which there is a general view of the city extending eastward to the Temple Mount. To the north can be seen the Second Wall and Agrippa I's Third Wall, with an extensive unbuilt-on area between them. At the north-west corner is the octagonal Tower of Psephinus. Half way along the west side are the three towers of Herod's Citadel ("David's Tower"). In front is the square tower named Phasael after Herod's elder brother, with two storeys rising above the lower wall-walk; beyond this is the tower named Hippicus after a friend of Herod's, with tall pillars round its four sides and a round upper section topped by a small dome; and to the south of this is the tower named Mariamne after Herod's wife, a Hasmonean princess, with a square base, three storeys of varying height surrounded by columns and a pointed conical top.

To the north of the Citadel is the tomb of the Hasmonean high priest John Hyrcanus (135–104 B.C.), with a pyramidal roof. To the south (in what is now the Armenian Quarter) is the rectangular palace of Herod with its gardens and suites of rooms. The adjoining upper town is laid out as an elegant residential district, with a rectangular grid of streets in accordance with the principles of Hippodamus of Miletus. Built against the wall running from the Citadel to Temple Mount (on the line of present-day David Street and Chain Street) is the rectangular complex of the Hasmonean palace. To the south of this (against the wall between the upper and lower town) is the Roman-style theatre built by Herod.

Going round the model in an anti-clockwise direction, we come to the south and then to the east side. Here we see the lower town, reconstructed as a huddle of small houses. In this area were shops, craftsmen's workshops and industrial establishments. To the east of this is the cramped area of the original City of David on Mount Ophel, into which Michael Avi-Yonah fitted a Roman hippodrome and a number of palatial mansions. To the north of this is the Temple Mount, separated from the city to the west by the Valley of the Cheesemakers (Tyropoeon), which is now filled in. At the south-west corner are the steps leading up the hill over Robinson's Arch; farther north is Wilson's Arch. In the south wall can be seen the Huldah Gates, one of the main entrances to the Temple (brought to light by recent excavations). Above the south wall rises the Royal Stoa (Stoa Basilike). Other colonnaded halls can be seen on the other sides of the large platform, the centre of which is occupied by the Herodian Temple with its courtyards on the east side. The exterior of this tall and massive structure is decorated with half-columns, pilasters, richly ornamented pediments and stepped battlements.

On the north the Temple platform is dominated by the mighty Antonia Fortress with its four corner towers, another Herodian building. To the north, within the inner wall (the Second Wall), are various markets. Beyond the outer wall (the Third Wall) the most notable feature is the Pool of Bethesda, surrounded by four Hellenistic porticoes, with a fifth dividing it into two halves. Here as elsewhere the model makes clear that in the 1st century A.D., in the time of Jesus, Jerusalem was largely a Hellenistic town. Here, as elsewhere in the Near East in this period Greco-Roman and Eastern were combined in a characteristic mixed culture.

Surroundings of Jerusalem

Hebron Road (Derekh Hevron) runs south from the railway station to Bethlehem (see entry). In 6.5km/4 miles the Greek Orthodox monastery of

Bethlehem, Hebron

St Elias (Elijah), founded in the 12th century and rebuilt in the 17th, is seen on higher ground to the left of the road. 1.5km/1 mile beyond this, on the right, is the Tomb of Rachel, a small domed building possibly dating from the 12th century. Soon after this, at a junction, the road to the right continues to Hebron (see entry), while the road to the left leads to Bethlehem (2km/1¼ miles).

Abu Ghosh, Latrun

Leave Jerusalem on the expressway to Tel Aviv. In 10km/6 miles a road goes off to the Arab hill village of Abu Ghosh (see entry). 15km/9 miles beyond this is the monastery of Latrun (see entry).

Givat Shaul

On the road to Ramallah, 5km/3 miles north of Jerusalem, is the hill of Givat Shaul (839m/2753ft), the site of Gibeath in the territory of the tribe of Benjamin (Joshua 18,28).
1km/⅔ mile south is the Biblical Zuph (now Shufat), home of the prophet Samuel (1 Samuel 9,5–6), where Samuel anointed Saul as first king of the Jews (1 Samuel 10,1).

Nabi Samwil

Shortly after Givat Shaul a road goes off on the left and comes in a few kilometres to Nabi Samwil (see entry), named after the prophet Samuel, whose tomb is revered here.

Gibeon/Jib

10km/6 miles north-west of Jerusalem (and only a few kilometres north of Nebi Samwil), in the hills of Judaea, is the Arab village of Jib, which is believed to be the Gibeon of the Old Testament. Excavations here brought to light a remarkable water supply system, with a large circular cistern of the Canaanite period and a tunnel linking it with a nearby underground spring.

El-Qubeiba

From Jib a narrow road runs west to the village of El-Qubeiba, a few kilometres away, which many people have believed since the Crusader period to be the Biblical Emmaus, where the risen Christ appeared to two of his disciples (Luke 24,13; but see also Latrun). There is a Franciscan church built in 1901 on the site of an earlier Crusader church.

El-Azariya, Wadi Qilt

The road east from Jerusalem runs past the village of El-Azariya/Bethany (see entry), where Christ raised Lazarus from the dead (John 11,1). At Ma'ale Am (16km/10 miles), in a bend to the right, a road goes off on the left into the Wadi Qilt (see entry), through which ran the Roman road to Jericho (see entry). From a viewpoint here a road runs down to the Greek Orthodox monastery of St George in the wadi.

Jezreel Plain/Emeq Yizre'el/HaEmeq   G/H 3

Districts: Northern, Haifa

Situation and characteristics

The large and fertile valley of the Jezreel plain, frequently referred to merely as HaEmeq (the Valley), extends south-eastward from the bay north of Haifa to the Jordan valley between the upland regions of Samaria and Galilee. The Arabs call it Marj Ibn Amr; its Old Testament name is the plain of Esdraelon.
The Jezreel plain is the largest valley in Israel and one of its most fertile regions. To the south-west the Iron valley forms a transition to the plain of Sharon (see entry). Megiddo (see entry), strategically situated on the Iron pass, was a place of great military importance from ancient times to the present century. As a zone of passage and an area of great fertility the Jezreel plain has been frequently fought over in the course of history, notably in the time of Deborah (Judges 5,19) and Gideon (Judges 7,5).

Settlements

The chief town and traffic junction point in the Jezreel plain is Afula (see entry).

In 1938 the kibbutz of Yizre'el was founded on the road between Afula and Jenin, which broadly follows the watershed between the eastern and western halves of the plain. It was one of the many Jewish settlements established after the Jewish National Fund began in 1910 to buy up land in the area, which since 1870 had belonged to Lebanese landowners. The kibbutz occupies the site of a palace of King Ahab of Israel, who had seized a vineyard belonging to Naboth the Jezreelite and built a palace on it (1 Kings 21). Here too Ahab's wife Jezebel and his son Joram were killed by his successor Jehu (2 Kings 9,27 and 33). Ahab's palace was later destroyed by the Persians.

On the tell adjoining the kibbutz are remains of the Crusader castle of Le Petit Gérin and its church; there are fine views from the top of the hill.

River Jordan/Yarden

H/J 2–4

The river Jordan (Hebrew Yarden), the longest (252km/157 miles) and most abundantly flowing river in Israel, is formed by the junction of three source streams, passes through the Sea of Galilee and after some meandering flows into the Dead Sea, bringing it a supply of fresh water.

Situation and characteristics

Although the Jordan is not particularly deep or wide, its significance for the Christian faith makes it one of the most famous rivers in the world.

The Jordan's three source streams are the Hazbani, which rises in Lebanon, the Dan, rising in the Dan Nature Reserve (see entry), and the Banyas, which rises at the village of that name (see entry). The three streams join in the Hule basin, and the Jordan then flows through a narrow valley into the Sea of Galilee, which it reaches after a course of 60km/37 miles.

Source streams

After emerging from the Sea of Galilee the Jordan is joined by the Yarmouk, which marks the frontier between Jordan and the Israeli-occupied Golan Heights. The Yarmouk was the scene of a dramatic historical event in August 636, when, during a violent sandstorm, the Arabs advancing from the south inflicted an annihilating defeat on the army of the Byzantine Emperor Heraclius. Palestine and Syria were lost to the Byzantine Empire and the period of Islamic rule began.

River Yarmouk

On the north bank of the Yarmouk is the spa of Hamat Gader (see entry), where Israeli archaeologists began excavating the site of the Roman settlement in 1967.

The riverine plain between the Sea of Galilee and the junction with the Yarmouk is broad and fertile. To the south the west bank becomes narrower, but opens out again at Bet Shean (see entry). In this area the Nahal Harod flows into the Jordan from the west.

Other tributaries

Farther south the Jordan is joined by the Nahal Tirza on the west bank and the Nahal Yaboq on the east. The east bank between Naharayim and Damiya was irrigated by the Jordanian government with aid from the United States, and more than 100,000 farmers have settled there since the 1960s.

South of Damiya the west bank of the river opens out into the Jordan plain, with the oasis of Jericho (see entry). Since 1967 numerous villages have been established in this area, whose inhabitants are able to harvest valuable agricultural crops out of season.

Jordan plain

Between the south end of the Sea of Galilee and the Dead Sea the Jordan follows a winding course. On the way to the Dead Sea it is spanned by the Adam (Damiya), Allenby and Abdullah Bridges. Between the Allenby and Abdullah Bridges is the spot, 8km/5 miles east of Jericho, where Jesus is believed to have been baptised.

The Jordan rift valley is part of the Syro-African Depression. In the Dead Sea (surface 398m/1306ft below sea level, bed up to 831m/2727ft below sea

Jordan rift valley

275

The Jordan as it leaves the Sea of Galilee

Place of baptism in the Jordan (Yardenit)

level) it reaches its deepest point, which is also the lowest point on the surface of the earth. The rift valley continues along the Arava depression and the Gulf of Aqaba into East Africa.

Judaea/Yehuda   F–H 4/5

Districts: Central, Tel Aviv, Jerusalem; West Bank

Situation and characteristics

Judaea extends from the Mediterranean in the west to the Jordan and the Dead Sea in the east and from the river Yarqon (which flows into the sea at Tel Aviv) in the north to a line between Gaza and En Gedi in the south. It is made up of the Shefela plain in the west, the central uplands (Har Yehuda) and the Judaean Desert (Midbar Yehuda) to the east. The southern part reaches a height of 1020m/3347ft at Hebron, the northern part 1016m/3333ft in the Bet El Hills.

Judaea is the most southerly of the three Biblical regions west of the Jordan (the others being Galilee and Samaria). In the south it was bounded in the time of Christ by Idumaea; it is now bordered by the Negev (see entry).

The northern part of the Judaean coastal plain has the highest population density in Israel. In the south, where the plain has been enlarged by deposits of sand carried down by the Nile, citrus fruits are grown, and farther inland wheat and vegetables. The Judaean Hills fall steeply down to the Dead Sea and form a rain barrier, so that the area to the east has become a desert which can be used only for grazing. Exceptions to this are a number of oases, like those of En Gedi on the Dead Sea and Jericho (see entries). Lying below sea level, the oases have a warm climate in which plants of many different species flourish.

History

Around 1200 B.C. the Philistines established themselves in the coastal plain, while the hills were occupied by the tribes of Judah and Benjamin, which

David united in a single kingdom after the death of Saul. Later David was recognised as king of all twelve tribes; but after the death of his son Solomon the ten northern tribes formed the kingdom of Israel and the two southern tribes the kingdom of Judah, which came to an end in 586 B.C. with the Babylonian conquest. Under Roman rule (from 63 B.C.) Judaea, along with Galilee and Samaria, fell within the territory ruled by Hyrcanus II and Herod, and thereafter was governed by Roman procurators.

The Diaspora of the Jews began after the destruction of Jerusalem in A.D. 70. In the 4th century Judaea was largely Christianised; then in the 7th century the process of Islamisation began. Small Jewish communities still survived, however, in Jerusalem and in Hebron and the surrounding area. After the War of Independence in 1948–49 western Judaea became part of the newly founded state of Israel and the eastern part of the region, with Hebron as its centre, passed to Jordan, which also received much of Samaria. In 1967 these territories, together with East Jerusalem, were occupied by Israeli troops.

Kefar Nahum

See Capernaum

Lachish   G 5

District: Southern
Altitude: 250m/820ft

The moshav of Lakhish, 10km/6 miles south-east of Qiryat Gat, to the south of the road from Ashqelon via Bet Guvrin and Bet Shemesh to Jerusalem, was founded in 1955 on the site of ancient Lachish and took its name. Along with the settlements of Bet Guvrin (see entry) and Tel Maresha (see Mareshah) a few kilometres north-east, Lachish is one of the most interesting archaeological sites in this area to the west of the Judaean Hills.

Situation and characteristics

The site was occupied as early as the 3rd millennium B.C., and in the 2nd millennium it was a Canaanite town. Letters found at Tell el-Amarna in Egypt show King Zimridu (1375–40 B.C.) defending himself against a charge of disloyalty to his Egyptian overlord, Pharaoh Akhenaten. In the 13th century B.C. Joshua, after his conquest of Jericho, Ai and Gibeon, captured five Amorite kings, including Japhia of Lachish, in a cave at Makkedah and put them to death; then in the following year he took Lachish and the neighbouring city of Mareshah (Joshua 10). The palace was rebuilt by David or Solomon in the 10th century B.C. Around 920 B.C. Solomon's son Rehoboam fortified the town, which had an area of 75,000sq.m/ 90,000sq.yds (2 Chronicles 11,11). In the 8th century B.C. King Amaziah of Judah, who had fled from Jerusalem, was killed here (2 Kings 14,19).

History

Lachish was captured in 701 B.C. by the Assyrian king Sennacherib (2 Kings 18,13–17), who depicted this event in reliefs in his palace in Nineveh. During Starkey's excavations a pit was found containing the skeletons of 1500 men who died on that occasion. In 588 B.C. Nebuchadnezzar conquered the town (two years before his conquest of Jerusalem). The period immediately before this catastrophe is documented in the Lachish Letters (now in the British Museum and the Rockefeller Museum in Jerusalem). The town was reoccupied after the Israelites' return from the Babylonian Captivity, and later a Persian fortress was built in the town. In the 2nd century B.C. it declined into an insignificant village.

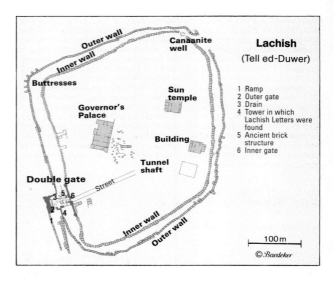

Lachish
(Tell ed-Duwer)

1 Ramp
2 Outer gate
3 Drain
4 Tower in which Lachish Letters were found
5 Ancient brick structure
6 Inner gate

© Baedeker

Excavations

Tel Lakhish, the site of ancient Lachish, was excavated by John L. Starkey (1932–36) and Yohanan Aharoni (1967–68). Starkey found nine occupation levels extending from the 3rd millennium to the 3rd century B.C.

To the north of the moshav were found remains of a double ring of walls and a massive gateway with a tower (inside the outer gate, on the right) in which the Lachish Letters (in Old Hebrew, written in ink on clay tablets) were found.

In the centre of the site was a palace, the seat of the governor; to the south-east was a well-shaft and to the north-east a sun temple (c. 1480 B.C.) which Kathleen Kenyon interpreted as the temple of a Canaanite divine triad. In the temple were found a three-pronged iron fork and a vessel for sacrificial flesh (9th c. B.C.) – pointing to the survival of the Canaanite cult into this late period.

Latrun   G 4

West Bank

Situation and characteristics

The monastery of Latrun, on the east side of the Ayalon valley, was built in 1927 by French Trappist monks. It lies – its long façade visible from a long way off – between the old road and the new expressway from Tel Aviv to Jerusalem, shortly before the two roads merge (28km/17 miles west of Jerusalem on the Israeli-occupied West Bank).

Until quite recent times this was a place of strategic importance. During the period of the mandate the British authorities had a fortified police post here which was handed over to the Arab Legion in 1948. The monastery and surrounding area were thus in Jordanian territory, and the road to Jerusalem was closed. It was reopened in 1967.

Sights

Monastery

In the beautifully laid out monastery garden is a collection of late antique and early Christian capitals and reliefs. In the monastery itself visitors can

The site of ancient Lachish

The monastery of Latrun, set amid luxuriant gardens

Lod (Lydda)

see the church. The monks are famed for their wine (sales point by the gate).

Crusader castle

On the hill behind the monastery (view) are the ruins of the Crusader castle of Toron des Chevaliers (12th c.). Hence the Arab name of El-Torun or Latrun, which led Christian pilgrims of the late medieval period to believe that this was the home of the Good Thief crucified with Christ (Latin *latro* = "thief").

Surroundings of Latrun

Amwas/Emmaus

1km/¾ mile north of Latrun, on the expressway, are the ruins of the Arab village of Amwas, a name derived from ancient Emmaus, the Greek name of several places in Palestine. The Emmaus in which the risen Christ appeared to two of the disciples (Luke 24,13) lay "three score furlongs" (60 stades: ie. 7 miles) from Jerusalem, which has led to its identification with El-Qubeiba, north-west of Jerusalem (see Jerusalem, Surroundings). Another tradition makes the distance from Jerusalem 160 stades (19 miles), which would fit in with Amwas. Excavations here have brought to light a Roman villa with mosaic pavements (2nd c.), a synagogue with an inscription in Greek and Hebrew (3rd c.) and two Byzantine churches (4th and 6th c.). A Crusader church was destroyed by Ibrahim Pasha in 1834.

Lod (Lydda)   G 4

District: Central
Altitude: 65m/215ft
Population: 38,000

Situation and characteristics

Lod (Lydda), 22km/14 miles south-east of Tel Aviv and 3km/2 miles north-east of Ramla, is now known mainly for its international airport, but it reaches far back into the past in history and myth.

History

The town was founded by the tribe of Benjamin after the Israelite occupation of the Promised Land (1 Chronicles 8,12). It was destroyed by the Assyrians in the 8th century B.C., rebuilt in the 5th century and occupied from the 4th century onwards by Greeks, who named it Lydda. The Hasmoneans captured the town in 143 B.C. (1 Maccabees 11,34). There was a Christian community here at a very early stage. Paul visited Lydda and healed a man who had been bedridden for eight years (Acts 9,32–34) before going on to Joppa (Jaffa: see Tel Aviv) and Caesarea (see entry). The Romans took the town during their advance on Jerusalem (A.D. 67) and renamed it Diospolis (City of Zeus). It still bears that name in the 6th century Madaba map.

After the destruction of Jerusalem in A.D. 70 there were still a few Jewish schools in the town, but in the 2nd century the rabbis left it because of its pagan character. In the time of Constantine (4th c.) it was predominantly Christian. It acquired special importance from its association with St George, who according to tradition was born in Lydda, served as a tribune in the Roman army and was martyred in 303, in the reign of Diocletian. His remains were brought back to Lydda, where from the 5th century onwards pilgrims were shown his tomb. The portrayal of the saint as a dragon-slayer seems, according to T. F. Meysels, to go back to the older myth of the dragon slain by Perseus when he freed Andromeda at Jaffa, farther up the coast; and it would appear that behind the dragon of the Perseus myth lurks the Philistine god Dagon.

St George, a megalomartyr of the Eastern church, also became a holy man revered by the Muslims – the bright spirit El-Chodr, who on the day of judgment will vanquish the demon Dajal outside the gates of Lod.

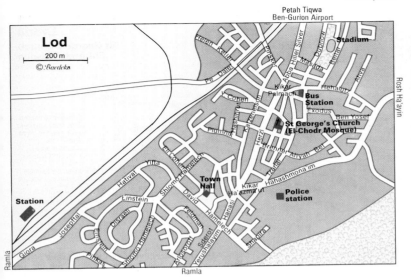

In Byzantine times a basilica dedicated to this warrior saint was built in Lod, but this was lost when the Omayyad Caliph Abd el-Malik destroyed Lod. The church was rebuilt by the Crusaders in the reign of Richard Coeur de Lion, and St George became the patron saint of England.

In the 13th century the Mamelukes used the church as a quarry of building stone for the El-Chodr Mosque, dedicated to the same St George as an Islamic holy man. Later the town sank into insignificance. In 1870 the Greek Orthodox community acquired the remains of the church and built a modern church on the site.

Most of the Arab inhabitants of the town left it in 1948 and were replaced by new Jewish immigrants. Lod now has a population of 4000 Arabs and 34,000 Jews.

During the British Mandate an airfield was constructed a few kilometres north of Lod, and soon after the foundation of the new Jewish state, in November 1948, this began to be used for civil aviation. In the following year the Israeli national airline, El Al, was established, and Lod became an international airport, which from 1975 bore the name of Israel's first prime minister, Ben-Gurion.

St George's Church/El-Chodr Mosque

When the minaret of the El-Chodr Mosque collapsed in 1927 it was replaced by the present white minaret, a prominent landmark drawing attention to this double shrine of the Christian saint and the Islamic holy man. The complex occupies the site of the 6th century Byzantine basilica and the Crusader church which replaced it in the 12th century. Columns and other elements from these earlier buildings have been preserved in the present structure.

The entrance to both the church and the mosque are at the west end of the complex. Between them are a number of shops.

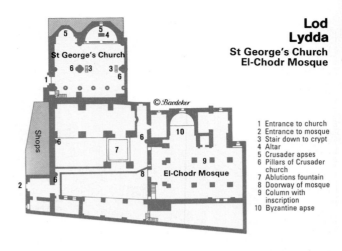

**Lod
Lydda**
**St George's Church
El-Chodr Mosque**

© *Baedeker*

1 Entrance to church
2 Entrance to mosque
3 Stair down to crypt
4 Altar
5 Crusader apses
6 Pillars of Crusader church
7 Ablutions fountain
8 Doorway of mosque
9 Column with inscription
10 Byzantine apse

St George's Church

To the left of the shops is the entrance to the Greek Orthodox church of St George, rebuilt in 1870. Over the doorway is a relief of St George and the dragon. The church occupies the north end of the nave and left-hand aisle of the Crusader church, from which there survive two apses – which, contrary to the normal rule, face north rather than east – and two columns. The painting of the interior rather spoils the imposing spatial effect. Between the two columns, in front of the iconostasis, are two flights of steps leading down to the crypt. This contains the sarcophagus of St George, on the lid of which (restored, as an inscription records, in 1871, in the time of Patriarch Cyril) is a likeness of the saint.

El-Chodr Mosque

The southern part of the complex is occupied by the El-Chodr Mosque. In the forecourt, to the left, is an ablutions fountain. At the north end of the prayer hall is an apse from the Byzantine church, and near the east side is a column, also from the church, with a Greek inscription.

Surroundings of Lod

Ramla

3km/2 miles south is the town of Ramla (see entry), with both Christian and Islamic monuments.

Mameluke bridge

On the road running north from Lod is a stone bridge with pointed arches. Between two lions similar to those on the Lion Gate (St Stephen's Gate) in Jerusalem is an Arabic inscription recording the contruction of the bridge by the Mameluke Sultan Baibars in 1273.

Tomb of Mazor

Continuing north on the same road and passing Lod Airport, we come (9km/6 miles from Lod) to a side road on the right. Turning into this road and in 5km/3 miles taking a road on the left signposted to Rosh Ha'Ayin (see entry), we come in another 4km/2½ miles to the Tomb of Hazor, a few kilometres west of the village of Hazor. This Roman (or Nabataean) temple-tomb of the 2nd or 3rd century, built of dressed stone, stands in the middle of an earlier necropolis. On the façade, between massive buttresses, are two Corinthian columns supporting the entablature. A staircase leads up on to the roof.

Makhtesh Hagadol

District: Southern

Makhtesh Hagadol (the "Great Mortar") is the middle one of three erosion craters in the Negev, smaller than Makhtesh Ramon (see entry). Like Makhtesh Haqatan, the "Little Mortar", it lies to the north of the Wilderness of Zin.

Situation and characteristics

From the development town of Yeroham (32km/20 miles south-east of Beersheba), founded in 1951, a road runs south-east and comes in 7km/4½ miles to the north-western edge of the crater. Continuing through the crater, we emerge from it through a gorge on the south-east side. Off the road to the right, 5km/3 miles south-west, are the Oron phosphate works, where many of the inhabitants of Yeroham work. A road to the left runs north and in 12km/7½ miles joins the road from Beersheba via Dimona to the Dead Sea at Mount Rotem, near the site of Mamshit (see entry).

Through the crater

From here it is possible, with an all-terrain vehicle, to go on to Makhtesh Haqatan. 3km/2 miles beyond Makhtesh Hagadol a narrow road branches off the Oron–Rotem road on the right and runs south-east to the kibbutz of Hazeva in the Arava depression (32km/20 miles). In 10km/6 miles this runs close to Makhtesh Haqatan (on left), which can be reached in a half-hour walk. On its south-east side is a gorge leading to the Wilderness of Zin. 4km/2½ miles farther on is the Scorpion Staircase (Ma'ale Aqrabbim), which Moses was told would be the southern border of the land to be settled by the Jews: "And your border shall turn from the south to the ascent of Akrabbim, and pass on to Zin: and the going forth thereof shall be from the south to Kadesh-barnea" (Numbers 34,4). The "staircase", rebuilt by the British authorities, leads steeply down 450m/1475ft into the Wilderness of Zin. The road continues to Hazeva, 137m/449ft below sea level, where it runs into the road from Elat to the Dead Sea.

Makhtesh Haqatan

Makhtesh Ramon

District: Southern

The largest of the three elliptical craters known as "mortars" (makhtesh) in the Negev is Makhtesh Ramon, which is 30km/19 miles long by 8km/5 miles wide. It lies 86km/53 miles south of Beersheba between the Wilderness of Zin and the Wadi Paran

Situation and characteristics

Makhtesh is not a volcanic crater but was formed 70 million years ago by the collapse of the land over underground cavities. Huge fossils of saurians which lived 150 million years ago were found here.

The road from Beersheba leads to the little town of Mizpe Ramon, founded in 1953. On the south side of the town is a viewing terrace (restaurant) from which there is an impressive view into the crater, the bottom of which is 500m/1640ft lower down.

★View

On the western edge of the crater Har Ramon rises to 1035m/3396ft, Har Ored on the south side to 935m/3068ft. On the east side are the remains of forts, notably Mezad Mishhor, built by the Nabataeans in the 1st century B.C. to protect the caravan route from their capital, Petra, to Avdat and via Subeita (Shivta: see entry) to Nizzana.

View of Makhtesh Ramon from the viewing terrace at Mizpe Ramon

Mamshit/Kurnub G 6

District: Southern
Altitude: 470m/1540ft

Situation and
characteristics

The remarkable ruins of ancient Mampsis (Hebrew Mamshit, Arabic Kurnub), the most northerly Nabataean town in the Negev, are prominently
situated on a hill 42km/26 miles south-east of Beersheba and 6km/4 miles
south-east of Dimona. Excavations by Abraham Negev between 1965 and
1973 brought to light a Nabataean settlement which had undergone little
change in Byzantine times, so that its original character is better preserved
than at Avdat (see entry), Nizzana or Shivta (see entry).

History

The town of Mampsis was founded during the period when the Nabataeans, from their capital at Petra, set out to colonise the Negev. It prospered in the 1st century A.D. as a trading town with a caravanserai, stables,
residential areas and administrative buildings. After the fall of Nabatene in
106 the Romans built barracks here. In Byzantine times (when Mampsis
featured on the mosaic map at Madaba) the old Nabataean system of
irrigation was brought into use again, as it was at Avdat, and two churches
were built. The town was destroyed during the Arab conquest in the 7th
century.

The ★Site

Administrative
buildings

The town is entered through the north gate in the town walls, from which
we continue along ancient streets between blocks of houses to two large
administrative buildings. Here, as in many of the houses, can be seen the
springing of the stone arches which supported the roof. There is little

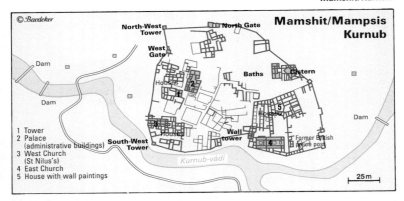

© Baedeker

North-West Tower
North Gate
Mamshit/Mampsis
Kurnub
West Gate
Baths
Cistern
Dam
Dam
Houses
2
1
5
Houses
Dam
3
Houses
Wall tower
4
Former British police post
South-West Tower
Kurnub-vádi

1 Tower
2 Palace (administrative buildings)
3 West Church (St Nilus's)
4 East Church
5 House with wall paintings

25 m

ornament. In one of the buildings the arches have been preserved and it is possible to climb to the upper floor, from which there is a fine general view of the site.

Keeping straight ahead, we come to the West Church, which is built against the town walls. This aisled basilica was built by St Nilus of Sinai about 400, as an inscription in the mosaic pavement of the nave records: "Lord, help thy servant Nilus, builder of this church. Amen". Also preserved are the columns between the nave and the aisles, the apses at the east end and part of the marble screen between the nave and the sanctuary.

West Church (St Nilus's)

Farther east, immediately in front of the ruins of a police post of the Mandate period, is the East Church, which was dedicated to the Holy

East Church

Mamshit: steps leading up . . .   *. . . to the East Church*

285

Mamshit: water channel . . .   *. . . and arched doorway*

Martyrs. It is approached by a broad flight of steps leading up from a square which from Nabataean to Byzantine times was the market square. Like the West Church, it is an aisled basilica. In the atrium is a large cistern. A mosaic pavement in the nave has been preserved; in the right-hand apse is the tomb of a martyr.

Other buildings

Other interesting buildings, identified by signs, include stables, a portico with Nabataean horn-capitals and a building with well preserved wall paintings.

Dams

To the west of the site, far below in the wadi, can be seen the dams (recently restored) which enabled the Nabataeans and Byzantines to store up water during the short rainy season for use during the arid summer months.

Cemetery

Outside the entrance to the site, on the right when leaving it, is a signpost pointing to a cemetery north-east of the town in which numerous tomb chambers have been excavated.

Mareshah

District: Southern
Altitude: 275m/900ft

Situation and
characteristics

The ancient city of Mareshah in Judaea lies 16km/10 miles east of Qiryat Gat and 2km/1¼ miles south of Bet Guvrin (see entry) on the road from Ashqelon via Qiryat Gat and Bet Shemesh to Jerusalem. The Arab name of the site, Tell Sandahanna, is derived from a church dedicated to St Anne. The special feature of Mareshah is the numerous caves round the tell, of which there are something like sixty in all. For a visit to this labyrinth it is advisable to take a guide from the local kibbutz.

Mareshah is assigned in the book of Joshua (15,44) to the tribe of Judah. The site is an irregular rectangle 160m/175yds by 150m/165yds; with an area of 24,000sq.km/29,000sq.yds, it is only a third of the size of neighbouring Lachish (see entry). About 920 B.C. it was fortified by Solomon's son Rehoboam along with Lachish and fourteen other towns, "which are in Judah and in Benjamin fenced cities" (2 Chronicles 11,8–10). It was destroyed by the Babylonians in 587 B.C. and after the Israelites' return from the Babylonian Captivity was not reoccupied by Jews: like other places in southern Judaea and the Negev, it was resettled by Edomites, who made it their capital. In the 4th century B.C. the Phoenicians founded a colony here – a departure from their usual practice of establishing their settlements on the coast. In the 3rd century B.C. the town was Hellenised and, under the name of Marissa, became the chief place in the province of Idumaea. Around 160 B.C. it was taken by Judas Maccabeus during his advance from Hebron to Ashdod (1 Maccabees 5,66), and about 115 B.C., in the reign of the Hasmonean ruler John Hyrcanus I, it was forcibly Judaised along with the rest of Idumaea. The town was finally destroyed in 40 B.C.

The site was identified as the Biblical city of Mareshah by an American scholar, Edward Robinson, in 1838 and was excavated by the Palestine Exploration Fund in 1900.

History

Sights

On the western slope of the tell is a burial cave of the 2nd century B.C., 32m/105ft long and 2.3m/7½ft wide. The walls contain no fewer than 1906 recesses for funerary urns, and accordingly the complex is known, on the analogy of similar Roman tombs, as a columbarium.

In the valley on the east side of the tell two tomb chambers of the 2nd century were discovered, one of which has wall paintings and carved urns and eagles on the front. The interior is in the shape of a reversed T, like some tombs at Palmyra, and contains 44 tomb recesses with Greek inscriptions. An inscription addressed by a girl to a young man suggests that the tomb had become a meeting-place for lovers.

Burial caves

Even more impressive than the burial caves is the "cave city" which also lies to the east of the tell. It consists of 44 bell-shaped caves lit by openings in the roof and linked with one another by underground passages. The origin and purpose of this underground town have not been established. It is supposed that the Phoenicians settled in Mareshah in the 4th century B.C. because it offered a supply of building stone for their port of Ashkelon and that they drove shafts through the hard surface rock to quarry the stone lying lower down.

Numbers of crosses scratched in the rock show that in Christian times the caves were occupied by hermits.

★Cave city

St Anne's Church, to the east of the road from Mareshah to Bet Guvrin, was built by the Crusaders in the 12th century. The central apse is well preserved.

St Anne's Church

Mar Saba/St Sabas's Monastery

H 5

West Bank. Altitude: 240m/785ft

The historic old Greek Orthodox monastery of St Sabas (Mar Saba) lies 18km/11 miles from Bethlehem (see entry) in the Judaean Hills, here sloping down towards the Dead Sea, on the Israeli-occupied west bank of the Jordan.

The monastery is reached by way of Bethlehem or from Jerusalem on a road which runs south-east via Abu Dis. Its watch-tower can be seen from afar rising amid the barren Judaean Hills. The last stretch of the road runs downhill, to end immediately in front of the entrance to the monastery.

Situation and characteristics

Mar Saba/St Sabas's Monastery

History

In the almost vertical rock walls of the Kidron gorge to the west of St Sabas's Monastery are innumerable caves which were inhabited by hermits in the early Christian centuries. One of these was occupied by the young Sabas, who – like the founder of the monastery of St Theodosius – was a native of Cappadocia (born 439). In 457 he entered a monastery in Jerusalem, but in 478 left it to seek solitude in the Kidron valley. Here there grew up a community of anchorites, and in 492 Sabas founded the monastery which bears his name on the slopes of the gorge opposite his first cave. Sabas gained a great reputation not only in Palestine but also in the capital of the Empire, Constantinople, and at the great age of 90 he travelled to that city and persuaded the Emperor Justinian to build the Church of the Nativity in Bethlehem. After his death in 532 at the age of 93 his tomb became a place of pilgrimage, and many daughter houses were founded by monks from his monastery.

The monastery was destroyed and its monks slaughtered by the Persians in 614 and the Arabs in 636. Nevertheless it survived, and in 712 it received within its walls a man whose impact on the world of Orthodox Christianity was no less powerful that that of Sabas. This was John of Damascus. Born about 650, the son of a noble Arab Christian family, John rose to high honour at the brilliant court of the Omayyad Caliph in Damascus, representing the Caliph's Christian subjects. At the age of about 50, however, he "preferred the humiliation of Christ to the treasures of Arabia", left Damascus and became a monk at Mar Saba. When an edict issued by the Emperor Leo III in 726 initiated the iconoclastic movement which resulted in the destruction of countless icons and was not finally brought to an end until 843, John of Damascus, from his base in St Sabas's monastery, became the most prominent defender of the veneration of images, for which he set out the theological justification in three famous speeches directed against the iconoclasts. Here too he wrote his treatises against Islam and against deviations from Christian orthodoxy (Nestorianism, Monophysitism). His most important theological work, the "Fount of Wisdom", was also written in the monastery. When John of Damascus died at a great age (according to tradition at 104) about 750 he was recognised as the greatest theologian of his day.

The monastery's two leading figures were not destined to remain undisturbed even in death. The remains of St Sabas were taken to Venice in the 12th century by the Crusaders; and when, in 1838, the Russians rebuilt the monastery after its destruction in the early 19th century they carried off the remains of St John of Damascus to Moscow. In 1965, however, in pursuance of his policy of reconciliation between the Roman Catholic and the Eastern churches, Pope Paul VI returned the relics of St Sabas to the monastery.

Sights

Women's Tower

Only men may enter the monastery. Women may climb a hill to the right of the monastery, with a tower in which female visitors used to be accommodated. An Austrian woman traveller, Ida Pfeiffer, gives a vivid account, in her "Visit to the Holy Land", of a night spent in the tower in 1842. From this tower, which contains a chapel and a dormitory, there is a good view of the monastery with its domes, courtyards and buildings ranged above one another on the slopes of the hill.

★Monastery

Male visitors enter the monastery precincts through a small doorway and go down a narrow stepped path to a courtyard containing a small domed building in which St Sabas's remains lay until their removal by the Crusaders. After their return in 1965 they were deposited in the monastery's principal church (Katholikon). The monks who guide visitors through the labyrinthine complex of the monastery take them into this domed cruciform church with its rich wall paintings and its icons and show them the saint's remains, which are relatively well preserved. Visitors are also taken into a chapel built on to St Sabas's Cave. Here, as in St George's Monastery in the Wadi Qilt (see entry), are preserved the skulls of the monks slaughtered by the Persians in 614. These victims of a long-past war, and still more St Sabas himself, the "Star of the Desert" – his life, the removal of his remains to Venice and their return to the monastery – are still immediately present to the monks. Finally visitors can look down from a balcony into the valley of the Kidron, 180m/590ft below, which is completely dry in summer. "Majestic rocky terraces," wrote Ida Pfeiffer in 1842, "piled one above the other by nature with such exquisite symmetry that the beholder gazes in silent wonder, overhang both banks of the stream in the form of galleries."

Surroundings of Mar Saba

From Bethlehem a good (though narrow) asphalted road runs east to Bet Sahur and then north-east to the monastery of St Theodosius (12km/7½ miles).

Monastery of
St Theodosius

Founded in 476 by St Theodosius, a native of Cappadocia in Asia Minor, the monastery had a population of 400 monks in its heyday. It was destroyed by the Persians in 614, along with Mar Saba and St George's Monastery in the Wadi Qilt (see entry). Around 1900 it was reoccupied and rebuilt by Greek Orthodox monks.

A short distance beyond the monastery of St Theodosius is the village of Ubeidiya ("Place of the Servants"), inhabited by the descendants of the guards and servants sent here by the Byzantine authorities to protect the monasteries of St Theodosius and St Sabas.

Ubeidiya

Masada

H 5

District: Southern
Altitude: 60m/200ft above sea level, 434m/1424ft above the level of the
Dead Sea

The massive rocky bulk of Masada (also spelt Mezada), rising steeply up above the Dead Sea, offered Jewish rulers an ideal site for a fortress; but in fact Masada was a place of historical importance for a mere hundred years, an impregnable place of refuge for Herod the Great and a stronghold in which Jewish Zealots were able to hold out against the Romans for three years after the fall of Jerusalem, until A.D. 73.

Situation and
characteristics

There are two routes to Masada. The road from Arad (19km/12 miles) ends at the foot of the Roman ramp, from which it is possible to climb to the West Gate, 100m/330ft higher up. (Since the road ends here it is necessary to return by the same route.) Much more impressive, however, is the approach from the Dead Sea. Cars can go up as far as the kibbutz 3km/2 miles from the shore of the lake (car park, restaurant, refreshments), from which there is a choice between climbing up the old "Snake Path" (restored 1954), a distance of 3km/2 miles with a height difference of 400m/1300ft, and taking the cableway which runs up to just below the East Gate.

The Jewish historian Flavius Josephus ascribes the first fortress erected on the hill to the high priest Jonathan – though this was clearly not the brother of Judas Maccabeus but his grand-nephew Alexander Jannaeus (103–76 B.C.), who also bore the name of Jonathan. Herod enlarged the original small fortress into a stronghold which combined royal magnificence with great defensive strength, so that Masada became *the* fortress (metsuda) par excellence. In the troubled year 40 B.C., when the Parthians chose the Hasmonean Antigonus as their leader, Herod brought his family and his betrothed wife Mariamne here for safety. Again in 31 B.C., when Octavian defeated Antony and Cleopatra's fleet in the battle of Actium and Herod travelled to Rhodes to swear allegiance to the new master of Rome, Herod's family sought the safety of Masada, though this time Mariamne,

History

The imposing bulk of Masada rising above the Dead Sea

along with her mother Alexandra, was taken separately to the fortress of Alexandreia in Samaria.

Between 37 and 31 Herod had turned Masada into an impregnable fortress. The summit plateau, covering an area 600m/660yds long by 200m/220yds wide, with its palaces, administrative buildings, store-rooms, barracks and cisterns, was enclosed by a 1300m/1420yd long casemate wall reinforced by 38 towers each 10m/33ft high. There were twelve cisterns, each with a capacity of 4000 cu.m/880,000 gallons, which together with the supplies of food in the store-rooms would enable the fortress to withstand a long siege.

This situation occurred some decades later, during the Jewish rising against Rome. In A.D. 66, even before the rising broke out, a group of Zealots – members of the radical party who had left Jerusalem as result of internecine conflicts among the Jews – had established themselves on Masada under the leadership of Menachem Ben Judah. Soon afterwards Menachem was murdered in Jerusalem and his nephew Eleazar Ben Yair assumed command on Masada. The Romans took the fortress of Herodeion (see entry), while the Zealot forces in the stronghold of Machaerus, on the east bank of the Jordan, surrendered in return for a promise of free passage and thereupon reinforced the garrison on Masada, which finally was occupied by a total of 967 men, women and children. After the fall of Jerusalem in the year 70 the defenders of Masada continued to hold out, and in 72 the Romans decided to overcome this last pocket of resistance by a siege. Their commander Flavius Silva enclosed Masada within a circumvallation (siege wall) with a total length of 4500m/4900yds and outside this built eight camps for the besieging forces; his headquarter camp, rhomboidal in plan, was on the west side. A great ramp was built up on the west side of the hill so that battering-rams and other siege engines might be deployed against the walls of the fortress. After an eight months' siege the Romans broke through the walls and set fire to the timber stockade behind them. Seeing that the situation was hopeless, Eleazar called on his com-

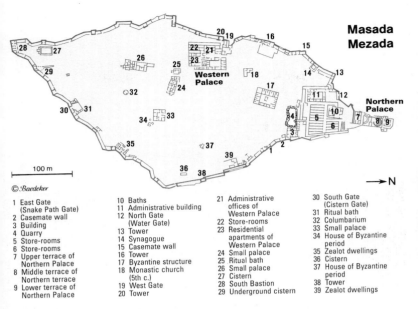

**Masada
Mezada**

Western Palace

Northern Palace

100 m

© Baedeker

→ N

1 East Gate
  (Snake Path Gate)
2 Casemate wall
3 Building
4 Quarry
5 Store-rooms
6 Store-rooms
7 Upper terrace of
  Northern Palace
8 Middle terrace of
  Northern terrace
9 Lower terrace of
  Northern Palace

10 Baths
11 Administrative building
12 North Gate
   (Water Gate)
13 Tower
14 Synagogue
15 Casemate wall
16 Tower
17 Byzantine structure
18 Monastic church
   (5th c.)
19 West Gate
20 Tower

21 Administrative
   offices of
   Western Palace
22 Store-rooms
23 Residential
   apartments of
   Western Palace
24 Small palace
25 Ritual bath
26 Small palace
27 Cistern
28 South Bastion
29 Underground cistern

30 South Gate
   (Cistern Gate)
31 Ritual bath
32 Columbarium
33 Small palace
34 House of Byzantine
   period
35 Zealot dwellings
36 Cistern
37 House of Byzantine
   period
38 Tower
39 Zealot dwellings

panions in arms, in a speech recorded by Flavius Josephus ("Jewish War", VII,8,6–8), to die rather than be taken prisoner. They burned all their possessions except the stores of food (there since Herod's time), in order to show the Romans that they had not been starved into surrender. Then, although Jewish law forbade suicide, they chose ten men who were to put the rest of the defenders to the sword and then kill themselves. When the Romans took the fortress on the following morning they found 960 bodies. Two women who had hidden in a water conduit along with five children told them what had happened. "But when they discovered the great numbers of bodies they did not rejoice over their defeat of their enemies but admired the noble resolution and the unshakeable defiance of death shown by all those involved in the deed" (VII,9,2). This heroism, irrational though it might be, has made Masada a symbol of Jewish determination to hold out even in an apparently hopeless situation. When recruits to the Israeli army are sworn in on Masada the oath includes the words "Never again shall Masada fall".

The site of Masada was identified by an American scholar, Edward Robinson, in 1838. Since then it has been investigated by American, British and German archaeologists and above all, in recent years, by Yigael Yadin (see Famous People) and Shemaria Gutmann.

The ★★ Site

From the East Gate (Snake Path Gate) we turn right past a watch-tower and other buildings to the large store-houses, with walls (thrown down in an earthquake and partly re-erected) separating the long, narrow store-rooms, in which numerous jars and amphoras were found.

Store-houses

The most monumental building is at the northern tip of the rock: Herod's Northern Palace, a boldly conceived structure on three levels. The upper-

Northern Palace

Masada

Masada Northern Palace

⊢ 10m ⊣

N ←

Section

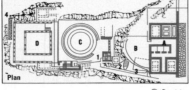

Plan

© *Baedeker*

A Residential apartments
B Semicircular terrace
C Middle terrace
D Lower terrace (peristyle)

1 Staircase
2 Bath
3 Cistern
4 Retaining wall

most part, with Herod's residential apartments, ends in a semicircle, from which there is a view of the two lower terraces, now reached on a modern flight of steps on the west side. On the way down cisterns for water can be seen in the rock. On the middle terrace (20m/65ft lower down), which Yadin concluded was designed to serve the purposes of leisure and relaxation, are two concentric rings of walls. 14m/46ft lower down is the square bottom terrace, a peristyle (courtyard surrounded by columns) with fluted Corinthian columns standing on a wall faced with painted plaster.

Baths

South of this palace is a bath-house on the Roman model. A courtyard surrounded on three sides by columns leads into a changing room (apodyterium) which was paved with black and white triangular tiles. Adjoining this were the tepidarium (warm room), also with a tiled floor, the frigidarium (cold bath) and the caldarium (hot bath). The caldarium, which has preserved its hypocaust (under-floor heating system), is particularly impressive. The small piers of the hypocaust, over 200 in number, originally supported a mosaic pavement.

From the roof of the baths there is a good view of the whole fortress.

Administrative building

South-west of the baths is a building which is believed to have housed Herod's work-rooms and offices. It contains a ritual bath (mikve) constructed by the Zealots between 66 and 73.

Synagogue

To the west of this building, against the fortress walls, the excavators found the remains of the oldest synagogue in the world and the only one dating from the period of the Temple. The roof was borne on columns, and in the time of Herod the building was divided into two parts by a wall. The Zealots altered the structure and installed stone benches. Here were found a number of scrolls, now in the Israel Museum in Jerusalem.

Byzantine church

South-east of the synagogue are another large complex of buildings and a church built by Byzantine monks in the 5th century. The church is entered through a porch or vestibule. The apse, at the east end, has a cavity in the floor which may have housed relics. On the north side of the nave was a

Byzantine church, Masada

Mosaic in the church

(partly preserved) mosaic pavement with representations of plants and fruits.

Continuing along the walls, we see to the south one of the towers of the West Gate (opposite the Roman ramp) and the large Western Palace. It can be seen how the Zealots altered the building to provide living accommodation and constructed another mikve to the south-east.

Western Palace

While the Northern Palace was Herod's private residence the Western Palace, which covers an area of some 4000sq.m/4800sq.yds, was his official residence. The north and west wings contained domestic and administrative offices and accommodation for officials and servants, and in the south wing were the king's residential and state apartments. In one room, apparently an audience chamber, the excavators found a well preserved mosaic pavement, the oldest ever discovered in Israel, with geometric designs and plant motifs (vine and fig leaves, olive-branches, etc.). At various points where the pavement has been destroyed can be seen the guide-lines used in laying the mosaic.

South-west of the Western Palace is a columbarium, a circular structure dating from the time of Herod with numerous niches for ash-urns, presumably to house the remains of non-Jewish members of Herod's garrison.

Columbarium

Going south from here, we pass two large open cisterns and come to the South Bastion at the southern tip of the plateau. On the way back along the eastern walls we pass a third mikve (at the South Gate), another cistern and houses dating from the Byzantine period (on left) and from the Zealot occupation (on right) before returning to the East Gate. From the eastern walls there are magnificent views of the Dead Sea and the hills beyond with their ever-changing play of colour.

Other buildings

Twice weekly (on Tuesday and Thursday) from April to October there is a fascinating sound and light show (*son et lumière*) on the history of Masada,

Sound and light show

293

with light effects and background music, in the Masada amphitheatre (which can be reached only on the road from Arad).

Megiddo   H 3

District: Northern
Altitude: 160m/525ft

Situation and characteristics

Megiddo, 12km/7½ miles west of Afula and 32km/20 miles south-east of Haifa, was an important stronghold in ancient times and, thanks to its strategic situation, retained its military importance into the 20th century. The old road from Egypt to Syria avoided Cape Carmel, leaving the coast near Caesarea and bearing north-east to run through the Iron valley into the Jezreel plain. Megiddo, situated at the mouth of the valley, where the road divides into a western branch heading for Tyre and Sidon and an eastern branch making for Damascus and Mesopotamia, controlled these important trade and military routes.

The tell of Megiddo, carefully and thoroughly excavated and now beautifully laid out by the National Parks Authority, is a fascinating and instructive site of great historical interest.

History

Excavation of the tell of Megiddo began in 1903–05 with the work of the German Palestine Society, when Schumacher cut the deep, wide trench on the east side which bears his name. Between 1925 and 1939 the site was systematically investigated by the Chicago Oriental Institute, and in 1960 Yigael Yadin began the excavations which established the chronology of the site. This work showed that after a period of occupation in the Neolithic era there was a Canaanite settlement here in the 4th millennium B.C. which continued in existence until the Israelite occupation of the Promised Land. From this period date a Chalcolithic shrine and another one nearby with a large circular altar. After a battle in 1479 B.C. in which Pharaoh Tuthmosis III gained control of the pass during his advance to the Euphrates the town was under Egyptian influence. In the Tell el-Amarna archives (14th c. B.C.) were found letters from the Egyptian governor Biridja asking for military reinforcements against the Habiru (Hebrews?). In the 13th century B.C. Joshua, after his triumph over the king of Hazor, also defeated the king of Megiddo (Joshua 12,21); but the Israelites held the town only for a short time, for in the 12th century the Philistines, thrusting inland from the coast, conquered Megiddo and the whole of the Jezreel plain as far as Beth-shean.

A new phase began around 1000 B.C., however, when David defeated the Philistines. In the 10th century Solomon made Megiddo the chief town of the fifth administrative region of Israel, extending as far as Beth-shean, with Baana son of Ahilud as its governor (1 Kings 4,12). Yigael Yadin's excavations brought to light, to the east of the main gate, a Northern Palace dating from this period, probably the royal residence, and one of the casemate walls characteristic of Solomon's time, like those at Hazor (see entry) and Gezer (see Ramla, Surroundings), as well as the formidable North Gate. On the south side of the site were the palace of the governor, Baana, and an administrative building. "This was not a mere fortress but a metropolis with imposing buildings designed for ceremonial purposes" (Yadin). The Solomonic city was destroyed in 923 B.C. by Pharaoh Seshonq (the Shishak of the Old Testament) and had to be rebuilt by King Ahab in the 9th century. On the site of the North and South Palaces were built stables for 450 horses (long known, erroneously, as "Solomon's Stables"). Ahab, who no doubt attached particular importance to Megiddo because of its situation on the road to Phoenicia, his wife's home country, renovated the Solomonic gate, built a strong new wall round the town and dug a large tunnel to ensure its water supply. Thereafter Megiddo enjoyed a period of prosperity, which ended in 733 B.C. with its conquest by the Assyrians in the reign of Tiglath-pileser III. In 609 B.C. King Josiah of Judah was killed at

Megiddo in a battle with Pharaoh Necho. After the Persian conquest in 538 B.C. the town was abandoned, but in Roman times a camp occupied by the 6th Legion was built 2km/1¼ miles south of the tell. This gave its name to the Arab village of Lajun, now the kibbutz of Megiddo.

In more recent times Napoleon (in 1799) and General Allenby (in 1917) won victories over Turkish armies at Megiddo, and here too in 1948 the Israelis defeated Arab forces which were threatening Haifa.

The ★Site

Near the car park is a building housing a refreshment stall and a museum which with its various displays and a large model of ancient Megiddo forms an excellent introduction to the site.

Museum

From here a footpath leads to the entrance on the north side of the tell, where, after passing a gate of the 15th century B.C. (on right), we come at a bend in the path to the gate of Solomon's time. The three chambers on either side of the entrance can be clearly distinguished.

Gates

Immediately south are extensive remains of buildings, in which a number of ivories of the 13th century B.C. were found.

View

The path now turns left (east) and runs past the remains of stables or chariot-sheds built by Ahab over the Northern Palace (on left) to a view-point from which there is a wide prospect northward over the fertile Jezreel plain to the Galilean hills round Nazareth.

On the other side of the platform there is a view down into the Schumacher Trench, in which a Canaanite shrine was excavated. A particularly notable feature is a large circular altar ("high place") dating from an earlier period

Circular altar

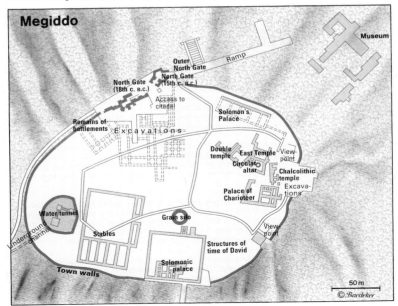

295

Canaanite shrine, Megiddo

which was renovated around 1900 B.C. when the immediately adjoining Eastern Temple (Level XV) was built. It is some 1.25m/4ft high and has a diameter of 7m/23ft, with steps on the east side leading up to the "high place".

Eastern Temple, Double Temple

The Eastern Temple consists – as is normal in Semitic temples – of a vestibule, the main chamber and the holy of holies. The rear wall of the holy of holies backs on to the temple with the circular altar. Built against the inner wall is a square altar approached by steps on the side. Adjoining this temple on the west, at an acute angle, are other cult buildings, presumed to be a double temple for a divine couple.

On the valley side are remains of walls from an older temple dating from the Chalcolithic period (4th millennium B.C.; Level XIX).

Grain silo

Returning from here and bearing left, we come to the southern section of the tell. In this area, sunk into the ground, is a large circular grain silo dating from the reign of King Jeroboam II (8th c. B.C.) On the inner walls are two flights of steps, so that people could go down one side and up the other at the same time.

Stables

Beyond this are two large complexes built by Ahab on the site of Solomon's palace. To the right is a courtyard with the famous stables, in which the stalls, feeding troughs and pillars with holes bored in them for tethering the horses can still be seen. The stables of Megiddo could accommodate 450 horses, together with the war chariots and their charioteers.

Water tunnel

The path now runs down to the large tunnel which guaranteed the town's water supply. This was formerly attributed to the 13th or the 11th century (the time of the Canaanites or Philistines), but Yadin's excavations have firmly dated it to the Israelite period, in the time of Ahab (9th c. B.C.). The source of Megiddo's water is a spring in a cave outside the confines of the town. In the time of Solomon a shaft 2m/6½ft high and 1m/40in. wide was cut through the walls to give access to the spring on the south-western slope of the tell. Ahab, who also provided Hazor with a water supply system, resolved to construct a conduit at Megiddo which would run from inside the town to the spring and in the event of a siege, would not be accessible to the enemy. A shaft was driven down through earlier occupation levels and then through the living rock to a depth of 60m/200ft, and from this a horizonal tunnel was cut through the rock to the spring, a distance of 120m/395ft. The original access to the spring was then closed. This monumental structure, one of the great engineering achievements of antiquity, has been made easy of access for visitors by the construction of staircases and walkways. The exit is through the original entrance to the cave which was closed in the time of Ahab.

Meron   H 2

District: Northern
Altitude: 670m/2200ft
Population: 300

The village of Meron in Upper Galilee, founded in 1949 to the north of the ancient city of that name, lies 9km/6 miles west of Safed on the eastern slopes of Mount Meron, the highest hill in Galilee (1208m/3963ft), at the point where the road to Nahariya branches off the road to Akko.
Situation and characteristics

Simeon Bar Yohai, one of the leaders of the Bar Kochba rising, was buried in Meron. He is credited in Jewish tradition with the authorship of the Kabbalistic work known as the "Zohar" ("Splendour"), which in fact was written in Spain in 1270. In his honour thousands of Jews come every year in spring to this place of pilgrimage and celebrate the festivity of Rashbi Hilula with a great procession, singing and dancing (April/May).

Joshua was victorious over a number of kings here (Joshua 11,7). During the Bar Kochba rebellion in the 2nd century A.D., the last Jewish rising against the Romans, Rabbi Simeon Bar Yohai and his son Eleazer hid in a cave which is shown to visitors at Peki'in, in the valley of the same name on the west side of Mount Meron.
History

Sights

In the centre of the village, in a building surrounded by a high wall, is the mausoleum containing the tombs of Simeon Bar Yohai and his son Eleazer, roofed with shallow white domes. On the roof are two tube-shaped copper sockets in which torches are set on the occasion of processions.
Tomb of Simeon Bar Yohai

On higher ground to the north of the tomb are the remains of a synagogue of the 3rd or 4th century which is also associated with the name of Simeon Bar Yohai. Of this building, which originally measured 27m/88ft by 13.5m/44ft, there survives little but the main front, facing south. It was divided into three aisles by two rows of eight columns.
Synagogue

Near the mausoleum of Simeon Bar Yohai are other tombs, including the rock-cut tomb of Rabbi Hillel and his disciples and, on the far side of the valley, the tomb of Rabbi Shammai. Both men founded Mishnah schools in the 1st century, Hillel teaching a liberal doctrine, Shammai a rigidly orthodox one.
Tombs

Mount Meron (Hare Meron) is reached from the village of Meron by taking the road which at first runs north and then bears west, coming in 9km/6 miles to the village of Sassa. 3km/2 miles farther on a road goes off on the left to Mount Meron, the summit region of which is a nature reserve.
Mount Meron

Mezada

See Masada

Modi'im
G 4

District: Central

Situation and characteristics

Modi'im, home of the Maccabees, lies 12km/7½ miles east of Lod, south-west of the Arab village of Midya, in an area near the Herzl Forest accessible only on very minor roads.

History

In 167 B.C. envoys from the Syrian ruler Antiochus IV Epiphanes, then pursuing a policy of Hellenisation, came to Modi'im and called on the people to sacrifice to the pagan gods. Mattathias, a priest, refused, and when another Jew showed himself ready to offer sacrifice Mattathias and his five sons killed the man and the king's envoys and fled into the hills. This was the beginning of the Maccabee rebellion which, under the leadership of Mattathias's sons, particularly Judas Maccabeus, led to the establishment of the Maccabean or Hasmonean state, which survived until Herod I put an end to it in 37 B.C. (1 Maccabees 2,15–30).

Rock-cut tombs

The lofty monument which the high priest Simeon, the last of the five brothers, erected over the tombs of his father and brothers (1 Maccabees 13,27) no longer exists, but the rock-cut tombs themselves, with their large grave slabs, can still be seen. Every year on the first night of the Hanukkah festival a torch is lit here and carried to Jerusalem, where the President of Israel kindles the Hanukkah lights with it. Hanukkah commemorates the victory of the Maccabees over the Assyrians who killed the Jews and prevented them practising their religion.

Montfort
H 2

District: Northern
Altitude: 200m/650ft

Situation and characteristics

The Crusader castle of Montfort, 14km/8½ miles east of Nahariya, is the largest ruin in western Galilee.
The castle can be reached only on foot, by either of two routes. One runs from the Goren Natural Forest, near the kibbutz of Elon (on the road going east from Rosh Haniqra close to the Lebanese frontier) and comes in 3km/2 miles to the castle (descent of 130m/427ft). The other starts from Mi'ilya, a village of Christian Arabs on the Nahariya–Safed road; 3km/2 miles north of this on a motorable road is a parking-place, from which it is a half-hour walk on a stony path running down through a wood (descent 250m/820ft). The castle stands on a spur of rock above the deep cleft of the Wadi Quren.

History

The castle was built by Comte Joscelin de Courtenay in the 12th century to protect Acre. In 1187 it was destroyed by Saladin; then in 1220 Hermann von Salza, Grand Master of the Teutonic Order, acquired the ruins with the idea of making the castle the Grand Master's residence. In 1271 the Teutonic Knights surrendered the castle to the Mameluke Sultan Baibars on the promise of free passage with their archives and the treasury of the Order. Since then the castle, which is known to the Arabs as Qalat Quren, has been abandoned. In 1926 the ruins were investigated by a team from the Metropolitan Museum in New York; finds from the site (capitals, a carved head) are in the Rockefeller Museum in Jerusalem. There are still substantial remains of the castle, since its remoteness saved it from being used as a quarry of building stone.

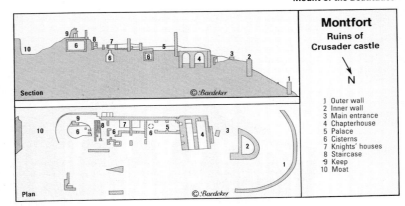

Montfort
Ruins of Crusader castle

N

1 Outer wall
2 Inner wall
3 Main entrance
4 Chapterhouse
5 Palace
6 Cisterns
7 Knights' houses
8 Staircase
9 Keep
10 Moat

Section   © *Baedeker*

Plan   © *Baedeker*

The ★castle

The castle, on a site which rises from east to west, was surrounded by a wall reinforced by square and round towers. The entrance is near the south-west corner. The most vulnerable part of the castle was the west end, which was given extra protection by a deep ditch and, beyond this, a massive tower, linked with the main castle by a drawbridge.

From one of the towers, still preserved to its original height of 18m/60ft, there is an impressive view of the wooded country round the castle, traversed by the rushing stream in the deep valley below. In the river-bed are remains of a dam, and on the banks is a ruined mill built by the Knights.

Mount of the Beatitudes

H 2

District: Northern

Situation and characteristics

On the northern shore of the Sea of Galilee, rising above the ruins of Tabgha and Capernaum (see entries), is the Mount of the Beatitudes, on which according to tradition Christ preached the Sermon on the Mount.
To reach the Mount of the Beatitudes from the Sea of Galilee, leave Tiberias on the road to Rosh Pinna. Soon after the road to Capernaum goes off on the right the commandingly situated domed church on the Mount of the Beautitudes can be seen to the right of the road. It is approached on a side road.

History

From a very early period this hill has been identified as the one on which Christ preached his Sermon on the Mount (Matthew 5–7). The event was originally commemorated by a church lower down near Tabgha (see entry), just north of the road to Capernaum. The new church, situated in a shady garden beside the Ospizio Monte de Beatitudine, was built in 1937.

Church of the Beatitudes

The Church of the Beatitudes is built of local basalt, using white Nazareth stone for the arches and Roman travertine for the columns. From the arcaded ambulatory round the church, which is octagonal in plan, there are magnificent views of the Sea of Galilee. The eight sides of the church are dedicated, as Latin inscriptions in the interior indicate, to the eight Beatitudes with which the Sermon begins (Matthew 5,3–10), blessing the poor in spirit, those who mourn, the meek, those who hunger and thirst after righteousness, the merciful, the pure in heart, the peacemakers and those who are persecuted for righteousness' sake. The dome symbolises the ninth Beatitude (Matthew 5,11–12), in which Christ addressed himself directly to those persecuted for his sake: "for great is your reward in heaven".

Church, Mount of the Beautitudes

Mount Gilboa/Har Gilboa

H 3

District: Northern
Altitude: 508m/1667ft

Situation and characteristics	Mount Gilboa, an outlier of the hills of Samaria, bounds the Jezreel plain on the south-east. Rising to a height of 508m/1667ft above sea level, its summit is 628m/2060ft above the town of Bet Shean, which lies 120m/393ft below sea level. From the Afula–Bet Shean road a winding track runs up to the summit. The summit itself is a military area closed to the public, but there are good views on the way up.
History	Mount Gilboa was the scene of a tragic event in Jewish history. Here King Saul assembled his army for battle with the Philistines, who were encamped at Shunam, and consulted the witch of Endor (see Afula). As the witch had foretold, the Israelites were defeated by the Philistines. Saul's sons Abinadab and Malchi-shua were killed; Saul, in despair, fell on his sword, and the victorious Philistines hung his body from the walls of Beth-shan (1 Samuel 31,1–12). David lamented over his death: "Ye mountains of Gilboa, let there be no dew, neither let there be rain, upon you . . . , for there the shield of the mighty is vilely cast away" (2 Samuel 1,21).
★Gan HaShelosha National Park	Under the north side of Mount Gilboa, between Bet Shean and Bet Alfa (see entries), is the Gan HaShelosha National Park (restaurant, picnic areas), with pools and natural waterfalls. The water of the falls was formerly used to drive a watermill. There is good swimming in the large pools above the falls.
Ma'ayan Harod National Park	10km/6 miles north-west on the road to Afula, on the wooded northern slopes of Mount Gilboa, is the Ma'ayan Harod National Park (youth hostel, camping site), in which is the source of the river Harod.

The spring at Harod is believed to be the "well of Harod" at which Gideon selected the three hundred men with whom he defeated the Midianites (Judges 7,5–7). In the Middle Ages this was the scene of another battle (1260), in which the Mameluke general Baibars won a decisive victory over the Mongols, who had advanced as far as Gaza, and drove them back into northern Syria. After this victory he became Sultan of Egypt and Syria.

Mount Tabor/Har Tavor H 3

District: Northern
Altitude: 588m/1929ft

Mount Tabor, which rises out of the Jezreel plain 21km/13 miles north-east of Afula, is frequently mentioned in the Old Testament and is believed to have been the scene of Christ's Transfiguration.

Situation and characteristics

The summit of Mount Tabor can be reached on a signposted road which branches off the Afula–Tiberias road at the south end of Kefar Tavor and runs north-west. Another road which goes off the Afula–Tiberias road farther to the south also runs up to the summit by way of the Arab village of Dabburiya. The last few kilometres of the winding road to the summit are not suitable for buses and caravans.

In the 2nd millennium B.C. there was a Canaanite shrine, a "high place", on Mount Tabor, as there was on other hills like Mount Carmel (see entry) and Mount Hermon. The god worshipped here was Baal, whose cult spread in the 2nd millennium, as a result of trading links, to the island of Rhodes, where he was worshipped on Mount Atabyrion (1215m/3986ft) under the name of Zeus Atabyrios. (Atabyrion was also the Greek name for Mount Tabor).

History

In the time of the Judges (12th c. B.C.) the prophetess Deborah and her general Barak mustered their forces on Mount Tabor before launching the victorious onslaught which annihilated Sisera, the king of Hazor's general, "and all his chariots and all his host" (Judges 4,12–16).

The significance of Mount Tabor in the history of Christianity began in the 4th century, when it became identified with the "high mountain apart" into which Christ went with his disciples Peter, James and John "and was transfigured before them: and his face did shine as the sun, and his raiment was white as the light. And, behold, there appeared unto them Moses and Elias talking with him" (Matthew 17; Mark 9,2–13; Luke 9,28–36). Jesus thus appeared to the disciples in his divine form, as the Christ and God's "beloved son". Together with the Resurrection, the Transfiguration became one of the central themes of the theology and iconography of the Eastern church. The appearance of the transfigured Christ in a glory of light also had a decisive influence on the mystical thought of Eastern monasticism: a form of mystical practice, still found on the "holy mountain" of Athos, which seeks through ascetic exercises to be blessed with the "uncreated light" of Mount Tabor and thus to achieve a mystical union with God.

The first churches on Mount Tabor were built before 422, and in 553 it became the see of a bishop. From this period dates the large mosaic of the Transfiguration in St Catherine's Monastery on Sinai (see entry). There was further building on Mount Tabor, both as a place of pilgrimage and as a fortress, during the Crusader period. The fortress withstood an attack by Saladin in 1191 but was destroyed by Baibars in 1263. In 1631 the Druze emir Fakhr ed-Din granted the summit of the hill to the Franciscans, whose monastery still exists. In 1911 the Greek Orthodox, to whom the northern part of the summit plateau belonged, built a church dedicated to St Elias (Elijah). The large Franciscan church (designed by Antonio Barluzzi) was built in 1921–23.

Sights

Church of St Elias

On the summit of the hill the road divides. The road to the left leads to the Greek Orthodox northern part of the plateau and the church of St Elias (1911), built on the site of an earlier Crusader church.

The courtyard, in which there is a deep open cistern, has ranges of cells along its north and east sides.

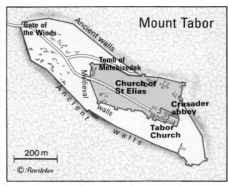

Mount Tabor — Gate of the Winds · Ancient walls · Tomb of Melchizedek · Church of St Elias · Medieval · Ancient walls · Crusader abbey · Tabor Church · 200 m · © Baedeker

★Church of the Transfiguration

The road to the right leads to the area occupied by the Franciscans, enters a walled courtyard and continues between the ruins of an older church on the left and the monastery garden on the right (memorial to the visit of Pope Paul VI in 1964, plaque commemorating the architect Antonio Barluzzi) to the Church of the Transfiguration (or Tabor Church).

Built of light-coloured limestone, it harks back to the style of church building which developed in Syria in the 4th–6th centuries. This architecture was no longer concerned only with the decoration and furnishing of the interior but for the first time sought to give the exterior a monumental stamp. This Syrian tradition (as found particularly at Qalb Lozeh near Aleppo) is reflected, for example, in the façade with its two projecting towers, between which a round-headed arch surmounted by a pediment frames the entrance to the church, and in the volute-like framing of the windows.
In the interior – again on the Syrian model – the nave is separated from the aisles by wide-spanned arches. The roof beams are born on short columns in the clerestory.

The church contains three grottoes which were described by Jonas Korte in 1751 as "three chapels, with a small altar; they are called tabernacles, and they are said to represent the three huts which Peter desired to build, one for his Master, the other two for Moses and Elias". The Grotto of Christ is in the eastern part of the church. Steps lead down to a lower level with a sanctuary enclosed by walls belonging to a Crusader church and roofed with a modern barrel vault. In the vaulting of the apse in the upper part of the church is a mosaic on a gold ground representing the Transfiguration. There are two other chapels in the towers on the west front: in the south tower the Chapel of St Elias, in the north tower the Chapel of Moses, with a mosaic pavement incorporating crosses in the design. This means that the mosaic must date from before 422, when the Emperor Theodosius II prohibited the representation of crosses in mosaic pavements so that this sacred symbol should not be trodden underfoot.

★View

To the north and south of the church walls belonging to older buildings are still standing. From the top of the walls there are views of much of the elliptical summit plateau with its remains of ancient buildings set in luxuriant gardens. Even more rewarding are the wider views of the hills of Nazareth to the west, the Jezreel plain and the hills of Samaria to the south, the Jordan rift valley and the hills of Jordan to the east and the green expanses of Galilee with the Horns of Hittim to the north.

Church of the Transfiguration, Mount Tabor

Surroundings of Mount Tabor

A few kilometres north-east of Mount Tabor is the village of Kafr Kama, established in 1880 by Circassian settlers. At that time many Circassians were leaving Russia because of their Muslim faith, and the Turkish authorities allowed them to settle in their Near Eastern territories, including Amman and Jerash (Gerasa) in what is now Jordan. In Israel, in addition to the village of Kafr Kama, there is another Circassian settlement in Upper Galilee, the village of Rihanya 13km/8 miles north of Safed. In 1948 the Circassians sided with Israel, and they now serve in the Israeli army.

Kafr Kama

Nabi Musa

H 4

West Bank

The Islamic shrine of Nabi Musa (= the Prophet Moses) lies in the Judaean Desert to the south of Jericho, on the Israeli-occupied west bank of the Jordan. It can be reached from Jerusalem by leaving on the road to the Dead Sea and in 28km/17 miles taking an asphalted road on the right which comes in 1km/¾ mile to the shrine.

Situation and characteristics

At the end of the Israelites' long journey from Egypt through Sinai, the wilderness of Zin and Paran and the land of the Edomites it was vouchsafed to Moses to see the Promised Land but not to enter it. From Mount Nebo (808m/2651ft), south-west of Amman, he looked down on the Dead Sea, 1200m/4000ft below, the Jordan valley and the oasis of Jericho, which was to be the first city west of the Jordan conquered by his people under the leadership of Joshua. Moses was buried "in a valley in the land of Moab, over against Beth-peor: but no man knoweth of his sepulchre unto this day" (Deuteronomy 34,1–6). According to an old tradition, however –

History

Nabi Musa

probably originating among Christian pilgrims in the Middle Ages and taken over by the Muslims – he was buried on the west bank of the Jordan at Nabi Musa. Saladin knew about this place in the 12th century, and the Mameluke Sultan Baibars (1260–77) built a mosque here with a large cenotaph for Moses. Accommodation for pilgrims was provided in the 15th century.

Mosque

The mosque with its associated buildings is commandingly situated on a hill, on the slopes of which is a large cemetery for Muslims who wish to be near the prophet even in death.

The Christian Easter and Jewish Passover is also the time when Muslims make the pilgrimage to Nabi Musa. As a result there were often anti-Christian riots during the period of Ottoman rule, while during the British Mandate hostility was frequently shown to the Jews.

Nabi Samwil   H 4

West Bank

Situation and characteristics

Nabi Samwil (= the Jewish Prophet Samuel), an Arab village in which Samuel's tomb is venerated, lies 9km/6 miles north-west of Jerusalem on the Israeli-occupied west bank of the Jordan.

It is reached from Jerusalem by leaving on the Ramallah road and turning left beyond Shufat, or by taking the road which runs north-west through the Mahanayim and Sanhedriya districts.

In 1948, during the Arab-Israeli war, Nabi Samwil was an Arab base. Since 1967 Jews as well as Arabs have been able to visit it.

Sights

The 885m/2904ft high hill near the village was known to the Crusaders in the 12th century as Mons Gaudii (Mount of Joy), since from here they could get their first glimpse of Jerusalem. They built a church – successor to an earlier church erected by Justinian in the 6th century – which was later converted by the Muslims into the present massive mosque, prominently situated on the hill. In the mosque is the cenotaph of Samuel, who lived in nearby Zuph (Givat Shaul: see Jerusalem, Surroundings) and according to tradition is buried here. The tomb, like the tombs of the patriarchs in Hebron (see entry), is in a cave under the mosque.

From the roof of the mosque there are wide views.

Nablus   H 4

West Bank
Altitude: 550m/1805ft
Population: 44,000

Situation and characteristics

Nablus (Shekhem to the Israelis) lies 42km/26 miles north-east of Tel Aviv and 60km/37 miles north of Jerusalem in the uplands of Samaria. An industrial town (soap-making), it is the main centre of Arab nationalism on the Israeli-occupied west bank of the Jordan. Since Nablus is subject to frequent outbreaks of violence (see History, below) it is advisable to enquire about the current situation before visiting the town.

History

In A.D. 72, two years after the destruction of Jerusalem, Titus founded the settlement of Flavia Neapolis (the "new city") 2km/1¼ miles north-west of the ruined town of Shechem. The town flourished, and in 244 was granted the status of a colonia. At first mainly populated by pagan veterans (time-served Roman soldiers) and Samaritans, it soon acquired a Christian community, which produced the philosopher and martyr Justinus (Justin Martyr, c. 100–165). In 521 the Samaritans killed the bishop and devastated the town's churches, whereupon Justinian had the rebels (except those who became converted to Christianity or managed to escape) executed or sold into slavery. In 636 the town of Neapolis was occupied by the Arabs and became known as Nablus. During the Crusader period Queen Melisande, widow of King Fulk, fortified the town against her son Baldwin III, who in 1152 excluded her from political life but left her in possession of Nablus, where she founded a number of churches. The Christian occupation of the town, however, was short-lived: in 1187 it was recovered by the Arabs and since then has remained a Muslim town.

In the 16th century Nablus was the centre of one of the four Ottoman administrative divisions of Palestine (the other centres being Gaza, Jerusalem and Safed). In 1936 it was the starting-point of a rebellion against the British Mandatory authorities. Jordan seized Nablus in 1948 but it was retaken by Israel in 1967. In 1980 the mayor of Nablus, Bassam Sheker, one of the most influential Palestinian politicians in the Israeli-occupied territories, lost both legs in a bomb attack, and in 1986 his successor Zafer el-Musri was murdered. The perpetrators of these terrorist acts have not been found, but are believed to have been either Israeli extremists or Palestinians who considered the mayors too pro-Israeli.

In the western part of the town is the district of Haret es-Samira, in which some 250 Samaritans live. The only other place where Samaritans are still to be found is Holon, near Tel Aviv, where there is a small community. | **Samaritan quarter**

The Samaritans were the result of the mingling of Jews who had escaped being deported after the fall of the northern kingdom of Israel in 721 B.C. with "men from Babylon and from Cuthah" who had settled here (2 Kings 17,24). They were, therefore, no longer recognised by official Jewry and began to develop their own particular faith. Their Torah scroll, which is believed to date from the 2nd century, contains only the five books of Moses, the only sacred writings they recognise. Their shrine is on Mount Gerizim (881m/2891ft), which rises on one side of Nablus; on the other is Mount Eval (the Biblical Ebal; 940m/3084ft).

Moses instructed the Israelites to "put the blessing upon mount Gerizim and the curse upon mount Ebal" (Deuteronomy 11,29). When they came into the Promised Land Joshua set up an altar on Mount Ebal (Joshua 8,30). In 168 B.C. the Samaritan shrine which had stood on Mount Gerizim since 350 B.C. was converted by the Hellenising Seleucid ruler Antiochus IV into a temple of Zeus. This was destroyed in 128 B.C. by the Hasmonean John Hyrcanus I, who desired to incorporate the Samaritans into his kingdom. The Samaritans were also persecuted under Pontius Pilate (A.D. 26–36), Vespasian and the Roman Emperors from Hadrian to Justinian II. In 486 their temple on Mount Gerizim was again destroyed by the Emperor Zeno and replaced by a Christian church.

In spite of their continuing persecution the Samaritans have survived to this day, though in very small numbers. They celebrate the Passover annually on the summit of Mount Gerizim, slaughtering seven lambs in precise accordance with the Mosaic prescriptions (Exodus 12,5–11).

The modern districts of Nablus with their tall office blocks are in sharp contrast to the maze of irregular streets and lanes in the old town. In the centre of the market area is the El-Nasser Mosque. The town's largest mosque is the El-Kebir Mosque, a few hundred yards east, which was built in 1168 on the foundations of a Frankish church. | **The town**

Shechem

The site of Old Testament Shechem is 2km/1¼ miles south-east of Nablus on the saddle between Mounts Gerizim and Eval. An important town in Canaanite times thanks to its situation at the intersection of important roads running east–west and north–south, Shechem was associated with many events in the Old Testament. | **Situation**

Nablus

History
Abraham set up camp here on his journey from Mesopotamia to Canaan and erected the first altar (Genesis 12,7). His grandson Jacob also pitched his tent outside the town after his return from Mesopotamia, bought land for a hundred pieces of money and also erected an altar (Genesis 33,18–20). Jacob's sons Simeon and Levi slew the men of Shechem and despoiled their city to avenge the dishonour of their sister Dinah (Genesis 34,1–29). In the 17th century B.C. the Hyksos built a fortress here. In the 13th century B.C. Joshua had the remains of Joseph brought from Egypt and buried in the field which his father Jacob had bought. Earlier he had set up a new altar on Mount Ebal (Joshua 8,30). After Joshua's death the Israelites "forsook the Lord, and served Baal and Ashtaroth" (Judges 2,12–13). At the end of the 12th century B.C. Abimelech, son of the first Judge, Gideon, was made king in the temple of Baal (Judges 9,6). In 928 B.C. the ten northern tribes called upon Jeroboam to be king of Israel, from Bethel to Dan (1 Kings 12). Later, when Omri founded the new capital of Samaria (see entry), Shechem lost its importance and declined into a village, until in 350 B.C. the Samaritans made it their capital. The history of the town came to an end with its conquest by John Hyrcanus I in 128 B.C.

Tell Balata
Remains of ancient Shechem were brought to light by German archaeologists, beginning with Ernst Sellin (1913), on Tell Balata. They included fortifications of the Hyksos period (17th c. B.C.), the foundations of a large Canaanite temple and a temple of Baal-Beelit dating from the 13th/12th century B.C., no doubt the scene of Abimelech's election as king.

Jacob's Well
On the eastern slopes of Mount Gerizim, some 500m/550yds south-east of Tell Balata, is a Greek Orthodox church within which is a 36m/118ft deep well traditionally believed to have been dug by Jacob. It is also believed to be the well at which Jesus met the woman of Samaria (John 4,5–9). Around 380 a cruciform church was built on the site which in later centuries was several times destroyed and rebuilt. In Crusader times a three-aisled church was built over the well. From the 15th century onwards this fell into ruin, but the crypt and the well have survived to the present day. In 1885 the site was acquired by the Greek Orthodox, who began in 1903 to rebuild the Crusader church – a project which has not yet been completed.

Joseph's Tomb
A few hundred yards north of Jacob's Well is a building with a white dome known as Joseph's Tomb. Here Joseph is said to have been buried in the field bought by his father Jacob (see History, above).

Surroundings of Nablus

Shiloh
36km/22 miles south of Nablus is the village of Sinjil, which takes its name from the Crusader Raymond de Saint-Gilles, Count of Toulouse. From here a poor road runs 6km/4 miles east by way of the village of Turmus-Aya to the site of ancient Shiloh (Hebrew Shillo, Arabic Khirbet Seilun). In the early period of Israelite settlement Shiloh was an important shrine, for it was here that the Tabernacle containing the Ark of the Covenant stood for a hundred years from about 1175 B.C. (Joshua 18,1). Here Samuel was called to be a prophet (1 Samuel 3). After the battle of Eben-ezer the Ark of the Covenant was carried off by the Philistines (1 Samuel 4,11) and the town was destroyed. In the 10th century B.C. Shiloh was the abode of the prophet Ahijah, who prophesied to Jeroboam that after Solomon's death he would be the first king of the northern kingdom of Israel (1 Kings, 29–37).
Excavations by Danish archaeologists from 1926 onwards brought to light a temple of the Canaanite period and a mosaic pavement from a Byzantine church. Adjoining the site is the Mosque of the Sixty (Djami Sittin).

Tel Tirza
15km/9 miles north-east of Nablus on the road to Tubas is Tel Tirza (Arabic Tell Faria). Excavations between 1946 and 1960 showed that there was a settlement here in the 4th millennium B.C. which was abandoned about 2500 B.C. Around 1700 B.C. the Canaanites established a new town, which was taken by Joshua in the 13th century B.C. (Joshua 12,24). In the 10th century Jeroboam, who had first resided in Shechem and later in Pnuel on the east bank of the Jordan, made Tirzah capital of his kingdom of Israel

(1 Kings 14,17). The town lost its importance when, about 880 B.C., Omri transferred his capital to Samaria (see entry). In 772 B.C. the town was destroyed by the Assyrians. Over the remains of the town the excavators found traces of Assyrian, Hellenistic and Roman settlement.

Two springs under the tell are the sources of the river Tirza. 24km/15 miles down the Tirza valley to the south-east (7km/4½ miles before Adam's Bridge over the Jordan) the road to Jericho goes off on the right. 6km/4 miles along this road, to the right, can be seen Mount Sartaba (alt. 377m/1237ft), rising some 700m/2300ft above the Jordan rift valley. Here in the 1st century B.C. the Hasmonean king Alexander Jannaeus built the fortress of Alexandreia, destroyed by the Romans and later rebuilt by Herod. In 31 B.C. it served as a place of confinement for Herod's wife.

It is a steep climb up the hill to the remains of the fortress destroyed by the Romans in A.D. 70, but the effort is rewarded by the magnificent views from the summit, extending south-westward to the Mount of Olives at Jerusalem (40km/25 miles) and north-eastward to the castle of Belvoir (see entry) on its hill (55km/35 miles). In the time of the Second Temple Sartaba, lying between these two points, was part of a chain of beacon stations which transmitted signals from Jerusalem to the boundaries of Israelite territory to announce the beginning of the month and of religious festivals.

Mount Sartaba

Nahariya

G 2

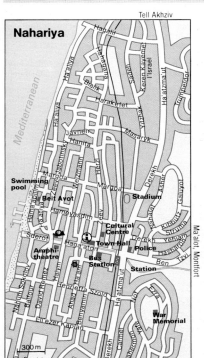

Shave Zion, Akko, Haifa

District: Northern
Altitude: 0–10m/0–35ft
Population: 30,000

Nahariya, 30km/19 miles north of Haifa on a beautiful stretch of the Mediterranean coast, was originally an agricultural settlement on the banks of the river Ga'aton founded in 1934 by Jews from Germany. It still bears the imprint of its original settlers, but has now developed into a popular seaside resort with beautiful scenery and many places of historical interest in the surrounding area.

Situation and characteristics

Nahariya takes its name from the river (Nahar) Ga'aton, which reaches the Mediterranean here. In the last section of its course before entering the sea it flows down the middle of the town's main street, Sderot Haga'aton, which is lined by eucalyptus trees. On the north side of the street is the Town Hall, in which are the tourist information office and

Sights

307

the Municipal Museum (modern painting on 5th floor, archaeology on 6th). On the south side of the street are the railway station and numerous cafés and restaurants. From the west end of the street Hama'apilim Street runs north to the boat landing-stages and the swimming pool. In the uncertain period before Israel became independent in 1948 Nahariya was cut off from its hinterland for many months and could be reached only by boat from Haifa. The Phoenicians built a harbour here which remained in use into Byzantine and perhaps early Islamic times. On a hill by the beach are remains of a temple of the 15th century B.C. dedicated to the Canaanite fertility goddess Astarte.

Surroundings of Nahariya

Akhziv

5km/3 miles north, at the mouth of the river Keziv, is the ancient site of Akhziv, lying close to a Club Méditerranée holiday village. The Old Testament city of Achzib had a mixed population, for "the Asherites dwelt among the Canaanites, the inhabitants of the land" (Judges 1,31–32). The Phoenicians obtained their famous purple dye from shellfish here. Excavation brought to light a cemetery which was used for burial from the 8th to the 6th century B.C. The place was known to the Crusaders as Castel Imbert. In more recent times, until 1948, there was a village of Arab fishermen here. The site is now a National Park, with a very beautiful beach, extensive areas of grass and a restaurant. Immediately north of the National Park is a rather unprepossessing wooden house which contains an interesting private museum of archaeological material. The owner purchased the property in 1952 and later declared it the independent state of Akhzivland, in which visitors can have their passport embellished by a very pretty stamp.

★Rosh Haniqra

7km/4½ miles north of Akhziv, on the Lebanese frontier, is the white chalk cliff of Rosh Haniqra ("Cape of the Caves"). In the course of his expedition

Akhziv: archaeological site and recreation area

to Egypt Alexander the Great, like many armies and merchants' caravans before and after him, passed this way and had steps cut in the cliff to make it easier to scale. This staircase in the rock later became known as the Ladder of Tyre. On top of the cliff there is now a viewpoint affording superb panoramic views, with a restaurant, souvenir shops and a cableway running down to the caves at the foot of the cliff.

15km/9 miles north-east of Nahariya is the kibbutz of Hanita, founded in 1938, with a guest-house and a small museum displaying finds from the surrounding area.

Hanita

1km/¾ mile south of Nahariya is the kibbutz of Evron, founded in 1938 and named after the Old Testament town of Hebron in the territory of the tribe of Asher (Joshua 19,28). Excavations in 1951 revealed traces of Palaeolithic settlement and the mosaic pavement of a 5th century Byzantine church.

Evron

2km/1¼ miles farther south is the village of Shave Zion, a seaside resort with a completely preserved mosaic pavement from an early Christian church.

Shave Zion

Farther south is the old port of Akko (see entry).

10km/6 miles south-east of Nahariya is the international Christian settlement of Nes Amim ("Signal to the Nations"), which seeks to promote Christian and Jewish co-operation. It was founded in 1963 by young Christians, mostly from the Netherlands.

Nes Amim

To reach Nes Amim, leave Nahariya on the coast road to the south and at the turn-off for Shave Zion (on right) take a road on the left which runs via Regba and then bears south for Nes Amim. By previous appointment (tel. 92 25 66) visitors can have a guided tour of the farm (rose-growing) or hear a talk on kibbutz life.

From Nahariya a road runs inland by way of Mi'ilya to the ruins of the Crusader castle of Montfort (14km/8½ miles: see entry), and south by way of the kibbutz of Yehi'am (11km/7 miles) to the ruined castle of Judin.

Montfort, Judin

Nathanya

See Netanya

Nazareth/Nazerat   H 3

District: Northern
Altitude: 350m/1150ft
Population: 39,000 (with Nazerat Illit 58,000)

Nazareth (Hebrew Nazerat, Arabic En-Nasra), the largest Arab town in Israel, lies on the southern edge of the Galilean uplands, above the Jezreel plain. Its inhabitants are mostly Christians, and the day of rest, on which most shops are closed, is Sunday and not the Sabbath. In fact, however, Sunday is usually a day of hectic activity, for many young couples are married in the Church of the Annunciation on that day, after which they drive about the town with the whole wedding party, horns blaring.

Situation and characteristics

As the place where the Archangel Gabriel announced the birth of Jesus to Mary and where Jesus spent most of his life, Nazareth has attracted Christian pilgrims for more than fifteen hundred years.

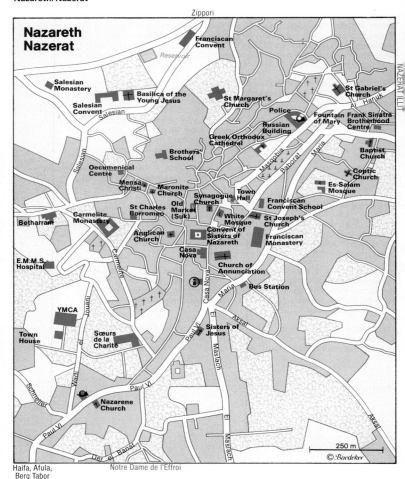

Nazareth
Nazerat

Zippori

Franciscan Convent

Reservoir

Salesian Monastery

Basilica of the Young Jesus

Salesian Convent

Salesian

St Margaret's Church

Police

Russian Building

Fountain of Mary

St Gabriel's Church

Frank Sinatra Brotherhood Centre

NAZERAT ILLIT

Al Hanuk

Greek Orthodox Cathedral

Brothers' School

Oecumenical Centre

Mensa Christi

Maronite Church

Old Market (Suk)

Synagogue Church

Town Hall

Franciscan Convent School

Baptist Church

Coptic Church

Es-Salam Mosque

St Charles Borromeo

White Mosque

St Joseph's Church

Carmelite Monastery

Betharram

Anglican Church

Casa Nova

Convent of Sisters of Nazareth

Franciscan Monastery

E.M.M.S. Hospital

Church of Annunciation

Bus Station

YMCA

Sœurs de la Charité

Sisters of Jesus

Town House

Paul VI

Paul VI

Nazarene Church

Schneller

Wadi

Carmelite

Casa Nova

Maria

El Aksal

El Maslach

El Aksal

Masqobia

Baborat

Maria

250 m

© Baedeker

Haifa, Afula, Berg Tabor

Notre Dame de l'Effroi

History

Nazareth is not mentioned in the Old Testament, and in pre-Christian times was probably an insignificant village. Excavations from 1955 onwards, however, showed that the hill on which the Church of the Annunciation and St Joseph's Church stand was inhabited from the time of the patriarchs (2nd millennium B.C.). The little houses of the village were built on top of tombs of the 2nd millennium and underground chambers hewn from the local tufa which had been used in the first half of the 1st millennium B.C. as store-rooms.

The name of Nazareth first appears in the New Testament in the account of the Annunciation (Luke 1,26–33). Jesus lived here until after his baptism by John (Luke 3,21), but after he began to teach spent most of his time round Capernaum (see entry).

View of Nazareth from the Salesian monastery

In the early Christian period the Grotto of the Annunciation became a much venerated place of pilgrimage, and the present church is the fifth built on the site. An early place of Christian settlement, Nazareth was taken in 614 by the Persians, who, in conjunction with the Jews, destroyed it.

Thereafter the Christian population declined. In 629, however, Nazareth was recovered by the Byzantines, who took their revenge by destroying the houses of the Jewish population. The place was not rebuilt until the time of Tancred, the Norman Crusader who took Nazareth in 1099 and ruled as Prince of Galilee.

Nazareth suffered further destruction in 1263 at the hands of Baibars and his Mamelukes. Thereafter no Christians were allowed to live in the town until the Druze ruler Fakhr ed-Din revoked the ban in 1620. The town developed in the 19th and 20th centuries under Ottoman and later British rule. In 1948 Nazareth became part of Israel, and the new Jewish settlement of Nazerat Illit (Upper Nazareth), with its own administration, grew up on the hills above the town.

Nazareth is a town of many churches, notably the Church of the Annunciation with its 37m/121ft high dome. Few, however, would describe it as a beautiful town. The churches are in busy streets, frequently overloaded with traffic, and surrounded by plain houses run up by high-speed building methods, with no open spaces or attractive squares.

The town

A convenient starting-point for a sightseeing tour of Nazareth is Casa Nova Street, in which is the Church of the Annunciation. From here almost all the other churches of interest can easily be seen on foot. It is also worth taking a stroll through the market area of the town, which lies to the north of Casa Nova Street.

★Church of the Annunciation

Earlier churches

Archaeological investigation has shown that the veneration of the Grotto of the Annunciation dates back to the 3rd century, when Jewish Christians built a first modest church (the Synagogue Church) modelled on the synagogues of the day.

The second church, a small building with a circular apse and an atrium at the west end, was built in the 4th century for the Empress Helen, Constantine the Great's mother, by a converted Jew called Joseph of Tiberias. An inscription records that this church was enlarged at some time before 427 by Conon of Jerusalem. On the south side of the church was a small monastery, which was destroyed by the Persians in 614.

The third church was built in the early 12th century by Tancred, Prince of Galilee, and was on a considerably larger scale than its predecessors. It was a three-aisled basilica 75m/246ft long by 30m/98ft wide. This church stood until 1263, when it was destroyed by Baibars, who spared only the grotto. Thereafter there was no church on the site until the Franciscans gained permission to build a new church in 1730. In contrast to the earlier churches, this was not oriented east–west but north–south, so that the choir stood directly over the grotto. The façade was added only in 1877.

In 1955 the Franciscan church was pulled down to make way for the fifth church on the site. This church, consecrated in 1969, is the most important modern church in Israel and the largest built in recent years.

The design by the Italian architect Giovanni Muzio was based on two principles. He wanted to present in visual form the history of the place from its earliest days and to depict the catholic nature of the Roman church; and, using modern means, he succeeded most convincingly in realising this concept. The lower church, offering a view of the lower and older levels of the structure, illustrates the historical continuity of the site, while the upper church shows the universality of the church in its decoration, which was the work of artists from many different countries.

The plan was based on the Crusader church. The side walls were built on top of the surviving courses of the older walls, and the apses at the east end of the Crusader church were incorporated in the new building. Only at the west end is the modern church shorter than its predecessor. Like the older church, the new one is a three-aisled basilica, but its distinctive characteristic is that it combines the basilican plan with a centralised structure. In the floor of the church is a large octagonal opening through which there is a

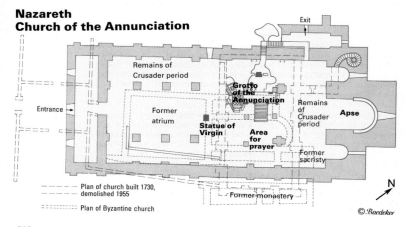

**Nazareth
Church of the Annunciation**

Exit

Remains of Crusader period

Grotto of the Annunciation

Entrance →

Former atrium

Remains of Crusader period

Apse

Statue of Virgin

Area for prayer

Former sacristy

Former monastery

— — — Plan of church built 1730, demolished 1955

:::::::: Plan of Byzantine church

N

© *Baedeker*

Church of the Annunciation: main doorway and tower

view of the lower level and the older structures below – the Grotto of the Annunciation and the remains of the earliest churches on the site. Over this area, which can also be seen from the upper church, is the dome.

The entrance gateway to the west leads into a courtyard with colonnades along the west and south sides. The west front of the church has ornamental friezes and a large relief of the Annunciation. The three bronze doors were the work of Roland Friederichsen of Munich. On the central door, top left, is the Nativity of Christ; bottom left the Flight into Egypt and Jesus as a boy; top right the Sermon on the Mount and the Crucifixion; bottom left the Baptism of Christ.
On the south doorway are scenes from the life of the Virgin by the American sculptor Frederick Shrady.

Exterior

The west doorway leads into the lower church. On the north side, to the left, is the wall of the Crusader church, articulated by semi-columns, with the wall of the modern church on top of it. Going east along the nave, we come to the octagon under the dome and can look down to the earlier levels. To the left is the Grotto of the Annunciation, with an altar bearing the inscription "Verbum hic caro factum est" ("Here the Word was made flesh": John 1,14). The copper canopy over the grotto was the work of a Belgian craftsman. The columns immediately in front of the grotto are ascribed to the 3rd century Synagogue Church. In the centre of the octagon is the modern altar. To the right can be seen the side wall and circular apse of the second church (4th–5th c.).
Farther east, beyond the octagon, are the three apses of the third (Crusader) church. Note particularly the richly decorated 12th century capitals in the right-hand apse.
Returning to the west end, we go up a staircase into the upper church. Like the lower church, this has aisles flanking the nave and an octagonal opening through which there is a view of the Grotto of the Nativity. The light dome over the octagon is in the form of a lily (an old symbol of the Virgin).

Interior

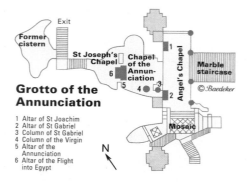

Grotto of the Annunciation

1 Altar of St Joachim
2 Altar of St Gabriel
3 Column of St Gabriel
4 Column of the Virgin
5 Altar of the Annunciation
6 Altar of the Flight into Egypt

The floor of the upper church is of inlaid marble (by Adriano Alessandrini), with scenes relating to the Virgin and to Marian councils. At the east end is the presbytery. Behind the white altar is a mosaic representing the Church, with Christ flanked by Mary and Peter and by saints. To the left is a chapel dedicated to saints of the Franciscan order, to the right the Chapel of the Sacrament.

On the walls of the upper church are images of the Virgin from all over the world. There are mosaics presented to the church by Australia, Britain, Cameroun, Czechoslovakia, Hungary, Ireland, Italy, Japan and Mexico; ceramics from Canada, Poland and Portugal; a fresco from Argentina; a

In the Grotto of the Annunciation

work in steel and silver from North America, a wood-carving from Venezuela.

Leaving the upper church by the north doorway, we come into a courtyard, on the right of which is the baptistery (by Bernd Hartmann and Ima Rochelle). Below it are excavations of ancient Nazareth.

Baptistery

Going north through the courtyard, we see on the right St Joseph's Church and come to the exit (to left).

Other Sights

St Joseph's Church (1914) is built over a cave known as Joseph's Workshop. It contains the remains of a cistern and storage pits which may date from the village that Christ knew.

St Joseph's Church

A little way west, through the market area, is the Synagogue Church, which belongs to the Melchites, a Greek Catholic community. To the left of the doorway is a door leading down to the synagogue which Jesus is said to have attended. In fact the scanty remains probably date from the 6th century.

Synagogue Church

A few hundred yards west of the Synagogue Church is the Franciscan Mensa Christi Church (1861), which contains a slab of stone 3.6m/12ft long and 3m/10ft wide, the Mensa Christi (Christ's Table), at which the risen Christ is said to have supped with his disciples.

Mensa Christi

From the Mensa Christi Church a path zigzags up to a commandingly situated monastery of French Salesians, with the Basilica of the Young Jesus. The church was built in 1918. Over the high altar is a figure of Jesus at the age of sixteen.

Salesian Monastery

From here there is a fine view of Nazareth.

Salesian monastery, Nazareth

Fountain of Mary

Negev

Fountain of Mary,
St Gabriel's
Church

1.5km/1 mile north-east of the Church of the Annunciation, near the main road to Tiberias, is the Fountain of Mary. In Orthodox tradition, based on an apocryphal gospel, the Archangel Gabriel first appeared to Mary at the village fountain. The present Fountain of Mary is modern and is on a different site from the original fountain, which is said to be under the altar of the Greek Orthodox church of St Gabriel, a little way north – also well worth a visit for the sake of its decoration.

Surroundings of Nazareth

Zippori,
Cana

5km/3 miles north-west is Zippori (see entry), with the ruins of a Crusader church. About the same distance north-east is Kafr Kanna (see Cana), scene of the marriage at Cana.

Afula,
Mount Tabor

11km/7 miles south of Nazareth is Afula (see entry), north-east of which is Mount Tabor (see entry).

Negev

F–H 5–8

District: Southern

Situation and
characteristics

The Negev ("desert", "arid land" in Hebrew), the most southerly part of Israel, is bounded on the west by the Egyptian–Israeli frontier and the Gaza Strip, on the east by the Arava depression and on the north approximately by a line running between Gaza and En Gedi. In terms of geographical structure it merges into Sinai to the south-west. The largest town in this huge triangle is Beersheba (Be'er Sheva), situated on the boundary

Desert landscape in the Negev

between the northern Negev, which has been made fertile by irrigation, and the arid Negev desert to the south.

The Negev seems to have become an arid area between 10,000 and 7500 B.C. In the 18th century B.C. Abraham came from the north to Beersheba. In the later 2nd millennium B.C. the Negev was occupied by three peoples – to the north, round Arad, those of the Canaanites who had advanced farthest south; to the south the Amalekites, whom David exterminated about 1000 B.C.; to the east, round the Arava depression, the Edomites, who moved north in the 6th century B.C., settled between Beersheba and Hebron and became known as the Idumaeans.

From the 1st century B.C. the Nabataeans sought to settle and cultivate the Negev from their capital at Petra. They achieved this with the help of ingenious methods of irrigation, and towns like Avdat (see entry), Subeita (see Shivta) and Mampsis (see Mamshit) were established. In the 4th–6th centuries the Byzantines took over from the Nabataeans and developed the region still further. After the coming of the Arabs, who in other countries had improved irrigation methods, the irrigation systems of the Negev broke down, and for more than a thousand years the Negev became an arid region inhabited only by Bedouin.

The situation changed when Jewish settlers came to the Negev. The decisive impulse to make the land fertile again was given by David Ben-Gurion, a member of the kibbutz of Sede Boqer (see entry), who established a university there for the study of the Negev. A scientific basis for the development of the region was provided by Michael Evenari (see Famous People), a botanist of German origin who established a farm at Avdat using Nabataean methods and founded a plant research institute in Beersheba. Of great importance for the resettlement of the Negev was the creation of the National Water Carrier, which brings water from northern Israel to the Negev.

Six different areas can be distinguished in the Negev: the north-western coastal plain, the Beersheba valley, the Negev Hills, a high plateau in the Wilderness of Paran, the Arava depression and the Elat Hills in the south. The north-western coastal plain, a densely populated region, also takes in the Gaza Strip. Well supplied with water, it forms a link between the Judaean coastal plain and the El-Arish plain in northern Sinai.

The Beersheba valley is divided into two by the Nahal Be'er Sheva, a river which is dry for most of the year. To the east, between Arad and Dimona, the plain is narrow, but it becomes wider in the area of the Haluza sand-dunes. With the help of irrigation this area can be brought into cultivation. To the south, in the Negev uplands, the land rises, reaching a height of 1035m/336ft in Mount Ramon. The central part of the area is dominated by the rugged Negev Hills, with their gorges and craters (see Makhtesh Ramon). Most of the rain which falls here is collected by the river Zin, which flows into the Arava depression and from there reaches the Dead Sea.

To the south-west is the Wilderness of Paran (Midbar Paran), part of a plateau which begins in Sinai at a height of 600m/2000ft and extends to the north-eastern reaches of the Arava depression. Through this area flows the river Paran, which is dry for most of the year but during the rainy season swells into a mighty torrent. To the east the Negev falls away to the Arava depression, which, like the Jordan and the Dead Sea, is part of the Syro-African rift valley system.

The Elat Hills belong geologically to the Sinai peninsula. From Elat they extend north for some 30km/20 miles, consisting of soft sandstones in shades of white, yellow and pink, with, here and there, veins of iron, copper and other ores. The famous Timna copper-mines are within this area.

In recent years the immigration of Jewish settlers, the provision of improved irrigation and the development of tourist facilities on the Gulf of Aqaba have led to a massive increase of population in the Negev. Whereas

Netanya (Nethanya, Nathanya)

during the British Mandate the population was around 12,000 (90% of them Bedouin and the remaining 10% settlers, mostly Jewish), it has now risen to over 230,000, including 38,000 Bedouin.

Touring the Negev

With Beersheba, Arad or Elat as a base, it is possible to see something of the scenery of the Negev and to visit its ancient sites – though there are few good modern roads. See Beersheba, Surroundings, and Elat, Surroundings. There are also organised trips in all-terrain vehicles.

Netanya (Nethanya, Nathanya)   G 3

District: Central
Altitude: 20m/65ft
Population: 105,000

Situation and characteristics

Netanya (Nethanya, Nathanya), situated on the Mediterranean coast 32km/20 miles north of Tel Aviv and 63km/39 miles south of Haifa, is a popular seaside and holiday resort with an agreeable climate and a beautiful sandy beach more than 10km/6 miles long. It has over 30 hotels, mostly in the middle and lower categories, and restaurants of corresponding quality.

History

Netanya was founded in 1928 amid the sand-dunes of the plain of Sharon by members of the organisation named Bene Binyamin in honour of Baron

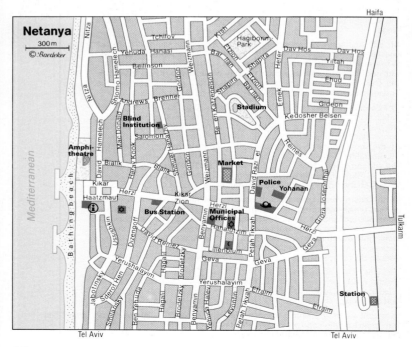

Ha'atzmaut Square in the centre of Netanya

Edmond (Binyamin) de Rothschild. Its name commemorates the American-Jewish philanthropist Nathan Strauss. Until the draining of the Hefer plain (see entry) from 1930 onwards and the building of roads the settlement, at first no more than a village, could be reached only on foot or on horseback from the Tulkarm railway station, 17km/10½ miles east.

During the Second World War immigrants from Antwerp established a diamond-cutting workshop which made a contribution to the war effort and after 1945 worked mainly for the jewellery industry. Since then Netanya has developed into a flourishing town with a sound infrastructure, an economically important industrial zone and excellent tourist facilities.

The town's principal street, named after Theodor Herzl, is lined with shops, restaurants and cafés. Herzl Street runs west from the main Tel Aviv–Haifa road, passing the Head Post Office (at the corner of David Raziel Street), the principal synagogue, the bus station (on Benyamin Boulevard), the central taxi rank (in Zion Square) and the Town Hall, to Ha'atzmaut Square (Kikar Ha'atzmaut) with its gardens and fountains. On the seaward side is the tourist information office, and along the north side is a small park with a modern amphitheatre facing the sea. There are numerous restaurants round the square, but the town's hotels are are to be found in the streets running north–south, almost all of them with a view of the sea.

The town's main north–south artery is a wide street known to the south of Herzl Street as Benyamin Boulevard and to the north as Weizmann Boulevard. In a parallel street to the east is the Market Hall, offering a wide range of fruit and vegetables, meat and fish. To the west of Weizmann Boulevard is a rehabilitation centre for the blind, established after the Second World War, with a library of books in braille and a museum (art exhibitions).

Also of interest are the diamond-cutting workshops, with showrooms, in the south of the town (Yahalom Street).

The town

Surroundings of Netanya

Jewish Legion Museum	In the moshav of Avihayil, 4km/2½ miles north of the town centre, is the Jewish Legion Museum, which illustrates the achievements of Jewish units in the British army during the First World War.
Caesarea	Some 25km/15 miles north of Netanya is the extensive archaeological site of Caesarea (see entry).
Tel Aviv	Tel Aviv (see entry) lies 30km/19 miles south of Netanya.

Paran   G/H 7

District: Southern

The river Paran (Nahal Paran) has the longest valley in the Negev. Initially flowing north, it turns east at the point where it is crossed by the road from Elat to Beersheba via Gerofit and Avdat and ends in the Arava depression to the south of the Dead Sea.

Waterless almost all year, the Paran turns into a "raging torrent" (the meaning of its Arabic name Wadi el-Jirafi) in the rainy season. Where it is crossed by the Elat–Beersheba road the wadi is a wild erosion valley, while lower down, where it is traversed by the road from Elat to the Dead Sea, it is wide and flat. From the moshav of Paran (founded 1971), near this road, the hills of Edom can be seen to the east, with the characteristic silhouette of Djebel Hor (Mount of Aaron; 1386m/4547ft), 60km/37 miles away above the Nabataean capital of Petra in Jordan.

History

The valley of the Paran and the surrounding desert, the wilderness of Paran, were an important staging-point in the Israelites' journey from Egypt to the Promised Land. From Sinai they came into the wilderness of Paran (Numbers 10,12), from which Moses sent out scouts, who entered the land of the Canaanites and came to Hebron. From there the Israelites journeyed farther north into the desert of Zin (Numbers 20,1), which extends between the spring of En Avdat (see entry) and the Arava depression. The king of Edom would not allow them to pass through his land, so they turned east, crossed the Arava and came to Mount Hor, on the summit of which Moses' brother Aaron died and was buried (Numbers 20,22–29); his tomb on Djebel Hor, above Petra, is still venerated. The Israelites then travelled on through the land of Moab, on the east side of the Jordan, and came into the land of the Ammonites, where Moses died, having been vouchsafed a sight of the Promised Land (Deuteronomy 34). In his final blessing of the Israelites Moses named Paran: "The Lord came from Sinai . . .; he shined forth from mount Paran" (Deuteronomy 33,2).

Qarne Hittim

See Horns of Hittim

Qumran   H 4

West Bank
Altitude: 330m/1080ft below sea level

Situation and characteristics

Qumran, 20km/12½ miles south of Jericho on the Israeli-occupied west bank of the Jordan, became famous in 1947 when a Bedouin boy found the

The Qumran caves, in which the Dead Sea scrolls were found ▶

first of the "Dead Sea scrolls" in a cave and the monastery-like settlement of the Essenes from which they came was excavated.

Discovery of the scrolls

Bedouin of the Ta'amira tribe, the first discoverers of the scrolls, took their finds in 1947 to Bethlehem, and from there were referred to Jerusalem. There Metropolitan Jeshue Samuel of the Syrian monastery of St Mark realised that the texts were written in Hebrew and acquired five scrolls, which he took to the United

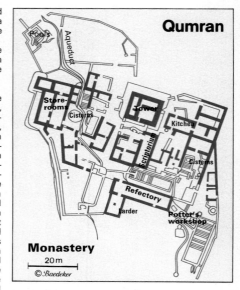

States after his monastery suffered damage during the Arab–Israeli war of 1948. In America, after exhibiting them publicly, he found a buyer, who at first was anonymous. This was the Israeli general and archaeologist Yigael Yadin, who bought the scrolls for 250,000 dollars and took them back to Israel, where the Shrine of the Book in the Israel Museum was built to house them. Yadin's father Professor E. L. Sukenik was able to buy five other scrolls from an antique dealer in Jerusalem. Two copper scrolls were acquired by the Jordanian government and are now in Amman Museum.

Altogether more than 500 Hebrew, Aramaic and occasionally also Greek manuscripts, ten of them almost completely preserved, have been found in eleven caves at Qumran. The scrolls were kept in pottery jars with lids. Almost all the texts are on parchment. Dating from the 1st century B.C. and the 1st century A.D., they are the oldest surviving manuscripts of the Bible. They include all the books of the Old Testament except Esther, together with apocrypha like the Hebrew text of the Book of Sirach, previously known only in translations, and various writings of the Qumran community, including a scroll over 3m/10ft long which contains the whole book of Isaiah in 54 columns and a 2m/6½ft long scroll with the "manual of discipline" of the Essenes of Qumran. There are also various private documents in Hebrew, Aramaic, Greek and, more rarely, Nabataean and Latin, and letters, including some from Bar Kochba, found in the wadis to the south of Qumran.

Not all the scrolls found between 1947 and 1956 have yet been deciphered and published. The more poorly preserved scrolls, which have disintegrated into hundreds of fragments, present particular problems for the team of twenty scholars at present working on the project. It is likely to take until the year 2000 to deal with this mass of material.

So far as it has gone the decipherment of the texts on the scrolls, which Albright already reckoned in 1948 to be "the greatest find of manuscripts in modern times", has made important contributions to knowledge in three respects. Comparison of the texts with later manuscripts of the Bible has shown the extraordinary reliability of the transmission of the Biblical text over the centuries; our knowledge of the Essene sect, previously known only from references by Jewish and Roman writers like Philo, Flavius Josephus and Pliny, has been widened and deepened; and it has been shown that Qumran was the centre of the Essene community.

The Essenes were the third of the main Jewish religious parties, after the Sadducees and Pharisees. The sect came into being about 150 B.C. in the course of conflicts in Jerusalem over the Temple and the service of the Temple. The Essenes were against the union in one person of both royal and priestly power, against the rigid and superficial Temple rites and against Hellenistic influence. They saw the religious community in Jerusalem as having fallen away from the faith and regarded themselves as the true people of Israel. The 4000 members of the sect scattered throughout the country established their centre at Qumran, where there was a community of some 200 Essenes.

History

The settlement at Qumran was established soon after 150 B.C. over the remains of an earlier settlement of the 9th–6th centuries B.C. It was destroyed in an earthquake in 31 B.C., rebuilt and then finally destroyed by Roman forces in A.D. 68 during the Jewish War. Before the destruction of their settlement the Essenes managed to hide their library, archives and other treasures in the neighbouring caves, where they survived the centuries. During the Bar Kochba rising of 132–135 Qumran was again briefly occupied.

During the 200 years of existence of their community the Essenes lived a strictly regulated communal life. Those who were admitted to the community by baptism after a novitiate of several years gave all their possessions to the community. After ritual purification the members ate their meals in common, with ceremonial breaking of bread and offering of wine. They devoted themselves to the study of the Bible and praised God with hymns of thanksgiving. They tilled the land at nearby En Gedi (see entry). Their objectives were extreme abstinence, piety and above all purity (white clothing, diet, baths). In Christoph Burchard's view the Essenes were neither an order nor a sect but "a strictly Jewish religious movement directed towards the attainment of sanctity, adhering strictly to the Torah, with a radical eschatology". The community was headed by the "Teacher of Righteousness", a priest descended from Zadok. The determinant elements in the theology of Qumran were the expectation of the coming of the Messiah and the dualist doctrine (set out in a scroll almost 3m/10ft long) of the conflict in the last days between the Sons of Light and the Sons of Darkness. It appears probable that John the Baptist belonged to the Essene community, at least for a time, and that the doctrines of Qumran had some impact on the New Testament and on the Jewish Karaite sect.

Sights

The monastery-like settlement of the Essenes was originally surrounded by a high wall. No living or sleeping accommodation was found within the complex (the Essenes presumably slept in the neighbouring caves), so there is some doubt whether it can in fact be regarded as akin to a monastery.

★Monastery

Near the entrance are the remains of a tower. Beyond this, to the left, is a courtyard, on one side of which (by the tower) is a kitchen and on the other the main building, which is 37.5m/123ft square. Along its south side is the refectory and assembly hall, 24m/79ft long by 4.5m/15ft wide. On the upper floor was a scriptorium. In an adjoining room were found 1700 pottery vessels and a jar with a lid like those in which the manuscripts were stored in the caves. The potters' workshop can be seen to the east of the main building, together with two cisterns damaged in the earthquake of 31 B.C. On the west side of the site are the remains of an aqueduct which fed the

Remains of monastery, Qumran

pools for ritual ablutions, as well as a cistern from the earlier Israelite period, a store-room, kilns and ovens.

Caves

From the open space beyond the remains of buildings there is a striking view over a deep gorge to the caves in which the scrolls were found; the caves themselves are accessible only to rock-climbers.

Ramallah
H 4

West Bank
Altitude: 870m/2855ft
Population: 15,000
(24,000 including Bira)

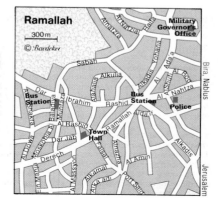

Situation and characteristics

Ramallah, a town with both Christian and Muslim inhabitants, lies 15km/9 miles north of Jerusalem on the Israeli-occupied west bank of the Jordan. It is a holiday resort, with many restaurants and cafés.

History

Ramallah was founded in the 14th century by Christians who had been driven out of Shobak (now in Jordan). In the 19th century the Roman Catholic church established a community here and built schools.

Ramallah now adjoins the Arab town of Bira; the population is partly Christian. As a result of the proximity of Jerusalem the town has developed considerably since the period of the Mandate. Thanks to its altitude (870m/2855ft) and its climate Ramallah has become a popular altitude resort.

North-west of the town centre, on the road to En Qinya, are the ruins of a church and monastery of the Byzantine period, and on a hill above the town are the remains of a Frankish church.

The town

Surroundings of Ramallah

4km/2½ miles north-east is the Arab village of Beitin, the Bethel ("House of God") of the Old Testament. To the east of Bethel Abraham, coming from the north, set up an altar (Genesis 12,8). After Joshua's conquest of the land Bethel belonged to the tribe of Benjamin (Joshua 18,13), and was later destroyed by the tribe of Ephraim (Judges 1,22). After the division of the kingdom Jeroboam, king of the northern kingdom of Israel, built shrines to a golden calf in Dan (see entry) and in Bethel. In 621 B.C. the shrine in Bethel was destroyed by King Josiah. In Roman times the troops who took Jerusalem in A.D. 70 were garrisoned here. In the 5th century Bethel was Christian. In 1892 a mosque was built over the remains of a Byzantine church. Excavations were carried out by American archaeologists to the north and east of the village. To the south-east are the ruins of a Crusader castle.

Beitin

Ramla/Ramleh

G 4

District: Central
Altitude: 70m/230ft
Population: 40,000

Ramla (Arabic Ramleh) lies 19km/12 miles south-east of Tel Aviv on the road to Jerusalem and on the north–south road between Haifa and Beersheba. It has a number of buildings of the Islamic and Christian periods, including the White Tower and the Great Mosque, which dates from the Crusader period.

Situation and characteristics

The town was founded in 716 by Caliph Suleiman, the second son of Abd el-Malik, builder of the Dome of the Rock in Jerusalem, and named Ramleh ("sand") after the type of soil in the area. Its palaces and mosques reflected the splendour of the Omayyad dynasty, whose capital was Damascus. When the Omayyads were succeeded in 750 by the Abbasids members of the Sufi sect left the new capital of Baghdad and came to Ramleh, where there were already Sunnite and Shiite Muslims, indigenous Jews and Jews of the Diaspora, as well as members of the Jewish Karaite sect, which came into existence in Babylon in the 8th century. The Karaites recognise only the Law as written down in the Torah but not the traditions collected in the Talmud. Their largest community is in Ramla, where 3000 of their approximately 11,000 members live.

History

In the 11th century Ramleh was pillaged (1025) and ravaged by earthquakes (1033, 1067). In 1099 it was taken by the Crusaders, who fought three battles with Fatimid forces here; in 1101 and 1105 they won, in 1102 they lost.

After Saladin's victory at the Horns of Hittim (see entry) in 1187 the Crusader period came to an end in Ramleh. The conquest of the town by

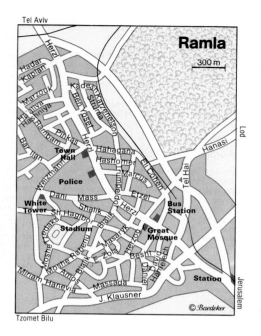

Baibars in 1267 marked the beginning of the Mameluke period, of which the White Tower is a relic. In the 14th century Ramleh's population included both Muslims and Jews as well as Christian monks. In the 17th century the town fell into decay. In 1799 Napoleon spent the night in Ramleh on the way to Akko. In 1917 a British military cemetery was laid out for 2000 of General Allenby's troops who had been killed in the fighting with the Turks. In 1936, during Arab riots, Ramleh's Jewish inhabitants left the town; then in 1948 it surrendered to Israeli forces without a fight. At that time there were only 1500 Arabs left in the town, but their numbers have since increased to over 5000.

Sights

Great Mosque	In the Oriental market quarter to the east of the town, on the south side of Herzl Street, is the Great Mosque, originally an aisled basilica built by the Crusaders in the 12th century, with a minaret built on the foundations of the church's bell-tower.
St Joseph's Church	Farther along Herzl Street to the north-west is the Franciscan church of St Joseph, dedicated to St Joseph of Arimathea, who offered his tomb for the burial of Christ.
Hospice of St Nicodemus	Adjoining is the Hospice of St Nicodemus with its clock-tower, which also belongs to the Franciscans.
★White Tower	Between this group of buildings and the police station farther west is a street which runs west to the White Tower, known to Muslims as the Tower

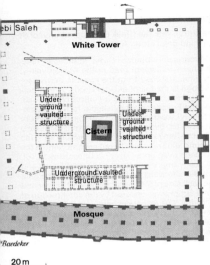

White Tower

of the Forty Companions of the Prophet, to Christians as the Tower of the Forty Martyrs.

This square tower in Gothic style, built by Baibars in 1267, is 27m/89ft high, with 128 steps leading to its upper platform. A German traveller called Anton von Prokesch-Osten, who described Ramleh in 1831 as "a very charming little town in rich surroundings with over 800 Greek and 200 Mohammedan inhabitants", also recounted how he waited on the top of the tower until sunset, "enjoying wide views over the fair land of the Philistines". Napoleon also climbed the tower in 1799, and in 1917 General Allenby used it as an observation post.

The White Tower stands on the north side of a spacious walled courtyard fully 500 years older than the tower. On the south side are substantial remains, measuring 90m/295ft by 12m/40ft, of a mosque built by Caliph Suleiman in 716. In the courtyard are three large underground vaulted structures, perhaps warehouses belonging to an old caravanserai or cisterns, which were used in the 17th century as a lunatic asylum and in the 19th as a house of the Whirling Dervishes.

Another of the sights of Ramla, which in chronological terms falls between the Great Mosque and the White Tower, is a large cistern dating from around 800 in a side street opening off Herzl Street to the east of the police station. The Crusaders gave it the name of Helen's Pools, ascribing it to the 4th century Empress, a great builder, who discovered the True Cross; but in fact it dates from the time of the fifth Abbasid Caliph, Haroun al-Rashid (766–809), famed for his connection with the "Arabian Nights" and for his diplomatic relations with Charlemagne. The cistern, with an area of 500sq.m/600sq.yds and a depth of 9m/30ft, is covered by 24 groined vaults, each with an opening on the top, so that 24 camels could be watered at the same time. Steps lead down into this subterranean world, with the vaulting reflected in the water.

St Helen's Pools

Surroundings of Ramla

Lod
3km/2 miles north is Lod (see entry), with the Greek Orthodox church of St George, the El-Chodr Mosque and Ben-Gurion Airport.

Gezer
7km/4½ miles south-east of Ramla is the kibbutz of Gezer, founded in 1945. It lies to the south of the Tel Aviv–Jerusalem road in the Ayalon valley, through which since ancient times the road from the coast to Jerusalem has run. South-west of the village is the tell of ancient Gezer. The importance of the place lay in its situation, which gave it control of the road. Excavations have shown that the Egyptians established a fortified settlement here, adjoining which the Hyksos built a fortress in the 18th century B.C. King Horam of Gezer was defeated by Joshua when he went to the help of Lachish (Joshua 10,33). Soon afterwards, in the 12th century B.C., the town fell to the Philistines. Around 1000 B.C. David went out and "smote the host of the Philistines from Gibeon even unto Gazer" (1 Chronicles 14,16). Solomon fortified the strategically important town and, as at Hazor and Megiddo (see entries), built casemate walls on the south side, with a gate flanked by three chambers on each side of the passageway. As at Hazor and Megiddo, too, the town's water supply was ensured by the construction of a tunnel leading to a hidden spring. In subsequent centuries the town was repeatedly destroyed and rebuilt. In the 2nd century B.C., during the Maccabean rebellion, Gezer was taken by Simon Maccabeus, cleansed of pagan idols and settled by orthodox Jews. The town was destroyed during the Jewish risings against Rome in the 1st and 2nd centuries A.D., and thereafter remained virtually uninhabited. The tell of Gezer has been thoroughly investigated by German archaeologists (1902–09), by an American team (from 1964) and by Yigael Yadin, and is well worth a visit by anyone with a particular interest in archaeology.

Latrun
7km/4½ miles south-east of the kibbutz of Gezer is the monastery of Latrun (see entry).

Rehovot   G 4

District: Central
Population: 58,000

Situation and characteristics
Rehovot, situated 21km/21 miles south-east of Tel Aviv in the coastal plain, lies in the centre of an orange-growing region. Its industries include pharmaceuticals and glass, and it is famed as the seat of the Weizmann Institute (named after Israel's first President), a large scientific complex of international repute.

History
Rehovot was originally a farming settlement founded in 1890 by Polish Jews, who dug a well and named the village Rehovot after the place of that name in the Negev where Isaac dug a well which he called Rehoboth (Genesis 26,22). The settlers originally grew vines, but at the turn of the century they switched to citrus fruits. In 1909 Yemeni Jews who had come to Israel in the second Aliyah established the suburb of Sha'araim.
When at the end of the First World War Rehovot was linked up with the Lod–Gaza railway line the rising town became an intermediary between the coastal plain and the Negev desert to the south. Its economy benefited as a result: the exports of citrus fruits increased, the orange-processing industry expanded and pharmaceutical factories were established.
Chaim Weizmann, born in Russia in 1873, studied chemistry at a number of European universities and in addition became deeply committed to the aims of the Zionist movement. Attracted by the pleasant surroundings, fragrant with orange-blossom, he settled in Rehovot in 1920 and established an agricultural research station. On the occasion of his 70th birthday in 1944 his friends and admirers established the Weizmann Institute. Weizmann died in Rehovot in 1952 and was buried near the Institute.

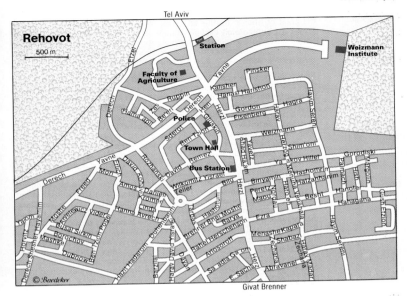

Rehovot

500 m

Tel Aviv

Station

Weizmann
Institute

Faculty of
Agriculture

Police

Town Hall

Bus Station

© Baedeker

Givat Brenner

Sights

The Weizmann Institute covers a broad spectrum of research in the natural sciences. It has several departments (biology, physics, chemistry) and a number of sub-departments (e.g. plant genetics, microbiology). Lectures are given here by scientists from all over the world. Some 1800 people work in the Institute, including some 500 students working for their final examinations.
Conducted tours of the Institute can be arranged by previous appointment.

Weizmann
Institute

On the northern outskirts of the town, near the Weizmann Institute, is the house in which Chaim Weizmann lived from 1949 to 1952. The building, which is open to the public, was designed by Erich Mendelsohn (1937). In the garden is Weizmann's grave.

Weizmann House

Surroundings of Rehovot

5km/3 miles south-east of Rehovot is the kibbutz of Givat Brenner (pop. 1700), founded in 1928. It is named after the writer Joseph Chaim Brenner, who was murdered by Arabs in Haifa in 1921. One of the largest kibbutzes in Israel, it produces canned foods, irrigation equipment and wood products. This was the home of the sculptor Jacob Loutchansky, whose work, inspired by events in the history of Israel, can be seen in squares and gardens in the kibbutz. In the cemetery is the grave of Yizhaq Sadeh (d. 1952), writer and officer in the Haganah, the Jewish underground movement.

Givat Brenner

Rosh Ha'ayin

G 4

District: Central
Population: 13,000

Situation and characteristics	The town of Rosh Ha'ayin ("Head of the Spring"; Arabic Ras el-Ain) lies in the plain of Sharon north-east of Tel Aviv, 4km/2½ miles beyond Petah Tiqwa and immediately east of the Lod–Hadera–Haifa railway line. Like the neighbouring old-established settlements of Tel Afeq and Migdal Afeq, it owes its prosperity to its situation near the source of the Yarqon, one of the few rivers in Israel which flow throughout the year.
History	About 1080 B.C. the Philistines mustered their army at Aphek (Afeq), while the Israelites gathered at Eben-ezer. In the battle that followed the Philistines captured the Ark of the Covenant, which had been brought from Shiloh (1 Samuel 4,1–4), and took it to Ashdod (see entry) but later returned it to Beth-shemesh (see Bet Shemesh).

In Hellenistic times Afeq was known as Pegai ("Springs", referring to the sources of the Yarqon). After being destroyed by the Hasmoneans the town was rebuilt by Pompey and given the name of the water nymph Arethusa. In 35 B.C. Herod built a square fort which he named Antipatris after his father. The Apostle Paul spent a night here while being taken from Jerusalem to Caesarea in the year 60 (Acts 23,31).

South-east of Afeq/Antipatris is the hill of Migdal Afeq or Migdal Zedeq, on which there were ancient and (on the evidence of a Greek inscription) Byzantine fortifications built to protect the sources of the Yarqon. The place became of major importance, however, only in the Crusader period, when the castle of Mirabel was held by Constable Manasses of Hierges. During Baldwin III's conflict with his mother Queen Melisande over his title to the throne he surprised and captured her supporter Manasses in Mirabel in 1152. Manasses was compelled to leave the country, Baldwin appointed his friend Humphrey, Lord of Toron, as Constable and Melisande was allowed to retire to Nablus (see entry) and was effectively excluded from political activity.

After the end of the Crusader period the fortress of Afeq/Antipatris was held by the Mamelukes and later by the Turks. In more recent times it has retained importance thanks to its abundance of water. In 1936 the British authorities built a pipeline to convey water from the springs to Jerusalem and established a military post to protect the supply. After Israel became independent in 1948 this developed into the town of Rosh Ha'ayin when numbers of new immigrants, mainly from Yemen, settled here. In 1955 the Israeli government laid a 100km/60 mile long pipeline from the Yarqon springs to the Negev, and in 1960 this was linked up with the National Water Carrier which cuts across Israel from the Jordan.

Sights

Tel Afeq	On Tel Afeq, to the west of the town, is a large square fortified caravanserai built by the Turks in the 17th century on the site of the Herodian fortress of Antipatris.
Mirabel	3km/2 miles south-east, on the hill of Migdal Afeq, are the overgrown ruins of the castle of Mirabel, of which substantial remains survive.

Rosh Pinna   H 2

District: Northern
Population: 1000

Situation and characteristics	Rosh Pinna, 26km/16 miles north of Tiberias and 10km/6 miles east of Safed, was the first Jewish village in Upper Galilee. It owes its present importance to its airport, which handles domestic flights. Immigrants from Romania settled in this rocky country in 1882, calling their village Rosh Pinna ("Cornerstone") after Psalm 118,22. With financial help from Baron Edmond de Rothschild they were able to cultivate the land and develop the area.

Surroundings of Rosh Pinna

2km/1¼ miles north is the town of Hazor HaGelilit, founded in 1953, which with its population of 550 has outstripped Rosh Pinna. It takes its name from Tel Hazor (see Hazor), 8km/5 miles north.

Hazor HaGelilit

A winding road runs west through beautiful scenery to Safed (10km/ 6 miles: see entry), once a centre of the Kabbalists.

Safed

From Rosh Pinna a road runs north-east, passing the kibbutz of Mishmar Hayarden (on left), to the Benot Ya'aqov ("Daughters of Jacob") Bridge over the Jordan (8km/5 miles).

Benot Ya'aqov

The bridge owes its name to a local legend that the patriarch Jacob passed this way with his family and that at Jacob's Ford his daughters foretold the fate of his son Joseph.
According to tradition Joseph was cast by his brothers into a well in the caravanserai of Gov Yosef (Jacob's Well) and then sold to Midianite merchants who carried him off to Egypt. Gov Yosef is the name of a ruined caravanserai near the kibbutz of Ammiad (6km/4 miles south of Rosh Pinna to the west of the road to Tiberias). The Bible, however, gives Jacob only one daughter, Dinah, and locates the event elsewhere: when Joseph was sent by Jacob to join his brothers in Shechem he travelled on the old royal highway through Samaria to Shechem and from there went on to Dothan, where he found his brothers and was sold by them to the merchants (Genesis 37,12–28).
The Crusaders, harking back to the old tradition, named the place Jacob's Ford and believed that it was here that Jacob wrestled with the angel – though this too was in contradiction to the Bible, which sets the incident at the ford on the river Jabbok (now Nahr ez-Zarqa), between Amman and Jerash in present-day Jordan (Genesis 32, 24f.). In 1178, to defend the crossing, King Baldwin IV built the castle of Chastellet, which was destroyed by Saladin only a year later.
On various occasions in the 20th century the Benot Ya'aqov Bridge, the only one over the upper Jordan, has been of strategic importance. From here British forces twice advanced into Syria, during the First World War, when Syria was held by the Turks, and in the Second World War, when it was controlled by Vichy France. In June 1946 the bridge was blown up, along with ten other bridges, by the Haganah, the Jewish underground organisation, in protest against British policy in the mandated territory.

A road now runs over the bridge to the Golan Heights (see entry).

Golan Heights

Safed (Zefat)

H 2

District: Northern
Altitude: 750–834m/2460–2736ft
Population: 17,000

The town of Safed (also spelt Zefat) lies 1000m/3300ft above the Jordan valley in the hills of Upper Galilee, 35km/22 miles from Tiberias and 50km/31 miles from Akko. From the 16th century it was a holy town to the Jews, a centre of the ancient mystical tradition of the Kabbalah. In the north of the town are a number of synagogues dating from that period. Safed is one of four cities holy to the Jews, the others being Tiberius, Hebron and Jerusalem.

Situation and characteristics

In more recent times, thanks to its beautiful setting and its agreeable, mild climate, Safed has developed into a summer holiday resort much frequented by the Israelis. Most foreign visitors spend only a day or two in the town in the course of a tour.

In the 1st and 2nd centuries A.D. a number of Mishnah and Talmud scholars lived in the Safed area. In 1102 the Crusaders built a castle here. After its

History

331

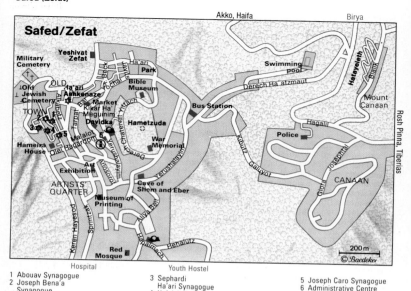

Safed/Zefat

1 Abouav Synagogue
2 Joseph Bena'a Synagogue

3 Sephardi Ha'ari Synagogue
4 Ha'alsheh Synagogue

5 Joseph Caro Synagogue
6 Administrative Centre (with tourist information office)

destruction in 1188 by Saladin it was rebuilt in 1240 by French Templars, who were forced to surrender it to the Mameluke Sultan Baibars in 1266. It became a Jewish town in the 16th century, under Ottoman rule, and for a time was a separate sanjak (administrative unit). Jews came from many parts of Europe and North Africa to settle here, and around 1550 the town had a population of over 10,000. Among its inhabitants were Rabbi Jakob Berab, who wanted to restore the Sanhedrin, Rabbi Joseph Caro, author of the "Shulhan Arukh", a collection of maxims (c. 1560), and Rabbi Izhak Luria (b. Jerusalem 1531), known as Ha'ari, the Lion. The first book in Hebrew was printed at Safed in 1578.

During the 18th century the population declined, although in 1778 Chassidist Jews from Poland came to Safed, as well as to Tiberias. In 1834 the town was pillaged by Druze raiders, and in 1837 it was destroyed by an earthquake. Towards the end of the 19th century new settlers came to Safed, bringing its population to 6000 Arab and 6000 Jewish families. By 1936, however, as a result of violent Arab rioting, the Jewish population had fallen to 1800, and when Israel became independent in 1948 there were 12,000 Arabs and only 1700 Jews. Then in May 1948 a group of Palmach fighters (Haganah commandos) stormed the Arab positions and drove the Arabs out of the town, which since then has been purely Jewish.

The ★town

Safed is built on a hilly site and there are many ups and downs in its topography. In recent decades new suburbs, widely spaced from one another, have sprung up round the old town centre. Tourist facilities are mainly concentrated on Mount Canaan (960m/3150ft), to the east of the town, where there are hotels, picnic areas and viewpoints.

Although the central area of Safed has no buildings of outstanding quality it is a friendly and attractive town. The main shopping street (partly pedestrianised) is Jerusalem Street (Rehov Yerushalayim), with a number of pavement cafés. Just off the south end of the street is the artists' quarter, to

Pedestrian zone, Safed

the north of which is the old part of the town with its numerous synagogues.

Sights

It is worth walking up the hill in the centre of the town, Hametzuda (834m/2736ft) for the sake of the fine views from the top. On the hill, which is laid out as a park, are the scanty remains of a Crusader castle and a memorial to those who died in the Arab–Israeli war in 1948.

Hametzuda

On the north side of the hill, in a house built in the second half of the 19th century as the residence of a Turkish pasha, is the Israeli Bible Museum, founded in 1985 on the initiative of the Jewish-American artist Philip Ratner. It displays hundreds of his paintings and works of sculpture representing scenes from the Bible, together with works by the painter and sculptor Enrico Glicenstein (1870–1942).

Bible Museum

To the west of the hill, beyond Jerusalem Street, is the Davidka Monument. The Davidka was a small and rather crudely constructed cannon, which at any rate made a very loud noise and drove the last Arabs out of Safed in 1948.

Davidka

Just off the south end of Jerusalem Street, to the west, is the artists' quarter, in a part of the town occupied until 1948 by Arabs – low houses, huddled closely together, in which there now live some sixty painters and sculptors. Many of them have their own galleries, and the former mosque serves as a showroom for them all.

★Artists' quarter

In this quarter is the Museum of Printing, illustrating the long tradition of printing in Safed (where the first Hebrew printing-press was installed in the 16th century). The museum also displays works of graphic art by leading Jewish artists.

Safed (Zefat)

Exhibition of sculpture in the artists' quarter, Safed

Synagogues
Between the artists' quarter and the old town to the north, with its many synagogues, is a broad flight of steps called Ma'alot Olei Hagardom. The name means "men who were hungry" – referring to the hardships suffered by the Jewish inhabitants of the town during the Arab siege.

Just above the steps is Hameira House, with a privately owned collection of material on the history of Safed and Jewish life in the town. Beyond this, in a maze of narrow winding lanes, are a number of synagogues which externally can hardly be distinguished from the surrounding houses. They are all named after well-known rabbis. Here, with a little luck, can be found the Joseph Caro Synagogue, built on the foundations of the house once occupied by the 16th century rabbi of that name. Nearby is the Ha'alsheh Synagogue.

Farther north are the Abouav Synagogue, which preserves, housed in a wooden shrine, a Torah written by Rabbi Abouav in the 15th century; the Joseph Bena'a Synagogue, also known as the Shrine of the White Holy Man; and the Ashkenazi Ha'ari Synagogue, with a vaulted roof borne on antique columns, which has an olive-wood Torah shrine carved at the end of the 19th century by a craftsman from eastern Europe. The Sephardi Ha'ari Synagogue, the oldest in Safed, lies on the lower western edge of the town; it has an enclosed recess in which the rabbi used to pray.

Jewish cemetery
Farther north, downhill, is the Jewish cemetery, with the graves of Rabbi Ari (d. 1573) and Joseph Caro (d. 1575).

Cave of Shem and Eber
Under the south side of the hill of Hametzuda is the Cave of Shem and Eber, in which tradition has it that Noah's son Shem and his grandson Eber studied the Torah.

Surroundings of Safed

9km/6 miles west of Safed is Meron (see entry) with its ancient tombs.

Meron

The village of Bar'am, now abandoned, has notable remains of an ancient synagogue. It is reached by taking the road which runs north from Meron to Sassa (9km/6 miles) and from there turning into a road on the right. According to tradition the prophet Obadiah and Esther, wife of the Persian king Xerxes, were buried in Bar'am.

★Bar'am

The site of the synagogue, now a National Park, lies above the kibbutz of Bar'am (founded 1948). The synagogue, which is preserved up to the second storey and has been well restored, dates from the 2nd or 3rd century and is thus one of the oldest buildings in the country. The entrance front with its three doorways faces in the direction of Jerusalem. In front of the entrance are some of the (originally eight) columns with Attic bases which supported a porch. The interior was divided by rows of columns into three aisles and an ambulatory.

100m/110yds from the synagogue is a small 19th century Maronite church (usually closed).

From Safed a winding road runs 10km/6 miles east to Rosh Pinna (see entry).

Rosh Pinna

St Sabas's Monastery

See Mar Saba

Samaria/Shomron

H 4

West Bank
Altitude: 430m/1410ft

The extensive remains of Samaria (Hebrew Shomron), capital of the kingdom of Israel from 880 to 721 B.C., lie above the Arab village of Sebastiya (11km/7 miles north-west of Nablus, 29km/18 miles east of Netanya) in the green hills of the land of Samaria, which is bounded by the Sharon plain on the west, the Jezreel plain on the north, the Jordan valley on the east and Judaea to the south. The area has been under Israeli occupation since 1967.

Situation and characteristics

After the division of the kingdom on Solomon's death in 928 B.C. the capital of the northern kingdom of Israel was at first Shechem (see Nablus), later Pnuel, on the east bank of the Jordan, and then Tirzah (see Nablus, Surroundings). After a series of short-lived rulers the fifth king of the northern kingdom, Omri (882–871 B.C.), founded a new capital "and called the name of the city which he built after the name of Shemer, owner of the hill, Samaria" (1 Kings 16,24). Omri and his son Ahab, who also did much building at Hazor and Megiddo (see entries), erected palaces and temples within a ring of walls. Under the influence of Ahab's wife Jezebel, who came from Sidon, the worship of Baal and Astarte, together with the refined culture of the Phoenicians, came to Israel. These developments were bitterly opposed by the prophet Elijah, who brought down the judgment of God on the pagan priests on Mount Carmel (see entry).

History

In 732 B.C. the kingdom of Israel fell under Persian control, and the authority of its last kings (Pekahiah, Pekah and Hoshea) was restricted to the capital and its immediate surroundings. With the conquest of Samaria by the Assyrian king Shalmaneser in 722 B.C. and the taking of the acropolis by Sargon II in the following year the kingdom ceased to exist. Many members of the upper classes were deported and replaced by "men from Babylon and from Cuthah" (2 Kings 17,24), and thereafter intermarriage between

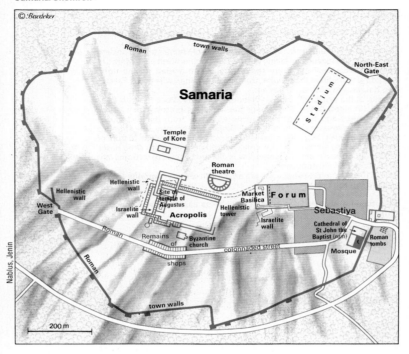

© Baedeker

Samaria

the incomers and the remaining Jews produced the people known as Samaritans.

Subsequently Samaria was used as a military base by Assyrians, Babylonians and Persians. At the end of the 4th century it was occupied by Macedonians and was Hellenised. When the Hasmonean ruler John Hyrcanus I took the town in 107 B.C. he had all non-Jews put to death.
Herod brought new splendour to Samaria, in which he married the Hasmonean princess Mariamne in 38 B.C. He rebuilt the town and renamed it Sebaste in honour of Augustus (in Greek Sebastos). Here too he had his wife Mariamne and her two sons put to death.
Sebaste's prosperity was short-lived. Jewish rebels set fire to the temple of Augustus, and soon afterwards, in A.D. 69, Vespasian razed the fortress to the ground. The foundation of Neapolis (Nablus: see entry) by Vespasian's son Titus in 72 set the seal on Sebaste's downfall.

The three disciples – Philip, Peter and John – who came to Samaria between A.D. 30 and 35 saw the town when it was still at the height of its splendour. Here they encountered Simon the sorcerer, who offered them money for the power to give the Holy Ghost (Acts 8,4–24). (Hence the term simony, the buying or selling of spiritual or church benefits).
Around 200 the Emperor Septimius Severus tried, unsuccessfully, to give new life to the town. Later a Christian community grew up in the town under their bishop, and when in the 5th century relics of St John the Baptist were found here (though he had not been beheaded here but in Machaerus

on the east bank of the Jordan) pilgrims began to come to the town. The cult of the saint's relics has continued down the centuries, and they are still revered in the mosque in the village of Sebastiya, which perpetuates the name of ancient Sebaste.

The ★ Site

There are two approaches to Samaria: either on a road which turns off at a white signpost and runs through the village of Sebastiya (cars only), or on a road (suitable also for buses) which goes off farther north at a yellow signpost pointing to the site and runs up the colonnaded street of the ancient town.

The route through the village runs past the mosque. As can be seen from a number of pillars and sections of wall, this was built on the remains of a Crusader church of 1160, which in turn was preceded by a Byzantine church of the 4th century. In a crypt under a domed roof are recesses in which the tombs of the prophets Elisha and Obadiah and the head of John the Baptist have been venerated since the 4th century. (Other relics of the Baptist have been preserved since the 4th century in the Omayyad mosque in Damascus.)

Mosque

From here the narrow lanes of the village lead up to the large rectangular area of the ancient forum, where the two approach roads to the site meet (car park; restaurant, in which small antiquities are sold). From the long north side of the forum, which measures 128m/140yds by 72m/80yds, there is a view of a depression in the ground marking the site of the ancient stadium. At the west end of the forum stood a three-aisled market basilica built about 200, during the reign of Septimius Severus; a few columns still stand erect, and the foundations and an exedra at the north end can be seen.

Forum

From the north-west corner of the forum a path runs up to the acropolis, partly excavated in 1908–11 and 1931–35. We come first to an Israelite wall (9th–8th c. B.C.), in front of which is a Hellenistic reinforcing wall with a massive round tower (3rd c.) and a Roman theatre. Continuing up to the left of the tower, we come to a monumental flight of steps, originally leading up to the Herodian temple of Augustus (c. 30 B.C.), of which no trace remains. The temple stood on the site of an earlier palace, begun by King Omri (882–871 B.C.) and extended in magnificent style by Omri's son Ahab (871–852 B.C.) and his Phoenician wife Jezebel. In the palace were a cult effigy of Astarte and a temple of Baal (1 Kings 16,32–33). The excavators of the palace found a number of pieces of ivory – confirming the reference by the prophet Amos (6,1–4) to "them that are at ease in Zion, and trust in the mountain of Samaria" who "lie upon beds of ivory" – and 75 pottery jars containing tax rolls dating from the time of King Jeroboam II (787–747 B.C.).

Acropolis

Continuing in an anti-clockwise direction round the walls enclosing this complex, we come on the south side of the hill to a well preserved little Byzantine church, built on the spot where, according to tradition, John the Baptist's head was found.

Byzantine church

Returning through an area laid out as a garden to the forum and turning right at the far end, we come into an ancient street, flanked by columns, of about A.D. 200 (also visible from the acropolis), which leads to the well preserved West Gate. This was originally built by Omri but dates in its present form from a later period. The round tower on the north side of the gate is Roman, but stands on square foundations of Hellenistic date.

West Gate

Sea of Galilee/Yam Kinneret

H/J 4–6

District: Northern
Altitude: 210m/690ft below sea level

Sea of Galilee/Yam Kinneret

Situation and characteristics

The Sea of Galilee or Lake Gennesaret (Hebrew Yam Kinneret) lies in the Jordan valley 210m/690ft below sea level. 21km/13 miles long by 12km/7½ miles across and up to 46m/150ft deep, with a total area of 170sq.km/65sq.miles, it is Israel's largest reservoir of fresh water. Its water is piped to various storage basins and from there to the Negev.

An important source of income for the people living round the lake is the tourist and holiday trade, which is concentrated mainly on the northern and western shores; the east side of the lake is quieter. Another source of revenue which has a long tradition behind it is fishing; a local speciality, offered in all the lakeside restaurants, is St Peter's fish, a species of perch indigenous to the Sea of Galilee.

Biblical history

The "sea of Chinnereth" is referred to in the Old Testament account of the distribution of land to the tribes of Israel after their arrival in Canaan (Numbers 34,11; Joshua 13,27). It is frequently mentioned in the New Testament: Jesus found his first disciples at Capernaum on the northern shore of the lake, where he spent most of his time after leaving Nazareth, and there is the familiar story of Jesus and Peter being caught in a storm on the lake (Matthew 14,22–33; Mark 6,45–56).

The ★lake

The Sea of Galilee is one of the most beautiful spots in Israel, its charm enhanced by the luxuriant subtropical vegetation.

Boat trips

There are regular boat services between Tiberias (see entry) and the kibbutz of En Gev (see entry) on the east side of the lake (crossing time about 45 minutes) and from Tiberias and En Gev to the archaeological site of Capernaum (see entry).

Sights

Round the lake are many places of artistic and religious interest like Capernaum, Tabgha and Tiberias (see entries).

View of the Sea of Galilee from the Mount of the Beatitudes

Tiberias, on the west side of the lake, is a popular holiday and health resort, with hot springs which have been used for medicinal purposes since ancient times (recommended in the treatment of rheumatism, disorders of the respiratory system, etc.). There are bathing stations on the lake and facilities for a variety of water sports.

Another spa, with springs which have also been frequented since ancient times, is Hamat Gader (see entry), near the east side of the lake in the lower Yarmouk valley.

Sede Boqer   G 6

District: Southern
Population: 600

The kibbutz of Sede Boqer ("Farmers' Field"), 50km/30 miles south of Beersheba, was founded by ex-soldiers on May 15th 1952 – the fourth anniversary of Israeli independence – in what was then a trackless waste in the Negev, near the Wadi Zin. The aim of its founders was to bring the desert into cultivation.

Situation and characteristics

The kibbutz has close associations with David Ben-Gurion, Israel's first prime minister (see Famous People). When Ben-Gurion resigned in 1953 he joined the young kibbutz in order, as he said, to do "what was really important": that is, to develop the Negev. Fourteen months later, however, he returned to politics, first as minister of defence and then as prime minister for a second time. In 1963, at the age of 77, he finally retired to Sede Boqer, which then became a focal point of Israeli political life. He died in 1973 and was buried in the kibbutz.

Sights

Turning off the main road 3km/2 miles south of the kibbutz (10km/6 miles north of Avdat), we come to the College of the Negev or Sede Boqer Institute (Midrashet Sede Boqer) of Arid Zone Research, founded by David Ben-Gurion. From modest beginnings as a secondary school and teachers' training college this has developed into a large establishment with over 400 students. The teaching here, in history, archaeology and sociology as well as in scientific subjects, always has reference to the special conditions of the Negev. A dominant feature in the extensive grounds of the Institute is the library building, which houses not only a large specialised library but also Ben-Gurion's archives, which contain much highly important material on the history of Jewry in the 20th century and of the state of Israel.

College of the Negev

In a carefully tended park adjoining the Library are the graves of David Ben-Gurion and his wife – two plain stone slabs in a square tree-shaded area on the edge of a sheer rock face falling down to the Wadi Zin. There is an impressive view into the gorge through which the river flows from its source in the Avdat spring (see En Avdat).

Ben-Gurion's Tomb

A few hundred metres north of the Sede Boqer College is the house (open to the public) in which Ben-Gurion and his wife lived. The interior, largely unchanged since Ben-Gurion died, is scarcely more luxurious than the houses of other members of the kibbutz. It contains a small collection of photographs and letters.

Ben-Gurion's House

Graves of David Ben-Gurion and his wife, Sede Boqer

Sepphoris

See Zippori

Sharon Plain/Emeq Sharon   G 3/4

Districts: Haifa, Central, Tel Aviv

Situation and characteristics

The plain of Sharon is the large coastal plain which extends for 60km/37 miles from the south side of Mount Carmel to the river Yarqon (Tel Aviv) and from the Mediterranean to the hills of Samaria.

Sharon owes its fertility to its abundance of water, supplied mainly by its perennial rivers. In all ages, however, the sand-dunes along the coast, have impeded the flow of water into the sea, leading to the formation of malaria-ridden swamps unless constant attention was given to drainage. The mouth of one of the old drainage canals can be seen at Herzliya (see entry). In modern times the drainage problem has been completely resolved, and as a result the region is intensively cultivated (citrus fruits) and densely populated.

History

The plain of Sharon was settled by man from early Canaanite times. Weapons and tools dating from that period were found in 1962 in the tell of Kefar Monash (9km/6 miles north-east of Netanya), a moshav founded by British ex-servicemen in 1946 and named after the Australian General Monash.

The old settlements were destroyed by the Assyrians and Babylonians (7th–6th c. B.C.); then in the 5th century B.C. the site was occupied by Phoenicians. Around 100 B.C. Sharon was incorporated in Judaea. In 25 B.C. Herod founded the port of Caesarea (see entry), which in Roman and

Byzantine times became capital of the province. After the Mameluke invasion in the 13th century the drainage system fell into disrepair and the plain reverted to marshland, which was almost completely uninhabited. The situation began to change when Jewish settlers established themselves in the area. In 1878 they founded Petah Tiqwa on the banks of the Yarqon to the south, and in 1890 Hadera (see entry) to the north. Thereafter the drainage of the area was systematically pursued, and since then numerous new settlements have been founded, including large towns like Herzliya and Netanya (see entries).

Shivta (Subeita)

F 6

District: Southern
Altitude: 350m/1150ft

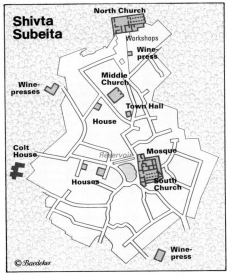

The ancient city of Subeita, now known as Shivta, lies 55km/34 miles south-west of Beersheba, on the south side of the road to the Egyptian frontier. Here can be seen the ruins, some of them astonishingly well preserved, of a Byzantine city of the 5th and 6th centuries, with three monastic churches, dwelling-houses, water cisterns and paved streets, which was still inhabited in Arab times.

Situation and characteristics

Subeita, lying between Avdat and Nizzana, was built by Nabataeans in the 1st century B.C. An unfortified town, it was taken over by the Byzantines and so radically altered and rebuilt that the British archaeologists who excavated the site in 1934 found no Nabataean but almost exclusively Byzantine remains.

History

The Site

On entering the site, which now lies within a National Park, we come first to the South Church, a three-aisled basilica with the apses still standing. To the left of the porch is the baptistery, with a cruciform font. Built against the church is a mosque dating from the 7th century.
A little way north of the church is the council house ("town hall"), which stands at the intersection of two streets. Taking the street to the left, we come to the Middle Church, also three-aisled, of which only a few sections of wall and the south apse survive. Continuing north, we come, just before the North Church, into the craftsmen's quarter, with a baker's oven or potter's kiln, a wine-press and other workshops.

Adjoining the North Church, which again is three-aisled, are conventual buildings. Next to the church are a baptistery, with steps leading down to the large immersion font, and a chapel, so that there are no fewer than five completely preserved apses standing side by side. At the entrance is part of an entablature with the chi-ro monogram (XP) and the Greek letters alpha (Λ) and omega (Ω).

Surroundings of Shivta

Nizzana

17km/10½ miles south-east of Shivta is the site of Nizzana, another Nabataean town which continued to exist in Byzantine and Arab times until the 9th century. Excavations here in 1935 brought to light churches and other buildings. One of the churches has a mosaic pavement. Near the Bedouin well of Auja el-Hafir the Turks built a frontier post in 1907, and during the period of the Mandate the British authorities sited a prison camp here. In 1948 the Egyptian army used Nizzana as a base for an attack on Beersheba.

Sinai Peninsula   A–G 5–8

Egyptian territory
Altitude: sea level to 2642m/8668ft

Situation and characteristics

The Sinai peninsula, bounded on the north by the Mediterranean, on the west by the Gulf of Suez, on the south by the Red Sea and on the east and south-east by the Jordan rift valley and its southern continuation the Gulf of Elat (Aqaba), forms a link between Africa and Asia. The peninsula is Egyptian territory. Under the Egyptian–Israeli peace treaty of September 1978 the Israeli forces which had occupied Sinai since 1967 evacuated the peninsula in stages, completing their withdrawal by April 1982. The frontier between Egypt and Israel now runs north–south from Rafiah (Rafah) on the Mediterranean to Taba on the Gulf of Aqaba.
Since many visitors to Elat (see entry) take day trips or longer excursions to Sinai, particularly to St Catherine's Monastery with its rich collection of icons, this Guide includes a description of the peninsula and the monastery.

★Scenery

The Sinai peninsula, an area more than twice the size of Sicily, is an almost uninhabited region of steppe and desert, with cultivable land only in the north, along the sea and in a few small oases – a land of barren high plateaux dissected by wadis. The most important of these dry valleys are the much ramified Wadi el-Arish, which ends on the Mediterranean coast, and the Wadi Feiran, which runs south into the Gulf of Suez. The mountains bordering the peninsula consist of granite, gneiss, porphyry and syenite. The hills in the north rise to no more than 1000m/3300ft, those in the south to over 2000m/6600ft (Gebel Serbal, 2057m/6749ft; Gebel Musa, 2285m/7497ft; Gebel Katerin, 2642m/8668ft).
In spite of its barrenness the Sinai peninsula is a region of great fascination, with its rugged mountains, remote valleys, picturesque rock formations and magnificent and ever-changing views.

Access

For short trips from Israel to southern Sinai and St Catherine's Monastery an entry permit valid for up to seven days can be obtained on payment of a fee.
The regional airline Air Sinai flies from Tel Aviv and Elat to the Mount Sinai airport. The road from the airport to the monastery is asphalted as far as a fork where the road into the Wadi Feiran goes off on the right and then a road to the left leads to the monastery.
There are bus services from Elat into Sinai and to the monastery, and it is also possible for visitors to take their own car (maximum 7 days); cars rented in Israel are not admitted.

Mountain landscape in the south of the Sinai peninsula

Since the earliest times the Sinai peninsula has been an area of passage between North Africa and western Asia. As early as the 3rd millennium B.C. the Egyptians were mining turquoise and copper here, as is evidenced by rock inscriptions and the remains of a temple of Hathor at Serabit el-Khadim in the west of the peninsula. The "Sinai inscriptions" discovered by Flinders Petrie in 1905 date back to the 2nd millennium B.C. and are attributed to Western Semitic tribes who in the course of their wanderings had visited Egypt and developed from the Egyptian hieroglyphics a system of consonantal signs which was later taken over by the Canaanites.

The Old Testament also tells of wanderings between Palestine and Egypt. Sinai, known to the Israelites as Mount Horeb, acquired particular importance as the place where Moses received his divine revelation and thus became the leader of the Jews in their journey out of Egypt towards the Promised Land and the founder of one of the three great monotheistic world religions. It was on Mount Horeb, where God had already appeared to him in the burning bush (Exodus 3,1–2), that Moses received the Ten Commandments (Exodus 20) and other divine injunctions. In the 9th century B.C. the prophet Elijah, fleeing from Ahab and Jezebel, sought refuge on Mount Horeb (1 Kings 19).

Sinai gained fresh significance as a holy place in Christian times. The first historian of the Christian church, Eusebius (c. 260–339), a native of Palestine, believed that Sinai was the mountain on which Moses received the Tables of the Law. In his time there were already monks and hermits in the Sinai area. In 324, according to a plausible tradition, the Empress Helen, mother of Constantine the Great, founded a monastery of the Burning Bush (Vatos) on the site of the Spring of Moses, the spot where he saw the burning bush. In the middle of the 6th century, in order to give the monks greater security, Justinian, whose empire included Sinai as well as Syria and Egypt, built the fortified monastery which still exists.

During his Egyptian expedition Napoleon gave the monastery his protection, and in the 19th century the Tsars of Russia began to take an interest in

Sinai. In 1840 the Sinai peninsula, which had belonged to the Ottoman Empire since 1517, became part of Mehmed Ali's independent territory of Egypt. In 1903 Britain marked out the boundary between Egypt, which it then occupied, and Turkey in a straight line running from Rafiah on the Mediterranean to Elat; and after the First World War this became the international frontier.

In the 20th century a new economic aspect came to the fore when oil was discovered on the west coast of Sinai and coal in other parts of the peninsula. This increased the importance of Sinai in the conflicts between Israel and Egypt. Israel occupied part of the peninsula in 1948 and the whole of it in 1967. In 1957 Israel returned the Sinai for a promise of peace and free and open travel through the Suez Canal. Egypt reneged on this agreement in 1967 and Israel recaptured the Sinai. When it was returned Israel gave Egypt oil fields which they had developed and air fields and 10,000 Jews gave up their homes. Under the Camp David agreements of September 1978, however, Israel withdrew all its forces from Sinai by April 1982.

★★St Catherine's Monastery

St Catherine's Monastery, situated at an altitude of 1528m/5013ft at the foot of the 2285m/7500ft high Mount of Moses (Gebel Musa), stands on the spot traditionally identified from the 4th century as the place where Moses saw the burning bush and where he watered the flocks of his father-in-law Jethro. The site is known to the Arabs as Wadi Shueib (Shueib being their name for Jethro) and as Wadi ed-Deir ("Valley of the Monastery").

History

The French nun Aetheria, who visited the Holy Land about 400 and wrote an account of her journey in her "Peregrinatio", which was rediscovered in Arezzo in 1885, noted that on Sinai "there were the cells of many holy men

St Catherine's Monastery, Sinai

344

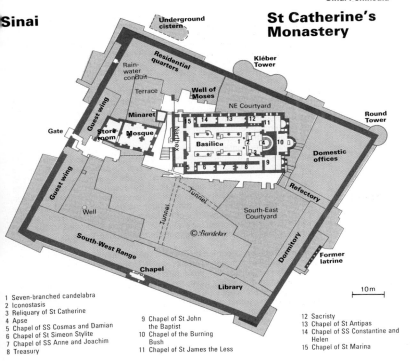

St Catherine's Monastery

1 Seven-branched candelabra
2 Iconostasis
3 Reliquary of St Catherine
4 Apse
5 Chapel of SS Cosmas and Damian
6 Chapel of St Simeon Stylite
7 Chapel of SS Anne and Joachim
8 Treasury

9 Chapel of St John the Baptist
10 Chapel of the Burning Bush
11 Chapel of St James the Less

12 Sacristy
13 Chapel of St Antipas
14 Chapel of SS Constantine and Helen
15 Chapel of St Marina

and a church built on the spot where the Burning Bush stands . . . In front of the church is a very fair garden with an abundance of good water, and the Burning Bush is in the garden". The church she mentions was the one said to have been founded by the Empress Helen in 324.

On the site of the original church Justinian built the present church within a fortified monastery. The building of the church can be precisely dated to between 548 and 565, on the evidence of inscriptions on the original ceiling beams, which still survive, recording that Justinian (d. 565) had it built by the master builder Stephen of Aila in memory of the Empress Theodora, who died in 548. Procopius, the historian of Justinian's reign, tells us ("De Aedificiis" V,8) that the church was dedicated to the Mother of God.

In the 10th or 11th century the church was re-dedicated to St Catherine of Alexandria, who was martyred in the reign of the Emperor Maxentius (306–312). Her remains were said to have been transported by angels to Sinai, where monks later found them on the Mount of St Catherine (Gebel Katerin) and took them to their monastery. Catherine had steadfastly defended her virginity, and this no doubt contributed to making the Burning Bush, originally a symbol of the young Moses' meeting with God, also a symbol of the Virgin Immaculate.

In its heyday the monastery was occupied by up to 400 monks, among whom were some particularly notable figures. About the year 400 Nilus (later canonised), a high dignitary at the court of the Emperor Arcadius in Constantinople, came to Sinai with his son. Over a thousand of his letters, which make an important contribution to our knowledge of monastic life in his time, have been preserved, together with various treatises and maxims.

In the 7th century John Climacus spent forty years on Sinai as a hermit and became abbot of the monastery; the name Climacus refers to his important devotional work, the "Klimax tou Paradisou" ("Ladder of Paradise"). Another outstanding figure was Simeon of Sinai, whom Archbishop Poppo of Trier met during his visit to Palestine. Simeon followed Poppo to Trier, where he had himself walled up in the Porta Nigra, the town's old Roman gate, died after a rigorous ascetic life in 1035 and was canonised only seven years later.

The number of monks declined in the 11th century, when under the harsh rule of the Seljuks in the Holy Land fewer pilgrims travelled to Sinai and offerings to the monastery fell. Nevertheless it has survived to the present day in a country which has been Muslim since the 7th century, recognising the existence of another faith to the extent of having a mosque within the precincts of the monastery.

The monastery continued to maintain relations with Europe. In the 13th century Roman Catholic monks built a chapel dedicated to St Catherine of the Franks. Monks from Sinai travelled to France, particularly to Rouen, to collect gifts of money and to sell relics: hence the numerous relics of St Catherine possessed by Rouen Cathedral. European pilgrims to Sinai in the 14th to 16th centuries left evidence of their presence in the coats of arms in the refectory (trapeza). Later Slav influences began to make themselves felt, first from the principalities of Moldavia and later, in the 17th century, from Russia. The monastery's material situation improved in the 19th century, when it received rich gifts from the Russian Tsars.

Monastic life

The monastery is occupied by Greek Orthodox monks, mainly from Crete and Cyprus. The number of monks, which in the heyday of the monastery was between 300 and 400, has now dwindled to around 50, of whom only 20 live in the monastery itself, the others in *metokhia* (outstations). The monastery is autocephalous: that is, it has the right, granted in 1571, to appoint its own abbot, who has the rank of an archbishop and is enthroned, after his election by the monks, by the Greek Orthodox Patriarch of Jerusalem. He normally resides in a *metokhion* of the monastery in Cairo and is represented in the monastery itself by four archimandrites.

The monastery

The monastery is in the form of an irregular rectangle measuring 85m/93yds by 75m/82yds. The granite wall surrounding it ranges in height between 12m/40ft and 15m/50ft, and in spite of earthquake damage in 1312 still preserves considerable stretches of the original 6th century walls, particularly on the south-west side. After the original entrance was walled up on grounds of security the only access for many centuries was by means of a winch on the north side. The present entrance on the west side was opened up in 1801 by a French expedition led by Kléber, which also restored large sections of the walls. Visitors can also enter the monastery through a new gate on the north side.

The interior of the monastery is a maze of alleys, staircases, passages, flights of steps and buildings huddled closely together on several levels round the church. The tourist entrance leads through a room with a sales counter into a courtyard on the north side of the church. On the left is a bush, behind the Chapel of the Burning Bush, to the right the Well of Moses.

Church of the Transfiguration

We now enter the narthex of the Church of the Transfiguration, which contains a collection of valuable icons, and can go a little way into the nave of the church: visitors are not as a rule allowed into the east end of the church or certain other parts of the monastery precinct.

The church and the Courtyard of the Burning Bush are situated in the lowest part of the precinct. The church built by Justinian is a three-aisled basilica, with a tower added by Tsar Alexander II in 1871. The doorway of the narthex, with carved figures of the Virgin and angels, dates from the Fatimid period (11th c.). The doorway into the nave is 3.63m/12ft high by 2.40m/8ft wide; the four doors of cypress-wood date from the original 6th century church. The nave has two rows of six granite columns coated with plaster, which, combined with the whitewashed walls, give the interior an air of coolness. The capitals are also of granite. Both aisles have chapels opening off them; those in the north aisle are dedicated to St Marina, SS Constantine and Helen and St Antipas, those in the south aisle to SS Cosmas and Damian, St Simeon Stylite and St Anne.

The interior has largely preserved the spatial effect of Justinian's church. The floor, of porphyry and marble, dates from the 18th century, as does the flat timber ceiling inserted below the original open roof structure. Huge candelabra, a gift in 1799 from Matthäus Bleyel of Nuremberg, hang in front of the gilded iconostasis, created by artists from Crete in 1612, in the time of Archbishop Lawrence. The position of the iconostasis would originally be occupied by a lower stone screen with columns, the templon, allowing an unobstructed view of the sanctuary.

In the sanctuary, immediately behind the iconostasis, are two reliquaries presented by the Tsars, and to the right, under a canopy, is another reliquary containing the remains of St Catherine. The original marble altar in the centre of the sanctuary was encased in wood in 1675 by Stamatios of Athens; this, like the contemporary canopy over the altar, is richly decorated with mother-of-pearl intarsia work.

The apse of the sanctuary has a synthronon (semicircular benches for the priests) characteristic of the Justinianic period. The abbot's throne, in the centre, is now occupied by a tabernacle. The apse is dominated by a fine 6th century mosaic of the Metamorphosis, Christ's Transfiguration on Mount Tabor: a theme of great significance to the Eastern church as the occasion on which Christ appeared to the disciples in his divine form. Christ is depicted between the prophets Elijah and Moses, with the disciples John, Peter and James below. Below this is a row of medallions of sixteen Old Testament prophets, with David in the centre; above it are apostles and saints, with the Cross in the centre.

On the east wall above the apse, flanking the double window, are two scenes connected with Sinai: Moses in front of the burning bush and the handing down of the Law (in the form of a scroll). In the spandrels Christ appears again, this time as the Lamb of God, with two angels offering him a sceptre and an orb – a theme clearly derived from the figures of Victory on Roman triumphal arches. Below the angels are medallions of John the Baptist and the Virgin, forming along with the Lamb the earliest representation of a theme which later became common, the Deisis (the Virgin and John interceding with Christ for the world). The apse is flanked by two chapels, the one on the left dedicated to St James, the one on the right to the Holy Fathers (or John the Baptist).

From the north aisle a doorway in the iconostasis leads into St James's Chapel, which has 15th century wall paintings. In the centre is Christ, with the Virgin in the Burning Bush below him. This central scene is flanked by the figures of two fathers of the church, St John Chrysostom on the left and St Basil on the right, and by representatives of the New and the Old Testament, St James the Great on the left and Moses on the right.

From here a passage leads to the most sacred place in the monastery, the Chapel of the Burning Bush behind the sanctuary, before entering which visitors must remove their shoes. Originally this was an open courtyard behind the apse of the church, which was made into a chapel at some time before 1216. In that year a German pilgrim called Thietmar saw the chapel and noted that "the bush was removed and distributed as relics among the Christians". The chapel, which is decorated with bluish-green tiles and a mosaic of a simple cross on a gold ground in the apse, marks the spot where the angel of the Lord appeared to Moses and God called to him out of a burning bush when he was looking after his father-in-law's sheep at a well (the Well of Moses on the north side of the church): "And he looked, and behold, the bush burned with fire, and the bush was not consumed . . . And when the Lord saw that he turned aside to see, God called unto him out of the midst of the bush, and said . . . Draw not nigh hither: put off thy shoes from off thy feet, for the place whereon thou standest is holy ground"

Chapel of the Burning Bush

(Exodus 3,2–5): hence the prohibition on wearing shoes in the chapel. An eternal flame in a lamp under the altar marks the place, now covered with a silver plate, where the burning bush grew. The rose and broom bush growing against the outside of the chapel is believed to have been a cutting from the original bush.

Mosque

In front of the church is the mosque, built in the 11th century in a former guest-house to meet the needs of the local Bedouin.

Refectory

Going along the south side of the church, we come to the long, narrow refectory (trapeza), with a fresco of the Last Judgment (Cretan work, 1573) and coats of arms and inscriptions by European pilgrims of the 14th–16th centuries.

Charnel-house

In the crypts under St Tryphon's Chapel, on the north-west side of the monastery precinct, is the charnel-house, in which the bones of thousands of monks are preserved. Guarding the entrance is the body, clad in a monk's cowl and robe, of a monk called Stephen who in the 6th century heard the confessions of pilgrims on their way up the Mount of Moses.

Museum

In the new guest wing built between 1932 and 1942 along the 6th century wall on the south-west side of the monastery (half way along which is a tiny wall chapel) are the Museum and Library.

The Museum contains over 2000 icons – in terms of both quality and quantity the world's finest collection of icons. It is of particular importance because it includes icons of the 5th and 6th centuries, which elsewhere were destroyed in the iconoclastic period, during the controversy (726–843) over the veneration of images. The collection includes, for example, three encaustic icons (produced by fusing wax colours to the surface) of Christ, Christ Pantocrator and the Virgin between the military saints George and Theodore.

The museum also has a fine collection of liturgical utensils, vestments, episcopal crowns and crosiers, as well as magnificent gifts from the Tsars and a chalice presented to the monastery by King Charles VI of France in 1411.

Library

Equally important is the Library, with a collection of some 3500 manuscripts – Greek (2289), Arabic (580), Syriac (276), Georgian (98), Slavonic (41), Ethiopian (6) and Armenian (1) – as well as an archive of some 2000 documents of the 12th–19th centuries. There is only one manuscript in Latin, suggesting that the monks systematically destroyed "Frankish" manuscripts. Among manuscripts of particular importance are two lectionaries (containing readings from the Gospels) dated to 967 and about 1000, an 11th century Book of Job, the writings of John Climacus (12th c.) and sixteen homilies by St Gregory of Nazianzus (c. 1150).

When visiting the monastery in the mid 19th century a German theologian called Konstantin von Tischendorf found a 4th century Greek Bible, the Codex Sinaiticus, and acquired 347 pages of the manuscript. Some of these came into the possession of Leipzig University Library but most of them went to St Petersburg and were bought by the Tsar for 27,000 gold marks. In 1933 the Soviet authorities sold these to the British Museum for £100,000. Some years ago a number of additional pages from the Codex are said to have been discovered in a walled-up cell in the monastery. A facsimile of the Codex is displayed in the room at the entrance to the monastery containing the sales counter, along with Napoleon's guarantee of protection and a similar guarantee (whether genuine or not) from Mohammed.

★Mount of Moses

There are two routes up the Mount of Moses (Gebel Musa; 2285m/7500ft), a formidable flight of over 3000 steps and a winding track, negotiable by camels, which was constructed for the convenience of a 19th century pasha; either way the climb takes at least three hours there and back. The "Pasha's Path", which begins to the east of the monastery, is to be preferred. After an hour's climb a path goes off on the right to St Stephen's Hermitage, situated beside a spring, with chapels dedicated to Moses and Elijah. A stepped path to the left (734 steps) leads up to the summit.

On the summit are a small chapel, built in 1930 on the site of an earlier chapel which had been destroyed, and a small mosque much venerated by the Arabs. At the north-east corner of the rocky plateau on which the chapel stands visitors are shown the hollow in which Moses was standing when God appeared to him. Near the mosque is a cavity in the rock in which, according to Muslim tradition, Moses remained fasting for forty days while he wrote down the Law on two stone tablets.

From the summit of Gebel Musa there are magnificent views of the wild and barren landscape of Sinai, extending south-westward over the highest hills in the peninsula to the Red Sea and the Gulf of Aqaba, north-westward over the mountains to the low hills in the north of the peninsula.

The descent by the flight of 3000 steps to the monastery almost 800m/2600ft below is only for the most athletic. It passes the Gate of Faith and the Gate of St Stephen, where the monk whose skeleton is preserved in the charnel-house of the monastery heard the confessions of pilgrims making their way up the mountain.

Mount of St Catherine

The Mount of St Catherine (Gebel Katerin; 2642m/8609ft), 6km/4 miles south of the monastery, can be climbed on a waymarked path in five hours. A motorable road runs past a chapel dedicated to Aaron, Moses' brother, and a monastery garden to a rest-house (originally begun in the 19th century as a country mansion) beside the small Monastery of the Holy Apostles. Beyond this is the Monastery of the Forty Martyrs, after which the climb to the summit begins. The chapel on the summit is built on the spot where according to the legend monks, guided by a vision in a dream, found the remains of St Catherine.

Subeita

See Shivta

Tabgha/En Sheva   H 2/3

District: Northern
Altitude: 200m/650ft below sea level.

The "place of the seven springs", known in Arabic as Tabgha and in Hebrew as En Sheva, is the traditional site of the miracle of the multiplication of the loaves and fishes (Mark 8,1–9).
The access to the site (12km/7½ miles from Tiberias) is on the right of the road to Capernaum, which turns right off the road running north from Tiberias.

Situation and characteristics

The first church on the site, an aisleless building measuring 15.50m/51ft by 9.50m/31ft, was built in the 4th century. In the 5th century it was replaced by a larger three-aisled cruciform basilica. The mosaics of this second church, excavated by Mader and Schneider in 1932, were housed in a new church built over them, adjoining which a monastery was founded by German Benedictines in 1956. The third church in turn was demolished and replaced by a new one, built in 1980–82 by the German Holy Land Association of Cologne.

History

Sights

Church of the
Multiplication
of the Loaves

The new Church of the Multiplication of the Loaves was designed by the Cologne architects Anton Goergen and Fritz Baumann.

The mosaics in the nave and north aisle are in simple geometric designs, while those in the five spaces between the columns depict a variety of birds (geese, herons, etc.). The most interesting mosaics, however, are in the transepts, those in the north transept being almost completely preserved. The artist was evidently familiar with the Nile delta, and may even have come from there, for he depicts the flora and fauna of that region – flamingoes, snakes, herons and ducks, in a setting of lotus flowers, reeds, etc. The mosaics in the south transept, which are only partly preserved, are on similar themes, and also show a Nilometer, a device for measuring the level of the river.

The altar in the sanctuary is built over the stone on which tradition has it that Christ stood during the multiplication of the loaves. In front of it is a mosaic depicting a basket containing loaves flanked by two fishes.

Chapel of
the Primacy
(St Peter's
Church)

200m/220yds farther along the road to Capernaum a footpath goes off on the right and, passing a Byzantine structure enclosing a spring, runs down to the shores of the Sea of Galilee and the Chapel of the Primacy, also known as St Peter's Church. A chapel built here in the 4th century was destroyed in 1263; the present chapel, in black basalt, was built by the Franciscans in 1933. This simple aisleless building commemorates the appearance of the risen Christ to his disciples on the shores of the lake, when he gave Peter primacy over the church with the thrice repeated injunction: "Feed my lambs . . . Feed my sheep . . . Feed my sheep" (John 21,15–16). The rock at the east end of the chapel is supposed to be the table

Church of the Multiplication of the Loaves, Tabgha

Chapel of the Primacy on the shores of the Sea of Galilee

at which Christ dined with the disciples. The rock-cut steps leading down to the lake on the south side of the chapel were described by the pilgrim Aetheria about 400 as "the steps on which the Lord stood".

Between the roads leading to the Church of the Multiplication of the Loaves and the Chapel of the Primacy, immediately north of the Capernaum road, are the remains of the small Monastery of the Sermon on the Mount, founded in the 4th century at about the same time as the first Church of the Multiplication and Chapel of the Primacy. On the south side of the complex are the conventual buildings, on the north side the church, the apse of which, with benches for the priests, projects beyond the enclosure wall. This little aisleless church measures only 7.20m/24ft by 4.48m/15ft. The narthex and nave had mosaic pavements (remains in the archaeological park at Capernaum: see entry). The square sacristy on the north side is entirely hewn from the native rock. The church, built of basalt, with an altar of white marble, existed until the beginning of the Muslim period (7th c.); in 1938 it was replaced by a new church higher up on the Mount of the Beatitudes (see entry).

Monastery of the Sermon on the Mount

Surroundings of Tabgha

A few kilometres from Tabgha, at the north end of the Sea of Galilee, is Capernaum (see entry), with the Octagon of Peter and an ancient synagogue.

Capernaum

Tabor, Mount

See Mount Tabor

Tel Aviv, Israel's modern metropolis

Tel Aviv–Jaffa (Yafo) G 4

District: Tel Aviv
Altitude: sea level
Population: 320,000 (conurbation 1.55 million)

Situation and
characteristics

The double town of Tel Aviv–Jaffa (Yafo), on the Mediterranean coast
65km/40 miles north-west of Jerusalem, is Israel's largest conurbation and
its principal economic centre. Most countries have their embassies in Tel
Aviv, since they do not recognise Jerusalem as capital of Israel.

Whereas the origins of Jaffa reach far back beyond the Christian era, Tel
Aviv ("Hill of Spring") is a young city. In recent years the two towns have
grown into one, now surrounded by a common girdle of residential
suburbs.

Although Tel Aviv can claim no great monuments of art and architecture
and its townscape is not uniformly attractive, it has an appealing character
of its own and is regarded as the "most Israeli" of Israel's towns. It has also
the widest range of cultural activities and entertainment facilities in Israel
and has extensive sandy beaches which attract many visitors.

Mythology
and legend

In Jewish tradition Jaffa (Joppa) was founded by Noah's son Japheth after
the Flood, in Greek legend by Joppa, daughter of the wind god Aeolus. The
Greeks also believed that a rock in the sea outside the harbour was the rock
to which Joppa's daughter Andromeda was chained at the mercy of a
sea-monster and from which she was released by Perseus. Jewish tradition
held that it was here in the 8th century B.C. that the prophet Jonah, seeking
to evade God's command to preach in Nineveh, boarded a ship from which
he was cast into the sea by the crew during a violent storm, and was then
swallowed by a great fish and later "vomited out . . . upon the dry land"
(Jonah 1 and 2). According to the New Testament it was in Jaffa that Tabitha

was raised from the dead by Peter, who then stayed in the house of Simon the Tanner (Acts 9,36–43).

During building work in northern Tel Aviv, near the corner of Ibn Gvirol and Nordau Streets, the earliest known traces of settlement were found – tombs dating from the Chalcolithic, the period of transition between the Stone and Bronze Ages (4000–3150 B.C.).

The first remains of a settlement which has been continuous into our own day were found on the 37m/120ft high hill above Jaffa's natural harbour. Excavations in recent years have brought to light a wall dating from the Hyksos period (18th–16th c. B.C.). In 1486 B.C. Pharaoh Tuthmosis III conquered Jaffa; and the excavators found a stone door with an inscription in the name of Pharaoh Ramesses II (13th c. B.C.). Around 1200 B.C. Philistines settled in Jaffa and on Tell Qasileh (north of the river Yarqon). About 1000 B.C. the town was captured by David, and his son Solomon imported cedarwood from Lebanon for the construction of the Temple in Jerusalem through the port of Jaffa or the harbour near Tell Qasileh (2 Chronicles 2,15). In later centuries, however, the population of Jaffa was predominantly Phoenician and from the 3rd century B.C. predominantly Greek. In the 2nd century B.C. there were conflicts between the Greek population and the Maccabees, who in 142 B.C. set fire to Jaffa (2 Maccabees 12,3–8) and settled numbers of Jews in the town. In the 1st century B.C. the port of Jaffa lost its leading place to the newly founded town of Caesarea.

The Christian era in Jaffa began with the visit of the apostle Peter (Acts 9,36–43). In the 4th century it was the see of a bishop. In 636 it was conquered by the Arabs, and in the 7th and 8th centuries enjoyed a period of prosperity under the Omayyad and Abbasid Caliphs. The Crusaders destroyed the town in 1099 and then rebuilt the walls; and thereafter the port was used by pilgrims visiting the Holy Land. The walls were strengthened by King Louis IX of France in 1251. The Crusader occupation came to an end, however, with the capture of the town by the Mameluke Sultan Baibars in 1267. Thereafter for many centuries Jaffa lay desolate.

From 1520 Palestine was ruled by the Ottomans, who in 1650 gave permission to Franciscan friars to build a church and pilgrim hospice. In 1799 Napoleon stayed in Jaffa on his way from Egypt to Akko. In 1807 Mahmud, whose severity earned him the name of Abu Nebut ("Father of the Cudgel"), became Pasha of Gaza and made Jaffa his capital. From his time date the Seraglio (now a museum), the nearby Hammam, the Mahmudiye Mosque and the Abu Nebut Fountain. In 1818 Jaffa had a population of 6000. In 1834 Ibrahim Pasha captured the town and founded the suburb of Abu Kabir a little way inland.

A new period of development under European auspices began in the mid 19th century. In 1852 American Adventists established a farm on the "Mount of Hope" near the river Ayalon, but in 1857 this was pillaged and thereafter abandoned. (The site is now occupied by the Shevah College in Hamasger Street.)

The "capitulations" agreed with the Turkish government ensured great influence for the European powers in Palestine. The French built hospitals and enlarged monasteries and churches. The Russians built a church dedicated to St Peter at the "Tomb of Tabitha" on the hill of Abu Kabir. In 1866 members of the American Church of the Messiah founded a colony, which failed because of Arab hostility and the unfavourable climate. In 1869 the German Society of the Temple took over the abandoned site and established the agricultural settlement of Jaffa-Valhalla; then in 1871 they founded another settlement at Sarona, north-east of Jaffa. Farther north the Jewish settlements of Newe Tzedek and Newe Shalom were established. In 1892 French engineers built a railway line between Jaffa and Jerusalem.

In 1909 immigrants from Russia founded the purely Jewish suburb of Ahuzat Bayit, with the Herzl Grammar School (on a site now occupied by the Shalom Tower). This marked the beginning of the modern town, which was named Tel Aviv in 1910 and, following Arab riots in 1921, broke away from Jaffa and became an independent city. During the British Mandate (1920–48) wide new streets were cut through Jaffa's maze of alleys to make it easier to control disorder. By 1924 the town had a population of 35,000. A power station was built in Tel Aviv, which became the first town in the country to have an electricity supply. In 1929 renewed Arab riots led many Jews to move from Jaffa to Tel Aviv. In 1936 the port of Jaffa was closed down, and Tel Aviv built its own port at Tell Qasileh.

The United Nations plan for the partition of Palestine (1947) proposed that Jaffa (population 100,000, including 30,000 Jews) should remain Arab and Tel Aviv (population 230,000) become Jewish. In 1948, following Arab attacks, Israel forces captured Jaffa. On May 14th 1948 David Ben-Gurion proclaimed the state of Israel in the former house of the first mayor of Tel Aviv, Meir Dizengoff. In 1950 the old town of Jaffa was amalgamated with the new Jewish town under the name of Tel Aviv–Yafo.

The ★town

Opinions on Tel Aviv differ widely. To some it is a noisy and unbeautiful city, to others the lively modern metropolis of Israel. It is true that some parts of the city, particularly the outer districts, are not particularly attractive; but the central area between the sea and Ibn Gvirol Street, with its functional buildings in the international style, is handsome and imposing.

Most of the hotels – all of them in the luxury category – are on Hayarkon Street, which runs parallel to the coast, and its continuation to the south, Herbert Samuel Street (though farther south the hotels begin to become less exclusive). The principal business and shopping quarter is round Dizengoff Street and Circle. There are also numbers of smaller shops in Allenby Street, south-west of which is the Newe Tzedek quarter, the oldest part of the town, with narrow little streets and low houses. Farther south is the old town of Jaffa (Yafo). The northern part of Tel Aviv, beyond the river

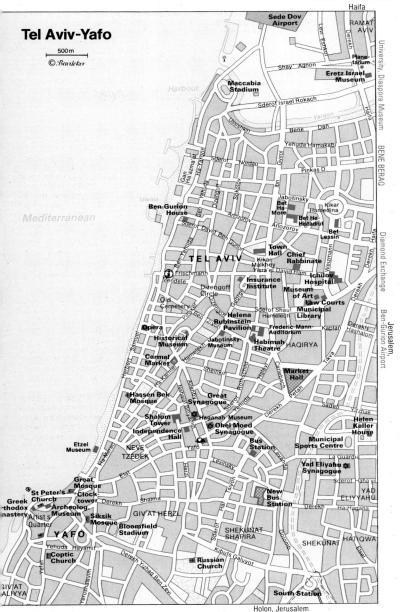

Tel Aviv-Yafo

500 m

©Baedeker

Haifa

Sede Dov
Airport

RAMAT
AVIV

Shay Agnon

Planetarium

Eretz Israel
Museum

Maccabia
Stadium

Harbour

Sderot Israel Rokach

Yarqon

University, Diaspora Museum

Ussishkin

Bene Dan

Haifa

Yehuda Hamakabi

Gan Ha-azma'ut

HaYarqon

Sderot

Nordau

Gvirol

Ibn

Pinkas D.

BENE BERAQ

Marina

Dizengoff

Sokolov

Ben-Gurion
House

Ben-Yehuda

Arlozorov

Jabotinsky

Bet
Ha
More

Kikar
Hamedina

Bet Ha-
Histadrut

Mediterranean

Sderot David Ben Gurion

Arlozorov

Bet
Lessin

Weizmann

Diamond Exchange

TEL AVIV

Ben-Yehuda

Frischmann

Mendele

Dizengoff

Kikar
Malkhey
Yisra'el David Ham

Town
Hall

Chief
Rabbinate

Ichilov
Hospital

Derekh

Jerusalem, Ben-Gurion Airport

Insurance
Institute

Museum
of Art

Pinsker

Dizengoff
Circle

George

Law Courts
Municipal
Library

Derekh Hashalom

Old
Cemetery

Sderot Shaul
Hamelech

Kaplan

Ben

Opera

Helena
Rubinstein
Pavilion

Frederic-Mann-
Auditorium

Tikva

Allenby

Historical
Museum

Jabotinsky-
Museum

Habimah
Theatre

HAQIRYA

Carmel
Market

Ha-Karmel

Hamelech

Sheinkin

Carlebach

Rothschild

Yehuda

Petah

Market
Hall

Hassen Bek
Mosque

Nahalat Binyamin

Great
Synagogue

Allenby

Derekh

Saden

Yizhak

Helen
Keller
House

Shalom
Tower
Independence
Hall

Haganah Museum

Ohel Moed
Synagogue

Bus
Station

Municipal
Sports Centre

Etzel
Museum

Frenkel

Eilat

NEVE
TZEDEK

Herzl

Yafo

Levinsky

La Guardia

Yad Eliyahu
Synagogue

Sderot Haha yil

Great
Mosque

Clock-
tower

Derekh

Shalma

New
Bus
Station

Ha

Tsiyon

Ha-Hagana

Derekh

YAD
ELIYYAHU

St Peter's
Church

Greek
Orthodox
Monastery

Archeolog.
Museum

Saksik
Mosque

GIV'AT HERZL

Sderot

Kibus Galuyot

Catlanb

SHEKUNAT
HATIQWA

Etsel

Artist's
Quarter

YAFO

Bloomfield
Stadium

SHEKUNAT
SHAPIRA

Coptic
Church

Yehuda Hayamit

Yefet

Derekh Yizhaq Ben Zevi

Russian
Church

Yerushalayim

GIV'AT
ALIYYA

South Station

Holon, Jerusalem

Yarqon, is very different, with handsomely laid out residential districts and large parks and gardens.

Opening Times

Archaeological Museum
10 Mifraz Shelomo Street, Jaffa
Open: Sun.–Fri. 9am–2pm (Tues. also 4–7pm), Sat. 10am–2pm

Art Museum
See Tel Aviv Museum of Art

Ben-Gurion House
17 Ben-Gurion Boulevard
Open:Sun. and Tues.–Thurs. 8am–2pm, Mon. 8am–5pm, Fri. 8am–noon
The interior of the house has been left largely as it was when David Ben-Gurion and his wife Paula lived there. It also displays part of his library and numbers of his letters.

Bialik House
(Bet Bialik)
22 Bialik Street
Open: Sun.–Thurs. 9am–7pm, Fri. 9am–1pm

Carmel Market
Corner of Allenby Street and Hakarmel Street
Open: daily until sunset, except on Fridays, Saturdays and public holidays

Diamond Museum
See Harry Oppenheimer Diamond Museum

Diaspora Museum
(Beit HaTefuzot)
University Campus, Ramat Aviv
Open: Sun.–Tues. and Thurs. 10am–5pm, Wed. 10am–7pm

Dizengoff House
See Independence Hall

Eretz Israel Museum
University, Ramat Aviv
Open: Sun.–Thurs. 9am–2pm (Tues. also 4–7pm), Sat. 10am–2pm

Etzel Museum
Herbert Samuel Esplanade
Open: Sun.–Thurs. 8am–4pm, Fri. 8am–1pm
The museum contains a small collection of material on the occupation of Jaffa by the Israelis.

Haganah Museum
23 Rothschild Boulevard
Open: Sun.–Thurs. 8am–3pm (Sun. and Tues. to 4pm), Fri. 8am–12.30pm

Harry Oppenheimer Diamond Museum
in Diamond Exchange
1 Jabotinsky Street, Ramat Gan
Open: Sun., Mon., Wed. and Thurs. 10am–4pm, Tues. 10am–7pm

Helena Rubinstein Pavilion
6 Tarsat Boulevard (Habimah Square)
Open: Sun.–Wed. 10am–5pm, Thurs. 10am–10pm, Sat. 10am–3pm

Historical Museum
27 Bialik Street
Open: Sun.–Thurs. 9am–2pm (Tues. also 4–7pm)

Israel Experience
4 Pasteur Street, Jaffa
Presentations (in English): daily at 9am, noon and 6, 8 and 9pm
A multi-media show

Jabotinsky Museum
38 King George Street
Open: Sun., Tues. and Thurs. 10am–6pm, Mon. and Wed. 10am–1pm and
6–8pm, Fri. 10am–1pm
A museum (attached to the Jabotinsky Research Institute) on Jewish resistance to the British Mandate authorities.

Rubin House
14 Bialik Street
Open: Sun., Mon., Wed. and Thurs. 10am–2pm, Sat. 11am–2pm
The house of the artist Reuven Rubin, now a museum, with a collection of his works.

Safari Park
Ramat Gan
Open: Sun.–Thurs. 9.30am–2pm, Fri. 8.30am–1pm, Sat. 9am–3pm

Shalom Tower (Migdal Shalom)
Herzl Street (north end)
Viewing platform and wax museum open: April–September, Sun.–Fri.
9am–7pm; October–March, Sun.–Thurs. 9am–4.30pm, Fri. 9am–1.30pm

Tel Aviv Museum of Art
27 King Saul Street
Open: Sun.–Wed. 10am–5pm, Thurs. 10am–10pm, Sat. 10am–3pm

Tell Qasileh
See Eretz Israel Museum

Zoological Gardens
See Safari Park

Sights

Central Area

The best starting-point for a tour of Tel Aviv is the Dizengoff Circle, named after Meir Dizengoff, Tel Aviv's first mayor after its separation from Jaffa in 1921. It is laid out on two levels, with a raised area for pedestrians above the carriageway. In this higher area is the striking "Fire and Water Fountain", designed by the well-known Israeli artist Yaacov Agam. At regular intervals (on the hour, except at 2 and 3pm) the fountain is illuminated from within, its coloured aluminium rings begin to revolve and the jets of water, computer-controlled, move rhythmically in time to the music.

Dizengoff Circle

From the Dizengoff Circle Dizengoff Street runs south-east to Habimah Square, the cultural centre of the city.
In this square is Israel's National Theatre, the Habimah Theatre, built in 1935. Originally founded in Moscow in 1917, the theatre moved to Tel Aviv in 1928. There are two houses, seating respectively 1000 and 300. Plays are normally performed in Hebrew, with simultaneous translation available on headphones.

Habimah Theatre

Tel Aviv–Jaffa (Yafo)

Frederic Mann Auditorium

Helena Rubinstein Pavilion	Immediately north of the theatre, in the Helena Rubinstein Pavilion, is a branch of the Tel Aviv Museum of Art, which puts on temporary exhibitions of works by modern artists both Israeli and foreign.
Frederic Mann Auditorium	Adjoining the Helena Rubinstein Pavilion is the Frederic Mann Auditorium (Hekhal Haturbut), home of the Israeli Philharmonic Orchestra. With seating for 3000, it is Israel's largest concert hall.
Tel Aviv Museum of Art	Some 700m/770yds north-east of Habimah Square, in Sderot Shaul Hamelech (King Saul Boulevard), is the Tel Aviv Museum of Art (by J. Yashar and D. Eitan, 1971), which contains works by leading Israeli and foreign artists, including Degas, Monet, Pissarro, Chagall, Kokoschka, Léger, Henry Moore and Picasso.
Old Cemetery	Going south-west from the Dizengoff Circle along Pinsk Street and turning right into Trumpeldor Street, we come to the Old Cemetery, with a common grave containing the remains of victims of the 1921 troubles and the tombs of leading Zionists like Chaim Arlosoroff, Meir Dizengoff and Max Nordau and the poets Chaim Nahman Bialik and Shaul Tchernikowsky.
Historical Museum	South-east of the cemetery, in Bialik Street, is the former Town Hall, now housing the Historical Museum (documents on the history of Tel Aviv).
Carmel Market	Continuing south down Bialik Street, we come to the busy and colourful Carmel Market, just south-west of the intersection with Allenby Street,
Haganah Museum	Returning to Allenby Street, we follow it south to the Great Synagogue (1926), at the corner of Ahad Ha'am Street, and the Haganah Museum, in a house at 23 Rothschild Boulevard once occupied by the Haganah commander Eliahu Golomb, which displays weapons used by the Jewish army during the British Mandate.

Tel Aviv Museum of Art

Close by, at 16 Rothschild Boulevard, is Bet Dizengoff, the former residence of Tel Aviv's first mayor. Here can be seen the Independence Hall in which David Ben-Gurion proclaimed the state of Israel on May 14th 1948. There is a display of mementoes of the historic event.

Independence Hall

Rothschild Boulevard runs into Herzl Street, the first street built in 1909 in the newly founded town of Tel Aviv. At its north end was the Hebrew grammar school which bore the name of Theodor Herzl, pulled down in 1958 to make way for Tel Aviv's first high-rise building, Migdal Shalom (Peace Tower). Mainly an office block, this also houses a shopping centre and a wax museum. From the viewing platform at 132m/433ft there are wide panoramic views.

Shalom Tower

Northern Tel Aviv

The northern districts of Tel Aviv lie beyond the Yarqon (the "green" river), which in ancient times marked the boundary between the tribes of Ephraim to the north and Dan to the south. The lawns bordering the river are a popular place of resort, particularly on the Sabbath (boat hire).

River Yarqon

The Eretz Israel Museum (Land of Israel Museum) occupies a large complex of buildings, the entrance to which is in University Road. By the car park is the Numismatic Museum. Also in the complex are the Museums of Ceramics, Glass, the History of Writing, the History of Science, Ethnography and Folklore and a department on "Man and his Work". Each of these collections covers its field from the earliest times to the present day. There is also a Planetarium.

★Eretz Israel Museum

In the centre of the area is Tell Qasileh with its excavations and a pavilion displaying finds from the site. The Israeli archaeologist B. Mazar identified

Tell Qasileh

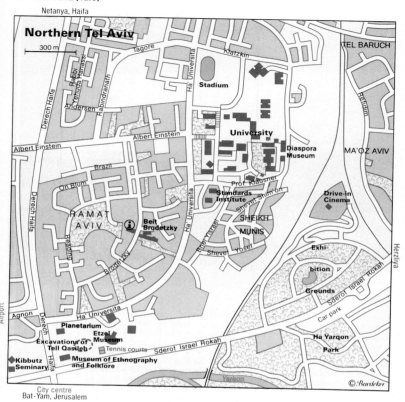

Netanya, Haifa

Northern Tel Aviv

300 m

TEL BARUCH

Tagore

Klatzkin

Rabbi Yehuda Hamassi

Rabindranath

Ha Universita

Andersen

Stadium

Albert Einstein

University

Derech Haifa

Albert Einstein

Brazil

Diaspora Museum

MA'OZ AVIV

On Blum

Prof. Klausner

Petahim

R A M A T
A V I V

Standards Institute

Shevet Shim'on

Drive-in Cinema

Derech Haifa

Beit Brodetzky

Ha Universita

B'nei Yisrael

SHEIKH

MUNIS

Herzliya

Reading

Brodetzky

Shevet Yosef

Exhi-

bition

Sderot Israel Rokah

Airport

Agnon

Ha Universita

Grounds

Car park

Planetarium

Etzel Museum

Excavations of
Tell Qasileh

Tennis courts

Sderot Israel Rokah

Ha Yarqon

Park

Derech Haifa

Kibbutz
Seminary

Museum of Ethnography
and Folklore

Yarqon

© Baedeker

City centre
Bat-Yam, Jerusalem

twelve occupation levels on the tell, the earliest dating back to the 12th century B.C. A brick building of that period was found in stratum XII and a strong wall and two copper-smelting furnaces of the 11th century in stratum XI. These two levels are attributed to the Philistines. Stratum X dates from the 10th century, when, after David's conquest of the area, the kings of Israel had a port here. Recently some scholars have suggested that the cedarwood from Lebanon which Solomon required for the building of the Temple was landed here, at the mouth of the Yarqon, rather than in the port of Jaffa. The discovery of store-rooms and storage jars here have shown that at that period the agricultural produce of the region was shipped from Tell Qasileh. After its destruction by Egyptian forces the settlement was rebuilt by the kings of Israel in the 9th century B.C., but it was again destroyed by the Assyrians in 732 B.C. In the 5th century B.C. cedarwood from Lebanon was again landed here for the building of the Second Temple (Ezra 3,7). The later strata show that Tell Qasileh was still occupied in Hellenistic, Roman, Byzantine and Islamic times, after which it was abandoned in favour of Jaffa.

University

From the Eretz Israel Museum University Road leads to the University of Tel Aviv, which offers the widest range of disciplines in Israel.

At the south-east corner of the University campus is the Diaspora Museum (Beit HaTefuzot, the "House of the Dispersion"), founded in 1979, which illustrates the life and culture of Jews in different countries at different times with the help of films, recordings, models, a computer and a wide variety of exhibits.

★Diaspora Museum

Eastern Tel Aviv

To the east of the city centre is the hilly suburb of Ramat Gan ("Garden Hill"), an industrial settlement laid out in 1920 and well provided with open space. Napoleon's Hill (Tel Gerisa), on the western outskirts, is so called because of the erroneous belief that French cannon were stationed here for the bombardment of Jaffa in 1799. The hill was inhabited as early as the 18th century B.C.

Ramat Gan

In Ramat Gan, housed in the Diamond Exchange, is the Harry Oppenheimer Diamond Museum, with an interesting collection which is supplemented from time to time by valuable items displayed on loan. The process of diamond-cutting is explained in a film show.

Diamond Museum

The Safari Park is an area of 100 hectares (250 acres) in which African animals roam freely. (Visitors can drive through the park in closed vehicles.)

Safari Park

To the east of Ramat Gan is the suburb of Bene Beraq, founded by orthodox Jews from Poland. Education in line with their beliefs is provided in a number of Talmudic schools.

Bene Beraq

Shalom Road (Derekh Hashalom) runs 3km/2 miles south to the campus of Bar Ilan University, founded in 1955 and named after a leader of orthodox Jewry. In all faculties particular importance is attached to Jewish religious studies.

Bar Ilan University

★Jaffa (Yafo)

Jaffa, to the south of the city centre, preserves something of the atmosphere of an old Arab town, very different from the European air of Tel Aviv. It is particularly lively in the evening, when the restaurants in the heart of the old town are thronged with people.
Jaffa has undergone great changes in the 20th century. During the 1921 riots, in the interests of maintaining order, the British authorities cut wide modern streets through the maze of alleys; then in 1948, following the mass flight of the Arab population, extensive slum clearance and redevelopment was necessary. Although part of the bazaar has been preserved, some streets have been widened, destroyed buildings have been cleared away and others have been restored. Many of them are now bars, restaurants and artists' quarters. The ancient remains on the acropolis, the site of the earliest settlement, have also been preserved. In recent years the historic buildings in the old town have been excellently restored.

The town

The Clock-Tower in the centre of Jaffa was built in 1906 to mark the 50-year jubilee of Sultan Abdul Hamid II. On the tower is a plaque commemorating the Israelis killed in the battle for the town in 1948.

Clock-Tower

Immediately west is the Great Mosque or Mahmudiye Mosque, built in 1810 by the Ottoman governor Mahmud Pasha, known as Abu Nebut ("Father of the Cudgel"). The builders re-used antique columns from Ashqelon and Caesarea but mistakenly set them upside down, with the capitals at the foot.

Great Mosque

South-west of the Great Mosque, set in gardens, is the Archaeological Museum. Housed in the old Turkish Seraglio, it has an interesting collection of local finds.

Archaeological Museum

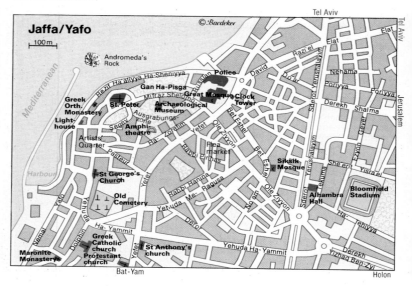

Jaffa/Yafo

© *Baedeker*

Mediterranean

Tel Aviv

Andromeda's Rock

Greek Orth. Monastery

Light-house

Artists' Quarter

Harbour

St. Peter

Gan Ha-Pisga

Archaeological Museum

Ausgrabungs-zone

Amphi-theatre

Police

Great Mosque Clock Tower

Flea market

St George's Church

Old Cemetery

Siksik Mosque

Alhambra Hall

Bloomfield Stadium

Maronite Monasterys

Greek Catholic church

Protestant church

St Anthony's church

Bat-Yam

Holon

Jaffa: Clock-Tower . . .

. . . and St Peter's Monastery

Excavations outside St Peter's Monastery

A few hundred metres beyond this is the acropolis (37m/121ft), on which is the Franciscan monastery of St Peter, built in 1654 on the site of a 13th century Crusader castle. Its name recalls the apostle Peter's visit to Jaffa (Acts 9,36–43), as does the so-called tomb of Tabitha in the Russian Monastery (see below). From the courtyard of the monastery steps lead down to the vaulted chambers, still intact, of the Crusader castle.

St Peter's Monastery

In the square in front of the monastery and the hill to the east, now laid out as an attractive park (Gan Hapisga), are the excavations which brought to light earlier occupation levels, with a 6m/20ft thick wall of the Hyksos period (18th–16th c. B.C.), a town gate bearing the name of Pharaoh Ramesses II (1290–24 B.C.), remains of a Canaanite town and a Jewish settlement of the 4th century B.C. and relics of the Maccabean and Roman periods.

Excavations

From the hill above St Peter's Monastery there is a fine view of the harbour. A place of importance from the 2nd millennium B.C. onwards, it was later superseded by Ashdod and Haifa and is now only a fishing and boating harbour.
Round the harbour are cliffs and isolated rocks, on one of which, according to Greek legend, Andromeda, daughter of the mythical foundress of the town, Joppa, was chained until her release by Perseus.

Harbour

If we now head southward in the direction of the old lighthouse through the narrow lanes of the town, passing picturesque old houses, we come to a small mosque built in 1730. It is believed to occupy the site of the house of Simon the Tanner, with whom Peter stayed after raising Tabitha from the dead.

Mosque

Some 2km/1¼ miles south-east of old Jaffa can be seen the slender tower of the Russian Monastery in its setting of palms. The Russian government

Russian Monastery

bought the hill of Abu Kabir in 1860 and built a monastery dedicated to St Peter with accommodation for pilgrims. Under the courtyard of the monastery is an underground chamber with numerous recesses for burials. It is part of a Jewish cemetery of the 1st–4th centuries A.D., but in Christian tradition is believed to be the tomb of Tabitha, whom Peter raised from the dead.

Surroundings of Tel Aviv–Jaffa

Rishon LeZion

14km/8½ miles south of the city is Rishon LeZion (pop. 95,000), one of the earliest Jewish agricultural settlements, founded in 1882.

Petah Tiqwa

A few kilometres east of Tel Aviv is Petah Tiqwa ("Gate of Hope"), the first modern Jewish farming village, founded in 1878. From difficult beginnings in an area of marshland it has developed into a flourishing city of 122,000 inhabitants.

In the centre of the town is the Founders' Garden (Gan Hameyasdim), commemorating the early settlers. Adjoining are the first synagogue built in the town and the new Town Hall. At the near end of the town on the road from Bene Beraq, on right, is a stone arch erected in honour of Baron Edmond de Rothschild and the financial assistance he gave to the founders of the village.

Rosh Ha'ayin

5km/3 miles north-east of Petah Tiqwa, near the sources of the river Yarqon, is the town of Rosh Ha'ayin (see entry).

Tel Arad

See Arad

Tel Dan

See Dan

Tiberias/Teverya   H 3

District: Northern
Altitude: 212m/696ft below sea level
Population: 30,000

Situation and characteristics

Tiberias (Hebrew Teverya), 70km/45 miles east of Haifa on the western shore of the Sea of Galilee, with the newer parts of the town reaching up the slopes above the lake, is a holiday resort much frequented in the cooler months of the year. Its hot springs have been used for medicinal purposes since ancient times, and the town is now equipped with modern spa facilities.

One of the four holy cities of the Jews, along with Jerusalem, Hebron and Safed, Tiberias is rich in historical and religious interest, as are the towns and villages on the shores of the lake and in the surrounding area.

History

Herod Antipas, son of Herod I and ruler of the country in the time of Jesus, founded Tiberias in A.D. 17 and named it after the Roman Emperor Tiberius. The new town lay between Hammat (Hammath) and Raqqat (Rakkath), which are mentioned in the Old Testament as fortified cities in the territory

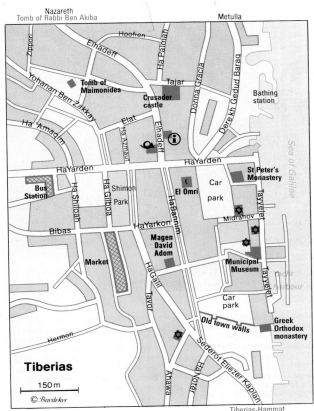

Nazareth
Tomb of Rabbi Ben Akiba

Metulla

Tiberias

150 m

© Baedeker

Tiberias-Hammat

of the tribe of Naphtali (Joshua 19,35). Since it was built over the cemetery of Hammath it was regarded by pious Jews as unclean, and at first the town was inhabited only by pagans. Jesus himself, who did much of his teaching in this area, seems never to have come here. Herod Antipas's successor Agrippa II also had his residence in Tiberias, which he embellished with paved streets, a palace and a bath-house. After the end of the Jewish War, in A.D. 70, he moved his capital to Sepphoris (see Zippori)

At the end of the 2nd century Rabbi Simeon Bar Yohai (see Meron) declared the town clean, and it then became the seat of the Sanhedrin. The head of the Sanhedrin, who had the style of Nasi (Prince), was the highest spiritual authority of Jewry until the office was abolished by the Emperor Theodosius II in 429. From the 3rd century onwards Tiberias was the spiritual centre of the Jews. It was now known as Teverya, a name which the Jews derived not from the Emperor Tiberius but from the Hebrew word *tabur* ("navel"), since they regarded the town as the navel of the world. It was here that the Mishnah (c. 200) and the Jerusalem Talmud (c. 400) were completed and the vocalic signs of the Hebrew alphabet were devised. Here too were – and are – the tombs of a number of famous rabbis.

Tiberias, on the Sea of Galilee

In the 4th century a Jewish convert to the Christian faith, Joseph of Tiberias, built churches in his native town and in other places, and there is known to have been a Christian bishop here in the 6th century. After the Persian conquest in 614 and the Arab conquest in 636 Jewish scholars joined the community in Babylon or went to Jerusalem. From 1099 to 1187 Tiberias lay within the dominions of Tancred, Prince of Galilee, and the kings of Jerusalem. Then in 1247 the Mameluke Sultan Baibars destroyed the town, which thereafter remained uninhabited until the time of the Ottomans (from 1517 onwards).

In 1562 Sultan Suleiman the Magnificent granted the town to a Jewish refugee from Spain, Don Joseph Hanassi, whom he had previously created duke of the Greek island of Naxos, and his aunt Gracia Mendes. They established a Jewish state in Galilee under Ottoman overlordship, but this was short-lived. In the 17th century Tiberias fell into ruin, and was not reoccupied until the Druze emir Daher el-Amr rebuilt the town and its citadel in 1738 and resettled it with Jews. Soon afterwards, in 1765, a first group of Jewish immigrants from Poland also settled here. Many inhabitants lost their lives in an earthquake in 1837, but after the disaster Tiberias was once again rebuilt. Around 1940 the town had a population of 12,000, half of them Arabs and half Jews. Since 1948 the population has been entirely Jewish.

The town

Tiberias consists of the old town, the large new district of Qiryat Shmuel to the north and the district of Hammat to the south with its hot springs. The principal streets of the old town – in which, however, there are few old buildings – are HaGalil Street and HaBannim Street, both running parallel to the shore of the lake.

There is a very attractive lakeside promenade with numerous restaurants and cafés and magnificent views of the Sea of Galilee (see entry).

Sights

On the northern edge of the old town are an art centre and a restaurant built over the remains of a Crusader castle which Daher el-Amr rebuilt in the local black basalt in 1738.

Crusader castle

Going south-east from here in the direction of the lakeside promenade, we pass the Franciscan monastery of St Peter, built in the second half of the 19th century over the remains of a Crusader castle. There is a beautiful cloister. The apse of the church projects like the bow of a ship – a reference to Peter's fishing-boat.

St Peter's Monastery

A few hundred metres south of the monastery, housed in a former mosque of about 1880, is the Municipal Museum, with a collection of archaeological material from Tiberias and the surrounding area. The museum is at present closed for restoration.

Municipal Museum

Continuing south on the lakeside promenade, we come to the Greek Orthodox Monastery. The present building was erected in 1862, but it had several predecessors, the earliest of which dated back to the 3rd or 4th century.

Greek Orthodox Monastery

Some 300m/330yds from the north end of HaGalil Street are a number of old tombs, including that of the great philosopher and physician Maimonides (Rabbi Mose Ben Maimon, also known as Rambam after the initial letters of these names). Born in Córdoba in 1135, Maimonides left Spain because of religious persecution, went to Cairo and became Saladin's personal physician. There too he became a rabbi, and later the spiritual head of the Jews in Egypt. He wrote very influential commentaries on the Mishnah, and Albertus Magnus and Thomas Aquinas thought highly of his philosophical work "Dalalat el-Hairin" ("Guide of the Doubters"). After his death in Cairo in 1204 his remains were taken to Tiberias.

Tomb of Maimonides

Nearby is the tomb of Yohanan Ben Zakkai, who after the destruction of Jerusalem in A.D. 70 founded a Jewish school in Yavne (see entry) and transferred the seat of the Sanhedrin to that town.

Tomb of Yohanan Ben Zakkai

Higher up on the neighbouring hill, in a new residential area, is the tomb of Rabbi Ben Akiba, who believed that Bar Kochba was the Messiah and was executed after his rising in A.D. 135. It is reached on a road which branches off the main road at the police station in the district of Qiryat Shmuel and runs south.

Tomb of Rabbi Ben Akiba

Tiberias-Hammat

Taking a street which runs south from the old town and following the lakeside road, we pass various bathing stations and come to Tiberias-Hammat with its hot springs. On the right of the road is the Tiberias Hot Springs spa establishment, which treats skin conditions. To the left of the road, on the shore of the lake, is the Young Tiberias Hot Springs establishment, with thermal baths which are open to the general public.

Spa treatment centre

Immediately south of the spa treatment centre is the entrance to an excavation site whose main attraction is a synagogue with a well preserved mosaic pavement. The archaeological park is entered through a small museum containing exhibits of folk and religious interest.
There was a synagogue on this site in the 3rd or 4th century, and in the 6th or 7th century a new synagogue was built over its remains, on a higher level. Both synagogues were three-aisled. On the south side of the earlier one is a square recess for the Torah shrine; the later one has a semicircular apse.
Of particular importance is the completely preserved mosaic pavement of the older synagogue, which is unusual in having figural representations.

★Synagogue

Synagogue, Tiberias-Hammat

The mosaics in the lateral aisles have simple ornamental designs, but the mosaic in the central aisle is richly patterned. It consists of three parts. At the near end is a dedicatory inscription which mentions the name of one Severus, son of the head of the Sanhedrin: a Roman name, which, like the use of the Greek alongside the Hebrew script and the figural representations in the main part of the mosaic, betray the influence of Hellenistic and Roman culture even on pious Jews during this period. In the centre of the principal mosaic is a head-and-shoulders figure of the sun god Helios surrounded by the signs of the Zodiac and, in the corners, the four Seasons. At the south end a Torah shrine is depicted between two seven-branched candlesticks, along with incense scoops and shofars (rams' horns). The themes of these mosaics are very similar to those of the mosaics at Bet Alfa (see entry), but the Hammat mosaics are of distinctly higher artistic quality.

Tomb of
Rabbi Meir

Above the synagogue (not accessible from the archaeological park) is the domed tomb of the legendary Rabbi Meir (2nd c.), which is in two parts, one Ashkenazi and the other Sephardi.

Surroundings of Tiberias

Bet Yerah

10km/6 miles south of Hammat on the lakeside road is the archaeological site of Bet Yerah ("House of the Moon"): a name which suggests that the original inhabitants worshipped the moon. To judge from the size of the tell Bet Yerah must have been an important Canaanite town, although it is not mentioned either in the Bible or in Egyptian records. Evidence of settlement was found here ranging from the Bronze Age to the period of Arab rule.

There are excellently preserved remains of baths of the 4th or 5th century A.D. In the centre of the frigidarium (cold bath), which had a domed roof, was a pool 2m/6½ft wide of which only the foundations survive. The excavations also revealed the remains of a Roman fort of the 3rd century A.D. Within this complex, which was abandoned in the 4th century, the Jewish community built a three-aisled synagogue oriented towards Jerusalem in the 5th or 6th century. There are remains of a mosaic depicting plants, animals and a man with a horse.

In the northern part of the tell the excavators found the foundations of a 5th century Byzantine church which was much altered in the 6th and 7th centuries.

1km/¾ mile west of Bet Yerah is a place of baptism in the Jordan, laid out in 1981. Although this is not the place where Jesus was baptised many pilgrims come here to be baptised in the sacred waters of the Jordan (illustration, page 276).

Yardenit (place of baptism)

2km/1¼ miles south of Bet Yerah, at the point where the Jordan emerges from the Sea of Galilee, is the kibbutz of Deganya. This was the very first kibbutz, founded in 1909 by Russian immigrants. The original kibbutz is now known as Deganya A, its more recently founded neighbour as Deganya B.

Deganya

At the main entrance to Deganya A is a Syrian tank which in 1948 advanced as far as the kibbutz but was then knocked out by a Molotov cocktail. Within the territory of the kibbutz is Gordon House (named after Aharon D. Gordon, one of the founders of the kibbutz), a research institute with an archaeological, natural history and agricultural museum.

A few kilometres west of Tiberias on the road to Nazareth, to the right, can be seen the Horns of Hittim (see entry). It is a half-hour walk to the hill (Qarne Hittim).

Horns of Hittim

An attractive short trip from Tiberias is to the area north of the Horns of Hittim, reached by taking the Nazareth road and after a wide bend to the left (still within the town) turning right into a road which soon comes into the Arbel valley. To the right of the road is the kibbutz of Arbel. From the hill above the kibbutz there is an impressive view of the Wadi el-Hammam, enclosed by sheer rock walls.

Arbel valley

Continuing to the end of the Arbel valley, we come (10km/6 miles from Tiberias) to Nabi Shueib, under the north side of the Horns of Hittim. This is an important holy place for the Druzes, for here they venerate the tomb of Moses' father-in-law Jethro, housed in a domed shrine. Annually in April they celebrate the memory of the man whom they regard as the first of their seven prophets. The last of the prophets was Caliph el-Hakim (11th c.), a contemporary of Darazi, who formulated the secret religion of the Druzes. The Druzes believe that the remains of Jethro, whom they call Nabi Shueib (*nabi* = "prophet"), were brought here from the land of the Midianites when his descendants came to Kedesh, south of the Sea of Galilee (Judges 4,11).

Nabi Shueib

Migdal (Magdala), 5km/3 miles north of Tiberias, was the home of Mary Magdalene. According to Flavius Josephus, the people of Migdal fought against Herod I and against the Romans, and finally sought refuge in the innumerable caves in the Wadi el-Hammam, a canyon-like valley to the west of Migdal. Once an important town, in which the Crusaders built a church in the 12th century, it later fell into ruin. The present farming village was established in 1910.

Migdal

3km/2 miles north of Migdal on the shores of the Sea of Galilee is the kibbutz of Ginnosar, founded in 1937. Its principal attraction is the fishing-boat of the time of Jesus which is displayed here. The remains of the boat, buried in mud near the edge of the lake, were discovered in 1986 after a long period of drought led to a sharp fall in the water level. The boat, 8.20m/27ft long by 2.30m/7½ft wide, has been dated to between 70 B.C. and

Ginnosar

A.D. 90, and was used for fishing just off the shores of the lake. In order to preserve it for posterity the water which had soaked into the wood is being replaced by wax – a process which it is expected will take until 1995 to complete.

In a cave in the Amud valley, which reaches the lake at Ginnosar, the skull of Galilee Man, who lived 100,000 years ago, was found in 1925.

En Gev

There are boat services from Tiberias to En Gev (see entry), on the east side of the Sea of Galilee.

Timna

G 8

District: Southern

Situation and characteristics

Some 30km/20 miles north of Elat is Timna Park, an area of 60sq.km/23sq.miles of fascinating desert landscape, with copper-mines which have been worked from ancient times into the 20th century. An asphalted road runs through the park, leading to bizarre rock formations like the famous Solomon's Pillars, Egyptian copper workings and rock engravings.

The area is reached by turning left off the main north–south road 27km/17 miles north of Elat, 2km/1¼ miles beyond a road on the left leading to the modern mines. Tickets are issued at the entrance to the park, together with a leaflet of information which contains a site plan.

History

Excavations by Benno Rothenberg of Jerusalem University (1959 onwards) showed that copper was being systematically mined in this area as early as 3000 B.C. (following earlier centuries in which nomads had been picking up lumps of copper ore in the desert and smelting them to obtain the metal) and that, on the evidence of inscriptions, the Egyptians were achieving particularly high outputs of copper in the 14th and 13th centuries B.C. (i.e. under the 18th and 19th Dynasties). The mines were also worked in Israelite times, particularly in the reign of Solomon, and also under Roman and Arab rule. The Israelis began mining here in 1955 but closed the mines down in 1976 as a result of the fall in world copper prices. Mining was resumed in 1980 in workings to the south of the ancient copper-mines.

Sights

★Solomon's Pillars

Bearing left from the entrance to the park, we come in a few kilometres to Solomon's Pillars, a wall of sandstone 50m/165ft high, glowing red in the sun, which in the course of thousands of years has been carved by erosion into the form of massive pillars. The name, catchy but historically in-accurate, was given to them by the American archaeologist Nelson Glueck, who investigated the copper-mines of Timna in the 1930s. A flight of steps leads up to a relief at a height of 30m/100ft in which Pharaoh Ramesses III (1184–53 B.C.) is depicted making an offering to the goddess Hathor.

Temple of Hathor

On the east side of this huge rock formation are the remains, now sur-rounded by railings, of a temple dedicated to the goddess Hathor (13th/12th c. B.C.).

Hill of the Slaves

Opposite Solomon's Pillars is the so-called Hill of the Slaves. This was a camp in which the miners were housed between the 14th and 12th cen-turies B.C. The entrance to the camp was protected by two gate-towers. Within the camp (still partly surrounded by walls) were found the remains of houses and workshops.

Lake Timna

In order to enhance the tourist attractions of Timna Park a small artificial lake has been created in the barren landscape to the east of Solomon's Pillars, with a restaurant and picnic areas. It is planned to open a museum.

Solomon's Pillars in Timna Park

Lake Timna, in a desolate desert setting

Returning along the same road and turning off to the left, we come to the **Mushroom Rock**, a 6m/20ft high rock with something of the shape of a mushroom. Round it are the remains of houses, workshops, smelting ovens (copy: original in Eretz Israel Museum in Tel Aviv) and food storage pits of the 14th–12th centuries B.C.

Mushroom Rock

Continuing on the road past the Mushroom Rock, we come to a car park from which a path is signposted to the Egyptian Copper-Mines. This leads in 200m/220yds to a large natural sandstone arch, from which a steep path leads up to old shafts, the deepest of which tunnels down for 37m/120ft. From a viewing platform can be seen light-coloured circles on the ground marking the position of shafts which have been filled in.

Egyptian
copper-mines

In a cleft in the rock to the north of the Egyptian copper-mines (now accessible by rock-cut steps) are Egyptian rock engravings of the 13th and 12th centuries B.C. They depict a group of hunters armed with bows and arrows, other figures carrying shields and axes and still others in war chariots drawn by animals.

Rock engravings

Wadi Qilt   H 4

West Bank

The Wadi Qilt, a romantic canyon-like valley on the Israeli-occupied west bank of the Jordan, runs eastward through the hills of Judaea into the plain of Jericho. Herod the Great built an aqueduct here which was repaired during the British Mandate and still carries water for most of the year.

Situation and
characteristics

The Romans built a road, parts of which can still be traced, along this ancient route between Jerusalem and Jericho. In early Christian times hermits lived in caves in this wild mountain country, and this led to the foundation in Byzantine times (5th–6th c.) of St George's Monastery.

History

★ St George's Monastery

20km/12½ miles from Jerusalem on the road to Jericho a side road sign-posted to the monastery goes off on the left. This leads to a car park on the left of the road, from the rather higher north side of which there is a first view into the gorge of the Wadi Qilt. From the car park a track suitable only for all-terrain vehicles runs north-east (about 1¼ hours on foot) to a hill with a cross, from which there is a view of the Greek Orthodox monastery of St George and, far to the left, a rivulet flowing down the hillside from a spring, water from which is channelled to the monastery. The stony track continues (another half-hour's walk) to the entrance to the monastery, which clings precariously to the sheer north face of the gorge (it lies in shadow from the early afternoon).

The monastery, originally dedicated to the Virgin, was founded about 480. It flourished in the 6th century but was destroyed by the Persians in 614 and thereafter was abandoned. The present buildings were erected between 1878 and 1901. The church dedicated to the Mother of God has fine icons and wall paintings; the church of St John and St George preserves a 6th century mosaic pavement. In a cave are the remains of the monks who were killed during the Persian advance on Jerusalem.

Yafo

See Tel Aviv–Jaffa

◄ *St George's Monastery in the Wadi Qilt*

Yam Hamelach

See Dead Sea

Yam Kinneret

See Sea of Galilee

Yarden

See River Jordan

Yavne

G 4

District: Central
Population: 11,200

Situation and characteristics

The town of Yavne, founded in 1946 on the site of an abandoned Arab village, lies 30km/19 miles south of Tel Aviv on the road to Ashqelon. It is best known for its nuclear research centre, with Israel's first atomic reactor.

History

First recorded in early Canaanite times (3000 B.C.), Yavne (Jabneel or Jabneh) was captured by Joshua in the 13th century B.C. and by the Philistines in the 12th century, and thereafter became part of the kingdom of Judah. In Persian times Phoenicians and Greeks settled here, calling the town Jamnia. The Maccabees destroyed the town, but in 147 B.C. rebuilt it, together with its port, and populated it with Jews. After the future Emperor Vespasian captured the town in A.D. 68 he gave Rabbi Yohanan Ben Zakkai permission to establish a Jewish school, in which the foundations of the Mishnah (completed about 200 in Tiberias) were laid.

After the destruction of Jerusalem in A.D. 70 Yavne became the seat of the Sanhedrin. Rabbis Gamaliel II and Ben Akiba taught in the school along with Yohanan. In 135 the Romans crushed the Bar Kochba rebellion and destroyed the school at Yavne, which had supported Bar Kochba. The Sanhedrin then moved to Usha (1km/¾ mile east of Qiryat Ata on the Bay of Haifa, now the site of a kibbutz) and later to Tiberias (see entry).

Sights

On a hill to the east of the main road is a Crusader church (12th c.) which was later converted into a mosque.
To the west of the road is a tomb which is believed by the Jews to be that of Rabbi Gamaliel and the Muslims to be that of Hureira, a friend of Mohammed.

Yavne Yam

7km/4½ miles north-west, immediately south of the kibbutz of Palmahim, is the old port of Yavne Yam, where remains of a fortress built of stone and brick were found.

Yehuda

See Judaea

Yeriho

See Jericho

Yerushalayim

See Jerusalem

Yodefat   H 3

District: Northern

The Galilean village of Yodefat (ancient Jotbah, Jotapata), situated   Situation and
20km/12½ miles south of Akko under the north side of Mount Azmon   characteristics
(548m/1798ft), was founded in 1926 as a reafforestation centre.
To reach the village from Akko, leave on the road to Ahihud (8km/5 miles),
take a road on the right to Yavor (3km/2 miles), turn into a narrow road on
the left and then beyond Segev (9km/6 miles) turn right for Yodefat.

The town played a part in the Jewish rising of A.D. 66–70, as Flavius   History
Josephus relates in two chapters of the "Jewish War" (III,7–8). The town
lay, he says, "almost entirely on a steep-sided crag, surrounded by gorges
so deep that a man looking down into them is dizzy before his eye reaches
the foot. The town is accessible only on the north side, where it extends
down a sloping hillside." The site was thus eminently suited for a fortress.
In A.D. 67 a large party of Jewish rebels entrenched themselves in this
stronghold under the leadership of a young priest from Jerusalem, Joseph
son of Mattathias, who defended Jotapata so successfully against the
Romans that Vespasian himself hastened to the scene and threw a double
ring of troops round the town. As at Masada (see entry) six years later, the
Romans built up a ramp on the more easily accessible north side, to which
the defenders responded by increasing the height of the walls. The rebels'
situation became critical, however, when they ran out of food and the
cisterns which were their only source of water dried up. Many of the
defenders, too, were killed on sorties or by missiles from catapults. Finally
on the 47th day of the siege the Romans breached the walls with a batter-
ing-ram, stormed the town and, "knowing neither mercy nor compassion",
slaughtered great numbers of the defenders and took 1200 prisoners.
Joseph, commander of the defenders, had hidden in a cistern, but came out
and gave himself up a few days later. His life was spared because he
prophesied to Vespasian that he would become Emperor, as in fact he soon
did. In A.D. 70 – now in the service of the Roman conqueror, Titus – he
witnessed the conquest of Jerusalem. Thereafter he took the Roman name
of Flavius Josephus under which he is now known and wrote his "Jewish
War" and "Jewish Antiquities", the most important sources for the events
of this period in Palestine (see Famous People).

Near the village are some remains of the ancient town, which can be seen   Sights
from an observation tower.
There are wide views from the summit of Mount Azmon (548m/1798ft), to
the south of the village.

Zefat

See Safed

Zikhron Ya'aqov   G 3

District: Haifa
Altitude: 50m/165ft
Population: 5000

Situation and characteristics	Zikhron Ya'aqov, founded by Romanian immigrants in 1882 on the southern slopes of Mount Carmel (see entry), 33km/21 miles south of Haifa, is now one of Israel's most important wine-producing towns.

The growing of vines and almond-trees was introduced by Baron Edmond de Rothschild in 1887, and a bottle factory was established at Nahsholim, 9km/6 miles west. The settlers showed their gratitude by naming the village and its synagogue, built in 1885 at the expense of the Rothschild family, after Edmond de Rothschild's father Jacob (James).

Sights

In the main street is Bet Aaronsohn, the house of Aharon Aaronsohn (1876–1917), a distinguished botanist who during the First World War founded an underground organisation to fight the Turkish rulers of Palestine. The house contains a small natural history museum with a large collection of Palestinian plants and a library.

One great tourist attraction in Zikhron Ya'aqov is a conducted tour of the Carmel winery, followed by a wine-tasting.

Surroundings of Zikhron Ya'aqov

Ramat Hanadiv (Rothschild Mausoleum)

On the southern outskirts of the town a road goes off on the right to Ramat Hanadiv ("Hill of the Benefactor"), on which Baron Edmond de Rothschild had expressed the wish to be buried; and in 1954 his remains and those of his wife Ada were brought from France to Israel in an Israeli warship and given a state burial here. The entrance to the luxuriant and carefully tended park containing the Rothschild Mausoleum is on the south side. To the west is a map carved in stone showing all the settlements in Israel founded by Edmond de Rothschild. In the centre of the park, entered through a rectangular courtyard, is his mausoleum, impressive in its simple monumentality.

Binyamina

5km/3 miles south of Zikhron Ya'aqov is the settlement of Binyamina, named after Edmond (Benjamin) de Rothschild, which was founded in 1922 as an offshoot from Zikhron Ya'aqov.

Bet Hananya

2km/1¼ miles west of Binyamina is the moshav of Bet Hananya, founded in 1950. Here there are two Roman aqueducts which carried water to Caesarea. Excavations on Tel Mevorakh, to the north of the village, have shown that there was a Hyksos fortress here (18th–16th c. B.C.). On the eastern slopes of the tell was found a mausoleum of the Roman period, probably belonging to a family from Caesarea. Two sarcophagi from this site are now in the Rockefeller Museum in Jerusalem.

Nahal Hataninim

If we now go west from Bet Hananya to the coast road and turn north we come to the "Crocodile River" (Nahal Hataninim), which was the habitat of crocodiles until around 1900. The area round the mouth of the river is now a nature reserve with a wide range of flora and fauna.

Ma'agan Mikhael

Beyond this, on a sandstone ridge, is the kibbutz of Ma'agan Mikhael, founded in 1949. Stone for Herod's buildings in Caesarea (see entry) was quarried here and water was conveyed to the city in a channel which was partly hewn from the rock and partly carried on aqueducts.

Zippori (Sepphoris) H 3

District: Northern

Situation and characteristics

The moshav of Zippori, founded in 1949, lies 6km/4 miles north-west of Nazareth in an area well supplied with springs. On a hill 1km/¾ mile north are the remains of ancient Zippori (Sepphoris).

The town is not mentioned in the Old Testament. Unlike neighbouring Yodefat (see entry), it took no part in the Jewish rebellion of A.D. 66 and was therefore spared by the Romans. Excavations by American archaeologists brought to light remains of the Roman period, when the town was known as Diocaesarea. The place became of some importance in 135, when, after the failure of the second Jewish rebellion against Rome, the Sanhedrin moved from Yavne (see entry) to Galilee and established its headquarters in Sepphoris and for a time in Bet Shearim (see entry), with Rabbi Judah Hanassi as its supreme spiritual authority. After his death the Sanhedrin moved to Tiberias (see entry).

In the 4th century a converted Jew named Joseph built a church here (as he also did in his native town of Tiberias). The Crusaders found a Christian community here and built a church dedicated to St Anne (the mother of the Virgin, who was believed to have been born here). The crusading army assembled here on July 2nd 1187 before their march to Hittim (see Horns of Hittim), where they suffered an annihilating defeat at the hands of Saladin two days later.

In and around an abandoned village are the remains of a Crusader castle (finely decorated doorway), the foundations of a Byzantine church and a Roman theatre excavated in 1931. St Anne's Church (built 1860) contains a mosaic from an earlier church on the site. From the little fort on the hill (built about 1745) there are fine panoramic views.

To the west are remains of the old water conduit and the large cisterns now known as the "Caverns of Hell".

Practical Information

Accommodation

See Hotels; Youth Hostels; Camping; Pilgrimages; Christian Hospices

Airlines

84 Ha'atzmaut Street, Haifa
Tel. (04) 64 33 71

Klal Center, Jerusalem
Tel. (02) 23 48 55

Sede Dov Airport, Tel Aviv
Tel. (03) 5 41 22 22

11 Frishman Street, Tel Aviv
Tel. (03) 24 02 20

Arkia

80 Ha'atzmaut Street, Haifa
Tel. (04) 37 06 70

12 Hillel Street, Jerusalem
Tel. (02) 23 33 34/5

32 Ben Yehuda Street, Tel Aviv
Tel. (03) 64 12 22

El Al

84 Ha'atzmaut Street, Haifa
Tel. (04) 67 07 56/7

Beit Yoel, Jaffa Road, Jerusalem
Tel. (02) 25 61 11/2

British Airways

7 Azzahra Street, East Jerusalem
Tel. (02) 28 36 02

1 Ben Yehuda Street, Tel Aviv
Tel. (03) 5 10 15 81/5

Airports

Israel's most important airport is Ben-Gurion International Airport at Lod, near Tel Aviv, to which there are direct flights from cities throughout the world.

Ben-Gurion Airport

◄ Yacht harbour, Tel Aviv

Airports

Other airports   For charter flights and domestic traffic the most important airport after Ben-Gurion is Elat. The airport in the centre of the town can handle only small aircraft, and larger ones have hitherto had to use the military airfield at Uvda, 60km/37 miles away.
For domestic flights there are also airfields at Tel Aviv, Jerusalem, Rosh Pinna, Haifa, Beersheba and Sodom.

Departure from Israel   See entry

Security controls   See Departure from Israel

Air Services

See Public Transport

Antiques

Antiques are defined by law as man-made objects fashioned before A.D. 1700. Such items may not be taken out of Israel (whether personally or by mail) without the written approval of the Director of the Antiquities Authority. A 10% duty is levied on the purchase price.
Many so-called antiques offered for sale are fakes. The most reliable shops are those which display the Ministry of Tourism emblem – an elaborate blue bow with two little men carrying a bunch of grapes, surrounded by the legend "Recommended by the Ministry of Tourism".
The Antiquities Authority cannot accept responsibility for the authenticity of antiques.

Information:
The Antiquities Authority
Rockefeller Museum, P.O. Box 586, 91004 Jerusalem
Tel. (02) 29 26 27 and 29 26 07

Beaches

Israel is not a country to come to for a bathing holiday alone, except perhaps in winter, since it lacks the endless sandy beaches of other Mediterranean countries; but for visitors who come to Israel for other reasons a few days in one of the coastal resorts is an agreeable addition to their trip. There are numerous resorts along Israel's Mediterranean coast; and Elat, at the northern tip of the Red Sea, attracts many holidaymakers looking for the sun. There are also beaches on the Dead Sea, though they are more likely to appeal to visitors "taking a cure" than to ordinary holidaymakers (see Spas).
The principal bathing beaches in Israel are briefly described below, going from north to south.

Akhziv   Akhziv, to the north of Nahariya, has a long and well kept sandy beach. Adjoining the beach is a National Park, with extensive areas of grass, picnic places and restaurants. There is no place of any size here, but a Club Méditerranée holiday village.

Nahariya   A long, broad sandy beach extends north and south of Nahariya. It is one of the most beautiful in Israel, but sometimes suffers from oil pollution near the town. There is also a swimming pool on the beach.

Shave Zion   Within the territory of the moshav of Shave Zion is a beautiful beach, with showers, changing cabins and refreshment stalls.

The beautiful beach of Ashqelon

Argaman Beach ("Purple Beach"), to the south of Akko, draws large numbers of Israeli and foreign visitors. The beach is lined with large hotels.   Akko

The beach at the west end of Haifa, lying close to the city and the port, is not particularly attractive.   Haifa

The beautiful beach on the moshav of Dor is comparatively quiet and unfrequented. Offshore are four small islands, now nature reserves. This is a popular diving area, particularly with underwater archaeologists.   Dor

There is an attractive beach to the north of the archaeological site at the aqueduct. It is popular with wind-surfers, since wind conditions here are usually ideal.   Caesarea

Netanya has become one of the most popular holiday resorts in Israel thanks to its beautiful long sandy beach. The stretch of beach in the centre of the town is well kept but during the season tends to be crowded. The beaches to north and south of the centre are quieter, but are frequently not particularly clean.   Netanya

The Herzliya beaches are popular with Israelis, and are particularly busy on Fridays and Saturdays.   Herzliya

The beach of Tel Aviv is always the scene of lively activity: it is a place to see and be seen. For a city beach it is astonishingly clean. The beach is lined by large hotels belonging to international chains.   Tel Aviv

There are sandy beaches north and south of Ashqelon, among the finest of which is the beach by the archaeological site (now a National Park). There are extensive areas of grass, sanitary facilities, picnic areas and restaurants.   Ashqelon

Solitude on the beach at Caesarea . . .   *. . . and rather more people at Elat*

Elat

Elat's guaranteed sunshine draws thousands of holidaymakers to this Red Sea resort, particularly in winter. The North Beach close to the town is shingly and usually overcrowded. More attractive is the Coral Beach to the south of the town (now a nature reserve). The waters off this beach of fine sand are a happy hunting ground for snorkellers and scuba divers.

Nude Bathing

Nude bathing is frowned on in Israel, and topless bathing is very much the exception, both in hotel pools and on the beach. Only at Elat can occasional visitors be seen sunbathing without their bikini top.

Breakdown Assistance

Road patrols

The patrols of the Automobile and Touring Club of Israel (MEMSI) operate throughout Israel from 8am to 5pm. Towing for a distance of up to 25km/15 miles is free; for assistance after 5pm there is a charge.
The emergency call number is (03) 62 29 61/2.

Addresses of Automobile Club

Head office:
Automobile and Touring Club of Israel (MEMSI)
19 Petah Tiqwa Street
Tel Aviv
Tel. (03) 62 29 61/4

Branch offices:

Uneco House, Room 35
Beersheba
Tel. (057) 3 62 64

c/o Ya'alat, New Shopping Centre
Elat
Tel. (059) 7 21 66

1 Palmer's Gate
Haifa
Tel. (04) 66 18 79

31 King George Street
Jerusalem
Tel. (02) 24 48 28

6 Shmuel Hanatziv Street
Netanya
Tel. (053) 3 13 43

23 Yohanan Ben Zakkai Street
Tiberias
Tel. (06) 79 07 15

Business Hours

Banks are open Sun., Tues. and Thur. 8.30am–12.30pm and 4–7 or 7.30pm, Mon. and Wed. 8.30am–12.30pm, Fri. 8.30am–noon.
Some banks have branches in the larger hotels which also operate outside normal banking hours. | Banks

Chemists' shops are open Sun.–Thur. 9am–1pm and 4–7pm, Fri. 9.30am–2pm. Outside these hours some chemists' shops are open on a rota basis: see Chemists. | Chemists

Most museums and archaeological sites are open Sun.–Thur. from 9 or 10am to 4 or 5pm. There are frequently restricted opening hours on Friday and Saturday. | Museums and archaeological sites

Head post offices are open Sun.–Tues. and Thur. 8am–6pm, branch offices 8am–12.30pm and 3.30–6pm; Wed. 8am–1.30pm and Fri. 8am to 1 or 2pm. | Post offices

Petrol stations are usually open all day and in the evening. It is sometimes difficult to get petrol on Friday afternoons and Saturdays, when there are likely to be only a few petrol stations open on main roads. | Petrol stations

Most restaurants are open at midday and in the evening, many remaining open until 11pm or midnight. Some restaurants are closed from midday on Friday until Saturday evening. | Restaurants

The usual opening hours for shops are 8am–1pm and 4–7pm. Small food-shops open even earlier in the morning, and department stores stay open all day, with no break at lunchtime.
Jewish shops open on Fridays (and on the day before feast days) from 8.30am to 1pm and thereafter remain closed until Sunday morning. Christian shops are closed on Sundays, Muslim ones on Fridays.
Since the outbreak of the *intifada* Arab shops in the occupied areas and in East Jerusalem tend to stay open only until noon. | Shops

Buses

See Public Transport

Calendars

The starting-point of Jewish chronology is the creation of the world, which is dated to 3761 b.c. The Hebrew calendar is based on a lunar year of 353, | Hebrew calendar

354 or 355 days. Since the lunar year is shorter than the solar year, there are seven intercalary years with a thirteenth month of thirty days in each cycle of nineteen years, thus bringing the lunar year into line with the solar year.

Months of the Hebrew calendar		
	Tishri	September/October
	Heshvan	October/November
	Kislev	November/December
	Tevet	December/January
	Shevat	January/February
	Adar	February/March
	Nisan	March/April
	Iyyar	April/May
	Sivan	May/June
	Tammuz	June/July
	Av	July/August
	Elul	August/September

Days of week		
	Yom rishón	Sunday
	Yom shení	Monday
	Yom shlishí	Tuesday
	Yom revií	Wednesday
	Yom hamishí	Thursday
	Yom shishí	Friday
	Shabát	Saturday

Muslim calendar

The starting-point of Muslim chronology is the Hegira, Mohammed's flight from Mecca to Medina on July 15th 622. The year is lunar, with months of 30 and 29 days. A normal year has 354 days, an intercalary or "leap" year 355 days.

Public holidays

See entry

Camping and Caravanning

Official camping sites in Israel offer full sanitary facilities, electric power, restaurants and/or food shops, telephones, postal services, first aid, shaded picnic and camp-fire areas, on-site or nearby swimming and round-the-clock security.

Tents, cabins, fully equipped caravans and small flats with showers, as well as camping equipment can be hired at camping sites.

Almost all camping sites are affiliated to the Israel Chalets and Camping Union, P.O. Box 53, 22100 Nahariya, tel. (04) 92 53 92. Information can also be obtained from Israel Government Tourist Offices or tourist information offices in Israel (see Information).

All-in packages

The Chalets and Camping Union offers "all-in" packages covering accommodation and transport, with the choice between three types of accommodation (tents, caravans and chalets) and two forms of transport (hired car or unlimited bus travel).

Car Rental

To rent a car it is necessary only to produce a national driving licence. The hirer must be over 21 and have driven for at least a year.

Car rental agencies are usually closed on Friday afternoons and Saturdays, except in Nazareth and East Jerusalem; car rental desks at Ben-Gurion Airport are open 24 hours a day.

Cars can be booked before leaving home through local offices of the main international hire companies.

Camping Sites

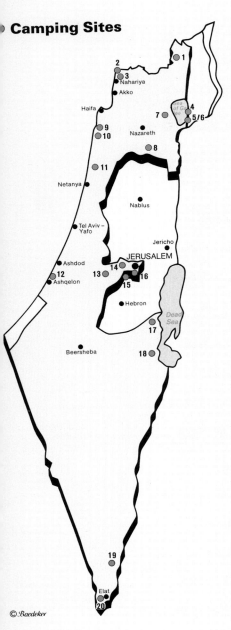

1 Tal
at Qiryat Shemona

2 Lehmann
in moshav of Lehmann

3 Akhziv
in Akhziv (5km/3 miles north
of Nahariya)

4 En Gev
in kibbutz of En Gev

5 Ha'on
in kibbutz of Ha'on (7km/4½
miles south of En Gev)

6 Ma'agan
in kibbutz of Ma'agan

7 Kefar Hittim
in moshav of Kefar Hittim

8 Harod
at Gidona

9 Dor
at kibbutz of Hof Dor

10 Newe Yam
in kibbutz of Newe Yam

11 Biton Aharon
at Netanya

12 Ashqelon
in Ashqelon

13 En Hemed
Bet Neqofa, Hare Yehuda
(west of Jerusalem)

14 Bet Zayit
in moshav of Bet Zayit

15 Mevo Betar
south-west of Jerusalem

16 Ramat Rahel
in kibbutz of Ramat Rahel

17 En Gedi
in kibbutz of En Gedi

18 Newe Zohar
at Arad

19 Ye'elim (Yotvata)
20km/12½ miles north of Elat

20 Elat
Sun Bay, on Gulf of Aqaba

Car Rental

Avis

Beersheba
11 Hanesim Street, tel. (057) 7 17 77

Elat
Elat Airport, tel. (059) 7 31 64

Haifa
28 Nathanson Street, tel. (04) 67 46 88

Jerusalem
22 King David Street, tel. (02) 24 90 01
19 Saladin Street (East Jerusalem), tel. (02) 28 10 20

Nazareth
6 Paul VI Street, tel. (06) 56 54 75

Netanya
1 Ussishkin Street, tel. (053) 33 16 19

Tel Aviv
12 Hamasger Street, tel. (03) 37 32 44
Ben-Gurion Airport, tel. (03) 9 71 10 80

Tiberias
Nahar Hayarden Hotel, tel. (06) 70 01 99

Budget

Beersheba
1 Ha'atzmaut Street, tel. (057) 7 66 81

Elat
Etzion Hotel, tel. (059) 7 61 39
King Solomon Palace Hotel, tel. (059) 7 91 11

Haifa
145 Jaffa Street, tel. (04) 53 85 58

Jerusalem
14 King David Street, tel. (02) 24 89 91

Netanya
2 Gad Makhnes Street, tel. (053) 33 06 18

Tel Aviv
99 Hayarkon Street, tel. (03) 24 52 33
Ben-Gurion Airport, tel. (03) 9 71 15 04

Tiberias
3 Elhadeff Street, tel. (06) 79 23 93

Europcar
(InterRent)

Beersheba
Hebron Road, tel. (057) 3 61 66

Elat
Shalom Center, tel. (059) 7 40 14

Haifa
3 Allenby Street, tel. (04) 67 13 48

Jerusalem
8 King David Street, tel. (02) 24 84 64

Nazareth
Hatzafon Garage, Afula Road, tel. (06) 57 20 46

Netanya
4 King David Street, tel. (053) 61 01 62

Tel Aviv
75 Hayarkon Street, tel. (03) 66 28 66
Ben-Gurion Airport, tel. (03) 9 72 10 97

Tiberias
Elhadeff Street, tel. (06) 72 27 77

Beersheba
5A Ben Zvi Street, tel. (057) 7 38 78

Hertz

Elat
HaTmarim Boulevard, tel. (059) 7 50 50

Haifa
90 Ha'atzmaut Street, tel. (04) 53 12 34

Jerusalem
18 King David Street, tel. (02) 23 13 51

Netanya
8 Ha'atzmaut Square, tel. (053) 2 88 90

Tel Aviv
88 Hahashomniam Street, tel. (03) 5 62 21 21
Ben-Gurion Airport, tel. (03) 9 71 17 07

Tiberias
Jordan River Hotel, HaBannim Street, tel. (06) 79 18 22

Chemists

Sun.–Thu. 9am–1pm and 4–7pm, Fri. 9.30am–2pm.

Opening hours

A list of chemists' shops open on a rota basis outside normal hours is
published in the press, and can also be obtained in hotels and from Magen
David Adom (Red Star of David, the Israeli equivalent of the Red Cross).

Out-of-hours
service

Consulates

See Diplomatic and Consular Offices

Credit Cards

See Currency

Currency

The unit of currency is the New Israeli Shekel (NIS), which is made up of 100
agorot. There are banknotes for 5, 10, 20, 50 and 100 shekels and coins in
denominations of 1, 5 and 10 agorot and ½ and 1 shekel.

The exchange rate of the shekel is subject to considerable fluctuations. The
current rate (Jan. 1995) is about 4.50 shekels to the £ sterling and 3 shekels

Exchange rates

Currency

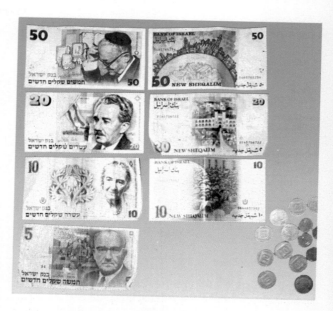

Israeli money

to the US dollar. The exchange rate is likely to be more favourable within Israel than outside the country, though rates vary from bank to bank.

Changing money

As in other countries with a weak currency, it is preferable to change money in the country itself, in small quantities at a time.

Money can be changed only in banks (which frequently have branches in the larger hotels). Shekels can be changed back up to a maximum value of US $100, or to a higher amount on production of exchange receipts.

Payment in foreign currency

Goods and services can often be paid for in foreign currency. (Many shops, indeed, price their goods not in shekels but in dollars.) There is, however, no obligation on shops, etc., to accept foreign currency. Since change is usually given in shekels it is advisable to have plenty of small notes. Where hotel, airline, car rental and other bills are paid in foreign currency no value-added tax (see entry) is payable.

Import and export of currency

There are no restrictions on the import or export of foreign currency. There is no limit on the amount of Israeli currency that can be brought in, but it can be exported only by arrangement with a bank.

Eurocheques

Eurocheques are accepted up to a maxim of 350 shekels per cheque. Holders of Eurocheque cards (and of Eurocards and Mastercards) can obtain money round the clock from the automatic tills at 150 branches of the Hapoalim Bank.

Credit cards

Banks, the larger hotels, good restaurants and many shops accept most international credit cards.

Loss of cards

The loss of Eurocheques, Eurocheque cards or credit cards should be reported at once by telephone to the issuing authority, with confirmation in writing, so that payment can be blocked.

Customs Regulations

The dual-channel customs clearance system is in operation at Israeli airports and at the Rafiah terminal. Visitors with no goods to declare may pass through the green channel on leaving the arrivals hall. Persons bringing in other items, even if they are exempt from duty, must use the red channel and declare them.

In the green channel the following items need not be declared: personal clothing and toilet articles; up to 1 litre of spirits and 2 litres of wine (persons over 17 only); up to ¼ litre of alcoholic perfumes like eau de cologne; up to 250 grams of tobacco or 250 cigarettes (persons over 17 only); and gifts up to a value of US $125. In addition the following items may be taken in duty-free if portable and appreciably used: typewriter, still and ciné cameras (but not video cameras, which must be declared), radio, tape recorder, binoculars, personal jewellery, musical instruments, gramophone, a pram, camping or sports equipment, bicycle (without auxiliary motor) and similar travellers' effects.

In the red channel the following items must be declared and the owners must put down a deposit for duties and taxes, which will be refunded when the items are taken out of Israel on departure: video equipment, personal computer, portable tools up to a value of $1650, boat, caravan trailer, diving equipment. Deposits may be paid by bank draft payable to the Collector of Customs or by credit card (Visa, Mastercard/Eurocard or Diners' Club).

Fresh meat or fruit, narcotics, pornographic literature, publications from Arab countries, firearms and other weapons may not be taken into Israel. *Prohibited items*

Visitors may bring in a motor vehicle for personal use or buy one in Israel tax-free provided they undertake to take it out on leaving the country within a year of its entry or purchase. To obtain this exemption they should present a foreign driving licence and an insurance certificate or "green card" valid in Israel. *Motor vehicles*

Cycling

See Sport

Departure from Israel

Visitors should check their flight reservations through a travel agency or the airline at least 72 hours before departure to make sure that there has been no change. For information about last-minute changes telephone (03) 9 71 24 84. Passengers must check in at Ben-Gurion Airport two hours before departure. *By air*

Passengers flying with El Al can check in their luggage, pay the airport tax and get their boarding cards at El Al offices on the day before departure, and need then arrive at Ben-Gurion Airport only an hour and a half before departure.

El Al check-in offices:

Jerusalem
49 Yirmiyahu Street, tel. (02) 38 31 66
Open: Sun.–Thur. 4–11pm, Sat. from an hour after sunset

Tel Aviv
Railway Station, Arlosorov Street, tel. (03) 21 71 98
Open: Sun.–Thur. 4–11.30pm

Haifa
80 Ha'atzmaut Street, tel. (04) 67 01 70
Open: Sun.–Thur. 6.30–10pm

Security
checks

On leaving Israel, as on entering it, visitors are subject to a thorough check of their person and their luggage (remember to take films out of cameras before reaching the security control!). As a rule all items of luggage are opened and thoroughly examined, and passengers are asked about where they stayed in Israel, whether they have met relatives or acquaintances, whether they have been given any packages or parcels to carry, and so on.

Transfer
to airport

In Jerusalem the Nesher Sherut Taxi Service (21 King George Street, tel. (02) 22 72 27 and 23 12 31) and the Tal Limousine Service (tel. (02) 24 58 45) run taxi services to Ben-Gurion Airport round the clock at fixed rates. Egged Buses run a shuttle service to the airport from the Central Bus Station every 20 minutes from 6.15am to 8pm.

In Tel Aviv there are buses from the railway station to the airport every half hour, and a shuttle bus service (No. 222) in run by United Tours from various pick-up points hourly from 4am to midnight.

By road

Visitors can travel by road to either Egypt or Jordan. For frontier crossing points and their opening times see Getting to Israel.
Egged Buses run a service to Cairo daily except Saturdays, departing from the Central Bus Station in Jerusalem. Travellers from Israel to Egypt must apply for a visa to the Egyptian Embassy in Tel Aviv (54 Basel Street, tel. (03) 22 41 51) – though it is simpler to get the visa before leaving home. (For visits to the Sinai peninsula a visa valid for seven days can be obtained at the frontier.)
Sherut (shared) taxis run from the Damascus Gate in Jerusalem to the Allenby Bridge, the frontier crossing point into Jordan. Visitors must have a Jordanian visa and a permit from the Jordanian authorities allowing them to cross the bridge, and must pay an entry tax in the form of fiscal stamps (obtainable in Israeli post offices and at the frontier).

Diplomatic and Consular Offices

Israeli Embassies

United Kingdom
2 Palace Green
London W8
Tel. (0171) 937 8050

United States
3514 International Drive
Washington DC 20008
Tel. (202) 364 5500

Canada
410 Laurier Avenue, Suite 601
Ottawa, Ontario K1R 7I3
Tel. (613) 237 6450

Embassies and Consulates in Israel

United Kingdom
Embassy:
192 Hayarkon Street
63405 Tel Aviv
Tel. (03) 24 91 71/8

Consulates:

Migdalor Building (6th floor)
1 Ben Yehuda Street, Tel Aviv
Tel. (03) 6 38 01

14 Tsofit Villas
Elat
Tel. (059) 7 23 44 and 7 49 08

Embassy: United States
71 Hayarkon Street
63903 Tel Aviv
Tel. (03) 65 43 38

220 Hayarkon Street   Canada
63405 Tel Aviv
Tel. (03) 22 81 22/6

Distances

See Motoring in Israel

Diving

See Sport

Dress

For the Israeli summer, which lasts around nine months, light clothing
(cotton or other natural fibres) is required, with something warmer for the
evening in the inland regions. Protection against the strong sun (hat,
sun-glasses) is essential. Stout footwear is advisable for site visits and
sightseeing in towns. In winter warmer clothing and protection against rain
are required except at Elat and in the Dead Sea area, where summer
clothing can still be worn.
Israelis are fairly casual dressers. Men need to wear a jacket and tie only on
ceremonial or business occasions. Visitors should be more careful in their
dress, however, when visiting holy places. Shorts are better avoided, and
women should make sure that their arms and shoulders are covered; at
some places it is possible to hire a scarf or other covering.

Electricity

The power supply in Israel is 220 volts AC. Since most power sockets are for
three-pin plugs a suitable adapter for razors, etc., should be taken or can be
obtained in Israel.

Embassies

See Diplomatic and Consular Offices

Emergencies

In the larger towns an ambulance can be called by dialling 101, the number   Ambulance
of Magen David Adom (Red Star of David), the Israeli equivalent of the Red

Cross, which runs an ambulance service, first aid stations and the Israeli blood bank.
The main Magen David Adom first aid station in Jerusalem is at 7 Ha-Mem Gimel Street in the Romema district. The station also gives emergency treatment. It is open on Fridays and the day before feast days from 4 to 7pm and on Saturdays and public holidays from 10am to 1pm and 3 to 6pm.

Dental emergencies

A dental emergency service is provided in Tel Aviv at 25 Achimeir Street, Ramat Aviv Gimmel (tel. (03) 42 58 32), Sunday to Friday 10am–1pm and 4.30–11pm, Saturdays and public holidays 6–11pm.

Fire

Dial 102.

Police

Dial 100

Breakdown assistance

See entry

Events

Information

Brochures listing events in the current week (e.g. "Hello Israel", "This Week in Israel", "Your Jerusalem", "Tel Aviv Today") can be obtained in hotels and at tourist information offices (see Information). Travel agencies also distribute leaflets about local events.

Since the Jewish and Muslim calendars are based on the phases of the moon and many of the Christian festivals are movable feasts, only approximate dates can be given for the events listed below.

January/February

Country-wide:
Tu B'Shevat, the "New Year of the Trees", when Jews eat the fruit of fifteen different trees. There are tree-planting ceremonies all over the country, particularly in the John F. Kennedy Peace Forest, at the Tombs of the Sanhedrin in Jerusalem and in the Martyrs' Forest in the Judaean Hills.

February/March

Country-wide:
Purim, the Feast of Lots, commemorating the deliverance of the Jews of Persia from the edict of destruction by Haman, when Esther, the Jewish wife of Xerxes I, intervened to prevent the planned persecution. In many towns throughout Israel there are colourful parades and other celebrations; children dress up and there is much singing and dancing and giving of presents.
In Ashkenazi communities plays are performed in Yiddish, usually burlesque one-act pieces on Biblical themes.

March/April

Akko:
Pesach. On the occasion of the Passover, which commemorates the night before the Israelites' departure from Egypt, there are concerts by Israeli choirs in the Crusader castle.

En Gev:
Pesach. Celebration of the Passover in the kibbutz of En Gev, with music, dancing and other entertainments.

Tel Aviv–Jaffa:
Pesach. Celebration of the Passover, with singing by Israeli and international choirs against the picturesque backdrop of the old harbour of Jaffa.

Jerusalem:
Palm Sunday, with a splendid procession from the village of Bethphage on the Mount of Olives to the Church of the Holy Sepulchre.

Jerusalem:
Easter, celebrated separately by the various Christian churches, which have different methods for calculating the date of Easter. The most spectacular celebrations are those of the Armenian and Greek Orthodox churches, with the lighting of the "holy fire" in the Church of the Holy Sepulchre.

Jerusalem:
International Book Fair.

Country-wide:
Holocaust Day, a memorial day for the martyrs and heroes of the Holocaust. The date for this commemoration was fixed in 1951 as the 27th day of the Jewish month of Nisan. In many towns throughout Israel sirens sound to mark the beginning of a few minutes of silent remembrance: traffic comes to a halt and work stops in offices, workshops and shops.

Netanya: April/May
Spring Festival

Jerusalem, Tel Aviv, Haifa:
Independence Day (5th day of the month of Iyyar). The celebrations of the foundation of the state of Israel on May 14th 1948 begin on the previous day with a rally at the tomb of Theodor Herzl in Jerusalem. On the day itself there are firework displays and open-air concerts in the large towns.

Jerusalem and elsewhere: May/June
Israel Festival. This is the cultural high point of Israel's year, centred particularly in Jerusalem: three weeks of concerts, theatre and ballet, with the participation of international artistes.

Jerusalem:
International Film Festival in the Cinémathèque, with contributions from forty countries.

Zemach (Sea of Galilee):
Shavuot, the festival of the First Fruits at the end of the fifty days of mourning after the Passover. At Zemach, at the south end of the Sea of Galilee, there is a folk dancing festival in which both professionals and amateurs take part.

Tiberias: July
Summer Festival, with musical, dancing and dramatic performances in the old town and at various places on the shores of the Sea of Galilee.

Netanya and Haifa:
International Folklore Festival.

Elat: July/August
Jazz Festival, with groups from many countries.

Netanya:
"Summer Nights" in the main square.

Tel Aviv–Jaffa:
"Jaffa Nights", with concerts and dramatic performances against the picturesque backdrop of the old harbour of Jaffa.

Akko: August/September
Festival of Alternative Theatre in the Crusader castle.

Country-wide: September/
Rosh Hashanah, the Jewish New Year (celebrated on the 1st and 2nd days   October
of the month of Tishri) and the first of the ten days of fasting at the

beginning of the year. During these ten days visitors will frequently hear the sound of rams' horns (shofars), the call to fasting and reflection. Many Jews wear white garments as a symbol of the transitoriness of man and of trust in God. At the Pool of Siloam in Jerusalem the ceremony of Tashlih, the symbolic casting of sins into the water, is performed.

Country-wide:
Sukkot (Succoth) and Simhat Tora. During the seven days of the Feast of Tabernacles (Sukkot, Succoth) Jews build huts in their gardens, in court-yards or on balconies in which they take their meals; orthodox Jews also sleep in the huts. At the end of the Feast of Tabernacles is the Rejoicing of the Torah (Simhat Tora), when in many towns there are processions carry-ing the Torah.

December	Sea of Galilee: International Marathon.
December/ January	Christmas, celebrated by Catholics and Protestants on December 24th and 25th, by the Orthodox on January 7th and by the Armenians on January 19th. There is little sign of a Christmas atmosphere in Jerusalem. In the Church of the Nativity in Bethlehem there is a midnight mass on Christmas Eve, relayed to the crowd in Manger Square by loudspeakers.

Food and Drink

Israel has no national cuisine: the dishes on the Israeli menu are either western European or Arab. The range is wide, from Russian borshch to American hamburgers, from pizza to German sausages.

Kosher

Kosher food is food prepared in accordance with Jewish dietary laws. The original reason for the laws was a concern with hygiene. No kosher restau-rant serves the meat of carnivorous animals, and certain species of fish are also banned (for example eels, on the ground that they are a kind of fish without scales). Dairy products, including cream and cheese, may not be served along with meat. A period of at least five hours must be allowed to pass between eating meat and drinking a dairy product.
The common idea that kosher food is tasteless can be disproved by experi-ment, for there are many excellent and tasty kosher dishes.

Meals

Breakfast in Israel is traditionally a substantial meal, and in most of the better hotels guests will be confronted by a substantial buffet, with fresh fruit and vegetables, various kinds of cheese, small pieces of fish, eggs, curds and an assortment of jams and preserves.
For lunch and dinner hotels usually serve three or four courses. The main course is usually fish or meat, cooked in accordance with Jewish dietary prescriptions.

Israeli
specialities

Baklava	Sweet puff pastry with honey and nuts, served as a dessert and also sold from stalls in the streets.
Blintzes	Pancakes with a sweet cheese filling.
Burekas	Flaky pastries filled with cheese, potatoes or spinach.
Cholent	A stew of beans, potatoes and fat meat prepared on Friday, simmered overnight and eaten on the Sabbath.
Felafel	A ball of ground chick peas and spices. Many street stalls sell felafel on slices of pitta bread along with salad – an ideal mid-morning or mid-afternoon snack.

A tempting display of olives

Gefilte fish	Small pieces of fish rolled into balls along with onions, matzo meal, eggs and spices and then boiled, fried or poached in fish bouillon.
Gilderne yoch	Chicken soup, traditionally eaten on the Sabbath.
Hallah	A traditional type of twisted loaf eaten on the Sabbath.
Hamentashen	Small triangular pastries with a walnut, poppy seed or apple filling. There are other variants.
Holishkes	Minced beef wrapped in cabbage leaves and braised in a sweet-sour sauce. Traditionally eaten on the Feast of Tabernacles.
Humus	Boiled chick peas puréed with garlic, oil and lemon juice. Often served with pitta bread.
Kebab	Small pieces of beef or mutton, well spiced and grilled on the spit.
Kunafa	A pastry with syrup, almonds, pistachios and walnuts.
Latkes	Potato fritters, often served with cinnamon sugar, apple sauce and/or sour cream. Traditionally eaten on the Feast of Lights (Hanukkah).
Mahallebi	Round-grain rice with attar of roses, sugar and nuts.
Mazza	Meze: a plate of hors d'oeuvres, usually including humus, aubergine salad, vine leaves, olives, etc.

St Peter's fish: a speciality of the Sea of Galilee

Of sum-sum	Chicken tossed in sesame seed and cooked in oil.
Pitta	A flat rounded, slightly leavened bread.
Seniya	Beef or lamb baked in the oven with tahina.
Shashlik	Grilled slices of beef or lamb.
Tahina	A paste made from sesame seeds with oil, lemon juice and garlic.

Beverages

In the past the Israelis drank very little mineral water, but this now seems to be changing. Two locally produced brands are Eden and Memi, which come from two of the Jordan's source springs in the north of the country. They are both still, with a slight mineral content. Most of the other soft drinks found in western Europe are also available in Israel; for almost all of them there is a "light version".
Freshly pressed fruit juices are also widely available.

Coffee, tea

The most popular drinks in Israel are coffee and tea. Many Israelis prefer their tea black (and usually fairly weak), but it is also served with lemon or milk. A request for coffee will normally produce Turkish coffee, but instant coffee (Nescafé) is also available. In the better restaurants and cafés it is possible also to get an espresso or a cappuccino.

Alcohol

In Israel there is no breath-testing of motorists – not because Israelis are better drivers but because practically no alcohol is drunk in Israel. On social occasions the party may begin with a tiny glass of brandy, but that concludes the consumption of alcohol for the evening.
There are in fact excellent Israeli wines. The main wine-growing areas are Rishon LeZion, between Tel Aviv and Jerusalem, and round Zikhron Ya'aqov and Beersheba. The vines are mostly French black grapes (Carignan

and Alicante-Grenache); the main types of white grapes are Muscat, Semillon and Clairette.
Israeli beers are light and sweet. The most popular brand is Maccabee.

See entry   Restaurants

Frontier Crossings

See Getting to Israel

Getting to Israel

The great majority of visitors to Israel go by air. There are direct flights to   By air
Ben-Gurion Airport, Tel Aviv, from London Heathrow (flying time 4½
hours), and many flights from cities in North America – some direct, some
via London or Amsterdam but without a change of aircraft, others via Paris
(flying time from New York 9–11 hours direct, 14–15 hours with change in
Paris). In addition to the normal scheduled fares the airlines offer a variety
of economy, off-peak, excursion and APEX rates. Even cheaper are the
charter flights to Tel Aviv, and also to Elat on the Red Sea from many
European cities.
For those who want to combine a holiday in Egypt with a visit to Israel there
are flights from Cairo by El Al and the Egyptian airline Air Sinai.

The Arkadia and Stability Lines run car ferry services once or twice weekly   By sea
between Piraeus (Greece) and Haifa. Information in United Kingdom: Via-
mare Travel Ltd, 33 Mapesbury Rd, London NW2 4HT, tel. (0181) 452 8231.

There are the following frontier crossing points between Egypt and Israel   By road
(private cars only, not rented cars):

Nizzana, 60km/37 miles west of Beersheba (the main crossing point)
Open: daily 8am–4pm

Rafiah, 50km/31 miles south-west of Ashqelon
Open: daily 9am–5pm

Netafim (crossing from Ras en-Naqb International Airport to Elat)
Open: daily round the clock

Taba (immediately south of Elat)
Open: daily round the clock

The frontier crossing point between Jordan and Israel is the Allenby
Bridge, 40km/25 miles east of Jerusalem.
Open on the Israeli side: Sun.–Thur. 8am–1pm, Fri. 8–11am; closed on
Saturdays and Jewish public holidays.
Private cars, motorcycles and bicycles are not allowed over the bridge. Film
must be removed from cameras.

Golf

See Sport

Help for the Disabled

In Britain the main sources of information and advice on travel by the   Information
disabled are the Royal Association for Disability and Rehabilitation

Hotels

(RADAR), 25 Mortimer Street, London W1N 8AB, tel. (0171) 637 5400; the Spinal Injuries Association, 76 St James's Lane, London N10 3DF, tel. (0181) 444 2121; and Mobility International, 62 Union Street, London SE1, tel. (0171) 403 5688.

Useful publications

"Holiday and Travel Abroad – A Guide for Disabled People", published by RADAR.

"The World Wheelchair Traveller", published by the AA for the Spinal Injuries Association.

"Low Cost Travel Tips for People Using Wheelchairs", published by Mobility International.

The AA also publishes a "Guide for the Disabled Traveller" (free to members).

Major sources of information in the United States are Louise Weiss's "Access to the World: A Travel Guide for the Handicapped" (available from Facts on File, 460 Park Avenue South, New York NY 10016) and the Society for the Advancement of Travel by the Handicapped, 26 Court Street, Penthouse Suite, Brooklyn NY 11242.

Group travel

For people with a severe physical disability it is advisable to travel in a group. The Israeli Government Tourist Office can supply information about tour operators who run tours for the disabled.

Hotels

The following hotels are suitable for wheelchair users: the Sheraton Plaza, Sonesta, Ariel and Eyal Hotels in Jerusalem; the Sinai, Tal, Sheraton and Moriah Plaza in Tel Aviv; the Dan Panorama Hotel in Haifa; the Moon Valley, Edomit, Shulamit Gardens, Americana, Queen of Sheba, Neptune, King Solomon's Palace, Lagoona, Sport and Moriah Hotels in Elat; and the Seasons, Sironit and Blue Bay Hotels in Netanya. (For addresses, see Hotels.) There are also many hotels in the Dead Sea spas and in Tiberias, as well as many kibbutz hotels, with facilities for disabled people.

Ben-Gurion Airport

The facilities for disabled passengers at Ben-Gurion Airport have been improved (lower payphones, wider entrances to shops, ramps for wheelchairs, etc.). There is also a special lift to facilitate entry to and exit from aircraft by wheelchair users.

Hotels

Tariffs

Tariffs vary according to season; they are highest round Christmas and Easter, at the Jewish New Year and in the summer months. In general it is cheaper to book a holiday in advance through a tour operator. Booked locally, a double room with breakfast in a luxury hotel is likely to cost up to US $250 a night, in a good-class hotel up to $150, in a middle-range hotel up to $100. The address and telephone number of each hotel is followed by the number of rooms (r.). SP = swimming pool; K = kosher cuisine.

Akhziv

Club Méditerranée, tel. (04) 92 32 41, 250 r., SP

Akko

Argaman, Acre Beach, tel. (04) 91 66 91, 75 r., SP, K
Palm Beach, Acre Beach, tel. (04) 81 58 15, 120 r., SP, K

Arad

Arad, 6 Hapalmach Street, tel. (057) 95 70 40, 51 r., K
Margoa, Moav Street, tel. (057) 95 70 14, 160 r., SP, K
Nof Arad, Moav Street, tel. (057) 95 70 56, 117 r., SP, K

Ashdod

Miami, 12 Nordau Street, tel. (08) 52 20 85, 38 r., K
Orly, Nordau Street, tel. (055) 3 15 49, 29 r., SP, K

Club Ashqelon, north of the National Park, tel. (051) 3 67 33, 196 r., SP
Samson's Gardens, 38 Hatamar Street, tel. (051) 3 66 41, 22 r., K
Shulamit Gardens, 11 Hatayassim Street, tel. (051) 71 12 61, 108 r., SP, K

Ashqelon

Arava, 37 Hahistadrut Street, tel. (057) 7 87 92, 27 r., K
Aviv, 40 Mordechai Hageta'ot Street, tel. (057) 7 80 59, 22 r., K
Desert Inn, Touviahu Road, tel. (057) 42 49 22, 160 r., SP, K
Hanegev, 26 Ha'atzmaut Street, tel. (057) 7 70 26, 13 r., K

Beersheba

Bethlehem Star, Al Baten Street, tel. (02) 74 32 49, 54 r.

Bethlehem

Dan Caesarea Golf Hotel, tel. (06) 36 22 66, 116 r., SP, K

Caesarea

Guest Farm Vered Hagalil, tel. (06) 93 57 85, 10 r., SP

Chorazin

See En Boqeq

Dead Sea

Americana, North Beach, tel. (07) 33 37 77, 107 r., SP, K
Bel Hotel, North Beach, tel. (07) 37 61 21, 84 r., K
Caesar, North Beach, tel. (07) 33 31 11, 240 r., SP, K
Carlton Coral Sea, Coral Beach, tel. (07) 33 35 55, 143 r., SP, K
Dalia, North Beach, tel. (07) 33 40 04, 52 r., K
Edomit, Tourist Center, tel. (07) 37 95 11, 85 r., SP, K
Etzion, Hatmarim Street, tel. (07) 37 41 31, 91 r., SP, K
Galei Elat, North Beach, tel. (07) 33 42 22, 107 r., SP, K
King Solomon's Palace, North Beach, tel. (07) 33 41 11, 403 r., SP, K
Lagoona, North Beach, tel. (07) 33 36 66, 256 r., SP, K
Moon Valley, North Beach, tel. (07) 33 38 88, 178 r., SP, K
Moriah Plaza Elat, North Beach, tel. (07) 33 21 11, 165 r., SP, K
Neptune, North Beach, tel. (07) 33 43 33, 273 r., SP, K
Queen of Sheba, North Beach, tel. (07) 33 41 21, 95 r., SP, K

Elat

King Solomon Hotel, Elat

Hotels

Red Rock, North Beach, tel. (07) 37 31 71, 119 r., SP, K
Shulamit Gardens, North Beach, tel. (07) 33 39 99, 224 r., SP, K
Sport, North Beach, tel. (07) 33 33 33, 225 r., SP, K
St Tropez Beach, North Beach, tel. (07) 37 61 11, 128 r., SP, K

En Boqeq

En Boqeq, tel. (057) 58 43 31, 105 r., SP, K
Galei Zohar, tel. (057) 58 43 11, 260 r., SP, K
Hod, tel. (057) 58 46 44, 205 r., SP, K
Lot, tel. (057) 58 43 21, 190 r., SP, K
Moriah Dead Sea (4km/2½ miles from town), tel. (057) 58 42 21, 220 r., SP, K
Moriah Gardens, tel. (057) 58 43 51, 184 r., SP, K
Sonesta, tel. (057) 58 41 52, 214 r., SP, K
Tsell Harim, tel. (057) 58 41 21, 160 r., SP, K

Haifa

Beth Shalom, 110 Hanassi Boulevard, tel. (04) 37 74 81, 30 r.
Carmelia, 35 Herzliya Street, tel. (04) 52 12 78, 50 r., K
Dan Carmel, 85–87 Hanassi Boulevard, tel. (04) 38 62 11, 219 r., SP, K
Dan Panorama, 107 Hanassi Boulevard, tel. (04) 35 22 22, 228 r., SP, K
Dvir, 124 Yafe Nof Street, tel. (04) 38 91 31, 35 r., K
Marom, 51 Hapalmach Street, tel. (04) 25 43 55, 29 r., K
Nesher, 53 Herzl Street, tel. (04) 64 06 44, 15 r., K
Nof, 101 Hanassi Boulevard, tel. (04) 35 43 11, 93 r., K
Shulamit, 15 Qiryat Sefer Street, tel. (04) 34 28 11, 84 r., K
Yaarot Hacarmel, Carmel National Park, tel. (04) 22 91 44, 103 r., SP, K

Herzliya

Dan Accadia, Herzliya on Sea, tel. (052) 55 66 77, 191 r., SP, K
Daniel, Herzliya on Sea, tel. (052) 54 44 44, 210 r., SP, K
Eshel Inn, Herzliya on Sea, tel. (052) 57 02 08, 48 r., K
Sharon, Herzliya on Sea, tel. (052) 57 57 77, 160 r., SP, K
Tadmor, 38 Basel Street, tel. (052) 57 23 21, 59 r., SP, K

Jerusalem

Alcazar, 6 Almutanbi Street, tel. (02) 28 11 11, 38 r.
Ambassador, Nablus Road, Sheikh Jarrah, tel. (02) 82 82 11, 118 r.
American Colony, Nablus Road, tel. (02) 28 51 71, 98 r., SP
Ariel, 31 Hebron Road, tel. (02) 71 92 22, 125 r., K
Caesar, 208 Jaffa Road, tel. (02) 38 21 56, 84 r., K
Capitol, 17 Saladin Street, tel. (02) 28 25 61, 54 r.
Central, 6 Pines Street, tel. (02) 38 41 11, 77 r., K
Christmas, Saladin Street, tel. (02) 28 25 88, 24 r.
Commodore, Suwaneh, Mount of Olives, tel. (02) 28 48 45, 45 r.
Eilon Tower, 34 Ben Yehuda Street, tel. (02) 23 32 81, 72 r., K
Eyal, 21 Shamai Street, tel. (02) 23 41 61, 71 r., K
Gloria, 33 Latin Patriarchate Street (Jaffa Gate), tel. (02) 28 24 31, 64 r.
Har Aviv, 16A Bet Hakerem Street, tel. (02) 52 15 15, 14 r.
Holyland, Bayit VeGan, tel. (02) 78 81 18, 115 r., SP, K
Holyland East, 6 Reshid Street, tel. (02) 28 48 41, 105 r.
Hyatt Regency Jerusalem, 32 Lehi Street, tel. (02) 82 13 33, 503 r., SP, K
Jerusalem Gate, 43 Yirmiyahu Street, tel. (02) 38 31 01, 298 r., K
Jerusalem Hilton, Givat Ram, tel. (02) 53 61 51, 415 r., SP, K
Jerusalem Meridian, 5 Ali Ibn Abi Taleb Street, tel. (02) 28 52 12, 74 r.
Jerusalem Panorama, Hill of Gethsemane, tel. (02) 28 48 86, 74 r.
Jerusalem Tower, 23 Hillel Street, tel. (02) 22 21 61, 120 r., K
King David, 23 King David Street, tel. (02) 25 11 11, 257 r., SP, K
Kings, 60 King George Street, tel. (02) 24 71 33, 187 r., K
King Solomon, 32 King David Street, tel. (02) 24 14 33, 150 r., K
Knesset Tower, 4 Wolfson Street, tel. (02) 53 11 11, 204 r., SP, K
Knight's Palace, 4 Javalden Street (near Church of Holy Sepulchre), tel: (02) 28 25 37, 40 r.
Laromme, 3 Jabotinsky Street, tel. (02) 69 77 77, 302 r., SP, K
Moriah Plaza Jerusalem, 39 Keren Hayassod Street, tel. (02) 23 22 32, 294 r., SP, K
Mount of Olives, Mount of Olives Road, tel. (02) 28 48 77, 63 r.

Hotels in Jerusalem: King David . . .   *. . . and Knesset Tower*

Mount Scopus, Sheikh Jarrah, tel. (02) 82 88 91, 65 r.
Mount Zion, 17 Hebron Road, tel. (02) 72 42 22, 150 r., SP, K
National Palace, 4 Azzahra Street, tel. (02) 27 32 73, 108 r.
Neve Shoshana, 5 Beit Hakerem Street, tel. (02) 52 17 40, 27 r., K
New Metropole, 6 Saladin Street, tel. (02) 28 38 46, 30 r.
Palatin, 4 Agrippas Street, tel. (02) 23 11 41, 28 r., K
Pilgrims Inn, Al Rashid Street, tel. (02) 28 48 83, 15 r.
Pilgrims Palace, 28 Sultan Suleiman Street, tel. (02) 28 33 37, 95 r.
Ramada Renaissance, 6 Wolfson Street, tel. (02) 52 81 11, 650 r., SP, K
Reich, 1 Hagai Street, Beit Hakerem, tel. (02) 52 31 21, 57 r., K
Ritz, 8 Ibn Khaldun Street, tel. (02) 27 32 33, 103 r.
Rivoli, 3 Saladin Street, tel. (02) 28 48 71, 31 r.
Ron, 44 Jaffa Road, tel. (02) 25 34 71, 22 r., K
St George International, Saladin Street, tel. (02) 28 25 71, 144 r., SP
Seven Arches (formerly Intercontinental), Mount of Olives,
tel. (02) 89 44 55, 200 r., SP
Shalom, Bayit VeGan, tel. (02) 42 31 11, 400 r., SP, K
Sheraton Jerusalem Plaza, 47 King George Street, tel. (02) 25 91 11, 414 r.,
SP, K
Sonesta Jerusalem, 2 Wolfson Street, tel. (02) 52 82 21, 172 r., K
Strand, 4 Ibn Jubeir Street, tel. (02) 28 02 79, 93 e.
Tirat Bat Sheva, 42 King George Street, tel. (02) 23 21 21, 70 r., K
Victoria, 8 Masudi Street, tel. (02) 28 62 20, 54 r.
Windmill, 3 Mendele Street, tel. (02) 66 31 11, 133 r., K
YMCA, 26 King David Street, tel. (02) 22 71 11, 70 r., SP
Zohar, 47 Leib Jaffe Street, tel. (02) 71 75 57, 110 r., K

Arazim, tel. (06) 94 41 43, 28 r., K	Metulla
Hamavri, tel. (06) 94 01 50, 18 r., K	
Nof Ramon, 7 Nahal Meishar, tel. (057) 8 82 55, 20 r.	Mizpe Ramon

Hotels

Sonesta Hotel, Jerusalem

Nahariya	Astar, 27 Haga'aton Boulevard, tel. (04) 92 34 31, 26 r., K
	Carlton, 23 Haga'aton Boulevard, tel. (04) 92 22 11, 200 r., SP
	Eden, 17 Jabotinsky Street, tel. (04) 92 32 46, 80 r., SP
	Frank, 4 Ha'aliya Street, tel. (04) 92 02 78, 50 r., K
	Kalman, 27 Jabotinsky Street, tel. (04) 92 03 55, 15 r., K
	Pallas Athene, 28 Hama'apilim Street, tel. (04) 92 23 81, 53 r., K
	Rosenblatt, 59 Weizmann Street, tel. (04) 82 00 69, 35 r., SP, K
Nazareth	Grand New, St Joseph Street, tel. (06) 57 33 25, 92 r.
	Hagalil, Paul VI Street, tel. (06) 57 13 11, 90 r.
Netanya	Atzmaut, Ha'atzmaut Square, tel. (053) 2 25 62, 20 r., K
	Bet Amin, 41 King Solomon Street, tel. (053) 61 12 22, 85 r., SP, K
	Blue Bay, 31 Hamelachim Street, tel. (053) 62 33 22, 194 r., SP, K
	Galil, 18 Nice Boulevard, tel. (053) 62 44 55, 84 r., K
	Goldar, 1 Ussishkin Street, tel. (053) 33 81 88, 151 r., K
	Grand Yahalom, 15 Gad Makhnes Street, tel. (053) 62 48 88, 48 r., SP, K
	Hof, 9 Ha'atzmaut Square, tel. (053) 62 44 22, 30 r., K
	King David Palace, 4 King David Street, tel. (053) 34 21 51, 51 r., K
	King Koresh, 6 Rav Kook Street, tel. (053) 61 35 55, 29 r., K
	King Solomon, 18 Ma'apilim Street, tel. (053) 33 84 44, 99 r., K
	Maxim, 8 King David Street, tel. (053) 62 10 62, 90 r., K
	Metropol Grand, 17 Gad Makhnes Street, tel. (053) 62 47 77, 65 r., SP, K
	Orly, 20 Maapilim Street, tel. (053) 33 30 91, 66 r., K
	Palace, 33 Gad Makhnes Street, tel. (053) 62 02 22, 71 r., K
	Park, 7 King David Street, tel. (053) 62 33 44, 90 r., SP, K
	Princess, 28 Gad Makhnes Street, tel. (053) 62 26 66, 147 r., K
	Residence, 18 Gad Makhnes Street, tel. (053) 62 37 77, 96 r., K
	Seasons, Nice Boulevard, tel. (053) 61 85 55, 82 r., SP, K
	Sironit, 18 Gad Makhnes Street, tel. (053) 34 06 88, 60 r., K
Qiryat Shemona	North, tel. (06) 94 47 02, 90 r., SP, K

David, Mount Canaan, tel. (06) 92 00 62, 42 r., K
Nof Hagalil, Mount Canaan, tel. (06) 93 15 95, 32 r., K
Rimon Inn, Artists' Colony, tel. (06) 92 06 55, 36 r., SP, K
Ron, Hativat Yiftah Street, tel. (06) 97 25 90, 50 r., SP, K
Ruckenstein, Mount Canaan, tel. (06) 92 00 60, 26 r.

Beit Hava, tel. (04) 92 23 91, 90 r., SP, K

Ambassador, 56 H. Samuel Esplanade, tel. (03) 5 10 39 93, 51 r., K
Astor, 105 Hayarkon Street, tel. (03) 22 31 41, 69 r., K
Avia, International Airport Area, tel. (03) 5 36 02 21, 104 r., SP, K
Aviv, 88A Hayarkon Street, tel. (03) 65 54 86, 20 r.
Basel, 156 Hayarkon Street, tel. (03) 5 24 41 61, 138 r., SP, K
Carlton Tel Aviv, 10 Eliezer Peri Street, tel. (03) 29 12 91, 284 r., SP, K
City, 9 Mapu Street, tel. (03) 5 24 62 53, 96 r., K
Dan Panorama, 10 Kaufman Street, tel. (03) 5 19 01 90, 523 r., SP, K
Dan Tel Aviv, 99 Hayarkon Street, tel. (03) 5 24 11 11, 290 r., SP, K
Dizengoff Square, 2 Zamenhof Street, tel. (03) 29 61 81, 59 r., K
Florida, 164 Hayarkon Street, tel. (03) 5 24 21 84, 52 r., K
Grand Beach, 250 Hayarkon Street, tel. (03) 5 46 65 55, 212 r., SP, K
Imperial, 66 Hayarkon Street, tel. (03) 65 70 02, 48 r.
Maxim, 86 Hayarkon Street, tel. (03) 5 17 37 21, 60 r., K
Moriah Plaza Tel Aviv, 155 Hayarkon Street, tel. (03) 5 27 15 15, 341 r., SP, K
Moss, 6 Ness Ziona Street, tel. (03) 5 17 16 55, 70 r., K
Ora, 35 Ben Yehuda Street, tel. (03) 65 09 41, 54 r., K
Park, 75 Hayarkon Street, tel. (03) 65 15 51, 99 r.
Ramada Continental, 121 Hayarkon Street, tel. (03) 5 27 26 26, 340 r., SP, K
Ramat Aviv, 151 Haifa Road, tel. (03) 6 99 07 77, 118 r., SP, K
Shalom, 216 Hayarkon Street, tel. (03) 5 24 32 77, 48 r.
Sheraton, 115 Hayarkon Street, tel. (03) 5 28 62 22, 354 r., SP, K
Sinai, 11–15 Trumpeldor Street, tel. (03) 65 26 21, 136 r., SP, K
Tal, 287 Hayarkon Street, tel. (03) 5 44 22 81, 126 r., K
Tel Aviv Hilton, Independence Park, tel. (03) 5 20 22 22, 633 r., SP, K

Ariston, Herzl Boulevard, tel. (06) 79 02 44, 75 r., SP, K
Astoria, 13 Ohel Ya'aqov Street, tel. (06) 72 23 51, 56 r., K
Caesar Tiberias, 103 Hatayelet Street, tel. (06) 72 33 33, 236 r., SP, K
Daphna, Ussishkin Street, tel. (06) 79 22 61, 72 r., K
Eden, 4 Nazareth Street, tel. (06) 79 00 70, 82 r., K
Gai Beach, Hamerchatzaot Road, tel. (06) 79 07 90, 120 r., SP, K
Galei Kinneret, 1 Kaplan Street, tel. (06) 79 23 31, 107 r., SP, K
Galilee, Elhadeff Street, tel. (06) 79 11 66, 84 r., K
Ganei Hammat, HaBannim Street, tel. (06) 79 28 90, 286 r., K
Golan, 14 Ahad Ha'am Street, tel. (06) 79 19 01, 78 r., SP, K
Hartman, 3 Ahad Ha'am Street, tel. (06) 79 15 55, 73 r., SP
Jordan River, HaBannim Street, tel. (06) 72 11 11, 401 r., SP, K
Kinar, Kinar Holiday Village, tel. (06) 73 26 70, 120 r., K
Laromme Tiberias Club Hotel, Ahad Ha'am St, tel. (06) 79 18 88, 310 r., SP
Peer, 2 Ohel Ya'aqov Street, tel. (06) 79 16 41, 69 r., K
Ron Beach, Gdud Barak Road, tel. (06) 79 13 50, 74 r., K
Sara, 7 Zeidel Street, tel. (06) 72 08 26, 17 r., K
Tiberias Plaza, HaBannim Street, tel. (06) 79 22 33, 272 r., SP, K
Washington, 13 Zeidel Street, tel. (06) 79 18 61, 107 r., K

Kibbutz Hotels

Many of Israel's 250 kibbutzes have guest-houses equipped with modern
amenities and frequently with a bathing beach or swimming pool. All
kibbutz hotels have either three or four stars and offer the same standards
of comfort as other hotels in the same categories, but they often have a
more personal atmosphere. Some of them run excursions in the surrounding area, and there may be talks about life in the kibbutz and a variety of
cultural events.

● **Kibbutz Hotels**

1 Kfar Giladi
  Tel. (06) 94 14 14, 158 r., SP

2 Hagoshrim
  Tel. (06) 95 62 31, 121 r., SP

3 Kfar Blum
  Tel. (06) 94 36 66, 59 r., SP

4 Ayelet Hashahar
  Tel. (06) 93 26 11, 144 r., SP

5 Nof Ginnosar
  Tel. (06) 79 21 61, 170 r.

6 Ramot
  Tel. (06) 73 26 36, 80 r., SP

7 En Gev
  Tel. (06) 75 80 27, 80 r.

8 Ha'on
  Tel. (06) 75 75 55, 42 r.

9 Ma'agan
  Tel. (06) 75 37 53, 96 r., SP

10 Lavi
   Tel. (06) 79 94 50, 124 r., SP

11 Gesher Haziv
   Tel. (04) 82 57 15, 48 r., SP

12 Beit Oren
   Tel. (04) 22 21 11, 67 r., SP

13 Nir Etzion
   Tel. (04) 84 25 41, 74 r., SP

14 Nahsholim
   Tel. (06) 39 95 33, 80 r.

15 Hof Shonit
   Tel. (06) 36 29 27, holiday village

16 Shefayim
   Tel. (052) 54 72 34, 110 r.

17 Shoresh
   Tel. (02) 34 11 71, 114 r., SP
   (The hotel caters for people with
   heart conditions and
   diabetics)

18 Ma'ale Hahamisha
   Tel. (02) 34 25 91, 121 r.

19 Qiryat Anavim
   Tel. (02) 34 89 99, 94 r., SP

20 Neve Ilan
   Tel. (02) 34 12 41, 25 r., SP
   (suitable for disabled people)

© Baedeker

Guest-house in the kibbutz of Ayelet Hashahar

21 Mizpe Rachel
    Tel. (02) 70 25 55, 79 r., SP

22 Hafetz Haim
    Tel. (08) 59 38 88, 57 r., SP
    (classed as a sanatorium)

23 Metzoke Dragot
    Tel. (02) 22 81 14, 48 r.

24 En Gedi
    Tel. (057) 58 47 57, 120 r., SP

25 Yelim
    Tel. (07) 37 43 62, 50 r., SP

Independent Travel

There is no difficulty about touring Israel on your own. You can either find your own accommodation in hotels, kibbutz hotels, youth hostels (see entries) or Christian hospices (see Pilgrimages) or on camping sites (see Camping and Caravanning), or you can book a "fly-drive" holiday covering the hire of a car (usually picked up at the airport) and accommodation at convenient places on your route.

In spite of the *intifada* visitors travelling in a hired car are unlikely to encounter any problems in the Israeli heartland, where there has been little trouble, but it is advisable to seek advice about the current situation before touring on the Israeli-occupied West Bank. The Gaza Strip is at present best avoided.

For those who like bus travel the Egged bus company issues round-trip tickets at reduced rates and also runs organised trips. (Head office at 15 Frishman Street, Tel Aviv, tel. (03) 5 27 12 12; branch offices in major towns.)

Women travelling on their own may sometimes find themselves in awkward situations. Even if modestly dressed they are liable to be approached and pestered by either Arabs or Israelis. They should, therefore, be particularly wary about where they go and how they behave.

Information

Information outside Israel

United Kingdom
Israel Government Tourist Office
18 Great Marlborough Street
London W1V 1AF
Tel. (0171) 434 3651

ישראל
ISRAEL

United States
Consulate-General of Israel
1100 Spring Street NW
Atlanta GA 30309
Tel. (404) 875 9924

Israel Government Tourist Office
5 South Wabash Avenue
Chicago IL 60603
Tel. (312) 782 4306

Israel Government Tourist Office
12700 Park Central Drive
Dallas TX 75251
Tel. (214) 991 9097

Israel Government Tourist Office
6380 Wilshire Boulevard 1700
Los Angeles CA 90048
Tel. (213) 658 7462

Israel Government Tourist Office
25 SE 2nd Avenue, Suite 745
Miami FL 33131
Tel. (305) 539 1919

Israel Government Tourist Office
350 Fifth Avenue (19th floor)
New York NY 10118
Tel. (212) 560 0650

Canada
Israel Government Tourist Office
180 Bloor Street West, Suite 700
Toronto, Ontario M5S 2V6
Tel. (416) 964 3784

Information in Israel

The Israel Government Tourist Office runs tourist information offices in the larger towns and in places of tourist interest, at which visitors can obtain information about local sights and events, accommodation and excursions in the locality. Town plans and brochures in English are issued free of charge.

El-Jazzar Street, Old City, tel. (04) 91 17 64	Akko
Commercial Centre, P.O. Box 222, tel. (057) 95 81 44	Arad
Commercial Centre, Afridar, tel. (051) 3 24 12	Ashqelon
43 Ben-Gurion Boulevard, tel. (03) 58 97 66	Bat Yam
6A Ben Zvi Street (opposite bus station), tel. (057) 3 60 01	Beersheba
Manger Square, tel. (02) 74 25 91	Bethlehem
Rechter Commercial Centre, tel. (059) 7 67 37	Elat
HaTmarim, tel. (059) 7 22 68	
Neptune Hotel, tel. (059) 7 42 33	
18 Herzl Street, tel. (04) 66 65 21	Haifa
Municipality Building, 14 Hassan Shukri Street, tel. (04) 35 62 00	
119 Hanassi Boulevard, tel. (04) 38 36 83	
23 Hanevi'im Street, tel. (04) 66 30 56	
24 King George Street, tel. (02) 24 12 81 Open: Sun.–Thur. 8.30am–5pm, Fri. 8.30am–1pm	Jerusalem
Jaffa Gate (Old City), tel. (02) 28 22 95 Open: Sun.–Thur. 8.30am–5pm, Fri. 8.30am–1pm	
17 Jaffa Road, tel. (02) 22 88 44 Open: Sun.–Thur. 9am–1pm	
Municipal Building, Haga'aton Boulevard, tel. (04) 92 21 21	Nahariya
Casa Nova Street, tel. (06) 57 30 03	Nazareth
Ha'atzmaut Square, tel. (053) 2 72 86	Netanya
50 Jerusalem Street, tel. (06) 93 06 33	Safed
7 Mendele Street, tel. (03) 2 23 26 66	Tel Aviv
6 Elhadeff Street, tel. (06) 72 09 92	Tiberias

Kibbutzes

See Facts and Figures, Population; Hotels, Kibbutz Hotels; Working Holidays

Language

The official languages of Israel are Modern Hebrew (Ivrit) and Arabic, which both belong to the Semitic language family. Since Israel is a country of

Hebrew Alphabet

Letter	Name	Pronunciation (Ivrit)	Numerical value
א	alef	silent (preceding vowel)	1
ב	bet	b, v	2
ג	gimel	hard g	3
ד	dalet	d	4
ה	he	h	5
ו	vav	v	6
ז	zain	z	7
ח	het	ch (as in "loch")	8
ט	tet	t	9
י	yod	y (as in "yet")	10
כ	kaf	k	20
ל	lamed	l	30
מ	mem	m	40
נ	nun	n	50
ס	samekh	s (unvoiced)	60
ע	ain	gutteral	70
פ	pe	p	80
צ	tzadi	ts	90
ק	kof	k	100
ר	resh	r	200
שׂ	sin	s (unvoiced)	300
שׁ	shin	sh	
ת	tav	t	400

vowel sign	Name	Transcription
־	pathah	a
ָ	kamets	ạ
ָ	kamets-hatuf	ọ
ֶ	segol	ẹ
ֵ	sere	e
ִ	hirek	i
ֹ	holem	o
ֻ	kibuts	u
ֲ	hatef-pathah	ä
ֱ	hatef-segol	ë
ֳ	hatef-kamets	ö
ְ	schwa	ë

Arabic Alphabet

Letter	Name	Pronunciation
ا	alif	glottal stop
ب	ba	b
ت	ta	t
ث	tha	th (as in "thing")
ج	jim	j
ح	ha	h (strongly aspirated)
خ	kha	ch (as in "loch")
د	dal	d
ذ	dhal	th (as in "the")
ر	ra	r (rolled)
ز	za	z
س	sin	s (unvoiced)
ش	shin	sh
ص	sad	s (emphatic)
ض	dad	d (emphatic)
ط	ta	t (emphatic)
ظ	za	ts (emphatic)
ع	ain	similar to glottal stop
غ	ghain	gh (like a French r)
ف	fa	f
ق	kaf	k (emphatic)
ك	kaf	k
ل	lam	l
م	mim	m
ن	nun	n
ه	ha	h
و	waw	w
ى	ya	y (as in "yet")

Most letters in the Arabic alphabet have four forms, depending on whether they are on their own (independent), are joined only to the preceding or following letter (final, initial) or are between two letters (medial). The letters shown above are in the independent form.

immigrants, however, visitors will encounter Israelis speaking a wide variety of European languages. The language of business is English. Only in remote parts of the country not usually visited by tourists are visitors likely to encounter road signs, etc., written only in Hebrew and Arabic script.

Ivrit, the modern version of Hebrew, is based on the Hebrew of the Old Testament but differs considerably from it.
Hebrew has an alphabet of 23 letters. Since Hebrew words have a more or less rigid consonantal structure, while the vowels can vary, written Hebrew was originally confined to the consonants which gave the word its meaning. Later the vowels came to be indicated by vocalic signs, written under the consonantal sign which they followed. The phonetic quality of the vowels is very variable. Each consonant also has a numerical value, and this played an important part in the numerical mysticism of the Kabbalah.

Hebrew, like Arabic, is written from right to left. The written script is similar to the printed alphabet, which is notable for its "square" forms (making some of the letters difficult to distinguish from one another at first sight).

Modern Arabic evolved from the northern form of Arabic spoken in antiquity and accompanied the spread of Islam throughout large areas round the southern and eastern Mediterranean. Many dialects have developed in the course of the centuries; here we give the Egyptian form of Arabic.

In Arabic long vowels are denoted by the letters alif, waw and ya; short vowels are usually omitted or indicated by particular signs above or below the consonants. The pronunciation of the short vowels varies considerably according to the neighbouring consonants and the educational level of the speaker.

Ivrit

Arabic

Useful Expressions

English	*Hebrew*	*Arabic*
Good morning	Bóker tov	Sabah el-kher
Good afternoon	Shalóm	Es-salamu alekum
Good evening	Erev tov	Misa el-kher
Good night	Láyla tov	Lela saida
Goodbye	Shalóm, lehitraót	Allalah, ma'as-salama
I do not understand	Aní lo mevín (m.), aní meviná (f.)	Ana mish fahmak
Excuse me	Slihá	Asif
yes	ken	aiwa
no	lo	la
please	bevakashá	min fadlak
thank you	todá	shokran
yesterday	etmól	embarih

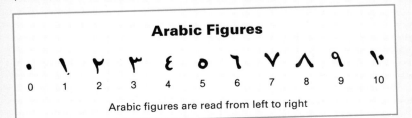

Arabic Figures

•	١	٢	٣	٤	٥	٦	٧	٨	٩	١٠
0	1	2	3	4	5	6	7	8	9	10

Arabic figures are read from left to right

Language

English	Hebrew	Arabic
today	hayóm	en-nahar-da
tomorrow	mahár	bukra
What time is it?	Ma hasha'á?	Es-sa'a kam?
When is . . . open?	Matái potkhím . . .?	Mata yaftah . . .?
When does . . . close?	Matái sogrím . . .?	Mata yiqifil . . .?
chemist's shop	beir merkáhad	agsahana
doctor	rofé klali	doktor, tabib
dentist	rofé shináyim	tabib asnan

Numbers

0	–	sifr
1	ehád	wahid
2	shnáyim	itnen
3	sloshá	talata
4	arbaá	arba'a
5	hamishá	khamsa
6	shishá	sitta
7	shivá	Saba
8	shmoná	tamanya
9	tishá	tisaa
10	asará	ashara
11	ahád-asár	hadashar
12	shnéym-asár	itnashar
13	shloshá-asár	talatashar
14	arbaá-asár	arbaatashar
15	hamishá-asár	hamastashar
16	shishá-asár	sittashar
17	shivá-asár	sabaatashar
18	shmoná-asár	tamantashar
19	tishá-asár	tisaatashar
20	esrím	ishrin
21	esrím veehád	wahid wa ishrin
22	esrím ushnáyim	itnen wa ishrin
30	shloshím	talatin
40	arbaím	arba'in
50	hamishím	khamsin
60	shishím	sittin
70	shivím	sabin
80	shmoním	tamanin
90	tishím	tisin
100	meá	miya
200	matáyim	miten
300	shlosh meót	toltomiya
1000	élef	alf
10,000	aséret alafím	asharat alaf
100,000	meá élef	mit alf

Fractions

a half	hatzí	noss
a third	shlish	tilt
a quarter	réva	rob
a tenth	asirít	oshr

In a Hotel

single room	héder leyahíd	gorfa bisirir wahid
double room	héder kafúl	gorfa bisiriren

English	Hebrew	Arabic
What's the price of a room with breakfast?	Kamá olé héder im aruhát bóker?	Qadd-e bitsavi el-oda bil-akl?
When is breakfast?	Matái magishím et aruhár habóker?	Imte haikun el-fitar?

Travelling

English	Hebrew	Arabic
aircraft	avirón	tayyara
airport	sde teufá	matar
arrival	biá, hagaá	wusul
baggage	mitán	shunat
baggage check	shovér hafazím	vasl el-afsh
bus	otobús	otobis
city tour	siyúr ir	rikhle lisiyarit el-balad
compartment	mahleká	divan
conductor	mevakér kartisim	kumsari
connection	késher	muwasla
departure	yeziá, haflagá	safar
dining car	kerón misnón	arabiyit akl
exchange office	hilúf ksafim	taghyir el-fulus
hotel	malón	fondok
passport	darkón	basbort
platform	razif	rasif
porter	sabál	shayal
ship	oniyá	bakhira
sleeping car	kerón shená	arabiyit nom
station	tahanát harakévet	makhatta
stop	shehiyá	wukuf
taxi	monít, táksi	taxi
ticket	kartisnesiá	taskara
timetable	lúah sman im	mawaid el-kitar
toilet	beit kise	mirhad
train	rakévet	katr
travel agency	misrád nésiot	maktab es-siyakha
waiting room	ulam hamtana	salit intisar
window seat	makóm leyád hahalón	makan biganib esh-shibbak

At the Post Office

English	Hebrew	Arabic
address	któvet	unwan
air mail	bedóar avir	berid gawi
counter	eshnáv	shibbak
express mail	mesirá meyuhédet, exprés	gawab mustaagil
letter	mihtáv	gawab
long-distance call	siha beinironít	muhadse kharigiye
packet	havilá ktaná	tard sighayar
parcel	havilá	tard
postage	ta'arif mishlóah	ugrit berid
post-box	tevát mihtavím	sanduk gawabat
postcard	gluyá	taskara
post office	beit dóar	maktab berid
poste restante	mihtavím shmurím	makhfus
stamp	bulím	warakit posta
telegram	mivrák	taligraf
telephone	telefón	telefon
telephone booth	ta hatelefón	kabina telefon

411

English	*Hebrew*	*Arabic*
telephone directory	madrih telefón	daftar telefon
telephone number	mispár hatelefón	nimri telefon

Motoring Terms

English	*Hebrew*	*Arabic*
accelerator	davshát délek	davasit bensin
axle	zir	aks
brakes	hablamím	farmala
bumper, fender	meamém	eksdam
car	mehonít, óto	sayara
carburettor	meayéd	karborater
clutch	mazméd	debriash
cylinder	galíl	silindr
engine	manóa	motor
exhaust	zinór plitá	il-adim
garage	beit melahá	warshit arabiyat
gear lever	hilúf mahalahím	en-nakl
headlights	sarkór	kashafat
horn	zofár	kalaks
inner tube	zinór	kharum
jack	jek	korek
lights	panasím	lamba
motorcycle	ofanóa	motosikl
oil	shémen	set
petrol	bensín, gasolín	bensin
petrol station	tahanát délek	makhatit bensin
petrol tank	meyhal	tank
radiator	mezanén-máyim	radiater
repair	tikún	taslikh
screw	bóreg	kalawus
spanner	maftéah beragím	samula
spare can	pah resérvi	safikha ikhtiati
spare wheel	galgál hilúf	agala stepn
sparking plugs	hamazatím	shama
speedometer	madmehirút	adad es-sura
starter	matnéa	marsh
steering	higúi	suwaka
steering wheel	hége	folan
tyre	ramíg	kawitsh
valve	shastóm	simam

Road Signs

Intersection	Hitzalvút	Mafraq et-turuq
One-way street	Rehov ben kivún ehád	Tariq fi ittigah wahid
Parking	Mekóm haniyá	Makhal wuquf es-sayarat

Hebrew Topographical Terms

Hebrew	*English*
agam	lake
ain	spring
atar	archaeological site
bayit, beit	house
beer	well
bereiha(t)	pool

Hebrew	English
bika(t), biqa(t)	valley
derekh	road, street
emeq	valley, plain
eretz	land
gan	garden
gay	gorge
gesher	bridge
gevul	frontier
giva(t)	hill
har	hill
hava	farm
hof	coast
hurba(t)	ruin
ir	town
iriya	municipal administration
kefar	village
kerem	vineyard
kever	tomb
kevish	main road
kibbutz	communal settlement: see page 26
kikar	square
kiryat, qiryat	district, town
ma'abara	transit camp for immigrants
ma'ale	pass, ascent
ma'ayan	spring
mathaf	hotel
mayim	water
metsuda(t)	castle, fortress
mifrats	gulf, bay
migdal	tower
misada	restaurant
mishtara	police
mo'etsa	council meeting
moshav	cooperative settlement: see page 28
moshava	village
mughara	cave
nahal	stream
nahar	river
newe	oasis; home
nir	field
pardess	grove of citrus trees
qiryat	district, town
rama(t)	hill, plateau
rehov	street
rova	district in town
sderot	boulevard, avenue
sha'ar	entrance, gate
sharav	desert wind
shehuna	district in town
simta	lane, alley
tel	settlement mound
ya'ar	wood, forest
yad	memorial
yam	sea

Arabic Topographical Glossary

Arabic	English
abu	father
ain	spring

Language

Arabic	English
bab	gate, door
bahr	sea
balad	town, village
beit, bet	house
bilad	land
bir	well
birke(t)	pond, pool
burj	tower, fort
dahr	pass
darb	road, track
deir	monastery
djami, jami	mosque
djebel, jebel, gebel	hill, mountain
djisr, jisr	bridge
djubb, jubb	cistern
ein	spring
fondok, funduk	hotel
ghab	wood, forest
hamma	hot springs
haram	shrine
kaber	tomb
kafer	village
karem	vineyard
khamsin	desert wind
khan	caravanserai
khirbe(t)	ruin
madni	minaret
mai	water
mar	holy man, saint
masjid	small mosque
mauristan	hospital
medina	town
medrese	Koranic school
mihrab	prayer niche in mosque
mina	harbour
minbar	pulpit in mosque
nabi, nebi	prophet
nahr	river
naqb	pass
qalaat	fortress
qantara	bridge
qasr	castle
qubba	domed tomb or other building
quneitra	small bridge
ras	head, headland, summit
sahel	plain
sahara	desert
seraglio	palace, council house
shari(a)	street
sheikh	sheikh, old man
sherif	nobleman
suk	market, market alley
tell	settlement mound
wadi	(usually dry) river valley
wali	holy man, holy man's tomb
zeitun	olive-tree

Markets

In all the larger towns in Israel there are markets and streets of shops in the old part of the town selling a wide range of commodities – fruit and vegetables, foodstuffs of all kinds, household articles, clothing and much else besides. In these areas prices are as a rule settled by bargaining.

In this section we list a selection of markets of most interest to visitors. (It should be remembered that since the beginning of the *intifada* Arab dealers have been opening their shops and stalls only in the mornings.)

Jerusalem

The Arab market in the Old City (which begins just inside the Jaffa Gate in David Street) is a shopper's paradise, with an extraordinary variety of wares to tempt the visitor.
The colourful Mahane Yehuda market in Jaffa Road deals mainly in foodstuffs (fruit and vegetables, fish and meat, bread, cakes and pastries). It is particularly busy on Thursday and Friday mornings.
Another fascinating scene is the sheep market held every Friday at the north-east corner of the city walls, when large numbers of Bedouin from the Judaean Desert come into the city to sell their stock.

Tel Aviv

The Carmel Market in Allenby Street offers an overwhelming abundance of fruit and vegetables. Here too, among much else, is an enormous range of other foodstuffs and kitchen articles of all kinds.
For those who like looking around junk markets in search of treasures there is the flea market in the centre of Jaffa. Here, among a great deal of kitsch and furniture doctored to look old, there is always the chance of finding genuine antiques and curios.

Beersheba

The Bedouin market held every Thursday morning in Beersheba attracts large numbers of Israelis as well as visitors. In recent years, however, it has become increasingly commercialised.

Fruit market, Jericho

In the Akko bazaar

Akko

The market in the narrow bazaar streets of Akko, with its Arab and Oriental atmosphere, is a particular favourite with tourists.

Medical Aid

Visitors to Israel require no protective inoculations, and the country presents no particular health risks.

Medical care

Medical care is good in all parts of the country. Most doctors speak English and other foreign languages.

Medicines

All medicines in regular use are available in Israel. Visitors who require to take special drugs should carry a supply with them.

Medical insurance

Israel has no social security agreement with Britain, and medical treatment must be paid for on the spot. Visitors are therefore strongly advised to take out short-term medical insurance before leaving home.

Private nurses

Private nurses can be engaged to provide nursing care or accompany visitors through the privately run organisation called Nursing. Telephone numbers:

Jerusalem: (02) 63 65 05
Tel Aviv: (03) 73 79 47
Haifa: (04) 38 11 11

Emergencies

See entry
The daily press (including foreign-language newspapers) carries daily listings of duty rosters for emergency hospitals, dental clinics and pharmacies open at night and on weekends and holidays.

Meet the Israeli

Israelis in general are outgoing people who like human contact and are friendly and helpful to visitors. The best way to get to know them is to meet them as guests in their own homes, and many Israeli families are happy to give hospitality to visitors, welcoming them with refreshments and lively conversation. Arrangements for visits of this kind can be made through any tourist information office (see Information). Visitors and their hosts can be matched for common interests (professional, cultural, etc.).

Visits to Israeli families can also be arranged through the Voluntary Tourist Service, representatives of which are on duty daily in the arrivals hall of Ben-Gurion Airport. The organisation can also be contacted through its local offices:

Jerusalem: Jaffa Gate, tel. (02) 28 81 40
Haifa: 10 Ahad Ha'am Street, tel. (04) 67 16 45
Elat: 14 Zofit Street, tel. (059) 7 23 44
Nahariya: 18 Sokolov Street, tel. (04) 92 01 35
Tiberias: P.O. Box 191, tel. (06) 79 50 72

Motoring in Israel

Israel has some 4000km/2500 miles of well engineered and well maintained trunk roads. There are four-lane highways between Tel Aviv and Haifa, Tel Aviv and Jerusalem and Tel Aviv and Ashdod, and a southward extension to Beersheba is under construction.
Round the larger cities, however, the present road system has difficulty in coping with the increasing volume of traffic, and during the morning and

Roads

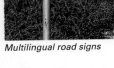
Multilingual road signs

Motoring in Israel

Road distances in kilometres between selected places in Israel	Akko	Ashdod	Ashqelon	Beersheba	Betlehem	Elat	Haifa	Hebron	Jerikó	Jeruzsálem	Lod (Ben-Gurion Airport)	Nahariya	Názáret	Netanya	Rehovot	Tel-Aviv	Tiberias	Safed	Zikhron Ya'apov
Akko		159	174	231	191	474	23	218	161	181	135	10	65	86	140	118	56	51	58
Ashdod	159		33	90	142	333	136	114	102	72	40	169	146	73	24	41	176	212	105
Ashqelon	174	33		63	145	306	151	117	115	75	54	184	161	88	39	56	191	227	120
Beersheba	231	90	63		76	243	208	48	119	83	98	241	218	145	85	113	248	284	177
Betlehem	191	142	145	76		319	168	26	43	10	61	193	145	105	63	73	208	244	128
Elat	474	333	306	243	319		451	291	364	326	341	484	461	388	328	356	491	527	420
Haifa	23	136	151	208	168	451		168	146	158	112	33	38	63	117	95	70	74	33
Hebron	218	114	117	48	26	291	168		67	37	88	217	172	132	88	100	201	237	153
Jerikó	161	102	115	119	43	364	146	67		35	86	174	126	122	92	98	181	217	151
Jeruzsálem	181	72	75	83	10	326	158	37	35		51	191	135	95	50	63	198	234	127
Lod (Ben-Gurion Airport)	135	40	54	98	61	341	112	88	86	51		145	122	49	17	18	152	188	85
Nahariya	10	169	184	241	193	484	33	217	174	191	145		55	96	146	128	66	52	69
Názáret	65	146	161	218	145	461	38	172	126	135	122	55		73	127	105	32	57	46
Netanya	86	73	88	145	105	388	63	132	122	95	49	96	73		54	32	103	139	32
Rehovot	140	24	39	85	63	328	117	88	92	50	17	146	127	54		21	157	193	81
Tel-Aviv	118	41	56	113	73	356	95	100	98	63	18	128	105	32	21		135	171	64
Tiberias	56	176	191	248	208	491	70	201	181	198	152	66	32	103	157	135		36	78
Safed	51	212	227	284	244	527	74	237	217	234	188	52	57	139	193	171	36		103
Zikhron Ya'apov	58	105	120	177	128	420	33	153	151	127	85	69	46	32	81	64	78	103	

afternoon rush hours, particularly in the Tel Aviv and Jerusalem conurbations, long delays and tailbacks are common.

Traffic regulations

Traffic goes on the right, with overtaking on the left. Traffic regulations are similar to those in western countries. Road signs and markings are in line with international standards; directions are given in Hebrew, English and occasionally in Arabic as well.

Priority

Traffic on main roads marked with a black-and-white-bordered yellow square set at an angle has priority over side roads. Otherwise traffic coming from the right has priority.

Speed limits

The speed limit in built-up areas is 50km/31 miles an hour; outside built-up areas it is 80km/50 miles an hour (90km/56 miles an hour where so marked) for private cars, 60km/37 miles an hour for cars with trailers and 70km/43 miles an hour for motorcycles.

Alcohol

Driving under the influence of alcohol is prohibited.

Safety belts

Safety belts must be worn.

Petrol

Filling stations in Israel supply standard-grade petrol (91 octane), premium grade (96 octane) and diesel fuel. Prices are generally rather higher than in Europe.

National Parks

Breakdown
assistance

Driving in
occupied
territory

See entry

Official Israeli maps make no distinction between the heartland of Israel
and the occupied territories. Visitors travelling in their own car or a rented
car, however, should carry a map showing the boundaries between the
two, and it is advisable, before entering any of the occupied territories, to
check up on the current political situation. In and around Hebron and round
Nablus and Ramallah few Israeli-registered private cars are to be seen (they
are distinguished by a yellow number-plate, while cars registered on the
West Bank have a blue plate and in the Gaza Strip a silver one).
Road blocks will sometimes be encountered on the West Bank, particularly
round Jericho, but visitors will usually be allowed through without
difficulty.

National Parks

Israel has 39 National Parks – not to be confused with nature reserves (see
entry) – in areas of archaeological, historical or scenic interest. They are
administered by the National Parks Authority, 4 Rav Aluf Maklef Street,
Hakirya, Tel Aviv, tel. (03) 25 22 81.
Visitors can obtain a reduced ticket entitling them to admission to three
National Parks over a period of two weeks.

1 Nimrod's Castle
   (Crusader castle)

2 Horeshat Valley
   (Recreation area with lake)

In Ashqelon National Park

○ **National Parks**

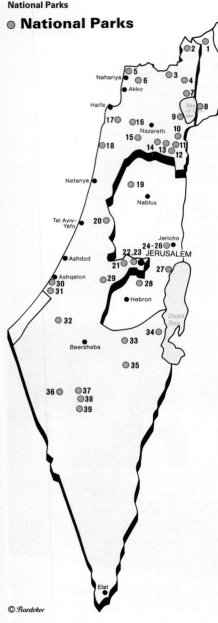

3 Bar'am
(Archaeological site)

4 Tel Hazor
(Archaeological site)

5 Akhziv
(Excavations, beach)

6 Yehiam
(Crusader castle)

7 Chorazin
(Archaeological site)

8 Kursi
(Archaeological site)

9 Tiberias-Hammat
(Archaeological site and spa)

10 Belvoir
(Crusader castle)

11 Bet Shean
(Archaeological site)

12 Gan HaShelosha
(Recreation area with waterfalls)

13 Bet Alfa
(Synagogue with fine mosaic)

14 Ma'ayan Harod
(Recreation area with artificial
lake)

15 Megiddo
(Archaeological site)

16 Bet Shearim
(Necropolis)

17 Carmel Park
(Mount Carmel)

18 Caesarea
(Archaeological site)

19 Samaria
(Archaeological site)

20 Tel Afeq
(Archaeological site)

21 Aqua Bella
(Archaeological site and
recreation area)

22 Jerusalem: Citadel

23 Jerusalem: Walls of Old City

24 Jericho: Tel Jericho
(Archaeological site)

© Baedeker

25 Jericho: Synagogue
   (Archaeological site)

26 Jericho: Hisham's Palace
   (Archaeological site)

27 Qumran
   (Archaeological site)

28 Herodeion
   (Archaeological site)

29 Bet Guvrin
   (Archaeological site)

30 Ashqelon
   (Archaeological site and
   recreation area with beach)

31 Yad Mordekhay
   (Memorial site)

32 Eshkol
   (Recreation area)

33 Arad
   (Archaeological site)

34 Masada
   (Archaeological site)

35 Mamshit
   (Archaeological site)

36 Shivta
   (Archaeological site)

37 Sede Boqer
   (David Ben-Gurion's tomb)

38 En Avdat
   (Spring in the desert)

39 Avdat
   (Archaeological site)

Nature Reserves

There are some 160 nature reserves in Israel, with a total area of 370,000 hectares/900,000 acres, containing 3000 species of plants (some 150 of them endemic to Israel), 430 species of birds, 70 mammals and 80 reptiles. The nature reserves extend from Tel Dan in the extreme north of Israel, with its luxuriant vegetation, by way of the marshlands of the Hule nature reserve and the oasis region of En Gedi to the bizarre desert landscapes of the Negev (Timna Park, Bai Har Wild Life Centre).
The nature reserves are administered by the Nature Reserve Authority, 78 Yirmiyahu Street, Jerusalem, tel. (02) 53 62 71.

The Society for the Protection of Nature in Israel (SPNI), founded in 1953, has as its objectives the preservation of the country's natural landscape and the inculcation in both Israelis and foreign visitors of respect for, and

Israel Nature Trails

love of nature. In pursuance of the latter objective the society has a special department ("Nature Trails") which runs well organised conducted visits and tours in selected areas of interest. In addition to ordinary sightseeing tours (e.g. to En Gedi, Masada and the Dead Sea) the programme includes more unusual outings such as a camel trip in the Negev or a moonlight excursion in the Judaean Desert.

SPNI offices

Beersheba
Tuvla Street, tel. (057) 3 21 56

Haifa
8 Menahem Street, tel. (04) 66 41 35

Jerusalem
13 Heleni Hamalka Street, tel. (02) 22 23 57

Tel Aviv
4 Hashfela Street, tel. (03) 37 50 63

"Plant a Tree"

The "Plant a Tree with your own Hands" campaign was launched by the Jewish National Fund (Keren Kayemet) in order to extend Israel's forest cover. For a nominal contribution visitors may plant trees and receive a certificate and pin badge to commemorate the event.
Information from the Jewish National Fund, 1 Keren Kayemet Street, Jerusalem, tel. (02) 70 74 11, or 96 Hayarkon Street, Tel Aviv, tel. (03) 23 44 49.

Newspapers and Periodicals

Of Israel's twenty or so daily newspapers about half are in Hebrew; in addition to papers in Arabic there are others in almost every European language. The English-language "Jerusalem Post" is one of the country's most respected journals.
British papers and magazines and the International Herald Tribune are usually available in Israel the day after publication.

Night Life

Israel's night life is concentrated mainly in Tel Aviv, where, particularly during the summer months, there are lively goings-on throughout the night round the old harbour of Jaffa and on Dizengoff Street. There are numerous discos, bars and night spots which stay open until the small hours.
There is also a wide range of after-dark entertainment at Elat on the Red Sea. The Mediterranean resorts are much quieter, and Jerusalem itself is not exactly a place for night owls.

Photography

It is forbidden to take photographs or use ciné cameras or videos from an aircraft, and to photograph military objectives (a term which includes airfields and airports, railway stations, bridges and frontier crossing points).

Ten films per person can be taken into Israel duty-free. It is advisable to take in as many as you expect to need, since films and other photographic material are extremely dear.

You should have no film in your camera when entering or leaving Israel, since cameras may be opened by security officers.

Newspapers and magazines in many languages

Pilgrimages

A high proportion of visitors to Israel go there as pilgrims. Most pilgrims go in organised groups; very few travel on their own. This is no doubt because to go on your own is considerably dearer and involves a good deal of preparatory paper work. Many tour operators offer package tours for pilgrims, for example Inter-Church Travel, The Saga Building, Middelburg Square, Folkestone, Kent CT20 1BL, tel. (0800) 300 444.

Israel Pilgrimage Committee
P.O. Box 1018
91009 Jerusalem
Tel. (02) 23 73 11

Information

Christian Information Centre
P.O. Box 14309
Jerusalem (in the Old City, by the Jaffa Gate)
Tel. (02) 28 76 47
Open Mon.–Fri. 8.30am–12.30pm and 3–6pm (in winter to 5.30pm), Sat. 8.30am–12.30pm.

Pilgrimage Promotion Division, Ministry of Tourism
23 Hillel Street
94262 Jerusalem
Tel. (02) 24 79 62 and 23 73 11

The principal places of pilgrimage are listed on a Pilgrims' Map of the Holy Land obtainable from the Israel Government Tourist Office.

Pilgrims' Map

Christians on a pilgrimage to the Holy Land can obtain accommodation (sometimes in dormitories) at reasonable prices in hospices run by various

Christian Hospices

Christian denominations. A list of such hospices can be obtained from the Israel Government Tourist Office.

Post, Telegraph, Telephone

Post offices
Post offices are identified by the leaping figure of a white stag on a blue ground. Head post offices are open Sun.–Thur. 8am–6pm, (branch offices 7–10am and 3.30–6pm) and Fri. from 8am to 1 or 2pm.

Stamps
Stamps can be bought in stationery and souvenir shops, bookshops and the larger hotels as well as in post offices.
The minimum charge for letters within Israel and to Europe applies to those weighing less than 20g. At present an airmail letter to Europe costs 1 NIS, a postcard 80 agorot. A letter can take up to 10 days.

Poste restante
Mail can be sent poste restante to any head post office (in Jerusalem at 23 Jaffa Road, in Tel Aviv at 132 Allenby Street).

Post-boxes
Post-boxes are either yellow (for local mail) or red (for all other destinations), with the leaping stag logo.

Telegrams
Telegrams can be sent from all post offices (round the clock from head post offices), by hotel reception desks or by telephone (dial 171).

Telephone
Calls within Israel can be dialled on public payphones, using special telephone tokens (*asimonim*) which can be bought in post offices and, at higher prices, from kiosks and in hotels. Some payphones are operated by magnetic cards, obtainable from post offices. Charges vary according to the time of day: highest rates from 8.30am to 1pm, medium rates from 1 to 9pm, cheap rates from 9pm to 8am, on Friday from 1pm and on Saturday.

Post-boxes for out-of-town and local mail

It is not usually possible to make international calls from public telephones, but they can be dialled direct from all private telephones and from hotels, the larger post offices and international telephone centres (at 3 Koresh Street and 236 Jaffa Road, Jerusalem; at 13 Frishman Street, Tel Aviv; at 14 Ha'atzmaut Square, Netanya; in the Hatmarim Boulevard Shopping Centre, Elat; and in the Pedestrian Mall, Tiberias). Charges are reduced by 25% on weekdays from 9pm to 1am and from Saturday at 7am to Sunday at 1am, and are reduced by 50% daily between 1 and 7am.

From the United Kingdom to Israel: 0010 972
From the United States or Canada to Israel: 011 972
From Israel to the United Kingdom: 00 44
From Israel to the United States or Canada: 00 1

International
dialling codes

In dialling to Israel or from Israel to the United Kingdom the zero of the local dialling code should be omitted.

Jerusalem 02
Afula 06
Ashdod 055
Ashqelon 051
Beersheba 057
Elat 059
Haifa 04
Netanya 053
Rehovot 08
Sharon area 052
Tel Aviv 03
Tiberias 06

Local dialling
codes in Israel

Public Holidays

The system of public holidays in Israel is complicated, since there are Jewish, Christian and Muslim holidays, and within the Christian communities there are differences between the western churches (Roman Catholic and Protestant) and the eastern churches (Greek Orthodox and Armenian). Exact dates cannot usually be given, since Jewish and Muslim festivals are regulated by lunar calendars (so that from year to year they occur at different dates in the Gregorian calendar) and because some of the Christian festivals are movable. See Calendars.

Jewish shops are closed and services like buses and railways close down on Friday afternoon and Saturday, the Jewish Sabbath. For Jews the day begins in the evening, so that a Jewish festival begins at sunset on the previous day and ends at sunset on the day of the festival, following Genesis 1,5: "And the evening and the morning were the first day."
For further information on Jewish festivals see Events.

The Sabbath;
Jewish festivals

Festivals date	Hebrew date	Gregorian	Dates of festivals
Rosh Hashanah (New Year)	1/2 Tishri	Sept./Oct.	
Yom Kippur (Day of Atonement)	10 Tishri	Sept./Oct.	
Sukkot[2] (Feast of Tabernacles)	15–21 Tishri	Sept./Oct.	
Simhat Tora (Rejoicing of the Torah)	22 Tishri	Sept./Oct.	
Hanukkah[1] (Feast of Lights)	24 Kislev to 2 or 3 Tevet	Nov./Dec.	

Public Transport

Tu B'Shevat[1] (New Year of the Trees)	15 Shevat	Jan./Feb.
Purim[1] (Feast of Lots)	14 Adar	Feb./Mar.
Pesach[2] (Passover)	15–21 (22) Nisan	Mar./Apr.
Independence Day	5 Iyyar	Apr./May
Lag Ba'Omer[1] (Feast of the Number 33)	18 Iyyar	Apr./May
Day of Liberation of Jerusalem	28 Iyyar	May/June
Shavuot (Feast of Weeks)	6 Sivan	May/June
Tisha B'Av[1]	9 Av	July/Aug.

[1] On these days shops are mostly open and public services operating.
[2] The first and last day of Sukkot and the first and seventh days of Pesach are days of rest.

Christian festivals

Christian shops and services are, in general, closed on Sunday. The principal Christian holidays are New Year's Day (celebrated by the western churches on January 1st, by the eastern churches on January 14th), Epiphany, Palm Sunday, Good Friday, Easter Day, Ascension, Pentecost and Christmas (celebrated by the western churches on December 24th/25th, by the eastern churches on January 7th).

Muslim festivals

Muslim shops and services are closed on Friday. The principal festivals are:

Id el-Adha, the Feast of Sacrifice, in December or January
New Year's Day in January or February
Mohammed's Birthday in April
First Day of Ramadan in October
Id el-Fitr (the last three days of Ramadan) in October or November

Public Transport

Public transport services (buses, *sherut* communal taxis and railways) do not operate on the Sabbath (Saturday), on the eve of the Sabbath (Friday evening) and on Jewish public holidays and the eve of holidays. Only buses and sherut taxis operated by Arabs run on these days (e.g. in East Jerusalem and Nazareth).

Buses

The most important means of passenger transport in Israel, both in towns and in the country, are the buses; the fares on the country services are particularly cheap. From the central bus stations in Jerusalem (Harakevet Street) and Haifa (2 Hahagana Street) there are fast services to all parts of the country. For journeys of any length it is advisable to book seats in advance.
Something like 90% of bus traffic is in the hands of two companies, Egged and Dan. Jerusalem's city buses, painted red and white, are run by Egged; Tel Aviv's, mostly painted blue and white, by Dan. The buses run by Arab companies in Jerusalem and on the West Bank are blue and white or green and white.
Country buses are in excellent condition, usually clean and sometimes air-conditioned.
Country buses almost everywhere start running at 5am and continue into the early evening. Only on the most important routes (Tel Aviv–Jerusalem and Tel Aviv–Haifa) do services continue until 11.30pm. Within the larger towns bus services continue until midnight.
Within towns buses stop only when required. Passengers who want to get off must press the bell in plenty of time.
On city buses multi-journey tickets are available at reduced prices; season tickets are usually not worth while for visitors. On long-distance buses there are reduced fares for school-children and students.

Sherut taxis are shared or communal taxis seating seven passengers which run on fixed routes in towns and between towns. For inter-city travel they are about 20% dearer than buses but more convenient. Fares are officially fixed, with a supplement for travel at night. The taxi ranks used by different sherut companies are listed in local telephone directories under "Taxi-cabs".	Sherut taxis
Railway services in Israel are run by a state-owned company, Israel Railways. Since the cancellation of services on the Jerusalem–Tel Aviv line, which was losing money, the Tel Aviv–Haifa–Nahariya line is for all practical purposes the only one of any importance for passenger traffic. Fares are lower than for buses.	Railways
Since distances within Israel are short, domestic air services – mainly flown by the airline Arkia – are of relatively minor importance. There are scheduled flights from Jerusalem to Tel Aviv, Haifa, Rosh Pinna and Elat; from Tel Aviv to Jerusalem, Rosh Pinna and Elat; and from Elat to Tel Aviv, Haifa and Jerusalem. Arkia and other private charter companies fly to many other airfields in the country, depending on demand; the demand for flights to Masada, for example, has increased considerably in recent years.	Air services
There are regular ferry services on the Sea of Galilee between Tiberias, En Gev and Capernaum, and boats for round trips on the Sea of Galilee can be chartered from the Kinnereth Sailing Company in En Gev (tel. (06) 72 02 48). There are also special evening cruises with dinner and an entertainment programme. In the Red Sea observation cruises in glass-bottomed boats are run from Coral Beach, to the south of Elat (Tour Yam Ltd, tel. (059) 7 21 11; departures from the landing-stage opposite the Coral Sea Hotel). There are also half-day excursions from Elat to Taba and short cruises in the Gulf of Elat.	Boat services
See entry	Taxis
See entry	Car rental

Radio and Television

Radio Kol Israel (Voice of Israel) transmits news in English at 7am and 1, 5 and 8pm on short waves (1170 kHz; in the north of the country 576 kHz).	Radio
Television programmes are almost exclusively in Hebrew and Arabic; only a few films are shown in the original language with subtitles. Israel Television transmits news bulletins in English at 8pm Sunday to Thursday and 7.15pm Friday and Saturday.	Television

Railways

See Public Transport

Restaurants

While hotel restaurants, except those under Arab management, usually serve kosher food, there are many restaurants which do not observe Jewish dietary prescriptions.
Most restaurants are open for both lunch and dinner, usually closing at 11pm or midnight. Many are closed on Friday afternoon and Saturday.

Restaurants

Akko
El Basha, 14 Saladin Street, tel. (04) 91 37 38 (Oriental cuisine)
Monte Carlo, Saladin Street, tel. (04) 91 61 73 (international cuisine)
Ptolemais, on harbour, tel. (04) 91 61 12 (fish specialities)

Ashqelon
Furama, 24–26 Ort Street, Afridar, tel. (051) 3 84 97 (Chinese)
Shanghai, New Tourist Center, tel. (051) 7 53 06 (Chinese)

Beersheba
Bar Sheva, 32 Kfar Darom Street, tel. (057) 7 71 91 (international cuisine)
Jade Palace, 79 Histadrut Street, tel. (057) 7 53 75 (Chinese)
Papa Michel, 95 Histadrut Street, tel. (057) 7 72 98 (Moroccan)

Caesarea
Harbour Citadel, Old Caesarea, tel. (06) 36 19 88

Elat
Au Bistrot, Bistrot Center, Elat Street, tel. (059) 7 43 33 (French)
Au Rendezvous, 14 Ye'elim Street, tel. (059) 7 95 04 (French and international cuisine)
Casa Italiana, Coral Beach (opposite Caravan Hotel), tel. (059) 7 63 03 (Italian)
Eddie's, 68 Almogim Street, tel. (059) 7 11 37 (steaks and seafood American style)
Jack Azoulai's Stagecoach, Ophira Park (opposite Shulamit Garden Hotel), tel. (059) 7 13 66 (Italian and French cuisine; expensive)
La Barracuda, Coral Beach, tel. (059) 7 34 42 (fish specialities)
Mai Thai, Yotam Road (New Tourist Centre), tel. (059) 7 25 17 (Chinese)
Mandy's Coral Beach, tel. (059) 7 22 38 (Chinese)
Oasis, at yacht harbour (near bridge), tel. (059) 7 24 14 (Israeli cuisine)
Pago Pago, Elat Lagoona (at King Solomon Hotel), tel. (059) 7 66 60 (floating restaurant)
Papa Michel, 1 Hatmarim Street, tel. (059) 7 41 31 (Moroccan)

En Gev
En Gev Fish Restaurant, tel. (06) 75 11 66 (lakeside terrace)

Haifa
Bankers' Tavern, 2 Bank Street, tel. (04) 52 84 39 (European cuisine)
Chin Lung, 126 Hanassi Boulevard, tel. (04) 38 13 08 (Chinese)
Dolphin, 13 Bat Galim Avenue, tel. (04) 52 38 37 (fish specialities)
Hipopotam, 116 Hanassi Boulevard, tel. (04) 37 43 66 (French)
La Trattoria, 119 Hanassi Boulevard, tel. (04) 38 20 20 (Italian and French cuisine)
Mathamim, 24 Herzl Street, tel. (04) 66 51 72 (Jewish cuisine)
Misadag, 29 Margolin Street, tel. (04) 52 44 41 (fish specialities)
Pagoda, 1 Bat Galim Avenue, tel. (04) 52 45 85 (Chinese)
Peer, 1 Atlit Street, tel. (04) 66 57 07 (Oriental specialities)

Herzliya
Henry VIII, De Chalit Square, Herzliya Pituah, tel. (052) 57 55 86 (Italian and French cuisine; live music on Fridays)
L'Auberge, 29 Hama'apilim Street, Herzliya Pituah, tel. (052) 57 21 79 (French)
Sechang, 87 Medinat Heyehudim Street, Herzliya Pituah, tel. (052) 57 35 00 (Chinese)

Jerusalem
Agam, 121 Agrippas Street, tel. (02) 22 24 45 (Middle Eastern cuisine)
Alla Gondola, 14 King George Street, tel. (02) 22 59 44 (Northern Italian cuisine; expensive)
Au Sahara, 17 Jaffa Road, tel. (02) 23 32 39 (Moroccan; expensive)
Charlie Chan, 2 Lunz Street, tel. (02) 24 24 64 (Chinese; simple, reasonably priced restaurant)
Chez Simon, 15 Shammay Street, tel. (02) 22 56 02 (French; expensive)
El Gaucho, 22 Rivlin Street, tel. (02) 22 66 65 (Argentinian grill-restaurant)
Feferberg's, 53 Jaffa Road, tel. (02) 22 48 41 (Jewish and East European cuisine)
Goulash Inn, En Karem, tel. (02) 41 92 14 (Hungarian; expensive; pleasant atmosphere)

Kamin, 4 Rabbi Akiva Street, tel. (02) 23 48 19 (French and international cuisine)
La Scala, 31 Jaffa Road, tel. (02) 22 80 65 (French)
Mandarin, 2 Shlomzion Hamalka Street, tel. (02) 22 28 90 (rated the best Chinese restaurant in Jerusalem)
Mishkenot Sha'ananim, Yemin Moshe (by Montefiore Windmill), tel. (02) 23 34 24 (French; elegant atmosphere)
Jerusalem Skylight, 34 Ben Yehuda Street, in Eilon Tower (21st floor), tel. (02) 23 32 81 (international cuisine; magnificent views)
Yesh Veyesh, 48 Emeq Refaim Street, German Colony, tel. (02) 63 00 98 (Mediterranean dishes; with garden restaurant)

Ahakura, in main street, tel. (06) 94 05 15 — Metulla

Chinese Inn, 28 Haga'aton Street, tel. (04) 92 37 09 (Chinese) — Nahariya
Donau, 32 Haga'aton Street, tel. (04) 8 92 86 99 (international cuisine)
El Gaucho, Haga'aton Street, tel. (04) 92 00 27 (grill-restaurant)

Astoria, 1 Casa Nova Street, tel. (06) 57 79 65 (Oriental cuisine) — Nazareth
Israel, Paul VI Street, tel. (06) 55 41 14 (Oriental cuisine)
Nof Nazareth, 23 Carmel Street, tel. (06) 55 43 66 (Hungarian)

Casa Mia, 10 Herzl Street, tel. (053) 34 72 28 (pizzeria) — Netanya
Chung Shing, Herzl Street, tel. (053) 3 23 04 (Chinese)
Diamond, 2 Jabotinsky Street, tel. (053) 61 95 04 (Chinese)
Hagozal, 95 Herzl Street, tel. (053) 33 53 01 (Jewish cuisine)
Lido, 3 Herzl Street, tel. (053) 33 48 34 (Oriental and European cuisine)
Pundak Hayam, 1 Harav Kook Street, tel. (053) 34 12 22
Renaissance, 9 Ha'atzmaut Square, tel. (053) 2 86 53 (Oriental cuisine)
Tandoori, 5 Ha'atzmaut Square, tel. (053) 61 00 17 (Indian)

Dag Al-Hadan, Banyas Road, tel. (06) 94 92 51 (fish restaurant on river Dan) — Qiryat Shemona

Misouyan, 59 Jerusalem Street, tel. (06) 93 04 28 (Chinese) — Safed
Pinati, 81 Jerusalem Street, tel. (06) 93 08 55 (Oriental cuisine)

Allegro, 29 Hamered Street, tel. (03) 65 13 18 (French) — Tel Aviv
Baiuca, 103 Yehuda Hayamit Street, on Jaffa harbour, tel. (03) 82 72 89 (Brazilian)
Cardo, 2 Allenby Street, tel. (03) 5 10 39 94 (French)
Casba, 32 Yirmiyahu Street, tel. (03) 44 26 17 (high standard of international cuisine; expensive)
Dolphin-Stern, 189 Dizengoff Street, tel. (03) 23 24 25 (fish specialities)
Keton, 145 Dizengoff Street, tel. (03) 23 36 79 (traditional Jewish cuisine)
La Prima Donna, 33 Yirmiyahu Street, tel. (03) 5 46 10 41 (Italian and French cuisine)
L'Entrecote, 195 Ben Yehuda Street, tel. (03) 5 46 67 26 (steak-house)
Le Relais, 13 Dolphin Street, Jaffa, tel. (03) 81 06 37 (French)
Maganda, 26 Rabbi Meir Street, tel. (03) 65 99 90 (Middle Eastern cuisine)
Maredo, 17 Petah Tiqwa Road, tel. (03) 61 47 59 (steak restaurant; fish specialities)
Peking, 265 Dizengoff Street, tel. (03) 45 34 23 (Chinese)
Pirozki, 30 Yirmiyahu Street, tel. (03) 45 75 99 (Russian)
Pundag, 8 Frishman Street, tel. (03) 22 29 48 (fish specialities)
Shaul's Inn, 11 Elyashiv Street, tel. (03) 65 33 03 (Oriental cuisine)
Shazam, 10 Marmorek Street, tel. (03) 5 61 60 07 (Indian)
Shmulik Cohen, 146 Herzl Street, tel. (03) 82 00 00 (traditional Jewish cuisine)
Taboon, Jaffa harbour, tel. (03) 81 11 76 (fish specialities)
Triana, 12 Carlebach Street, tel. (03) 5 61 49 49 (Greek)

Avi's Pub and Restaurant, HaKishon Street, tel. (06) 79 17 97 (Oriental cuisine) — Tiberias

Crimson Flower, 32 HaBonnim Street, tel. (06) 79 02 21 (Chinese)
Karamba, on Sea of Galilee, tel. (06) 79 15 46 (fish specialities)
Lido Kinneret, Gdud Barak Street (on shores of lake), tel. (06) 72 15 38 (fish specialities)
Nof Kinneret, Hayarkon Street, tel. (06) 72 07 73 (Oriental cuisine)
Panorama, Hagalil Street, tel. (06) 79 04 41 (Oriental cuisine)
Tiberius, Dona Grazia Street, tel. (06) 79 24 77 (international cuisine)

Zikhron Ya'aqov   The Well, on the old road to Haifa, tel. (06) 39 90 47 (international cuisine; expensive)

Riding

See Sport

Safety and Security

Insurance

Make sure that you have adequate insurance cover (health insurance, insurance against loss and theft of property, car insurance if you are taking your own car).

Organising your Trip

Good organisation, starting before you leave home, is important. If you know that everything is in order at home this will allow you to enjoy a relaxed holiday.

It is helpful to draw up a check list of what requires to be done, ticking off each item as it is dealt with.

Don't forget:
passports;
insurance documents;
tickets (air, rail, ferry) and confirmation of bookings;
photocopies of important documents (in luggage);
traveller's cheques, Eurocheques, credit and cheque cards, cash;
road maps;
first aid kit, and any medicine which you take regularly;
spare glasses if worn, and sun-glasses;
and, if you are taking your car –
driving licence and car registration document;
spare parts for the car.

Safety on the Road

Hiring a car   If you want to hire a car in Israel it is best to go to one of the internationally known car rental firms, since then you will have a reasonable assurance that the vehicle is properly maintained and in good condition for driving. Make sure that you are fully insured, taking out additional insurance if necessary to ensure that you have comprehensive cover.
Some car rental firms will give a discount to members of a motoring organisation like the AA. A credit card may enable you to avoid putting down a deposit in cash.

Seat-belts   Make sure that you have your seat-belt on and that your passengers, in both the front and the rear seats, have theirs on too. The belts should be properly adjusted – taut and not twisted. A loosely fitting belt can cause additional injury in an accident.

Seat-belts are most effective when used with properly adjusted head-restraints. These should have their upper edge at least as high as the level of the eyes: only then do they give protection to the cervical vertebrae.

Spectacle-wearers drive more safely at night if they have special non-reflective glasses. Tinted glasses should not be worn after dark. Since all glass reflects part of the light reaching it, even a clear windscreen lets through only some 90% of the available light; and spectacle-wearers lose another 10%. Tinted windscreens and tinted glasses allow only about half the available light to reach the eye, and safe driving is no longer possible.

Spectacle-wearers

If you have an accident in Israel

However carefully you drive, accidents can happen. If you are involved in an accident, the first rules are: whatever the provocation, don't get angry; be polite; and keep calm. Then take the following action:

1. Warn oncoming traffic by switching on your car's warning lights if you have them and setting your warning triangle (and, if you have one, a flashing light) some distance before the scene of the accident.

2. Look after anyone who has been injured, calling an ambulance if necessary.

3. Inform the police.

4. Record full particulars of the accident. These should include:
(a) names and addresses of witnesses (independent witnesses are particularly important);
(b) damage to the vehicles involved;
(c) name and address of the other driver, and of the owner if different;
(d) name and address of the other party's insurance company and, if possible, the number of the insurance certificate;
(e) registration number of the other vehicle;
(f) damage or injury to yourself or other persons;
(g) number of police officer or address of police station if involved;
(h) date, time and location of the accident;
(i) speed of the vehicles involved;
(j) width of the road, any road signs and the condition of the road surface;
(k) any marks on the road relevant to the accident;
(l) the weather and the manner of the other driver's driving.

5. Draw a sketch of the accident, showing the layout of the road, the direction in which the vehicles were travelling and their position at the time of impact, any road signs and the names of streets or roads. If you have a camera, take photographs of the scene.

Make no admission of responsibility for the accident, and above all do not sign any document in a language you do not understand.

On your return home you should of course report the accident to your insurance company and give them the full particulars.

Shopping, Souvenirs

Visitors to Israel will find a tempting variety of articles in all price ranges to take home as a reminder of their holiday. Israel has a large diamond and

431

jewellery industry, whose products can be bought in special shops or in the factories themselves. For those who are prepared to spend more there are Oriental carpets, furs and leather goods. Attractive smaller souvenirs are embroidery and needlework, pictures, ceramics and various arts and crafts. Characteristic Oriental products can be found in the Arab towns of Akko, Bethlehem, Hebron and Nazareth and the Druze villages on Mount Carmel. Very typical of Israel are the carved olive-wood figures of the Nativity group sold in Bethlehem. Hand-blown glassware can be bought in Hebron, small genuine antiques in Samaria.

Shops approved by the Ministry of Tourism as selling a range of well made craft products and souvenirs display a special symbol – a blue bow with two little men carrying a bunch of grapes and the legend "Recommended by the Ministry of Tourism" – and are graded with between one and three stars.

Antiques	See entry
Opening times	See Business Hours
Value-added tax	See entry

Social Conduct

The Sabbath	Visitors should pay particular regard to the customs of the country on the Sabbath and on special festivals. They should avoid smoking in public (and smoking is banned in the public rooms of hotels on these days). At the Western Wall (Wailing Wall) in Jerusalem, one of the Jews' holiest spots, photography is prohibited. Most forms of public transport cease operating on the Sabbath and on feast days, and practising Jews leave their cars at home.
Visiting holy places	Visitors should be suitably dressed when visiting churches, synagogues and mosques (no shorts, no sleeveless dresses, no décolletés), and should not enter them during services. Jews cover their heads in the synagogue, and visitors should do the same. Shoes must be taken off when entering mosques.

Spas

The principal spa resort on the Sea of Galilee is Tiberias, with numerous large hotels and a variety of treatment facilities. The main resorts on the Dead Sea are En Boqeq and Newe Zohar.

The therapeutic qualities of the climate and the water of the Dead Sea, with its high mineral content, are widely recognised. Thanks to the unique combination of high air pressure, strong sunshine and dry air considerable success has been achieved in the treatment of skin diseases, particularly psoriasis and neurodermatitis, disorders of the muscles and joints (polyarthritis and degenerative disorders) and psychosomatic complaints.
Tiberias, on the Sea of Galilee, has 17 hot springs at a temperature of around 60°C/140°F, with water containing a rare and complex combination of minerals which is recommended for the treatment of diseases of the muscles and joints, sinusitis, physical rehabilitation and psychosomatic complaints.
Asthmas and allergies have been successfully treated at the desert town of Arad.

Sport

In Israel all sport is amateur. Most international sporting events take place in Tel Aviv. The most popular sport is association football, followed by basketball.

Israel Cyclists' Touring Club
Kfar Saba, tel. (052) 2 37 16
The Club will help in the planning of cycle trips, and will also provide guides for touring groups.

Jerusalem Cyclists' Club
P.O. Box 7281, tel. (02) 81 65 22
The Club organises excursions for groups of cyclists.

The coasts of the Red Sea off Elat, with their beautiful banks of coral and their abundance of fish, offer magnificent tropical diving grounds, with visibility of up to 40m/130ft. Here diving is possible throughout the year. The range of possibilities extends from diving on the coral reef by way of exploring underwater caverns to archaeological exploration. Various diving schools offer courses for beginners and more experienced divers. Snorkelling and scuba diving equipment can be hired on Coral Beach.

The diving season on the Mediterranean coast of Israel extends from March to May, with visibility of up to 10m/35ft. This is a particularly good area for underwater archaeology. At Rosh Haniqra in northern Israel there is interesting diving in underwater caverns.

Diving schools:

Andromeda Diving Centre
Jaffa harbour, Tel Aviv
Tel. (03) 82 75 72

Snapir Diving Centre
Jaffa harbour, Tel Aviv
Tel. (03) 3 56 29

Shiqmona Diving Club
Kishon harbour, Haifa
Tel. (04) 23 39 08

Caesarea Diving Club
Roman Harbour
Tel. (06) 36 17 87

Aqua Sport Red Sea Diving Centre
Coral Beach, Elat
Tel. (059) 7 27 88

Red Sea Sport
King Solomon Quay, Elat
Tel. (059) 7 91 11

The only golf-course in Israel is the Caesarea Golf and Country Club (18 holes), near the site of ancient Caesarea (tel. (06) 26 11 74). Visitors can be admitted to temporary membership.

A good river for kayak trips is the Banyas, one of the three source streams of the Jordan.
Trips are organised by the kibbutz of Kfar Blum (tel. (06) 94 87 55).

Sport

Riding

Some riding clubs organise guided treks, others hire out horses. Upper Galilee in particular offers good riding country. The holiday village (with bungalows, swimming pool and tennis court) of Wered HaGalil (tel. (06) 93 57 85) 13km/8 miles north of Tiberias, near the Sea of Galilee, offers riding holidays. It runs two- to five-day treks (e.g. a three-day trip round the Sea of Galilee).

Riding schools:

Havat Amir
Atarot, Jerusalem, tel. (02) 85 21 90

King David's Riding Stables
Newe Ilan (near Jerusalem–Tel Aviv motorway), tel. (02) 78 28 98

Bacall Riding School
Ben Zvi Boulevard, Nahariya, tel. (04) 82 15 34

Green Beach Ranch
Netanya, tel. (053) 5 14 66

Bat Ya'ar Ranch
near Safed, tel. (06) 93 17 88

Sailing

Sailing boats can be hired, for example in the yacht harbours of Elat, Haifa, Tel Aviv–Jaffa and in Tiberias at Lido Beach and Tchelet Beach.

Skiing

Unlikely as it may seem, there is skiing to be had in the Holy Land. Israel's winter sports area is in the north of the country, on Mount Hermon, which rises to 2600m/8500ft on the Israeli side. The season is from December/January until about the middle of April. In the moshav of Newe Ativ (founded 1969) there is a ski school and skis can be hired. Although the pistes are not particularly testing, they are very popular with Israelis.

Surfing

Surfing can be practised all along Israel's Mediterranean coast. A particularly popular area is round Nahariya, where the world championships were held in 1980. There are also good conditions for surfing at Elat on the Red Sea and on the Sea of Galilee.

Tennis

Many of the large hotels have their own tennis courts. In addition there are the courts belonging to the Israel Tennis Centre, which offer facilities for visitors:

Ramat Hasharon (24 courts), tel. (03) 5 44 72 22
Jerusalem (19 courts), tel. (02) 41 38 66
Tel Aviv (17 courts), tel. (03) 83 00 38
Ashqelon (17 courts), tel. (051) 2 22 86
Haifa (24 courts), tel. (04) 52 27 21
Arad (7 courts), tel. (057) 95 68 77
Qiryat Shemona (8 courts), tel. (06) 94 90 34
Tiberias (6 courts), tel. (06) 73 15 68

Walking

Various tour operators offer walking holidays in Israel. Day trips and longer trips lasting several days are organised by the Society for the Protection of Nature in Israel, 3 Hashfela Street, Tel Aviv, tel. (03) 37 50 63.
There is also, of course, plenty of scope for walking on your own. There is a long-distance trail between Mount Hermon in the north of the country and Elat on the Red Sea.

Surfing

See Sport

Taxis

Taxis can be called by telephone (e.g. by dialling 22 32 23 in Jerusalem, 25 42 54 in Tel Aviv and 38 27 27 in Haifa) or hailed in the street.
For inter-city journeys the fares are officially fixed, and taxi-drivers are obliged to show the list of fares on request. Within towns the fare is shown on the meter; there is a supplement of 25% during the night.

For journeys to the West Bank it is advisable on security grounds to take a taxi with an Arab driver. The rank for Arab taxis in Jerusalem is at the Damascus Gate.

In occupied territories

See Public Transport

Sherut taxis

Telephone

See Post, Telegraph, Telephone

Television

See Radio and Television

Tennis

See Sport

Theatres, Concerts

Israel's most famous orchestra, the Israel Philharmonic, gives some 150 concerts every year, frequently under the baton of internationally famed conductors. Its home is the Frederic Mann Auditorium in Tel Aviv.
During the winter the Jerusalem Symphony Orchestra of the Israel Broadcasting Authority gives regular concerts (mainly of works by Israeli composers) in the Henry Crown Symphony Hall in Jerusalem's Art Centre.

Concerts are also given by the Haifa, Ramat Gan and Beersheba Orchestras, the Israel Chamber Ensemble and various trios and quartets, and there are recitals by renowned international and Israeli soloists.

The best known theatres in Israel are the Habimah Theatre (Israel's National Theatre), the Cameri Theatre and the Municipal Theatre in Tel Aviv, the Municipal Theatres of Haifa and Beersheba and the Khan Theatre in Jerusalem. Touring companies from these theatres in the larger towns give performances all over Israel.
While numerous classical and contemporary plays are performed in Hebrew, many small companies put on plays in English, Yiddish and other languages. The Habimah Theatre in Tel Aviv provides simultaneous translation facilities for foreign visitors.

Theatres

Habimah Theatre, Tel Aviv

Ballet
The Israel Classical Ballet, as its name indicates, specialises in classical ballet, while the Bat Dor and Bat Sheva Dance Companies perform modern works. These companies also put on performances in towns and sometimes kibbutzes throughout Israel.

Folk evenings
In addition to concerts, plays and ballet Israel offers a variety of other events which enable visitors to get to know the country and its people. Among them are the folk evenings which are regularly organised in Jerusalem, Tel Aviv, Haifa and Tiberias and frequently also in the large hotels in the tourist centres of Ashqelon, Netanya and Elat and the resorts on the Dead Sea.

Theft

Although Israel has not an unusually bad reputation in this respect, thefts do occur, and it is wise to take precautions against them. Visitors should be particularly wary in places where there are large numbers of people crowded together, for example in markets. If travelling in the occupied territories they should never leave anything in a parked car. They should deposit anything of value in the hotel safe or carry it on their person in an inner pocket or belt.

Time

Israel is two hours ahead of Greenwich Mean Time and seven hours ahead of Eastern Standard Time in the United States.
Israeli Summer Time (three hours ahead of GMT) is in force from mid April to the end of September.

Tipping

Hotel bills include a service charge, but it is usual to give porters and chambermaids a little extra.
A service charge is also usually added to restaurant bills; if it is not, this will be indicated. If there is no service charge a tip of 10–15% is usual.
Taxi-drivers may be tipped if they have given good service. It is usual to round up the metered fare to the nearest convenient amount.

Travel Documents

Visitors to Israel must have a passport valid for not less than six months beyond their date of arrival. A visa is also required, but this is issued free of charge to citizens of the United States, Canada and numerous other countries at the point of entry into Israel. Citizens of the United Kingdom do not require an entry visa.
Young people under 18 travelling on their own must have an officially certified statement by their parent or guardian giving permission for them to travel.

Personal papers

There are at present no vaccination requirements for visitors entering Israel.

Vaccinations, etc.

National driving licences and car registration documents are recognised in Israel and must be carried by the driver of the car.
Third party insurance is compulsory in Israel. An international insurance certificate ("green card") is accepted; visitors who cannot produce a green card must obtain cover from the Israel Insurance Association in Tel Aviv (113 Allenby Road) or Haifa.

Car papers

Visitors who want to visit the Sinai peninsula from Israel can obtain an entry visa at the Taba frontier crossing (south of Elat) on payment of a fee. Those who want to travel farther into Egypt must obtain a visa in advance from an Egyptian diplomatic or consular office.

Entry to Egypt

Value-Added Tax

Value-added tax (VAT) at the rate of 18% is charged on all goods and services and is included in the price.
VAT is not charged on the following services when they are paid for in foreign currency: flights on Israeli airlines; organised tours, including meals taken en route; accommodation in hotels and meals taken in hotel restaurants provided that these are entered on the bill; car rentals, either self-drive or with guide/driver.

Visitors who make purchases to the value of over US $50 in a shop recommended by the Ministry of Tourism and pay for them in foreign currency are entitled to a reduction of at least 5% and to reimbursement of VAT at the airport (or seaport) of departure. Shops operating this scheme display a notice to that effect in the window, as well as the "Recommended by the Ministry of Tourism" symbol (see Shopping, Souvenirs).
These arrangements do not apply to tobacco goods, electrical appliances or apparatus, films and other photographic requisites.

Reductions

The following is the procedure for reimbursement of VAT. You must obtain a receipt showing the amount of VAT paid and must make sure that a copy of this is enclosed along with your purchases in a transparent carrier bag, which is closed with sealing tape and stamped by the shop so as to show

Reimbursement of VAT

that it has not been opened. At Ben-Gurion Airport you must present the package along with the original of the receipt to the customs official. He will then stamp the receipt, and on presentation of this to the bank in the departures hall you will be reimbursed the amount of VAT paid.

If for any reason you cannot obtain immediate reimbursement you must print your name and address in the bottom left-hand corner of the receipt and put it into a box beside the bank. The money will then be sent to your home address.

Expenses will be deducted from the amount of VAT at the rate of US $2 when the amount is under $30 and $5 when it is over $30.

Walking

See Sport

Water Parks

Water parks have been laid out as a tourist attraction on the Sea of Galilee, on the Mediterranean coast of Israel and at Elat. Children in particular will be delighted by the huge water-chutes and flumes and other water effects. Some water parks also offer a range of other water sports, including water-skiing and parasailing, and many of them have pedalos and kayaks for hire.

Sea of Galilee   Luna Gal Beach
at Golan Beach on the north-east side of the lake, north of Kursi

Zemach Beach
on the south shore of the lake, south of Kinneret

Red Sea   Rhapsody in White, North Beach, Elat

Mediterranean   Kibbutz of Newe Yam, near Atlit

Kibbutz of Shefayim, north of Herzliya

Bat Yam, south of Tel Aviv

Ashqeluna, in Ashqelon

Water Sports

See Sport

Weather

See Facts and Figures, Climate; When to Go

When to Go

Although Israel is crowded with visitors in the summer months this is not the ideal time to go. It is very hot, with temperatures of over 30°C/86°F, and it is often oppressively muggy, particularly on the Mediterranean coast. The climate is more tolerable in Jerusalem, which lies high, but is almost unendurable on the Dead Sea and the Red Sea.

It is pleasanter to travel in Israel in spring (March/April) or autumn (October) – though both these seasons are very short. The country is particularly

Weather in Israel

Air temperature (A; in °C), water temperature (W; in °C) and number of days with sun (S) at selected places in Israel during the main holiday months

Place		January	February	March	April	September	October	November	December
Haifa (Mediterranean)	A	8–17°	9–18°	8–21°	13–26°	20–30°	16–27°	13–23°	9–18°
	W	18°	18°	18°	19°	29°	28°	23°	19°
	S	16	16	22	25	29	27	22	19
Tel Aviv (Mediterranean)	A	9–18°	9–19°	10–20°	12–22°	20–31°	15–29°	12–25°	9–19°
	W	18°	18°	18°	19°	29°	27°	23°	19°
	S	17	16	23	26	29	28	22	19
Tiberias (Sea of Galilee)	A	9–18°	9–20°	11–22°	13–27°	22–35°	19–32°	15–26°	11–20°
	W	17°	15°	17°	21°	30°	28°	24°	22°
	S	19	18	25	27	30	30	25	23
Sodom (Dead Sea)	A	12–21°	13–22°	16–26°	22–32°	27–36°	24–32°	19–27°	14–22°
	W	21°	19°	21°	22°	31°	30°	28°	23°
	S	30	26	31	30	30	31	30	29
Elat (Red Sea)	A	10–21°	11–23°	13–27°	17–31°	24–36°	20–33°	16–28°	11–23°
	W	22°	20°	21°	22°	27°	26°	25°	24°
	S	30	27	29	29	30	31	29	30
Jerusalem (Uplands)	A	6–11°	7–14°	8–16°	12–21°	18–28°	16–26°	12–19°	7–15°
	S	19	19	23	27	30	29	23	22
Safed (Uplands)	A	4–10°	5–11°	6–13°	9–19°	17–27°	15–24°	12–16°	5–9°
	S	18	13	26	27	20	21	20	19

beautiful in spring, when northern Israel has a luxuriant and colourful growth of vegetation.

A pleasant place for a winter holiday is Elat, where the climate is usually pleasantly warm even in December and January and the sky is often brilliantly blue. The northern parts of the country also have their attractions in winter, though constant good weather cannot be guaranteed. Even at this time of year there are relatively warm and absolutely clear days, though cool and rainy days predominate and there may sometimes even be snow in the hill country.

Visitors whose interest in Israel is not primarily religious should avoid the periods of the great Christian festivals, when large numbers of pilgrims flock to the holy places, particularly in Jerusalem. During the main Jewish public holidays (see entry) and the school holidays (mid June to the beginning of September) many bathing resorts are overcrowded.

Working Holidays

Most kibbutzes accept volunteers to work for varying periods of time. Volunteers should be aged between 18 and 32 and should be prepared to work for at least three weeks, six days a week for a minimum of six hours per day. In return they get free accommodation, board and pocket money.

Work in a kibbutz

Information:

Kibbutz Representative
1A Accommodation Road, London NW11
Tel. (0181) 450 9235

Youth Hostels

Jewish Agency
Kibbutz Aliyah Desk
515 Park Avenue
New York NY 10022
Tel. (212) 688 4134

United Kibbutz Movement
82 Hayarkon Street, Tel Aviv
Tel. (03) 65 17 10

Work in a moshav

Volunteers can also work in a moshav. They must be prepared to work an eight-hour day, six days a week. The work is usually harder than in a kibbutz; the pay is better, but volunteers must usually provide their own board.

Information:

Moshav Volunteer Department
19 Leonardo da Vinci Street
Tel Aviv
Tel. (03) 25 84 73

Archaeological digs

During the summer volunteers can work on archaeological sites. They are expected to work for a minimum period of at least one or two weeks; usually there is no pay, but food and accommodation (in tents, youth hostels or hotels, depending on the site) are often provided.

Information:

Department of Antiquities and Museums
P.O. Box 586
Jerusalem
Tel. (02) 27 86 03

Youth Hostels

The Israel Youth Hostels Association (IYHA), which is affiliated to the International Youth Hostels Association, operates some 30 youth hostels throughout the country. The hostels are open to all, regardless of age. All offer dormitory accommodation and most also provide meals and self-service kitchen facilities. Some hostels also have family accommodation for parents accompanied by at least one child.
Individual reservations should be booked directly at specific hostels, group reservations with the IYHA.
Further information can be obtained from national youth hostels associations or from the Israel Youth Hostels Association, 3 Dorot Rishonim Street, P.O. Box 1075, 94625 Jerusalem, tel. (02) 25 27 06. A youth hostels brochure is available from Israel Government Tourist Offices and tourist information offices in Israel.

Youth hostel tours

The IYHA also arranges individual package tours, called "Israel on the Youth Hostel Trail", for two, three or four weeks. These include overnight stays in any of 25 hostels, with breakfast and dinner, unlimited bus travel, a half-day guided tour, free admission to National Parks, a map and other informative material.

Akko

Old City (by lighthouse), P.O. Box 1090, tel. (04) 91 19 82, 120 beds

Arad

Blue-White Hostel, P.O. Box 34, tel. (057) 95 71 50, 150 beds

Bet Yatziv, P.O. Box 7, tel. (057) 7 74 44, 164 beds — **Beersheba**

P.O. Box 152, tel. (059) 7 23 58, 200 beds — **Elat**

Bet Sara, Post Dead Sea, tel. (057) 8 41 65, 200 beds — **En Gedi**

Carmel, Mobile Post Hof Hacarmel, tel. (04) 53 19 44, 250 beds — **Haifa**

Hadarom, Hof Gaza Mobile Post 79725 (west of Beersheba), tel. (051) 4 75 97, 220 beds — **Hevel Katif**

Beit Shmuel, 13 King David Street, tel. (02) 20 34 66, 160 beds — **Jerusalem and surroundings**

Bet Bernstein, 1 Keren Hayessod Street, tel. (02) 22 82 86, 80 beds

Bet Meir, Ramot Shapira, P.O. Box 7216, Jerusalem (20km/12½ miles from city centre), tel. (02) 91 32 91, 200 beds

En Karem, P.O. Box 17013 Jerusalem, tel. (02) 41 62 82, 90 beds

Jerusalem Forest, P.O. Box 3353, Jerusalem, tel. (02) 41 60 60, 98 beds

Kfar Etzion, Mount Hebron (25km/15 miles from city centre), tel. (02) 93 51 33, 150 beds

Louise Waterman Wise Hostel, 8 Hapisga Street, Bayit VeGan, tel. (02) 42 33 66, 250 beds

Old City, Jewish Quarter, P.O. Box 7880, Jerusalem, tel. (02) 28 86 11, 80 beds

Qiryat Anavim, Haezrahi, Mobile Post Hare Yehuda (12km/7½ miles from city centre), tel. (02) 34 27 70, 100 beds

Yoram, Mobile Post Korazim (at north end of Sea of Galilee), tel. (06) 72 06 01, 180 beds — **Kare Deshe**

Emeq Hefer (half way between Tel Aviv and Haifa), tel. (053) 66 60 32, 200 beds — **Kfar Vitkin**

Hankin, Mobile Post Gilboa, tel. (06) 53 16 60, 140 beds — **Ma'ayan Harod**

Isaac H. Taylor Hostel, Masada Mobile Post Dead Sea, tel. (057) 8 43 49, 130 beds — **Masada**

Bet Noam, P.O. Box 2, tel. (057) 8 84 43, 160 beds — **Mizpe Ramon**

Yad Labanim, Yahalom Street, tel. (03) 9 22 66 66, 150 beds — **Petah Tiqwa**

Taiber, Tiberias, P.O. Box 232, tel. (06) 75 00 50, 140 beds — **Poria**

Young Judea, Post Kfar Makkabi (18km/11 miles north-east of Haifa), tel. (04) 44 29 76, 180 beds — **Ramat Yohanan**

Rosh Haniqra, Mobile Post, Western Galilee (north of Nahariya), tel. (04) 82 13 30, 200 beds — **Rosh Haniqra**

Nature Friends (26km/16 miles north of Tiberias), tel. (06) 93 70 86, 100 beds — **Rosh Pinna**

Bet Benyamin, P.O. Box 1139, tel. (06) 93 10 86, 120 beds — **Safed**

32 Bnei Dan Street, tel. (03) 5 46 07 19, 300 beds — **Tel Aviv**

Tel Hai, Mobile Post Upper Galilee, tel. (06) 94 00 43, 120 beds — **Tel Hai**

Yosef Meyouhas Hostel, P.O. Box 81, tel. (06) 72 17 75, 220 beds — **Tiberias**

Index

Index

The Principal Sights at a Glance

(continued from page 6)

Sources of Illustrations

Bader: pp. 82(left), 94, 146(2), 147, 324, 327, 333, 334.

Bildagentur Schuster: pp. 159, 192.

Bilderdienst Süddeutscher Verlag: p. 73(left).

Borowski: pp. 8, 11, 12, 13(right), 20(2), 21(left), 29, 40, 41, 43, 44(2), 45(2), 78, 79(3), 82(right), 97, 98, 101, 103, 107(2), 109, 112, 116(2), 117, 121(2), 125, 133(3), 135(right), 136, 141, 142, 151, 155, 159, 162, 163, 168, 175, 177, 184(2), 189, 190, 195, 1197, 199, 204, 206(2), 210/11, 216, 220, 223(2), 224, 226, 230, 232, 233(3), 239, 241, 243, 245(left), 247(2), 248, 249(2), 250, 251, 253(3), 256, 258(2), 261, 262(2), 264, 265, 267(2), 269, 270(2), 271(2), 279(2), 284, 285(2), 286(2), 290, 292, 293(2), 296, 308, 311, 313(2), 314, 315, 316, 319, 338, 340, 350, 351, 352/53, 358, 359, 362, 363, 366, 368, 371(2), 378, 381, 382(2), 388, 395, 399, 401, 402, 405, 416(2), 419, 423, 424, 436.

Brödel: pp. 167, 321, 372.

CESA Diaarchiv: pp. 165, 186, 343.

Hoene: pp. 13(left), 21(right), 27, 91, 99, 135(left), 139, 151, 170, 183, 245(right), 272, 276(2), 303, 396.

Lade (Fotoagentur): pp. 81, 300.

Rudolph (Diaarchiv): p. 344.

Sperber: pp. 24(9), 238(2), 417(2).

Steller: p. 415.

Ullstein Bilderdienst: pp. 69(3), 73(middle and left).